AIRLINERS
OF THE WORLD

Stewart Wilson

INTRODUCTION

Welcome to *Airliners of the World*, a comprehensive directory of the commercial aircraft that have carried airline passengers to all four corners of the earth from 1914 to the present day.

My intention with this book has been to create a single volume which provides information on a large number of aircraft in an easy to access manner, with sufficient data to answer most questions but also to encourage more detailed research into a particular aircraft.

All the major airliners are covered along with many of the minor ones plus some of the more interesting one-offs and prototypes which didn't achieve production for various reasons. Although comprehensive with 300 entries, *Airliners of the World* makes no claim as to being definitive, as the constraints of time and space have to be considered. Nevertheless, I hope there is much of interest for readers within these pages.

The entries are arranged alphabetically by manufacturer and chronologically within that format. Specification, performance and production data is presented along with a concise history of each type. Many aircraft have multiple entries to cover their variants and allow their evolution to be traced.

One of the problems has been deciding under which manufacturer's name some aircraft should be listed, given the mergers and rationalisations that have taken place over the years. The decision has been made, therefore, to present aircraft under the manufacturer by which they are best known, or under which the bulk of production took place.

Taking Douglas aircraft as an example: up to and including the DC-8, they are listed under the Douglas heading; the DC-9, DC-10, MD-11 and MD-80/90 families are under McDonnell Douglas but the latest DC-9 derivative, the MD-95, is listed under the Boeing 717 heading as that is the company which has assumed development and production responsibility for the aircraft. Many British aircraft have the same problem – is the 748 turboprop an Avro, Hawker Siddeley or British Aerospace product? For the purposes of this book, it's listed under Hawker Siddeley, its primary manufacturer.

As for the latest aircraft, the book includes aircraft which have flown by the cut-off date of mid-1999. Some airliners which will fly at a later date are therefore not included but are usually mentioned in the text. Look for them in the next edition of *Airliners of the World*!

Finally, I would like to thank Don Stephens and Juanita Franzi for their cover artwork, and as always, my thanks go to Jim Thorn and the crew at Aerospace Publications for their ongoing and much valued support. In particular thank you to Gerard Frawley for allowing me access to some of his research material, Ian Hewitt for starting the arduous process of sourcing the photographs – and Scott Mason for finishing it – and production manager Gayla Wilson, who has worked with me for the first time in that capacity and done an excellent job.

Stewart Wilson
Buckingham 1999

Published by Aerospace Publications Pty Ltd (ACN: 001 570 458) PO Box 1777, Fyshwick, ACT 2609, Australia.
Phone (02) 6280 0111, fax (02) 6280 0007, e-mail mail@ausaviation.com.au and website
www.ausaviation.com.au – publishers of monthly *Australian Aviation* magazine.
Production Manager: Gayla Wilson

ISBN 1 875671 44 7

Proudly Printed in Australia by Pirie Printers Pty Ltd, 140 Gladstone St, Fyshwick, ACT 2609.
Distributed throughout Australia by Network Distribution Company, 54 Park St, Sydney, 2000. Fax (02) 9264 3278
Distributed in North America by Motorbooks International, 729 Prospect Ave, Osceola, Wisconsin, 54020, USA.
Fax (715) 294 4448. Distributed throughout Europe and the UK by Airlife Publishing Ltd, 101 Longden Rd,
Shrewsbury SY3 9EB, Shropshire, UK. Fax (743) 232944.

FRONT COVER: Don Stephens' especially commissioned painting depicts (from left to right, top to bottom): Junkers Ju 52/3m, Douglas DC-3, Boeing 747-400, Fokker F27 Friendship, Handley Page HP.42 'Hannibal', de Havilland DH.114 Heron 2, BAC-Aerospatiale Concorde, Short S.23 Empire, Vickers Viscount 700, Lockheed L.1049 Super Constellation, Tupolev Tu-124, Boeing 707-120, de Havilland Comet 4, Airbus A300B.

MILESTONES OF COMMERCIAL AVIATION

An airliner which can be described as truly revolutionary, the Boeing 747 was the world's first widebody jet and ushered in the age of mass air travel. The prototype first flew on 9 February 1969 and Pan American began services – with the aircraft in January 1970. (Boeing)

1 January 1914: The world's first scheduled commercial aeroplane service (between St Petersburg and Tampa, Florida) is conducted by the appropriately named St Petersburg-Tampa Airboat Line using a Benoist Type XIV flying boat. The pilot was Anthony Jannus and the single passenger – Mr A Phiel – paid $US5 for the 16nm (29km) journey.

9 May 1917: The Boeing Airplane Company established on Lake Union near Seattle. William (Bill) Boeing and his partner Conrad Westervelt had previously established the Pacific Aero products Company in July 1916.

5 February 1919: Deutsche Luft-Reederei starts the world's first sustained daily passenger airline service between Berlin and Weimar.

1 May 1919: Publication of the Air Navigation Regulations in Britain allows civil aviation activities to resume.

15 May 1919: The first section of the US transcontinental airmail service (between Chicago and Cleveland) is inaugurated by the US Post Office. Full transcontinental mail flights between San Francisco and New York start on 22 February 1921 using DH.4Ms and taking 1½ days in 14 sectors. Daily scheduled flights between the two cities begin on 1 July 1924.

31 May 1919: Lt Cdr A C Read USN commands the first trans-Atlantic crossing by air in a Curtiss NC-4 flying boat stopping at Nova Scotia, Newfoundland, the Azores, Portugal, Spain and ending at Plymouth, England.

January 1914 – the Benoist Type XIV prepares for the world's first scheduled commercial aeroplane service between St Petersburg and Tampa, Florida.

14-15 June 1919: The first non stop crossing of the Atlantic by air, between St John's, Newfoundland and Clifden, Ireland, completed by Capt John Alcock and Lt Arthur Whitten Brown in a Vickers Vimy. Flying time is 16hr 27min.

25 June 1919: The world's first all metal airliner, the Junkers F 13, records its first flight.

25 August 1919: Aircraft Transport and Travel Ltd inaugurates the world's first scheduled daily international airline service between Hounslow (England) and Le Bourget (France). The aircraft is a DH.16.

7 October 1919: The world's oldest surviving airline, *Koninklijke Luchtvaart Maatschappij voor Nederland an Kolonien* (KLM Royal Dutch Airlines) is formed.

1 November 1919: The first American scheduled international passenger service is inaugurated by Aeromarine West Indies Airways between Key West (Florida) and Havana (Cuba).

10 December 1919: Australian brothers Capt Ross and Lt Keith Smith complete the first England to Australia flight in a Vickers Vimy.

1 November 1920: Aeromarine West Indies Airways is awarded the first contract for foreign mail by the US Post Office.

14 December 1920: Britain suffers its first scheduled commercial airline fatal accident when a Handley Page O/400 crashes in fog at Cricklewood shortly after taking off.

19 March 1921: The British Government introduced subsidies to help Handley Page Air Transport and Instone Air Lines to compete with French carriers on the London-Paris route.

7 April 1922: The first mid air collision between passenger carrying airliners on scheduled services between a Daimler Airways DH.18 and a Grands Express Aériens Farman Goliath over Thieuloy-Saint-Antoine, France. All seven passengers and crew die.

1 April 1924: Formation of Imperial Airways, Britain's first national airline company. It is established by combining Handley Page Air Transport, Daimler Airways, Instone Air Lines and the British Marine Air Navigation Company.

28 September 1924: Two Douglas World Cruisers return to Seattle after completing the first around the world flight in a flying time of 371hr 11min. Four DWCs had left Seattle on 6 April of which one crashed in Alaska early in the flight and another force landed in the Atlantic near the Faeroe Islands.

The Vickers Vimy was responsible for two epochal aviation events in 1919: the first non stop crossing of the Atlantic by air (Alcock and Brown), and the first England to Australia flight (the Smith brothers).

The world's first all metal airliner, the Junkers F 13, first flown on 25 June 1919.

First flown on 4 September 1925, the Fokker F.VII/3m was the first trimotor airliner. This is an F.VIIb/3m privately owned by Belgian financier Albert Loewenstein.

The largest aircraft in the world before WWII, the Dornier Do X flew with a staggering 169 people on board on 21 October 1929 – nine of whom were stowaways!

Arguably the most significant airliner of them all, the Douglas DC-3 (first flight 17 December 1935).

4 September 1925: First flight of the Fokker F.VII/3m, the first trimotor airliner.

16 June 1926: Imperial Airways' London-Paris service becomes fully self supporting with the introduction of the Armstrong Whitworth Argosy on the route. In May 1927 the airline introduced the world's first luxury air service on the same route and with the same aircraft, offering 'Silver Wing' lunches and other attractions.

20-21 May 1927: Capt Charles Lindbergh completes the first non stop solo crossing of the Atlantic in his Ryan NYP *Spirit of St Louis*. The flight from Long Island, New York to Paris takes 33hr 39min.

31 May-9 June 1928: Capt Charles Kingsford Smith and Charles Ulm complete the first trans-Pacific flight in their Fokker F.VIIB/3m *Southern Cross*, travelling from San Francisco to Brisbane via Honolulu and Suva. Flying time is 83hr 38min.

21 October 1929: The Dornier Do X flying boat (first flight July 1929) and the largest aircraft of its type built before WWII, takes off with 169 people on board: ten crew, 150 passengers – and nine stowaways!

13 October 1930: First flight of the Junkers Ju 52 all metal single engined transport. The important Ju 52/3m trimotor version flies in April 1931.

1932: The Soviet national airline *Grazdansiy Wozdusniy Flot* or Aeroflot is formed out the previous airline Dobroflot.

8 February 1933: First flight of the Boeing 247, regarded by many as the first 'modern' airliner with its all metal monoplane construction and retractable undercarriage. It enters service with United Air Lines in March 1933 but loses in the marketplace to the Douglas DC-2.

I July 1933: The first 'Douglas Commercial', the DC-1, flies for the first time. It leads to the first of the series, the DC-2 (first flight 11 May 1934).

18 January 1934: Qantas Empire Airways joins Imperial Airways to fly the final leg of the Empire air service route from England to Australia. Operations begin on 10 December 1934 and weekly scheduled services between Brisbane and London begin on 13 April 1935, Qantas flying the early sectors.

The Boeing 247, regarded by many as the first 'modern' airliner. First flown on 8 February 1933, it was of all metal construction and featured retractable undercarriage.

In one of the most significant but often unheralded long distance flights, this Focke-Wulf Fw 200S-1 Condor flew non stop from Berlin to New York in August 1938, the journey taking 25 hours.

The Boeing 307 Stratoliner, the first pressurised airliner. First flown on 31 December 1938, it entered service with TWA in April 1940.

The world's first turboprop airliner, the Vickers Viscount. First flown on 16 July 1948, it entered regular service with BEA in April 1953. This is a later V.806 variant. (Dave Fraser)

The prototype de Havilland Comet, the first jet airliner. First flown on 27 July 1949, BOAC began jet services in May 1952 but the early model Comets were grounded two years later after a series of accidents.

The origin of the Boeing jet airliner species. The Model 367-80 ('Dash 80') first flew on 15 July 1954, serving as the prototype for the commercial 707 and the military C-135 families. This shot was taken during the aircraft's final flight in 1981. (Boeing)

20 October 1934: Start of the MacRobertson England to Australia Air Race to celebrate the centenary of Australian state Victoria's foundation. The race is won by Charles Scott and Tom Campbell-Black in the DH.88 Comet racer *Grosvenor House*, but a KLM Douglas DC-2 proves the viability of commercial air transport by finishing second outright and first in the handicap section.

22 November 1935: Pan American Airways operates the first scheduled trans-Pacific airmail service from San Francisco to the Philippines via Honolulu, Midway Island, Wake Island and Guam. The aircraft used is the Martin M.130 flying boat *China Clipper*.

17 December 1935: First flight of the Douglas DC-3, one of the true revolutionary milestones of commercial aviation.

30 October 1936: Imperial Airways introduces the Short S.23 C-Class 'Empire' flying boat to service.

21-22 July 1938: The upper part of the Short-Mayo composite, the *Mercury* seaplane, flies the Atlantic non stop carrying mail and newspapers after having detached from its mother aircraft *Maia*, a modified Empire flying boat. The destination was Montreal, Canada.

August 1938: A Deutsche Luft Hansa Focke-Wulf Fw 200 Condor flies non stop from Berlin to New York in 25 hours.

31 December 1938: First flight of the Boeing 307 Stratoliner, the world's first pressurised airliner. It enters service with TWA in April 1940.

20 May 1939: Pan American Airways starts the first regular trans-Atlantic airmail service, from New York to Lisbon and Marseilles with the Boeing 314 flying boat *Yankee Clipper*.

3 August 1939: The state owned British Overseas Airways Corporation (BOAC) is formed by an Act of Parliament, amalgamating Imperial Airways and British Airways.

4 August 1939: The BOAC Short Empire flying boat *Caribou* performs the first British trans-Atlantic airmail service between Britain, Canada and the USA. Flight refuelling from a Handley Page Harrow tanker is used (the first for a commercial flight), the technique having been tested earlier in the year.

Late 1942: First meetings of the Brabazon Committee, established to determine Britain's postwar commercial aviation needs and define specifications for the necessary aircraft. From this came the world's first pure jet and turboprop airliners, the de Havilland Comet and Vickers Viscount plus other types such as the de Havilland Dove.

1 January 1946: Britain's wartime ban on civil aviation lifted.

February 1946: Britain's state owned European carrier, the British European Airways Corporation (BEA), established.

6 April 1948: First flight of Vickers Viking powered by two Rolls-Royce Nene turbojets instead of the usual Bristol Hercules piston engines – in effect the world's first jet airliner.

16 July 1948: First flight of the Vickers Viscount, the world's first purpose built and production turboprop airliner.

27 July 1949: First flight of the de Havilland Comet, the world's first purpose built jet airliner.

10 August 1949: First flight of the world's second purpose

The de Havilland Comet 4, first commercial jet across the Atlantic in October 1958. (Bill Dougan)

The Boeing 707, the airliner which introduced jet travel on a large scale. Pan American operated its first 707 commercial flight in October 1958.

built jet airliner, the Avro Canada Jetliner. It did not go into production.

29 July 1950: The prototype Vickers Viscount conducts the first turboprop airliner flight with fare paying passengers on board. The trip is between London (Northolt) and Paris (Le Bourget). Of the 26 passengers, 14 were fare paying and the remainder guests of the BEA and Vickers.

22 January 1952: The de Havilland Comet 1 is awarded its Certificate of Airworthiness by the British Ministry of Civil Aviation, officially becoming the world's first jet airliner.

2 May 1952: The world's first commercial jet passenger service flown, a BOAC Comet 1 travelling from London Heathrow to Johannesburg via Rome, Cairo, Khartoum, Entebbe and Livingstone. Thirty passengers were on board for the 23hr 37min journey.

18 April 1953: BEA inaugurates the world's first regular turboprop airliner service between London and Cyprus via Rome and Athens. A London to Istanbul service started the next day.

15 July 1954: First flight of the Boeing 367-80 ('Dash 80'), prototype for the 707/C-135 series of airliners and military tanker/transports.

27 May 1955: First flight of the Sud Aviation Caravelle, the first airliner specifically designed for short haul jet services and the first with widely copied rear mounted engines. Air France introduced it to service in May 1959.

17 June 1955: First flight of the Soviet Union's first jet airliner, the Tupolev Tu-104.

15 September 1956: The world's second jet airliner to be put into service, the Tupolev Tu-104, begins operations with Aeroflot on the Moscow-Irkutsk route.

19 December 1957: BOAC inaugurates the first trans-Atlantic passenger service with a turboprop aircraft, the Bristol Britannia.

20 December 1957: Maiden flight of the first 'proper' Boeing 707, a -121 for Pan American.

14 January 1958: Qantas starts the first around-the-world scheduled airline service, with Lockheed Super Constellations.

4 October 1958: A BOAC Comet 4 conducts the world's first trans-Atlantic commercial jet service between London

and New York via Gander, beating Pan American's Boeing 707 service by three weeks.

26 October 1958: Pan American introduces the Boeing 707 to service on the trans-Atlantic route, the inaugural flight between New York and Paris.

1959: For the first time, more passengers cross the Atlantic by air than by sea.

19 May 1959: First flight of the Boeing 707-420 with Rolls-Royce Conway turbofans, the initial production application for this type of jet engine. The first airliner with Pratt & Whitney JT3D turbofans flew in June 1960.

29 July 1959: Qantas inaugurates the first jet airliner service across the Pacific with Boeing 707s.

10 October 1959: Pan American introduces the first jet around-the-world service with Boeing 707s.

15 October 1959: Qantas launches the first jet service between Australia and Europe with Boeing 707s.

1960: The rationalisation of the British aircraft industry: Hawker Siddeley (already comprising Armstrong Whitworth, Avro, Gloster and Hawker) acquires Blackburn, Folland and de Havilland in accordance with government policy. Bristol,

The Tupolev Tu-144, the world's first supersonic transport to fly (31 December 1968), the first to exceed Mach 1 and the first to enter limited service. Unfortunately the Tu-144 failed to achieve its design aim of operating regular passenger services. This is a later model Tu-144D with numerous changes over the earlier versions.

English Electric, Vickers and Hunting are grouped together under the British Aircraft Corporation (BAC) banner.

21 August 1961: A Rolls-Royce Conway powered Douglas DC-8 Srs.40 becomes the first airliner to exceed the speed of sound, reaching Mach 1.012 during a planned dive from 52,090ft (15,877m), itself a record for airliners. The aircraft was delivered to Canadian Pacific three months later.

2 October 1962: The Soviet Union's first turbofan powered airliner, the Tupolev Tu-124, enters service with Aeroflot.

9 February 1963: First flight of the Boeing 727 trijet, which became the world's best selling jet airliner (1832 built) until usurped by the same company's 737.

The Anglo-French Concorde was and remains the only supersonic transport to enter full, scheduled service. The prototype flew on 2 March 1969 and the type entered service with British Airways and Air France in January 1976.

Europe's Airbus Industrie was established in December 1970 and its first product – the A300 – flew on 28 October 1972. The A300 was also the world's first widebody twin and entered service with Air France in May 1974. (Airbus)

April 1967: Facing a cashflow crisis, Douglas Aircraft succeeds in finding an equity partner and is taken over by McDonnell to form the McDonnell Douglas Corporation.

8 August 1967: First flight of the Boeing 737 short to medium range twinjet, developed through three generations and numerous variants to become by far the world's best selling jet airliner with more than 4200 ordered and 3200 delivered by 1999.

31 December 1968: First flight of the Tupolev Tu-144, the world's first supersonic transport (SST).

9 February 1969: First flight of the Boeing 747, the first widebody airliner and one which revolutionised air travel, its large capacity reducing seat-mile operating costs and allowing airfares to be more affordable than ever before. The 747 was also the first civil aircraft to use the new generation of high bypass turbofans.

2 March 1969: First flight of the Anglo-French BAC-Sud Concorde supersonic transport.

15 June 1969: Aeroflot and Pan American inaugurate joint services between Moscow and New York using an Aeroflot Ilyushin Il-62.

22 January 1970: The Boeing 747 enters service with Pan American, the inaugural flight on the New York to London route.

December 1970: Establishment of the European airliner manufacturing consortium Airbus Industrie, the five partners and their financial interest comprising France's Aerospatiale (37.9%), Deutsche Aerospace Airbus (DASA, now DaimlerChrysler Aerospace 37.9%), Hawker Siddeley (now British Aerospace, 20%) and Spain's CASA (4.2%).

28 October 1972: First flight the Airbus A300, Airbus Industrie's first product and the world's first widebody twin engined airliner.

May 1974: The Airbus A300 enters service with Air France.

December 1975: The Tu-144 supersonic transport enters limited service carrying mail and freight between Moscow and Alma Ata in Kazakstan. Passenger services commence in November 1977 but the aircraft is withdrawn in June 1978.

21 January 1976: British Airways and Air France conduct the world's first commercial supersonic passengers services, simultaneously launching flights from London to Bahrain and Paris to Rio de Janeiro.

The Airbus A320, first flown on 22 February 1987 and the first airliner with digital fly-by-wire flight controls and advanced 'glass' cockpit. (Keith Gaskell)

Fokker – one of the world's oldest manufacturers and a name synonymous with airliners over more than seven decades – went bankrupt in March 1966. The Fokker 70 was its last design to enter production.

17 March 1977: The final rationalisation of the British aircraft industry: Hawker Siddeley Aviation, Hawker Siddeley Dynamics, the British Aircraft Corporation and Scottish Aviation merged to form a single state owned entity, British Aerospace (BAe). The company was floated on the Stock Exchange in January 1981 and fully privatised by 1985.

27 March 1977: The world's worst aviation disaster occurs when a Pan American 747 and a KLM 747 collide on the runway of Santa Cruz airport on Tenerife. 578 are killed.

22 November 1977: After a lengthy legal battle, Air France and British Airways inaugurate regular Concorde services from London and Paris to New York.

August 1984: Lockheed withdraws from the commercial aircraft business with the delivery of the final L-1011-500 TriStar, for the Algerian Government.

22 February 1987: First flight of the Airbus A320, the European consortium's first narrowbody airliner and the world's first airliner with digital fly-by-wire flight controls, sidestick controllers and advanced 'glass' cockpit.

28 September 1988: First flight of the Ilyushin Il-86, initial version of the Soviet Union's first (and so far only) family of widebody airliners which includes the improved Il-96.

17 August 1989: Qantas 747-400 VH-OJA *City of Canberra* sets a world record for civil aircraft by flying non stop from London to Sydney. It covered the distance of 9694nm (17,953km) in 20 hours 9 minutes.

10 May 1991: First flight of the Canadair Regional Jet, the first of a new generation of low capacity jet airliners for regional routes and a threat to the previous dominance of turboprops on these services.

12 June 1994: First flight of the Boeing 777 widebody twinjet, the company's first aircraft with fly-by-wire flight controls.

1996: The first global airline strategic alliance, the Star Alliance, is established, early members including United, Lufthansa, SAS, Thai International and Air Canada.

March 1996: One of the world's oldest established manufacturers, Fokker, is declared bankrupt. A few aircraft are completed afterwards, the last in April 1997.

4 August 1997: Boeing's takeover of McDonnell Douglas is completed, resulting in the disappearance of the Douglas name. All but one of MDC's airliner products are axed over the next few months, the surviving DC-9 derived MD-95 renamed the Boeing 717.

June 1999: The Ilyushin Il-96T becomes the first Russian airliner to be awarded US FAA certification.

June 1999: Boeing predicts a market for 20,150 new jet airliners with more than 50 seats over the next 20 years. Airbus predicts a need for 15,500 new jet airliners with more than 70 seats over the same period.

Powered by Pratt & Whitney PW2337 engines, the Ilyushin Il-96T freighter became the first Russian airliner to achieve US FAA certification, in June 1999. This is the prototype Il-96M passenger version. (Paul Merritt)

Aero Spacelines Guppy

Country of origin: USA.

Powerplants: 201 – four 4912ehp (3663kW) Allison 501-D22C turboprops; four bladed propellers.

Performance: 201 – max cruise 250kt (463km/h) at 20,000ft; economical cruise 220kt (407km/h) at 20,000ft; max payload range 440nm (815km); max range 2540nm (4705km).

Weights: 201 – operating empty 45,360kg (100,000lb); max takeoff 77,112kg (170,000lb); max payload 24,494kg (54,000lb).

Dimensions: 201 – wing span 47.62m (156ft 3in); length 43.84m (143ft 10in); height 14.78m (48ft 6in); wing area 182.5m^2 (1965sq ft).

Capacity: Hold volume 1104m^3 (39,000cu ft); length 33.98m (111ft 6in); max width 7.64m (25ft 1in); max height 7.77m (25ft 6in).

Production: 1 Pregnant Guppy, 1 Super Guppy, 1 Mini Guppy, 1 Guppy-101, 4 Guppy-201, total 8 conversions.

History: Best known in recent years for its role in transporting large aircraft components from the Airbus Industrie production centres in Europe and the UK to the final assembly lines at Toulouse and Hamburg, the Guppy family of outsize cargo transports originated in the early 1960s. All were conversions based on the Boeing Model 377 Stratocruiser/C-97 Stratofreighter, a perhaps delightful irony considering the current rivalry between Boeing and Airbus.

Jack Conroy's Van Nuys, California based Aero Spacelines conceived the idea and with two exceptions the Guppy conversions were performed on its behalf by neighbours On Mark Engineering. First to fly was the B-337PG Pregnant Guppy on 19 September 1962, the conversion involving lengthening the donor Stratocruiser's fuselage by 5.08m (16ft 8in) and adding a 6.20m (20ft 4in) circular section 'bubble' in place of the normal upper fuselage lobe. The original 3500hp (2610kW) Pratt & Whitney R-4360 Wasp Major engines were retained. The Pregnant Guppy entered service in July 1963 operating under contract to NASA and carrying items such as Saturn S-IV rocket stages.

The B-337SG Super Guppy (based on a C-97J) flew in August 1965. This represented a more extensive conversion with the fuselage further lengthened, wing span increased, an even larger fuselage upper lobe fitted, a taller fin installed and the piston engines replaced by 7000shp (5220kW) P&W T34 turboprops. The B-337MG Mini Guppy (first flight May 1967) retained the piston engines but had a smaller upper lobe and swing tail. The Guppy-101 (March 1970) was the first with Allison 501 turboprops and featured the largest lobe size, taller fin and a hinged nose for straight-in loading.

The Guppy-201 was similar but intended for the carriage of large airframe components. The first example flew on 24 August 1970 and the second two years later. Both were purchased by Aerospatiale for operation by Aeromaritime to transport Airbus components. A further two conversions were subsequently performed for Airbus by France's UTA Industries in 1982-83. Airbus began replacing its four Guppys with A300-600ST Super Transporters (which see) from late 1995 and the last was disposed of at the end of 1998.

Photo: Guppy-201 (Airbus).

Airbus A300B2/4

Country of origin: European consortium.

Powerplants: Two 51,000lb (226.8kN) General Electric CF6-50C or 53,000lb (235.7kN) Pratt & Whitney JT9D-9 turbofans.

Performance: B2-200 – High speed cruise 496kt (917km/h), typical long range cruise 457kt (847km/h); range with 251 passengers 1850nm (3426km). B4-200 – range with 269 passengers 2900nm (5372km); max fuel range 3400nm (6300km).

Weights: B2-200 – operating empty 85,910kg (189,395lb), max takeoff 142,000kg (313,051lb). B4-200 – operating empty 88,500kg (195,106lb), max takeoff 165,000kg (363,756lb).

Dimensions: Wing span 44.84m (147ft 1in), length 53.62m (175ft 11in), height 16.53m (54ft 3in); wing area 260.0m^2 (2799sq ft).

Accommodation: Typically 269 passengers in two classes or up to 336 economy class passengers eight abreast.

Production: 520 A300Bs of all models ordered by July 1999 of which 483 delivered. A300B1/2/4 – 251 built.

History: The Airbus A300 is significant not only for being a commercial success in its own right, but for being the first design of Europe's most successful postwar airliner manufacturer.

After several years of design studies and preliminary work, Aerospatiale of France, CASA of Spain, the forerunners of Germany's DaimlerChrysler Aerospace (DASA) and British Aerospace formally established the Airbus Industrie consortium in 1970 specifically to develop a twin engined 300 seat widebody 'air bus' to fill an identified market gap.

The original design evolved into a smaller 250 seater, the A300 designation gaining a 'B' suffix to denote the change. Two prototype A300B1s were built, the first of these flying from Toulouse, France on 28 October 1972, the second on 5 February 1973. The General Electric CF6 was the powerplant choice for initial A300s. Following the prototype A300B1s was the 2.65m (8ft 8in) longer A300B2, the first production version of which first flew in April 1974. The B2 entered service with Air France in May 1974 but sales were slow for some years and it was not until 1978 (and a substantial order from the USA's Eastern Airlines) that the critical breakthrough was made and the programme took off.

Variants are the B2-200 with Krueger leading edge flaps and different wheels and brakes; B2-300 with increased weights for greater payload and multi stop capability; the B4-100 longer range version of the B2 with Krueger flaps; and the increased max takeoff weight B4-200 which featured reinforced wings and fuselage, improved landing gear, additional fuel and much improved payload-range performance. Small numbers of A300C convertibles were also built with a main deck freight door. An optional two crew flight deck (without flight engineer) was offered late in the A300B4's production life as the A300-200FF.

Production of the A300B4 ceased in May 1984, with manufacture switching to the improved A300-600. Older A300s are now finding a useful niche as freighters, with a number of companies, in particular DaimlerChrysler Aerospace Airbus and British Aerospace offering conversion programmes.

Photo: Airbus A300B4-200 (Airbus).

Airbus A300-600

Country of origin: European consortium.

Powerplants: Two 59,000lb (262.4kN) General Electric CF6-80C2A1; 61,500lb (273.6kN) CF6-80C2A5; 56,000lb (249.1kN) Pratt & Whitney PW4156 or 58,000lb (258.0kN) PW4158 turbofans.

Performance: A300-600R – max cruise 484kt (897km/h); long range cruise 472kt (874km/h); range with 267 passengers and standard fuel and CF6 engines 4050nm (7500km), 4070nm (7540km) with PW4000s. A300-600 – range with 267 passengers 3600nm (6670km). A300-600F – max payload range 2650nm (4908km).

Weights: A300-600 – operating empty with CF6s 90,065-90,115kg (198,556-198,666lb); max takeoff 165,900kg (365,740lb). A300-600R – operating empty 90,965-91,040kg (200,550-200,700lb); max takeoff 170,500kg (375,880lb) or optionally 171,700kg (378,527lb). A300-600F – (CF6) operating empty 78,335kg (172,6960lb); max takeoff 170,500kg (375,880lb).

Dimensions: Wing span 44.84m (147ft 1in); length 54.08m (177ft 5in); height 16.62m (54ft 6.5in); wing area 260.0m² (2799sq ft).

Accommodation: Typically 266 passengers in two classes; maximum 375 passengers in high density layout. A300-600F – max payload 55,017kg (121,290lb).

Production: 520 A300s of all models ordered by July 1999 of which 483 delivered. A300-600 – 269 ordered and 232 delivered by June 1999.

History: The A300-600 family followed on from the earlier A300B4 and incorporated a number of significant improvements and refinements, foremost being a two crew flight deck with EFIS displays and fly-by-wire secondary control surfaces. The A300-600 is in many ways a very different aircraft to earlier models, taking advantage of the technical developments which had become available and borrowing several design and construction ideas from the A310.

Other changes include a slight increase in length and incorporation of the rear fuselage and smaller tailplane of the A310, space for two more seat rows, revised and simpler flaps, new digital avionics, small winglets (optional from 1989, standard from 1991), simplified systems, greater use of composites, new brakes and APU, more efficient engine options and improved payload/range performance through an extensive drag reduction programme on the airframe. The A300-600 was first flown on 8 July 1983 and deliveries began in March 1984 to Saudia.

The A300-600 was further developed into the longer range A300-600R, its extended range resulting from a fuel trim tank in the tailplane and higher maximum takeoff weight. First flown on 9 December 1987, American Airlines was the -600R's initial customer, receiving its first aircraft in April 1988.

Convertible freight/passenger versions of all variants of the A300 have been offered, as has the all freight A300F4-600. The first new build pure freighter A300, one of 36 on order for Federal Express, flew in December 1993. Airbus also offers conversion packages of existing passenger A300s into freighters with a port side forward freight door, strengthened floor and associated freight handling equipment.

Photo: Aibus A300-600R.

Airbus A300-600ST

Country of origin: European consortium.

Powerplants: Two 59,000lb (262.4kN) General Electric CF6-80C2A8 turbofans.

Performance: Max cruising speed 421kt (780km/h); range with 40 tonnes (88,183lb) payload 1296nm (2400km); range with 30 tonnes (66,138lb) payload 2160nm (4000km).

Weights: Max takeoff 155,000kg (341,700lb).

Dimensions: Wing span 44.83m (147ft 1in); length 56.16m (184ft 3in); height 17.22m (56ft 6in); wing area 260.0m² (2799sq ft).

Capacity: The A300-600ST's maximum payload of 47 tonnes (103,615lb) is unlikely to be fully utilised, as the emphasis of the design is on volume rather than payload. The internal main cabin volume is 1400m³ (49,442cu ft), and can carry a range of oversize components, such as a fully equipped A330 or A340 wing shipset, or two A320/321 wing shipsets, or two A310 fuselage sections (front and rear). Internal useable length 37.70m (123ft 8in), diameter 7.39m (24ft 3in).

Production: Original order for four delivered to Airbus Industrie by late 1998 with option on fifth converted to firm order for delivery in 2001.

History: The A300-600ST Super Transporter was designed to replace Airbus Industrie's Super Guppy (Boeing 377 conversions) transports, used by the manufacturer to ferry oversize components such as wings and fuselage sections between the Airbus partners' plants throughout western Europe.

Development of the A300-600ST (nicknamed Beluga and also Super Flipper) began in August 1991. The A300-600ST's tight development programme – for what in many ways is effectively a new aircraft – resulted in the transport being rolled out in June 1994, with first flight on 13 September of that year.

The A300-600ST then entered a 400 hours flight test programme which culminated in the awarding of certification in September 1995. The first delivery and entry to service with Airbus occurred in January 1996.

All of the first four on order had been delivered by mid 1998 which allowed retirement of the Super Guppy in October 1997. The fifth Super Transporter is scheduled to be delivered in 2001.

The A300-600ST is based on the A300-600 airliner, with which it shares the wing, lower fuselage, main undercarriage and cockpit. The fuselage has been extensively modified incorporating a bulged main deck, new forward lower fuselage, enlarged tail with winglets and an upwards opening main cargo door.

A design study for a similarly configured A340, the A340ST Mega Transporter, to carry components for the A3XX very large airliner was being undertaken in 1998-99.

Programme management of the A300-600ST is the responsibility of the Special Aircraft Transport Company, or SATIC, an economic interest grouping formed on a 50/50 basis by Aerospatiale and DASA operating on behalf of Airbus Industrie. While much of the work on the aircraft is performed by the Airbus partners, other European companies are also involved in the programme.

Photo: Airbus A300-600ST (Airbus)

Airbus A310

Country of origin: European consortium.

Powerplants: Two 48,000lb (213.5kN) Pratt & Whitney JT9D-7R4D1; 50,000lb (222.4kN) General Electric CF6-80A3; 53,500lb (238.0kN) CF6-80C2A2; 59,000lb (262.4kN) CF6-80C2A8; 52,000lb (231.2kN) PW4152 or 56,000lb (249.1kN) PW4156 turbofans.

Performance: A310-200/300 – max cruise 484kt (896km/h); long range cruise 459kt (850km/h). A310-200 – range with 218 passengers 3670nm (6798km). A310-300 – range with 218 passengers and CF6 engines 4310nm (7983km) or 5170nm (9576km) at high gross weight option.

Weights: A310-200 with CF6-80C2A2s – operating empty 80,142kg (176,680lb); max takeoff 142,000kg (313,050lb). A310-300 with CF6-80C2A8s – operating empty 81,205kg (179,025lb); max takeoff 150,000kg (330,690lb) standard or up to 164,000kg (361,552lb) optional.

Dimensions: Wing span 43.89m (144ft 0in); length 46.66m (153ft 1in); height 15.80m (51ft 10in); wing area 219.0m² (2357sq ft).

Accommodation: Max passenger capacity 280 in nine abreast high density layout; typical two class arrangement for 212 passengers in two classes.

Production: 261 ordered by July 1999, of which 255 delivered.

History: The A310 first began life as the A300B10, one of a number of projected developments and derivatives of Airbus' original A300B airliner.

While based on the larger A300, the A310 introduced a number of major changes. The fuselage was shortened by 13 frames compared to the A300B reducing seating to typically 200-220 passengers and a new, highly efficient and higher aspect ratio wing of smaller span and area was developed by Airbus partner British Aerospace.

A new rear fuselage design, smaller horizontal tail surfaces and a two crew EFIS flight deck were incorporated as were fly-by-wire secondary flight controls, upgraded systems and the use of advanced construction materials in some areas. The engine pylons are common to suit the powerplant options – Pratt & Whitney JT9D, PW4000 or General Electric CF6.

The first A310 (with Pratt & Whitney engines) flew on 3 April 1982 following programme launch in July 1978. The first GE powered A310 flew in August 1982 while deliveries of both models began in March 1983 to Lufthansa and Swissair. Early production A310-200s lacked the small winglets that became a feature of later aircraft and were standard on the longer range A310-300 which carries an additional 7000kg (15,430lb) fuel load in the tailplane in combination with higher operating weights.

The first A310-300 (with Pratt & Whitney engines) flew in July 1985 and deliveries (to Swissair) began the following December. GE powered A310-300s entered service from April 1986, initially with Air India. The A310-200F freighter is available new build or as a conversion of existing aircraft. Thirteen A310s were converted to freighters for Federal Express by Airbus partner Daimler Benz (now DaimlerChrysler) Aerospace Airbus. The A310-200C convertible passenger/freighter first entered service with Dutch operator Martinair in November 1984.

Photo: Airbus A310-300. (Airbus)

Airbus A319

Country of origin: European consortium.

Powerplants: Two 22,000-23,500lb (97.8-104.5kN) CFM International CFM56-5A or International Aero Engines IAE V2500-A5 turbofans.

Performance: Max cruise 487kt (902km/h); economical cruise 454kt (841km/h); range with 124 passengers 1831nm (3391km) at standard takeoff weight, 3967nm (6848km) at increased maximum weight.

Weights: Operating empty 39,884kg (87,928lb); standard max takeoff 64,000kg (141,093lb) or optionally 75,500kg (166,446lb).

Dimensions: Wing span 33.91m (111ft 3in); length 33.84m (111ft 0in); height 11.80m (38ft 8½in); wing area 122.4m² (1318sq ft).

Accommodation: 124 passengers in a typical two class configuration; maximum 142 passengers six abreast.

Production: 603 ordered by July 1999 of which 145 delivered.

History: The A319 is in 1999 the smallest member of Airbus' highly successful single aisle airliner family currently in service, and competes with Boeing's 737-300 and 737-700.

The A319 programme was launched at the Paris Air Show in June 1993 on the basis of just six orders placed by International Lease Finance Corporation (ILFC) in late 1992 and the predicted better prospects of the commercial airliner market, which were subsequently realised. The first A319 airline order came from French carrier Air Inter (since merged into Air France), whose order for six was announced in February 1994.

Since then Swissair, Air Canada, Lufthansa, Northwest, United, US Airways and British Airways are among the major customers to order more than 550 A319s. All also operate or have A320s on order. The A319 flew for the first time on 25 August 1995 from the Airbus facility in Hamburg, Germany. European JAA certification and initial service entry with Swissair took place in April 1996.

The A319 is a minimum change, shortened derivative of the highly successful A320. The major difference between the two is that the A319 is shorter by seven fuselage frames, while in most other respects the A319 and A320 are identical.

Like the A321, A330 and A340, the A319 features Airbus' common two crew glass cockpit with sidestick controllers first introduced on the A320. There are significant crew training cost benefits and operational savings from this arrangement as the A319, A320 and A321 can all be flown by pilots with the same type rating, meaning that the same flight crew pool can fly any of the three types. Further, the identical cockpit means reduced training times for crews converting to the larger A330 and A340.

Like the A321, A319 final assembly takes place in Hamburg with DaimlerChrysler Aerospace Airbus. Final assembly of all other Airbus airliners, including the A320, is conducted at Toulouse A long range corporate version (the Airbus Corporate Jetliner) was launched in 1998 while the A319 also forms the basis for the new baby of the Airbus family, the further 'destretched' A318 107 seater which was under development in 1999 for first deliveries in 2002.

Photo: Airbus A319. (Airbus)

Airbus A320

Country of origin: European consortium.

Powerplants: Two 25,000-27,000lb (111.2kN-120.1kN) CFM International CFM56-5A1; 26,500lb (117.9kN) CFM56-5A3; 27,000lb (120.1kN) CFM56-5B4; 25,500lb (113.4kN) International Aero Engines IAE V2500-A1 or 26,500lb (117.9kN) V2500-A5 turbofans.

Weights: A320-200 – operating empty 42,175-42,220kg (92,978-93,078lb); max takeoff 73,500kg (162,037lb), 75,500kg (166,445lb) or 77,000kg (169,753lb).

Performance: A320-200 – max cruise 487kt (902km/h); economical cruise 454kt (841km/h); range with 150 passengers and CFM56s 2615-3045nm (4844-5640km) depending on maximum weight; range with V2500s (same conditions) 2632-3065nm (4875-5677km).

Dimensions: Wing span 34.09m (111ft 10in); length 37.57m (123ft 3in); height 11.760m (38ft 7in); wing area 122.4m^2 (1318sq ft).

Accommodation: Up to 179 passengers in six abreast high density layout; typical two class arrangement for 150 passengers.

Production: 2087 A319/320/321 ordered by July 1999 of which 1024 delivered. A320 – 1220 ordered and 743 delivered by July 1999.

History: A major contributor to Airbus Industrie's status as one of the world's two major airliner manufacturers, the A319/320/321 family is a significant sales success and a technological trailblazer. The 150 seat A320 is the original and so far most commercially successful member of the family.

The A320 is perhaps best known as the first airliner to introduce a fly-by-wire flight control system, where control inputs from the pilot are transmitted to the flying surfaces by electronic signals rather than mechanical means.

Apart from a small weight saving, the main advantage of fly-by-wire is that it is computer controlled, providing flight envelope protection (including stall protection) which makes it virtually impossible to exceed certain flight parameters such as 'g' limits and the aircraft's maximum operating speed and angle of attack.

Also integral to the A320 is the advanced electronic flight deck, with six fully integrated EFIS colour displays and innovative side stick controllers in place of conventional control columns.

The A320 also employs a relatively high percentage of composite materials compared to earlier designs. Two engines are offered, the CFM56 and IAE V2500.

The A320 was launched in March 1982 and the first of four CFM56 powered flight test aircraft flew on 22 February 1987. Certification was awarded in February 1988 with launch customer Air France taking delivery of its first aircraft in March that year. The first V2500 powered A320 flew in July 1988 and deliveries (to Cyprus Airways) began in May 1989.

The initial production version was the A320-100 of which only 21 were built before production switched to the definitive A320-200 with increased weights and fuel capacity, greater range and winglets. The first A320-200 delivery was to Ansett in November 1988.

The stretched A321 and shortened A319 are described separately. All three share a common pilot type rating.

Photo: Airbus A320-200. (Airbus)

Airbus A321

Country of origin: European consortium.

Powerplants: A321-100 – two 30,000lb (133.4kN) International Aero Engines V2530-A5 or CFM International CFM56-5B1 turbofans; 31,000lb (139.7kN) CFM56-5B2 optional. A321-200 – as for -100 or 32,000lb (142.3kN) CFM56-5B3 or 33,000lb (146.8kN) V2533-A5 turbofans.

Performance: A321-100 – max cruise 488kt (904km/h); economical cruise 447kt (828km/h); range with 186 passengers and V2530 engines 2350nm (4353km). A321-200 – range with 186 passengers 2650nm (4908km).

Weights: A321-100 – operating empty 47,776-47,900kg (105,326-105,600lb); max takeoff 83,000kg (182,980lb) or 85,000kg (187,390lb). A321-200 – operating empty 48,024-48,139kg (105,873-106,127lb); max takeoff 89,000kg (196,208lb).

Dimensions: Wing span 34.09m (111ft 10in); length 44.51m (146ft 0in); height 11.81m (38ft 9in); wing area 123.0m^2 (1320sq ft).

Accommodation: Maximum 220 passengers in high density layout six abreast; 199 in standard single class layout; typical two class arrangement 186 passengers.

Production: 2087 A319/320/321 ordered by July 1999 of which 1024 delivered. A321 – 264 ordered and 136 delivered by July 1999.

History: Like the shortened A319, the A321 is a minimum change, in this case stretched, development of the successful A320. The first aircraft flew on 11 March 1993 (as the first Airbus assembled in Germany) and deliveries to Lufthansa began in January 1994.

The A321's major modification over the A320 is the incorporation of a stretched (by 13 frames) fuselage with forward and rear plugs totalling 6.93m (22ft 9in) of which 4.26m (14ft 0in) is immediately forward of wing and 2.67m (8ft 9in) immediately aft.

Other changes include strengthening of the undercarriage to cope with higher weights, the option of more powerful engines, a simplified and refined fuel system and larger tyres for improved braking performance. The fly-by-wire control system and method of construction is identical to the A320.

A slightly modified wing with double slotted flaps and modifications to the flight controls allows the A321's handling characteristics to closely resemble the A320's. The A321 also features an identical flight deck to that of the A319 and A320, and shares the same type rating as the two smaller aircraft.

One compromise associated with the 'minimum change' concept applied to the basic A321-100 is that it has reduced range compared to the A320 as fuel tankage was not increased to compensate for the extra payload.

To overcome this Airbus launched the longer range, heavier A321-200 in 1995 with transcontinental USA range with full passenger load. This is achieved through fitting higher thrust V2533-A5 or CFM56-5B3 engines, minor structural strengthening and 2900 litres (766US gal/638Imp gal) greater fuel capacity with the installation of an additional centre section tank.

The A321-200 first flew from Daimler Benz (now DaimlerChrysler) Aerospace's Hamburg facility in December 1996.

Photo: Airbus A321-200. (Airbus)

Airbus A330-300

Country of origin: European consortium.

Powerplants: A330-300 – two 67,500lb (300.2kN) General Electric CF6-80E1A2; 64,000lb (284.7kN) Pratt & Whitney PW4164; 68,000lb (302.4kN) PW4168; 68,000lb Rolls-Royce Trent 768; 72,000lb (320.2kN) Trent 772 or 73,000lb (324.7kN) PW4173 turbofans.

Performance: A330-300 – max cruise 475kt (880km/h); economical cruise 464kt (859km/h); range with 335 passengers 4500-4640nm (8335-8595km); extended range version 5500nm (10,188km).

Weights: A330-300 – operating empty 121,870-122,460kg (268,673-269,973lb); max takeoff 212,000kg (467,372lb). Extended range version – operating empty 122,210-122,780kg (269,422-270,679lb); max takeoff 217,000kg (478,395lb).

Dimensions: Wing span 60.30m (197ft 10in); length 63.68m (208ft 11in); height 16.74m (54ft 11in); wing area 363.1m² (3908sq ft).

Accommodation: Typical seating for 295 passengers in three classes or 335 in two classes; maximum 440 passengers in high density configuration.

Production: 257 A330s of all models ordered by July 1999 of which 108 delivered. A330-300 – 187 ordered by July 1999.

History: The A330-300 is the largest member of the Airbus widebody twinjet family and is closely related to the four engined long range A340 with which it shares near identical systems, airframe, flight deck and wings, the major difference being the twin (versus four) engine configuration.

The A340 and A330 were launched simultaneously in June 1987 after an evaluation period which saw various innovations examined including the use of variable camber 'adaptive' wings in which the wing profile could be varied in flight to suit different phases of it through adjusting the Fowler flaps. This interesting idea was eventually dropped.

Although developed in parallel, the first A330-300 recorded its maiden flight more than a year after the A340, on 2 November 1992. It was the first aircraft to gain simultaneous European Joint Airworthiness Authorities (JAA) and US FAA certification, achieving this milestone in October 1993. Initial deliveries were made near the end of the same year with French domestic operator Air Inter inaugurating commercial services in January 1994.

Differences between the A330 and A340 (apart from the number of engines) revolve around slight changes to the wing and internal systems, including fuel tankage. The A330 (like the A340) takes advantage of a number of technologies first pioneered on the A320, including the common advanced EFIS flight deck with side stick controllers and fly-by-wire computerised flight control system.

While the standard A330-300 shares the same fuselage length as the A340-300, Airbus has studied various stretched (A330-400) and shortened (A330-100 and -200) versions of the aircraft. The shortened A330-200 was formally launched in 1996 as a long range 767-300ER competitor, and is described separately.

Photo: Airbus A330-300. (Airbus)

Airbus A330-200

Country of origin: European consortium.

Powerplants: Two 67,500lb (300.2kN) General Electric CF6-80E1A2; 64,000lb (284.7kN) Pratt & Whitney PW4164; 68,000lb (302.5kN) PW4168; 68,000lb (302.5kN) Rolls-Royce Trent 768 or 72,000lb (320.3kN) Trent 772 turbofans.

Performance: Max cruise 475kt (880km/h); economical cruise 464kt (859km/h); range with max passengers 6400nm (11,855km).

Weights: Operating empty 120,150-120,750kg (264,880-266,204lb) depending on engines; max takeoff 230,000kg (507,055lb).

Dimensions: Wing span 60.30m (197ft 10in); length 59.00m (193ft 7in); height 16.81m (55ft 2in); wing area 363.1m² (3908sq ft).

Accommodation: Typically 256 passengers in three classes or 293 passengers in two classes.

Production: 257 A330s of all models ordered by July 1999 of which 108 delivered. A330-200 – 70 ordered by July 1999.

History: The A330-200 is the newest member of Airbus Industrie's widebody twinjet family and swaps reduced passenger capacity with a shortened fuselage for increased range. It was developed in part as a replacement for the A300-600R and also as a competitor to the Boeing 767-300ER.

Airbus launched development of the A330-200 in November 1995 and International Lease Finance Corporation (ILFC) placed the first order (for 13) in February 1996. First flight was recorded on 13 August 1997 and certification awarded in April 1998. Initial deliveries took place in the same month.

The A330-200 is based on the A330-300 and shares near identical systems, airframe, flight deck and wings, the only major difference being the fuselage length. Compared with the A330-300 the A330-200 is 10 frames or 4.68m (15ft 4in) shorter. This allows the A330-200 to accommodate 256 passengers in a three class configuration, or alternatively 293 in two classes but carry them over a notably longer range.

Because of its decreased fuselage length the A330-200 features enlarged horizontal and vertical tail services to compensate for the loss of moment arm with the shorter fuselage. Another important change is the addition of a centre fuel tank, which increases the A330-200's range with typical passenger load by between 900nm and 1900nm (1665-3520km) over the various A330-300 powerplant and maximum weight combinations.

As with the A330, engine options are the General Electric CF6-80, Pratt & Whitney 4000 series and the Rolls-Royce Trent 700.

The General Electric powered A330-200 was the first to enter service, with Canada 3000 in May 1998, followed by the Pratt & Whitney version (with Austrian Airlines) in August 1998 and the Rolls-Royce powered model shortly afterwards. Other A330-200 customers by late 1998 (covering all three engine options) included ILFC, Korean Airlines, Emirates, Swissair, Sabena, Monarch, Asiana, TAM, Air Lanka and Leisure International.

Photo: Airbus A330-200. (Airbus)

Airbus A340

Country of origin: European consortium.

Powerplants: Four 31,200lb (138.8kN) CFM International CFM56-5C or 32,550lb (144.7kN) CFM56-5C3 turbofans.

Performance: A340-200 – max cruise 494kt (915km/h); economical cruise 475kt (880km/h); range with 263 passengers 7450nm (13,800km). A340-300 – range with 295 passengers 6700nm (12,410km).

Weights: A340-200 – operating empty 126,000kg (277,778lb); max takeoff 260,000kg (573,192lb). A340-300 – operating empty 129,800kg (286,155lb); max takeoff 260,000kg (573,192lb). A340-300E – operating empty 129,300-130,200kg (285,053-287,037lb); max takeoff 271,000kg (597,4443lb) or 275,000kg (606,261lb).

Dimensions: A340-200 – wing span 60.30m (197ft 10in), length 59.39m (194ft 10in); height 16.74m (54ft 11in); wing area 363.1m² (3908q ft). A340-300 – length 63.70m (209ft 0in).

Accommodation: A340-200 – typical three class arrangement for 263 passengers or 303 in two classes. A340-300 – typical three class accommodation for 303 passengers or 335 in two classes; maximum 440 in high density single class layout. Underfloor sleepers optional for both versions.

Production: 270 A340s of all models ordered by July 1999 of which 162 delivered.

History: The A340-200 and -300 are the initial variants of the four engined A340 family of long range widebodies. The A340 and closely related A330 were launched in June 1987, with the A340's first flight (a -300) occurring on 25 October 1991. The first A340-200 flew on 1 April 1992 and service with Lufthansa and Air France began in March 1993.

The A340 shares the flight deck (including side stick controllers and EFIS), plus fly-by-wire, basic airframe, systems, fuselage and wing with the twin engined A330 series. The four engined configuration is regarded as more efficient for long range flights (as twins need more power for a given weight for engine out takeoff performance) and is free from ETOPS restrictions.

The A340-300 has the same fuselage length as the A330-300, while the shortened A340-200 trades seating capacity for greater range. The A340-300E is available with increased maximum takeoff weights has a range of up to 7300nm (13,520km) with 295 passengers. The first A340-300Es were delivered to Singapore Airlines in April 1996.

The 275,000kg (606,260lb) maximum takeoff weight A340-8000 is based on the -200 but has extra fuel in three additional rear cargo hold tanks and offers an 8100nm (15,000km) range with 232 three class passengers. One has been built for the Sultan of Brunei.

In 1997 Airbus announced two new A340 variants, the stretched, heavier, ultra long range and much more powerful -500 and -600. Both will be powered by four 56,000lb (249.1kN) Rolls-Royce Trent 556 turbofans and have a larger wing and typical three class accommodation for 316 and 372 passengers, respectively. The A340-500 will be the longest range airliner in the world, capable of travelling 8500nm (15,745km), while the higher capacity -600 will have a range of 7500nm (13,890km). First flight (a -600) is planned for 2001 with first deliveries the following year.

Photo: Airbus A340-200. (Airbus)

Airco DH.4A

Country of origin: United Kingdom.

Powerplant: One 350hp (261kW) Rolls-Royce Eagle VIII V12; four bladed propeller.

Performance: Max speed 105kt (195km/h); range 217nm (402km).

Weights: Empty 1179kg (2600lb); max takeoff 1687kg (3720lb).

Dimensions: Wing span 12.92m (42ft 4½in); length 9.30m (30ft 6in); height 3.35m (11ft 0in); wing area 40.3m² (434sq ft).

Accommodation: Pilot and two passengers.

Production: 6295 DH.4s of all models of which 1449 built in Britain and 4846 in the USA. DH.4A – 22 conversions; numerous other civil conversions of ex military DH.4s.

History: Generally regarded as the best day bomber of World War I, the DH.4 was designed for the Aircraft Manufacturing Company (Airco) by chief designer and test pilot Geoffrey de Havilland, who later established his own firm under his own name when Airco failed, creating one of the most famous companies in aviation history.

The first DH.4 flew in August 1916 and the type was subsequently mass produced in Britain and the USA for the Royal Flying Corps and the US Army, the majority of production in fact performed in the USA. Apart from DH.4s built by Airco, manufacture was widely subcontracted: Berwick & Co, Glendower Aircraft, Palladium Autocars, Vulcan, Warring & Gillow and Westland in Britain; the Dayton Wright Airplane Co, Fisher Body Corp and Standard Aircraft in the USA. Rolls-Royce Eagle, BHP and Liberty engines were the usual powerplants.

Postwar, numerous conversions for civil use were performed in Britain and the USA for a variety of roles ranging from passenger transport to crop dusting. The 'formal' civil conversion was designated the DH.4A and originated in late 1918 when 13 were modified for use by 2 Squadron RAF for daily communications flights carrying a government official and his secretary between London and Paris during Treaty of Versailles negotiations.

The conversion involved fitting a hinged and glazed cabin roof over the rear fuselage under which two facing passengers sat. The upper mainplanes were moved 30cm (1ft) aft to maintain centre of gravity.

The RAF aircraft were subsequently sold to Handley Page but four other purely civil DH.4A conversions were performed by Airco for the Aircraft Transport & Travel Company. One of these was used for the first British commercial passenger service from Hounslow to Le Bourget. Other services (including to Amsterdam) were operated by AT&T before it ceased operations at the end of 1920.

Handley Page also produced DH.4As for use by its own airline (Handley Page Transport) and for Belgian operator SNETA. The final DH.4A conversion was produced by A V Roe & Co for shipping firm Instone & Co which first used it for the fast carriage of ships' papers and then – following the introduction of subsidies – on services to Paris operating as Instone Air Line. This aircraft made history in September 1922 when it won the first King's Cup race, Captain F L Barnard flying it from Croydon to Renfrew and back at an average speed of 123mph (198km/h).

Photo: Airco DH.4A of Instone Air Line.

Airco DH.16

Country of origin: United Kingdom.

Powerplant: One 320hp (239kW) Rolls-Royce Eagle VIII V12 or 450hp (335kW) Napier Lion W12; four bladed propeller.

Performance: Max speed 118kt (219km/h); cruising speed 87kt (161km/h); initial climb 1000ft (305m)/min; service ceiling 21,000ft (6400m); range 304-369nm (563-684km).

Weights: Empty 1431kg (3155lb); max takeoff 2155kg (4750lb).

Dimensions: Wing span 14.17m (46ft 6in); length 9.68m (31ft 9in); height 3.45m (11ft 4in); wing area 45.5m² (490sq ft).

Accommodation: Pilot and four passengers.

Production: 9 DH.16 conversions plus more than 110 other civil conversions of DH.9/9A.

History: The DH.16 was an extensive cabin conversion of the DH.9A day bomber, itself an improved variant of the DH.9 which was in turn a development of the original DH.4. The first DH.9 (converted from a DH.4) flew in July 1917 and the DH.9A in March 1918. Combined production exceeded 5500.

The DH.9 models formed the basis of several post World War I conversions along the lines to those which had been performed to create the DH.4A (see separate entry) with accommodation for a pilot and two passengers. Conversions were performed for a decade from 1919 by Airco, the Aircraft Disposal Co, the newly established de Havilland Aircraft Co (from 1920) and others. Operators included Aircraft Transport & Travel, Instone Air Lines, QANTAS, Handley Page Transport and many others around the world.

The DH.16 was a considerably more extensive conversion which doubled the civil DH.9's passenger capacity from two to four, in effect halving the seat-mile operating costs. The major modifications were the installation of a Rolls-Royce Eagle initially and a Napier Lion later, moving the pilot's cockpit forward to under the centre section and widening the rear fuselage to allow two facing pairs of passengers to be carried in a glazed cabin.

The first DH.16 flew in March 1919 and immediately entered service with Air Transport & Travel on joyriding flights. On 25 August 1919 it made air transport history by inaugurating British commercial operations by flying the first international passenger service between London and Paris. Noteworthy is the fact that the DH.16 entered commercial service a year before the DH.4A conversion.

Only nine DH.16s were produced up to June 1920, used mainly by AT&T from London/Croydon to Paris, Amsterdam and other points. The company only survived until December 1920 when its seven surviving aircraft were sold to the recently established KLM Royal Dutch Airlines. Previously, a chartered DH.16 had flown the inaugural KLM service in May 1920.

The de Havilland Aeroplane Hire Service took over two of the surviving ex AT&T/KLM DH.16s from July 1922 and operated them until January 1923 when one crashed. Another aircraft was supplied to the River Plate Aviation Company of Buenos Aires in April 1920 and remained in service until 1925.

Photo: Airco DH.16.

Airco/de Havilland DH.18

Country of origin: United Kingdom.

Powerplant: One 450hp (336kW) Napier Lion W12; three bladed propeller.

Performance: DH.18B – max speed 111kt (206km/h); cruising speed 87kt (161km/h); initial climb 660ft (201m)/min; service ceiling 16,000ft (4877m); range 348nm (644km).

Weights: DH.18A – empty 1833kg (4040lb); max takeoff 2956kg (6516lb). DH.18B – empty 1955kg (4310lb); max takeoff 3228kg (7116lb).

Dimensions: 15.61m (51ft 2³/₄in); length 11.89m (39ft 0in); height 3.96m (13ft 0in); wing area 57.7m² (621sq ft).

Accommodation: Pilot and up to eight passengers.

Production: 1 DH.18, 3 DH.18A, 2 DH.18B, total 6.

History: The first Airco product specifically designed for commercial passenger carrying and the company's last product before its liquidation, the DH.18 wire braced biplane of wooden construction resulted from the realisation that the growing number of air travellers and airlines were going to need better aircraft than just rough conversions of WWI types. It featured a relatively spacious cabin for eight passengers immediately behind the engine while the pilot sat in an open cockpit aft.

The DH.18 was important for the newly established de Havilland Aircraft Company. The prototype first flew in February 1920, built by Airco and just one month before the failing company's assets were taken over by the Birmingham Small Arms Company (BSA) and its activities wound down. Geoffrey de Havilland established his own firm in September 1920. As a result, the remaining five DH.18s were completed by de Havilland Aircraft, the first two from Airco components and the others from scratch.

The prototype entered service with Aircraft Transport & Travel in April 1920 on the Croydon to Paris route but was damaged beyond repair in August 1920 following an engine failure after takeoff from Croydon. AT&T itself failed in December 1920 and disappeared into BSA.

The next three aircraft were designated DH.18A and delivered to AT&T during 1920. These were purchased by the Air Council and transferred to Instone Air Line from March 1921 for services to the Continent. The Air Council was empowered to purchase aircraft and allocate them following the introduction of government subsidies for air services.

The final two aircraft were DH.18Bs with plywood covered fuselages, emergency exits and increased weights. They were delivered to Instone Air Line in December 1921 and January 1922. One was dismantled in 1923 and the other lost after a deliberate ditching off Felixstowe in May 1924 during a test to determine how long it could remain afloat – 25 minutes, sufficient to recover the Lion engine but the airframe was deemed expendable.

Daimler Hire operated one ex AT&T DH.18A for just two days in April 1922 on its Croydon-Paris service, the aircraft colliding with a Farman Goliath in bad visibility over northern France. This was the world's first collision between airliners. The last surviving aircraft was the first DH.18A, ending its days as a test bed at Farnborough until late 1927.

Photo: Prototype Airco DH.18.

Airspeed Ferry

Country of origin: United Kingdom.

Powerplants: Three 120hp (89kW) de Havilland Gipsy II/III or 120hp (89kW) Gipsy Major four cylinder inline engines; two bladed propellers.

Performance: Max speed 97kt (180km/h); cruising speed 87kt (161km/h); initial climb 800ft (244m)/min; service ceiling 15,500ft (4724m); range 265nm (547km).

Weights: Empty 1497kg (3300lb); max takeoff 2449kg (5400lb).

Dimensions: Wing span 16.76m (55ft 0in); length 12.09m (39ft 8in); height 4.34m (14ft 3in); wing area 56.7m² (610sq ft).

Accommodation: Pilot and 10 passengers.

Production: Four.

History: Although ordered for pleasure flying rather than airline operations and built in very small numbers (only four), the Ferry was significant in that it 'sold' the concept of safe, comfortable and fast — for the time — airline flying to thousands of Britons who paid for rides in aircraft operated by Sir Alan Cobham's 'flying circus'.

Cobham's National Aviation Day Displays were held all over the United Kingdom between 1932 and 1935, promoting aviation in general and the role of the airliner in particular. Cobham wanted a mini airliner specifically for short range 'joyflights' as part of this, capable of carrying a reasonable number of passengers and operating from small fields near the communities his shows visited.

Two A.S.4 Ferry aircraft were ordered in June 1931 at a price of £5195 each. A large three engined, 10 passenger biplane of wooden construction with plywood fuselage covering and fabric wing skinning, the Ferry was built specifically to Sir Alan's requirements. The Gipsy engines originally comprised two upright units on the lower wings and an inverted one on the upper wing centre section but inverted Gipsy Majors subsequently became the standard fitting.

The first Ferry – G-ABSI *Youth of Britain II* – flew on 5 April 1932 and was delivered just over two weeks later. A second Ferry (G-ABSJ *Youth of Britain III*) followed in early June. The aircraft were an immediate hit, visiting more than 200 towns and villages in their first season, between them making more than 9000 flights and carrying 92,000 passengers.

Two more aircraft were built in the first half of 1933 for Midland and Scottish Air Ferries, these aircraft operating services from Renfrew to Campbelltown, Belfast and Speke (Liverpool) over the next two years before the airline closed down and the aircraft disposed of.

Alan Cobham's second Ferry was sold to the Himalaya Air Transport and Survey Company in 1934, operating in India until it was destroyed by vandals at Delhi in October 1936. The National Aviation Day Displays ended in 1935 and the three British based Ferries ended up spending the next few years performing joyriding duties for company's such as C W A Scott's Air Displays and Air Publicity.

After that they faded away as Certificates of Airworthiness expired although the original Ferry was briefly used by Isle of Wight based Wight Aviation for its shuttle service before being impressed into RAF service with the outbreak of war in September 1939. It flew until late 1940.

Photo: Prototype A.S.4 Ferry.

Airspeed Envoy

Country of origin: United Kingdom.

Powerplants: I – two 185hp (138kW) Wolseley AR.9 Mk.1 nine cylinder, 220hp (164kW) Armstrong Siddeley Lynx IVc or 277hp (206kW) Armstrong Siddeley Cheetah V seven cylinder radials. II – Lynx IVc. III – two 260hp (194 kW) Walter Castor nine cylinder, 290hp (216kW) Wolseley Scorpio nine cylinder or 350hp (261kW) Cheetah IX radials; two bladed propellers.

Performance: I – max speed 148kt (274km/h); cruise speed 130kt (241km/h); initial climb 850ft (259m)/min; ceiling 17,000ft (5180m); range 347nm (644km). III – max speed 176kt (327km/h); cruise speed 148kt (274km/h); ceiling 22,000ft (6705m); range 539nm (998km).

Weights: I – empty 1561kg (3442lb); max takeoff 2404kg (5300lb). III – empty 1969kg (4340lb); max takeoff 2994kg (6600lb).

Dimensions: Wing span 15.95m (52ft 4in); length 10.51m (34ft 6in); height 2.90m (9ft 6in); wing area 31.5m² (339sq ft).

Accommodation: Pilot and 6-8 passengers.

Production: 16 Srs.I, 8 Srs.II, 26 Srs.III, 1 Viceroy, total 51 by Airspeed plus 10 by Mitsubishi.

History: Evolved from the single engined Airspeed A.S.5 Courier of 1933 (the first production British aircraft with retractable undercarriage), the A.S.6 Envoy twin was of the same wooden construction with plywood and fabric covering and powered by a large variety of different radial engines.

The prototype first flew on 26 June 1934 powered by Wolseley AR.9 radials but this engine was subsequently cancelled and most British and many export Envoys had Armstrong Siddeley Lynx or Cheetah engines. Four Series III aircraft sold to Czechoslovenske Statni Aerolinie (CSA) in 1935 were powered by local Walter Castor radials. Three series of Envoys were produced: the initial A.S.6/A Envoy I, A.S.6D Envoy II of 1936 with flaps and Lynx engines; and A.S.6E/J/K Envoy III models (1936) with split flaps and stressed ply wing skinning.

The sole A.S.8 Viceroy with windows blanked out and long range fuel tanks installed in the cabin was built for the 1934 MacRobertson England-Australia air race but only got as far as Athens. Following the delivery of six Envoy Is to the Japanese Air Transportation Co in mid 1935 for use on its Japan-Manchuria services, 10 were built under licence by Mitsubishi as the *Hina-Zuru* (Young Crane). Some of these were powered by Mitsubishi built Lynx engines and delivered to Japanese Air Transportation, Manchuria Air Transport and the Japanese military.

Other customers for the Envoy included Britain's North Eastern Airways, Olley Air Service, IOW Aviation and Cobham Air Routes, France's Air Pyrenees, Czechoslovakia's Victorise Mill and Steel Co and the Maharajahs of Jaipur and Indores. Perhaps the best known example was the A.S.6J Envoy III delivered to the King's Flight while the South African Air Force and South African Airways jointly purchased seven for military and civil use. These were convertible between roles and could be fitted with a dorsal turret and light bomb racks.

Australian aviation pioneer Charles Ulm and his copilot were lost in a Cheetah powered Envoy I when it went missing on the first stage of a trans-Pacific flight in December 1934. Fitted with cabin tanks, the aircraft had a range of up to 3100nm (5740km).

Photo: A.S.6 Envoy I.

Airspeed Consul

Country of origin: United Kingdom.

Powerplants: Two 395hp (295kW) Armstrong Siddeley Cheetah 10 seven cylinder radials; two bladed propellers.

Performance: Max speed 165kt (306km/h); cruising speed 136kt (251km/h); initial climb 1180ft (360m)/min; service ceiling 19,000ft (5790m); range 782nm (1448km).

Weights: Empty 2743kg (6047lb); max takeoff 3742kg (8250lb).

Dimensions: Wing span 16.25m (53ft 4in); length 10.77m (35ft 4in); height 3.38m (11ft 1in); wing area 32.3m^2 (348sq ft).

Accommodation: Pilot and passenger in cockpit plus six passengers in cabin.

Production: Approximately 150 conversions from Oxfords.

History: The Airspeed A.S.65 Consul was a civilian conversion of the wartime Oxford aircrew trainer and light transport, itself a derivative of the prewar Envoy and sharing that aircraft's wooden construction.

The first Oxford flew on 19 June 1937 and 8586 were subsequently built by Airspeed, de Havilland, Percival and Standard Motors for use as multi engined, bombing, gunnery, radio and navigation trainers plus communications, ambulance, anti aircraft calibration and radio/ radar trainer calibration roles during World War II. Several variants were built powered by Armstrong Siddeley Cheetah or Pratt & Whitney Wasp Junior radial engines.

The Consul conversions were performed by the manufacturer between 1946 and 1948, modifications for civil use including redesigning the cabin to accommodate six passengers, adding cabin windows, providing baggage space at the rear of the cabin, adding a partition between the cockpit and cabin, fitting a longer nose for the carriage of luggage and resetting the tailplane to help provide an extended centre of gravity range.

The prototype conversion first flew in early 1946 and achieved certification in March of the same year. Despite its lack of refinement, the Consul proved to be very popular with and suitable for British and overseas air taxi and local service operators trying to establish their industries in the aftermath of the war and while the arrival of more modern equipment was awaited.

Useful size and low initial purchase price coupled with reliability and low maintenance requirements were the Consul's main attributes along with ready availability. Of the approximately 150 conversions performed, over 100 initially went to some of the many British operators which sprung up from 1946 such as Morton Air Services, British Air Transport, Lancashire Aircraft, Air Enterprises, British Aviation Services and Steiner's Air Service. These aircraft were used extensively within the British Isles and also on longer distance charters which took them throughout Europe, the Near and Middle East and even South America.

Deliveries were also made to several overseas customers, especially in the Near East, French Colonial Africa and French Indo-China. Others were operated on behalf of the United Nations Commission in Israel, while Air Malta, Malayan Airways, Iberia, Union of Burma Airways, Aer Lingus and Airways (India) were all Consul operators. Some export Consuls were also used as ambulances and aerial survey aircraft.

Photo: A.S.65 Consul.

Airspeed Ambassador

Country of origin: United Kingdom.

Powerplants: Two 2625hp (1957kW) Bristol Centaurus 661 18-cylinder radials; four bladed propellers.

Performance: Max speed 271kt (502km/h); cruise speed 226-236kt (418-438km/h); initial climb 1250ft (381m)/min; range with 5285kg (11,650lb) payload 478nm (885km); max range 1365nm (2495km).

Weights: Empty 16,230kg (35,780lb); loaded 23,814kg (52,500lb).

Dimensions: Wing span 35.05m (115ft 0in); length 25.00m (82ft 0in); height 5.56m (18ft 3in); wing area 111.5m^2 (1200sq ft).

Accommodation: 47-60 passengers.

Production: 3 prototypes and 20 production aircraft.

History: Built to the Brabazon Committee's Requirement IIA of 1943 for a medium range type with twice the capacity of the Douglas DC-3 for use on postwar European routes, the Airspeed A.S.57 Ambassador sold in very small numbers despite being profitable and popular with passengers. Delays in getting the aircraft into production cost it orders from several operators and by the time it was available, the turboprop Vickers Viscount had taken centre stage.

Of all metal construction and pressurised, the prototype made its first flight on 10 July 1947 powered by Bristol Centaurus 130 engines. Production aircraft were powered by uprated Centaurus 661s with two-stage superchargers, fitted with split flaps and referred to as the Ambassador 2.

The second and third prototypes flew in August 1948 and May 1950, respectively, the latter to the full production standard. Meanwhile, in August 1948, British European Airways had placed what was to be the only order for the Ambassador, for 20 aircraft.

BEA received its first aircraft in August 1951 and following crew training and proving flights the first scheduled service was flown (to Paris) on 13 March 1952. By the end of 1955 it had achieved the highest utilisation rate of any BEA aircraft at an average 2230 hours per annum.

BEA's Ambassadors were named 'Elizabethan Class' in honour of the succession of Queen Elizabeth II and were fitted with 47 passenger seats. In later service with smaller operators this could increase to 60. The last Ambassador was delivered to BEA in March 1953 and the airline operated its final service with the type – from Cologne to London – in July 1958.

After that, the Ambassadors flew with several British independent operators including Autair, BKS Air Transport and Dan-Air. Foreign operators included Switzerland's Globe Air, Norway's Norronafly, the Royal Jordanian Air Force, the Sultan of Morocco and Australia's Butler Air Transport. Others ended their days as engine testbeds for Bristol and Rolls-Royce, and with the Decca Navigator Co as a flying laboratory.

One of the Ambassador's less fortunate claims to fame was the February 1958 crash of a BEA aircraft on takeoff from Munich Airport with the Manchester United football team on board. Most surviving Ambassadors were withdrawn from service in the 1967-69 period but two – the Decca aircraft and one operated by Dan-Air – survived until late 1971.

Photo: Prototype A.S.57 Ambassador.

Antonov/PZL Mielec An-2

Countries of origin: Soviet Union/Poland.

Powerplant: One 1000hp (746kW) Shvetsov ASh-62IR or PZL-Kalisz ASz-62IR nine cylinder radial; four bladed propeller.

Performance: An-2P – max speed 136kt (253km/h); cruising speed 103kt (191km/h); initial climb 710ft (216m)/min; service ceiling 14,435ft (4400m); max range 488nm (904km).

Weights: An-2P – empty 3450kg (7606lb); max takeoff 5500kg (12,125lb).

Dimensions: Wing span (upper) 18.18m (59ft 8in); wing span (lower) 14.24m (46ft 8½in); length 12.74m (41ft 9½in); height 4.01m (13ft 2in); wing area 71.5m² (770sq ft).

Accommodation: An-2P – 12 passengers three abreast or 1497kg (3300lb) freight.

Production: 3596 in Soviet Union, approximately 12,000 in Poland by PZL-Mielec by 1999 and about 1000 in China as Y-5, total approximately 16,600 by 1999.

History: One of the most remarkably versatile postwar aircraft, the An-2 has been in production in its various forms for more than five decades, fulfilling a multitude of civil and military roles.

The largest biplane still in operational service, the An-2 has proved itself to be one of the toughest and most reliable aircraft ever built and capable of operating from just about any cleared piece of land – or water and snow. It has served widely with Aeroflot and other airlines aligned with the Soviet *Bloc* including on scheduled services.

Oleg Antonov worked as a designer with the Yakovlev bureau but after WWII decided to establish his own organisation to design and develop a 'go anywhere, do anything' utility aircraft to meet a Soviet Agriculture and Forestry Ministry requirement. The resulting An-2 (NATO reporting name 'Colt') first flew on 31 August 1947 powered by a 760hp (567kW) Shvetsov ASh-21 radial engine. Production aircraft were fitted with the more powerful ASh-62.

The An-2 has excellent STOL performance thanks to its low speed flight capabilities helped by the large wing area and the electrically actuated automatic leading edge slots on the upper wings, and trailing edge slotted flaps and ailerons which can be used conventionally for roll control but can also droop to 20 degrees to complement the lower wings' full span slotted trailing edge flaps.

Production of the An-2 began at Kiev in September 1949, continuing there until 1962. Further production was undertaken in the Soviet Union at Dolgoprudnyi (Russia) in 1964-65 but most aircraft have been built by PZL-Mielec in Poland, the first example from that source flying in 1960. Low rate production continues in 1999. Chinese production as the Y-5 began in 1957 at Nanchang and remained there until 1968; current Chinese production is at Shijiazhuang. Of the PZL production total, more than 10,600 have been delivered to the Soviet Union/Russia/CIS.

Some of the civil An-2 variants produced over the years include the An-2P (passenger/freight), An-2L (firefighting), An-2S (agricultural), An-2V (floatplane), An-2M (Polish floatplane), An-2PK (executive version), An-2P-Photo (photo survey), An-2PR (television relay), An-2S (ambulance) and An-2T (Polish general purpose model). The turboprop powered An-3 was not proceeded with.

Photo: Antonov An-2P. (Bill Lines)

Antonov An-10 and An-12

Country of origin: Soviet Union.

Powerplants: An-10/12 – four 4015ehp (2994kW) Ivchenko AI-20K turboprops; four bladed propellers.

Performance: An-10A – max cruise 367kt (679km/h); economical cruise 340kt (629km/h); initial climb 1960ft (597m)/min; max payload range 658nm (1220km); max range 2200nm (4072km). An-12 – max cruise 361kt (668km/h); economical cruise 297kt (550km/h); max payload range 1080nm (2000km); max range 3075nm (5696km).

Weights: An-10A – max takeoff 54,000kg (119,048lb). An-12 – operating empty 35,100kg (77,381lb); max takeoff 61,000kg (134,480lb).

Dimensions: An-10A – wing span 38.00m (124ft 8in); length 34.00m (111ft 6in); height 9.83m (32ft 3in); wing area 121.7m² (1310sq ft). An-12 – length 33.10m (108ft 7in).

Accommodation: An-10A – normally 100 passengers five/six abreast, up to 130 passengers six/seven abreast. An-12 – max payload 20,000kg (44,092lb).

Production: Approximately 500 An-10/A and 1243 An-12.

History: Direct developments of the twin engined An-8 which appeared in 1956, the An-10 and An-12 (NATO reporting names 'Cat' and 'Cub') are civil and military versions, respectively, of the same basic design and were developed more or less in parallel. The An-12 in its standard form differs primarily in having a redesigned rear fuselage incorporating a loading ramp and a freight interior.

The first An-10 flew in March 1957 with Kuznetsov NK-4 turboprops but these were replaced by the more economical Ivchenko AI-20 in production aircraft. Development was protracted due to serious stability problems which resulted in the fitting of anhedral outer wing panels and the addition of various vertical and ventral fins.

Aeroflot began services from Simferopol in the Ukraine to Moscow and Kiev in July 1959 with the basic An-10 which accommodated 84 passengers and even had (for a very short time) a children's play room at the rear. The major production An-10A with 2.00m (6ft 7in) fuselage stretch entered service in February 1960 and served exclusively with Aeroflot until May 1972 when it was withdrawn following a crash.

The first An-12 flew in December 1957 and entered military service the following year to become the standard Soviet medium range paratroop and cargo transport. Elint and ECM versions were also developed and many were fitted with rear defensive guns. About one-third of the An-12's production run was of civil freighters delivered to Aeroflot, Polish Air Lines, Air Guinee, Iraqi Airways, Bulair and Egyptair. Production ended in 1972.

China's Shaanxi Aircraft Company builds several military and civil developments of the An-12 under the designation Y-8. Powered by four 4250shp (3169kW) Zhuzhou WJ6 turboprops, the prototype flew in December 1974. Civil models are the unpressurised Y-8B freighter, pressurised Y-8C for export (developed with the help of Lockheed), Y-8F livestock transport (up to 500 sheep or goats can be carried) and Y-8K 121 seat airliner with the rear loading ramp deleted.

Photo: Antonov An-12. (Keith Anderson)

Antonov An-22 Antheus

Country of origin: Soviet Union.

Powerplants: Four 15,000shp (11,185kW) Kuznetsov NK-12MA turboprops; eight bladed counter-rotating propellers.

Performance: Max speed 400kt (740km/h); cruise speed 313-345kt (580-639km/h); max payload range 2700nm (5000km); max range with 45,000kg (99,200lb) payload 5905nm (10,940km).

Weights: Operating empty 118,727kg (261,743lb); max takeoff 250,000kg (551,146lb).

Dimensions: Wing span 64.41m (211ft 4in); length 57.91m (190ft 0in); height 12.53m (41ft 1½in); wing area 345.0m² (3714sq ft).

Capacity: Unpressurised main cabin volume 3000m³ (22,600cu ft); max payload 80,000kg (176,367lb); pressurised cabin for 28-29 passengers on upper deck behind cockpit.

Production: Approximately 65.

History: The largest and heaviest aircraft in the world when it first appeared, the An-22 was intended as both a strategic military and commercial heavy lift freighter capable of carrying very large loads such as T-62 tanks and oil drilling equipment.

Design work began in 1962 and part of the An-22's design brief was that it should be able to operate from unprepared fields in remote areas of the Soviet Union such as Siberia. As a result, the aircraft features a 24 wheel main undercarriage design with each pair of wheels independently sprung. Tyre pressures can be changed from the cockpit to suit different airfield conditions.

For freight handling, the design incorporates winches and travelling gantries, while when the rear loading ramp is lowered a large door (which forms the underside of the rear fuselage) retracts upwards inside the fuselage to facilitate the loading of large vehicles.

A proposed airliner variant capable of carrying 724 passengers did not progress beyond the drawing board. The An-22 was allocated the NATO reporting name 'Cock'.

The prototype flew on 27 February 1965 and the first production aircraft the following year. After the completion of State Acceptance Trials, deliveries to the Soviet Air Force began in 1969. Early aircraft were dubbed simply An-22 and featured transparent nose glazings but most were built to An-22A standard with 'solid' noses and modifications to the fuel and other systems plus upgraded equipment. Production for the Soviet Air Force and Aeroflot was undertaken at a new assembly facility at Tashkent in Uzbekistan and ended in 1974.

The An-22 set 14 payload to height records in 1967 including one in which 100 tonnes (220,458lb) was carried to 25,748ft (7848m). Another was maximum payload lifted to an altitude of 2000m (6561ft) with a load of 104,444kg (230,256lb).

Of interest is the fact that despite the majority of An-22s being built for the military, almost all flew in 'civilian' Aeroflot markings. In the days of the Cold War, this gave the aircraft access to airports and overfly rights which would have been denied had military colours been carried. The An-22 had been largely superseded by the An-124 Ruslan by the mid 1990s but about 30 remained in service in 1999.

Photo: Antonov An-22. (D Fraser)

Antonov An-24

Country of origin: Soviet Union.

Powerplants: An-24V Srs I – two 2500ehp (1864kW) Ivchenko AI-24 turboprops. An-24V Srs II/P/T – two 2550ehp (1901kW) AI-24A turboprops. An-24RV/RT – AI-24A turboprops plus 1985lb (8.8kN) thrust RU 19-300 auxiliary turbojet in starboard nacelle; four bladed propellers.

Performance: An-24V Srs II – cruise speed 243kt (450km/h) at 19,685ft (6000m); initial climb 1515ft (462m)/min; service ceiling 27,560ft (8400m); max payload range 296nm (548km); max fuel range 1293nm (2395km).

Weights: An-24V Srs II – empty 13,300kg (29,321lb) max takeoff 21,000kg (46,296lb).

Dimensions: Wing span 29.20m (95ft 9½in); length 23.53m (77ft 2½in); height 8.32m (27ft 3½in); wing area 75.0m² (807sq ft).

Accommodation: An-24V – 44-52 passengers four abreast. An-24T – max payload 5700kg (12,566lb).

Production: Approx 1200 An-24s in USSR plus Xian Y7 in China.

History: Designed to a 1957 Aeroflot requirement for a 32-40 seat turboprop airliner to replace the airline's piston engined Ilyushin Il-14s on short haul regional services, the An-24 was also intended to be operated from short and/or unpaved airfields. Short field performance was achieved by the incorporation of wide span Fowler flaps, double slotted outboard of the engines and single slotted inboard. The pressurised semi monocoque fuselage used a bonded/welded method of construction. The NATO codename 'Coke' was applied.

By the time the An-24 first flew in April 1960 the aircraft had become a 44 seater, achieved by rearranging the cabin. A second prototype and five preproduction aircraft followed and the first aircraft was handed over to Aeroflot for training and route proving in September 1962. Aeroflot inaugurated regular services between Moscow, Voronezh and Saratov a year later.

Early aircraft were to the basic An-24 standard but were quickly supplanted by the 50 seat An-24V Series I. The An-24V Series II appeared in 1968 with slightly more powerful water injection engines and in passenger, mixed passenger/freight, convertible cargo/passenger, freight and executive versions. Other variants were the An-24T freighter with a ventral cargo door under the rear cabin (which could also be used for airdropping); the An-24RT freighter with an auxiliary turbojet in the starboard engine nacelle for engine starting and improved takeoff performance in hot and high conditions; the An-24RV (similar to the Series II aircraft but with the auxiliary turbojet); and the An-24P which was equipped to drop firefighters onto forest fires. An-24 production ended in 1978.

Apart from Aeroflot, the An-24 has been widely operated by airlines in countries allied to the former Soviet Union including Air Guinee, Air Mali, Balkan Bulgarian, Cubana, China's CAAC, Egyptair, Iraqi Airways, East Germany's Interflug, Mongolian Airlines, Polish Airlines, Lot and Tarom. Others were delivered to a number of air forces.

China's Xian Aircraft Company has been building developed versions of the An-24 as the Y-7 since 1970, later models continuing in production with winglets, more powerful engines and upgraded Western avionics and systems.

Photo: Antonov An24V Series II. (Rob Finlayson)

Antonov An-26 and An-32

Country of origin: Soviet Union/Ukraine.

Powerplants: An-26 – two 2780ehp (2073kW) Ivchenko AI-24VT turboprops and one 1765lb (7.85kN) thrust RU 19A-300 auxiliary turbojet. An-32 – two 4192ehp (3126kW) Ivchenko AI-24M or 5109ehp (3810kW) AI-24D turboprops; four bladed propellers.

Performance: An-26 – cruise speed 237kt (439km/h); initial climb 1575ft (480m)/min; service ceiling 24,600ft (7500m); max payload range 594nm (1100km); max fuel range 1434nm (2656km). An-32 – cruise speed 248-286kt (449-530km/h); service ceiling 30,840ft (9400m); max payload range 459nm (850km); max fuel range 1080nm (2000km).

Weights: An-26 – operating empty 16,914kg (37,289lb); max takeoff 24,000kg (52,910lb). An-32 – operating empty 16,800kg (37,037lb); max takeoff 27,000kg (59,524lb).

Dimensions: Wing span (both) 29.20m (95ft 9½in). An-26 – length 23.80m (78ft 1); height 8.57m (28ft 1½in). An-32 – length 23.67m (77ft 8in); height 8.75m (28ft 8½in).

Accommodation: An-26 – up to 40 passengers/troops or 5500kg (12,125lb) freight. An-32 – up to 50 passengers/troops or 6700kg (14,770lb) freight.

Production: An-26 – 1410. An-32 – 450 by 1999.

History: The military and further civil potential of the An-24 airliner was realised in the development of new variants with a rear loading ramp. The first was the An-26 (NATO codename 'Curl') based on the An-24RT specialist freighter with auxiliary turbojet. The prototype first flew on 21 May 1969 and entered service with the Soviet Air Force in the early 1970s.

Apart from the rear loading ramp, the An-26 also featured more powerful AI-24VT engines and a restressed airframe for heavier operating weights. Variants include the An-26B of 1978 with improved freight handling equipment and An-26P firefighting version. Other variants for ambulance, research, training and electronic warfare were created by conversion. Deliveries were made to the Soviet military and Aeroflot plus civil and military operators in 27 countries. By 1999 about 400 remained in military service worldwide plus another 440 in civil hands of which some 300 were operated by Aeroflot and its successors in the CIS.

The An-30 'Clank' was a specialist aerial survey version developed from the An-26 with an extensively glazed nose for a navigator and raised flight deck. First flown in 1974, small numbers were built for military or quasi-military use.

The final development of the basic design is the An-32 'Cline', originally designed to meet an Indian Air Force requirement with considerably more powerful engines for operation in extreme hot and high conditions. The engines are mounted in new overwing cowlings and aerodynamic refinements include triple slotted flaps outboard of the engines, automatic leading edge slats and enlarged ventral fins. The prototype flew on 9 July 1976 and deliveries of 123 aircraft to India began in 1984. Series production ended in 1992 but the An-32 was still available to order in 1999. The An-32B with 5300ehp (3952kW) engines was offered from 1993.

Photo: Antonov An-32 firebomber. (Keith Anderson)

Antonov/PZL An-28 and M-28

Country of origin: Soviet Union/Ukraine and Poland.

Powerplants: An-28/M-28 – two 960shp (716kW) PZL built Glushenkov TVD-10B turboprops; three bladed propellers. M-28PT Skytruck – two 1100shp (820kW) Pratt & Whitney Canada PT6A-65B turboprops; five bladed propellers.

Performance: An-28/M-28 – max cruise 189kt (350km/h); economical cruise 181kt (335km/h); max payload range 275nm (509km); max fuel range 736nm (1245km). Skytruck – max cruise 181kt (335km/h); initial climb 2657ft (810m)/min; service ceiling 20,340ft (6200m); max fuel range 765nm (1417km).

Weights: An-28/M-28 – empty equipped 3900kg (8598lb); max takeoff 6500kg (14,330lb). Skytruck – empty equipped 3917kg (8635lb); max takeoff 7000kg (15,432lb).

Dimensions: Wing span 22.07m (72ft 5in); length 13.10m (43ft 0in); height 4.90m (16ft 1in); wing area 39.7m² (427sq ft).

Accommodation: 15-18 passengers three abreast or 20 in high density layout; folding seats in utility/military versions.

Production: Approximately 200 An-28/M-28s ordered by late 1998 including about 15 M-28TP Skytrucks. About 100 of all models in commercial service.

History: The winner of a 'fly off' competition against the Beriev Be-30 to find a replacement for the Antonov An-2 biplane and piston engined An-14 operating Aeroflot's short haul routes, the An-28 was derived from the latter retaining its high wing and twin fins layout but with a new and enlarged fuselage (retaining the original rear clamshell doors) and turboprop engines.

The prototype (as the An-14M) first flew in September 1969 followed by the first pre-production An-28 in April 1975 after the original 810shp (604kW) TVD-850 turboprops were replaced by more powerful TVD-10Bs. PZL-Mielec in Poland was named as the sole source of production in 1978 but it wasn't until July 1984 that the first Polish built example flew. Soviet certification was awarded in February 1986.

About 160 had been delivered to the USSR by 1989, at which time production for that market was terminated. PZL continued development of the basic design, by now under the designation M-28.

Marketing and production of the TVD-10B powered standard model continued, variants including the M-28A Polar region transport with increased fuel capacity, M-28P firefighting version, M-28TD military transport/paratroop model first flown in 1992 and M-28RM maritime patrol version, the latter pair for the Polish Air Force and Navy, respectively.

A westernised model with PT6A-65B engines and Bendix-King avionics first flew on 28 July 1993 as the M-28PT Piryt and is now marketed as the Skytruck PT. It is in limited production and was certificated to the Polish equivalent of FAA Part 23 standards in 1996.

The An-28 also forms the basis of the Antonov developed An-38 with a stretched fuselage for up to 27 passengers and 1760shp (1312kW) AlliedSignal TPE331-14GR or 1300shp (969kW) Rybinsk TVD-1500 turboprops. The prototype first flew on 16 December 1994 and the first delivery was made to Russia's Vostok Airlines in October 1996.

Photo: PZL M-28 Skytruck.

Antonov An-72 and An-74

Country of origin: Soviet Union/Ukraine.

Powerplants: Two 14,330lb (63.7kN) Lotarev/ZMKB Progress D-36 turbofans.

Performance: An-72 – max speed 381kt (706km/h); cruising speed 297-374kt (550-693km/h); service ceiling 35,105ft (10,700m); max payload range 432nm (800km); max fuel range 2592nm (4800km). An-74 – max cruise 324kt (600km/h); max range 2321nm (4300km).

Weights: An-72 – operating empty 19,500kg (42,990lb); max takeoff 34,500kg (76,058lb). An-74 – max takeoff 36,500kg (80,467lb).

Dimensions: Wing span 31.89m (104ft 7¹/₂in); length 28.07m (92ft 1in); height 8.65m (28ft 5in); wing area 98.7m² (1062sq ft).

Accommodation: An-72 – max payload 10,000kg (22,046lb) freight or up to 68 passengers on removable and/or folding seats; VIP and combi versions available. An-72G – max payload 10,500kg (23,148lb).

Production: More than 160 by 1998, mostly for military customers.

History: Development of the An-72 began in 1972, initially to meet an Aeroflot requirement for a multirole STOL transport to replace the An-24, or the An-26 in military use. Most have been built for military or quasi-military use in a variety of roles but some have been delivered as commercial freighters.

The most significant design feature of the An-72 and An-74 is the use of the Coanda effect to improve STOL performance, utilising engine exhaust gases blown downwards over the wings' upper surfaces and multi slotted flaps, the flow 'sticking' to them and therefore boosting lift. Other features of the An-72 include a rear loading ramp and multi unit landing gear capable of operations from unprepared strips.

The first of seven An-72 prototypes (two of which were static test airframes) flew on 31 August 1977 at Kiev, although it was not until December 1985 that the first production model flew from Kharkov, the transfer of production and modifications to the design causing significant delays.

Included in the pre series batch were two An-74s, a variant originally developed for operation in Polar regions by Aeroflot's Arctic and Polar Directorates. Limited production of the An-72/74 family continues and about 30 An-72s and six An-74s were in commercial service in 1998.

Versions of the An-72 family (NATO codename 'Coaler') include the standard An-72 'Coaler-C' with extended wings and lengthened fuselage compared to the prototypes; An-72S 38 passenger military VIP transport; An-72AT freighter; An-72G with increased weights; and An-72P maritime patrol aircraft.

An-74 variants include the standard model; An-74T civil freighter; An-74TK convertible cargo/passenger model with 52 folding seats; An-74TK-100 and -74TK-200 combis; and An-74P 16 seat VIP transport. The -100 suffix to a designation indicates the fitting of a navigator's station in the aircraft; 'TK' indicates a combi version.

Most An-72s and An-74s have been built at Kharkov in the Ukraine but production was transferred to Omsk in Russia during 1993.

Photo: Antonov An-74T-100. (Keith Anderson)

Antonov An-124 Ruslan

Country of origin: Soviet Union/Ukraine.

Powerplants: Four 51,654lb (229.7kN) Lotarev/ZKMB Progress D-18T turbofans.

Performance: Cruising speed 405-459kt (750-850km/h); max payload range 2430nm (4500km); range with 40,000kg (88,183lb) payload 6480nm (12,000km); max fuel range 8688nm (16,093km); max endurance 20 hours.

Weights: Operating empty 175,000kg (385,802lb); max takeoff 405,000kg (892,857lb).

Dimensions: Wing span 73.30m (240ft 6in); length 69.10m (226ft 8¹/₂in); height 21.08m (69ft 2in); wing area 628.0m² (6760sq ft).

Capacity: Upper deck cabin for up to 88 passengers; main (lower deck) cargo hold volume 1000m³ (35,314cu ft), max length (including ramps) 43.46m (142ft 7in), max width 6.68m (21ft 11in), max height 4.40m (14ft 5in); max payload 150 tonnes (330,690lb).

Production: About 60 by 1998.

History: The largest aircraft in the world at the time of its introduction (at least in terms of wing span and weight – the Lockheed C-5 Galaxy is longer), the An-124 (NATO codename 'Condor') was developed from 1977 as a successor to the An-22 heavy lift turboprop, primarily as a military strategic freighter but also with possible civil applications.

The Ruslan (a mythical giant from Russian folklore), features nose and tail loading doors, a upper and lower decks (the latter the main cargo area), travelling cranes and winches, five double wheel high flotation 'kneeling' main undercarriage units per side (each of which is independent), four wheel nosewheel and powered quadruple redundant fly-by-wire controls. Possible loads include heavy battle tanks, construction vehicles, industrial generators, missiles and other very large items.

The prototype first flew on 26 December 1982 and deliveries to Soviet Military Transport Aviation began in February 1987. The second prototype made the An-124's first appearance in the West at the 1985 Paris Air Show. The standard An-124 was joined by the purely civilian An-124-100 with lower maximum weight of 392,000kg (864,197lb), civil certification of which was awarded in December 1992.

The An-124 has set several payload records including lifting 171.2 tonnes (377,473lb) to 35,270ft (10,750m) in July 1985. In 1993 a 135.2 tonnes (298,060lb) powerplant generator and its purpose built load spreading cradle was carried from Dusseldorf to New Delhi, at that time the heaviest single load ever transported by air.

The Ruslan is or has been flown by several civilian operators for heavy freight commercial charters including Antonov itself, Aeroflot, Volga Dnepr and British operators Air Foyle and HeavyLift, which lease Russian registered aircraft. Volga Dnepr and HeavyLift operate An-124s in co-operation with each other and the Russian organisation has been responsible for improvements and upgrades to the aircraft including raising the time between overhauls (TBO) of the engines to 4000 hours. It has also looked at fitting the aircraft with Rolls-Royce RB211s.

The An-124's reign as the 'world's largest aircraft' ended in late 1991 with the first flight of the so far one-off stretched, rewinged and six engined derivative, the An-225 Mriya.

Photo: Antonov An-124.

Armstrong Whitworth Argosy

Country of origin: United Kingdom.

Powerplants: I – three 385hp (287kW) Armstrong Siddeley Jaguar III 14-cylinder radials. II – three 420hp (313kW) Jaguar IVA; two bladed propellers.

Performance: Max speed 96kt (177km/h); cruising speed 78kt (145km/h); time to 3000ft (914m) 4.5min; range 360-452nm (667-837km).

Weights: I – empty 5443kg (12,000lb); max takeoff 8165kg (18,000lb). II – empty 5484kg (12,090lb); max takeoff 8709kg (19,200lb).

Dimensions: I/II – wing span 27.53m (90ft 4in); length 20.42m (67ft 0in); height 6.10m (20ft 0in).

Accommodation: Two pilots in open cockpit and 18-20 passengers in cabin.

Production: 3 Argosy I, 4 Argosy II, total 7.

History: The largest British airliner at the time of its appearance and the first Armstrong Whitworth civil aircraft, the three engined Argosy resulted from an Imperial Airways policy to use only multi engined aircraft for reasons of safety to replace the various single engined types inherited from its predecessors.

Although slow and old fashioned (especially compared with contemporary Junkers and Fokker designs), the Argosy proved to be economical and reliable to operate and the enclosed, spacious cabin gave the passengers a semblance of 'luxury'. Construction of the Argosy (which had no Armstrong Whitworth model number) was of fabric covered steel tube fuselage and mainly wooden wings with fabric covering.

The Argosy established its reputation on the prestigious London (Croydon) to Paris 'Silver Wings' lunchtime service, later expanding to other points in Europe including Basle, Brussels and Cologne. In June 1928 an Argosy flew from Croydon to Turnhouse via the east coast of England in a race against the famous *Flying Scotsman* express train, winning by 15 minutes.

Three Argosies were initially ordered, the first of them flying on 16 March 1926. These aircraft were powered by direct drive Jaguar III engines and later designated Argosy I when a further batch of four was ordered in 1928. They entered service in August and September 1926 on the London-Paris route, for which they were fitted with 18 passenger seats and a bar at the rear of the cabin. The high standard of catering on these flights became famous.

The four Argosies of the second batch were known as the Mk.II models and differed from the earlier aircraft in having more powerful Jaguar IVA engines initially housed in ring cowlings, additional fuel, servo operated ailerons and Handley Page slats on the leading edges of the upper wings. These 20 seaters were delivered between May and August 1929 and the three Mk.I aircraft were subsequently re-engined with Jaguar IVAs.

An Argosy was used to fly the inaugural London-India mail services in March 1929, the route involving carrying the mail by air to Basle from where it travelled to Genoa by rail and thence to Karachi via numerous air stages. Argosies also saw service on South African routes. Imperial Airways kept the Argosy in service until 1935-36 when the survivors were scrapped.

Photo: Argosy I.

Armstrong Whitworth Atalanta

Country of origin: United Kingdom.

Powerplants: Four 340hp (253kW) Armstrong Siddeley Serval III 10-cylinder radials; two bladed propellers.

Performance: Max speed 135kt (251km/h); cruise speed 102-113kt (190-209km/h); initial climb 700ft (213m)/min; range 348nm (644km).

Weights: Empty 6323kg (13,940lb); max takeoff 9526kg (21,000lb).

Dimensions: Wing span 27.43m (90ft 0in); length 21.79m (71ft 6in); height 4.57m (15ft 0in).

Accommodation: 3 crew and 9 passengers (plus mail/freight) on African services or up to 17 passengers on European routes.

Production: 8.

History: Sometimes described as the 'art deco airliner', the A.W.15 Atalanta was built to a 1930 Imperial Airways specification for a four engined airliner to carry nine passengers plus mail and freight on the Nairobi-Cape Town and Karachi-Singapore sectors of the airline's trunk routes to South Africa and Australia.

A streamlined cantilever monoplane in the biplane age, the Atalanta was of mixed construction but basically plywood covered metal. The spatted mainwheels attached to an undercarriage structure housed within the fuselage, providing a shallow ground angle and low ground clearance. In service, the spats were removed to facilitate easier servicing and replaced by simple stone guards. The A.W.15 was regarded as an advanced design for its time, and its four Serval radials were originally known as the Double Mongoose.

The first Atalanta flew on 6 June 1932 and all eight aircraft had been completed by April 1933. Initial services were within Europe, the inaugural London (Croydon) to Brussels and Cologne service flown on 26 September 1932. The A.W.15 was subsequently used to link London with Paris, Basle and Zurich.

Proving flights to destinations further afield began in early January 1933 when one aircraft departed London for Cape Town, arriving the following month after delays caused by engine troubles and the need to conduct familiarisation flights for Imperial Airways pilots on the way. Three others then went to Africa for use on the Kisumu-Cape Town route.

In early May 1933 another Atalanta departed England for Australia as part of a proving flight preliminary to London-Singapore services, from where Qantas would complete the service to Australia using de Havilland DH.86s. The proving flight continued to Australia, however, although the aircraft was forced down in a jungle clearing on Bathurst Island near Darwin on the way due to adverse headwinds reducing fuel margins. It eventually reached Melbourne at the end of June. The inaugural Karachi-Singapore service was flown in July 1933, this subsequently being operated by Trans-Continental Airways, an Imperial Airways subsidiary, whose two aircraft carried Indian registration.

The Atalantas continued to efficiently ply the African and Far East routes for eight years, during which time three were lost in accidents. In March 1941 the five survivors (two Indian and three Imperial Airways) were impressed for service with the Indian Air Force.

Photo: A.W.15 Atalanta.

Armstrong Whitworth Ensign

Country of origin: United Kingdom.

Powerplants: Mk.1 – four 800hp (596kW) Armstrong Siddeley Tiger IX or 850hp (634kW) Tiger IXC 14-cylinder radials. Mk.2 – four 950hp (708kW) Wright R-1820-G102A Cyclone nine cylinder radials; three bladed propellers.

Performance: Mk.1 – max speed 178kt (330km/h); cruise speed 148kt (273km/h); initial climb 700ft (213m)/min; service ceiling 18,000ft (5485m); range 747nm (1384km). Mk.2 – max speed 182kt (338km/h); cruise speed 156kt (290km/h); initial climb 900ft (274m)/min; service ceiling 24,000ft (7315m); max range 1190nm (2205km).

Weights: Mk.1 – empty 14,932kg (32,920lb); max takeoff 22,226kg (49,000lb). Mk.2 – empty 16,595kg (36,586lb); max takeoff 25,175kg (55,500lb).

Dimensions: Wing span 37.49m (123ft 0in); length 34.75m (114ft 0in); height 7.01m (23ft 0in); wing area 227.6m² (2450sq ft).

Accommodation: Empire routes – 27 seated or 20 berthed passengers. Europe – 40 passengers.

Production: 12 Mk.1 and 2 Mk.2, total 14 (eight Mk.1 converted to Mk.2).

History: Of all metal stressed skin construction and featuring retractable undercarriage, the A.W.27 Ensign was the largest landplane built for Imperial Airways before the war. Designed to a 1934 specification for use on the land sections of Empire routes to South Africa and Australia, an initial order for 12 was placed in May 1935.

Changes to the specification resulted in delays, the prototype flying some two years late on 24 January 1938. Early flight tests revealed problems including a lack of power from the Tiger IX engines. The first service was flown from London (Croydon) to Paris (Le Bourget) in October 1938. Three Ensigns were used to fly the Christmas mail to Australia in the same year, but all failed to reach their destination due to engine and other problems. That was the extent of service on prewar Empire routes due to ongoing problems.

Two standards of Ensign were built: the 'European' model (four aircraft) with 40 seats and the 'Empire' or 'Eastern' version with accommodation for 27 seated or 20 berthed passengers. The sixth aircraft was the first to feature more powerful Tiger IXC engines driving constant-speed propellers, while the last two A.W.27s (built in 1941) had more powerful and reliable Wright Cyclones. These were designated Mk.2 and eight 'Mk.1s' were converted to the new standard.

Imperial Airways merged with British Airways to form the British Overseas Airways Corporation (BOAC) in November 1939. Early wartime service saw camouflaged Ensigns carrying food, ammunition and other supplies to British forces in France while some later flew a shuttle service linking East and West African ports and other transport duties. Three were lost to enemy action, several suffered battle damage while two fell into German hands and were used as VIP transports, one subsequently fitted with Daimler-Benz engines.

The nine survivors ended their operational days flying the Cairo-Calcutta section of the route to Australia for BOAC, continuing until retirement in 1945 when they returned to Britain for disposal and scrapping. The final Ensign flight (from Cairo to Hurn) was in June 1946.

Photo: Prototype Ensign 1.

Armstrong Whitworth Apollo

Country of origin: United Kingdom.

Powerplants: Four 1135ehp (846kW) Armstrong Siddeley Mamba Mk.503 or 1475ehp (1100kW) Mamba Mk.504 turboprops; three or four bladed propellers.

Performance: Max speed 287kt (531km/h); cruising speed 240kt (444km/h); range 817nm (1513km).

Weights: Empty 14,062kg (31,000lb); max takeoff 20,412kg (45,000lb).

Dimensions: Wing span 28.04m (92ft 0in); length 21.78m (71ft 5¹/₂in); height 7.92m (26ft 0in); wing area 91.6m² (986sq ft).

Accommodation: 26-31 passengers.

Production: 2.

History: Like the Vickers Viscount, the AW.55 Apollo was designed to meet the Brabazon Committee's Type II requirement for a postwar short-medium range airliner for European operations, this later specifying the carriage of 24-30 passengers over a range of 1000 statute miles (1609km) at a speed of 300mph (483km/h).

Unlike the enormously successful Viscount, the Apollo failed to achieve production. A series of development problems mainly associated with its powerplants resulted in the programme being abandoned and handing a potentially lucrative market to its rival.

Construction of two flying prototypes and a static test specimen began in early 1948, the overall length of the aircraft having grown from 19.66m (64ft 6in) to the final 21.78m (71ft 5¹/₂in) during the design process. The names Achilles and Avon were considered for the aircraft before Apollo was chosen.

The first aircraft – with a Ministry of Supply military serial number – flew on 10 April 1949, flight testing quickly revealing longitudinal and directional instability and serious problems with the engines.

The stability problems were easily fixed by modifying the tail unit but those associated with the engines were more difficult to solve.

The axial flow Mamba 503 turboprops fitted to the prototype proved to be not only unreliable but also incapable of delivering the promised power. 1135ehp (846kW) was anticipated but only about 800ehp (597kW) was being produced.

Development continued, the prototype assuming civil registration in 1950 and from October of that year embarking on a series of proving flights which were generally successful even though the engine problems had not been fully solved.

The more powerful and supposedly more reliable Mamba Mk.504 became available in July 1951 but even this was subject to operational restrictions which inhibited the development of the aircraft.

This forced a decision in June 1952 to cancel the Apollo. Despite this, the second prototype was completed and flown on 12 December 1952. The first aircraft went to the Aeroplane and Armament Experimental Establishment (A&AEE) at Boscombe Down before being scrapped in 1955.

The second flew with the Empire Test Pilots' School (ETPS) at Farnborough until 1957 before it was also 'converted to components'.

Photo: First prototype Apollo.

Armstrong Whitworth AW.650 Argosy

Country of origin: United Kingdom.

Powerplants: Srs.100 – four 2020ehp (1506kW) Rolls-Royce Dart 526 turboprops. Srs.222 – four 2230ehp (1663kW) Dart 532/1; four bladed propellers.

Performance: 100 – normal cruise 240kt (444km/h); initial climb 900ft (274m)/min; service ceiling 20,000ft (6096m); max payload range 287nm (532km); max fuel range (5443kg/12,000lb payload) 1400nm (2592km). 222 – normal cruise 243kt (450km/h); initial climb 900ft (274m)/min; service ceiling 21,000ft (6400m); max payload range 421nm (780km); max fuel range (7710kg/17,000lb payload) 1529nm (2833km).

Weights: 100 – operating empty 21,773kg (48,000lb); max takeoff 39,917kg (88,000lb). 222 – operating empty 22,190kg (48,920lb); max takeoff 42,185kg (93,000lb).

Dimensions: Wing span 35.05m (115ft 0in); length 26.44m (86ft 9in); height 8.91m (29ft 3in).

Capacity: 100 – max payload 12,700kg (28,000lb). 220 – max payload 14,098kg (31,080lb). Freight hold volume 104.2m³ (3680cu ft).

Production: 10 Series 100, 56 C.1, 7 Series 200, total 73 (plus three incomplete airframes).

History: The last aircraft to carry the Armstrong Whitworth name (before becoming a Hawker Siddeley product from 1963), the Argosy resulted from 1955 studies into a freighter for the RAF. Further development resulted in the private venture AW.650 (later HS.650) Argosy medium range freighter with twin booms and podded fuselage with rear loading ramp powered by four Rolls-Royce Dart turboprops for both civil and military use.

With some commercial interest being shown, Armstrong Whitworth laid down a batch of 10 aircraft plus two structural test airframes. As the Argosy Series 100, the prototype first flew on 8 January 1959. Deliveries of the first of seven Srs.101s ordered by the USA's Riddle Airlines began in December 1960 following a series of route proving flights. All were delivered by August 1961. The remaining three Argosies from the original batch (including the prototype) were delivered to British European Airways in late 1961 as Srs.102s.

The bulk of Argosy production was for the RAF, which received the first of 56 HS.660 Argosy C.1s with redesigned 'beaver tail' rear fuselage doors/ramp, nose radome, 2680ehp (1998kW) Dart 101s and increased weights. The first aircraft flew on 4 March 1961, deliveries began at the end of that year and were completed in April 1964.

The final civil variant was the Series 200, of which seven were built, a prototype (first flight 11 March 1964 and retained by the manufacturer) and six Srs.222s for BEA. These featured more powerful Darts, increased weights, integral instead of bag fuel tanks, a redesigned wing spar box, and wider front and rear loading door apertures. The first BEA aircraft flew in January 1965 and the five covered by the initial order had been delivered within six months. One crashed early in its career and was replaced by another aircraft in November 1966. BEA operated its Argosies until early 1970. Subsequent operators included Capitol, Zantop, Universal, Air Bridge, Sagittair, IPEC, Safe Air and Aer Turas. The last were retired by 1992.

Photo: Argosy 100.

ATR 42

Countries of origin: France and Italy.

Powerplants: ATR 42-300 – two 1800shp (1342kW) Pratt & Whitney Canada PW120 turboprops. ATR 42-320 – two 1950shp (1454kW) PW121; four bladed propellers. ATR 42-500 – two 2400shp (1790kW) PW127E; six bladed propellers.

Performance: 300 – max cruise 265kt (491km/h); economical cruise 243kt (450km/h); max operational ceiling 25,000ft (7620m); range with 48 passengers 920nm (1704km). 320 – max cruise 269kt (498km/h). 500 – max cruise 305kt (565km/h); max payload range 1010nm (1871km).

Weights: 300 – operating empty 10,285kg (22,674lb); max takeoff 16,700kg (36,817lb). 320 – operating empty 10,290kg (22,685lb); max takeoff 16,700kg (36,817lb). 500 – operating empty 11,250kg (24,802lb); max takeoff 18,600kg (41,005lb).

Dimensions: Wing span 24.57m (80ft 7in); length 22.67m (74ft 4¹/₂in); height 7.59m (24ft 11in); wing area 54.5m² (587sq ft).

Accommodation: 300/320 – 42-50 passengers four abreast; nine containers and 4000kg (8818lb) payload in all freight version.

Production: Approximately 343 ATR 42s ordered by late 1998.

History: France's Aerospatiale and Italy's Aeritalia (now Alenia) established Avions de Transport Regional as a Groupement d'Intéret Economique (GIE) under French law to develop a family of turboprop regional airliners. The ATR 42 was the consortium's first aircraft and was launched in October 1981.

The first of two ATR 42-200 prototypes flew on 16 August 1984 and the second aircraft followed two months later. The first production standard ATR 42-300 with higher operating weights and improved payload/range performance than the prototypes flew in April 1985 and following Italian and French certification in September 1985 the first aircraft entered airline service with Air Littoral in December 1985. Other early customers included Finnair, Cimber Air and Holland Aero Lines. The first US customer was Command Airways, which received its initial aircraft in January 1986.

The ATR 42-300 remained the standard production version until 1996 although it was joined from 1989 by the -320 with more powerful PW121 engines for improved hot and high performance. The ATR 42 Cargo is a quick change freight/passenger version of the ATR 42-300.

The ATR 42-500 is the first significantly improved version of the aircraft and features a revised interior, more powerful PW127E engines driving six bladed propellers, EFIS cockpit, the elevators and rudders of the stretched ATR 72 (described separately), plus new brakes and landing gear and strengthened wing and fuselage for higher weights. The first ATR 42-500 flew in September 1994 and the initial delivery was to Aeromar in June 1995.

ATR became part of Aero International (Regional), the regional airliner consortium established by Aerospatiale, Alenia and British Aerospace in January 1996 to incorporate ATR, Avro and Jetstream. AI(R) handled sales, marketing and support for ATR plus the Avro RJ and the Jetstream 41 until its disbandment in mid 1998 when ATR regained its independence. An agreement which could see the ATR 42 assembled in India by HAL was signed in February 1999.

Photo: ATR 42-300.

ATR 72

Countries of origin: France and Italy.

Powerplants: ATR 72-200 – two 2160shp (1610kW) Pratt & Whitney Canada PW124B turboprops. ATR 72-210 – two 2480shp (1849kW) PW127; four bladed propellers.

Performance: 200 – max cruise 279kt (517km/h); economical cruise 248kt (459km/h); max operational ceiling 25,000ft (7620m); range with 66 passengers 1200nm (2223km); max payload range 645nm (1195km).

Weights: 200 – operating empty 12,500kg (27,557lb); max takeoff 21,500kg (47,399lb).

Dimensions: Wing span 27.05m (88ft 9in); length 21.17m (89ft 1½in); height 7.65m (25ft 1in); wing area 61.0m² (657sq ft).

Accommodation: 64-74 passengers four abreast. Freighter with large forward freight door – max payload 7200kg (15,873lb) in 13 containers.

Production: Approximately 569 ATRs of all models ordered by late 1998 including about 225 ATR 72s.

History: The ATR 72 is a stretched development of the ATR 42 and was launched in January 1986. The first of three development aircraft flew on 27 October 1988, followed by the awarding of French and then US certification in late 1989. Entry to service was in October 1989 by Kar Air of Finland.

Significant differences between the ATR 72 and the smaller ATR 42 include a 4.50m (14ft 9in) fuselage stretch and reworked wings. The ATR 72's wings are new outboard of the engine nacelles and have 30 per cent of their structure made of composite materials including the spars and skin panels and a carbon fibre wing box.

Aside from the baseline ATR 72-200, three developments have been offered, the ATR 72-210, ATR 72-210A and the proposed ATR 52C. The ATR 72-210 is the current major production model and is optimised for operations in hot and high conditions. It has more powerful PW127 engines for better takeoff performance. Certificated in December 1992, the launch customer was American Airlines which ordered 60 for US regional services.

The ATR 72-210A (for a time called the ATR 72-500) is a further improved hot and high model and was certificated in early 1997. It features another boost in power with PW127F engines driving six bladed composite propellers.

The ATR 52C is an as yet unlaunched derivative intended for both civil and military operators with a redesigned tail to incorporate a rear loading ramp. As with the ATR 42, a military maritime patrol version known as the Petrel has also been offered.

The ATR 72 was planned to form the basis of the ATR 82, a 78 seat stretched development. If built, the ATR 82 would have been powered by two heavily derated Allison AE 2100 turboprops (or similar) and have a cruising speed of up to 335kt (620km/h). Despite reaching the advanced definition stage, the ATR 82 project was suspended when AI(R) was formed in early 1996.

The ATR 42 and 72 have also provided the basis for various regional jet studies utilising their fuselages in combination with a new wing and turbofan engines.

Photo: ATR 72-200.

Aviation Traders Carvair

Country of origin: United Kingdom.

Powerplants: Four 1450hp (1081kW) Pratt & Whitney R-2000-7M2 Twin Wasp 14-cylinder radials; three bladed propellers.

Performance: Max speed 217kt (402km/h); max cruise 185kt (343km/h); normal cruise 160-169kt (296-314km/h); initial climb 650ft (198m)/min; service ceiling 18,700ft (5700m); max payload range 1477nm (2736km); range with max fuel, no reserves and 4536kg (10,000lb) payload 3000nm (5557km).

Weights: Empty 18,763kg (41,365lb); max takeoff 33,476kg (73,800lb).

Dimensions: Wing span 35.81m (117ft 6in); length 31.27m (102ft 7in); height 9.09m (29ft 10in); wing area 135.8m² (1462sq ft).

Capacity: Cabin volume 131.1m³ (4630cu ft); max payload 8770kg (19,335lb). Max seating for 85 passengers or up to five cars and 22 passengers.

Production: 21 conversions from Douglas DC-4/C-54s.

History: A car/passenger ferry and freighter conversion of the Douglas DC-4/C-54, the Carvair was the brainchild of the often far sighted Freddie Laker, managing director of engineering and overhaul firm Aviation Traders and its associated company Channel Air Bridge. This needed a replacement for its fleet of Bristol Freighters used to transport cars and passengers from Britain to the Continent. Development of an entirely new design was too expensive, so the readily available, cheap and well supported DC-4 was selected as the basis for a conversion programme.

The conversion involved replacing the entire forward fuselage with a new lengthened and enlarged section which incorporated a hydraulically operated sideways hinging nose door which facilitated straight in loading of cars or freight. The flight deck was moved to the top of the new structure, DC-6 brakes and a larger DC-7 fin and rudder were fitted and the nosewheel retracted into an external blister. The conversion was given the model number ATL.98 and the name Carvair was a contraction of 'Car-Via-Air'.

A full scale mockup was built around a derelict KLM DC-4 in 1960 and the prototype conversion – from a former World Airways C-54B – first flew on 21 June 1961. Channel Air Bridge began scheduled services between Southend and Rotterdam in March 1962. It merged with Silver City Airways later in the same year to form British United Air Ferries (BUAF), these organisations between them taking delivery of 11 of the 21 conversions.

Other customers were Luxembourg's Intercontinental/Interocean (2), Aer Lingus (3 – the last of which was modified to carry horses), Spain's Aviaco (2) and Ansett (3). Series 'production' of the Carvair ended with the 20th aircraft (for Ansett) in late 1965 but the Australian carrier ordered a third example two years later. This first flew in July 1968 and brought the programme to an end.

Similar conversions of the DC-6 and DC-7 (some with Rolls-Royce Dart turboprops) were proposed but not developed, while in 1999 only two Carvairs remained in service with Hawkair in Canada and Custom Air Services in the USA. Another example in South Africa is believed flyable. All three are former Ansett aircraft.

Photo: ATL.98 Carvair.

Avro 618 Ten

Country of origin: United Kingdom.

Powerplants: Three 240hp (179kW) Armstrong Siddeley Lynx IVB or IVC radials; two bladed propellers.

Performance: Max speed 100kt (185km/h); cruising speed 87kt (161km/h); initial climb 675ft (205m)/min; service ceiling 16,000ft (4877m); range 348nm (644km).

Weights: Empty 2731kg (6020lb); max takeoff 4808kg (10,600lb).

Dimensions: Wing span 21.72m (71ft 3in); length 14.48m (47ft 6in); height 3.88m (12ft 9in); wing area 71.7m² (772sq ft).

Accommodation: 2 crew and 8 passengers.

Production: 14.

History: A V Roe and Co Ltd acquired a licence to build the successful Fokker F.VIIB/3m three engined transport in 1928 and with it sales rights for throughout the British Empire with the exception of Canada. Avro dubbed its version the Type 618 Ten, after the aircraft's seating capacity including crew.

Differences between the British and Dutch versions were minimal except in detail where local airworthiness requirements had to be met. An example was the centre engine, which on the Ten had its thrust line tilted downwards compared to the original.

Of the 14 Tens built from 1929, five were delivered to Charles Kingsford Smith's Australian National Airways (ANA) including the prototype which became VH-UMF *Southern Cloud*. This aircraft was subject to considerable mystery when it was lost over the rugged southern New South Wales mountain ranges on a flight between Sydney and Melbourne in March 1931 and the wreckage not found until 27 years later. This accident had a significant effect on the introduction of upgraded airline operating standards in Australia and also contributed to the demise of ANA.

Other ANA Tens of note include VH-UMG *Southern Star* in which Kingsford Smith flew the Christmas mail from Australia to England in 1931 and VH-UMI *Southern Moon* which Charles Ulm used for long distance flights. This aircraft was later used for casualty evacuation in New Guinea in the early days of the Pacific War when operated by Stephens Aviation. Another ANA aircraft was re-engined with 330hp (246kW) Wright Whirlwind engines.

Other Avro Ten customers were Imperial Airways which purchased two in 1930 for general charter work initially in the Near East and then Europe, while of the four built for Indian State Airways in 1931, none were delivered to the customer. One went to the Viceroy of India for his personal use, two to the Egyptian Air Force and the last to Midland and Scottish Air Ferries, delivered in 1933. One of the Egyptian aircraft eventually found its way into Indian National Airways service.

Two others were delivered to Australia to the Queensland Air Navigation Co for the Brisbane-Narromine section of the Empire air route while these and one of the ANA aircraft were taken over by New England Airways in 1934. The last Ten was delivered to the Wireless and Equipment Flight of the Royal Aircraft Establishment (RAE) at Farnborough in July 1936.

Photo: Australian National Airways Avro Ten.

Avro 619 Five and 624 Six

Country of origin: United Kingdom.

Powerplants: Five/Six – three 105hp (78kW) Armstrong Siddeley Genet Major 1 radials; two bladed propellers.

Performance: Five – max speed 102kt (190km/h); cruising speed 82kt (153km/h); initial climb 750ft (228m)/min; service ceiling 15,000ft (4572m); range 348nm (644km). Six – max speed 98kt (182km/h); cruising speed 82kt (153km/h); initial climb 600ft (183m)/min; service ceiling 14,000ft (4267m); range 348nm (644km).

Weights: Five – empty 1266kg (2790lb); max takeoff 2005kg (4420lb). Six – empty 1361kg (3000lb); max takeoff 2268kg (5000lb).

Dimensions: Five – wing span 14.33m (47ft 0in); length 10.90m (35ft 9in); height 2.90m (9ft 6in); wing area 30.9m² (333sq ft). Six – wing span 15.54m (51ft 0in); length 10.97m (36ft 0in); height 2.90m (9ft 6in); wing area 33.4m² (360sq ft).

Accommodation: Five – one crew and four passengers. Six – two crew and four passengers.

Production: Five – 4; Six – 3.

History: Ostensibly a scaled down Type 618 Ten for four passengers, the Avro Type 619 Five was in reality a new design by Roy Chadwick. As had been the case with the larger aircraft, the name reflected the number of seats including crew as it did in the following Type 624 Six with provision for a second crew member in the cockpit and other modifications.

Both were trimotors powered by 105hp (78kW) Genet Major radials, providing an extraordinary ratio of passengers per engine (1.33 to 1!) along with a relatively meagre carrying capacity considering the size of the aircraft.

The prototype Five first appeared in 1929 as G-AASO and was used as a demonstrator before being entered in the 1930 King's Cup Race, in which it was less than spectacularly successful, retiring during the event. This aircraft was taken over by Wilson Airways in Kenya later in the same year, following two others (VP-KAD and VP-KAE) which had been delivered in 1929. In Australia, a single Five (VH-UNK) was purchased by the Queensland Air Navigation Co to supplement the two Tens it had in service.

The Type 624 Six was a variant of the same basic design but slightly enlarged with a widened cockpit fitted with side-by-side seats and dual controls, a deeper cabin, bigger wing, higher weights and in the case of the first aircraft, the underwing engines mounted directly to the structure rather than underslung on short struts as on the Five. The earlier configuration was quickly reverted to.

The first Six (G-AAYR) appeared in May 1930 and after being used as a demonstrator was sold in 1931 to the Far East Aviation Company in Hong Kong, which later sold it to the Chinese Government.

The third and final aircraft also went to Far East Aviation (as VR-HBF) and thence the Chinese Government while the second Six (G-ABBY) flew as a navigation trainer with Air Service Training at Hamble until it was impressed into RAF service and issued to the RAF's No 11 Air Observers' Navigation School in early 1940.

Photo: Avro 619 Five.

Avro 642

Country of origin: United Kingdom.

Powerplants: 642/2m – two 450hp (335kW) Armstrong Siddeley Jaguar VID 14-cylinder radials; four bladed propellers. 642/4m – four 240hp (179kW) Armstrong Siddeley Lynx IVC radials; two bladed propellers.

Performance: 642/2m – max speed 135kt (251km/h); cruising speed 117kt (217km/h); initial climb 970ft (295m)/min; service ceiling 15,500ft (4724m); range 521nm (965km). 642/4m – max speed 130kt (241km/h); service ceiling 15,000ft (4572m); range 486nm (900km).

Weights: 642/2m – empty 3338kg (7360lb); max takeoff 5352kg (11,800lb). 642/4m – empty 3960kg (8731lb); max takeoff 5556kg (12,250lb).

Dimensions: Wing span 21.72m (71ft 3in); length 16.61m (54ft 6in); height 3.50m (11ft 6in); wing area 67.6m² (728sq ft).

Accommodation: 2 crew and 16 passengers.

Production: 1 Type 642/2m and 1 Type 642/4m.

History: The final and largest development of the Avro Type 618 Ten – a licence built version of the Fokker F.VIIB/m trimotor – the Type 642 took the wooden wing from that aircraft and married it to a new, enlarged and considerably redesigned fabric covered steel tube fuselage which was aerodynamically much cleaner. The wing was lowered to a shoulder position and the aircraft was built in both twin and four engined versions with the previous nose mounted powerplant eliminated. In both cases the engines were neatly faired into the wing leading edges.

The result was a completely different looking aircraft compared to its predecessor with improved performance. Capable of carrying 16 passengers in addition to two flight crew, the 642 was sometimes referred to as the 'Eighteen' in reference to its seating capacity and following on from the tradition established by earlier Avro airliners. Only a single example of each of the two versions was built.

The twin engined Type 642/2m with Armstrong Siddeley Jaguar radials was the first to appear as G-ACFV. Originally fitted with a rounded nose section, this was immediately changed to a more conventional nose with stepped windscreen. First flown at the beginning of 1934, the 642/2m was delivered to Midland and Scottish Air Ferries in April of the same year and thence to Commercial Air Hire at Croydon in March 1935 for use on morning newspaper delivery flights to the Continent.

The aircraft was sold to W R Carpenter Airlines for mail services in New Guinea in 1936 and remained there until destroyed by Japanese forces in 1942 while in the service of Carpenter subsidiary Mandated Airlines.

The second aircraft was the sole four engined Type 642/4m, built as a seven seat VIP transport for the Viceroy of India, Lord Willington, to replace an Avro Ten. Apart from its powerplants, this aircraft featured elongated rather than individual cabin windows. Delivered in late 1934 as VT-AFM *Star of India*, the 642/4m was transferred to the RAF in India at the beginning of 1938 and attached to Air Headquarters, Delhi. It was withdrawn from service in early 1940.

Photo: Avro 642/2m.

Avro 652A Nineteen

Country of origin: United Kingdom.

Powerplants: Two 420hp (313kW) Armstrong Siddeley Cheetah XV seven cylinder radials; two bladed propellers.

Performance: Srs.2 – max speed 149kt (275km/h); cruise speed 135kt (249km/h); initial climb 730ft (222m)/min; service ceiling 15,000ft (4572m); range 573nm (1062km).

Weights: Srs.1 – empty 3365kg (7419lb); max takeoff 4717kg (10,400lb). Srs.2 – empty 2983kg (6576lb); max takeoff 4717kg (10,400lb).

Dimensions: Srs 1 – wing span 17.22m (56ft 6in); length 12.88m (42ft 3in); height 4.22m (13ft 10in); wing area 43.0m² (463sq ft). Srs.2 – wing span 17.52m (57ft 6in); area 40.9m² (440sq ft).

Accommodation: 1-2 crew and 9 passengers.

Production: 10,996 Type 652/652A/Ansons of all models including 25 Mk.18, 325 Mk.19 (140 Srs.1, 185 Srs.2, civil and military), 60 Mk.20, 252 Mk.21 and 34 Mk.22.

History: Only two examples of the original Avro 652 six seat civil transport (first flight January 1935) entered service before the design was modified to become the Type 652A for the Royal Air Force and Commonwealth air arms. As the Anson, the aircraft went on to be produced in several miliary versions and in very large numbers in Britain and Canada for wartime use as coastal patrol, light transport and navigator, wireless and air gunner training aircraft.

The Anson Mks.XI and XII of 1944 served as the basis for the postwar Mk.XIX (or 19 and sometimes Nineteen) transport for civil use. These featured the raised cabin roofline of later models, fewer cabin windows, hydraulically rather than manually operated retractable undercarriage and (on the XII) Cheetah XV engines driving constant-speed propellers. The prototype Mk.19 was a Mk.XII converted to the new standard with oval cabin windows and seating for nine passengers. It first flew in early 1945 and formed the basis of the military C.19, T.20, T.21 and T.22 for the RAF and Mk.18 for export. The last Anson built was a T.21 delivered in May 1952.

Two versions of the Nineteen were built, the Series 1 which retained the construction method of earlier aircraft and the Series 2 with tapered fabric covered metal (rather than wood) wings of slightly greater span and a metal tailplane. Production of civil versions amounted to 48 aircraft. The largest user was Britain's Railway Air Services which flew 14 on routes from Croydon to Dublin, Belfast, the Isle of Man and northern England. The airline was taken over by British European Airways in early 1947 and the aircraft withdrawn from service soon after.

Other Avro Nineteen operators included the British Ministry of Civil Aviation (six for airports radio calibration), Decca Navigator company, the College of Aeronautics as a flying classroom, Misrair in Egypt, the British Colonial Office for pest control in East Africa, Indian Air Survey and Transport and the Irish Air Corps. Several hundred demobbed Anson Is also found postwar civilian work as airline and charter transports, freighters, survey aircraft and even agricultural aircraft in Britain, Canada, India, Africa, the Americas, New Zealand and elsewhere. Australian operators were major users of ex RAAF Ansons in the immediate postwar years with 18 companies flying them in a variety of roles.

Photo: Avro 652A Anson I.

Avro Lancastrian

Country of origin: United Kingdom.

Powerplants: Four 1635hp (1219kW) Rolls-Royce Merlin T.24/4 or 500 V12s; three bladed propellers.

Performance: Max speed 274kt (507km/h); cruising speed 200kt (370km/h); initial climb 950ft (290m)/min; service ceiling 25,500ft (7772m); max range 3606nm (6680km).

Weights: Empty 13,800kg (30,426lb); max takeoff 29,484kg (65,000lb).

Dimensions: Wing span 31.09m (102ft 0in); length 23.42m (76ft 10in); height 5.94m (19ft 6in); wing area 120.5m² (1297sq ft).

Accommodation: 3 flight crew and 9-13 passengers or freight.

Production: Lancastrian – 23 Mk.1, 33 Mk.2, 18 Mk.3 and 8 Mk.4 (total 82) conversions by Avro plus 4 Mk.4 by Skyways. Lancaster XPP – 9 conversions by Victory Aircraft. Lancaster Transport – approximately 20 conversions.

History: The Lancaster bomber's reliability, handling, performance and ready availability made it an obvious choice for conversion to a transport in the late war and immediate postwar years, pending the arrival of more modern and comfortable aircraft. Two streams of development were pursued, the Lancaster Transport (which retained the Avro Type number – 683 – of the bomber) and the Type 691 Lancastrian. Both had their gun turrets removed and streamlined fairings fitted but the Lancastrian had cabin windows cut into the rear fuselage.

The first Lancaster transport conversions were performed in Canada by Victory Aircraft when the pattern aircraft delivered in 1941 as a prelude to local production as the B.X was modified to Lancaster XPP ('Mk.X Passenger Plane') standards. It was used by Trans-Canada Airlines for experimental freight flights from early 1943 and then (after modification to carry 10 passengers and additional fuel) trans-Atlantic passenger, mail and freight services between Montreal and Prestwick. Eight other XPPs were converted in 1944-45.

The winding down of British Lancaster production from late 1944 made airframes available for Avro to produce its own version under the name Type 691 Lancastrian, the first of which flew on 17 January 1945.

Four versions were built: the Mk.1 with cabin windows on the starboard side only and accommodation for nine passengers plus mail and freight for use on the England-Australia route by BOAC and Qantas (services from Hurn began on 31 May 1945, Qantas inaugurated flights in the reverse direction from Sydney two days later); the similar C.2 for the RAF; the Mk.3 developed for British South American Airways (BSAA) as a shorter range 13 seater, Alitalia, Qantas and Silver City Airways; and the equivalent C.4 for the RAF of which most went to Skyways and Flota Aerea Mercante Argentina. The Skyways aircraft played a major part in the Berlin air lift and the operator performed four of its own Lancastrian 4 conversions in 1947-48.

Many of the Lancaster Transport conversions were used as engine and equipment test beds or for experimental work by Flight Refuelling Ltd (which also used them to transport fuel during the Berlin Airlift), although BSAA took six in early 1946, four of them freighters.

Photo: Lancastrian Mk.1. (Qantas)

Avro York

Country of origin: United Kingdom.

Powerplants: Four 1640hp (1228kW) Rolls-Royce Merlin T.24 or 502 V12s; three bladed propellers.

Performance: Max speed 259kt (480km/h) at 21,000ft (6400m); cruising speed 194kt (358km/h); service ceiling 26,000ft (7925m); max range 2346nm (4345km).

Weights: Empty 19,070kg (42,040lb); max loaded 30,845kg (68,000lb).

Dimensions: Wing span 31.09m (102ft 0in); length 23.93m (78ft 6in); height 5.03m (16ft 6in); wing area 120.5m² (1297sq ft).

Accommodation: 24-50 passengers or 4535kg (10,000lb) freight.

Production: 257 including 1 by Victory Aircraft, Canada.

History: Developed over a period of only six months in 1942, the York combined the Lancaster bomber's wings, tail unit (with a third central fin), Rolls-Royce Merlin engines and undercarriage with a new, more capacious slab sided fuselage suitable for the carriage of freight and passengers. The wings were shoulder mounted rather than in the mid position of the Lancaster.

The first York was flown on 5 July 1942, this and the second aircraft fitted with twin fins and 1280hp (958kW) Merlin XXs. The first aircraft subsequently had 1650hp (1236kW) Bristol Hercules radial engines installed to become the sole York Mk.II.

The third prototype went on to have a colourful career after it was converted to a VIP transport in 1943 for the personal use of Winston Churchill. The only York to feature square windows, this aircraft was operated by No 24 Squadron RAF and carried the British Prime Minister and other cabinet ministers on many trips including to summit meetings in Moscow, Yalta and Tehran. It also took King George VI on a North African tour in 1943.

Production York C.1s were built in VIP, freighter, passenger/freighter and first class passenger variants. Five early aircraft were diverted to BOAC in 1944 as 12 seaters (plus freight) for use on the UK-Morocco-Cairo route. A further 32 were delivered to the airline from August 1945 while others were delivered to British South American Airways (12) and Flota Aerea Mercante Argentina (5) in 1946.

As the York had a low production priority, deliveries did not get into full swing until 1945 with the establishment of the first fully operational RAF squadron. As a result, most were delivered postwar, the last in April 1948. Postwar RAF service continued until 1957 and achievements in the meantime included substantial involvement in the Berlin Airlift of 1947-48. Some gained civil identities when used on joint RAF/BOAC services.

Many ex RAF Yorks also found their way into commercial service including with South African Airways in 1946-47 while awaiting the delivery of Douglas DC-4s. Many former BOAC Yorks were flown by British independent carriers after their withdrawal from passenger services in 1950. The last BOAC York freight service was flown in October 1957. During 13 years of service, BOAC's Yorks flew 226,996 hours and carried 90,000 passengers. Operators such as Eagle Aviation, Skyways, Scottish Airlines and Air Charter continued operating Yorks until the early 1960s, often on trooping charters on behalf of the British military.

Photo: Avro Type 685 York.

Avro Tudor 1, 3 and 4

Country of origin: United Kingdom.

Powerplants: Four 1770hp (1320kW) Rolls-Royce Merlin 621 V12s; four bladed propellers.

Performance: Mk.1 – max speed 226kt (418km/h); cruising speed 182kt (338km/h); initial climb 700ft (213m)/min; service ceiling 26,000ft (7925m); max range 3154nm (5842km). Mk.4 – max speed 245kt (454km/h); cruising speed 182kt (338km/h); initial climb 800ft (244m)/min; service ceiling 27,400ft (8350m); max range 3476nm (6438km).

Weights: Mk.1 – empty 21,755kg (47,960lb); max takeoff 32,205kg (71,000lb). Mk.4 – empty 22,426kg (49,441lb); max takeoff 36,288kg (80,000lb).

Dimensions: Mk.1 – wing span 36.57m (120ft 0in); length 24.23m (79ft 6in); height 6.37m (20ft 11in); wing area 132.0m² (1421sq ft). Mk.4 – length 25.98m (85ft 3in).

Accommodation: Mk.1 – 12-24 passengers. Mk.3 – nine seat VIP layout. Mk.4 – 32 passengers.

Production: 33 Tudors of all models completed including 8 Mk.1, 2 Mk.3 and 12 Mk.4.

History: Conceived in 1944 as a trans-Atlantic airliner using the Lincoln bomber as a basis but with a new, pressurised fuselage, the first British airliner with this feature. It was beset with problems throughout its life, many resulting from sponsoring customer BOAC insisting on hundreds of changes.

The fact that only 33 Tudors were completed in no fewer than seven marks speaks for itself, while the construction of other airframes was abandoned and others scrapped after little or no use. Two basic families were produced, the short fuselage Type 688 Mks.1, 3 and 4 (as described here) and the long fuselage Type 689.

The prototype Tudor 1 first flew on 14 January 1945, testing quickly revealing serious aerodynamic problems which resulted in the fitting of a taller fin and rudder, extended wing root fillets and inner engine nacelles and shorter undercarriage. BOAC ordered 14 Tudor 1s (plus six for British South American Airways) but cancelled them in 1947.

BSAA used its Tudor 1s as freighters including successful service on the Berlin Airlift. Most Type 688 airframes were completed as Tudor 4s with a slightly longer fuselage and deletion of the flight engineer's station for an increase in passenger capacity. It was introduced into BSAA service on the South Atlantic route in October 1947 but following the loss of two aircraft under mysterious circumstances it was decreed that from early 1949 the Tudor should not be used for passenger flights. This ban remained in force until 1954, following Aviation Traders' purchase of 11 Tudor 1, 2 and 3 freighters (plus a stock of components from scrapped aircraft) and after substantial modification (including disabling the pressurisation system) and recertification used some of them for charter work with 42 seats. Others received large freight doors as Super Trader freighters.

Other Type 688 Tudors were the Mk.3 VIP transport for the British Government (converted to freighters shortly after completion); Mk.4B conversion of the Mk1 for BSAA with flight engineer's station retained; and Mk.8, the second Mk.1 prototype fitted with four Rolls-Royce Nene turbojets and reflown in September 1948 as a testbed.

Photo: Tudor 4.

Avro Tudor 2, 5 and 7

Country of origin: United Kingdom.

Powerplants: Mk.2/5 – four 1770hp (1320kW) Rolls-Royce Merlin 621 V12s; four bladed propellers.

Performance: Mk.2/5 – max speed 256kt (475km/h); cruising speed 204kt (378km/h) at 20,000ft (6096m); initial climb 740ft (225m)/min; service ceiling 25,550ft (7787m); range 2025nm (3750km).

Weights: Mk.2/5 – empty 21,000kg (46,300lb); max takeoff 36,288kg (80,000lb).

Dimensions: Wing span 36.57m (120ft 0in); length 32.18m (105ft 7in); height 7.39m (24ft 3in); wing area 132.0m² (1421sq ft).

Accommodation: 44 seated or 36 berthed passengers planned, 52 in later use.

Production: 33 Tudors of all models completed included 4 Mk.2, 6 Mk.5 and 1 Mk.7.

History: While the long range Tudor 1 was being developed, a BOAC requirement also existed for a larger aircraft capable of carrying more passengers but over the shorter stage lengths of the Empire Air Routes. The result was the long fuselage Type 689 Tudor 2 with a new fuselage 7.6m (25 feet) longer and of wider cross section than the Mk.1. It retained the Mk.1's wings, powerplants, tail surfaces and undercarriage and at one stage 79 were on order for BOAC, Qantas and South African Airways.

The prototype flew on 10 March 1946 but flight testing revealed the same problems as had inflicted the earlier aircraft. The incorporation of modifications (including enlarged tail surfaces) resulted in performance degrading weight penalties, both Qantas and SAA cancelling their combined order for 29, instead purchasing Constellations and DC-4s, respectively. Subsequent trials revealed further deficiencies with the result that BOAC also cancelled its orders leaving only six aircraft for British South American Airways as the Mk.5.

Eleven long fuselage Tudors were completed: four Mk.2s (used for research from early 1949); six basically similar (except for circular rather than square windows) Mk.5s originally intended for BSAA (one for Airflight in 1948 and used in the Berlin airlift, five for BSAA and converted to tankers also for the Airlift); a single Mk.7, and a Mk.2 with Bristol Hercules radial engines instead of the usual Rolls-Royce Merlins. It first flew in April 1947 and was operated by the Telecommunications Research Establish and then Flight Refuelling Ltd.

Other Type 689 Tudor models were unbuilt including the Mk.6, six of which were ordered by Argentinian operator FAMA but cancelled, leaving the airframes unfinished and joining many others which had a similar fate. The Type 711 Trader was a 1949 project for a freighter which combined the Tudor 2's wings, tail and centre fuselage mated to the nose of the Mk.4 and new forward and rear fuselage sections.

The Tudor 5s were successful in the Berlin Airlift and had brief subsequent careers as 52 seat charter aircraft operated by William Dempster Ltd. Sadly, the Tudor is undoubtedly best remembered for the August 1947 crash of the Mk.2 prototype which took the lives of all on board including Avro's chief test pilot 'Bill' Thorn and famed chief designer Roy Chadwick. The crash was caused by the aileron control circuits being incorrectly assembled.

Photo: Tudor 2 prototype.

Avro RJ70 and BAe 146-100

Country of origin: United Kingdom.

Powerplants: 146-100 – four 6970lb (31.0kN) Textron Lycoming ALF 502R-5 turbofans. RJ70 – four 6130lb (27.3kN) or 7000lb (31.1kN) AlliedSignal LF 507-1F turbofans.

Performance: 146-100 – cruise speed 361-425kt (669-787km/h); range with 80 passengers 1200nm (2222km); max payload range 880nm (1630km). RJ70 – cruise speed 356-432kt (659-800km/h); range with 70 passengers and standard fuel 1175nm (2176km) or 1550nm (2871km) with optional fuel.

Weights: 146-100 – operating empty 23,288kg (51,340lb); max take-off 38,102kg (84,000lb). RJ70 – operating empty 23,723kg (52,300lb); max takeoff 38,102-43,092kg (84,000-95,000lb).

Dimensions: Wing span 26.21m (86ft 0in); length 26.20m (85ft 11½in); height 8.61m (28ft 3in); wing area 77.3m² (832sq ft).

Accommodation: Normally single class seating for 70 passengers five abreast or 82 passengers six abreast; high density arrangement for up to 94 passengers six abreast.

Production: 221 BAe 146s of all models built up to 1994 including 37 146-100s. 132 RJs of all models built by June 1999 including 12 RJ70s.

History: The BAe 146-100 and Avro RJ70 are the smallest of this family of regional jet airliners which are unique in their class in having four engines. The 146 was the last aircraft to be designed and built at the famous Hatfield works of the old de Havilland company.

In August 1973 the then Hawker Siddeley Aviation announced it was designing a short range and very quiet airliner with modest airfield requirements powered by four small turbofans. As the HS.146, full scale development was brief before a worsening world economic recession induced by the oil crisis caused the project to be shelved in October 1974.

Despite this, some low key development and design work continued, but it was not until July 1978 that the project was officially relaunched (albeit with no orders booked), by which time Hawker Siddeley had been absorbed into the newly created British Aerospace.

The resulting BAe 146-100 made its first flight on 3 September 1981 and initial delivery was to Dan-Air in May 1983. Other early 146-100 customers included Pacific Southwest Airlines and the Royal Air Force Queen's Flight. EFIS instead of analogue cockpits were offered from 1986 on all 146s.

BAe first offered the improved RJ70 and RJ80 in 1990, both of which are based on the 146-100. Seating 70 and 80 passengers respectively, these designs were optimised as regional jets and have matured into the RJ70 with improved FADEC equipped LF 507 engines and digital avionics. First RJ70 deliveries occurred in late 1993 but the type was out of production by 1998, marketing concentrating on the larger RJ85 and RJ100 instead.

The RJ models were originally marketed and manufactured by Avro Aerospace, a separate BAe company, and so named because production of the 146/RJ was moved to the Manchester facility formerly occupied by Avro. Plans for a partnership with Taiwan Aerospace fell through and Avro subsequently became part of the Aero International (Regional) consortium. AI(R) was disbanded in mid 1998 and the Avro RJ again became a BAe product.

Photo: Avro RJ70.

Avro RJ85 and BAe 146-200

Country of origin: United Kingdom.

Powerplants: 146-200 – four 6970lb (31.0kN) Textron Lycoming ALF 502R-5 turbofans. RJ85 – four 7000lb (31.1kN) AlliedSignal LF 507 turbofans.

Performance: 146-200 – cruise speed 377-425kt (698-787km/h); range with 85 passengers and standard fuel 1310nm (2426km) or 1510nm (2797km) with optional fuel. 146-200QT – range with 11.3 tonnes (25,000lb) payload 1120nm (2075km). RJ85 – cruise speed 364-432kt (674-800km/h); range with 85 passengers and standard fuel 1290nm (2389km) or 1450nm (2685km) with optional fuel; range with 100 passengers (standard-optional fuel) 1145-1390nm (2120-2575km).

Weights: 146-200 – operating empty 23,882kg (52,650lb); max take-off 42,185kg (93,000lb). RJ85 – operating empty 24,600kg (54,239lb), max takeoff 43,998kg (97,000lb).

Dimensions: Wing span 26.21m (86ft 0in); length 28.60m (93ft 10in); height 8.59m (28ft 2in); wing area 77.3m² (832sq ft).

Accommodation: Typically 80-85 passengers five abreast or 100 six abreast; up to 112 passengers six abreast. 146-200QT – max payload 11,825kg (26,070lb).

Production: 221 BAe 146s of all models built to 1994 including 116 146-200s (incl 4 QC and 14 QT); 132 RJs of all models delivered by June 1999 including 71 RJ85s.

History: The BAe 146-200 is a simple stretch of the 146-100, while the Avro RJ85 in turn is a modernised version of the 146-200. The 146-200 is essentially similar to its smaller stablemate, but has a 2.41m (7ft 11in) longer fuselage for increased passenger and under-floor cargo volume and increased weights.

The 146-100's powerplants are retained, resulting in slightly degraded airfield performance but better economics due to reduced seat-mile costs. The first BAe 146-200 flew on 1 August 1982, while UK Type Certification was awarded in February 1983. Deliveries began in May 1983 to Air Wisconsin, the first of several US regional airlines to operate the 146 as its quietness allowed it into airports other jets were banned from, or had to operate with reduced payload in order to meet noise requirements.

Versions of the 146-200 include the Quiet Trader (QT) freighter with large cargo door, often used for night freight operations due to its low noise (TNT was the major customer for services in Europe and Australia), and the QC passenger or freight convertible.

The improved Avro RJ85 (the first of the RJ line) first flew on 23 March 1992, and like the small RJ70 and larger RJ100, is a modernised development of the basic 146 with improvements including more efficient FADEC equipped AlliedSignal LF 507 engines, enhanced cabin and a digital flight deck and avionics. Deliveries of the RJ85 began in April 1993 to Switzerland's Crossair.

With more than 370 of all 146/RJ models on order by late 1998, the aircraft continues to sell in modest numbers and was just over 70 sales short of matching Britain's biggest selling airliner, the Vickers Viscount. Further improvements to the basic design (particularly involving a twinjet version with new engines) were being investigated in 1999.

Photo: Avro RJ85. (D McIntosh)

Avro RJ100 and BAe 146-300

Country of origin: United Kingdom.

Powerplants: 146-300 – four 6970lb (31.0kN) Textron Lycoming ALF 502R-5 turbofans. RJ100 – four 7000lb (31.1kN) AlliedSignal LF 507 turbofans.

Performance: 146-300 – cruise speed 377-425kt (698-787km/h); range with 100 passengers and standard fuel 1220nm (2260km) or 1370nm (2358km) with optional fuel. 146-300QT – range with 12.2 tonnes (27,000lb) payload 1060nm (1963km). RJ100 – cruise speed 371-432kt (687-800km/h); range with 100 passengers 1210nm (2241km) with standard fuel or 1355nm (2510km) with optional fuel.

Weights: 146-300 – operating empty 24,878kg (54,846lb); max takeoff 44,226kg (97,500lb). RJ100 – operating empty 25,362kg (55,913lb); max takeoff 44,225kg (97,500lb) or optional 46,040kg (101,500lb).

Dimensions: Wing span 26.21m (86ft 0in); length 30.99m (101ft 8in); height 8.59m (28ft 2in); wing area 77.3m² (832sq ft).

Accommodation: RJ100 – typically 100 passengers five abreast. RJ115 – standard arrangement 116 passengers six abreast; maximum 128 passengers six abreast. 146-300QT – max payload 12,480kg (27,513lb).

Production: 221 BAe 146s of all models built to 1994 including 70 146-300s (incl 10 QT); 132 RJs of all models built by June 1999 including 49 RJ100s.

History: The 146-300, RJ100 and RJ115 are the largest members of the four engined BAe 146 and Avro/Aero International (Regional) Regional Jet families.

The original 146-300 as proposed in 1984 featured a 3.20m (10ft 6in) fuselage stretch over the -200 for 122-134 passengers six abreast, winglets and more powerful ALF 502R-7engines, but the US market in particular wanted a spacious five abreast 100 seater with better operating economics. The resulting 146-300 therefore had a more modest stretch of 2.44m (8ft 0in), no winglets, increased weights and the same engines as the 146-100 and -200.

The prototype was converted from the original 146-100 and flew for the first time on 1 May 1987 with certification granted the following September. The first true 146-300 flew in June 1988 and deliveries to launch customer Air Wisconsin began in December 1988.

The RJ100 is an improved derivative of the 146-300, sharing the latter's fuselage length but with the same more efficient LF 507 engines of the RJ70 and RJ80, improved interior, digital flight deck and avionics plus other upgrades. First flight was on 13 May 1992 and first delivery to THY Turkish Airlines in July 1993. Like the 146-200 and RJ85, freighter versions of the 146-300 and RJ100 are known as Quiet Trader (QT) and a convertible passenger/freight model is also available.

Other customers for the 146-300 and RJ115 have included Jersey European, Ansett NZ, TNT (QT), Thai International, Ansett Australia, China Northwest and SAM Colombia.

The RJ100 has also been marketed as the RJ115 with mid cabin emergency exits allowing up to 128 passengers to be carried in a high density six abreast seating configuration. None had been sold by early 1999.

Photo: BAe 146-300.

Avro Canada Jetliner

Country of origin: Canada.

Powerplants: Four 3600lb (16.0kN) Rolls-Royce Derwent 5 turbojets.

Performance: Max speed 434kt (804km/h) at 30,000ft (9144m); cruising speed 373kt (691km/h) at 30,000ft (9144m); service ceiling 37,300ft (11,370m); design range with typical payload 1085nm (2010km).

Weights: Empty 15,150kg (33,400lb); max takeoff 29,484kg (65,000lb).

Dimensions: Wing span 29.90m (98ft 1in); length 24.61m (80ft 9in); height 8.06m (26ft 5½in); wing area 107.5m² (1157sq ft).

Accommodation: 40-52 passengers four abreast.

Production: 1 prototype only.

History: Although built only as a single prototype, the Avro Canada C-102 Jetliner was a significant aircraft in that it was the world's second jet airliner (flying for the first time just two weeks after the pioneering de Havilland Comet) and the first on the American Continent, beating the Boeing 'Dash 80' prototype by nearly five years.

The Jetliner's commercial prospects were defeated in the end by its engines. The intended power source – two Rolls-Royce Avon axial flow turbojets – was not approved for civil use at the time and were therefore not available. A quartet of the relatively primitive Rolls-Royce Derwent centrifugal flow turbojets had to be substituted with resulting penalties in fuel consumption, overhaul life and operating costs.

Design work on the C-102 began in January 1946 in response to a broad requirement issued by Trans-Canada Airlines (TCA) for a 36 seater with trans-Atlantic range. Avro Canada's parent company in Britain also conducted some design studies to meet the same requirement under the designation Avro 703.

The design evolved during 1946 as an aircraft intended more for short and medium range services, especially those linking city pairs in the USA and Canada. In that sense it was therefore a decade ahead of its time. TCA gave the project its backing in April 1946 by issuing a Letter of Intent covering the construction of two prototypes, but in March 1947 the design had to be revised so the intended but unavailable two Avons could be replaced by four Derwents.

Jetliner design features included a circular pressurised fuselage, a straight wing of similar section to the Lancaster bomber (which had been built in Canada) with simple split flaps and no leading edge devices, integral fuel tanks in the outer wings, retractable tricycle undercarriage, hydraulically powered flight controls and the engines mounted in paired nacelles on the inner wings.

The one and only Jetliner recorded its first flight on 10 August 1949, early testing revealing no major technical problems but higher than expected drag. This in combination with the high fuel consumption of the Derwents was the Jetliner's downfall. Demonstration flights were carried out in the USA and Canada over the next two years, but no orders eventuated. TCA's interest ended in 1951 and after being used for various tests and trials, the aircraft was grounded in November 1956 after logging 452 flying hours.

Photo: The sole prototype Jetliner.

BAC One-Eleven 200/300/400

Country of origin: United Kingdom.

Powerplants: 200 – two 10,410lb (46.3kN) Rolls-Royce Spey Mk.506 turbofans. 300/400 – two 11,400lb (50.1kN) Spey Mk.511.

Performance: 200/300/400 – max cruise 440kt (871km/h); economical cruise 400kt (742km/h); max operational ceiling 35,000ft (10,668m). 200 – initial climb 2500ft (762m)/min; max fuel range 1850nm (3428km); range with typical capacity load 760nm (1408km). 300/400 – initial climb 2580ft (786m)/min; max fuel range 2103nm (3895km); range with typical capacity load 1243nm (2300km).

Weights: 200 – operating empty 21,049kg (46,405lb); max takeoff 35,834kg (79,000lb). 300/400 – operating empty 22,492kg (49,587lb); max takeoff 39,463kg (87,000lb).

Dimensions: Wing span 26.97m (88ft 6in); length 28.50m (93ft 6in); height 7.47m (24ft 6in); wing area 93.2m² (1003sq ft).

Accommodation: Typically 65 passengers in two classes four and five abreast; or 74-89 single class passengers five abreast.

Production: 235 One-Elevens of all models in UK including 58 Srs.200, 9 Srs.300 and 70 Srs.400.

History: Britain's most commercially successful airliner of the 1960s and early '70s, the One-Eleven has its origins in the Hunting H.107 project of 1956, a 32 seater powered by two rear mounted Bristol Orpheus turbojets. The project lay dormant for four years by which time Hunting had become part of the British Aircraft Corporation. As the BAC.107 and now a 59 seater, the design was revived but further enlarged to accommodate 79 passengers as the BAC.111 (marketed as the One-Eleven) powered by two Spey turbofans.

The first order (for 10 aircraft) was placed by British United Airways in May 1961 and in October 1961 Braniff International became the first US airline to order a British product 'off the drawing board' by placing a contract for six. By the time of the prototype One-Eleven's first flight, BAC had 60 orders in the book.

The prototype first flew on 20 August 1963 but crashed two months later with the loss of all on board including test pilot Mike Lithgow. The cause of the accident was the phenomenon known as 'deep stall', the result of airflow to the T-tail being blocked by the wings at high angles of attack and making stall recovery impossible under certain circumstances. From this accident came the modern stick shaker and stick pusher stall protection systems.

Three versions of the original 'short fuselage' One-Elevens were built: the basic short range Srs.200; the heavier, more powerful and longer ranging Srs.300 with increased fuel; and the similar Srs.400 for the US market but with reduced maximum weight to comply with the then US two man crew regulations. The 400's weight was later increased so that eventually it and the 300 were indistinguishable. The 400 was launched against an order for 15 (plus 15 options) from American Airlines in July 1963. The 200 entered service with BUA in April 1965, the 400 with American in early 1966 and the 300 with British Eagle in June 1966. The final delivery of this series of One-Elevens was a 400 to Bavaria Fluggesellschaft in December 1970.

Photo: One-Eleven 400. (Keith Gaskell)

BAC One-Eleven 500

Country of origin: United Kingdom.

Powerplants: Two 12,550lb (55.8kN) Rolls-Royce Spey Mk.512 DW turbofans.

Performance: Max cruise 470kt (871km/h); economical cruise 400kt (742km/h); initial climb 2280ft (695m)/min; max operational ceiling 35,000ft (10,668m); max fuel range 1880nm (3484km); range with typical capacity payload 1480nm (2741km).

Weights: Operational empty 24,758kg (54,582lb); max takeoff 45,201kg (99,650lb) standard or 47,401kg (104,500lb) optional.

Dimensions: Wing span 28.50m (93ft 6in); length 32.61m (107ft 0in); height 7.47m (24ft 6in); wing area 95.8m² (1031sq ft).

Accommodation: Typically 97-109 passengers single class five abreast or up to 119 passengers five abreast in high density layout.

Production: 235 One-Elevens of all models in UK including 86 Srs.500.

History: Although the One-Eleven in its original forms had sold well, large scale production was concentrated over the relatively short period of the second half of the 1960s, after which it declined to a relative trickle. Part of the reason for this was the lack of early availability of a larger capacity variant, allowing the Douglas DC-9 and Boeing 737 to dominate the market. Although it had been the first of the trio to fly, the One-Eleven was the last to be stretched.

The One-Eleven 500 for around 100 seats was launched by a January 1967 order for 18 from British European Airways. Compared to the 400, the 500 was 4.11m (13ft 6in) longer, had wings of extended span, more powerful Spey 512 engines, strengthened undercarriage and increased weights. Like all One-Eleven variants, the maximum weight of the 500 grew, from the original 41,950kg (92,483lb) of BEA's aircraft to 47,401kg (104,500lb) in later versions equipped for high density inclusive tour operations.

The prototype Srs.400 (first flown in July 1965) also served as the Srs.500 aerodynamic prototype and after modification flew in its new guise on 30 June 1967. The first true 500 was flown in June 1968, BEA taking delivery of its first aircraft two months later.

Other customers for the 500 included British Caledonian, British Midland, Philippine Airlines, Transbrasil, Bahamasair, Germanair, Court Line, Cyprus Airways, British Airways (BOAC and BEA merged) and Romania's Tarom, the latter ahead of a deal which would lead to Romanian production of the aircraft (see next entry). The last British built One-Eleven 500 was delivered to Tarom in February 1982. Interestingly, none were sold to the USA.

Other versions of the One-Eleven were proposed but not built including the original stretched Srs.600 of 1968 for up to 130 passengers; the later Srs.600 (1977) as proposed for British Airways for the order eventually won by the Boeing 737-200 (basically a 500 with a new wing and engine silencers); the Srs.700 (1974) for up to 134 passengers and powered by reworked, quieter and more fuel efficient Speys; the Srs.800 (1975) with substantial stretch to carry up to 160 passengers and fitted with CFM56 turbofans; and the almost completely redesigned X-Eleven (1976) for 130-160 passengers in a wider, six abreast cabin and also powered by CFM56s.

Photo: One-Eleven 500. (Dave Fraser)

BAC One-Eleven 475/Rombac One-Eleven

Countries of origin: United Kingdom/Romania.

Powerplants: 475 – two 12,550lb (55.8kN) Rolls-Royce Spey Mk.512 DW turbofans.

Performance: 475 – max cruise 470kt (871km/h); economical cruise 400kt (742km/h); initial climb 2480ft (760m)/min; max operational ceiling 35,000ft (10,668m); max fuel range 1998nm (3702km); range with typical capacity payload 1619nm (3000km); max range (executive version) with optional fuel 2550nm (4723km).

Weights: 475 – operating empty 23,465kg (51,731lb); max takeoff 41,731kg (92,000lb) or 44,680kg (98,500lb) optional.

Dimensions: Wing span 28.50m (93ft 6in); length 28.50m (93ft 6in); height 7.47m (24ft 6in); wing area 95.8m^2 (1031sq ft).

Accommodation: Up to 89 passengers five abreast in high density layout.

Production: 235 One-Elevens of all models in UK including 12 Srs.475. Romanian production – 9 Srs.561.

History: The final One-Eleven variant developed was the Srs.475, intended for operation from secondary airports with low strength and short runways. It combined the short fuselage of the Srs.200/300/400 with the extended wings and more powerful engines of the Srs.500 along with a modified undercarriage using low pressure tyres. The well used Srs.400/500 prototype was once again put to use as the prototype for the 475 and after modification (including 'destretching') reflew in its latest form on 27 August 1970.

The first production 475 flew in April 1971 and the initial delivery was to Faucett of Peru in July 1971. Only 12 were built between then and 1981 with two aircraft stored and not completed and until 1984. Customers were Faucett, Air Malawi, Air Pacific, Oman Air Force (with large freight doors), Sheikh L Al Midani, McAlpine Aviation and Tarom.

The Srs.670 was a development of the 475 for the Japanese market with extended wings, larger flaps and hushkitted engines. The Srs.475 prototype was converted to serve as the development and demonstration 670 in 1977 but no orders were forthcoming.

In 1981, the newly established British Aerospace and the state run Romanian industrial organisation Grupul Aeronautica Bucaresti concluded a technology and trade transfer agreement which would see the One-Eleven built in Romania. The national airline Tarom had already ordered One-Elevens from British production. A new organisation called ROMBAC was established and several kits were supplied to start the programme. The original plan was to build the Srs.475 and 500 in Romania with the programme covering 80 aircraft at a rate of about six per annum of which the 23rd onwards would be entirely built in that country.

As it happened, political and social unrest in Romania restricted the programme to just nine aircraft, all of them Srs.500s (as the Srs.561). The first one flew in September 1982 and the last in April 1989, by which time Romania's troubles had overtaken events.

The One-Eleven has been subject to several planned engine conversions programmes involving replacing the noisy and thirsty Speys with later generation Rolls-Royce Tays. Only one has been flown as a prototype, the Dee Howard 2400 (based on a Srs.400) in 1990.

Photo: ROMBAC One-Eleven 561.

BAC/Aerospatiale Concorde

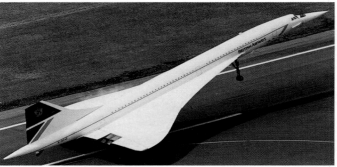

Countries of origin: France and United Kingdom.

Powerplants: Four 38,050lb (169.2kN) Rolls-Royce SNECMA Olympus 593 Mk 610 afterburning turbojets.

Performance: Max cruising speed Mach 2.04 or 1176kt (2178km/h) at 51,000ft (15,545m); initial climb 5000ft (1524m)/min; service ceiling 60,000ft (18,288m); range with typical payload 3550nm (6575km).

Weights: Operating empty 78,700kg (173,500lb); max takeoff 185,069kg (408,000lb).

Dimensions: Wing span 25.56m (83ft 10in); length 62.17m (203ft 9in); height 11.40m (37ft 5in); wing area 358.2m^2 (3856sq ft).

Accommodation: Normally 100 passengers four abreast, maximum 128.

Production: 2 prototypes, 2 preproduction and 16 production aircraft, total 20.

History: A technological and engineering masterpiece, Concorde is the only supersonic transport in service. Its genius lies in its ability to routinely transport 100 passengers in safety and comfort over long distances at twice the speed of sound.

The aircraft survived despite intense lobbying against it by environmentalists, politicians and the US industry, the latter mainly because of the 'not invented here' attitude when the USA cancelled its own SST programme. Despite more than 70 options from 17 airlines being held at one stage, in the end only the two flag carriers of the sponsoring nations (British Airways and Air France) bought Concordes.

Concorde emerged from a major collaborative effort between the aviation industries of Britain and France. It resulted from design work for a supersonic airliner carried out by Sud Aviation and Bristol, whose respective Super Caravelle and Bristol 233 designs had many similarities. The high cost of these programmes led to a 1962 agreement between France and Britain resulting in the British Aircraft Corporation (into which Bristol had been merged) and Sud Aviation (part of Aerospatiale from 1970) joining to design and develop such an aircraft. Rolls-Royce and SNECMA jointly developed the Olympus 593 afterburning turbojet.

Design work concentrated on an aircraft with trans-Atlantic range despite Sud initially preferring a shorter range version. The advanced airframe design features a highly complex delta wing featuring cambering and ogival leading edges with pairs of engines mounted in pods under the wing. The fuel system is designed to trim the aircraft longitudinally by transferring fuel between tanks to counter changes in the centre of pressure as the aircraft accelerates and decelerates. Another feature is the variable geometry nose which is lowered while taxiing and during the lower speed flight regimes to improve visibility from the cockpit.

The first (French assembled) Concorde flew on 2 March 1969 followed by the first from the British line on 9 April 1969. Two preproduction examples followed in late 1971 and early 1973, then the first of 16 production models in December 1973. The final Concorde flew in April 1979. Airline service began in January 1976 after a lengthy development period and the Concorde has been flying safely and reliably ever since. Relatively low utilisation and fatigue management programmes should see it remain in service until at least 2010.

Photo: 12th production Concorde.

Beechcraft 99

Country of origin: USA.

Powerplants: 99 – two 550shp (410kW) Pratt & Whitney Canada PT6A-20 turboprops. A99/B99 – two 680shp (507kW) PT6A-27. C99 – two 715shp (533kW) PT6A-36; three bladed propellers.

Performance: C99 – max cruise 249kt (461km/h); initial climb 2221ft (677m)/min; service ceiling 28,080ft (8558m); range with 15 passengers 450nm (833km); max fuel range 707nm (1310km) at 8000ft (2438m).

Weights: B99 – max takeoff 4944kg (10,900lb). C99 – operating empty 2994kg (6600lb); max takeoff 5126kg (11,300lb).

Dimensions: Wing span 13.98m (45ft 10^1/$_2$in); length 13.58m (44ft 6^3/$_4$in); height 4.38m 14ft 4^1/$_4$in); wing area 26.0m^2 (280sq ft).

Accommodation: 15 passengers two abreast.

Production: 147 Model 99/99A, 17 Model B99 and 75 Model C99, total 239.

History: The emergence of the third level or commuter airline market in the USA during the second half of the 1960s encouraged Beechcraft to develop an aircraft specifically to meet this market's needs.

The resulting Model 99 Airliner for 15 passengers plus flight crew was basically the combination of a stretched version of the unpressurised, piston engined Queen Air fuselage with the wings, powerplants, undercarriage and tail surfaces which would subsequently be applied to the King Air 100 turboprop, itself a stretched development of the existing King Air 90 series.

The prototype Model 99 first flew in July 1966 and deliveries began in July 1968 to the appropriately named US operator Commuter Airlines. Production of the Models 99, 99A and A99 (the latter with more powerful PT6A-27 engines) continued until 1971, by which time 147 had been built, the production peak being reached in 1969 when 82 were delivered.

After that the market slowed dramatically but Beechcraft nevertheless introduced the Model B99 with PT6A-27s in 1972 but only 17 were built between then and the suspension of production in 1975. The Chilean Air Force received eight 99s in 1971 but of the 164 99/A99/B99s built, the vast majority of their 64 purchasers were American. A corporate version of the B99 was also offered as the 'Executive'.

A revival in what was by now called the 'regional airline' market in the late 1970s resulted in the development of the Model C99 Airliner with further increased weights, more powerful PT6A-36 engines and other detail refinements. The C99 was launched in conjunction with the Model 1900 pressurised 19 seater, as described in the next entry.

The first C99 (converted from a B99) was flown on 20 June 1980 and the first production examples delivered to US carriers Sunbird Airlines and Christman Air System in July 1981. Other C99 purchasers included Air Kentucky, Transwestern, Bar Harbor Airlines and Wings West.

Production of the C99 ended in 1986 with the 75th and last example handed over to Rio Airways in February 1987 only to be repossessed two months later and subsequently purchased by Bar Harbor Airlines.

Photo: Beechcraft C99. (E Daw)

Beechcraft 1900

Country of origin: USA.

Powerplants: 1900C – two 1100shp (820kW) Pratt & Whitney Canada PT6A-65B turboprops. 1900D – two 1280shp (954kW) PT6A-67D; four bladed propellers.

Performance: 1900C-1 – max cruise 267kt (494km/h); economical cruise 231kt (428km/h); initial climb 2360ft (719m)/min; operational ceiling 25,000ft (7620m); max range with 10 passengers 1569nm (2906km). 1900D – max cruise 285kt (528km/h); long range cruise 230kt (426km/h); initial climb 2625ft (800m)/min; operational ceiling 25,000ft (7620m); range with 19 passengers 571nm (1058km); max range with 10 passengers 1498nm (2775km).

Weights: 1900C – empty 4327kg (9540lb); max takeoff 7530kg (16,600lb). 1900D – operating empty 4785kg (10,550lb); max takeoff 7688kg (16,950lb).

Dimensions: 1900C – wing span 16.60m (54ft 6in); length 17.63m (57ft 10in); height 4.55m (14ft 11in); wing area 28.1m^2 (303sq ft). 1900D – wing span 17.67m (57ft 11^3/$_4$in); length 17.63m (57ft 10in); height 4.57m (15ft 0in); wing area 28.8m^2 (310sq ft).

Accommodation: 19 passengers two abreast in airliner versions.

Production: 1900C – 248. 1900D – over 300 ordered by early 1999.

History: Beech decided to re-enter the regional airliner market in the late 1970s with three products: the upgraded 15 seat unpressurised C99 Airliner, the Model 1300 13 seat variant of the King Air 200 pressurised corporate turboprop and the Model 1900, a 19 seater with stretched King Air fuselage, more powerful engines, cargo door at the rear and modified tail incorporating 'tailets' on the tailplane tips and 'stabilons' under the rear fuselage.

The prototype 1900 flew on 3 September 1982 and the first delivery (as the 1900C) was to US operator Bar Harbor Airlines in February 1984. Military and corporate versions were also offered, the first example of the latter (as the Exec-Liner) delivered to the General Telephone Company of Illinois in mid 1985. Airline customers included Cascade Airways, Business Express, Continental Air Lines, Texas Air, Great Lakes Aviation, Mesa Airlines, Ontario Express and Conquest Airlines.

Military customers included the USAF (six as the C-12J mission support aircraft), Taiwan (12) and Egypt (eight) for electronic surveillance and maritime patrol duties.

The only major change in the 1900C's basic specification occurred in 1986 when a 'wet' wing with increased fuel capacity was introduced from the 75th aircraft as the 1900C-1. The last example was delivered in November 1991.

The 1900C was replaced on the production line by the 1900D with raised fuselage roofline for 'stand up' headroom, more powerful engines, winglets and additional aerodynamic devices around the tail. First flight was on 1 March 1990 and initial delivery to Mesa Airlines (which has ordered more than 100) in November of the same year.

Since then, the 1900D has dominated the 19 seat regional airliner market with over 300 ordered by early 1999. A corporate version is also offered, the first one delivered to Ghana's Ashanti Goldfields in April 1995.

Photo: Beechcraft 1900D.

Bellanca Airbus and Aircruiser

Country of origin: USA.

Powerplants: Airbus/C-27 – one 650hp (485kW), 675hp (503kW) or 750hp (559kW) Wright R-1820 Cyclone nine cylinder; or 550hp (410kW) or 650hp (485kW) Pratt & Whitney R-1860 Hornet nine cylinder radial; three bladed propeller. Aircruiser – one 550hp or 650hp (410-485kW) Hornet or one 850hp (634kW) Cyclone; three bladed propeller.

Performance: Airbus with 650hp (485kW) R-1860-S3D1-G Hornet – max speed 140kt (259km/h); cruising speed 122kt (227km/h); service ceiling 16,000ft (4877m); max range 565nm (1046km). C-27C with 750hp (559kW) R-1820-25 Cyclone – max speed 143kt (265km/h); max range 956nm (1770km).

Weights: Airbus – empty 2450kg (5400lb); max takeoff 4613kg (10,170lb). C-27C – max takeoff 4380kg (9655lb).

Dimensions: Wing span 19.81m (65ft 0in); length 13.03m (42ft 9in); height 3.52m (11ft 5½in); wing area 60.6m² (652sq ft).

Accommodation: 11-15 passengers.

Production: 30 of all models.

History: A series of large single engined transports developed from the Bellanca Model K of 1928, the Airbus and Aircruiser were distinguishable by their unusual wing configuration – a kind of 'sesquiplane' arrangement in which the company's concept of lift producing wing struts was expanded to provide very wide struts which were in fact lifting surfaces which acted as both wings and struts for the conventional upper wing.

From the fuselage, these joined the spatted main wheels and then tapered to a point where they joined the undersurface of main wing at about two-thirds span and from head on looked like a flattened 'w'.

The 14 seat prototype Model P-100 Airbus flew in 1930 powered by a 600hp (447kW) Curtiss Conqueror inline engine but the unreliability of this engine resulted in a switch to the Wright Cyclone or Pratt & Whitney Hornet radials. Very few found their way into commercial service although the 12 passenger P-200 and 15 passenger P-300 were built. New York and Suburban Airways operated a float equipped Airbus in 1934.

The major customer for the Airbus was the US Army Air Corps which ordered 14 as the C-27 with 12 seats and large cargo door. Four service evaluation Y1C-27s with 550hp (410kW) Hornets were built followed by 10 C-27As with 650hp (485kW) versions of the same engine. The designations C-27B and C-27C were applied to aircraft subsequently converted to Wright Cyclone engines.

The closely related Models 66-70, 66-75 and 66-76 Aircruiser followed with either Cyclone or Hornet power and delivered in small numbers from 1935 mainly to Canadian operators including Central Northern Airways, Mackenzie Air Service and Canadian Pacific Airlines. These operated on either wheels or floats and the last example remained flying until the early 1970s. One Aircruiser was fitted with an 850hp (634kW) Cyclone for improved payload and performance.

Photo: Bellanca Aircruiser. (Keith Myers)

Benoist Type XIV

Country of origin: USA.

Powerplant: One 75hp (56kW) Roberts four cylinder inline piston engine or 70hp (52kW) Sturtevant piston engine; two bladed propeller.

Performance: Max speed 56kt (105km/h); cruising speed 39kt (72km/h); range 43nm (80km).

Weights: Maximum loaded 637kg (1404lb).

Dimensions: Wing span 12.80m (42ft 0in); length 7.92m (26ft 0in).

Accommodation: Pilot and one passenger.

Production: Approximately 10.

History: One of the most important aircraft in the history of commercial aviation – despite only carrying one passenger – the Benoist Type XIV flying boat was responsible for operating the world's first scheduled airline service with a heavier-than-air machine on New Year's Day 1914.

The service was between the Florida centres of St Petersburg and Tampa, a distance of just 16 nautical miles (29km) and the first passenger – Mr A C Pheil – paid the standard fare on the route of $US5 for the privilege of being part of history. The pilot on that flight was Mr Anthony Jannus and the operator was the appropriately named St Petersburg-Tampa Airboat Line.

The aircraft and the airline resulted from some forward thinking by two men – Thomas Benoist and Paul Fansler. Benoist had made a considerable fortune in the automobile industry and had a dream that aircraft could be successfully used for commercial operations and so established himself as an aircraft manufacturer in St Louis, Missouri.

A series of small floatplanes resulted, the Type XIV used on the inaugural commercial service being a biplane pusher using the Curtiss design philosophies as its basis.

Benoist and Fansler got together to create the St Petersburg-Tampa Airboat Line, the route considered ideal for what the two men had in mind because St Petersburg was at that stage two hours away from the nearest shopping establishments by boat, 12 hours by rail and a day trip away by car over bad roads.

The airline was formed on 4 December 1913, Benoist providing the aircraft for the enterprise (and much of the financial backing) while Fansler looked after the business side of things. He was able to negotiate a three months contract with the city of St Petersburg to provide a subsidy for the service to the tune of $US50 per day in January 1914 and $US25 per day over the following two months.

Two round trips between St Petersburg and Tampa were flown each day and the service was quickly profitable such was its demand during the Florida tourist season. The airline was able to repay much of the subsidy by the end of the first month and put a slightly larger Benoist aircraft into service at the end of January 1914.

The $US5 fare was for a one way trip and passengers weighing more than 200lb (91kg) had to pay a surcharge. The contract with St Petersburg expired at the end of March 1914, by which time 1204 passengers had been carried. The operation continued into April 1914 but the end of the tourist season saw a hefty decline in passenger numbers and it ended that month.

Photo: Benoist Type XIV.

Bloch M.B.120

Country of origin: France.

Powerplants: Three 300hp (224kW) Lorraine Algol 9Na nine cylinder radials; two bladed propellers.

Performance: Max speed 140kt (260km/h); cruising speed 124kt (230km/h); service ceiling 20,670ft (6300m); max range approx 700nm (1300km).

Weights: Empty 3700kg (8157lb); max takeoff 6000kg (13,227kg).

Dimensions: Wing span 20.54m (67ft 5in); length 15.30m (50ft 2¹/₂in); wing area 61.0m² (657sq ft).

Accommodation: Typically four passengers plus mail and/or freight or a maximum of 10 passengers two abreast; typical payload 800kg (1764lb).

Production: 12.

History: Marcel Bloch's (later Marcel Dassault) three engined all metal, high wing transport with fixed and spatted main undercarriage was developed during 1933 to meet a requirement for a robust transport for operation in France's overseas colonies, notably those in Africa.

The new transport was to fulfil passenger, freight and mail transport duties plus general military activities. A significant part of the requirement was for an aircraft which would allow France to develop regular air services in Africa and in May 1934 the government owned Air Afrique was established to meet this end.

The M.B.120 prototype was first flown in early 1934, followed by 10 series production aircraft of which six were for civil use and four for the Armée de l'Air. All were used in Africa and a fifth military aircraft was subsequently added to the total.

Commercial services began on 7 September 1934, the Air Afrique M.B.120s operating on a route from Algiers to the French Congo via Niamey and Fort Lamy with numerous refuelling stops in between. The longest leg was 652nm (1207km) between Aoulef and Gao, a flight of some five-and-a-half hours in the M.B.120.

Only mail and freight were carried initially but after experience was built up, passengers were able to join the service from April 1935. The high temperatures and heavy fuel loads associated with the route meant that only three or four passengers plus some freight could normally be carried.

The French Government made one of the M.B.210s available to Service de la Navigation Aérienne de Madagascar for use on its Tananarive (Madagascar) to Broken Hill (South Africa) route from May 1935. A second aircraft was added two months later to meet increasing demand for the service.

This operator extended the service from Madagascar to the Congo in November 1935 and exchanged loads with Air Afrique, allowing mail to be flown over the entire route and then on to and from France. Air Afrique took over the entire African operation in September 1937 and continued flying the M.B.120s until September 1939, although one was reportedly in service as late as 1942.

The Armée de l'Air's M.B.120s were also put to good use in France's African colonies with one or two remaining in use until well into 1942.

Photo: Bloch M.B.120.

Bloch M.B.220 and 221

Country of origin: France.

Powerplants: 220 – two 985hp (734kW) Gnome-Rhône 14N 16/17 14-cylinder radials. 221 – two 1200hp (895kW) Wright R-1820-97 Cyclone nine cylinder radials; three bladed propellers.

Performance: 220 – max speed 178kt (330km/h); economical cruise 151kt (280km/h); service ceiling 22,965ft (7000m); range 756nm (1400km).

Weights: 220 – empty 6807kg (15,007lb); max takeoff 9500kg (20,944lb).

Dimensions: Wing span 22.82m (74ft 10¹/₂in); length 19.25m (63ft 2in); height 3.90m (12ft 9¹/₂in); wing area 75.0m² (807sq ft).

Accommodation: 16 passengers two abreast.

Production: 17.

History: First flown in the same month as the DC-3, the M.B.220 is regarded by some as being the French equivalent of the famous Douglas transports of the time, although in terms of passenger capacity and maximum weight it is closer to the smaller DC-2 which preceded it by 18 months. With only one prototype and 16 production aircraft built, the M.B.220 came nowhere near matching the Douglas airliners' commercial success and its performance was somewhat inferior.

A monoplane of all metal construction, the M.B.220 was intended for use on Air France's main European routes. The prototype first flew in December 1935 and revealed modern features including retractable undercarriage, controllable pitch propellers, low drag engine cowlings and split flaps. Rubber boot de-icing equipment was fitted to the wing, tailplane and fin leading edges after the aircraft entered service.

Air France ordered 14 M.B.220s and inaugurated services in late 1937 on the Paris-Marseilles route with Paris-London flights added in March 1938. Ten had been delivered by mid 1938 by which time the aircraft was operating to other more distant ports including Stockholm and Bucharest. Air France ordered two more at this time, bringing its total to 16. No more were ordered by any operator.

The outbreak of World War II in September 1939 interrupted Air France's commercial use of the M.B.220 and the subsequent invasion of France by Germany saw five of the aircraft seized and handed over to Lufthansa. The remainder spent the war years operated by both the Free and Vichy French in Europe, North Africa and the Middle East.

These aircraft returned to Air France service later in 1945 and were re-engined with more powerful and reliable Wright R-1820 Cyclone radials. The aircraft had been used only lightly since they were built – especially by comparison with modern airliner utilisation – with none showing more than 3000 flying hours in its logbook.

With the new engines installed and now redesignated as Bloch 221s, the aircraft returned to service with Air France in the early postwar years, flying on short range European routes such as between Paris, Strasbourg, Prague and Geneva. They were sold to the Société Auxiliaire de Navigation Aérienne (SANA) in 1949 but all had been withdrawn from service by the end of 1950.

Photo: Bloch M.B.220.

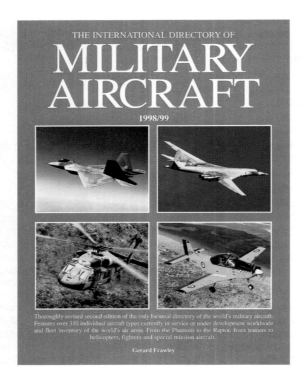

Boeing 40

Country of origin: USA.

Powerplant: 40A/C – one 420hp (313kW) Pratt & Whitney Wasp nine cylinder radial. 40B – one 525hp (391kW) Pratt & Whitney Hornet nine cylinder radial; two bladed propeller.

Performance: 40A – max speed 111kt (206km/h); service ceiling 14,500ft (4420m); max range 565nm (1046km). 40B-4 – max speed 119kt (220km/h); cruising speed 108kt (201km/h); service ceiling 16,100ft (4907m); range 465nm (861km).

Weights: 40A – empty 1602kg (3531lb); max takeoff 2722kg (6000lb). 40B-4 – empty 1688kg (3722lb); max takeoff 2756kg (6075lb).

Dimensions: Wing span 13.47m (44ft 2¼in); length 10.12m (33ft 2¼in); height 3.74m (12ft 3¼in); wing area 50.8m² (547sq ft).

Accommodation: 40A – pilot, two passengers and mail. 40B/C – pilot and four passengers.

Production: 1 Model 40, 25 Model 40A, 43 Model 40B-4 (including 4 in Canada), 10 Model 40C, 2 Model 40X/Y, total 81.

History: Boeing began a period of considerable expansion in the 1920s based on the success of its fighters and the 1926 decision by the US Post Office to transfer transcontinental mail services from the government to the private sector.

The company had already designed and built a specialist mailplane – the Model 40 single engined biplane – the previous year, but its effectiveness was hampered by its heavy 400hp (298kW) Liberty V12 engine. The installation of much more efficient Pratt & Whitney Wasp or Hornet radials on production versions helped Boeing win the contract for the San Francisco-Chicago mail service.

A new company, Boeing Air Transport (BAT), was formed to operate the service, flying from the newly acquired Boeing Field at Seattle. Further expansion followed with the acquisition of Pacific Air Transport, the combination dubbed The Boeing System.

The original Liberty engined Model 40 first flew on 7 July 1925. Of mixed metal, wood and fabric construction, the aircraft could carry a 454kg (1000lb) load of mail.

The improved Model 40A with Wasp engine and completely redesigned steel tube (rather than wooden) fuselage flew on 20 May 1927 and was responsible for BAT winning the contract because it could not only carry the required load of mail, but also two passengers.

The extra revenue generated by the passengers allowed Boeing to bid lower than its rivals for the contract. BAT flew its first service on 1 July 1927.

Model 40 variants were: the basic 40A (of which 24 went to Boeing Air Transport and one to Pratt & Whitney as a testbed); 40B-2 (40As converted to Hornet engines); 40B-4 (first flight early 1928, production version with Hornet, four passenger seats in fuselage); 40C (mid 1928, four passengers, Wasp engine, later re-engined with Hornets, nine to Pacific Air Transport and one to National Park Airways); 40X (one-off executive version for Associated Oil, Wasp engine); and 40Y (also a one-off executive model for Standard Oil but with Hornet engine).

Photo: Model 40B-4. (Boeing)

Boeing 80 and 226

Country of origin: USA.

Powerplants: 80 – three 410hp (306kW) Pratt & Whitney Wasp nine cylinder radials. 80A/B/226 – three 525hp (391kW) Pratt & Whitney Hornet nine cylinder radials; two bladed propellers.

Performance: 80 – max speed 111kt (206km/h); service ceiling 14,000ft (4267m); range 473nm (877km). 80A – max speed 120kt (222km/h); cruising speed 108kt (201km/h); service ceiling 14,000ft (4267m); range 400nm (740km).

Weights: 80 – empty 4187kg (9231lb); max takeoff 6929kg (15,276lb). 80A – empty 4800kg (10,582lb); max takeoff 7938kg (17,500lb).

Dimensions: 80A – wing span 24.38m (80ft 0in); length 17.22m (56ft 6in); height 4.65m (15ft 3in); wing area 113.3m² (1220sq ft). 80 – length 16.74m (54ft 11in).

Accommodation: 80 – 12 passengers three abreast. 80A – 18 passengers three abreast or 12 passengers and 519kg (1145lb) mail or freight.

Production: 4 Model 80, 10 Model 80A, 1 Model 80B, 1 Model 226, total 16.

History: The success of Boeing Air Transport's operations with its single engined Model 40 on the Chicago-San Francisco route with both mail and passengers prompted Boeing to develop a larger aircraft to meet growing traffic needs. In particular, passenger growth needed to be catered for and the resulting Model 80 three engined unequal span biplane was aimed primarily at that market.

Of steel and alloy construction with fabric covering, the first Model 80 powered by three 410hp (306kW) Pratt & Whitney Wasps flew in August 1928 and three more were built for Boeing Air Transport during the course of the year. Accommodating 12 passengers, BAT's Boeing 80s introduced a world first – a stewardess, who sat on a jump seat at the rear of the cabin. All were registered nurses and the first to fly was Ellen Church in May 1930.

The improved Model 80A with more powerful Hornet engines, redesigned tail unit, higher weights, slightly lengthened fuselage and accommodation for up to 18 passengers appeared in 1929. Ten were delivered to BAT and subsequently redesignated Model 80A-1 when reconfigured for mixed passenger/freight operations with 12 seats plus a 519kg (1145lb) cargo or mail payload. They also acquired small auxiliary fins and rudders on the tailplane and reduced fuel capacity.

Two other aircraft in the series were built, the oneoff Models 80B and 226. The original Model 80's enclosed cockpit was greeted unenthusiastically by some pilots who were used to the wind on their faces, resulting in the sole Model 80B with open cockpit, although this quickly reverted to standard. The Model 226 was an 80A built as an executive aircraft for the Standard Oil Company and equipped with six seats, toilet, stove and luxury furnishings.

Production of the Model 80 ended in 1930. BAT began replacing its aircraft from 1933 with the arrival of the more advanced Boeing 247, although successor United Air Lines kept four of them until as late as 1937. One of these was subsequently fitted with a large freight door on the starboard side of the rear fuselage and used by an Alaskan operator who kept it in service carrying mining equipment and other heavy freight until 1945.

Photo: Model 80. (Boeing)

Boeing 247

Country of origin: USA.

Powerplants: Two 550hp (410kW) Pratt & Whitney R-1340-S1D1 (247) or R-1340-S1H1-G (247D) Wasp nine cylinder radials; three bladed propellers.

Performance: 247 – max speed 158kt (293km/h); cruising speed 135kt (250km/h); service ceiling 18,400ft (5608m); range 421nm (780km). 247D – max speed 174kt (322km/h); cruising speed 164kt (304km/h); service ceiling 25,400ft (7742m); range 647nm (1200km).

Weights: 247 – empty 3810kg (8400lb); max takeoff 5783kg (12,650lb). 247D – empty 4148kg (9144lb); max takeoff 6191kg (13,650lb).

Dimensions: 247 – wing span 22.55m (74ft 0in); length 15.65m (51ft 4in); height 4.70m (15ft 5in); wing area 77.7m^2 (836sq ft). 247D – length 15.72m (51ft 7in).

Accommodation: 10 passengers two abreast.

Production: 61 Model 247, 1 Model 247A, 13 Model 247D, total 75.

History: Boeing had developed expertise in the 1930s with modern, all metal cantilever monoplanes with retractable undercarriage through its single engined Monomail and twin engined B-9 bomber. The lessons learnt were applied to the Model 247 twin engined airliner, at the time the most advanced airliner in the world.

In many ways the 247 was a victim of its own technical success. Some 50 knots (93km/h) faster than the trimotors it was intended to replace, 59 were ordered before first flight by United Air Lines but the operator's insistence that they should all be delivered before any other customers got theirs, meant they had to look elsewhere. Most looked to Douglas, notably American Airlines, which issued the requirement that resulted in the DC-3. Superior to the 247, the DC-3 (and its predecessor, the DC-2) sold in very large numbers, while 247 production was restricted to just 75.

There was no prototype as such, the first 247 flying on 8 February 1933 and deliveries beginning only seven weeks later. The 30th 247 was completed as an executive and research aircraft for Pratt & Whitney. Fitted with 625hp (466kW) Twin Wasp Junior engines it first flew in September 1933, while two other standard aircraft were delivered to Deutsche Luft Hansa.

The only other production variant was the 247D, developed to overcome performance shortcomings at high elevation airfields. Although similarly rated, a geared version of the Wasp engine was fitted along with controllable-pitch propellers, the result being markedly improved performance. Other changes included more streamlined engine cowlings and conventional rather than forward sloping windscreens. Production ended in 1935.

Most early 247s were upgraded and 12 247Ds were delivered to United in 1934 with another going to China for the personal use of a warlord as the Model 247Y with machine guns and a plush six seat cabin! The last United 247 was retired in July 1942 while some served with the USAAF in WW2 as the C-73.

The 247's career is perhaps best summed up by its performance in the 1934 England to Australia air race. Flown by Roscoe Turner and Clyde Pangborn, it did well, finishing third outright and second in the transport category... behind a Douglas DC-2.

Photo: Model 247D.

Boeing 307 Stratoliner

Country of origin: USA.

Powerplants: Four 1100hp (820kW) Wright GR-1820-G102 or GR-1820-G105A Cyclone nine cylinder radials; three bladed propellers.

Performance: Max speed 214kt (395km/h); cruising speed 191kt (354km/h); service ceiling 26,200ft (7985m); range 1520-2077nm (2815-3847km).

Weights: Empty 13,749kg (30,310lb); max takeoff 19,051-20,412kg (42,000-45,000lb).

Dimensions: Wing span 32.69m (107ft 3in); length 22.65m (74ft 4in); height 6.32m (20ft 9in); wing area 138.0m^2 (1486sq ft).

Accommodation: 33-38 seated passengers or 16 berthed and nine seated passengers.

Production: 4 S-307, 5 SA-307B, 1 SB-307B, total 10.

History: The world's first pressurised transport to achieve production, the Stratoliner combined the wings (with added leading edge slots), powerplants and tail surfaces of the B-17C Flying Fortress bomber with a new circular section and lightly pressurised fuselage.

Despite being built only in very small numbers, the Stratoliner enjoyed a lengthy career, with some still earning their keep well into the 1960s. Three versions were built: the S-307 (four for Pan American with G102 Cyclone engines); SA-307B (five for TWA with G105A engines incorporating two-speed superchargers); and a single SB-307B for Howard Hughes.

The SB-307B was originally fitted with additional fuel tanks in the cabin for an around the world record attempt which was thwarted by the outbreak of war. Delivered in July 1939, the aircraft was then converted to a 'flying palace' for Hughes' personal use (at a cost of $US250,000) and fitted with 1600hp (1193kW) R-2600 Twin Cyclones. Rarely used, it subsequently passed through several owners and by 1963 had only amassed 500 flying hours in 24 years.

The first aircraft (a Pan Am S-307) flew on 31 December 1938 but crashed three months later while being flown by a KLM pilot. The aircraft entered an unintentional spin, the accident resulting in subsequent Stratoliners being fitted with a larger fin and rudder which was also applied to Fortresses from the B-17E onwards.

The remaining Pan Am aircraft and those for TWA were delivered in 1940, the former basing its 307s in Miami for services to Latin America. Pan Am's aircraft, flown by its own pilots, were extensively used on military transport flying from Miami, Havana and Nassau after the USA's entry into the war before resuming normal duties in 1944.

TWA's five Stratoliners were impressed as C-75s in 1942 and were extensively used on trans-Atlantic services (also flown by the airline's pilots), crossing the ocean some 3000 times. On their return to TWA in 1944 they were rebuilt as SA-307B-1s with B-17G wings and tail surfaces, modified electrical systems and 1200hp (895kW) GR-1820-G666 Cyclones. With pressurisation systems disabled they operated with TWA until 1951 mainly between New York and Kansas City, averaging better than 10 hours utilisation per day.

They were then sold to France's Aigle Azur and subsequently flew with Airnautic of France, Air Laos and in Vietnam. The Pan Am aircraft later flew in Ecuador and with the Haitian Air Corps as a Presidential transport.

Photo: Model 307 Stratoliner.

Boeing 314 'Clipper'

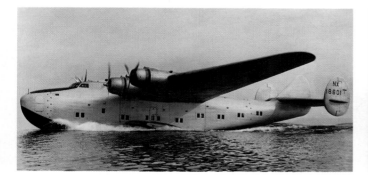

Country of origin: USA.

Powerplants: 314 – four 1500hp (1118kW) Wright GR-2600 Double Cyclone 14-cylinder radials. 314A – four 1600hp (1193kW) Double Cyclones; three bladed propellers.

Performance: 314 – max speed 168kt (311km/h); cruising speed 159kt (294km/h); service ceiling 13,400ft (4084m); range 3041nm (5634km). 314A – cruising speed 163kt (303km/h); range 3202nm (5930km).

Weights: 314 – empty 22,800kg (50,268lb); max takeoff 37,422kg (82,500lb). 314A – max takeoff 38,102kg (84,000lb).

Dimensions: Wing span 46.33m (152ft 0in); length 32.31m (106ft 0in); height 8.41m (27ft 7in); wing area 266.3m² (2867sq ft).

Accommodation: 74 day passengers in four cabins or 40 with sleeping berths.

Production: 6 Model 314 and 6 Model 314A, total 12.

History: Designed to meet a Pan American Airways requirement for a high capacity, long range flying boat with trans-Atlantic capability, the Model 314 combined the wing and horizontal tail surfaces of the one-off Model 294/XB-15 very large bomber (development of which began in 1934) with a capacious fuselage. The 314 was of all metal stressed skin construction and featured large lower fuselage sponsons for stability on the water. These contained fuel which was pumped up into the main wing tanks.

Pan Am ordered six 314s in July 1936 and the first aircraft flew on 7 June 1938. Originally fitted with a single fin and rudder, a twin unit was subsequently installed to help cure directional control problems. A third, centre fin (the same as the original single unit) was also added before the problem was finally solved and this became standard. All six 314s were delivered to Pan American between January and June 1939 and given fleet names including the word 'Clipper' (*Yankee Clipper*, *Dixie Clipper*, *American Clipper* etc), the aircraft universally becoming known as 'Boeing Clippers', although this was never officially adopted.

The first of six improved Model 314As with more powerful engines, larger diameter propellers and increased fuel capacity flew on 20 March 1941 and five of the original Model 314s were upgraded in 1942. Of the 314As, three were delivered to BOAC for service on the wartime trans-Atlantic route. The last 314A was delivered in January 1942.

The Clipper was the largest airliner in the world when it entered service with Pan American. Initial operations were across the North Atlantic, starting with a mail service on 20 May 1939 followed by the world's first trans-Atlantic passenger service from 28 June 1939. They subsequently flew across the Pacific from San Francisco to Hong Kong. With the USA's involvement in World War II, four of Pan American's aircraft were put into military service as C-98s, flown by Pan Am crews. Likewise, the BOAC Clippers were flown by crews from the airline.

Both Winston Churchill and Franklin Roosevelt used Clippers to attend overseas conferences during the war. Pan Am flew its aircraft until April 1946 while BOAC's last Clipper service (Bermuda to New York) was in January 1948. Most were scrapped in 1950-51.

Photo: Model 314.

Boeing Fortress Transport

Country of origin: USA.

Powerplants: B-17F/G – four 1200hp (895kW) Wright R-1820-97 Cyclone nine cylinder radials; three bladed propellers.

Performance: B-17G – max speed 250kt (462km/h); normal cruise 158kt (293km/h); long range cruise 139kt (257km/h); service ceiling 35,600ft (10,850m) max range with standard fuel 2958nm (5471km).

Weights: B-17G – basic empty 16,390kg (36,135lb); normal max takeoff 29,711kg (65,500lb); max overload 32,659kg (72,000lb).

Dimensions: Wing span 31.62m (103ft 9in); length 22.78m (74ft 9in); height 5.82m (19ft 1in); wing area 131.9m² (1420sq ft).

Accommodation: Swedish conversions – 14 passengers.

Production: 12,731 B-17s of all models. Transport conversions include 3 XC-108, 1 YC-108, 8 Fortress Transports by Saab and 1 Model 299AB for TWA; others converted for various civil roles.

History: Boeing's famous B-17 Flying Fortress bomber was widely used postwar in various civil roles but several were converted for purely transport duties. The first was the XC-108 VIP transport for General Douglas MacArthur in 1943.

Converted from a B-17E, it had its armament and armour deleted, bomb bay sealed and a five seat passenger compartment installed in the forward waist area. The XC-108 was used in the Pacific area and a similar conversion from a B-17F (as the YC-108) was performed for use in Europe and the Middle East.

The XC-108A (ex B-17E) and XC-108B (B-17F) were both single conversions for freight transport in New Guinea and fuel carriage over 'The Hump' (Himalayas) route between Burma and China, respectively.

More than 60 B-17Fs and Gs made forced landings in neutral Sweden during WWII. Of these, most were returned to the USAAF in mid 1945 but eight were purchased from the US Government for the nominal sum of $US1.00 each and converted into airliners by Saab.

Gun turrets were removed and faired over, windows fitted in the fuselage sides and 14 passenger seats installed. An elevator was fitted for loading freight into the bomb bay.

The converted Fortresses were operated by Sweden's ABA airline in partnership with Denmark's DDL on trans-Atlantic services. The first Stockholm to New York (via Iceland and Canada) service was flown on 27 July 1945 and the route network was soon expanded to include Rio De Janeiro, Addis Ababa, Cairo, Moscow, Paris and Zurich.

Trans World Airlines had an executive conversion of a B-17G (Model 299AB) which it used for commercial services operating under a Limited Type Certificate for a brief period from 1946 while other users of civil Fortresses included France's l'Institute Geographique National which had a dozen on its books from 1947 for photographic mapping survey work, the last of them not retiring until 1989.

Other B-17s found themselves put to work as executive transports, freighters and water bombers while one of the latter was converted to Rolls-Royce Dart turboprops in 1969.

Photo: Model 299AB Fortress Transport. (Boeing)

Boeing 377 Stratocruiser

Country of origin: USA.

Powerplants: Four 3500hp (2610kW) Pratt & Whitney R-4360-B6 Wasp Major 28-cylinder radials; four bladed propellers.

Performance: Max speed 326kt (603km/h); max cruise 295kt (547km/h); normal cruise 261kt (483km/h); service ceiling 32,000ft (9754m); max range 3650nm (6760km).

Weights: Empty 37,876kg (83,500lb); max takeoff 67,133kg (148,000lb).

Dimensions: Wing span 43.05m (141ft 3in); length 33.63m (110ft 4in); height 11.66m (38ft 3in); wing area 164.3m² (1769sq ft).

Accommodation: Up to 100 passengers on main deck plus 14 in lower deck lounge; typical seating for 63 or 84 passengers or 28 berthed and five seated passengers.

Production: 56 Model 377 Stratocruisers (plus 888 military Model 367/K/C-97).

History: A civil derivative of the Model 367 Stratofreighter built in large numbers for the US Air Force, the Model 377 Stratocruiser was rather less successful with only 55 built. Although offering considerable luxury for passengers thanks to its spacious two deck layout with lounge and bar, the Stratocruiser's commercial prospects suffered by its military origins and extremely complex turbocharged Wasp Major engines, although these problems were no worse than those which grounded the rival Douglas DC-7 and Lockheed Constellation.

Design work on a transport derivative of the B-29 Superfortress bomber began in 1942, the resulting Model 367 combining the B-29's wings, powerplants, tail surfaces and undercarriage with a capacious new 'double bubble' fuselage, of which the lower lobe was the same diameter as the B-29's fuselage. The prototype flew on 15 November 1945 but production models had the more powerful Wasp Major engines, revised structure and taller tail of the B-50 Superfortress. Deliveries (as the C-97 Stratofreighter) to the USAF began in early 1948 and of the 888 built between then and 1956, 811 were as KC-97 tankers.

The first Model 377 Stratocruiser flew on 8 July 1947 against a launch order from Pan American for 20 aircraft placed in June 1946. Other orders were subsequently placed by American Overseas Airlines (8), Northwest (10), BOAC (6), SAS (4) and United Air Lines (7). Pan Am also acquired the prototype and six of the AOA aircraft (for a total of 27) all of which were later fitted with upgraded turbochargers and ten with increased fuel capacity.

BOAC eventually operated 17 — its original six plus four taken over from the cancelled SAS order, six acquired from United and one from Pan Am. BOAC urgently needed more when its Comet fleet was grounded in 1954. The last new Stratocruiser was delivered to BOAC in March 1950.

Pan Am inaugurated Stratocruiser services in September 1948 and like BOAC used its aircraft mainly on the trans-Atlantic route, usually with some berthed accommodation. Those built for Northwest and United differed externally by having square rather than round cabin windows. Pan Am traded many of its aircraft for 707s in 1958-59 while most other operators swapped theirs for more efficient DC-7s or Super Constellations after relatively brief careers. Second hand users included Transocean Airlines and Venezuela's RANSA.

Photo: Model 377-10-30 Stratocruiser.

Boeing 707-120 and -220

Country of origin: USA.

Powerplants: 120 – four 13,500lb (60.0kN) Pratt & Whitney JT3C-6 turbojets. 120B – four 17,000lb (75.6kN) P&W JT3D-1 or 18,000lb (80.1kN) JT3D-3 turbofans. 220 – four 15,800lb (70.3kN) P&W JT4A-3 turbojets.

Performance: 120 – cruise speed 455-496kt (843-919km/h); initial climb 1400ft (427m)/min; service ceiling 31,500ft (9600m); max payload range (no reserves) 2670nm (4945km); max fuel range (no reserves) 4040nm (7483km). 120B – cruise speed 466-535kt (863-991km/h); initial climb 3240ft (987m)/min; service ceiling 39,000ft (11,887m); max payload range (no reserves) 3680nm (6816km); max fuel range (no reserves) 5540nm (10,262km).

Weights: 120 – operating empty 53,525kg (118,000lb); max takeoff 116,575kg (257,000lb). 120B – operating empty 55,590kg (122,553lb); max takeoff 116,575kg (257,000lb). 220 – max takeoff 112,039kg (247,000lb).

Dimensions: Wing span 39.88m (130ft 10in); length 44.04m (144ft 6in); height 12.80m (42ft 0in); wing area 226.0m² (2433sq ft).

Accommodation: Typically 110 passengers in two classes, maximum 174 six abreast.

Production: 856 707s of all models (incl military derivatives) including 56 707-120, 72 707-120B, 7 707-138, 6 707-138B and 5 707-220.

History: The USA's first jet airliner, the 707 was at the forefront of the jet travel revolution, benefiting from the failure of the early model de Havilland Comets and from the large orders placed by the USAF for the related Model 717 (K/C-135) tanker/transport. Both the K/C-135 and 707 evolved from the original Model 367-80 prototype launched in May 1952 and first flown on 15 July 1954.

The K/C-135 family with wider fuselage than the 'Dash 80' and other changes was built first, flying in August 1956 and entering service in April 1957. Production amounted to 820.

The commercial Model 707 featured a further slightly widened fuselage, the initial 707-120 with the same JT3C (military J57) turbojets as most K/C-135s first flying on 20 December 1957. Certification was awarded in September 1958 and by the end of that year launch customer Pan American had six in service. Although intended mainly for domestic routes, Pan Am initiated services on the prestigious trans-Atlantic route on 26 October 1958, three weeks after BOAC's historic first service on that route with a Comet 4. Other 707-120 customers were Continental, American, TWA and the USAF (as the VC-137A).

Performance and operating efficiency increased considerably from May 1961 with the introduction to service of the 707-120B with quieter, more powerful and much more fuel efficient JT3D turbofans for Pan Am and TWA. Most of the earlier aircraft were upgraded.

Other 'short fuselage' 707 variants were the -138 and -138B exclusively for Qantas with fuselage shortened by 3.05m (10ft) and swapping passenger capacity (typically 90 in two classes or 120 all economy) for range on its long trans-Pacific routes; and the 707-220 for Braniff's 'hot and high' South American services with more powerful JT4A turbojets, lower weights and notably improved rate of climb and airfield performance.

Photo: 707-138B.

Boeing 707-320 and -420

Country of origin: USA.

Powerplants: 320 – four 15,800lb (70.3kN) Pratt & Whitney JT4A-3, 16,890lb (75.1kN) JT4A-9 or 17,500lb (77.8kN) JT4A-11 turbojets. 420 – four 17,500lb (77.8kN) Rolls-Royce Conway 508 turbofans.

Performance: 320 – cruise speed 455-522kt (843-967km/h); initial climb 2890ft (881m)/min; service ceiling 37,200ft (11,338m); max payload range (no reserves) 3820nm (7076km); max fuel range (no reserves) 5350nm (9910km). 420 – cruise speed 454-515kt (841-954km/h); initial climb 2100ft (640m)/min; service ceiling 37,000ft (11,278m); max payload range (no reserves) 3980nm (7373km); max fuel range (no reserves) 5850nm (10,836km).

Weights: 320 – operating empty 61,236kg (135,000lb); max takeoff 141,523kg (312,000lb). 420 – operating empty 60,329kg (133,000lb); max takeoff 141,523kg (312,000lb).

Dimensions: Wing span 43.41m (142ft 5in); length 46.61m (152ft 11in); height 12.80m (42ft 0in) or 12.93m (42ft 5in); wing area 268.7m² (2892sq ft).

Accommodation: Typically 121 passengers in two classes; maximum 189 six abreast.

Production: 856 707s of all models (incl military derivatives) including 69 707-320 and 37 707-420.

History: As the first 707-120s were entering service, the pressure was on Boeing to produce a longer range, genuinely intercontinental version of the airliner to meet airline demands and to counter increased competition from the Douglas DC-8.

Work on such a variant had started as early as 1955 following discussions with Pan American and Air France and resulted in the 707-320 'Intercontinental' with stretched fuselage, more powerful JT4A turbojets, increased wing span and fuel capacity and heavier weights. Early aircraft featured the -120's 'short' fin and rudder but later aircraft had taller vertical tail surfaces.

The first -320 (the 13th 707 off the line) flew on 11 January 1959 and the aircraft entered service with Pan American shortly after being awarded certification six months later. Other operators were Air France, Sabena, South African Airways and TWA, the 707-320 'holding the fort' for Boeing until the turbofan powered -320B entered service in 1962.

A turbofan powered version was, however, offered in the meantime. The 707-420 with Rolls-Royce Conways was available two years before the Pratt & Whitney JT3D powered -320B. It was ordered by BOAC, Air India, Cunard Eagle, El Al, Lufthansa and Varig, albeit in relatively small numbers as most operators opted to wait for the later generation JT3D.

Apart from its powerplants and some associated equipment, the 707-420 was identical to the -320. The first example (the 35th 707) for BOAC was flown on 19 May 1959 and deliveries began in April 1960. The 37th and last -420 was handed over to El Al in February 1962.

Despite its brief production life, the -420 pioneered 707 turbofan operations and had one lasting effect on the 707 programme as a whole – it was the first variant to feature the taller fin, rear fuselage ventral fin and powered rudder which were applied to 707s generally, the result of British certification requirements relating to directional control standards in engine out conditions.

Photo: 707-436.

Boeing 707-320B and -320C

Country of origin: USA.

Powerplants: 320B – four 18,000lb (80.1kN) Pratt & Whitney JT3D-3/3B turbofans. 320C – four JT3D-3/3B or 19,000lb (84.5kN) JT3D-7 turbofans.

Performance: 320B/C – cruise speed 462-525kt (856-972km/h); initial climb 2300ft (701m)/min; service ceiling 35,600ft (10,850m). 320C – range with 36,288kg (80,000lb) payload and reserves 3150nm (5835km); max fuel range (with reserves) 5000nm (9262km).

Weights: 320B – operating empty 63,504kg (140,000lb); max takeoff 150,141kg (331,000lb). 320C – operating empty 66,407kg (146,400lb); max takeoff 151,320kg (333,600lb).

Dimensions: Wing span 44.42m (145ft 9in); length 46.61m (152ft 11in); height 12.93m (42ft 5in); wing area 283.3m² (3050sq ft).

Accommodation: Typically 121-147 passengers in two classes or 189-199 in one class six abreast; up to 215 passengers in 707-320C high density arrangement.

Production: 856 707s of all models (incl military derivatives) including 174 707-320B and 337 707-320C; 93 military E-3/E-6/E-8 based on 707-320B/C airframe.

History: Sales of the 707 increased markedly with the introduction of the 707-320B and -320C powered by Pratt & Whitney JT3D turbofans, these models bringing together the elements which would make the 707 the great airliner it always promised to be.

The 707-320B shared the same fuselage, fuel capacity and general systems as the basic -320 in combination with JT3D turbofans, structural modifications which allowed increased operating weights and a substantially modified wing of increased span incorporating low drag tips, full span leading edge slots and larger trailing edge flaps.

Pan American was once again the launch customer and the first -320B flew on 31 January 1962 with services beginning the following June. The airline eventually took delivery of 60, while 18 other customers also ordered new -320Bs.

The 707-320C was the definitive commercial version and the most produced with 337 delivered to 46 civil operators and eight governments or air forces. It differed externally in featuring a large cargo door on the forward port side of the fuselage allowing pure cargo or mixed passenger/freight operations. Revised operating weights and various structural and undercarriage modifications allowed greater payloads to be carried, while Boeing developed a cargo loading system for the aircraft using pallets or containers. Of the approximately 125 707s still in service by early 1999, the vast majority were used for freight work.

The first 707-320C flew on 19 February 1963 and deliveries began four months later. The last 'pure' 707 to be built and delivered was a -320C to the Moroccan Government in March 1982, although this aircraft had first flown in April 1977 as the one-off 707-700 test bed for the CFM56 advanced turbofan. This engine was never adopted for commercial 707s although some military variants have it and large numbers of KC-135 tankers were subsequently re-engined. The 707-320C airframe served as the basis for the E-3 Sentry AWACS and E-6 Mercury command post military variants and as such remained in production until 1991.

Photo: 707-331C.

Boeing 720

Country of origin: USA.

Powerplants: 720 – four 12,000lb (53.4kN) Pratt & Whitney JT3C-7 or 13,000lb (57.8kN) JT3C-12 turbojets. 720B – four 17,000lb (75.6kN) P&W JT3D-1 turbofans.

Performance: 720 – cruise speed 463-522kt (857-967km/h); initial climb 2100ft (640m)/min; service ceiling 38,500ft (11,735m); max payload range (no reserves) 3680nm (6817km); max fuel range (no reserves) 4550nm (8428km). 720B – max cruise 540kt (1001km/h); initial climb 3700ft (1128m)/min; service ceiling 40,500ft (12,344m); max payload range (no reserves) 3570nm (6613km); max fuel range (no reserves) 5600nm (10,373km).

Weights: 720 – operating empty 50,259kg (110,800lb); max takeoff 103,874kg (229,000lb). 720B – operating empty 52,164kg (115,000lb); max takeoff 106,142kg (234,000lb).

Dimensions: Wing span 39.88m (130ft 10in); length 41.50m (136ft 2in); height 12.72m (41ft 9in); wing area 226.0m² (2433sq ft).

Accommodation: Typically 112 passengers in two classes, maximum 149 six abreast.

Production: 65 720, 89 720B, total 154.

History: Boeing introduced a third different structural and engineering standard to the Dash 80 prototype's offspring in 1959 with the Model 720. Although outwardly similar to the 707, the 720 (or 707-020 as it was originally known) differed in several significant ways.

Intended as a simplified 'lightweight' and lower cost 707 derivative for use on short and medium haul routes, the 720 was 2.54m (8ft 4in) shorter than the 707-120, had lower rated JT3C turbojets, reduced weights and modified wings incorporating full span Krueger leading edge flaps, greater wing area, and a 'glove' between the inner engines and fuselage which in effect increased the wing sweep in that area, the result being higher cruising and lower approach speeds.

The first 720 (for launch customer United Airlines) flew on 23 November 1959 and services began in July 1960. Other customers were American, Aer Lingus, Braniff, Eastern, Pacific Northern and the US Federal Aviation Administration.

A turbofan variant was introduced in 1960, the 720B with JT3Ds, bringing the same benefits of lower noise and fuel consumption and increased performance to the 720 as had the 707-120B. Apart from its turbofan engines, the 720B introduced a higher maximum takeoff weight and substantially increased maximum zero fuel weight which increased the weight limited payload by no less than 45 per cent.

And improved power-to-weight ratio gave the 720B the most modest runway requirements of any 707/720 variant and the aircraft's low purchase price saw ordered by 11 operators in the USA and overseas, the nickname 'Bargain Basement Jet' was quickly applied.

The first 720B (for American Airlines) flew on 6 October 1960 and certification was awarded in March 1961. Many 720s were converted to 720B standards and the final example was delivered to Western Air Lines in September 1967. The 720 was important to Boeing as part of the 707/720 'family' (with attendant marketing benefits), and it established a useful customer base in the short-medium haul market for the 727 trijet when it came along a few years later.

Photo: 720-022. (Boeing)

Boeing 727-100

Country of origin: USA.

Powerplants: Three 14,000lb (62.2kN) Pratt & Whitney JT8D-7 or 14,500lb (64.5kN) JT8D-9 turbofans.

Performance: Max speed 547kt (1014km/h); max cruise 526kt (974km/h); economical cruise 495kt (917km/h); initial climb 2940ft (896m)/min; service ceiling 37,400ft (11,400m); max payload range 1390nm (2575km); max fuel range 2989nm (5537km).

Weights: Operating empty 38,556kg (85,000lb); max takeoff 64,411-76,658kg (142,000-169,000lb).

Dimensions: Wing span 32.92m (108ft 0in); length 40.59m (133ft 2in); height 10.36m (34ft 0in); wing area 157.9m² (1700sq ft).

Accommodation: Typically 114 passengers in two classes, maximum 131 six abreast.

Production: 1832 727s of all models including 572 727-100 (of which 164 -100C and QC).

History: The world's most produced jet airliner until overtaken by the 737, serious development of the 727 began in 1959 for an airliner to fill the growing need for a short-medium haul jet with better operating economics and more modest airfield requirements than the 720.

The resulting design combined the same fuselage upper structure (and cross section) as the 707/720 with three economical and quiet (for the time) rear mounted JT8D turbofans, a T-tail and new wing incorporating high lift devices such as outer leading edge Krueger flaps and triple slotted main flaps plus high and low speed ailerons and flight and ground spoilers, the latter for lift dumping on landing. Thrust reversers were fitted to all three engines.

Similar in configuration to Britain's Hawker Siddeley Trident (which flew 19 months before the 727), the Boeing aircraft trounced its rival in the marketplace mainly due to interference to the Trident's design by sponsoring airline BEA, this causing delays and reducing its market appeal and therefore allowing the 727 to dominate.

The initial 727-100 was launched against orders for 40 each from Eastern and United, the prototype flying on 9 February 1963. A further 20 had flown by the end of the year. After certification, the 727 entered service with Eastern Air Lines on 1 February 1964; United began 727 services four days later.

The basic design was developed to incorporate the options of higher operating weights and more powerful engines, each improvement offering customers a choice of configurations to meet individual needs. As a result, more than 50 airlines ordered over 570 727-100s, the last of which was flown in August 1971 and delivered to the ITT Corporation.

A convertible passenger/freight model with cargo door, strengthened floor and freight handling system was developed, entering service with Northwest Orient in April 1966. The 727C's configuration could be changed from passenger to freight (or *vice versa*) or mixed in less than two hours, but the introduction of a quick change (QC) kit with seats, toilets, galleys and floor coverings on pallets allowed this to be reduced to about half an hour.

About 380 727-100s remained in service in early 1999, mostly as freighters and many with hushkits or in the case of 44 UPS 727QFs, re-engined with Rolls-Royce Tay turbofans.

Photo: 727-41. (Boeing)

Boeing 727-200

Country of origin: USA.

Powerplants: Three 14,500lb (64.5kN) Pratt & Whitney JT8D-9A, 15,500lb (68.9kN) JT8D-15, 16,000lb (71.1kN) JT8D-17 or 17,400lb (77.4kN) JT8D-17R turbofans.

Performance: 727-200 Advanced – max speed 549kt (1017km/h); max cruise 514kt (952km/h); economical cruise 471kt (872km/h); initial cruise altitude 33,000ft (10,058m); range with 18,144kg (40,000lb) payload 1530-2160nm (2834-4000km); max fuel range 2370nm (4390km).

Weights: Operating empty 45,360kg (100,000lb); max takeoff 83,825-95,029kg (184,800-209,500lb).

Dimensions: Wing span 32.92m (108ft 0in); length 46.69m (153ft 2in); height 10.36m (34ft 0in); wing area 157.9m² (1700sq ft).

Accommodation: Typically 145 passengers in two classes, maximum 189 six abreast. 727-200F – max payload 28,623kg (63,102lb).

Production: 1832 727s of all models including 1260 727-200s.

History: Announced in August 1965, the 727-200 consolidated Boeing's trijet as the best (and fastest) selling airliner of its time, extending the customer base for operators of the aircraft to no fewer than 104 airlines, corporations and governments. By early 1999 over 900 of the 1260 built remained in service carrying passengers or freight, many fitted with hushkits or other modifications allowing them to operate under the strict Stage 3 noise limitations of the 1990s and beyond.

Compared to the 727-100, the -200 featured a 6.10m (20ft 0in) fuselage stretch allowing as many as 58 additional passengers and increased weights. In its original form the JT8D-9 engines of later 727-100s were retained, and compared to the original, the increased payload resulted in reduced range. Subsequent development of the 727-200 Advanced would see more powerful engine options, higher weights and greater fuel capacity offered in various combinations.

The first 727-200 flew on 27 July 1967 and the first customer – Northeast – inaugurated services in December of the same year. Others in the impressive list of operators included Singapore Airlines, Pacific Southwest, United, Pan American, Continental, American, Eastern, Braniff, Icelandair, Lufthansa, Air France, Iberia, Alitalia, TWA, Delta, Western, Northwest, USAir and numerous others all over the world.

The development of more powerful versions of the JT8D turbofan by Pratt & Whitney led to the 727-200 Advanced with weight, powerplant and fuel capacity options as mentioned above. A redesigned and more modern interior was incorporated, and from 1976, an automatic reverse thrust system for the engines. The result was a highly capable airliner flown by most of the world's domestic trunk route airlines.

The first 727-200 Advanced flew on 3 March 1972 and entered service with All Nippon Airways in July 1972. Convertible and freighter models were later offered and the final 727, a -200F freighter for Federal Express, was flown in August 1984 and delivered the following month. The proposed further stretched 727-300 of 1973 with JT8D-200 engines remained a study only and the 757 was developed in its place.

Photo: 727-224. (Gary Gentle)

Boeing 717-200

Country of origin: USA.

Powerplants: Two 18,500lb (82.3kN) BMW Rolls-Royce BR715 turbofans.

Performance: Cruising speed 438kt (811km/h); range with 106 passengers 1375nm (2547km) or 1812nm (3356km).

Weights: Operating empty 31,298-31,706kg (69,000-69,900lb); max takeoff 51,710kg (114,000lb) or 54,885kg (121,000lb).

Dimensions: Wing span 28.45m (93ft 4in); length 37.80m (124ft 0in); height 8.86m (29ft 1in); wing area 93.0m² (1001sq ft).

Accommodation: Typically 106 passengers in two classes, maximum 117 five abreast.

Production: 115 firm orders held by March 1999, first deliveries scheduled for late 1999.

History: The only Douglas airliner not to be axed following the 1997 takeover of McDonnell Douglas by Boeing, the 100 seat 717 (formerly the MD-95) is the latest development of the DC-9/MD-80/MD-90 family and is designed for high frequency, short range regional airline operations. The 717 model number was previously used for Boeing's K/C-135 family of military tankers and transports.

McDonnell Douglas originally announced the MD-95 at the 1991 Paris Air Show, ahead of an anticipated formal launch later in the same year, first flight in July 1994 and deliveries from October 1995. As it happened, McDonnell Douglas did not offer the MD-95 to potential customers until mid 1994 and the official programme launch was delayed until October 1995 when US discount airline ValuJet (now AirTran Airlines) ordered 50 and optioned a further 50. A late 1998 order for 50 (plus 50 options) by TWA gave the programme a much needed boost.

In January 1998 Boeing relaunched the aircraft as the 717-200. The prototype first flew on 2 September 1998 and service entry with AirTran is scheduled for September 1999.

McDonnell Douglas initially proposed powering the MD-95 with Pratt & Whitney JT8D-218 or Rolls-Royce Tay turbofans, but in February 1994 it was announced that the completely new BMW Rolls-Royce BR715 had been selected ahead of those and an engine from the proposed 'Project Blue' teaming of General Electric, Snecma, MTU and Pratt & Whitney.

Apart from its advanced engines, the basic 717-200 features a fuselage 1.45m (4ft 9in) longer than the DC-9-30's, a wing based on the DC-9-34's, an advanced six LCD screen Honeywell EFIS flight deck and a cabin interior similar to that developed for the MD-90. It is offered in standard 717-200BGW (Basic Gross Weight) and heavier, extended range 717-200HGW (High Gross Weight) forms.

Other 717 variants under study in early 1999 included the shortened 80 seat 717-100 (formerly MD-95-20) and stretched 120 seat 717-300 (formerly MD-95-50).

Partner companies participating in the 717 programme include Alenia (fuselage), South Korea's Hyundai Space & Aircraft Co (wings), Korean Air (nose), AIDC of Taiwan (empennage), ShinMaywa of Japan (engine pylons and horizontal stabilizers), Israel Aircraft Industries (undercarriage), and Fischer of Austria (interior). A 1994 plan for Dalfort Aviation of Dallas, Texas, to perform final assembly of the MD-95 was abandoned.

Photo: 717-200. (Boeing)

Boeing 737-100/200

Country of origin: USA.

Powerplants: 737-100 – two 14,000lb (62.2kN) Pratt & Whitney JT8D-7 turbofans. 737-200 – two 14,500lb (64.5kN) JT8D-9A, 15,500lb (68.9kN) JT8D-15, 16,000lb (71.1kN) JT8D-17 or 17,400lb (77.4kN) JT8D-17R turbofans.

Performance: 100 – economical cruise 460kt (852km/h); max payload range 1000nm (1852km); max fuel range 1540nm (2852km). 200 Advanced – max cruise 462kt (856km/h); economical cruise 430kt (796km/h); range with 115 passengers 1855nm (3436km) standard or 2530nm (4686km) optional; range with 130 passengers (high takeoff weight) 2255nm (4177km).

Weights: 100 – empty 25,855kg (57,000lb); max takeoff 49,896kg (110,000lb). 200 Advanced – typical operating empty 27,692kg (61,050lb); maximum takeoff 52,391-58,106kg (115,500-128,100lb).

Dimensions: 200 – wing span 28.35m (93ft 0in); length 30.53m (100ft 2in); height 11.28m (37ft 0in); wing area 91.0m² (980sq ft). 100 – length 28.65m (94ft 0in).

Accommodation: 100 – typically 100 passengers in one class six abreast. 200 – typically 115-120 passengers in one class six abreast or maximum of 130.

Production: 4250 737s of all models ordered by March 1999 of which 3303 delivered. 737-100 – 30 built. 737-200 – 1114 built including 104 737-200C.

History: A relatively late starter in the short haul jetliner market, the 'Baby Boeing' survived a slow start to be developed over three generations and become by far the biggest selling jet airliner in history. It differed from its rival DC-9 and BAC One-Eleven in having a wider cabin for six abreast seating (utilising the same cross section as the 707 and 727) and rejecting the fashionable rear mounted engines for an underwing engine configuration.

The original short fuselage, 100 seat, 737-100 was announced in February 1965. The prototype first flew on 9 April 1967 and the -100 entered service with launch customer Lufthansa in February 1968. Only 30 737-100s were built including the prototype, ordered by Lufthansa (22), Avianca (2) and Malaysia-Singapore Airlines (5). The last was delivered to MSA in October 1969.

The stretched 737-200 appeared only slightly later, first flying on 8 August 1967 followed by the first delivery to United Airlines the following December. Sales of the -200 built up to very high levels, especially after the introduction of the Advanced models, the first of which flew in April 1971 and entered service with All Nippon Airways the next month.

The -200 Advanced took advantage of more powerful versions of the JT8D engine being developed by Pratt & Whitney, these offered in combination with several optional increased maximum takeoff and operating weights configurations and fuel capacities. By the time the last 737-200s were delivered to China Airlines and Ethiopian Airlines in July 1988, no fewer than 118 operators had ordered them.

Convertible (-200C) and quick change (-200QC) models with large freight doors were also offered, as was a rough field kit. The USAF took delivery of 19 737-200 navigation trainers in 1973-74 as the T-43A.

Photo: 737-236. (Boeing)

Boeing 737-300/400

Country of origin: USA.

Powerplants: 737-300 – two 20,000lb (88.9kN) CFM International CFM56-3B-1 or 22,000lb (97.8kN) CFM56-3B-2 turbofans. 737-400 – two 22,000lb (97.8kN) CFM56-3B-2 or 23,500lb (105.5kN) CFM56-3C-1 turbofans.

Performance: 300 – max cruise 491kt (909km/h); economical cruise 429kt (794km/h); range with 128 passengers 1625nm (3010km) standard or 2520nm (4668km) optional. 400 – max cruise 492kt (911km/h); economical cruise 439kt (813km/h); range with 146 passengers 1960nm (3630km) standard or 2500nm (4630km) optional.

Weights: 300 – operating empty 32,705kg (72,100lb); max takeoff 56,473kg (124,500lb) standard or 62,824kg (138,500lb) optional. 400 – operating empty 34,564kg (76,200lb); max takeoff 62,824kg (138,500lb) standard or 68,040kg (150,000lb) optional.

Dimensions: 300 – wing span 28.88m (94ft 9in); length 33.40m (109ft 7in); height 11.13m (36ft 6in); wing area 105.4m² (1135sq ft). 400 – length 36.45m (119ft 7in).

Accommodation: 300 – typically 120-128 passengers in two classes or up to 149 single class six abreast. 400 – typically 146 passengers in two classes or up to 172 single class six abreast.

Production: 4250 737s of all models ordered by March 1999 of which 3303 delivered. 737-300 – 1106 ordered and 1088 delivered; 737-400 – 486 ordered and 477 delivered by March 1999.

History: The second generation 737 family has been hugely successful for Boeing since it was announced in 1981, the 737-300/400/500 models between them accounting for nearly 2000 sales by early 1999 and taking the overall 737 tally well past the previous record of 1832 held by the Boeing 727.

Compared to earlier versions, all feature efficient and quiet CFM56 turbofans (a joint General Electric/Snecma project) mounted in distinctive nacelles with flattened bottoms, increased use of composites in the airframe, EFIS flight decks, extended dorsal fin and aerodynamic improvements. Various combinations of engine thrust rating, fuel capacity and operating weights are offered optionally.

The first of the new generation was the 120-149 seat 737-300 which recorded its maiden flight on 24 February 1984. Despite the list of modifications it retains 80 per cent airframe spares commonality with the 737-200, which remained in production until 1988. The first -300 deliveries were to USAir and Southwest Airlines in November 1984, the latter becoming a very substantial operator of the type with no fewer than 150 ordered.

The further stretched 737-400 with accommodation for 146-172 passengers first flew on 19 February 1988. It has a fuselage 3.05m (10ft 0in) longer than the -300, more powerful engines and higher weight options. Deliveries began in October 1988, Piedmont taking the first production aircraft.

Although the larger Boeing 757 (refer later entry) was developed to replace the venerable 727 trijet, the 737-400 has to a large extent taken over this role. The -400 has also proven to be popular with charter and holiday package tour operators, flying in a single class, high density arrangement.

Photo: 737-4Y0. (Boeing)

Boeing 737-500

Country of origin: USA.

Powerplants: Two 18,500lb (82.3kN) CFM International CFM56-3B-1 or 20,000lb (88.9kN) CFM56-3C-1 turbofans.

Performance: Max cruise 492kt (911km/h); economical cruise 430kt (795km/h); range with 108 passengers 1520nm (2815km) standard or 2400nm (4445km) optional.

Weights: Operating empty 31,983kg (70,510lb); max takeoff 52,391kg (115,500lb) standard or 60,555kg (133,500lb) optional.

Dimensions: Wing span 28.88m (94ft 9in); length 31.01m (101ft 9in); height 11.13m (36ft 6in); wing area 105.4m² (1135sq ft).

Accommodation: Typically 108-110 passengers in two classes or 132 single class six abreast.

Production: 4250 737s of all models ordered by March 1999 of which 3303 delivered. 386 737-500s ordered and 385 delivered by March 1999.

History: The smallest and last to appear of the second generation 737 family, the -500 is very close in size to the previous -200 but with the upgrades of the new models including CFM56 engines, increased use of airframe composites, aerodynamic improvements and EFIS cockpit. Like the others of the family, engine thrust rating, weight and fuel capacity options are available and all share a common air crew type rating.

The 737-300 is just 0.48m (1ft 7in) longer than the -200 but 2.38m (7ft 10in) or three seat rows shorter than -300 and can be considered a direct replacement for the earlier model. The first aircraft flew on 20 June 1989, certification was awarded in February 1990 and initial customer Southwest Airlines inaugurated services in the same month.

Other 737-500 customers include Aer Lingus, Air France, Air Nippon, Asiana, Braathens SAFE, Continental, Egyptair, Garuda, Hapag-Lloyd, LOT Polish Airlines, Lufthansa, Luxair, Malaysia Airlines, Royal Air Maroc, Sabena, Tunisair, United and several of the major leasing companies. Most also operate 737-300s and -400s and a large proportion have also contracted for the Next Generation (737-600/700/800/900) models.

The surge in orders for the 737 in the second half of the 1990s created substantial problems for Boeing, which was forced to massively increase production. 737 deliveries of all models had dropped from a peak of 218 in 1992 to just 76 in 1996 but in 1998 this leapt to 281 with a further increase to 320 planned for 1999 before reducing again to the still very substantial figure of 282 in 2000.

The production increase resulted in a logistical nightmare creating problems with the supply of components from both within the company and from external suppliers. The production process got out of synchronisation as a result, meaning delivery delays (and associated financial penalties) and a slowdown in anticipated cashflow. The company expended considerable effort sorting it out and things appeared to be once again on track by 1999. With the Next Generation models dominating the order book, production of the 737-300/400/500 will wind down with 114 delivered in 1998, 44 in 1999 and only two planned for 2000.

Photo: 737-59D. (Boeing)

Boeing 737-600/700

Country of origin: USA.

Powerplants: 737-600 – two 18,530lb (82.4kN), 20,000lb (88.9kN) or 22,000lb (97.8kN) CFM International CFM56-7B turbofans. 737-700 – two 22,000lb (97.8kN) or 24,000lb (106.7kN) CFM56-7B.

Performance: Typical cruise speed 450kt (833km/h); max certificated altitude 41,000ft (12,497m). 600 – range with 108 passengers 1505nm (2788km) standard or 3230nm (5983km) optional. 700 – range with 128 passengers 1585nm (2936km) standard or 3300nm (6112km) optional.

Weights: 600 – operating empty 36,955kg (81,470lb); max takeoff 56,246kg (124,000lb) standard or 65,092kg (143,500lb) optional. 700 – operating empty 38,007kg (83,790lb); max takeoff 60,329kg (133,000lb) standard or 70,081kg (154,500lb) optional.

Dimensions: 600 – wing span 34.31m (112ft 7in); length 31.24m (102ft 6in); height 12.57m (41ft 3in); wing area 124.9m² (1344sq ft). 700 – length 33.60m (110ft 4in).

Accommodation: 737-600 – typically 108 in two classes or 132 single class six abreast. 737-700 – typically 126 in two classes, max 149.

Production: 4250 737s of all models ordered by March 1999 of which 3303 delivered. 737-600 – 133 ordered and 13 delivered; 737-700 – 456 ordered and 113 delivered by March 1999.

History: The 737-600 and -700 are the smaller members of Boeing's already enormously successful 'Next Generation' 737-600/700/800/900 family. Among the many changes introduced, the new 737s feature more efficient CFM56-7 turbofans. The CFM56-7 combines the core of the CFM56-5 with the CFM56-3's low pressure compressor and a 1.55m (61in) fan. The new wing has greater chord, span and area, while the tail surfaces are also larger.

The new engines and wings allow the 737 to cruise at Mach 0.78 to Mach 0.80, while the larger wing also allows greater fuel tankage providing transcontinental USA range. Other features include an optional 777 style EFIS flight deck with six flat panel LCDs which can be programmed to present information to suit the type of aircraft involved (including the 737-300/-400/-500 series), allowing a common pilot type rating for the two 737 families.

The Next Generation Boeing 737 family (originally covered by the 737-X designation) was launched in November 1993, starting with the 737-700. It is based on the 737-300, while the smaller 737-600 is based on the 737-500. The first 737-700 flew on 9 February 1997, certification was awarded in November 1997 and launch customer Southwest put the new airliner into service the following month.

The 737-600 first flew on 22 January 1998 and entered service with SAS in September of the same year. Production of all 737 models was running at record rates in 1999 with 320 scheduled to be delivered during the year.

The Boeing Business Jet is based on the fuselage of the 737-700 with the larger 737-800's strengthened wings, centre section and undercarriage. With greatly increased fuel capacity in belly tanks it has a range of up to 6000nm (11,115km). First flight was on 4 September 1998. A convertible passenger/freighter variant of the -700, the 737-700QC, has been ordered by the US Navy as the C-40A with first delivery scheduled for 2000.

Photo: 737-7H4. (Boeing)

Boeing 737-800/900

Country of origin: USA.

Powerplants: 737-800/900 – two 24,000lb (106.7kN) or 26,400lb (117.4kN) CFM International CFM56-7B turbofans.

Performance: Typical cruise speed 450kt (833km/h); max certificated altitude 41,000ft (12,497m). 800 – range with 162 passengers 1925nm (3565km) standard or 2925nm (5418km) optional. 900 – range with 177 passengers 1925nm (3565km) standard or 2728nm (5053km) optional.

Weights: 800 – operating empty 41,554kg (91,610lb); max takeoff 70,535kg (155,500lb) standard or 78,246kg (172,500lb) optional. 900 – max takeoff 74,390kg (164,000lb) standard or 79,017kg (174,200lb) optional.

Dimensions: 800 – wing span 34.31m (112ft 7in); length 39.47m (129ft 6in); height 12.55m (41ft 2in); wing area 124.9m^2 (1344sq ft). 900 – length 42.11m (138ft 2in).

Accommodation: 800 – typically 162 passengers in two classes or up to 189 single class six abreast. 900 – typically 177 passengers in two classes or 189 in single class six abreast.

Production: 4250 737s of all models ordered by March 1999 of which 3303 delivered. 737-800 – 493 ordered and 82 delivered by March 1999; 737-900 – 45 ordered (first delivery 2001).

History: The 737-800 and 737-900 are the largest members of the 'Next Generation' (in effect third generation) 737 family, introducing longer fuselage lengths which increase maximum seating capacity to 189.

Like the smaller -600 and -700 models, the -800 and -900 feature numerous improvements including more efficient CFM56-7 turbofans, a new wing with greater chord, span and area, larger tail surfaces and an optional 777 style EFIS flight deck with six flat panel LCDs which can be programmed to present information to suit the type of aircraft involved (including the 737-500/600/700 series), allowing a common pilot type rating for the two 737 families.

Until its launch in September 1994 the 737-800 was known as the 737-400X Stretch. Compared with the -400 it is 3.02m (9ft 11in) longer, increasing typical two class seating from 147 to 162, while range is also significantly increased. As with other 737 models, various options of engine thrust rating, operating weights and fuel capacity are available.

As of early 1999, the 737-800 was the best selling of the Next Generation 737s which between them had attracted 1114 orders. Of those, the -800 accounted for 494, ahead of the -700 (447), -600 (133) and -900 (40). First flight of the 737-800 was on 31 July 1997 and the first delivery (to Hapag-Lloyd) in April 1998.

The 737-900 is the latest and largest member of the 737 family, launched in September 1997 on the strength of an order for 10 from Alaska Airlines. Compared to the -800, the -900 has its fuselage stretched by a further 2.64m (8ft 8in), allowing an increase in seating to 177 passengers in two classes. First flight of the 737-900 is scheduled for 2000.

From its modest beginnings in the mid 1960s, the 737 family has been developed through three generations and become by far the best selling airliner of all time. On sheer weight of numbers alone it is therefore also one of the most significant.

Photo: 737-824. (Gary Gentle)

Boeing 747-100

Country of origin: USA.

Powerplants: Initially four 43,500lb (193.5kN) Pratt & Whitney JT9D-3 turbofans then choice of 46,950lb (208.8kN) JT9D-7A; 48,000lb (213.5kN) JT9D-7F; 46,500lb (206.8kN) General Electric CF6-45A2; 52,500lb (233.5kN) CF6-50E2 or 53,110lb (236.2kN) Rolls-Royce RB211-524D4.

Performance: Max cruise 522kt (967km/h); economical cruise 490kt (907km/h); operational ceiling 45,000ft (13,716m); range with 442 passengers 4500nm (8335km); range with 366 passengers 5500nm (10,187km).

Weights: Operating empty 169,420-171,869kg (373,500-378,900lb); max takeoff 322,056kg (710,000lb), 333,396kg (735,000lb) or 340,200kg (750,000lb).

Dimensions: Wing span 59.64m (195ft 8in); length 70.66m (231ft 10in); height 19.33m (63ft 5in); wing area 510.9m^2 (5500sq ft).

Accommodation: Typically 366 passengers in three classes or up to 442 single class and ten abreast; high density arrangement for up to 498 passengers in 747-100SR.

Production: 1289 747s of all models ordered by March 1999 of which 1197 delivered. 747-100 production 205 (166 -100, 10 -100B, 29 -100SR).

History: The importance of the Boeing 747 to the history of air transport cannot be understated as it revolutionised the industry. Far bigger than anything preceding it, the 747's passenger capacity reduced seat-mile operating costs to a level which allowed airlines to offer considerably cheaper fares than before.

The 747's sheer size brought with it several then innovative features including a twin aisle widebody cabin configuration, a small upper deck (incorporating the cockpit) above the main deck cabin, and use of the new generation of 'big fan' high bypass turbofan engines. As the 707 and DC-8 had done a decade earlier, the passenger appeal and operating economics of the 747 made it imperative for international airlines to buy what was quickly dubbed the 'Jumbo Jet' as it was as great an advance over these older jets as they had been over the piston engined airliners.

A Pan American requirement provided the impetus to build the aircraft which in some areas drew from design experience gained with the company's unsuccessful bid to win the 1965 contract for a very large transport for the USAF, a competition won by the Lockheed C-5 Galaxy. Pan Am ordered 25 747s in April 1966 to launch the programme.

The first 747 flew on 9 February 1969, by which time 160 had been ordered by 27 airlines. Type approval was gained amazingly quickly for such a major step forward (in December 1969) using five aircraft in the flight test programme. Pan Am inaugurated services with the initial production 747-100 between New York and London on 22 January 1970.

Various powerplant, weights and fuel capacity options were offered to the airlines. 747-100 variants were the -100B with strengthened structure and increased weights and -100SR optimised for high capacity, short range routes for All Nippon Airways and Japan Airlines. The last 747-100s were delivered in 1982.

Photo: 747-121. (Boeing)

Boeing 747-200

Country of origin: USA.

Powerplants: Four 54,750lb (243.5kN) Pratt & Whitney JT9D-7R4G2; 52,500lb (233.5kN) General Electric CF6-50E2; 56,700lb (252.2kN) CF6-80C2B1 or 53,110lb (236.2kN) Rolls-Royce RB211-524D4 turbofans.

Performance: 200B – max cruise 522-530kt (967-982km/h); economical cruise 490kt (907km/h); cruise ceiling 45,000ft (13,716m); range with 366 passengers 6350-6900nm (11,762-12,780km) depending on engine and maximum weight option; range with 442 passengers 5200nm (9630km); 200F – range with 90.2 tonnes (200,000lb) payload 4550-4900nm (8428-9076km).

Weights: Operating empty 169,964-174,000kg (374,700-383,600lb); max takeoff 351,540kg (775,000lb), 356,076kg (785,000lb), 362,880kg (800,000lb), 371,952kg (820,000lb) or 377,849kg (833,000lb).

Dimensions: Wing span 59.64m (195ft 8in); length 70.66m (231ft 10in); height 19.33m (63ft 5in); wing area 510.9m² (5500sq ft).

Accommodation: 200B – typically 366-397 passengers in three classes, 452 passengers in two classes or up to 516 passengers single class high density ten abreast. 200F – total cargo volume 687.0m³ (24,260cu ft); max payload 108.3-112.4 tonnes (238,900-247,800lb).

Production: 1289 747s of all models ordered by March 1999 of which 1197 delivered. 747-200 – 389 built comprising 226 -200B (incl 2 VC-25A for USAF), 13 -200C, 73 -200F and 77 -200M.

History: Heavier, more powerful versions of the 747 with greater fuel capacity featured in Boeing's early planning for the aircraft, as did freighter and convertible models to expand the versatility of the family. Originally designated 747B (passenger), 747C (convertible) and 747F (freighter) these were subsequently grouped together under the overall designation 747-200 as the -200B, -200C and -200F.

The 747-200F features an upwards hinging nose loading door and can carry 29 standard pallets or containers on its main deck (serviced by a fully mechanised powered handling system) while the lower cargo holds up to 30 smaller containers, also serviced by a mechanised loading system. A further variant, the 747-200M Combi was subsequently introduced, this featuring a large cargo door on the port side rear fuselage and allowing operators to carry a mixture of passengers and freight (or either exclusively) as required.

The first 747-200B flew on 11 October 1970 and the initial delivery was to KLM on 16 January 1971. Other first flights and initial deliveries in the series were: 200C – 23 March 1973 and 27 April 1973 to World Airways; 200F – 30 November 1971 and 9 March 1972 to Lufthansa; 200M – first delivery to Air Canada in March 1975.

Two 747-200Bs were built as VC-25A VIP aircraft for the US President in 1987 and four others were completed as E-4 Advanced Airborne Command Posts for the USAF. The last -200B was delivered to Air China in October 1990 and the last of the series was a -200F delivered to Nippon Cargo in November 1991. Many former passenger -200Bs are now being converted to freighters.

Photo: 747-227B. (Boeing)

Boeing 747SP

Country of origin: USA.

Powerplants: Four 46,500lb (206.8kN) General Electric CF6-45A2 or -50E2F; 46,250lb (205.7kN) Pratt & Whitney JT9D-7A; 50,100lb (222.8kN) Rolls-Royce RB211-52B2; 51,600lb (229.5kN) RB211-524C2 or 53,110lb (236.2kN) RB211-524D4 turbofans.

Performance: Max speed 538kt (996km/h); service ceiling 45,100ft (13,746m); range with 276 passengers 6650nm (12,318km); range with 331 passengers 5200nm (9632km); max ferry range 8000nm (14,818km).

Weights: Operating empty 151,457kg (333,900lb); max takeoff 285,768kg (630,000lb), 299,376kg (660,000lb), 303,912kg (670,000lb), 312,984kg (690,000lb), 315,705kg (696,000lb) or 317,520kg (700,000lb).

Dimensions: Wing span 59.64m (195ft 8in); length 56.31m (184ft 9in); height 19.94m (65ft 5in); wing area 510.9m² (5500sq ft).

Accommodation: Typically 276-316 passengers in two classes or maximum of 440 in single class ten abreast.

Production: 1197 747s of all models ordered by March 1999 of which 1197 delivered. 747SP – 44 built.

History: A long range version of the 747 developed to meet a requirement for non stop long haul sectors such as New York-Tokyo, New York-Dhahran and Los Angeles-Sydney, the SP ('Special Performance') is so far the only 747 variant to feature a revised fuselage length.

Fundamentally, the SP swapped payload for additional range with its fuselage shortened by 14.35m (47ft 1in) compared to other 747 models with resultant reduction in passenger capacity. The vertical tail surfaces were enlarged (and fitted with a double hinged rudder) to compensate for the shorter fuselage and a lightened structure in parts of the wing, fuselage and landing gear was incorporated. Maximum weights were reduced (although several options were offered) and redesigned trailing edge wing flaps fitted.

The first 747SP flew on 4 July 1975, certification was awarded in February 1976 and Pan American took delivery of the first of 10 it would eventually receive the following month.

Despite its capabilities, the SP was a slow seller for Boeing, most of the 13 customers taking only two or three. Compared to the 747-200 the SP had poorer operating economics due to its lower seating capacity, but it nevertheless did pioneer several long haul services.

Apart from Pan Am, the only airline to order more than four was South African Airways with six. Other customers were the Abu Dhabi Government, Braniff, China's CAAC, China Airlines, Iran Air, Korean Air Lines, Qantas, the Saudi Government, Saudia, Syrian Arab Airlines and TWA. The final SP was delivered to Abu Dhabi in December 1989.

The 747SP set several long distance records in the mid 1970s, the most prominent of which was on the delivery flight of a South African Airways aircraft on 23-24 March 1976. With 50 passengers on board, it flew nonstop from Paine Field in Washington State to Cape Town, a distance of 8940nm (16,560km). This was a world record for a commercial aircraft and only beaten 13 years later when a Qantas 747-400 flew 9688nm (17,945km) nonstop from England to Australia on its delivery flight.

Photo: 747SP-38.

Boeing 747-300

Country of origin: USA.

Powerplants: Four 54,750lb (243.5kN) Pratt & Whitney JT9D-7R4G2; 53,110lb (236.2kN) Rolls-Royce RB211-524D4; 52,500lb (233.5kN) General Electric CF6-50E2 or 56,700lb (252.2kN) CF6-80C2B1 turbofans.

Performance: Max cruise 507kt (939km/h); economical cruise 490kt (907km/h); long range cruise 485kt (898km/h); range with 400 passengers 6100-6700nm (11,300-12,410km) depending on powerplant and maximum weight option.

Weights: Operating empty 174,137-178,174kg (383,900-392,800lb); max takeoff 351,540kg (775,000lb), 356,076kg (785,000lb), 362,880kg (800,000lb), 371,952kg (820,000lb) or 377,848kg (833,000lb).

Dimensions: Wing span 59.64m (195ft 8in); length 70.66m (231ft 10in); height 19.33m (63ft 5in); wing area 510.9m^2 (5500sq ft).

Accommodation: Typically 400 passengers in three classes or 470 in two classes.

Production: 1289 747s of all models ordered by March 1999 of which 1197 delivered. 747-300 production 81.

History: The 747-300 introduced the first increase in cabin area to the 747 by incorporating a stretched upper deck capable of accommodating up to 69 economy class passengers. It resulted from a number of Boeing studies which looked at increasing the 747's seating capacity.

Ideas examined included fuselage plugs fore and aft of the wing increasing seating to around 600, or running the upper deck down the entire length of the fuselage. Boeing finally launched a more conservative version initially known as 747SUD (Stretched Upper Deck) in June 1980.

The 747SUD designation was soon changed to 747EUD (for Extended Upper Deck), and then 747-300. It first flew on 5 October 1982 (with P&W JT9D engines) and the first delivery was to Swissair in March 1983. Other customers for the 747-300 were Air India, Cathay Pacific, Egyptair, International Lease Finance Corporation, Japan Asia, Japan Airlines, Korean Airlines, KLM, Malaysia Airlines, Qantas, Sabena, Saudia, Singapore Airlines, South African Airways, Thai International, UTA and Varig.

Many of these opted for the 747-300M Combi with large cargo door on the port side fuselage aft of the wing, while the -300SR version optimised for short stage lengths was purchased only by Japan Airlines. The last 747-300 (a Combi) was delivered to Sabena in September 1990.

Compared to the 747-200, the -300's upper deck is stretched aft by 7.11m (23ft 4in), increasing economy class seating from 32 to a maximum of 69. The lengthened upper deck features two new emergency exit doors and allows the fitting of an optional crew rest area immediately behind the flight deck.

The extended upper deck was also offered as a retrofit to existing 747-100/200s, although the only airline to take up this option was KLM. The airline has since converted two to freighters, creating the first 747 freighters with the stretched upper deck

Photo: 747-3B3. (Boeing)

Boeing 747-400

Country of origin: USA.

Powerplants: Four 57,100lb (254.0kN) Pratt & Whitney PW4056; 60,200lb (267.8kN) PW4060; 62,900lb (279.9kN) PW4062; 56,500lb (251.3kN) General Electric CF6-80C2B1F; 60,200lb (267.8kN) CF6-80C2B1F1; 62,100lb (276.2kN) CF6-80C2B7F; 58,000lb (258.0kN) Rolls-Royce RB211-524G; 60,600lb (269.5kN) RB211-524H or 59,000-60,000lb (262.4-266.9kN) RB211-524G/H-T turbofans.

Performance: 400 – max cruise 507kt (939km/h); typical cruise 488kt (904km/h); range with 420 passengers 5930-7270nm (10,984-13,466km) depending on powerplant and maximum weight option. 400F – range with 110.7 tonnes (244,000lb) payload 4300nm (7965km).

Weights: Operating empty 182,256-183,753kg (401,800-405,100lb); max takeoff 362,880kg (800,000lb), 377,849kg (833,000lb), 385,560kg (850,000lb) or 396,900kg (875,000lb).

Dimensions: Wing span 64.44m (211ft 5in); length 70.66m (231ft 10in); height 19.41m (63ft 8in); wing area 520.2m^2 (5600sq ft).

Accommodation: 400 – typically 420 passengers in three classes. 400D Domestic – typically 568 passengers in two classes. 400M Combi – typically six or seven pallets and 266 passengers in three classes. 400F Freighter – 30 pallets on the main deck and 32 LD1 containers in the lower hold; max payload 110.7 tonnes (244,000lb).

Production: 1289 747s of all models ordered by March 1999 of which 1197 delivered. 747-400 – 565 ordered and 473 delivered by March 1999, comprising 372 -400, 19 -400D, 26 -400F and 56 -400M.

History: The 747-400 is the latest, longest ranging and best selling model of the 747 family, launched in October 1985. The first development aircraft flew on 29 April 1988, US certification (with PW4000s) was awarded in January 1989 and initial deliveries were made to Northwest later in the same month. Certification of the GE CF6-80C2 powered version was awarded in May 1989 and that of the Rolls-Royce RB211-524G model in June 1989.

Significant changes over the -300 include a new, two crew digital flight deck with six large CRT displays, an increased span wing with winglets, more efficient engines, recontoured wing/fuselage fairing, upgraded interior design, heavier maximum takeoff weight options, increased fuel capacity and greater range.

Apart from the basic 747-400 passenger model, a number of variants have been offered: the 747-400D Domestic (without winglets) optimised for Japanese short haul domestic sectors; 747-400M Combi passenger/freight model with large cargo door on port side rear fuselage; and 747-400F Freighter which combines the 747-200F's fuselage including upwards hinging nose for straight in loading with the -400's wing. Several growth versions were under consideration in 1999 including the 413,150kg (910,825lb) max takeoff 747-400IGW (increased gross weight) version with a 7700nm (14,263km) range.

A production rate of four per month was maintained in 1998-1999 but this was scheduled to drop to only one per month in 2000 as the market slowed. Stretched and longer range versions remain under study.

Photo: 747-412. (Boeing)

Boeing 757-200/300

Country of origin: USA.

Powerplants: 200 – two 37,400lb (166.3kN) Rolls-Royce RB211-535C; 40,100lb (178.4kN) RB211-535E4s; 38,200lb (169.9kN) Pratt & Whitney PW2037 or 41,700lb (185.5kN) PW2040 turbofans. 300 – two 43,100lb (191.7kN) R-R RB211-535E4-B or 43,850lb (195.0kN) P&W PW2043 turbofans.

Performance: 200 – max cruise 493kt (913km/h); economical cruise 460kt (852km/h); range with 186 passengers 2550-3930nm (4723-7280km) depending on engine and weight option. 200PF – range with 22.68 tonnes (50,000lb) payload 3700-3885nm (6853-7196km). 300 – range with 243 passengers 3440nm (6374km).

Weights: 200 – operating empty 57,970-58,605kg (127,800-129,200lb); max takeoff 99,792kg (220,000lb), 108,864kg (240,000lb) or 115,668kg (255,000lb). 300 – operating empty 64,593kg (142,400lb); max takeoff 122,472kg (270,000lb).

Dimensions: Wing span 38.05m (124ft 10in); length 47.32m (155ft 3in); height 13.56m (44ft 6in); wing area 185.3m^2 (1994sq ft). 300 – length 54.43m (178ft 7in).

Accommodation: 200 – typically 178-201 passengers in two classes or up to 231 single class six abreast. 200PF – up to 15 standard pallets. 300 – typically 243 passengers in two classes, maximum 289 six abreast.

Production: 966 757s of all models ordered by March 1999 of which 845 delivered. 757-200 – 949 orders and 845 deliveries (766 -200, 1 -200M, 78 -200PF); 757-300 – 17 ordered by March 1999, first delivery March 1999.

History: Boeing considered a number of proposals for a larger successor to the 727 trijet during the 1970s (including a stretched 727-300) before settling on a new design initially called the 7N7 incorporating the familiar 707/727/737 fuselage cross section with a new wing, nose, EFIS flight deck, a T-tail (later dropped) and two underwing high bypass turbofans. As the 757-200 (there is no -100), the first orders were placed by Eastern Air Lines (21) and British Airways (19) in late 1978. Engine choices were the Rolls-Royce RB211 initially or Pratt & Whitney PW2000 (originally JT10D) from 1985.

First flight was on 19 February 1982 and the 757 entered service with Eastern in January 1983. Subsequent versions to be offered are the 757-200PF 'Package Freighter' with large cargo door (first delivery September 1987 to UPS) and 757-200M Combi (also with cargo door) with only one delivered, to Royal Nepal Airlines in September 1988.

After many years of offering only a single fuselage length for the 757, Boeing launched the stretched 757-300 in September 1996. Featuring a 7.11m (23ft 4in) longer fuselage, it is aimed mainly at the European inclusive tour market and can carry up to 289 passengers in a high density layout.

The first -300 flew on 3 August 1998, certification was awarded in January 1999 and first delivery to Lufthansa charter subsidiary Condor was in March 1999. By then, orders had also been received from Icelandair and Arkia Israeli Airlines and production of all 757 versions was running at over five per month.

Photo: 757-200.

Boeing 767-200

Country of origin: USA.

Powerplants: 767-200 – two 48,00E0lb (213.5kN) Pratt & Whitney JT9D-7R4D; 50,000lb (222.4kN) PW4050 or 52,500lb (233.5kN) General Electric CF6-80C2B2 turbofans. 767-200ER – two 50,000lb (222.4kN) P&W PW4050; 52,000lb (231.3kN) PW4052; 56,750lb (252.4kN) PW4056 or 57,900lb (257.5kN) GE CF6-80C2B4F turbofans.

Performance: 200 – max cruise 493kt (913km/h); economical cruise 461kt (854km/h); range with 216 passengers 3160-3850nm (5853-7131km) depending on engine and weight option. 200ER – range with 181 passengers 6625-6670nm (12,270-12,355km).

Weights: 200 – operating empty 80,514-80,922kg (177,500-178,400lb); max takeoff 136,080kg (300,000lb) or 142,884kg (315,000lb). 200ER – typical operating empty 84,642kg (186,600lb); max takeoff 175,543kg (387,000lb).

Dimensions: Wing span 47.57m (156ft 1in); length 48.51m (159ft 2in); height 15.85m (52ft 0in); wing area 283.3m^2 (3050sq ft).

Accommodation: Typically 181 passengers in two classes or 216 in three classes; maximum 290 passengers in single class eight abreast layout.

Production: 864 767s of all models ordered by March 1999 of which 736 delivered. 767-200 – 128 ordered and all delivered; 767-200ER – 111 ordered and 101 delivered by March 1999.

History: Developed under the project number 7X7 (originally as a trijet), the 767 medium range twin engined airliner was launched in July 1978 and developed in tandem with the narrowbody 757 with which it shares a common two crew EFIS flight deck and many systems. The 767 also features a unique width 'semi widebody' two aisle cabin seating seven abreast in economy class, although eight abreast is available in a high density layout.

The 767 programme included a high degree of international participation with Aeritalia and Japan's CTDC, Fuji, Kawasaki and Mitsubishi all contributing major components. Development of the 767 (and 757) was driven to a large extent by the realisation in the mid 1970s that environmental matters (fuel efficiency and noise) would become increasingly important criteria for the design of future airliners.

Boeing originally intended to offer two versions, the 767-200 and shorter fuselage 767-100, the latter abandoned as it was too close in capacity to the 757. United Air Lines launched the 767 with an order for 30 767-200s, first flight was on 26 September 1981 and the aircraft entered service with United in September 1982.

The longer range 767-200ER (Extended Range) version features higher weights and an additional wing centre section fuel tank. It first flew on 6 March 1984 and service entry with Ethiopian Airlines was two months later. The -200ER makes full passenger load nonstop flights such as London to Bombay or Miami, New York-Beirut, Tokyo-Sydney or Bangkok-Athens possible. As such, it has found a market as a replacement for Boeing 707s and Douglas DC-8s with some airlines.

The 767-200 went out of production in 1994 when all orders had been filled but a late 1998 order for 10 by Continental has revived the line.

Photo: 767-223. (Boeing)

Boeing 767-300/400

Country of origin: USA.

Powerplants: 300 – two 48,000lb (213.5kN) Pratt & Whitney JT9D-7R4; 50,000lb (222.4kN) JT9D-7R4E; 50,000lb (222.4kN) PW4050; 52,000lb (231.3kN) PW4052; 48,000lb (213.5kN) General Electric CF6-80A/A2; 52,500lb (233.5kN) CF6-80C2B2; 57,900lb (257.5kN) CF6-80C2B4F or 60,000lb (266.9kN) Rolls-Royce RB211-524G turbofans. 300ER – as -300 or 56,750lb (252.4kN) PW4056 or 60,000lb (266.9kN) CF6-80C2B6. 400ER – two 63,300lb (281.5kN) PW4062; 62,100lb (276.2kN) CF6-80C2B7F1 or 63,500lb (282.4kN) CF6-80C2B8F turbofans.

Performance: 300 – max cruise 486kt (900km/h); economical cruise 460kt (852km/h); design range with 218 passengers 4285nm (7937km). 300ER – design range with 218 passengers 6140nm (11,373km). 300F – max payload range 3000nm (5557km). 400ER – design range with 245 passengers 5630nm (10,428km).

Weights: 300 – typical operating empty 87,136kg (192,100lb); max takeoff 156,492kg (345,000lb) or 159,214kg (351,000lb). 300ER – typical operating empty 90,538kg (199,600lb); max takeoff 172,368kg (380,000lb) or 186,883kg (412,000lb). 400ER – operating empty 103,149kg (227,400lb); max takeoff 204,120kg (450,000lb).

Dimensions: 300 – wing span 47.57m (156ft 1in); length 54.94m (180ft 3in); height 15.85m (52ft 0in); wing area 283.3m² (3050sq ft). 400 – wing span 51.92m (170ft 4in); length 61.37m (201ft 4in); height 16.79m (55ft 1in).

Accommodation: 300 – typically 218 passengers in three classes or 269 in two classes; 290 passengers in single class seven abreast or maximum 350 single class high density eight abreast. 300F – max payload 50.8 tonnes (112,000lb). 400 – typically 245 passengers in three classes.

Production: 864 767s of all models ordered by March 1999 of which 736 delivered. 767-300 – 571 ordered and 507 delivered (99 -300, 379 -300ER, 29 -300F); 400ER – 54 ordered by March 1999.

History: Boeing announced it was developing a stretched development of the 767-200 in February 1982, the resulting 767-300 featuring a 6.43m (21ft 1in) longer fuselage and accommodation for up to 350 passengers. The flight deck and systems were carried directly over from the 767-200, other changes relating mainly to the increased length and more powerful engine options.

The 767-300 first flew on 30 January 1986 and entered service with Japan Air Lines the following September. The higher weight and increased fuel capacity -300ER flew on 19 December 1986 with initial delivery to American Airlines in February 1988. Rolls-Royce RB211-524G engines became available from 1989. In 1993 Boeing launched the 767-300F freighter with strengthened undercarriage and wing structure, a cargo handling system, no cabin windows and a main deck freight door. UPS introduced it to service in October 1995.

A further stretched version, the -400ER was launched in January 1997 with an order for 21 from Delta Airlines. Its fuselage is lengthened by a further 6.43m (21ft 1in), it has extended wings, 777 style advanced flight deck, strengthened structure, higher weights and taller undercarriage. First flight is scheduled for October 1999.

Photo: 767-375ER. (Boeing)

Boeing 777-200

Country of origin: USA.

Powerplants: 200 – two 74,000lb (329.1kN) Pratt & Whitney PW4074; 77,000lb (342.5kN) PW4077; 75,000lb (333.3kN) General Electric GE90-75B; 76,000lb (338.0kN) GE90-76B; 75,000lb (333.6kN) Rolls-Royce Trent 875 or 77,000lb (342.5kN) Trent 877 turbofans. 200ER – 84,000lb (373.6kN) PW4084; 85,000lb (378.1kN) GE90-85B; 84,000lb (373.6kN) Trent 884 or 90,000lb (400.3kN) class PW4090, GE90-90B1 or Trent 890 turbofans.

Performance: Typical cruise speed 490kt (908km/h). 200 – range with 305 passengers 3780-5150nm (7000-9540km) depending on engine and weight option. 200ER – range with 305 passengers 5960-7150nm (11,040-13,244km) depending on engine and weight option.

Weights: 200 – typical operational empty 139,165kg (306,800lb); max takeoff 229,522kg (506,000lb), 233,604kg (515,000lb) or 242,676kg (535,000lb). 200ER – operating empty 142,430-143,020kg (314,000-315,300lb); max takeoff 263,088kg (580,000lb) or 286,902kg (632,500lb).

Dimensions: Wing span 60.93m (199ft 11in) or folded 47.32m (155ft 3in); length 63.73m (209ft 1in); height 18.51m (60ft 9in); wing area 427.8m² (4605sq ft).

Accommodation: Typically 305 passengers in three classes or up to 440 in single class nine abreast.

Production: 419 777s of all models ordered by March 1999 of which 191 delivered. 777-200 – 376 ordered and 174 delivered by March 1999.

History: The 777 long range widebody twin incorporates more advanced technologies than any previous Boeing airliner. It was originally conceived as a stretched 767, but airline resistance to that configuration led to Boeing developing an all new design with wider fuselage.

Features include Boeing's first application of fly-by-wire controls, an advanced technology glass cockpit, comparatively large scale use of composites and advanced and extremely powerful engines. The 777 is also offered with optional folding wings where the outer 6.7m (22ft) of each folds upwards for operation at space restricted airports.

The 777-200 as launched in October 1990 was offered in two versions: the basic 777-200 (initially called 'A-Market') and the increased weight longer range 777-200IGW (Increased Gross Weight, initially 'B-Market'). The IGW has since been redesignated 777-200ER.

The first 777-200 flew on 12 June 1994, with joint US FAA and European JAA certification awarded on 19 April 1995. The FAA awarded full 180 minutes ETOPS clearance for PW4074 powered -200s the following month. Deliveries (to United Airlines) began in May 1995 with services starting in June. The first Rolls-Royce Trent powered 777-200ER was delivered to Emirates in April 1997.

The 777-100X was a proposed shortened ultra long range (8635nm/16,000km) model, dropped in favour of the 777-200X design study. If produced (for service entry in early 2002), the -200X will be the world's longest range airliner, carrying 298 passengers in three classes up to 8520nm (15,780km). It will have additional fuel, extended wings, a maximum weight of about 331,128kg (730,000lb) and power from two 100,000-112,000lb (445-498kN) thrust engines.

Photo: 777-200. (Boeing)

Boeing 777-300

Country of origin: USA.

Powerplants: Two 90,000lb (400.3kN) Pratt & Whitney PW4090; 98,000lb (435.9kN) PW4098; 92,000lb (409.2kN) Rolls-Royce Trent 892 or 92,000lb (409.2kN) General Electric GE90-92B turbofans.

Performance: Typical cruising speed 482kt (893km/h); range with 368 passengers 5700nm (10,558km).

Weights: Operating empty 160,393kg (353,600lb); max takeoff 263,088kg (580,000lb) standard or 299,376kg (660,000lb) optional.

Dimensions: Wing span 60.93m (199ft 11in) or folded 47.32m (155ft 3in); length 73.86m (242ft 4in); height 18.49m (60ft 8in); wing area 427.8m² (4605sq ft).

Accommodation: Typically 368-394 passengers in three classes, 400-479 in two classes or up to 550 in single class high density layout nine abreast.

Production: 419 777s of all models ordered by March 1999 of which 191 delivered. 777-300 – 43 ordered and 17 delivered by March 1999.

History: The Boeing 777-300 is the world's largest twin engined aircraft, powered by the world's most powerful turbofan engines, and is also the world's longest airliner. It was designed as a replacement for early generation 747-100s and -200s, offering comparable passenger capacity and range, but with a 33 per cent lower fuel burn and maintenance costs reduced by 40 per cent.

Compared with the basic 777-200, the -300 basically swaps increased capacity for range, although that capability remains very substantial. It features a 10.13m (33ft 3in) fuselage stretch, comprising plugs fore and aft of the wings. The longer fuselage allows seating for up to 550 passengers in a single class high density configuration.

To cope with the stretch and increased weights, the -300 has a strengthened undercarriage, airframe and inboard wing. Other changes over the 777-200 include a tailskid and ground manoeuvring cameras mounted on the horizontal tail and underneath the forward fuselage – necessary given the aircraft's extreme length. Changes have otherwise been kept to a practical minimum to maximise commonality. A single type rating covers all members of the 777 family.

Boeing publicly announced it was developing the 777-300 at the Paris Air Show in June 1995, at which time 31 firm orders from All Nippon, Cathay Pacific, Korean Airlines and Thai Airways had been secured. Production go ahead was given later in the same month.

The first 777-300 was rolled out in September 1997 with first flight following on 16 October. The aircraft made commercial aviation history in May 1998 when it was simultaneously awarded type certification by the US FAA and European JAA along with 180 minutes ETOPS approval. Service entry was with Cathay Pacific later in May 1998.

A longer range version was subject to a design study in 1999 as the 777-300X. If built, it will feature a maximum takeoff weight in the region of 324,324kg (715,000lb) and a range with 368 passengers of 6400nm (11,855km). Production of all 777 versions was running at seven per month in early 1999, dropping to five per month later in the year.

Photo: 777-367ER. (Boeing)

Bombardier de Havilland Dash 8-100/200

Country of origin: Canada.

Powerplants: 100A – two 2000shp (1491kW) Pratt & Whitney Canada PW120A turboprops. 100B – two 2150shp (1603kW) PW121A. 200 – two 2150shp (1603kW) PW123C. 200A – two 2150shp (1603kW) PW123D; four bladed propellers.

Performance: 100A – max cruise 265kt (491km/h); range cruise 237kt (439km/h); initial climb 1560ft (475m)/min; operational ceiling 25,000ft (7620m); range with 37 passengers 820nm (1519km); range with 30 passengers 1100nm (2037km). 100B – max cruise 270kt (500km/h); range with 37 passengers 1035nm (1917km). 200A/B – max cruise 295kt (546km/h); range with 37 passengers 935nm (1732km).

Weights: 100A – operating empty 10,251kg (22,600lb); max takeoff 15,649kg (34,500lb). 100B – operating empty 10,273kg (22,648lb); max takeoff 16,466kg (36,300lb). 200A/B – operating empty 10,435kg (23,004lb); max takeoff 16,465kg (36,300lb).

Dimensions: Wing span 25.91m (85ft 0in); length 22.25m (73ft 0in); height 7.49m (24ft 7in); wing area 54.3m² (585sq ft).

Accommodation: Typically 37 passengers four abreast; maximum 40.

Production: 590 Dash 8s of all models ordered by June 1999 of which 522 delivered. Dash 8-100 – 299 ordered and 296 delivered; Dash 8-200 – 88 ordered and 76 delivered by June 1999.

History: The first of the 'new generation' of efficient 30-40 seat regional turboprop airliners developed in the 1980s, the Dash 8's name derives from its de Havilland Canada DHC-8 designation, the eighth of a line of aircraft starting with the Chipmunk and progressing through the Beaver, Otter, Caribou, Buffalo, Twin Otter and Dash 7 airliner (see under DHC heading).

Development of the Dash 8 began in 1980 in response to what DHC saw as a considerable potential market for a new generation 30 to 40 seat commuter airliner. The first prototype flew on 20 June 1983, Canadian certification was awarded in September 1984 and the first Series 100 delivery was to Canadian operator norOntair the following month.

The Dash 8 has an advanced flight control system and large full length trailing edge flaps and although having modest runway requirements, is not a full STOL aircraft. The modern Pratt & Whitney Canada PW120 turboprops were originally designated PT7A.

Initial Dash 8 production was of the Series 100 with either PW120A or PW121 engines, followed by the Series 100A in 1990. The 100A introduced a revised interior with extra headroom and PW120A turboprops; first delivery was to Pennsylvania Airlines in July 1990. The Series 100B with more powerful PW121s for better climb and airfield performance was introduced in 1992.

Also announced in 1992 was the improved performance Series 200. Announced in 1992, the 200 features more powerful PW123C engines. The 200B derivative has PW123Ds for further improved hot and high performance. Surveillance Australia launched the 200 with an order for three, equipped with search radar and FLIR for Customs use and delivered from April 1995.

From the second quarter of 1996 all Dash 8s have been built with a noise and vibration suppression system, reflected in the changed designation Dash 8Q (Q for 'quiet').

Photo: Dash 8-200. (Bombardier)

Bombardier de Havilland Dash 8-300

Country of origin: Canada.

Powerplants: 300A – two 2380shp (1775kW) Pratt & Whitney Canada PW123A turboprops. 300B – two 2500shp (1864kW) PW123B; four bladed propellers.

Performance: 300 – max cruise 287kt (531km/h); initial climb 1800ft (549m)/min; operational ceiling 25,000ft (7620m); range with 50 passengers 830nm (1537km). 300B – max cruise 285kt (528km/h); range with 50 passengers 878nm (1626km) standard or 1228nm (2275km) with optional fuel. 300E – range 1528nm (2830km).

Weights: 300 – operating empty 11,667kg (25,720lb); max takeoff 18,643kg (41,100lb) standard, 19,505kg (43,000lb) optional. 300B – operating empty 11,719kg (25,836lb); max takeoff 19,505kg (43,000lb).

Dimensions: Wing span 27.43m (90ft 0in); length 25.68m (84ft 3in); height 7.49m (24ft 7in); wing area 56.2m² (605sq ft).

Accommodation: Standard single class seating for 50 passengers four abreast, maximum 56.

Production: 590 Dash 8s of all models ordered by June 1999 of which 522 delivered. Dash 8-300 – 161 ordered and 150 delivered by June 1999.

History: Following the success of the Dash 8-100 series, the Dash 8-300 stretched version was a logical development, taking the aircraft into the 50 seat class, a sector occupied by previous generation regional turboprops such as the Fokker F27.

De Havilland Canada launched full scale development of a 50 seat stretched version of its Dash 8 regional airliner during 1986. The company had become a Boeing subsidiary in January of that year following its purchase from the Canadian Government.

The first Series 300 aircraft was converted from the prototype Dash 8-100, flying in its new configuration on 15 May 1987. First delivery was to Time Air in February 1989. Other early customers included China's Zhejiang Airlines, Air Ontario, Air Nova and Presidential Airways.

The Dash 8-300's fuselage stretch comprises plugs forward and aft of the wing totalling 3.43m (11ft 3in) allowing 50-56 passengers to be carried. The wings are of greater span and other modifications include a larger and repositioned galley, larger toilet, additional wardrobe, dual air conditioning packs, a new galley service door and optional auxiliary power unit (APU).

The Dash 8-300 has been offered in a number of variants. The standard 300 was followed in 1990 by the 300A which introduced optional higher gross weights, interior improvements (as on the Dash 8-100A and including increased headroom) and standard PW123A engines with PW123Bs optional. The 300B was introduced in 1992 and has 2500shp (1864kW) PW123Bs as standard, plus the higher maximum weight offered as an option on the 300A. The 300E has 2380shp (1775kW) PW123Es flat rated to 40 degrees Celsius (104°F) for improved hot and high performance.

Like other Dash 8s, all -300s built since the second quarter of 1996 have been fitted with a noise and vibration suppression system (or NVS) and redesignated as the Dash 8Q-300.

Photo: Dash 8-300. (DHC)

Bombardier de Havilland Dash 8 Q400

Country of origin: Canada.

Powerplants: Two 4573shp (3410kW) Pratt & Whitney Canada PW150A turboprops; six bladed propellers.

Performance: Max cruising speed 350kt (648km/h); max certificated ceiling 25,000ft (7620m) standard or 27,000ft (8230m) optional; max range with 70 passengers 1296nm (2400km).

Weights: Operating empty 16,565kg (36,520lb); max takeoff 27,306kg (60,198lb) standard or 28,690kg (63,250lb) optional.

Dimensions: Wing span 28.42m (93ft 3in); length 32.84m (107ft 9in); height 8.36m (27ft 5in); wing area 63.1m² (679sq ft).

Accommodation: 70-78 passengers in single class four abreast.

Production: 590 Dash 8s of all models ordered by June 1999 of which 522 delivered. Dash 8 Q400 – 42 ordered by June 1999.

History: Bombardier's 70 seat de Havilland Dash 8 Series Q400 is the latest and longest member of the successful Dash 8 family, but is in many ways a new design with its with new engines, avionics and systems, modified wing and stretched fuselage.

The Q400 had a fairly protracted development. De Havilland was already working on a 60-70 seat stretch of the Dash 8 as a competitor for the European ATR 72 and the British Aerospace ATP when Bombardier acquired the company from Boeing in 1992. Studies had begun as early as 1986 and at one stage an in service date of 1992 was regarded as possible.

As it happened, the Q400 programme was not formally launched until June 1995 and the first aircraft flown on 31 January 1998 with certification in June 1999. Initial customers included UNI Airways (Taiwan), SAS Commuter and Tyrolean Airways.

The Q400 is aimed at the short haul regional airliner market for stage lengths of 300nm (550km) or less. Despite the recent proliferation of regional jets, Bombardier claims they have created their own market niche and are not replacing turboprops, which remain more economical over shorter stage lengths. The Q400's claimed break-even load factor for a 195nm (360km) stage length is 42 per cent or 30 passengers.

The Q400 features a new fuselage stretched by 7.16m (23ft 6in) over the Series 300 mated with the familiar Dash 8 nose section and vertical tail, while the horizontal tail is new. The fuselage's cross section and structure is based on the earlier Dash 8's but with entry and emergency exit doors rearranged. The Q400's wing centre section and wing/fuselage join are new, while the outer wing has been strengthened. Power is from two FADEC equipped 4573shp (3410kW) Pratt & Whitney Canada PW150A turboprops driving advanced six bladed Dowty propellers. The undercarriage is also new and a third hydraulic system is fitted.

The Q400 is fitted with Bombardier's NVS active noise and vibration system which reduces cabin noise to levels comparable to the CRJ jet airliner. This is achieved through the use of computer controlled active tuned vibration absorbers (ATVAs) mounted on the airframe. The flight deck features five large Sextant LCD colour screens which present information to the pilots in a similar format to earlier Dash 8s, allowing a common type rating.

Photo: Prototype Dash 8-Q400. (Bombardier)

Bombardier Canadair CRJ

Country of origin: Canada.

Powerplants: 100/200 – two 9220lb (41.0kN) General Electric CF34-3A1 or -3B1 turbofans. 700 – two 12,670lb (56.4kN) CF34-8C1 turbofans.

Performance: 100 – max cruise 459kt (850km/h); range cruise 424kt (785km/h); operational ceiling 41,000ft (12,497m) range with 50 pax 980nm (1815km). 100ER – range with 50 pax 1620nm (3000km). 100LR – range with 50 pax 1970nm (3649km). 200LR – range with 50 pax 2000nm (3705km). 700 – cruise speed 442-464kt (818-859km/h); range with 70 pax 1700nm (3149km). 700ER – range with 70 pax 2032nm (3764km).

Weights: 100 – operating empty 13,653kg (30,100lb); max takeoff 21,523kg (47,450lb). 200LR – operating empty 13,740kg (30,292lb); max takeoff 24,040kg (53,000lb). 700 – operating empty 19,732kg (43,500lb); max takeoff 32,886-34,020kg (72,500-75,000lb).

Dimensions: 100/200 – wing span 21.21m (69ft 7in); length 26.77m (87ft 10in); height 6.22m (20ft 5in); wing area 54.5m² (587sq ft). 700 – wing span 23.01m (75ft 6in); length 32.41m (106ft 4in).

Accommodation: 100/200 – 50-52 passengers in one class four abreast. 700 – 70-78 passengers.

Production: 647 CRJs of all versions ordered by June 1999 of which 313 delivered. CRJ100/200 – 439 ordered and 301 delivered by June 1999.

History: A pioneer of the new 50 seat jet class and based on the Challenger corporate jet, the Canadair Regional Jet (CRJ) is designed to offer the speed advantages of larger jets while simultaneously providing operating economics close to that of comparable size turboprops.

The concept of a stretched airliner derivative of the Challenger jet dates back to 1981 when Canadair first studied a 24 seat development of the original CL-600. Design studies for an airliner based on the improved CL-601 were first undertaken in 1987, Canadair launching the Regional Jet programme in March 1989. The first of three development aircraft flew on 10 May 1991. First customer delivery was to Lufthansa in October 1992.

Apart from the fuselage, major changes over the Challenger include a new advanced wing optimised for airline operations, higher weights, EFIS flight deck, new undercarriage, additional fuel capacity and slightly more powerful versions of the CF34 engine.

The original CRJ100 models – the Series 100, 100ER and 100LR (with progressively higher weights and more fuel) – were augmented by the Series 200 with more efficient engines in 1995. It is available in standard 200 and long range 200LR with optional greater fuel capacity forms. Corporate shuttle configurations are also available as the Corporate Jetliner and the SE (Special Edition).

The further stretched CRJ700 with more powerful engines, redesigned and extended span wing, modified fuselage with greater headroom, modified undercarriage and accommodation for 70-78 passengers first flew on 28 May 1999 with initial deliveries scheduled for early 2001. Customers include American Eagle, Lufthansa and Atlantic Southeast. All the CRJs are international projects with Mitsubishi (aft fuselage), Shorts (fuselage and engine nacelles), Avcorp (tail) and Westland (aft fuselage) involved in the manufacturing programme.

Photo: CRJ100. (Bombardier)

Boulton and Paul P.64/P.71A

Country of origin: United Kingdom.

Powerplants: P.64 – two 555hp (414kW) Bristol Pegasus I.M.2 nine cylinder radials. P.71A – two 490hp (365kW) Armstrong Siddeley Jaguar VIA 14-cylinder radials; two bladed propellers.

Performance: P.64 – cruising speed 149kt (277km/h); range 1086nm (2011km). P.71A – cruising speed 130kt (241km/h); range 521nm (966km).

Weights: P.64 – empty 2778kg (6125lb); max takeoff 4763kg (10,500lb). P.71A – empty 2767kg (6100lb); max takeoff 4309kg (9500lb).

Dimensions: P.64 – wing span 16.46m (54ft 0in); length 12.95m (42ft 6in); wing area 66.8m² (719sq ft). P.71A – wing span 16.46m (54ft 0in); length 13.46m (44ft 2in); wing area 66.8m² (719sq ft).

Accommodation: P.64 – two crew and mail load. P.71A – seven passengers in main cabin.

Production: 1 P.64 and 2 P.71A.

History: The British Air Ministry in 1932 issued a requirement for a high speed mailplane capable of carrying a 454kg (1000lb) load over a range of 1609km (1000 statute miles) at a cruising speed of not less than 241km/h (150mph). Apart from the payload weight requirement, up to 5.0m³ (175cu ft) of volumetric space had to be available for mail.

A single example of the twin engined Boulton and Paul P.64 Mailplane was ordered with the intention of testing it on Empire air routes. An equal span strut and wire braced biplane with a capacious fuselage for its overall size, the Mailplane was of fabric covered all metal construction with wheel spats and a single fin and rudder. Power was provided by a pair of Bristol Pegasus radials attached to the underside of the upper wing.

The sole example (G-ABYK) first flew in March 1933 and was touted as the fastest British civil aircraft by the manufacturer. Its life was short, however, the aircraft crashing during a test flight in October 1933 after entering an unexplained dive from which it failed to recover.

An Imperial Airways requirement for a high speed aircraft suitable for charter and secondary route operations while offering the same levels of passenger comfort as larger aircraft led to the revised P.71A.

Compared to the P.64 it had a lower maximum weight, less powerful Armstrong Siddeley Jaguar engines, a slightly longer and slimmer fuselage, metal fuselage skinning around the cabin area and triple vertical tail surfaces instead of the previous single unit. The P.71A's cabin was fitted out to accommodate seven passengers in a VIP layout or with seats removed it could be operated as light freighter or air ambulance.

Only two P.71As were built – G-ACOX *Boadicea* and G-ACOY *Britomart*, and both were delivered to Imperial Airways in February 1935. They attracted considerable press attention at the time because of their speed compared to contemporary British transports but neither had successful careers nor were they particularly liked by either passengers or crew.

Both had short lives: *Britomart* was damaged beyond repair in a landing accident at Brussels in October 1935 and *Boadicea* was lost in the English Channel in September 1936 during a mail flight, the role for which it had been most often used.

Photo: Boulton and Paul P.64 Mailplane.

Breguet 14 Salon

Country of origin: France.

Powerplant: One 300hp (224kW) Renault 12Fe V12 piston engine; two bladed propeller.

Performance: Bre 14 T.2 – cruising speed 68kt (126km/h) at 6562ft (2000m); range 248nm (460km).

Weights: Bre 14 T.2 – empty 1328kg (2928lb); max takeoff 1984kg (4374lb).

Dimensions: Wing span 14.36m (47ft 1¼in); length 8.99m (29ft 6in); height 3.30m (10ft 10in); wing area 50.0m² (538sq ft).

Accommodation: Two (three in some versions) passengers in forward fuselage.

Production: Approximately 7800 Bre 14s of all models including at least 135 civil models.

History: Regarded as the outstanding French day bomber/reconnaissance aircraft of World War I, the Breguet 14 was built in numerous military then civil versions. The prototype flew on 21 November 1916 and the type remained in production until 1928, built in nine factories. Of the production total, one-third were built after 1918.

The Bre 14 was a robust, single engined biplane with unequal span wings. Construction was of duralumin, steel and timber with fabric covering. Most were powered by the reliable 300hp (224kW) Renault 12F V12 but alternative powerplants included the 400hp (298kW) Renault 12K, 300hp (224kW) Fiat A.12bis, and 400hp (298kW) Liberty.

Military versions carried a crew of two with the pilot in the front cockpit and the observer/gunner behind with twin rear firing machine guns. A fixed forward firing gun was fitted and light bombs could be carried under the wings.

Service began in mid 1917 and wartime versions included the Bre 14 A.2 armed reconnaissance version with camera, Bre 14 B.2 bomber and Bre 14S ambulance. Postwar, the aircraft was extensively used by France in its overseas colonies until 1932 and exports were made to 11 nations in Europe and South America.

Commercial operations were preceded by a series of long distance flights in early 1919 including a double crossing of the Mediterranean plus Lyons-Rome-Nice and Le Bourget-Morocco flights.

The major purely civil version, the Bre 14T.2 Salon, entered service with Compagnie des Messageries Aériennes (CMA) in 1919. The fuselage was deepened so that two passengers could be accommodated forward, some windows were installed, a small door fitted to the starboard side and the pilot's cockpit moved back to where the observer/gunner's station had previously been.

The Bre 14Tbis differed in having more cabin windows, the Bre 14 Torpédo carried mail in two streamlined pods under the inner upper wing, and other aircraft (converted from military Bre A.2s) had their fuel tanks removed from the fuselage and relocated in external pods under the lower wings. Floatplane and ambulance versions were also developed and some carried three passengers.

CMA operated Salons from France to various parts of Europe including London while the largest fleet was operated by Lignes Aériennes Latécoère, whose 100 or so Salons of various types flew in Europe, Africa and South America. Other operators included Belgium's SNETA.

Photo: Bre 14 T.2 Salon.

Breguet 763 Provence

Country of origin: France.

Powerplants: Four 2400hp (1790kW) Pratt & Whitney R-2800-CA18 Double Wasp 18-cylinder radials; three bladed propellers.

Performance: Max cruise 210kt (389km/h); economical cruise 182kt (338km/h); service ceiling 23,950ft (7300m); max payload range 1169nm (2165km); max range 2535nm (4695km).

Weights: Operating empty 32,535kg (71,726kg); max takeoff 51,600kg (113,757lb).

Dimensions: Wing span 42.99m (141ft 0in); length 28.94m (94ft 11½in); height 9.55m (31ft 4in); wing area 185.4m² (1996sq ft).

Accommodation: Typically 117 passengers (59 on upper deck, 48 on lower deck); maximum 135 passengers.

Production: 1 Br 761 prototype, 3 Br 761S pre-production, 12 Br 763, 4 Br 765, total 20.

History: Ungainly but capable, the double decker Br 761-765 family gave sterling service to Air France and the Armée de l'Air. Capable of transporting either passengers or freight (including mixed loads), the aircraft could carry a 12.2 tonne (26,895lb) payload in the latter role. Freight (including vehicles) was loaded via clamshell doors in the lower rear fuselage.

The aircraft was known by several names: the manufacturer referred to it as the Deux Ponts (for 'two decks'), Air France called its fleet of Br 763s the Provence and in French military service it was known as the Sahara.

Design work on the Deux Ponts began in 1944 but the circumstances of the time dictated a lengthy delay and the first flight of the prototype Br 761 was not until 15 February 1949. Of all metal construction with tricycle undercarriage, this aircraft featured twin fins and rudders inset from the tips and was powered by four 1580hp (1178kW) SNECMA built Gnome-Rhône 14R radials.

Three pre-production Br 761Ss followed, differing from the prototype in having 2020hp (1506kW) Pratt & Whitney R-2800-B31 engines, modified wingtips and revised vertical tail surfaces with a third, smaller fin introduced above the rear fuselage. One Br 761S was leased to Air Algérie and another served briefly with Britain's Silver City Airways before all three were transferred to the Armée de l'Air.

Air France ordered 12 examples of an upgraded version, the Br 763, in 1951. Featuring more powerful R-2800-CA18 engines, a three rather than four crew cockpit and strengthened wings, the first example flew on 20 July 1951 and entered service in August 1952 as the Provence.

Provences were operated almost exclusively on services between France and Algiers and in 1964 six were transferred to the Armée de l'Air, joining four other new build Br 765s with removable cargo doors which had been delivered from 1958 and the three pre-production aircraft. Called the Sahara in military service, they were capable of carrying up to 146 equipped troops. The last was retired in late 1972.

Air France's six remaining Provences ended their days as freighters (with yet another name – Universal) and they were retired in 1971.

Photo: Br 763 Provence.

Bristol 170 Freighter

Country of origin: United Kingdom.

Powerplants: Mk.21 – two 1690hp (1260kW) Bristol Hercules 672 14-cylinder radials. Mk.31/32 – two 1980hp (1476kW) Hercules 734; four bladed propellers.

Performance: Mk.21 – max speed 169kt (314km/h); cruising speed 143kt (265km/h); max payload range 426nm (788km). Mk.31/32 – max cruise 168kt (310km/h); normal cruise 143kt (265km/h); max payload range 712nm (1320km).

Weights: Mk.21 – empty 12,013kg (26,484lb); max takeoff 18,144kg (40,000lb). Mk.31 – empty 12,206kg (26,910lb); max takeoff 19,958kg (44,000lb); max payload 5670kg (12,500lb). Mk.32 – empty 13,404kg (29,550lb); max takeoff 19,958kg (44,000lb).

Dimensions: Mk.21/31 – wing span 32.92m (108ft 0in); length 20.83m (68ft 4in); height 6.60m (21ft 8in); wing area 138.1m² (1487sq ft). Mk.32 – length 22.35m (73ft 4in); height 7.24m (23ft 9in).

Accommodation: Mk.I/21/31 – typically two small/medium cars and 15 passengers or up to 32 passengers or freight. Mk.32 – three small/medium cars and 23 passengers or maximum of 60 passengers in high density layout.

Production: 24 Mk.I, 19 Mk.II, 4 Mk.XI, 61 Mk.21, 88 Mk.31, 18 Mk.32, total 214.

History: Bristol began work on its Type 170 short range transport in 1944 as a private venture, the intention being to design a rugged and simple low cost workhorse for both civil and military applications. Features included an unobstructed rectangular section cabin of 66.8m³ (2360cu ft) volume with the flight deck mounted above it and clamshell doors in the nose for straight in loading, fixed undercarriage and the use of steel in the structure rather than expensive alloys.

Variants were the original Mk.I Freighter and Mk.II Wayfarer passenger transport with nose doors deleted, wing span of 29.87m (98ft 0in) and 1675hp (1249kW) Hercules 675s; Mk.XI mixed traffic version with definitive extended wing; Mk.21 with slightly more powerful Hercules 672s; and Mk.31 with Hercules 732s and extended fin fillet. Maximum weights grew with each model and both the Mk.21 and 31 were available in either basic Freighter form or as 21/31E convertible passenger/freight Wayfarers.

The final version was the Mk.32 developed for Silver City Airways with taller fin and lengthened nose so an additional car could be carried on cross-Channel car ferry services. Initial delivery was in March 1953, several were converted from earlier models on the production line.

The prototype Mk.I first flew on 2 December 1945 and the second aircraft (a Mk.II) in April 1946. The Type 170 was a commercial success with the long list of civil operators including Indian National Airways, Air Vietnam, Channel Island Airways, Silver City Airways, Channel Air Bridge, Air Charter, Hunting Air Surveys, Shell, Bharat Airways, Dan-Air, Iberia, Wardair, SAFE and Skytravel. Military customers included Australia, Canada, New Zealand, Burma and Pakistan which received 68 Mks.21/31 in 1950-55.

The last Freighter – a Mk.31 for New Zealand's Straits Air Freight – flew in February 1958 and only one remained in service by early 1999 with Canada's Hawkair Aviation Services.

Photo: Freighter Mk.31M.

Bristol Brabazon

Country of origin: United Kingdom.

Powerplants: Eight 2500hp (1864kW) Bristol Centaurus 20 18-cylinder radials in four coupled pairs; four sets of six bladed contra-rotating propellers.

Performance: Max speed 261kt (483km/h); cruising speed 217kt (402km/h) at 25,000ft (7620m); range 4780nm (8853km).

Weights: Empty 72,263kg (159,310lb); max takeoff 131,544kg (290,000lb).

Dimensions: Wing span 70.10m (230ft 0in); length 53.95m (177ft 0in); height 15.24m (50ft 0in); wing area 493.9m² (5317sq ft).

Accommodation: Planned to carry 100 passengers in standard long range layout, maximum 180 for short range operations.

Production: 1 completed and flown, construction of second abandoned.

History: In order to establish what types of aircraft would be needed to meet Britain's postwar commercial aviation requirements, a committee was established in December 1942 under the chairmanship of Lord Brabazon of Tara. This 'Brabazon Committee' identified the need to develop five types to fill roles ranging from short range local services to long range trans-Atlantic operations. Several successful aircraft resulted from this – notably the Viscount and Dove – but also some monumental failures including the Brabazon.

The Committee's Type I requirement was for an aircraft capable of non-stop services between London and New York and led to the design of the Bristol Type 167 Brabazon (named after the committee's chairman), which was and remains the largest landplane built in Britain.

The design of the Brabazon Mk.I had been largely settled by late 1944, features including a fuselage diameter of 5.11m (16ft 9in) – similar to today's Boeing 767 – tricycle undercarriage, cabin pressurisation and four coupled pairs of Bristol Centaurus radial engines buried in the wings driving six bladed contra-rotating propellers. A Mk.II version with four coupled pairs of 7000ehp (5220kW) Bristol Proteus turboprops, modified structure and bogie main undercarriage design was also planned. The fuselage, wing centre section and tailplane were built as an integral structure.

Construction of the prototype began in October 1945 but progress was slow. It was rolled out in December 1948 but first flight wasn't until 4 September 1949 after several postponements due to ongoing problems.

The Brabazon received a restricted Certificate of Airworthiness in June 1950 and some demonstration flights were undertaken with 30 seats fitted in the rear fuselage. The flight test programme revealed fatigue cracking in the propeller mounting structure and other problems with the result that the granting of an unrestricted C of A was refused.

This effectively killed the Brabazon and the programme – the whole concept of which was doubtful anyway – was abandoned after £3m had been spent. The prototype was grounded after logging fewer than 400 hours and scrapped in October 1953. Construction of the second aircraft – the turboprop powered Brabazon II – was halted when half completed and it was also scrapped in 1953.

Photo: Brabazon prototype.

Bristol Britannia

Country of origin: Great Britain.

Powerplants: Srs.100 – four 3870ehp (2886kW) Bristol Proteus 705 turboprops. Srs.300/310 – four 4120ehp (3072kW) Proteus 755 or 761. Srs.320 – four 4445ehp (3315kW) Proteus 765; four bladed propellers.

Performance: 100 – typical cruise 314kt (582km/h); max payload range with no reserves 2380nm (4410km); max fuel range with no reserves 3302nm (6116km). 310 – max cruise 352kt (652km/h); economical cruise 310kt (574km/h); max payload range with no reserves 3590nm (6647km); max fuel range with no reserves 4635nm (8586km).

Weights: 100 – empty 39,917kg (88,000lb); max takeoff 70,308kg (155,000lb). 310 – empty 42,230kg (93,100lb); max takeoff 83,916kg (185,000lb).

Dimensions: 100 – wing span 43.36m (142ft 3in); length 34.75m (114ft 0in); height 11.18m (36ft 8in); wing area 192.7m² (2075sq ft). 300/310/320 – length 37.87m (124ft 3in); height 11.43m (37ft 6in).

Accommodation: 100 – typically 68-76 passengers in two classes; up to 98 in single class six abreast. 300/310/320 – typically 81 passengers in two classes; maximum 139 in single class.

Production: 17 Srs.100, 23 Srs.250, 8 Srs.300, 35 Srs.310, 2 Srs.320, total 85.

History: An outstanding aircraft that was simply too late for commercial success, Bristol's 'Whispering Giant' missed its chance as entry to service was seriously delayed due to recurring flameout problems with the Proteus turboprop because of dry ice accretion. As a result, Britannia production was restricted to just 85 including 23 for the RAF. By the time it entered service, airlines were ordering jets.

The Bristol Type 175 was developed to meet a 1947 BOAC requirement for a medium range transport. Original plans were for the aircraft to be powered by Bristol Centaurus radials but of the three prototypes ordered in July 1948, two were intended to be convertible to the Proteus turboprop. In the event, all Britannias were powered by this engine, BOAC placing the first order for 25 Proteus powered and longer range Britannia 100s in July 1949.

The prototype Series 100 first flew on 16 August 1952 but it would not be until February 1957 that BOAC inaugurated Britannia services to South Africa and to Australia the following month. BOAC remained the only customer for the Srs.100, receiving 15.

Other models had fuselages stretched by 3.12m (10ft 3in), more powerful engines, and increased weights: the Srs.250 Britannia C.1 and C.2 mixed freight/passenger versions for the RAF (first flight March 1958 and built by Shorts); Srs.300 (first flight July 1956) for Aeronaves de Mexico, Air Charter and Ghana Airways; Srs.310 with increased fuel (first flight December 1956) for BOAC, Cubana, El Al, Canadian Pacific and Hunting Clan; and Srs.320 for Canadian Pacific (delivered late 1959) with more powerful engines. Production ended in 1960.

Britannias gave economical and reliable service for many years with smaller operators after they had been retired by the original customers. Most of the RAF aircraft found owners among freight operators from 1975. The last Britannia flight was recorded in October 1997 when a Transair Cargo (of Zaire) C.1 was ferried to the UK for preservation. The Britannia was also built under licence in Canada as the CL-44.

Photo: Britannia Srs.253/C.1.

Britten-Norman Islander

Country of origin: United Kingdom.

Powerplants: BN-2A/B – two 260hp (194kW) Lycoming 0-540-E or 300hp (224kW) IO-540-K six cylinder piston engines; two or three bladed propellers. BN-2T – two 320shp (231kW) Allison 250B-17C turboprops; three bladed propellers.

Performance: BN-2B (260hp) – max cruise 142kt (263km/h); economical cruise 126kt (233km/h); initial climb 860ft (262m)/min; service ceiling 13,600ft (4145m); range (standard/optional) 539-952nm (998-1763km). BN-2B (300hp) – max cruise 143kt (265kmh); economical cruise 128kt (237km/h); initial climb 1130ft (344m)/min; service ceiling 19,700ft (6005m); range (standard/optional) 503-896nm (932-1659km). BN-2T – max cruise 170kt (315km/h); economical cruise 150kt (278km/h); initial climb 1050ft (320m)/min; operational ceiling 25,000ft (7620m); range 590nm (1093km).

Weights: BN-2B – empty equipped 1914-1973kg (4220-4350lb); max takeoff 2994kg (6600lb). BN-2T – empty equipped 1837kg (4050lb); max takeoff 3175kg (7000lb).

Dimensions: BN-2B/T – wing span 14.94m (49ft 0in); length 10.87m (35ft 8in); height 4.42m (14ft 6in); wing area 30.2m² (325sq ft).

Accommodation: Pilot and nine passengers.

Production: 1150 of all models by early 1999.

History: Conceived by John Britten and Desmond Norman as a simple and inexpensive 10 seat short range transport for smaller operators, the BN-2 Islander resulted from the two partners' interest in Cameroon Air Transport, whose Piper Apache light twin was found to be underpowered for the prevailing hot and high conditions and had insufficient carrying capacity.

Design work began in 1963, the prototype with two 210hp (157kW) Continental IO-360 six cylinder engines flying from the company's Isle of Wight facility on 13 June 1965. Flight testing revealed the need for more power, the prototype re-engined with Lycoming 0-540s and the wing span increased. The first production aircraft flew in April 1967 and deliveries began the following August.

Progressive development saw numerous modifications and a multitude of subvariants introduced with increased weights and aerodynamic refinements. After the initial BN-2 series the major models were the BN-2A (1968) with the option of increased fuel in extended tips and either 260hp (194kW) or 300hp (224kW) engines; and BN-2B (1978) with detail improvements mainly relating to an improved cabin and cockpit environment and (later) the optional fuel capacity housed within the standard wing span.

The BN-2T Turbine Islander with Allison 250 turboprops first flew in August 1980 and deliveries began in December 1981, this and the piston engined versions remaining available since then. The Defender military version was introduced in 1971 and sold widely.

Islander production was at high levels in the early years (the 500th delivered in August 1974) but then started to decline. The early flurry of activity saw many delivered to their originally intended market in many countries including the USA but in later years most have been built for military and government customers in specialist role versions.

Photo: BN-2T Turbine Islander. (PBN)

Britten-Norman Trislander

Country of origin: United Kingdom.

Powerplants: Three 260hp (194kW) Lycoming O-540-E4C5 flat six piston engines; two bladed propellers.

Performance: Max speed 156kt (290km/h); max cruise 144kt (267km/h); normal cruise 138kt (255km/h); initial climb 980ft (298m)/min; service ceiling 13,150ft (4008m); range with 15 passengers 340nm (630km); max range 868nm (1608km).

Weights: Operational empty 2858kg (6300lb); max takeoff 4536kg (10,000lb).

Dimensions: Wing span 16.15m (53ft 0in); length 13.93m (45ft 8½in) or 15.01m (49ft 3in); height 4.32m (14ft 2in); wing area 31.3m² (337sq ft).

Accommodation: Pilot and passenger on flight deck plus 16 passengers two abreast in cabin.

Production: 82 completed by Britten-Norman plus 1 prototype converted from Islander; 11 others built as kits.

History: Based on the successful Islander utility twin, the Trislander resulted from company research which concluded there was a market for a higher capacity commuter airliner version of the Islander. Early investigations centred around a modest stretch with the second prototype rebuilt with an 83.8cm (33in) longer fuselage and seating for 12. Called the BN-2 Super, it first flew on 14 July 1968.

The Super was soon abandoned in favour of a more radical stretch for 18 seats with a 2.29m (7ft 6in) longer cabin with a completely new rear fuselage/tail section with a third engine mounted above a widened fin and rudder. The basic Islander's 260hp (194kW) Lycoming piston engines were retained and the optional wider span wings fitted, as was a new main landing gear with larger wheels and tyres.

Named the BN-2A Mk.III Trislander ('Tri-Islander') the first aircraft was another conversion of the second prototype Islander, flying for the first time in its new guise on 11 September 1970. Testing revealed the need to extend the fin above the centre engine and the first true Trislander flew in March 1971. British certification was awarded in May 1971 and the first delivery (to Aurigny Air Services) was made the following month. Channel Islands (Guernsey) based Aurigny remains the major Trislander operator in 1999.

Production versions were the basic Mk.III-1 with short nose, Mk.III-2 with lengthened nose for extra baggage space and Mk.III-3 with an autofeathering system. Also offered was the Mk.III-4 with a 350lb (1.5kN) thrust rocket motor mounted on the tail to provide extra thrust should an engine fail on takeoff.

Series production ran until 1977, by which time 79 Trislanders had been completed. A further three were completed in 1980-81 and 11 others were built as kits ahead of plans for the aircraft to be built in the USA as the Tri-Commuterair by the International Aviation Corporation. The kits were delivered in 1982 but never assembled.

Plans to complete the kits in Australia also failed. Parts from one of the kits were subsequently used in the rebuild of a damaged Aurigny Trislander in 1996 by subsidiary Anglo Normandy Aeroengineering and another was completed by that firm shortly afterwards. China Northern Airlines ordered three new Trislanders in 1999 for delivery in 2000-2001. Other orders were being sought to fully reopen the line.

Photo: Trislander Mk.III-1.

British Aerospace Jetstream 31/32

Country of origin: United Kingdom.

Powerplants: J31 – two 940shp (701kW) Garrett TPE331-10UG-513H turboprops. J32 – two 1020shp (760kW) TPE331-12-UAR turboprops; four bladed propellers.

Performance: J31 – max cruise 258kt (478km/h); range cruise 237kt (439km/h); initial climb 2000ft (610m)/min; operational ceiling 25,000ft (7620m); range with 18 passengers 620nm (1148km); max range 1050nm (1945km). J32 – max cruise 261kt (483km/h); range cruise 240kt (444km/h); initial climb 2240ft (683m)/min; operational ceiling 25,000ft (7620m); range with 19 passengers 629nm (1165km); max range 1080nm (2000km).

Weights: J31 – operating empty 4381kg (9659lb); max takeoff 6950kg (15,322lb). J32 – operating empty 4598kg (10,137lb); max takeoff 7350kg (16,204lb).

Dimensions: Wing span 15.85m (52ft 0in); length 14.36m (47ft 1½in); height 5.38m (17ft 8in); wing area 25.2m² (271sq ft).

Accommodation: 18-19 passengers three abreast in airliner layout.

Production: 220 Jetstream 31 and 161 Jetstream 32, total 381.

History: Derived from the original Turboméca Astazou powered Handley Page HP.137 Jetstream 10-18 seat light transport, the Jetstream 31 with Garrett TPE331-10 engines was launched in December 1978. Handley Page folded in early 1970 and the Jetstream project was taken over by Scottish Aviation which built further examples for the RAF and Royal Navy. Between them, Handley Page and Scottish Aviation completed 67 Jetstreams up to 1976.

One Handley Page aircraft was the prototype Jetstream 3M for the US Air Force (as the C-10A) with TPE331s. This first flew in November 1968 but the order for 11 was cancelled when Handley Page failed. The Mk.3 with its new engines, minor structural changes and increased weights formed the basis of the Jetstream 31 which would be built by Scottish Aviation, from 1977 part of British Aerospace.

The prototype J31 was converted from a Handley Page built airframe and first flew on 28 March 1980. The first new build J31 followed in February 1982 and the initial delivery – to German operator Contactair – was in December 1982. Although the J31 was offered in nine seat corporate and 12 seat 'executive shuttle' layouts, the vast majority were sold as 18-19 seat regional airliners. The aircraft was especially successful in the US market where it was ordered by many of the major airlines' regional associates, sometimes in large numbers.

The J31 was followed by the Jetstream 32 (marketed as the Super 31 for a few years) with more powerful TPE331-12 engines, increased weights, slightly greater fuel capacity, improved interior and better payload/range performance. The J32 first flew on 13 April 1988 and Big Sky Airlines (a Northwest Airlink operator) took first delivery the following October.

Production ended in November 1993 and since then BAe has offered the Jetstream 32EP (Enhanced Performance) upgrade conversion with aerodynamic improvements and revised operating procedures to provide better payload/range and hot/high performance.

Photo: Jetstream 32. (BAe)

British Aerospace Jetstream 41

Country of origin: United Kingdom.

Powerplants: Two 1500shp (1118kW) or 1650shp (1230kW) AlliedSignal TPE331-14GR/HR turboprops; five bladed propellers.

Performance: Max cruise 295kt (546km/h); economical cruise 260kt (482km/h); long range cruise 254kt (470km/h); initial climb 2200ft (670m)/min; operational ceiling 25,000ft (7620m); range with 29 passengers (early aircraft) 681nm (1261km), later aircraft 774nm (1434km); max fuel range 1500nm (2778km).

Weights: Operating empty 6416kg (14,144lb); max takeoff 10,478kg (23,100lb) or 10,886kg (24,000lb).

Dimensions: Wing span 18.42m (60ft 5in); length 19.25m (63ft 2in); height 5.74m (18ft 10in); wing area 32.4m² (349sq ft).

Accommodation: 27-29 passengers three abreast in airliner configuration.

Production: 106.

History: Thoughts of a stretched Jetstream had been discussed as early as 1979 by Scottish Aviation and continued through the 1980s under BAe's stewardship. The name Jetstream 41 was unofficially used during this period but it was not until May 1989 that the 29 seat passenger aircraft was formally launched by BAe in association with risk sharing partners Pilatus, Slingsby, Gulfstream and Field Aircraft.

The procrastination associated with its go ahead undoubtedly cost the J41 sales. Although less expensive to purchase and operate than its competitors, it was probably three or four years too late and by the time it appeared much of the market had already been captured. The prototype J41 first flew on 25 September 1991 and first deliveries to Loganair and Manx Airlines were made in November 1992.

The J41 differed considerably from its predecessor. The basic fuselage cross section was retained but stretched by 4.88m (16ft 0in), the increased span wing mounted below the fuselage (resulting in no main spar intrusion in the cabin), a new windscreen fitted, the cockpit fitted with EFIS displays, systems upgraded to the latest standards, the main loading door relocated to the forward fuselage and a large baggage door installed at the rear, an additional baggage compartment located in the rear wing root fairing, fuel capacity increased and more powerful TPE331-14 engines installed driving advanced five bladed propellers.

An uprated version with more powerful engines and increased weights was introduced in August 1994 but even this failed to stimulate better than modest sales. Apart from the airliner versions, the J41 was also offered in 10-16 seat corporate versions.

BAe established a separate Jetstream Division in 1993 and from January 1996 the J41 became part of the short lived Aero International (Regional) consortium comprising the former BAe Regional Aircraft and ATR. BAe's desire to remove itself from the regional turboprop market saw it announce in May 1997 that J41 production would end when existing orders had been fulfilled. The 106th and last aircraft was handed over to the Hong Kong Government Flying Service at the end of 1998.

Photo: Jetstream 41. (BAe)

British Aerospace ATP

Country of origin: United Kingdom.

Powerplants: ATP – two 2653shp (1978kW) Pratt & Whitney Canada PW126A turboprops. Jetstream 61 – two 2750shp (2050kW) PW127D turboprops; six bladed propellers.

Performance: ATP – max cruise 266kt (493km/h); long range cruise 236kt (437km/h); operational ceiling 25,000ft (7620m); range with 64 passengers 985nm (1825km); max payload range 619nm (1146km). Jetstream 61 – range with 70 passengers 777nm (1439km).

Weights: ATP – operational empty 14,243kg (31,400lb); max takeoff 23,678kg (52,200lb).

Dimensions: Wing span 30.63m (100ft 6in); length 26.01m (85ft 4in); height 7.59m (24ft 11in); wing area 78.3m² (843sq ft).

Accommodation: Typically 64-68 passengers four abreast, maximum 72.

Production: 63 ATP and 2 Jetstream 61, total 65.

History: Although consideration had been given to developing a stretched, higher capacity version of the successful Avro/Hawker Siddeley 748 regional turboprop as early as 1961 (as the 748E with a 1.83m/6ft fuselage extension), it wasn't until March 1984 and the launch of the BAe ATP (Advanced Turbo Prop) that the idea came to fruition.

After conducting a 'marketing launch' in 1982 and examining several options ranging from designing a completely new aircraft to simply stretching the 748, BAe decided on a 'middle course' route which ended up being a comprehensive reworking of the 748 as future needs were recognised.

The ATP combined the 748's fuselage cross section with a 5.58m (18ft 4in) stretch allowing accommodation for 60-72 passengers, a swept back fin and rudder and reprofiled nose to modernise the aircraft's appearance, new generation PW126 turboprops, slow turning six bladed propellers, EFIS cockpit and comprehensively revised systems, equipment and interior furnishings.

The prototype ATP flew on 6 August 1986 and British Midland Airways inaugurated revenue services in May 1988. Unfortunately for BAe, the ATP was always a slow seller, most customers for aircraft in its class opting for the much more successful ATR 72 and smaller stablemate, the ATR 42. Other orders trickled in from British Airways, United Feeder Services, Merpati, SATA and Bangladesh Biman but production in effect ended in 1993 with several airframes remaining unsold.

An attempt to 'rebrand' and revitalise the ATP was made in the same year with the announcement of the Jetstream 61 variant with more powerful engines, increased weights, revised 'wide body' interior (including innovative armrests incorporated in the cabin walls to allow wider seats) and other changes. The J61 was certificated in June 1995 but none were sold and the two examples built were scrapped, as were 11 ATP fuselages.

Marketing of the ATP ceased when BAe and ATR established the Aero International (Regional) consortium at the beginning of 1996, as it would have been a direct competitor to the ATR 72. The last three ATPs were finally delivered from storage at the end of 1998 – two for British World Airways and one for Sun-Air of Scandinavia.

Photo: BAe ATP. (BAe)

Canadair Four

Country of origin: Canada.

Powerplants: DC-4M-1 – four 1725hp (1286kW) Rolls-Royce Merlin 622 V12s. C-4 – four 1760hp (1312kW) Merlin 626; three or four bladed propellers.

Performance: C-4 – max cruise 262kt (486km/h); typical cruise speed 251kt (465km/h); service ceiling 26,400ft (8047m); max range 3370nm (6242km).

Weights: C-4 – empty 21,243kg (46,832lb); max takeoff 37,331kg (82,300lb).

Dimensions: Wing span 35.81m (117ft 6in); length 28.54m (93ft 7½in); height 8.39m (27ft 6¼in); wing area 135.3m² (1457sq ft).

Accommodation: Typically 40 first class or up to 62 economy class.

Production: 18 C-54GM, 1 DC-4M, 6 DC-4M-1, 19 DC-4M-2, 22 C-4, 4 C-4-1, 1 C-5, total 71.

History: Canadair was established in 1944 as a successor to the Canadian Vickers organisation. Its first product was the Canadair Four, a licence built development of the Douglas DC-4/C-54 transport incorporating substantial modification including replacing the original Pratt & Whitney R-2000 radial engines with Rolls-Royce Merlin V12s and in the civil models, adding cabin pressurisation.

The unpressurised prototype C-54GM first flew on 15 July 1946 followed by 23 similar aircraft of which 17 were delivered to the Royal Canadian Air Force as the C-54GM North Star and six were diverted to Trans Canada Airlines as the DC-4M-1 pending first deliveries of an order for pressurised DC-4M-2s. TCA took delivery of its first aircraft in November 1946 and its last in March 1947; services were inaugurated on the Montreal-London route in April 1947 and the survivors were returned to the RCAF in 1949.

TCA received 20 pressurised DC-4M-2s between October 1947 and June 1948. Powered by Merlin 622 or 624 engines driving either three or four bladed propellers, these differed externally from the earlier models by featuring square DC-6 style cabin windows in place of the previous round DC-4 units. The last TCA DC-4M was withdrawn from service in 1961.

BOAC ordered 22 similar C-4 variants with slightly more powerful Merlin 626s. Operating under the class name Argonaut, these were delivered between March and November 1949 and used on BOAC's world wide network until disposed of from 1958.

The final customer for the aircraft was Canadian Pacific Air Lines, which took delivery of four C-4-1s in 1949 but operated them only briefly. Similar to BOAC's aircraft, one crashed while landing in bad weather at Tokyo in February 1950 and the remaining three went to TCA the following year.

A single example of the larger C-5 with 2100hp (1566kW) P&W R-2800 radials was flown in 1950 and used by the RCAF as a long range crew trainer and VIP transport.

Smaller operators such as Aden Airways, British Midland, East African Airways, Transglobe and Lineas Aereas Unidas plus the air forces of Rhodesia and El Salvador flew second hand Canadair Fours but most had been scrapped by the late 1960s. One notable operator was the King of Burundi who had an ex TCA DC-4M-2 at his disposal in the early 1960s.

Photo: C-54GM first prototype.

Canadair CL-44

Country of origin: Canada.

Powerplants: Four 5730eshp (4273kW) Rolls-Royce Tyne 515/10 turboprops; four bladed propellers.

Performance: CL-44D-4 – max cruise 335kt (621km/h); economical cruise 320kt (592km/h); max payload range 2833nm (5247km). CL-44J – max cruise 339kt (628km/h); economical cruise 317kt (587km/h); range with 189 passengers 3042nm (5634km).

Weights: CL-44D-4 – empty equipped 40,348kg (88,950lb); max takeoff 95,256kg (210,000lb).

Dimensions: CL-44D-4 – wing span 43.37m (142ft 3½in); length 41.73m (136ft 10¾in); height 11.16m (36ft 8in); wing area 192.8m² (2075sq ft). CL-44J – length 46.33m (152ft 0in).

Capacity/Accommodation: CL-44D-4 – max freight payload 29,995kg (66,128lb) or up to 178 passengers. CL-44J – up to 214 passengers.

Production: 12 CL-44-6/CC-106, 27 CL-55D-4, total 39 including 3 CL-44J conversions.

History: Canadair acquired a licence to manufacture the Bristol Britannia airliner in March 1954. The company pursued two lines of development: the unpressurised CL-28 Argus maritime reconnaissance aircraft in which the original Bristol Proteus turboprops were replaced by Wright R-3350 Turbo Compound radials; and the CL-44 transport with Rolls-Royce Tyne turboprops, lengthened pressurised fuselage and increased weights. The first Argus flew in March 1957, 33 were delivered.

The prototype CL-44 flew on 15 November 1959. Intended mainly as a freighter but with secondary passenger carrying capability, initial production was of the CL-44-6 version for the RCAF with side loading freight doors. Deliveries to the RCAF as the CC-106 Yukon began in July 1960 and 12 were handed over including the prototype.

A prototype of the commercial version, the CL-44D-4, flew on 16 November 1960, this featuring the world's first 'swing tail' loading configuration on a production commercial aircraft and allowing the straight in loading of bulky objects into the full cross section of the main cabin, the tail area and rear underfloor hold.

Deliveries of the CL-44D-4 began in July 1961 when the first of seven for Seaboard World Airlines was handed over. Other original customers were Flying Tiger Line (12), Slick Airways (4) and Iceland's Loftleidir which took delivery of the prototype in 1965 and three others in 1963-65. Two of these were delivered as standard CL-44D-4s and used for low cost trans-Atlantic passenger flights with seating for 178.

The swing tail was retained and both were subsequently converted to CL-44J (Canadair 400) standard with the fuselage stretched by another 3.99m (13ft 1in) and passenger accommodation increased to a maximum of 214. Loftleidir's third CL-44J was delivered in its modified form and was the last of the line, flying in March 1965.

Second hand sales – including of former RCAF Yukons – saw several other operators fly the CL-44 over the years including Cargolux, Aeronaves del Peru, Heavylift, Transmeridian, Transglobe, Tradewinds and Airlift International. One was converted to a high volume freighter by Conroy Aircraft in 1969 as the CL-44-0 with a substantially enlarged upper fuselage.

Photo: CL-44-D-6.

Cant Z.506 Airone

Country of origin: Italy.

Powerplants: Three 750hp (559kW) Pratt & Whitney R-1690 Hornet, 760hp (567kW) Wright GR-1820-F52, 800hp (597kW) Alfa Romeo 126 RC 10 or 750hp (559kW) Alfa Romeo 126 RC 34 nine cylinder radials; three bladed propellers.

Performance: Cruising speed 173kt (320km/h); range 702nm (1300km).

Weights: Empty 7200kg (15,873lb); max takeoff 10,500kg (23,148lb).

Dimensions: Wing span 86ft 11in (26.49m); length 18.92m (62ft 1in); height 6.77m (22ft 2¹/₂in); wing area 85.0m² (915sq ft).

Accommodation: Up to 16 passengers.

Production: Approximately 40 civil Z.506/C plus 324 Z.506B.

History: Derived from the similar Cantieri Riuniti dell'Adriatico (Cant) Z.505 three engined, twin float mail carrying seaplane, the Z.506 Airone (Heron) was developed into successful civil and military versions.

A low wing monoplane of wooden construction, the Z.506 was regarded as being particularly seaworthy thanks to its wing design which incorporated watertight compartments and its large metal floats, each of which had a buoyancy equivalent to the maximum takeoff weight of the aircraft. The passenger cabin was divided into two sections fore and aft of the loading door on the port side.

The first Z.506 flew on 19 August 1935 powered by Pratt & Whitney Hornet engines but the first production batch for Ala Littoria had Wright GR-1820 Cyclones installed. The Alfa Romeo 126 radial was an alternative and aircraft fitted with these engines were dubbed Z.506C.

Ala Littoria was the major commercial operator of the Z.506, having a fleet of about 19 aircraft before World War II. They were flown on the Rome-Benghazi, Rome-Palma-Melilla-Cadiz, Rome-Genoa-Marseilles and Trieste-Brindisi routes. Z.506s operated by Ala Littoria set a substantial number of speed, altitude and distance records before the war.

The military Z.506B was the major production version. Powered by Alfa Romeo 126 engines, it entered Regia Aeronautica service in 1937 as a bomber and reconnaissance aircraft with defensive guns and a ventral bay capable of accommodating two torpedoes or a 1000kg (2205lb) bomb load. The only major sub variant was the Z.506S air-sea rescue conversion.

Z.506Bs saw early service with the Italian Legion during the Spanish Civil War and by the time Italy entered WWII in June 1940 about 95 were on strength with production continuing by both the parent company and Piaggio. Poland ordered 30 but only one had been delivered by the time of the German invasion in September 1939.

Some civil Z.506s flew in military colours during the war. The two Regia Aeronautica groups operating the Z.506B were initially used as bombers during the French and Balkans campaigns and against the Royal Navy's Mediterranean fleet. Losses were heavy and the aircraft was soon switched to secondary roles. One Z.506B achieved fame when it became the only aircraft to be hijacked by prisoners of war, RAF personnel taking it over and flying it to Malta.

Photo: Z.506.

CASA C-212 Aviocar

Country of origin: Spain.

Powerplants: 100 – two 776shp (589kW) Garrett AiResearch TPE331-5-251C turboprops. 200 – two 865shp (645kW) TPE331-10-501C. 300 – two 900shp (671kW) TPE331-10R-513C; four bladed propellers.

Performance: 100 – max speed 199kt (368km/h); economical cruise 170kt (315km/h); max payload range 258nm (478km); max range 950nm (1760km). 300 – max cruise 191kt (354km/h); economical cruise 162kt (300km/h); initial climb 1630ft (497m)/min; service ceiling 26,000ft (7925m); range with 25 passengers 237nm (440km); range with 19 passengers 765nm (1417km).

Weights: 100 – operating empty 3700kg (8157lb); max takeoff 6300kg (13,889lb). 200 – max takeoff 7450kg (16,424lb). 300 – operating empty 3780kg (8333lb); max takeoff 7700kg (16,975lb).

Dimensions: 100/200 – wing span 19.00m (62ft 4in); length 15.21m (49ft 11in); height 6.30m (20ft 8in); wing area 40.0m² (431sq ft). 300 – wing span 20.27m (66ft 6in); length 16.15m (53ft 0in); wing area 41.0m² (441sq ft).

Accommodation: 300 – up to 26 passengers three abreast or 28 if rear loading ramp deleted.

Production: Approx 450 C-212s of all models built by early 1999 (including about 100 by IPTN) of which approx 170 for commercial operators.

History: Originally developed as a light utility and multirole transport for the Spanish Air Force, the Aviocar has since found a steady market with more than 20 military customers for transport, training, photographic survey, patrol and other roles, and with commercial operators as a utility and commuter transports.

A simple unpressurised, high wing, fixed undercarriage and all metal design, the C-212 differs from most comparable aircraft in featuring a rear loading ramp allowing straight in loading to the box section fuselage.

The prototype flew on 23 March 1971 and deliveries to the Spanish Air Force began in March 1974. Initial production aircraft had TPE331-5 engines and a maximum takeoff weight of 5670kg (12,500lb); successive models introduced progressive increases in both weight and power.

The commercial C-212C 19 seater (subsequently 212-100) was introduced in 1975 with -5 engines and 6300kg (13,889lb) maximum weight. Indonesia's Pelita Air Services was an early customer for the civil version, prompting the arrangement of a licence production deal with IPTN. The first IPTN assembled Aviocar flew in July 1975.

The C-212-200 with more powerful TPE331-10 engines and increased weights first flew in April 1978 and this remained the major production version until the appearance of the 212-300 in 1987. The -300 features increased span wings with upturned tips, more power and weight, a lengthened nose for greater baggage capacity and an optional rear fuselage fairing in place of the loading ramp. This allows an increase in maximum passenger capacity to 28.

A further upgrade, the C-212-400 with 1100shp (820kW) TPE331-12 engines, first flew in April 1997.

Photo: C-212C. (S McCarthy)

CASA/IPTN CN-235

Countries of origin: Spain and Indonesia.

Powerplants: 100 – two 1750shp (1305kW) General Electric CT7-9C turboprops; four bladed propellers.

Performance: 100 – max cruise 244kt (452km/h); initial climb 1527ft (645m)/min; operational ceiling 25,000ft (7620m); max payload range 430nm (796km); range with 44 passengers 1079nm (1998km); max range 2291nm (4244km).

Weights: 100 – operating empty 9800kg (21,605lb); max takeoff 15,100kg (33,289lb).

Dimensions: Wing span 25.81m (84ft 8in); length 21.40m (70ft 2¹/₂in); height 8.18m (26ft 10in); wing area 59.1m² (636sq ft).

Accommodation: 100 – up to 44 passengers four abreast; max payload 4000kg (8818lb).

Production: 230 CN-235s of all versions ordered by early 1999 of which about 26 delivered to commercial operators.

History: The CN-235 military tactical transport and regional airliner was developed jointly by CASA of Spain and Indonesia's IPTN under the Aircraft Technology Industries (Airtech) banner.

Final assembly lines were established in both countries but the manufacture of components is not duplicated. CASA is responsible for the centre and forward fuselage, wing centre section, inboard flaps and engine nacelles while IPTN builds the outer wings and flaps, ailerons, rear fuselage and tail unit. The CN-235 is pressurised and features a rear loading ramp.

One prototype was built in both countries and these were simultaneously rolled out on 10 September 1983. The Spanish prototype flew first, on 11 November 1983, with the Indonesian aircraft following on 30 December of the same year. First delivery was from the Indonesian line to Merpati Nusantara in December 1986 and the first Spanish aircraft went to the Royal Saudi Air Force in February 1987.

The initial production CN-235-10 with 1700shp (1268kW) CT7-7A engines was replaced by the CASA CN-235-100 and IPTN CN-235-110 after 37 of the earlier model (including prototypes) had been built. The -100 series features CT7-9C engines housed in new composite nacelles and systems improvements. The first (Spanish built) -100 flew in March 1989 and the majority of deliveries have come from that source, mainly for military customers in a number of specialist role subvariants.

The CN-235-200 (CASA) and -220 (IPTN) with strengthened structure, increased weights and improved payload/range performance was announced in 1992 but although Merpati was reported to have ordered 16 in 1994, no deliveries are believed to have been made by 1999. CASA has also developed its own stretched variant, the C-295, for military use.

The small number of other civil customers for the CN-235 includes Austral, Binter Canarias and Binter Mediterraneo, all of which purchased CASA built aircraft. Several other Indonesian and Spanish operators placed options but none were converted to firm orders and the military versions developed by CASA account for the vast majority of sales.

Photo: CN-235-10.

Consolidated Commodore

Country of origin: USA.

Powerplants: Two 575hp (429kW) Pratt & Whitney R-1690 Hornet nine cylinder radials; three bladed propellers.

Performance: Cruising speed 94kt (174km/h); range 870nm (1610km).

Weights: Empty 4763kg (10,500lb); max takeoff 7983kg (17,600lb).

Dimensions: Wing span 30.48m (100ft 0in); length 20.73m (68ft 0in); height 4.77m (15ft 8in); wing area 103.1m² (1110sq ft).

Accommodation: 12 passengers on long distance flights, maximum 22-32 passengers.

Production: 14.

History: In February 1928 the US Navy ordered a single prototype of the Consolidated XPY-1 Admiral patrol flying boat. Powered by two 450hp (335kW) Pratt & Whitney Wasp radials, it was a parasol monoplane of metal construction with fabric covered wing and metal skinned hull.

First flight was in January 1929 but the nine production aircraft were built by Martin (as the P3M) after it successfully bid for the separate production contract by undercutting the design company. Consolidated later received orders for an updated version, the P2Y, of which 23 were built in 1932 and 1933.

In the meantime, the original XPY was considered to have commercial potential and development efforts along these lines were made during 1929. As the Model 16 Commodore, the aircraft was re-engined with more powerful Pratt & Whitney Hornet radials and the interior redesigned to accommodate 12 passengers in three well appointed cabins on long distance flights or up to 22 passengers over short distances.

The major physical characteristics of the Commodore remained as before: strut mounted constant chord parasol wing, engines strut mounted below the wing, outrigger floats mounted on prominent sponsons and strut braced twin vertical tail surfaces. The cockpit was originally open but was soon enclosed.

The first Commodore flew in September 1929 and 14 were ordered by the newly established but short lived New York, Rio and Buenos Aires Line (NYRBA), owned by a consortium of individuals and companies and planning commercial operations from Miami to the West Indies and onto ports in South America.

NYRBA began operations with the Commodore in February 1930, the aircraft proving well suited to the 7820nm (14,490km) route from Miami to Buenos Aires, which was completed in seven days. NYRBA had received 10 Commodores by September 1930, at which time it was taken over by Pan American. The last four aircraft went direct to Pan Am which began operating them on non stop services between Jamaica and the Panama Canal.

The 9th, 10th, 11th and 12th Commodores were completed as Model 16-1s with slightly longer hulls and accommodation for up to 32 passengers and the final two as Model 16-2s, similar but with cowled engines.

NYRBA set up a Brazilian subsidiary which became Panair do Brasil after the Pan American takeover and six Commodores were transferred to that operation.

Photo: Commodore of NYRBA.

Convair CV-240

Country of origin: USA.

Powerplants: Two 2400hp (1790kW) Pratt & Whitney R-2800-CA18 Double Wasp 18-cylinder radials; three bladed propellers.

Performance: Max speed 302kt (558km/h) at 16,000ft (4877m); normal cruise 235kt (435km/h); service ceiling 30,000ft (9144m); range with 40 passengers 1564nm (2897km).

Weights: Empty equipped 13,764kg (30,345lb); max takeoff 18,956kg (41,790lb).

Dimensions: Wing span 27.97m (91ft 9in); length 22.76m (74ft 8in); height 8.20m (26ft 11in); wing area 75.9m² (817sq ft).

Accommodation: Normally 40 passengers four abreast.

Production: 1 Model 110 and 176 CV-240 plus 364 T-29A/B/C/D.

History: One of the first postwar designs intended to fill the perceived need for a DC-3 replacement, the twin piston engined and pressurised CV-240 produced by the Consolidated-Vultee Aircraft Corporation (Convair – later part of General Dynamics) was arguably the most advanced short haul airliner of its day.

The CV-240 sold reasonably well despite a glut of cheap DC-3/C-47s becoming available immediately after the war. Further developed into the CV-340 and 440, production of all commercial versions exceeded 500, a figure doubled if sales to the US military are taken into account.

The series started with CV-110, the result of discussions between Convair and American Airlines in 1945. First flown in July 1946 it was a 30 seater, and although flight testing was successful it was deemed too small by American which asked for a larger aircraft. This was duly developed as the CV-240 with accommodation for 40 in a new, lengthened and marginally narrower fuselage. The project was launched with an order for 100 from American, subsequently reduced to 75.

The first CV-240 flew on 16 March 1947, advanced features including cabin pressurisation (the first in a short haul airliner); the use of fibreglass in the rudder and elevator trailing edges; the utilisation of exhaust augmented cooling of the Double Wasp engines, the system also producing some residual 'jet' thrust; and the incorporation of retractable ventral passenger loading stairs under the rear fuselage.

The CV-240 entered service with American Airlines in June 1948, other customers for new aircraft including Western Air Lines, Pan American, Trans Australia Airlines, KLM, Aerolineas Argentinas, Continental, Swissair, Northeast, Garuda Indonesia and Sabena. The Ford Motor Company set a trend which would follow the 'Convairliner' throughout its career by ordering a corporate version. The final CV-240 was delivered to Garuda in December 1950 and only a handful of CV-240s remained in service in their original piston engined form by 1999.

Military sales boosted the CV-240 programme with the USAF taking delivery of 364 T-29 navigator and bombardier trainers between March 1950 and August 1955. The first 46 – designated T-29A – had 2300hp (1715kW) R-2800-97 engines and lacked cabin pressurisation while the T-29B, C and D were pressurised and had 2500hp (1864kW) engines.

Photo: CV-240.

Convair CV-340 and 440

Country of origin: USA.

Powerplants: 340 – two 2400hp (1790kW) Pratt & Whitney R-2800-CB16 Double Wasp 18-cylinder radials. 440 – two 2400hp (1790kW) R-2800-CB16 or 2500hp (1864kW) R-2800-CB17 Double Wasps; three bladed propellers.

Performance: 340 – normal cruise 247kt (457km/h); range cruise 209kt (386km/h); initial climb 1190ft (363m)/min; max payload range 504nm (933km); max range 1750nm (3243km). 440 – max cruise 261kt (483km/h); economical cruise 251kt (465km/h); initial climb 1260ft (384m)/min; service ceiling 24,900ft (7590m); max payload range 248nm (459km); max range 1677nm (3106km).

Weights: 340 – empty equipped 14,697kg (32,400lb); max takeoff 21,319kg (47,000lb). 440 – operating empty 15,111kg (33,314lb); max takeoff 22,544kg (49,700lb).

Dimensions: 340 – wing span 32.10m (105ft 4in); length 24.13m (79ft 2in); height 8.58m (28ft 2in); wing area 85.5m² (920sq ft). 440 – length with radar nose 24.84m (81ft 6in).

Accommodation: Typically 44-52 passengers four abreast.

Production: 207 CV-340 and 177 CV-440 plus 152 C-131 and R4Y miliary variants.

History: By 1950, Convair had seen the need to further develop the CV-240 to meet changing market requirements and to counter the threat imposed by the Martin 4-0-4 which had received orders from Eastern Air Lines and TWA. The result was the stretched and refined CV-240A, subsequently named the CV-340.

Compared to the CV-240, the 340 featured a 1.37m (4ft 6in) fuselage stretch increasing standard passenger capacity to 44 (although up to 52 could be accommodated), increased span wings, additional fuel capacity, more powerful Double Wasps in lengthened nacelles and higher weights. United Air Lines launched the CV-340 with an order for 55.

The first aircraft flew on 5 October 1951 and deliveries to United began in March 1952. Other customers for the 340 included Braniff, Continental, Delta, Northeast, National, Aeronaves de Mexico, KLM and PAL.

The CV-440 was a refined development of the 340 and a response to the substantial impact Britain's Vickers Viscount turboprop was having on the domestic airliner market. Sometimes known as the Metropolitan, the 440 had the same dimensions as its predecessor but slightly increased weights and an integral air-stair door on the forward port side fuselage. Considerable effort was put into the exhaust system and other areas to reduce cabin noise, an area where the Viscount held a significant advantage.

The CV-440 first flew on 6 October 1955 and entered service with Continental in April 1956. Other customers included SAS, Sabena, Swissair, Alitalia, Iberia, Eastern, Lufthansa, Braniff, Delta and Eastern. Production ended in 1958 and some 180 were subsequently converted to CV-580s and CV-640s with turboprop engines (see next entry).

Military versions based on the CV-340/440 were designated C-131 for the USAF and R4Y for the USN and USMC and included the C-131A Samaritan casualty evacuation version, C-131B transport and flying laboratory, C-131D/VC-131D transport and C-131E ECM trainer.

Photo: CV-440.

Convair CV-540, 580, 600 and 640

Country of origin: USA.

Powerplants: 540 – two 3060ehp (2282kW) Napier Eland NE.1 turbo-props. 580 – two 3750ehp (2796kW) Allison 501-D13H turboprops. 600/640 – two 3025ehp (2256kW) Rolls-Royce Dart 542-2 turbo-props; four bladed propellers.

Performance: 580 – max cruise 297kt (550km/h); max payload range 1069nm (1980km); max fuel range 2490nm (4612km). 600 – cruising speed 278-291kt (515-539km/h); max range 1564nm (2897km). 640 – cruising speed 260kt (482km/h); max payload range 1069nm (1980km); max fuel range 1695nm (3140km).

Weights: 580 – operating empty 13,733kg (30,275lb); max takeoff 26,372kg (58,140lb). 600 – operating empty 13,699kg (30,200lb); max takeoff 21,319kg (47,000lb). 640 – operating empty 14,152kg (31,200lb); max takeoff 25,855kg (57,000lb).

Dimensions: 580 – wing span 32.10m (105ft 4in); length 24.84m (81ft 6in); height 8.89m (29ft 2in); wing area 85.5m² (920sq ft). 600 – wing span 27.96m (91ft 9in); length 22.76m (74ft 8in); wing area 75.9m² (817sq ft).

Accommodation: 600 – 40 passengers four abreast. 580/640 – 44-56 passengers four abreast.

Production: 10 CV-540, 153 CV-580, 38 CV-600, 27 CV-640 conversions.

History: The piston engined Convair CV-240/340/440 series has been subject to several turboprop conversion programmes, taking advantage of the airframe's reliability and long life to create new versions which continue to fly more than five decades after the original entered service. About 100 remained in service by early 1999.

The potential of turboprop power was investigated very early, Convair flying a CV-240 with Allison 501 engines in December 1950 as the Turboliner. The first of two CV-340s with Allison 501s flew in June 1954 under the designation YC-131C as part of a USAF general investigation into the use of turboprops on transport aircraft.

The first commercial conversions were by Britain's Napier engine company when a CV-440 was fitted with two Eland turboprops. First flown in February 1956 and dubbed the CV-540, six other conversions were performed between then and 1960 (for delivery to Allegheny Airlines) while Canadair also created three CV-540 conversions in 1959-60. Canadair also built 10 new aircraft for the RCAF from 1960.

The most numerous conversion was the CV-580 with Allison 501Ds, based on the CV-340/440 and performed by Pacific Airmotive (PacAero) in California on behalf of Allison. The first conversion flew on 19 January 1960 but it was not until June 1964 that the 580 entered airline service with Frontier Airlines. Other major original users included Allegheny, Lake Central, North Central and Avensa. The final conversions were performed in 1969.

Convair's own conversion programme used the Rolls-Royce Dart under the designations CV-600 (based on the 240) and CV-640 (based on the 340/440). The first CV-600 flew in May 1965 and Trans Texas Airlines was the major customer, taking 25 of the 38 conversions. The first CV-640 flew in August 1965 and customers included Pacific Western, Zantop, Hawaiian, Martinair and Air Algerie. The last CV-640 was delivered in December 1968.

Photo: CV-580.

Convair 880

Country of origin: USA.

Powerplants: 880 – four 11,200lb (49.8kN) General Electric CJ-805-3A turbojets. 880-M – four 11,650lb (51.8kN) CJ-805-3B turbojets.

Performance: 880 – max cruise 530kt (983km/h); economical cruise 483kt (895km/h); range cruise 435kt (806km/h); normal cruise altitude 35,000ft (10,668m); service ceiling 41,000ft (12,497m); max payload range 2780nm (5150km); range with typical load 3000nm (5557km); max fuel range 3471nm (6429km). 880-M – max payload range 3258nm (6035km).

Weights: 880 – operating empty 41,958kg (92,500lb); max takeoff 83,689kg (184,500lb). 880-M – operating empty 42,638kg (94,000lb); max takeoff 87,545kg (193,000lb).

Dimensions: Wing span 36.58m (120ft 0in); length 39.42m (129ft 4in); height 11.07m (36ft 4in); wing area 185.8m² (2000sq ft).

Accommodation: 88 passengers four abreast in first class arrangement; typical all economy class layout 110 passengers five abreast.

Production: 48 Convair 880 and 17 Convair 880-M, total 65.

History: The Convair Division of General Dynamics conducted market surveys among US domestic trunk route operators in the mid 1950s and came up with the concept of a four engined jetliner which was smaller, lighter and faster than the competing Boeing 707 and Douglas DC-8.

The project was largely driven by the billionaire Howard Hughes, who controlled TWA at the time. It was launched in September 1956 on the basis of 30 orders from TWA and 10 from Delta. Hughes later greatly influenced the project in a negative way. Part of his company's deal with Convair for the TWA order was that it would control the first 40 delivery positions, regardless of whether or not they were for TWA aircraft. His delaying tactics and general recalcitrance cost Convair's salesmen numerous orders, especially after Boeing responded to the threat by offering the 'lightweight 707', the 720. The result was financial calamity for Convair.

What was finally called the Convair 880 began life as the Skylark, then Golden Arrow, then Convair 600 (for its speed in miles per hour) and finally 880 for its speed in feet per second! Powered by four GE CJ-805 turbojets (derived from the military J79), it featured five abreast seating compared to the six abreast of its competitors.

The prototype 880 first flew on 27 January 1959 and Delta flew the first services in May 1960. Sales remained poor with only 65 built including 17 of the improved 880-M from 1961 with leading edge slats, power boosted rudder, more powerful engines, increased weights and greater fuel capacity. A big financial loser for Convair despite being generally successful in service, the last 880s were delivered in July 1962.

Operators of new aircraft were TWA, Delta, Northeast, Viasa, Swissair, Civil Air Transport, JAL, Cathay Pacific, Alaska Airlines and the US FAA. Elvis Presley purchased an ex Delta 880 in 1975 and converted it into a luxurious 'flying hotel' suite. Named *Lisa Marie* after his daughter, it is now preserved at the Graceland Museum in Memphis. The FAA aircraft was used on various flight safety programmes, then the US Navy as testbed. Also equipped for flight refuelling, it was the last 880 in service, retired in 1995.

Photo: CV-880-22M.

Convair 990 Coronado

Country of origin: USA.

Powerplants: Four 15,850lb (70.5kN) General Electric CJ-805-23 or 16,050lb (71.4kN) CJ-805-23B turbofans.

Performance: Max cruise 540kt (1000km/h); economical cruise 484kt (896km/h); long range cruise 420kt (779km/h); service ceiling 41,000ft (12,497m); max payload range 2780-3124nm (5150-5785km); max fuel range 4730nm (8761km).

Weights: Operating empty 54,840kg (120,900lb); max takeoff 111,676kg (246,200lb) or 114,761kg (253,000lb).

Dimensions: Wing span 36.58m (120ft 0in); length 42.43m (139ft 2½in); height 12.01m (39ft 5in); wing area 209.0m² (2250sq ft).

Accommodation: 96 passengers four abreast in first class arrangement; typically 100-116 passengers in two classes or 121-131 five abreast all economy class, maximum 149.

Production: 37.

History: Faced with the fact that the Convair 880 was not selling, General Dynamics had the choice of either abandoning its jetliner programme and cutting its losses or trying to improve the product. It chose the latter course – unwisely as it turned out – deciding in 1958 to produce a stretched development of the 880 with more powerful engines, a revised wing incorporating greater sweep, more seating capacity, increased fuel capacity and higher weights.

Originally known as the Model 600 when launched against an order for 25 from American Airlines in July 1958, it was soon given the appellation Convair 990, recognition of its guaranteed cruising speed of 615 miles per hour expressed in kilometres per hour and a convenient progression – for marketing – from the 880. The name Coronado was later applied.

The 990 also had first generation turbofan engines. Although the general CJ-805 designation of the 880's turbojets was retained, the -23 version was redesigned to feature a rear fan to produce a higher bypass ratio with benefits in fuel consumption and noise. Another feature was the installation of aerodynamic anti shock bodies on the trailing edges of the wings, these intended to decrease drag at high subsonic speeds.

The first 990 was built on production tooling and flew on 24 January 1961. Flight testing quickly revealed some serious problems including oscillations in the outer engine pods (which necessitated shortening the pylons) and excessive drag which meant that speed and range guarantees could not be met. Two years of costly research and modification followed, the upgraded aircraft being redesignated Convair 990A. The problems caused SAS to cancel its order and Varig to refuse delivery until they were fixed.

The 990 (in unmodified form) entered service with American and Swissair in March 1962 but the original customer list remained small at those plus Varig and Garuda for a total of just 37 aircraft. The last one was delivered to Garuda in September 1963 and after sustaining enormous losses on the 880/990 adventure, Convair withdrew from the airliner market.

Several airlines flew leased or second hand 990s with Spanish charter operator Spantax the largest and last with 14, the final example of which was retired in March 1987.

Photo: Convair 990-30A-5. (Convair)

Curtiss F-5L/Aeromarine 75

Country of origin: USA.

Powerplants: Two 400hp (298kW) Liberty 12A V12 piston engines; two bladed propellers.

Performance: Max speed 78kt (145km/h); cruising speed 65kt (121km/h); range 720nm (1334km).

Weights: Empty 3955kg (8720lb); max takeoff 6508kg (14,348lb).

Dimensions: Wing span upper 31.62m (103ft 9in), lower 23.77m (78ft 0in); length 15.03m (49ft 4in); height 5.72m (18ft 9in); wing area 129.8m² (1397sq ft).

Accommodation: 12 passengers.

Production: 60 F-5Ls; number of Aeromarine conversions unknown.

History: Curtiss began licence production of the British Felixstowe F.5 patrol flying boat in 1918 for the US Navy as the F-5L. Compared with the original, the F-5L featured revised wings of marginally greater span but less area, increased maximum weight and replacement of the Rolls-Royce Eagle engines with Liberty 12s.

The first civilian F-5Ls were basic conversions by Aeromarine Airways which had begun operations in August 1919 between New York and Atlantic City, New Jersey, initially using war surplus Curtiss HS-2 flying boats modified to carry passengers and then converted F-5Ls. These services were successful and provided Aeromarine with the necessary encouragement and finance to undertake more extensive commercial conversions of the F-5L.

What was dubbed the Aeromarine Model 75 was a substantial modification of the Curtiss F-5L which involved incorporating an entirely new and considerably enlarged plywood upper hull/cabin for 12 passengers in two compartments fore and aft of the two man open cockpit located between the engines.

The unequal span wings, braced tailplane (of wooden with fabric covering construction) and lower hull remained as before, as did the floats mounted near the tips of the lower wing.

The first conversion flew in 1920 but the precise number performed is not known. At least two are confirmed but there could be several more. Similarly, the number of 'standard' F-5L conversions is open to conjecture.

Aeromarine purchased the assets of Florida West Indies Airways in 1920 and initially using a pair of F-5Ls, operated the Key West (Florida) to Havana service carrying mail and passengers. Flights were also made between Miami and Nassau. This service was extremely popular with US citizens who liked a drink and wished to avoid the restrictions imposed by alcohol prohibition at home!

Aeromarine expanded its operations in 1921 to include what was called its 'Highball Express' service from New York to Havana via Atlantic City, Beaufort (South Carolina), Miami and Key West. Seasonal demands meant these services were most popular in winter as northern USA residents sought warmer climes, with the result that from 1922 Aeromarine deployed some of its fleet of F-5Ls and Model 75s on commuter services between Cleveland and Ohio during summer.

Aeromarine remained in business for another year before it succumbed to falling traffic in September 1923.

Photo: Curtiss Aeromarine F-5L.

Curtiss Condor

Country of origin: USA.

Powerplants: AT-32 – two 720hp (537kW) Wright SGR-1820-2, -3 or F Cyclone nine cylinder radials; three bladed propellers.

Performance: T-32 – max speed 148kt (274km/h); cruising speed 130kt (241km/h). AT-32 – max speed 165kt (306km/h); service ceiling 22,000ft (6705m); range 622nm (1152km).

Weights: T-32 – empty 5096kg (11,235lb); max takeoff 7620kg (16,800lb). AT-32 – empty 5550kg (12,235lb); max takeoff 7938kg (17,500lb).

Dimensions: Wing span 25.00m (82ft 0in); length 14.81m (48ft 7in); height 4.98m (16ft 4in); wing area 112.2m² (1208sq ft).

Accommodation: Up to 12 sleeper berths or 15 day passengers.

Production: 21 T-32, 13 AT-32, 8 BT-32, 3 CT-32, total 45.

History: Curtiss built two twin engined biplane airliners under the name Condor in the late 1920s and early 1930s. The first was the Model 18, essentially a 1928 modification of the B-2 Condor bomber. Powered by two 625hp (466kW) Curtiss GV-1750 Conqueror V12s and capable of carrying up to 18 passengers, six were built but remained unsold until 1931 when they were bought by Eastern Air Transport, a Curtiss-Wright Corporation affiliate.

The second and better known Condor airliner was the T-32, sometimes known as the Condor II. This was also a biplane but a completely new design with two Wright Cyclone engines, semi retractable undercarriage, and generally more modern appearance. It was capable of carrying up to 15 seated or 12 berthed passengers in two compartments.

The first T-32 flew on 30 January 1933 and it entered service with American Airways (later Airlines) the following May. Twenty-one T-32s were built – nine for American, nine for Eastern Air Transport, two for the US Army as the YC-30 and one for the Byrd Antarctic Expedition of 1933, this Condor featuring fixed undercarriage which could be fitted with floats or skis.

The improved AT-32 models with supercharged engines, variable pitch propellers, low drag engine cowlings and increased fuel capacity appeared in 1934 and were built in several subvariants: AT-32A – three for American; AT-32B – three for American with a different version of the Cyclone engine; AT-32C – one day transport for Swissair; AT-32D – four for American with unsupercharged engines; AT-32E – two 12 passenger VIP transports for the US Navy/Marine Corps as the R4C-1; BT-32 – eight bomber versions sold to China, Colombia and Peru; and CT-32 – three military freighters for Argentina.

Ten T-32 Condors were modified to AT-32 standards and redesignated T-32C.

Although antiquated when compared to the contemporary Boeing 247 and Douglas DC-2 monoplanes, the Condor's appearance shortly before these types ensured it some orders. US scheduled airline service ended in 1936 but the Condor continued flying in other parts of the world.

Four Eastern Air Transport T-32s were sold to British operator International Air Freight in 1937 and were impressed into RAF service on the outbreak of war in September 1939. The last known user was the Peruvian Air Force, which operated a Condor until as late as 1956.

Photo: T-32 Condor.

Curtiss Commando

Country of origin: USA.

Powerplants: C-46A – two 2000hp (1491kW) Pratt & Whitney R-2800-51 Double Wasp 18-cylinder radials; three bladed propellers.

Performance: C-46A – max cruise 197kt (356km/h); normal cruise 162kt (300km/h); range cruise 150kt (278km/h); initial climb 1300ft (396m)/min; service ceiling 27,600ft (8412m); max payload range 773nm (1433km); max range 2737nm (5070km).

Weights: C-46A – operating empty 14,969kg (33,000lb); max takeoff 21,773kg (48,000lb).

Dimensions: Wing span 32.94m (108ft 0in); length 23.37m (76ft 4in); height 6.63m (21ft 9in); wing area 126.2m² (1358sq ft).

Accommodation: 40-62 passengers; max payload 5275kg (11,630lb).

Production: 1 CW-20/C-55 prototype, 25 C-46, 1491 C-46A, 2 XC-46C, 1410 C-46D, 17 C-46E, 234 C-46F, 1 C-46G, 160 R5C-1, total 3341.

History: Originally developed from 1936 as the CW-20, a modern 36 passenger pressurised airliner of all metal construction with a spacious 'double bubble' fuselage, what became the military C-46 Commando was an effective transport capable of carrying greater payloads than the ubiquitous Douglas DC-3/C-47 and with higher performance. World War II interrupted the CW-20's intended career as a commercial airliner, and all were built for the military.

The first CW-20 was flown on 26 March 1940 with 1700hp (1268kW) Wright R-2600 engines and twin fins. US military interest was immediate and the aircraft was ordered for the USAAC. The prototype was converted to military specifications as the C-55 and ended up in Britain, flying with BOAC in 1941-43.

A substantial redesign of the aircraft for military use was undertaken including deletion of the pressurisation system and incorporation of a single fin. A preliminary batch of 25 C-46s was delivered to the USAAF in 1942, these featuring the definitive Pratt & Whitney R-2800 engines and fewer cabin windows.

The major production versions which followed were the C-46A Commando with large cargo door, strengthened floor and folding seats along the cabin walls; C-46D with double cargo doors and modified nose; and the C-46F with more powerful 2200hp (1640kW) R-2800-75s and square wing tips. Other versions were either of limited production or experimental while the USMC's R5C-1 was equivalent to the C-46A.

Postwar, Curtiss attempted to market a new passenger transport version but the glut of relatively inexpensive war surplus C-47s, C-54s, C-46s and other types made it superfluous. Interestingly, most major US airlines chose to equip with the Douglas products, the Commando finding itself operating mainly with smaller carriers in the USA and overseas, often as a freighter.

Sales were particularly strong to South, Latin and Central America and more than 600 were flying in that part of the world by the late 1950s. Operating as 'aerial tramp steamers' these Commandos paid their way for many years, usually as freighters. By 1999 only about 20 remained in service.

Photo: CW-20D.

Dassault Mercure

Country of origin: France.

Powerplants: Two 15,500lb (68.9kN) Pratt & Whitney JT8D-15 turbofans.

Performance: Max cruise 500kt (926km/h); economical cruise 463kt (860km/h); max payload range 408nm (756km); max fuel range 1750nm (3242km).

Weights: Operating empty 31,800kg (70,106lb); max takeoff 56,500kg (124,559lb).

Dimensions: Wing span 30.55m (100ft 3in); length 34.84m (114ft 3½in); height 11.37m (37ft 3½in); wing area 116.0m² (1249sq ft).

Accommodation: Typically 120 passengers in two classes or maximum 162 six abreast.

Production: 12.

History: One of the great commercial failures in the history of aviation, the Mercure short haul airliner was a financial disaster for the parent company and its risk sharing partners. Only 12 were built including two prototypes and only one airline placed an order, the French domestic operator Air Inter, and then largely due to French government pressure.

Apart from Dassault, big losers on the Mercure were French taxpayers (the government provided loan support for 56 per cent of the total programme cost), Aeritalia (now Alenia), Spain's CASA, Belgium's SABCA, Switzerland's Federal Aircraft Factory and Canadair.

The Mercure's origins lie in a 1963 project for a 32 seater regional airliner called the Mystère 30, a scaled up development of the Mystère/Falcon 20 business jet. By 1964 the aircraft had grown to a 36-40 seater and by 1965 a 40-56 seater now called the Mercure after the Roman god Mercury.

By 1968 the size and general specification of the definitive and much larger 130-150 seat Mercure had been pretty much decided. It was decided to optimise the aircraft for short stages which reflected the sort of services most of the world's airline passengers flew. Short range capability only was decided on as a result, but what was missed by those involved was that a full load, multi-stage capability without refuelling was the real requirement with the option of longer single stages. Air France rejected it on the grounds of cost and lack of range.

Overall, the Mercure was uncomfortably close to the Boeing 737-200 in both specification (apart from range) and configuration, the Advanced versions of which would shortly be selling in huge numbers. Dassault always said it would not launch the Mercure unless it had 50 orders. It was in fact launched on the basis of just 10 orders from the one and only customer, Air Inter.

The prototype first flew on 28 May 1971 and deliveries to Air Inter began in May 1974, over a year behind schedule. The final aircraft was flown in November 1975. The Mercure's short range with a full load proved to be inadequate even for French internal services and Air Inter operated its Mercures with the help of a subsidy from the French government to offset the extremely high cost of spares. Technically, the Mercure was a perfectly good airliner, but the concept behind it was fatally flawed. Air Inter retired its Mercures in 1995-96.

A slightly larger Mercure 200 with CFM56 engines and considerably more range remained a project, as did plans for a joint venture development with McDonnell Douglas.

Photo: Mercure.

de Havilland DH.34

Country of origin: United Kingdom.

Powerplant: One 450hp (336kW) Napier Lion W12; three bladed propeller.

Performance: Max speed 111kt (206km/h); cruising speed 91kt (169km/h); service ceiling 10,000ft (3048m); range 317nm (587km).

Weights: DH.34 – empty 2075kg (4574lb); max takeoff 3266kg (7200lb). DH.34B – empty 2120kg (4674lb); max takeoff 3266kg (7200lb).

Dimensions: DH.34 – wing span 15.65m (51ft 4in); length 11.89m (39ft 0in); height 3.66m (12ft 0in); wing area 54.8m² (590sq ft). DH.34B – wing span 16.56m (54ft 4in); wing area 59.2m² (637sq ft).

Accommodation: Up to nine passengers.

Production: 11 plus one airframe not completed.

History: By the early 1920s airlines and aircraft manufacturers were beginning to better understand the economics of commercial operations and realised that faster aircraft capable of carrying a greater payload per horsepower was the way to go.

Following the introduction of subsidies for air services in Britain from March 1921 and the empowerment of the Air Council to oversee airliner development, the DH.34 was designed to fill a requirement of that organisation. Built of wood with a plywood covering, the DH.34 was not notably faster than its predecessors but embodied lessons learnt from earlier de Havilland designed types such as the Airco DH.16 and DH.18 (see earlier entries).

Powered by a single Napier Lion engine, it featured an open two man cockpit forward and a cabin for nine passengers in wicker chairs (or eight plus cabin boy) amidships. The cabin door was large enough to load a spare engine if necessary and inertia engine starting was fitted, ending the days of propeller swinging.

The DH.34 was launched against two orders: Daimler Hire (2) and the Air Council (7), the latter for lease to Instone Air Line and Daimler Hire. Instone eventually operated four and Daimler six, both flying from Croydon (London) to points in Europe. The first DH.34 flew on 26 March 1922 and, incredibly by modern standards, was delivered to Daimler Hire just five days later and flew its first Croydon to Paris service another two days after that!

The eight other British DH.34s were delivered over the next couple of months and the last of the initial batch of 10 aircraft was shipped to the Russian airline Dobrolet in June 1922. An additional aircraft was delivered to Daimler Hire later in 1922.

With the merger of existing operators to form Imperial Airways in April 1924, six DH.34s were inherited by the new airline. The survivors of these continued on the Brussels and Amsterdam routes until March 1926 when they were retired, Imperial having adopted a policy of using only multi engined aircraft.

Although the DH.34 gave solid service, it suffered from one flaw, a relatively high stalling speed. This made forced landings difficult and several crashes resulted. Three aircraft were therefore converted to DH.34B standards with increased wing span and area, reducing the stalling speed from 55kt (101km/h) to a more manageable 49kt (90km/h).

Photo: DH.34.

de Havilland DH.50

Country of origin: United Kingdom.

Powerplant: One 230hp (171kW) Armstrong Siddeley Puma inline; 300hp (224kW) ADC Nimbus, 385hp (287kW) Armstrong Siddeley Jaguar III radial; 420hp (313kW) Bristol Jupiter IV or 450hp (336kW) Jupiter VI radial; two bladed propeller.

Performance: DH.50/Puma – max speed 97kt (180km/h); cruising speed 82kt (153km/h); initial climb 605ft (184m)/min; service ceiling 14,600ft (4450m); range 325nm (603km). DH.50J/Jupiter – max speed 115kt (212km/h); cruising speed 95kt (177km/h); initial climb 1250ft (381m)/min; service ceiling 20,000ft (6096m); max range 570nm (1055nm).

Weights: DH.50 – empty 1022kg (2253lb); max takeoff 1769kg (3900lb). DH.50A/J – empty 1094-1148kg (2413-2532lb); max takeoff 1905kg (4200lb).

Dimensions: All models – wing span 13.03m (42ft 9in); height 3.35m (11ft 0in); wing area 40.3m^2 (434sq ft). DH.50/A – length 9.07m (29ft 9in). DH.50J – length 8.76m (28ft 9in).

Accommodation: Pilot and four passengers.

Production: 16 DH.50 (by de Havilland), 18 DH.50A (QANTAS 4, West Australian Airways 3, Larkin 1, SABCA 3, Aero 7), 4 DH.50J (QANTAS 3, de Havilland 1), total 38.

History: Designed as a replacement for the DH.9 civil conversions used by de Havilland Hire Service, the DH.50 carried four passengers in a forward enclosed cabin. Produced in three major versions and powered by a variety of engines, most of the 38 DH.50s were built overseas in Australia, Belgium and Czechoslovakia.

The Puma powered first aircraft flew on 3 August 1923 and only four days later it was taken to Sweden by Alan Cobham where it won the prestigious International Air Traffic Competitions against all the major European manufacturers. A year later Cobham won the King's Cup race in the same aircraft while he took the second aircraft on renowned pioneering long distance survey flights to South Africa and Australia in 1925-26, for which he earned a Knighthood.

The basic versions were the standard DH.50; DH.50A with slightly longer cabin, revised centre section strut geometry, additional radiator area and undercarriage set slightly forward; and DH.50J (from November 1926) with more powerful Jupiter engines. All were capable of operating on floats.

Manufacturing licences were acquired by several firms including QANTAS, West Australian Airways and Larkin Aircraft Supply for operations in Australia, QANTAS using its aircraft to link inland rail heads. One was used to inaugurate Royal Flying Doctor Service operations in August 1927 and several earlier models were upgraded to DH.50J standards.

Only four DH.50s were flown by British operators (Imperial Airways and Air Taxis), most of the production being exported. Three DH.50As were built by SABCA in Belgium for Sabena in the Belgian Congo, while seven DH.50As built by Aero in Czechoslovakia were for CLS. A single Jupiter engined DH.50J floatplane was built in Britain for the North Sea Aerial and General Transport Company. It was used on a pioneering mail service along the Nile between Khartoum and Kisumu from December 1926.

Photo: DH.50A.

de Havilland Giant Moth

Country of origin: United Kingdom.

Powerplant: One 500hp (373kW) Bristol Jupiter XI, 500hp (373kW) Armstrong Siddeley Jaguar VIC or 525hp (391kW) Pratt & Whitney Hornet radial; two bladed propeller.

Performance: Max speed 115kt (212km/h); cruising speed 96kt (177km/h); initial climb 900ft (274m)/min; service ceiling 16,000ft (4877m); range 565nm (1046km).

Weights: Empty 1656kg (3650lb); max takeoff 3175kg (7000lb).

Dimensions: Wing span 15.85m (52ft 0in); length 11.89m (39ft 0in); height 3.66m (12ft 0in); wing area 56.9m^2 (613sq ft).

Accommodation: Pilot and 6-8 passengers.

Production: 9.

History: Considering Imperial Airways' stated policy of using only multi engined aircraft, observers were surprised when de Havilland revealed its next airliner to be single engined. The DH.61 Giant Moth continued normal de Havilland practice – a wooden biplane with forward cabin – but on a larger scale with accommodation for up to eight passengers.

Originally developed to meet Australian requirements, the prototype was powered by a Jupiter VI engine pending availability of the more powerful Jupiter XI intended for production aircraft. It first flew in December 1927 and was named *Canberra* in honour of its major intended market. This served as the DH.61's type name for a short time until it was changed to Giant Moth.

The first aircraft was shipped to Australia in early 1928 and subsequently flew with MacRobertson Miller, Western Australian Airways and Guinea Airways. Three others also served in Australia, two of them used by QANTAS to carry mail on the last leg of the Britain to Australia route and a third by Larkin Aircraft Supply on internal mail flights.

Two Giant Months were sold to British operators – one to the *Daily Mail* newspaper as a mobile office complete with typewriters, darkroom and motorcycle for a reporter. It served with the newspaper for about 18 months, during which time it ranged widely around Britain and Europe.

The second British aircraft went to Sir Alan Cobham who used it on his 'Flying Circus' tours to encourage the development of commercial aviation. Powered by a Jaguar VIC engine, this aircraft visited countless communities in 1929 conducting joyflights which saw thousands of local authority dignitaries, businessmen, members of the public and schoolchildren take to the air, usually for the first time. This aircraft later served with Imperial Airways in Africa in January 1930 but was written off in a crash after only two weeks.

Two other Giant Moths were fitted with floats and delivered to Western Canada Airways and the Ontario Provincial Air Service for the carriage of firefighters and their equipment to forest fires.

The last Giant Moth was shipped to London Air Transport in Ontario in 1929 where it lay dormant for a time before re-emerging in 1932 fitted with floats and a Pratt & Whitney Hornet engine for service with the Ontario Provincial Government, again on firefighting duties.

Photo: DH.61 Giant Moth of Alan Cobham Aviation.

de Havilland Hercules

Country of origin: United Kingdom.

Powerplants: Three 420hp (313kW) Bristol Jupiter VI nine cylinder radials; two bladed propellers.

Performance: Max speed 111kt (206km/h); cruising speed 96kt (177km/h); initial climb 765ft (233m)/min; service ceiling 13,000ft (3962m); range 456nm (845km).

Weights: Empty 4110kg (9060lb); max takeoff 7076kg (15,600lb).

Dimensions: Wing span 24.23m (79ft 6in); length 16.92m (55ft 6in); height 5.56m (18ft 3in); wing area 143.7m² (1547sq ft).

Accommodation: Seven passengers and mail or 14 passengers and reduced mail.

Production: 11.

History: Designed to meet a 1925 Imperial Airways requirement for an aircraft to use on its subsidised fortnightly passenger, freight and mail service between Cairo and Karachi, the DH.66 Hercules marked a step forward for de Havilland in that its design incorporated a fabric covered tubular steel fuselage structure, although the wings remained fabric covered wood.

The cabin and aft baggage compartment were basically plywood 'boxes' within the main fuselage structure. Three engined so as to increase safety over remote areas, the Hercules (named following a competition in *Meccano Magazine*) was capable of carrying up to 14 passengers or typically seven plus mail in Imperial Airways service.

Imperial Airways ordered five DH.66s, the first of which flew on 30 September 1926. Deliveries began the following December and services were inaugurated in January 1927. The route was subsequently extended to Delhi and an additional aircraft ordered to cope with demand.

The first five Hercules had all been delivered by March 1927, the sixth entered brief service in October 1929 before being destroyed after stalling on approach to Jask in Iran. A replacement was ordered – the last Hercules built – this entering service in January 1930.

On the other side of the world, Western Australian Airways was awarded an Australian Government contract in 1928 to fly subsidised services between Perth and Adelaide. Four Hercules were ordered to fill this role of which the first was flown in March 1929. Services began two months later.

The Australian DH.66s differed from their British counterparts in having an enclosed cockpit and tail wheel (instead of skid), although this was subsequently replaced. Two of the Western Australian Airways Hercules were sold to Imperial Airways as attrition replacements in 1930-31.

Imperial Airways conducted two experimental mail flights to Australia using Hercules, the first of them – in April 1931 – resulting in the aircraft being damaged beyond repair in a forced landing near Koepang (Indonesia) in poor weather. The mail was retrieved by no less a personage than Charles Kingsford Smith, who took it on to Melbourne in his Fokker F.VII/3m *Southern Cross*. Kingsford Smith also flew the first leg of the return service.

Imperial Airways conducted a Hercules proving flight to South Africa in late 1932 with regular services starting the next year.

Photo: DH.66 Hercules.

de Havilland Dragon

Country of origin: United Kingdom.

Powerplants: Two 130hp (97kW) de Havilland Gipsy Major 1 inverted four cylinder inline engines; two bladed propellers.

Performance: Mk.1 – max speed 111kt (206km/h); cruising speed 95kt (175km/h); initial climb 612ft (186m)/min; service ceiling 12,500ft (3810m); range 400nm (740km). Mk.2 – max speed 116kt (215km/h); cruising speed 99kt (183km/h); initial climb 565ft (172m)/min; service ceiling 14,500ft (4420m); range 474nm (877km).

Weights: Mk.1 – empty 1043kg (2300lb); max takeoff 1905kg (4200lb). Mk.2 – empty 1060kg (2336lb); max takeoff 2041kg (4500lb).

Dimensions: Wing span 14.43m (47ft 4in); length 10.51m (34ft 6in); height 3.07m (10ft 1in); wing area 34.9m² (376sq ft).

Accommodation: Pilot plus 6-8 passengers.

Production: 149 Mk.1 (UK 62, Australia 87), 53 Mk.2 (UK), total 202.

History: Developed for British operator Hillman's Airways which wanted a low cost twin for its London to Paris service, the DH.84 Dragon biplane (originally known as the Dragon Moth) was of the well proven de Havilland wooden construction method. It exhibited good operating economics due to its ability to carry up to eight passengers on the power of only two 130hp (97kW) Gipsy Major engines.

The Dragon played a major part in developing air services in Britain as well as Australia, New Zealand, Canada, Africa and Egypt. It made profitable commercial services possible and quickly developed a reputation for ruggedness and reliability.

The prototype first flew on 24 November 1932 and Hillman's inaugurated services to Paris on April Fool's Day 1933. Other operators included Midland and Scottish Air Ferries, the Scottish Motor Traction Co, Northern and Scottish Airways, Jersey Airways, Aberdeen Airways, Railway Air Services, Canadian Airways, Aer Lingus, Misrair of Egypt, African Air Transport, Indian National Airways, Nairobi's Wilson Airways, Western Mining in Australia for survey work, the Royal Flying Doctor Service, MacRobertson-Miller and many others. Some Canadian Dragons operated from floats or skis.

DH.84M military versions with machine guns and light bomb load were delivered to Iraq, Denmark and Portugal, while Jim and Amy Mollison flew their Dragon (modified with cabin fuel tanks) on long distance non stop flights between Britain and North America.

A Mk.II Dragon with individually framed cabin windows in place of the previous 'glasshouse' arrangement, faired main undercarriage legs and increased maximum weight was introduced in September 1933.

British production ended in May 1937 but was resumed by De Havilland Aircraft in Australia with 87 built between September 1942 and June 1943 for the RAAF to meet an urgent need for radio and navigation trainers. Based on the Dragon I with glasshouse windows and no undercarriage fairings, these are sometimes referred to as Dragon IIIs.

Photo: DH.84 Dragon.

de Havilland DH.86

Country of origin: United Kingdom.

Powerplants: Four 200hp (149kW) de Havilland Gipsy Six inverted six cylinder inline engines; two bladed propellers.

Performance: DH.86A/B – max speed 144kt (267km/h); cruising speed 123kt (228km/h); initial climb 925ft (282m)/min; service ceiling 17,400ft (5303m); range 660nm (1223km).

Weights: DH.86 – empty 2859kg (6303lb); max takeoff 4536kg (10,000lb). DH.86B – empty 2943kg (6489lb); max takeoff 4649kg (10,250lb).

Dimensions: Wing span 19.66m (64ft 6in); length 14.05m (46ft 1in); height 3.96m (13ft 0in); wing area 59.5m² (641sq ft).

Accommodation: 10 passengers.

Production: 32 DH.86, 20 DH.86A, 10 DH.86B, total 62.

History: De Havilland's first four engined airliner, the DH.86 was designed for Qantas for use on the Singapore-Australia leg of the Empire Air Route from England. Multi-engined safety was a requirement, the aircraft therefore fitted with a quartet of de Havilland's new Gipsy Six engines, a six cylinder development of the four cylinder Gipsy Major.

The DH.86 continued the de Havilland biplane airliner tradition of fabric covered wooden construction. The wings were tapered and the undercarriage fully faired with 'trouser' spats. The prototype first flew on 14 January 1934 and like the next two aircraft featured a short nose and room for only one pilot. Qantas required two pilots with the result that a redesigned nose with side by side cockpit seating for two became standard.

The DH.86 entered service with Railway Air Services in August 1934. Other initial model DH.86s (sometimes called the 'Express') were built for Australia's Holyman Airways and Qantas, Imperial Airways, Jersey Airways, Egypt's Misrair and Wrightways.

The DH.86A with a modified windscreen, metal rudder, larger brakes and revised undercarriage was introduced in 1935, and saw service with Imperial Airways, Misrair, Blackpool and West Coast Air Services, British Airways and Railway Air Services.

A series of accidents and the criticism of the DH.86's rudder and aileron control characteristics which followed resulted in the final version, the DH.86B with large auxiliary fins on the end of the tailplane which had increased chord at the tips along with higher geared ailerons. The first was flown in February 1937 and nine others were built during the year with the last delivered to Turkey in December. All remaining DH.86As were modified to DH.86B standards.

Meanwhile, Qantas had been operating its six DH.86s on international services, the first one departing Brisbane on 25 February 1935 and arriving in Singapore 10 days later. Imperial Airways' six aircraft for European and Empire routes entered service in February 1936. By 1939 many of the original customers' aircraft had been sold to other operators and several flew in military colours during World War II. A few survived after 1945 and the last airworthy example – operated by the Hampshire Aeroplane Club – was destroyed at Madrid in September 1958 when its undercarriage collapsed on landing.

Photo: DH.86A. (Qantas)

de Havilland Dragon Rapide

Country of origin: United Kingdom.

Powerplants: DH.89A/B – two 200hp (149kW) de Havilland Gipsy Queen 2 or 3 six cylinder inverted inline engines; two bladed propeller.

Performance: DH.89A – max speed 136kt (252km/h); cruising speed 115kt (212km/h); initial climb 867ft (264m)/min; service ceiling 16,700ft (5090m); range 502nm (930km). Mk.4 – cruising speed 121kt (225km/h); initial climb 1200ft (365m)/min; range 452nm (837km).

Weights: DH.89A – empty 1486kg (3276lb); max takeoff 2495kg (5500lb). Mk.4 – max takeoff 2722kg (6000lb).

Dimensions: Wing span 14.63m (48ft 0in); length 10.51m (34ft 6in); height 3.12m (10ft 3in); wing area 31.2m² (336sq ft).

Accommodation: Up to eight passengers.

Production: 730 of all models including 469 DH.89B Dominie.

History: A replacement for the DH.84 Dragon, the DH.89 Dragon Rapide was the last de Havilland wooden biplane to enter production, combining the twin engined philosophies of the earlier aircraft with some of the design features of the four engined DH.86 including a smaller version of the tapered wing. It has often been described as a 'scaled down' DH.86.

The Rapide became a mainstay of the lighter end of commercial aviation all over the world in the 1930s. Postwar, the ready availability of ex military aircraft at relatively low cost enabled a large number of operators to establish (or re-establish) their businesses. Corporations and private owners also purchased the aircraft in numbers.

The prototype was flown on 17 April 1934 and the first civil customer was that de Havilland stalwart Hillman's Airways, which put the Rapide into service on its Paris and Belfast routes shortly afterwards. Wing flaps to improve airfield performance, a landing light in the nose and cabin heating were introduced with the DH.89A in 1936.

The outbreak of World War II saw most British civil operated Rapides impressed into RAF service. Deliveries of the DH.89B Dominie for the RAF began in September 1939 with production initially undertaken by de Havilland at Hatfield but then moved to Brush Coachworks in 1942 to make space for Mosquito production by the parent company.

The last Dominie was delivered in July 1946 and the aircraft was built as a radio or navigation trainer (Mk.I) and communications aircraft (Mk.II).

Postwar civil conversions were performed by the de Havilland Repair Unit and other organisations and the Rapide quickly became a commercial mainstay once again with charter operators, small airlines, flying clubs and private owners in scores of countries around the world. Some 'new' aircraft were built from spares.

Retrospective mark numbers were introduced to differentiate the versions: Mk.1 (surviving prewar examples); Mk.2 (eight seat Dominie civil conversions); Mk.3 (nine seat civil conversions); and Mk.4 (increased maximum weight and constant-speed propellers for improved performance). The one-off Mks.5 and 6 featured manually controlled variable-pitch and fixed-pitch metal propellers, respectively.

Photo: DH.89B Dragon Rapide.

de Havilland Albatross

Country of origin: United Kingdom.

Powerplants: Four 525hp (391kW) de Havilland Gipsy Twelve I inverted V12s; two bladed propellers.

Performance: Passenger version – max speed 195kt (361km/h); cruising speed 182kt (338km/h); initial climb 710ft (216m)/min; service ceiling 17,900ft (5455m); range 904nm (1674km). Mailplane – max speed 193kt (357km/h); cruising speed 177kt (328km/h); initial climb 550ft (167m)/min; service ceiling 15,100ft (4600m); max range 2867nm (5312km).

Weights: Empty 9630kg (21,230lb); max takeoff 13,381kg (29,500lb).

Dimensions: Wing span 32.00m (105ft 0in); length 21.79m (71ft 6in); height 6.78m (22ft 3in); wing area 100.1m² (1078sq ft).

Accommodation: Up to 23 seated or 12 berthed passengers.

Production: 7.

History: Designed in 1936 to an Air Ministry requirement for two trans-Atlantic mailplanes, the elegant and streamlined DH.91 Albatross represented a major step forward for de Havilland, incorporating retractable undercarriage, a cantilever monoplane wing and a new standard (for Britain) in aerodynamic efficiency.

Construction was all wood – fuselage of cedar ply laminations and balsa sandwich and a one piece wing built around a load bearing spar with two layers of diagonally applied spruce skinning. The same principal was later applied to the Mosquito fighter-bomber.

Power was provided by four of the new and untried Gipsy 12 inverted V12s in tight streamlined cowlings with air fed to the rear of the engines from intakes in the wing leading edges.

The first Albatross flew on 20 May 1937, flight trials resulting in the original inset and braced twin fins being redesigned and moved to the end of the tailplanes. The electrically operated undercarriage initially caused some problems and the second aircraft broke its back on landing during overload tests in May 1938. It was rebuilt with a strengthened fuselage.

The first two DH.91s were built to the original mailplane specification with greater fuel capacity than the five passenger versions which followed, these also having extra cabin windows and slotted rather than split flaps.

Deliveries of the passenger version to Imperial Airways began in October 1938 and the aircraft soon settled into service on the Croydon to Paris, Brussels and Zurich routes. The mailplanes built for the Air Ministry were never used for their intended role before the war and were instead allocated to crew training before joining Imperial Airways.

The outbreak of war in September 1939 ended any possibility of further orders. The two mailplanes were allocated to the RAF for use on courier flights between Britain and Iceland (with both destroyed in landing accidents in that country), while the five Imperial Airways machines continued in service flying mainly from Bristol to Shannon, Alexandria and Lisbon. Three were destroyed (one in an air raid, one by sabotage and another due to structural failure) and the remaining pair was scrapped in 1943.

Photo: DH.91 Albatross.

de Havilland Flamingo

Country of origin: United Kingdom.

Powerplants: Two 890hp (664kW) Bristol Perseus XIIC or 930hp (693kW) Perseus XVI nine cylinder radials; three bladed propellers.

Performance: Max speed 208kt (385km/h); max cruise 177kt (328km/h); normal cruise 160kt (296km/h); initial climb 1470ft (448m)/min; service ceiling 20,900ft (6370m); range 1051nm (1948km).

Weights: Empty 5137kg (11,325lb); max takeoff 8165kg (18,000lb).

Dimensions: Wing span 21.34m (70ft 0in); length 15.72m (51ft 7in); height 4.65m (15ft 3in); wing area 60.5m² (651sq ft).

Accommodation: Up to 17 passengers.

Production: 16.

History: De Havilland's first all metal, stressed skin aircraft, the DH.95 Flamingo finally went some way towards bridging the gap between British and US airliner technology.

A high wing monoplane, advanced features included hydraulically retractable undercarriage, split flaps and constant-speed propellers driven by two Bristol Perseus XIIC radials initially and then more powerful Perseus XVIs from the fifth aircraft.

The prototype first flew on 28 December 1938 with a triple fin configuration, the centre unit subsequently being removed.

Two versions were offered – with 12 seats for stage lengths up to 900nm (1667km) and 17 seats for shorter stages. Guernsey and Jersey Airways were the first customers, ordering three between them.

Jersey leased the prototype for proving flights in May 1939, operating from Heston and Eastleigh to the Channel Islands. During a two month period it carried 1373 passengers with an average load factor of 71 per cent.

The outbreak of war effectively killed the Flamingo's commercial career and an order from the Egyptian Government lapsed. BOAC ordered eight in early 1940, these being sent to Cairo where they formed the backbone of wartime local services to Addis Ababa, Aden, Jedda, Teheran and other points.

The Jersey/Guernsey machines were impressed into the RAF before entering commercial service, as was the prototype. One of the BOAC aircraft flew with the Royal Navy and three others were ordered by the RAF for communications duties and for the King's Flight. This was permanently retained on standby to evacuate the Royal Family if necessary in the early stages of the war.

One aircraft was completed as a Hertfordshire troop carrier for the RAF with accommodation for up to 22 soldiers. Although 40 were ordered only the prototype was built and it crashed in October 1940, four months after delivery.

Six DH.95s were lost in accidents (some as a result of control problems caused by the elevator shroud distorting), BOAC withdrew its aircraft in late 1943, the RAF in 1944 and the RN in 1945. Improved versions with Pratt & Whitney Twin Wasp engines and other refinements did not materialise. Only one of the survivors flew commercially after the war before scrapping, this briefly flying on charter work with British Air Transport in 1947.

Photo: DH.95 Flamingo.

de Havilland Dove

Country of origin: United Kingdom.

Powerplants: Srs.1/2 – two 330hp (246kW) de Havilland Gipsy Queen 70-3 inverted six cylinder engines. Srs.1B/2B – two 340hp (253kW) Gipsy Queen 70-4. Srs.5/6 – two 380hp (283kW) Gipsy Queen 70-2. Srs.7/8 – two 400hp (298kW) Gipsy Queen 70 Mk.3; three bladed propellers.

Performance: Srs.1 – normal cruise 143kt (265km/h); initial climb 750ft (228m)/min; service ceiling 20,000ft (6096m); max range 870nm (1400km). Srs.1B – normal cruise 155kt (288km/h); initial climb 850ft (259m)/min; max range 870nm (1400km). Srs.5 – max cruise 175kt (325km/h); normal cruise 155kt (288km/h); initial climb 920ft (280m)/min; range 795nm (1473km). Srs.8 – max cruise 182kt (338km/h); normal cruise 164kt (304km/h); initial climb 1135ft (346m)/min; range 634-886nm (1174-1641km).

Weights: Srs.1/1B – empty 2563kg (5650lb); max takeoff 3855kg (8500lb). Srs.5 – empty 2597kg (5725lb); max takeoff 3992kg (8800lb). Srs.7/8 – max takeoff 4060kg (8950lb).

Dimensions: Wing span 17.37m (57ft 0in); length 11.96m (39ft 3in); height 4.06m (13ft 4in); wing area 31.1m^2 (335sq ft).

Accommodation: 8-11 passengers in main cabin two abreast.

Production: 544 of all models.

History: Designed to meet a Brabazon Committee requirement for a postwar feederliner, the Dove found worldwide favour in this and many other roles including corporate transport, military communications, aerial survey, air ambulance and charter. It was produced in large numbers in the late 1940s and early 1950s (half the production run had been built by 1950 and 450 by the end of 1953) after which the rate reduced considerably. The 544th and last example was completed in 1967.

The prototype first flew on 25 September 1945 (the de Havilland company's 25th anniversary) and the aircraft was built in several series with progressively increased power, weights and performance: Srs.1 airliner (1946) and Srs.2 corporate equivalent (1948); Srs.3 stillborn high altitude survey variant; Srs.4 Devon (1947) for the RAF, RN and other air forces; Srs.1B/2B (1952); Srs.5 airliner and 6 executive (1953); and Srs.7/8 with raised Heron style cockpit (1960). By then, production was at a trickle and only 27 were built over the next seven years. Many earlier Doves were upgraded to later standards throughout the 1950s and '60s.

Although the Dove was aimed at small feeder and charter operators, its cost precluded many from ordering it, most turning to much less expensive Dragon Rapides and Airspeed Consuls. Despite this, the aircraft found a ready market with more affluent operators. The first customer to take delivery was British firm Skyways, which received its first aircraft in October 1946.

Other early customers included Sudan Airways, BOAC (for crew training), Iraq Petroleum, West African Airways, Hunting, Morton Air Services, Cambrian, British Midland, Channel Airways, Airlines of Western Australia and Central African Airways. The largest single customer was the Argentine Government which ordered 70 for transport, ambulance and other duties.

Photo: Dove 7. (Paul Merritt)

de Havilland Comet 1

Country of origin: United Kingdom.

Powerplants: Four 5050lb (22.5kN) de Havilland Ghost Mk.50-1 turbojets.

Performance: Max cruise 429kt (788km/h); normal cruise 392kt (724km/h); cruising altitude 35,000ft (10,668m); max payload range 1520nm (2816km); max range (no reserves) 3355nm (6213km).

Weights: 1 – max takeoff 48,535kg (107,000lb). 1A – max takeoff 52,164kg (115,000lb).

Dimensions: Wing span 35.05m (115ft 0in); length 28.35m (93ft 0in); height 8.65m (28ft 4^1/$_2$in); wing area 187.2m^2 (2015sq ft).

Accommodation: Typically 36 passengers four abreast; maximum 44 passengers.

Production: 114 Comets of all versions including 21 Comet 1/1A and 16 Comet 2.

History: The world's first pure jet airliner, the DH.106 Comet was designed to meet a 1943 Brabazon Committee requirement for a 'jet propelled mailplane' for the North Atlantic. The design evolved into a passenger carrier and for its day was highly advanced. Features included high pressure underwing refuelling and hydraulically powered flight controls with no manual backup. Construction used the new Redux metal-to-metal bonding method previously utilised in the Dove and the cabin pressurisation differential was twice that of any previous aircraft.

At the time of the first of two prototypes maiden flight on 27 July 1949, the Comet was five years ahead of any US jet airliner project but several accidents involving structural failure resulted in it being grounded in 1954. It would be four years before improved models again carried fare paying passengers. The subsequent accident investigation was ground breaking and taught the industry much about the previously largely unknown area of metal fatigue.

The first of nine production Comet 1s for BOAC flew in January 1951 and after a series of proving flights had been conducted, the world's first commercial jet passenger service took place on 2 May 1952 when 30 passengers travelled from London Heathrow to Johannesburg via Rome, Cairo, Khartoum, Entebbe and Livingstone. Production Comet 1s differed from the prototypes in having four wheel main undercarriage bogies instead of single main wheels.

Export models were built to Comet 1A standards with increased weight and fuel capacity and water injected engines. Deliveries were made between December 1952 and August 1953 to France's UAT (3), Air France (3), Canadian Pacific (2, of which one was transferred to BOAC and the other crashed on takeoff during its delivery flight) and the Royal Canadian Air Force (2).

The commercial career of the Comet 2 with more powerful Rolls-Royce Avon axial flow turbojets was thwarted by the groundings, all 34 orders from nine operators being cancelled. The prototype Mk.2 was flown in February 1952 and 16 were built, some for experimental work. Ten Comet C.2 transports with fully modified airframes (including round rather than square cabin windows) were delivered to RAF Transport Command in 1956-57, serving reliably for a decade. Three unpressurised and unmodified Comet 2Rs were also delivered to the RAF in 1957 and used for electronic intelligence gathering.

Photo: Comet 1A.

de Havilland Comet 4

Country of origin: United Kingdom.

Powerplants: Four 10,500lb (46.7kN) Rolls-Royce Avon Mk.524 turbojets.

Performance: Max cruise 457kt (846km/h); economical cruise 438kt (811km/h); service ceiling 42,000ft (12,800m); range with typical load and reserves 2366nm (4382km); max range (no reserves) 3823nm (7081km).

Weights: Operational empty 34,200kg (75,400lb); max takeoff 73,483kg (162,000lb).

Dimensions: Wing span 35.00m (114ft 10in); length 33.99m (111ft 6in); height 8.99m (29ft 6in); wing area 197.0m² (2121sq ft).

Accommodation: Typically 74-81 passengers in two classes; maximum 106 five abreast.

Production: 114 Comets of all versions incl 1 Comet 3 and 28 Comet 4.

History: The crashes and subsequent grounding of the early model Comets in 1954 gave the American manufacturers a chance to catch up, and through the Boeing 707 and Douglas DC-8, set the scene for US dominance of the jetliner market until Airbus began to exert some influence in the 1970s.

Before the groundings, de Havilland had announced the stretched – by 5.64m (18ft 6in) – and Avon powered Comet 3 with additional fuel housed in pinion tanks on the wing leading edges. It first flew in July 1954 – three months after the groundings and just four days after the Boeing 367-80 prototype – but orders for 16 aircraft from BOAC, Pan American and Air India lapsed. It was subsequently used for an around the world demonstration tour starting in late 1955 and served as an aerodynamic prototype for the improved Comet 4 with which it was dimensionally similar.

The Comet 4's design benefited from the lessons learned from the Comet 1 crash investigations and had a significantly modified structure. It was launched against a March 1955 order for 19 from BOAC but came to be overshadowed by the American jets which sold in large numbers. Although a capable and safe airliner, only 28 Comet 4s were built for BOAC, Aerolineas Argentinas (6) and East African Airways (3).

The first aircraft flew on 27 April 1958 and BOAC took initial delivery in September 1958 after several overseas proving flights had been undertaken. Although the Comet 4 had been designed for service on BOAC's African and Far East routes, the lure of the prestige associated with flying the first scheduled trans-Atlantic jet service was too great to ignore.

It was therefore between London and New York (via Gander) that the first BOAC Comet service was flown on 4 October 1958. This beat the inaugural Pan American Boeing 707-120 trans-Atlantic service by three weeks but commercially, Boeing was well ahead. BOAC itself became a 707 operator in 1959.

Aerolineas Argentinas received its first Comet 4 in March 1959 with East African Airways following in July 1960. BOAC flew its final Comet 4 revenue flight in November 1965 between Sydney and London while other operators of second hand and/or leased aircraft included Kuwait Airways, Malaysian Airways (later MSA), Ecuador's AREA, Air Ceylon and Dan-Air.

Photo: The first Comet 4. (de Havilland)

de Havilland Comet 4B and 4C

Country of origin: United Kingdom.

Powerplants: Four 10,500lb (46.7kN) Rolls-Royce Avon Mk.525/B turbojets.

Performance: 4B – max cruise 482kt (893km/h); economical cruise 452kt (837km/h); max payload range with reserves 1600nm (2964km); max range (no reserves) 3240nm (6000km). 4C – typical cruise 411-438kt (761-811km/h); range with 100 passengers and reserves 2250nm (4168km).

Weights: 4B – operational empty 35,653kg (78,600lb); max takeoff 71,669kg (158,000lb). 4C – operational empty 36,107kg (79,600lb); max takeoff 73,483kg (162,000lb).

Dimensions: 4B – wing span 32.87m (107ft 10in); length 35.97m (118ft 0in); height 8.99m (29ft 6in); wing area 191.3m² (2059sq ft). 4C – wing span 35.00m (114ft 10in); wing area 197.0m² (2121sq ft).

Accommodation: Typically 101 economy class passengers five abreast or up to 119 in high density layout.

Production: 114 Comets of all versions including 18 Comet 4B and 30 Comet 4C.

History: The final commercial developments of the Comet, the 4B and 4C were short and medium range versions, respectively, both featuring a 1.98m (6ft 6in) longer fuselage than the Comet 4. The 4B featured reduced span wings and lacked the pinion fuel tanks of the 4, while the 4C combined the new fuselage length with the original span wings and increased fuel capacity of its predecessor.

The Comet 4B was developed for British European Airways' Mediterranean services. It ordered six in March 1958 and eventually acquired 14. The only other customer was Olympic Airways which ordered four in July 1959.

The sole Comet 3 was converted to 3B standards to serve as the prototype for the 4B, first flying in this guise on 21 August 1958 in BEA livery. The first real Comet 4B was flown on 27 June 1959, while BEA inaugurated 4B services between London and Tel Aviv in April 1960. Olympic received its first aircraft in May 1960 and the two airlines operated the aircraft in close co-operation. The last Comet 4B was delivered to BEA in June 1961.

The first Comet 4C flew on 31 October 1959 and deliveries to launch customer Mexicana began in January 1960. The 4C was the most commercially successful Comet variant, customers for new aircraft comprising Mexicana (3), United Arab Airlines (9), Middle East Airlines (4), Sudan Airways (2), Aerolineas Argentinas (1), the Saudi Government (1), Kuwait Airways (2), RAF (5 as the Comet C.4) and the British A&AEE (1). The final delivery was in February 1964. The last two unsold 4C airframes were completed as prototypes for the Nimrod maritime reconnaissance aircraft, first flying in this guise in 1967.

Subsequent users of the Comet 4B/C were Channel Airways, BEA Airtours and most notably Dan-Air, the largest and last commercial operator of the Comet. Dan-Air acquired 48 Comet 4s, 4Bs and 4Cs between 1966 and 1975, modifying them to accommodate up to 119 passengers. The last Comet revenue flight was in November 1980 when Dan-Air flew a group of enthusiasts from Gatwick to Dusseldorf.

Photo: Comet 4C.

de Havilland Heron

Country of origin: United Kingdom.

Powerplants: Four 250hp (186kW) de Havilland Gipsy Queen 30 Mk.2 inverted six cylinder inline engines; two bladed propellers.

Performance: Srs.1 – normal cruise 143kt (265km/h); max climb 1060ft (323m)/min; service ceiling 18,500ft (5642m); range with 14 passengers 547nm (1014km). Srs.2 – normal cruise 159kt (295km/h); max climb 1140ft (347m)/min; range with 14 passengers 608nm (1126km); range with 10 passengers 1008nm (1867km).

Weights: Srs.1 – empty 3622kg (7985lb); max takeoff 5897kg (13,000lb) or 6124kg (13,500lb). Srs.2 – empty 3697kg (8150lb); max takeoff 5897-6124kg (13,000-13,500lb).

Dimensions: Wing span 21.79m (71ft 6in); length 14.78m (48ft 6in); height 4.75m (15ft 7in); wing area 46.4m² (499sq ft).

Accommodation: 14-17 passengers two abreast.

Production: 51 Srs.1 and 98 Srs.2, total 149.

History: The Heron was conceived as a feederliner incorporating many Dove components. Compared to the earlier aircraft it featured a stretched fuselage (with the upper lobe raised to provide more headroom), increased span wings and four direct drive and normally aspirated Gipsy Queens in place of the Dove's two geared and supercharged engines.

Two basic models were offered, the Srs.1 with fixed undercarriage for short stages where speed was not so important, and the Srs.2 with retractable undercarriage. Standard accommodation was for 14 passengers and up to 17 could be carried if the rear cabin toilet was removed and the baggage area reduced. An interesting feature was linked single lever controls for the throttles and propeller constant-speed units.

The prototype Heron 1 first flew on 10 May 1950 and the initial delivery was to New Zealand National Airways in April 1952. Norway's Braathens SAFE followed the next month. Other Srs.1 customers included UTA, Garuda, Jersey Airlines and BEA. Most were built as Srs.1Bs with increased maximum takeoff weight.

The first Heron 2 was flown on 14 December 1952 and the first three production aircraft were delivered to the Saudi Royal Family, South Africa's Anglo American Corporation and Canadian Comstock in June 1954 as VIP/corporate aircraft. Other Heron 2s were delivered for this role including to the Queen's Flight. The first airline delivery was to Braathens SAFE in January 1955. Some were also sold to military customers. Production effectively ended in 1963 and the last Heron was delivered from storage to its manufacturer as a company hack in 1967.

Heron 2 models varied little, the Srs.2C being an executive version and the 2D/E featuring increased maximum weight and feathering propellers. Many were converted to more reliable and economical US engines including those by Riley with 290hp (216kW) Lycoming IO-540s (20 in the USA and eight in Australia), Japan's Toa Airways (six Srs.1s with 260hp/194kW Continental O-520s) and Puerto Rican airline Primair which re-engined 20 Herons with 300hp (224kW) Continentals. The most radical conversion was the Saunders ST-27 (which see) with stretched fuselage and two turboprops.

Photo: Heron 2. (Lance Higgerson)

de Havilland Canada Twin Otter

Country of origin: Canada.

Powerplants: 100/200 – two 579shp (432kW) Pratt & Whitney Canada PT6A-20 turboprops. 300 – two 620shp (462kW) PT6A-27; three bladed propellers.

Performance: 300 – max cruise 181kt (335km/h); initial climb 1525ft (465m)/min; service ceiling 26,000ft (7925m); range with 20 passengers and reserves 100nm (185km); range with 13 passengers 520nm (963km); range with 10 passengers and optional fuel 700nm (1296km).

Weights: 300 – operating empty (20 seat commuter) 3375kg (7440lb); max takeoff 5670kg (12,500lb). 100/200 – max takeoff 5252kg (11,579lb).

Dimensions: 200/300 – wing span 19.81m (65ft 0in); length 15.77m (51ft 9in); height 5.94m (19ft 6in); wing area 39.0m² (420sq ft). 100 – length 15.09m (49ft 6in).

Accommodation: Up to 20 passengers three abreast.

Production: 115 Srs.100, 115 Srs.200 and 614 Srs.300, total 844.

History: One of the most successful and widely used postwar light transports, the DHC-6 Twin Otter was originally designed as a STOL bush aircraft for the Canadian north but quickly found a large number of customers worldwide for a wide variety of roles operating from wheels, floats or skis.

Of the 844 built and supplied to operators in over 80 countries, more than 500 were delivered to third level/commuter airlines; about 200 were for geophysical survey, corporate, medevac, search and rescue, utility, relief agency and other work; and over 80 were purchased by military forces.

The Twin Otter made a substantial impact on the regional airline industry in its 20 seat commuter version and was largely responsible for establishing the 'modern' era of those operations in the USA and elsewhere, led by US operators Pilgrim Airlines and Air Wisconsin.

The Twin Otter incorporated many components from the single engined DHC-3 Otter, including a stretched version of its fuselage and the same basic wing albeit in longer span form. A new rear fuselage and empennage was developed, fixed tricycle undercarriage fitted and the single Pratt & Whitney R-1340 in the nose replaced by two wing mounted PT6A turboprops. Double slotted full span trailing edge flaps provided good STOL performance.

The prototype Twin Otter first flew on 20 May 1965, the second and third aircraft following in April 1966. Deliveries began three months later, early customers including Trans Australia Airlines, Air Wisconsin, the Chilean Air Force, Pilgrim Airlines, East African Airways and Shell Canada.

The first 115 Twin Otters were built as Srs.100s with PT6A-20 engines, followed by a similar number of Srs.200s with lengthened nose for increased baggage capacity from March 1968. The definitive Srs.300 with more powerful PT6A-27 engines and increased maximum weight first flew in May 1969 and the last was delivered in December 1988.

Six Srs.300S Twin Otters with upper wing spoilers for steep approaches and upgraded brakes were built in 1973 for experimental services sponsored by the Canadian Government, linking short city 'STOLports' in Montreal and Ottawa.

Photo: Twin Otter 300.

de Havilland Canada Dash 7

Country of origin: Canada.

Powerplants: Four 1120shp (835kW) Pratt & Whitney Canada PT6A-50 turboprops; four bladed propellers.

Performance: 100 – max cruise 231kt (428km/h); initial climb 1220ft (372m)/min; service ceiling 21,000ft (6400m); range with 50 passengers 760nm (1408km); range with 33 passengers 1170nm (2167km). 150 – max cruise 230kt (426km/h); range with 50 passengers 1100nm (2037km).

Weights: 100 – operating empty 12,560kg (27,690lb); max takeoff 19,958kg (44,000lb). 150 – max takeoff 21,319kg (47,000lb).

Dimensions: Wing span 28.35m (93ft 0in); length 24.54m (80ft 6in); height 7.98m (26ft 2in); wing area 79.9m² (860sq ft).

Accommodation: Normally 50 passengers four abreast, maximum 54.

Production: 113.

History: Conceived in the early 1970s as a 'step up' regional airliner, aimed at existing operators of the Twin Otter, the DHC-7 or Dash 7 offered several unusual features for this class of aircraft to meet the perceived market requirements of the time.

Four engined, quiet and with high lift devices such as double slotted flaps over 80 per cent of the wing trailing edges (to take advantage of slipstream from the slow turning propellers), the Dash 7 had exceptional short takeoff and landing (STOL) characteristics in order to utilise the many city 'STOLports' which were then being planned.

Unfortunately, these did not develop at anything like the expected rate and the Dash 7's sales suffered as a result. Most regional carriers continued operating from normal airports where the Dash 7's STOL qualities and very low noise levels were less important than acquisition and running costs. Also, it was probably too large for many operators at the time.

The prototype Dash 7 flew on 27 March 1975 followed by the second aircraft three months later. Certification was awarded in May 1977. Deliveries to first customer Rocky Mountain Airways began in November 1977, with services inaugurated in February 1978. Rocky Mountain's route network was one which was ideally suited to the Dash 7 as it encompassed the "highest, hottest and shortest runways", according to its president.

Other Dash 7 customers included Spantax, Wardair Canada, Air Wisconsin, Ransome, Norway's Wideröe, Greenlandair, Henson Airlines, Time Air, Golden West, Tyrolean, Hawaiian, Arkia, Brymon (for services to London City Airport), Inex Adria, Air Niugini and the Canadian military.

Most were built as Srs.100 passenger or Srs.101 passenger/ freight versions, the latter with large cargo door. DHC marketed the Srs.150 with increased maximum weight and fuel capacity from 1985 but only one was built for the Canadian Department of the Environment for ice reconnaissance duties. The rise of the new generation regional turboprops such as DHC's own Dash 8 hastened the Dash 7's demise and the last was delivered to Tyrolean Airways in December 1988.

Photo: DHC-7-102.

Dewoitine D.332-338

Country of origin: France.

Powerplants: D.332/333 – three 575hp (429kW) Hispano-Suiza 9V (Wright Cyclone) nine cylinder radials. D.338 – three 650hp (485kW) Hispano-Suiza 9V 16/17; two bladed propellers.

Performance: D.332 – max speed 161kt (299km/h); cruising speed 135kt (249km/h); service ceiling 20,670ft (6300m); range 1080nm (2000km). D.338 – max speed 162kt (300km/h); cruising speed 140kt (259km/h); range 1053nm (1950km).

Weights: D.332 – empty 5280kg (11,640lb); max takeoff 9350kg (20,613lb). D.338 – empty 8053kg (17,753lb); max takeoff 11,150kg (24,581lb).

Dimensions: D.332 – wing span 29.00m (95ft 2in); length 18.95m (62ft 2in); wing area 80.0m² (861sq ft). D.338 – wing span 29.35m (96ft 3½in); length 22.13m (72ft 7¼in); height 5.56m (18ft 3in); wing area 99.0m² (1066sq ft).

Accommodation: D.332 – eight passengers. D.333 – 10 passengers. D.338 – up to 22 passengers.

Production: 1 D.332, 3 D.333, 31 D.338.

History: This series of low wing, cantilever monoplane, all metal trimotor airliners began with the one-off D.332 flown for the first time on 11 July 1933. Named *Emeraude* (Emerald) and fitted with a trousered fixed undercarriage, it was capable of carrying eight passengers and its modern design gave it good performance for its day.

The D.332 set several speed-with-payload records during the course of 1933 to various European capitals. In December 1933 the aircraft was on the return leg of a pioneering flight from Paris to Saigon (the route it was intended to serve for Air France) when it crashed during a violent thunderstorm only 215nm (400km) from home. Despite this, the aircraft had proven itself and Air France ordered three improved 10 passenger D.333s for use on the Toulouse-Dakar sector of its service into Africa. This first flew in 1934.

The most numerous of the series was the D.338 with more powerful engines, increased weights, retractable undercarriage and stretched fuselage with accommodation for up to 22 passengers on Air France's European services. D.338s used on African services carried 15 passengers and on Far East routes 12, of which six were accommodated in convertible sleeping berth seats.

The prototype D.338 first flew in the first half of 1936 and entered service with Air France on the Paris-Marseilles-Cannes route in the northern summer of the same year. Air France ordered 30 production D.338s, the first of which flew in August 1937. They were soon in widespread use throughout the airline's network.

D.338s operated a Paris to London service in the early months of WWII and during the conflict they were put to work as VIP and government liaison transports between France's overseas possessions. Nine survived the war and flew on Air France's Paris-Nice route for several months in 1946.

Other variations on the theme were the D.343 24 seater of 1939 with three 915hp (682kW) Gnome-Rhône 14N radials and the further stretched D.620 of 1936 for 30 passengers and also powered by Gnome-Rhône engines. Like the D.343, this was a one-off.

Photo: D.338.

Dornier Do J Wal

Country of origin: Germany.

Powerplants: Two tandem mounted piston engines of various types between 300hp (224kW) and 750hp (559kW) including 350hp (261kW) Rolls-Royce Eagle IV V12, 450hp (336kW) Napier Lion, 750hp (559kW) Fiat A.24R, and 600hp (447kW) BMW VI V12; two, three or four bladed propellers depending on version.

Performance: Do J II 8-ton Wal (BMW VI engine) – cruising speed 104kt (193km/h); range 1188nm (2200km). Do J II 10-ton Wal – cruising speed 99kt (183km/h); range 1943nm (3600km).

Weights: Maximum takeoff between 4000kg (8818lb) and 10,000kg (22,046lb).

Dimensions: Wing span 22.50-27.20m (73ft 10in-89ft 3in); length 18.20m (59ft 8½in); height 5.36m (17ft 7in); wing area (23.20m/76ft 1½in span) 96.0m² (1033sq ft).

Accommodation: Up to 12 passengers, mixed passengers-mail/freight or all mail/freight.

Production: Approximately 300.

History: One of the most important airliners of the 1920s and '30s, the Wal (Whale) flying boat was versatile and reliable, contributing a great deal to opening up air services to previously inaccessible regions. Of all metal construction, the Wal featured two engines mounted in tandem above the strut braced parasol wing and the trademark large Dornier stabilising sponsons on the fuselage sides.

Apart from the prototype, production was initially undertaken by Dornier subsidiary CMASA in Italy to circumvent a Treaty of Versailles ban on German manufacture of this type of aircraft. Wals were also built in Japan, the Netherlands, Spain and finally Germany but CMASA contributed about half the total. There were numerous variations on the basic theme with maximum weight more than doubling during the aircraft's life, four different wing spans used and no fewer than 20 different engine types installed.

The Do J Wal evolved from the Dornier Gs I of 1919 and uncompleted Gs II flying boats, the first example flying on 6 November 1922. The first German built model was the Do J II 8-ton Wal of 1932, followed by the 10-ton Wal (or Wal 33) with enclosed cockpit the following year. Production ended in 1936.

The larger Do R Super Wal for 21 passengers with either two 650hp (485kW) Rolls-Royce Condors or four 500hp (373kW) Siemens built Rolls-Royce Jupiter VIIIs in two tandem pairs flew in 1926 and 16 were built in Germany plus some in Spain.

Passenger, mail carrier and military versions were produced, Spain becoming the first operator of the type in 1923 with the latter version. One of these flew 5438nm (10,073km) between Spain and Argentina in early 1926, while Arctic explorer Roald Amundsen used two for his North Pole expeditions.

A Deutsche Luft Hansa Wal completed an around the world flight in 1932 as a prelude to its South Atlantic mail services between Stuttgart and Buenos Aires, operating from depot ships. These services started in February 1934. The Wal was also extensively used in the Mediterranean area. From 1934 the aircraft was redesignated as the Do 15.

Photo: Do R Super Wal.

Dornier Komet and Merkur

Country of origin: Germany.

Powerplant: Komet II – one 250hp (186kW) BMW IV six cylinder inline engine. Merkur – one 600hp (447kW) BMW VI V12; two bladed propeller.

Performance: Komet II – cruising speed 73kt (135km/h); range 270nm (500km). Merkur – max speed 103kt (191km/h); cruising speed 97kt (180km/h); service ceiling 13,123ft (4000m).

Weights: Komet II – empty 1500kg (3307lb); max takeoff 2200kg (4850lb). Merkur – empty 2100kg (4630lb); max takeoff 3600kg (7936lb).

Dimensions: Komet II – wing span 17.00m (55ft 9in); length 10.30m (33ft 9½in); wing area 50.0m² (538sq ft). Merkur – wing span 19.60m (64ft 3½in); length 12.50m (41ft 0in); wing area 62.0m² (667sq ft).

Accommodation: Komet II – 4 passengers. Merkur – 6 passengers.

Production: Merkur – 70.

History: This series of single engined, high wing monoplanes began with the Dornier Do C III Komet I of 1921, fundamentally a landplane development of the Delphin flying boat with the original planing hull replaced with a new lower fuselage set above short undercarriage legs. The cabin provided space for four passengers and the single seat open cockpit was located forward of the wing.

Powered by a 185hp (138kW) BMW III engine, the Komet I served with several German operators including Deutsche Luft Hansa (DLH) when it was established in 1926. The improved Komet II with lengthened fuselage (for an additional crew member) and more powerful engine first flew on 9 October 1922 and was more widely used with examples operated by Switzerland's Ad Astra Aero, Deutsche Luft Reederei, Deutscher Aero Lloyd and DLH. Others served in Spain, Colombia and the Soviet Union.

The further refined and enlarged Komet III first flew on 7 December 1924. This featured the wing raised above the fuselage on short struts and accommodation for six passengers plus two crew side by side in a cockpit below the wing leading edge. Power was from either a 360hp (268kW) Rolls-Royce Eagle IX V12 or 450hp (335kW) Napier Lion. It served with airlines in Germany, Denmark, Switzerland and the Ukraine while Kawasaki built some in Japan. The overall Komet production figure is not known.

The Do B Merkur was similar to the Komet III but with a wing of slightly increased span, unbraced and enlarged tail surfaces and more powerful BMW engine. A twin floatplane version was available. The prototype first flew on 10 February 1925 and deliveries were made to DLH plus operators in China, Switzerland, Japan, Brazil and Colombia. One Swiss Merkur floatplane flew from Zurich to Cape Town between December 1926 and February 1927.

Luft Hansa had a fleet of 36 Komet IIIs and Merkurs, most of which were used on the Berlin-Königsberg sector of the Moscow night flight service. Later, Russo-German operator Deruluft flew ex Luft Hansa aircraft out of Moscow. Two further developed models were built in small numbers, the Do B Bal with increased weights and the Do B Bal 2 with a 640hp (477kW) BMW VIu engine.

Photo: Komet III.

Dornier Do X

Country of origin: Germany.

Powerplants: First aircraft – originally twelve 525hp (391kW) Siemens built Bristol Jupiter nine cylinder radials then 640hp (477kW) Curtiss V-1750 Conqueror V12s. Second and third aircraft – twelve 580hp (432kW) Fiat A.22R V12s; four bladed propellers.

Performance: Conqueror engines – max speed 116kt (215km/h); cruising speed 95-102kt (176-189km/h); ceiling 4100ft (1250m); max range 1512nm (2800km).

Weights: Empty (Conqueror engines) 32,675kg (72,036lb); max take-off 56,000kg (123,457lb).

Dimensions: Wing span 48.00m (157ft 6in); length 40.05m (131ft 5in); height 9.60m (31ft 6in); wing area 450m² (4844sq ft).

Accommodation: 66-100 passengers for trans-Atlantic operations.

Production: 3 by the Swiss Dornier company.

History: By far the world's largest, heaviest and most powerful aircraft when it appeared (and for some time afterwards), the Do X was an attempt to produce a flying boat capable of carrying up to 100 passengers on trans-Atlantic services at a level of comfort equivalent to the ocean liners of the time.

Basically, it was a substantial scaling up of the formula established by the Wal series of flying boats with side sponsons, an enormous wing mounted above the fuselage and six pairs of tandem engines on pylons above that. These were large enough for an engineer to inspect the engines in flight, entering via a tunnel in the wing. Construction was all metal.

The hull contained three decks with passenger accommodation on the middle one complete with individual sleeping cabins, bathroom, kitchen, dining room and smoking room. The lower deck housed fuel and stores and the upper accommodated the cockpit, captain's cabin, radio office, navigation room and engine control room, the latter a considerable distance from the cockpit and the place from which the throttles and other engine controls were adjusted.

The first Do X flew on 25 July 1929 and three months later demonstrated its capabilities by taking 169 people aloft – nine of which were stowaways!

Flight testing revealed overheating problems in the rear Jupiter engines and the aircraft's ceiling was a mere 1378ft (420m) due to those engines never developing full power and the inefficient, low aspect ratio wing. A change to Curtiss Conqueror engines improved the ceiling slightly but their much greater weight made it impossible to carry an economical payload.

The Do X's one flight of note started in November 1930 when it departed Germany bound for New York via Holland, England, Portugal, the Canary Islands, Portugese Guinea, Cape Verde Islands, Fernando Noronha and Brazil. After a litany of misadventures it finally reached its destination more than nine months later! The return flight was completed in a more reasonable five days.

After that, the Do X was briefly used for research and then placed in a Berlin museum. It was destroyed during an air raid in WWII. Two other Do Xs were built by Dornier in Switzerland, powered by Fiat engines and supplied to the Italian Air Force for experimental purposes.

Photo: Dornier Do X.

Dornier 228

Country of origin: Germany.

Powerplants: 100/200 – two 715shp (533kW) Garrett TPE331-5 turboprops. 212 – two 776shp (579kW) Garrett/AlliedSignal TPE331-5-252D; four bladed propellers.

Performance: 100/200 – max cruise 231kt (428km/h); economical cruise 180kt (333km/h); initial climb 2025ft (617m)/min; service ceiling 29,600ft (9022m). 100 – range with 15 passengers 724nm (1341km). 200 – range with 19 passengers 323nm (598km). 212 – max cruise 234kt (433km/h); economical cruise 180kt (333km/h); initial climb 1870ft (570m)/min; service ceiling 28,000ft (8534m); range with 19 passengers 630nm (1167km); max range 1320nm (2445km).

Weights: 100 – operating empty 3413kg (7524lb); max takeoff 5700kg (12,566lb). 212 – operating empty 3742kg (8250lb); max takeoff 6400kg (14,109lb).

Dimensions: 100 – wing span 16.97m (55ft 8in); length 15.04m (49ft 4in); height 4.86m (15ft 11½in); wing area 32.0m² (344sq ft). 200 – length 16.56m (54ft 4in).

Accommodation: 100 – typically 15 passengers two abreast. 200 – typically 19 passengers two abreast; also air ambulance, freighter and specialist military/paramilitary layouts.

Production: Approximately 240 of all models by early 1999.

History: Work on what resulted in the Dornier 228 family of unpressurised light commuter airliner and utility turboprops began in the 1970s under a German Government funded research project for a 'new technology wing'. Called *Tragflügels Neuer Technologie* (TNT), the wing was of advanced supercritical section and unusual planform with sharply raked tips. It was tested on a Do 28D Skyservant from June 1979.

Further development resulted in the 15 passenger Do 28E-1 and 19 passenger Do 28E-2 (later Dornier 228-100 and -200, respectively) combining the basic Do 28D fuselage section in two lengths with the new wing, retractable tricycle undercarriage, the use of composites in secondary structural areas and TFE331 turboprops.

The two versions were developed simultaneously, the 100 first flying on 28 March 1981 and the 200 following on 9 May 1981. The 228-100 entered service with Norway's Norving Flyservice in April 1982; the first 228-200 went to Malaysia Air Charter the following November.

The 228 was progressively developed, new designations generally reflecting increased maximum weights and other detail changes for improved payload range performance. These are the 228-101 and corresponding 201 (1984) with reinforced structure and landing gear for higher weights; 228-202 (1987) with a further weight increase; and 203F dedicated freighter. Specialist maritime patrol, survey and pollution control versions were also offered. India's HAL began delivering licence built 228-101s and 201s for civil and military use in 1986.

The final version is the 228-212 (introduced from the 177th aircraft in 1989) with further increased maximum weight, lower empty weight, upgraded avionics, improved brakes and more powerful TPE331-5-252D engines.

In 1996 it was announced that HAL would become the sole source of 228 production.

Photo: Dornier 228-200.

Dornier (Fairchild) 328

Country of origin: Germany.

Powerplants: Two 2180shp (1625kW) Pratt & Whitney Canada PW119B/C turboprops; six bladed propellers.

Performance: 328-100 – max cruise 335kt (620km/h); initial climb 2420ft (738m)/min; design cruising altitude 25,000-31,160ft (7620-9500m); range with 30 passengers at max cruise 730nm (1352km). 328-110 – range with 30 passengers at max cruise 900nm (1667km).

Weights: 100 – operating empty 8810kg (19,422lb); max takeoff 13,640kg (30,070lb). 110 – operating empty 8920kg (19,665lb), max takeoff 13,990kg (30,842lb).

Dimensions: Wing span 20.98m (68ft 10in); length 21.23m (69ft 8in); height 7.24m (23ft 9in); wing area 40.0m² (431sq ft).

Accommodation: 30-33 passengers three abreast.

Production: 102 ordered by early 1999.

History: Development of the technologically advanced Dornier 328 began in the mid 1980s when market research indicated there existed a substantial market for regional airliners in the 30 seat class through to 2005. The Dornier board originally approved the launch of a 30 seat growth version of the 228 in late 1986 but the project was halted pending a clear market definition.

It was resumed in August 1988 and the prototype 328 first flew on 6 December 1991 followed by two more development aircraft in 1992. The first delivery was to Swiss regional carrier Air Engiadina in October 1993 immediately following European JAA certification. US FAA approval was given the following month, after which Horizon Air received its first aircraft.

The 328 design incorporates an all new pressurised fuselage for three abreast seating combined with the same basic supercritical wing of the earlier Dornier 228. Composite materials are used in a number of areas (particularly the tail) to reduce weight and the six blades of the advanced Hartzell propellers are also composite. The flight deck features a five screen Honeywell Primus 2000 EFIS avionics system, while with head up displays the 328 can be qualified for Cat IIIa instrument landings.

Industrial participation on the 328 comes from Daewoo Heavy Industries (fuselage), Aermacchi (nose), Westland (engine nacelles) and Israel Aircraft Industries (wing).

Variants of the 328 are the initial production standard 328-100; the 328-110 with heavier weights, enlarged dorsal and ventral fins, increased diameter propellers and improved payload-range (earlier aircraft were upgraded to this standard); 328-120 with PW119C engines and improved airfield performance (certified March 1996); and 328-130 with progressive rudder authority reduction with increasing airspeed, ground spoilers and an additional flap setting.

Fairchild Aerospace acquired 80 per cent of Dornier in mid 1986 to form Fairchild Dornier (now Fairchild Aerospace), resulting in a review of the relatively slow selling 328. Stretched versions with 50 seats have been studied but abandoned while Dornier has also studied a hydrogen powered version. The turbofan powered 328JET development is described under the 'Fairchild' heading.

Photo: Dornier 328-110.

Douglas DC-2

Country of origin: USA.

Powerplants: Two 710hp (529kW) SGR-1820-F3 Cyclone, 875hp (652kW) Wright SGR-1820-F52 Cyclone, or 720hp (537kW) Pratt & Whitney R-1690 Hornet nine cylinder radials; three bladed propellers.

Performance: SGR-1820-F52 engines – max speed 182kt (338km/h); cruising speed 172kt (319km/h); service ceiling 22,450ft (6843m); range 870nm (1610km).

Weights: Empty 5628kg (12,408lb); max takeoff 8419kg (18,560lb).

Dimensions: Wing span 25.91m (85ft 0in); length 18.89m (61ft 11³/₄in); height 4.97m (16ft 3³/₄in); wing area 87.2m² (939sq ft).

Accommodation: 14 passengers two abreast.

Production: 198 including 39 assembled by Fokker.

History: It's perhaps ironic that the indirect inspiration for the first Douglas Commercial (DC) aircraft was a Boeing product, the 247. This advanced monoplane airliner of 1933 had been subject to an order for 59 by United Air Lines, but the airline's insistence that they should all be delivered before others got theirs forced potential customers to look elsewhere.

One which did was Transcontinental & Western Air (TWA), which issued its own specification for a three engined all metal monoplane capable of carrying 12 passengers over a distance of 1080 miles (1738km) at a speed of 150mph (241km/h). Three engines were specified because part of the requirement was that the aircraft should be able to take off fully loaded with one engine out.

Douglas responded not with a trimotor but with a twin which could meet that requirement. The DC-1 was powered by two 690hp (514kW) Wright Cyclones, had retractable undercarriage and featured an extremely strong multi cellular wing structure designed by Jack Northrop.

The sole example first flew on 1 July 1933 and quickly demonstrated outstanding performance in a series of proving flights, often in TWA markings. One of them was a US coast-to-coast record of 13hr 4min between Los Angeles and Newark in February 1934.

TWA ordered 20 production aircraft in September 1933 under the designation DC-2 with 710hp (529kW) Cyclones and a slightly longer fuselage for 14 passengers. The first one flew on 11 May 1934 and was delivered to TWA just one week later.

The DC-2 was quickly adopted by many other major airlines in the USA and elsewhere including American, Eastern, Pan American, Australia's Holyman's Airways, Swissair and KLM. Fokker obtained a licence for the DC-2 and assembled 39 in 1934-37.

A KLM aircraft proved the DC-2's capabilities when it won the transport category of the 1934 England to Australia air race (ahead of a Boeing 247) and was second outright behind a purpose built racer, the DH.88 Comet. DC-2s were also ordered by the USAAC (C-33/C-39) and US Navy (R2D), while impressed aircraft flew with the USA, Australia, Finland and Britain in WWII. The last of the series (a C-39) was delivered in September 1939.

Photo: The Douglas Historical Foundation's restored DC-2 on a special photo flight over Catalina. (Douglas Historical Foundation/Harry Gann)

Douglas DC-3

Country of origin: USA.

Powerplants: Two 1000-1200hp (746-895kW) Wright R-1820 Cyclone nine cylinder or Pratt & Whitney R-1830 Twin Wasp 14-cylinder radials; three bladed propellers.

Performance: C-47 – max speed 199kt (368km/h); cruising speed 160-178kt (296-330km/h); initial climb 1130ft (344m)/min; service ceiling 23,200ft (7071m); normal max range 1303nm (2414km).

Weights: Empty equipped 8250kg (18,190lb); max takeoff 12,700kg (28,000lb).

Dimensions: Wing span 28.95m (95ft 0in); length 19.62m (64ft 5^{1}/$_{2}$in); height 5.15m (16ft 11in); wing area 91.7m^2 (987sq ft).

Accommodation: Prewar – typically 21 passengers three abreast or 14 berths. Postwar – up to 36 passengers four abreast.

Production: US production 10,665 of all models including 455 DC-3/DST. Approximately 2500 Lisunov Li-2 and 485 Nakajima L2D.

History: An extremely significant aircraft, the Douglas DC-3 and its military derivatives revolutionised prewar air travel (by being able to operate profitably without subsidy), served with distinction on every front during World War II, and then formed the basis of the world's civil transport industry after 1945. It went on to fight in several more wars and even at the end of the 20th century as many as 400 remain in commercial service with many more in military colours.

The DC-3 was developed from the DC-2 with a longer and wider fuselage, increased span wings, more powerful engines and greater weights. The catalyst was American Airlines, which wanted a larger airliner than the DC-2 with increased sleeper capacity for its transcontinental USA overnight services. Douglas' response was called the Douglas Sleeper Transport (DST).

The prototype DC-3/DST first flew on 17 December 1935 and American Airlines inaugurated services (initially as a day plane) on 25 June 1936. Two models were offered: the DC-3A with P&W Twin Wasps and the DC-3B with Wright Cyclones. The DC-3 was an immediate sales success and by the time the USA entered World War II in December 1941, 434 had been delivered to operators around the world.

The war resulted in many DC-3s being impressed into military service under various designations and also inspired the mass production of military variants. These accounted for the vast majority of aircraft built, production peaking in 1944 when no fewer than 4878 were completed. The most numerous was the Twin Wasp powered C-47 Skytrain (Dakota in British and Commonwealth service), which accounted for over 9000 in three major subvariants.

Demobbed C-47s equipped just about every airline in the world after the war and the type – generically referred to as the DC-3 regardless of origin – remained in service in very large numbers for decades afterwards. Even by the early 1960s some 1500 were still in airline service.

Douglas attempted to exploit the postwar market with the DC-3S or Super DC-3. First flown in August 1949 it featured more powerful engines, a lengthened fuselage, updated appearance and improved performance but it failed because it was competing with masses of cheap demobbed DC-3s and new, modern types such as the Convair 240.

Photo: Douglas DC-3.

Douglas DC-4E

Country of origin: USA.

Powerplants: Four 1450hp (1081kW) Pratt & Whitney R-2180-S1A1 Twin Hornet 14-cylinder radials; three bladed propellers.

Performance: Max cruise 174kt (322km/h); max range 1912nm (3541km).

Weights: Empty 21,087kg (46,488lb); max takeoff 30,164kg (66,500lb).

Dimensions: Wing span 42.14m (138ft 3in); length 29.74m (97ft 7in); height 7.48m (24ft 6^{1}/$_{2}$in); wing area 200.2m^2 (2155sq ft).

Accommodation: Up to 52 day passengers or 30 night passengers.

Production: 1.

History: In early 1936, before the Douglas DC-3 had entered service, Douglas and United Air Lines had begun discussing a four engined airliner with twice the capacity of the twin engined aircraft. Design of the aircraft began in February 1936 and the participation of five major airlines soon followed, United, Trans World, Pan American, Eastern and American each putting up $US100,000 to cover half the cost of developing the aircraft. Between them they also ordered 40.

The new airliner was dubbed DC-4, the redesignation DC-4E (for 'Experimental') being applied later when the programme was abandoned and development of the definitive smaller DC-4 (see next entry) began.

As originally proposed, the DC-4E was a 42 seater with a maximum takeoff weight of 22,680kg (50,000lb) but by the time it appeared the aircraft had grown to a 52 seater weighing 29,484kg (65,000lb) fully loaded, this figure subsequently also increasing slightly.

The DC-4E first flew on 7 June 1938 and for its time was a very large and advanced aircraft of all metal stressed skin construction with tricycle undercarriage, pressurised cabin, triple fins and rudders, powered controls and an APU. The fuselage was divided into several compartments including a main cabin, aft stateroom, separate amenities for men and women, a galley and provision for sleeper berths with small windows for them above the main cabin windows.

The DC-4E was awarded certification in May 1939 and handed over to United Air Lines for a series of demonstration and proving flights. It attracted large crowds wherever it went but it soon become clear the aircraft was not suitable for service at that time. It was considered too big for the market, performance was disappointing, operating economics were poor and it showed signs of being something of a maintenance nightmare.

The sponsoring airlines therefore lost interest in the DC-4E, asking Douglas to develop a smaller, unpressurised and less complex four engined airliner instead. The result was the more familiar DC-4 which first flew in February 1942.

The DC-4E was dismantled in October 1939 and sent to the Mitsui Trading Company in Japan, supposedly for operations with Greater Japan Airlines. It was in fact used for a bit of reverse engineering by the Japanese and used as the basis of the unsuccessful Nakajima G5N Shinzan bomber before crashing into Tokyo Bay in 1940.

Photo: The sole DC-4E.

Douglas DC-4

Country of origin: USA.

Powerplants: Four 1450hp (1081kW) Pratt & Whitney R-2000-2SD-13G Twin Wasp 14-cylinder radials; three bladed propellers.

Performance: Max speed 243kt (450km/h); cruising speed 198kt (367km/h); initial climb 880ft (268m)/min; service ceiling 22,300ft (6797m); max payload range 1460nm (2704km); max fuel range 3693nm (6840km).

Weights: Empty 19,641kg (43,300lb); max takeoff 33,113kg (73,000lb).

Dimensions: Wing span 35.81m (117ft 6in); length 28.63m (93ft 11in); height 8.38m (27ft 6in); wing area 135.6m² (1460sq ft).

Accommodation: Originally 44 passengers four abreast; later up to 86 in high density layout.

Production: 1244 of all versions comprising 1163 C-54, 1 C-114, 1 C-116 and 79 DC-4.

History: The original DC-4 (later DC-4E) was a one-off, large, pressurised airliner for 52 passengers powered by four P&W Twin Hornet engines and fitted with tricycle undercarriage. First flown in June 1938, its development was sponsored by several major US airlines but it proved to be too big and expensive for the market of the time.

Instead, attention turned to a completely new, smaller and unpressurised DC-4 capable of carrying 44 passengers over medium to long ranges but at considerably lower acquisition and operating costs. Powered by four P&W R-2000 Twin Wasps, the prototype first flew on 14 February 1942.

Designated DC-4A, the new aircraft was much more attractive to the airlines and orders for 61 had been placed before first flight, but the events of 7 December 1941 and Japan's attack on Pearl Harbour meant that these were taken over by the US military. As a result, the DC-4 would see no civil service until 1945 and the great bulk of production was of the C-54 (USAAF) and R5D (US Navy) Skymaster models.

Deliveries began in June 1942, the USAAF quickly putting the C-54 into service on regular routes around the world including across the Atlantic to Britain, the Pacific to Australia, the Indian Ocean between Australia and Ceylon, and to Africa, China, India and elsewhere. Both Franklin Roosevelt and Winston Churchill used Skymasters as VIP transports.

Postwar, the C-54 enjoyed a long career with military and commercial operators all over the world, the latter largely equipping from the approximately 500 sold or leased by the US military to the civilian market in 1945-46. By 1960 some 350 were still in airline service but by 1999 this had dropped to about 80, mostly as freighters.

Douglas marketed new civil DC-4s to the airlines after the war but the availability of relatively cheap former military C-54s inhibited sales. The company nevertheless built 79 as DC-4-1009s, the first of them delivered to Western Air Lines in January 1946 and the last to South African Airways in August 1947. Other customers included Sabena, KLM, Air France, Australian National, Northwest, National, SAS, Sabena, Iberia, Trans Australia and Swissair.

The DC-4 was built under licence by Canadair and also served as the basis for the Aviation Traders Carvair conversion (see separate entries).

Photo: DC-4-1009.

Douglas DC-5

Country of origin: USA.

Powerplants: Two 900hp (671kW) Wright R-1820-F62 or 1100hp (820kW) R-1820-44 Cyclone nine cylinder radials; three bladed propellers.

Performance: Max speed 192kt (355km/h); cruising speed 175kt (325km/h); initial climb 1500ft (457m)/min; service ceiling 23,700ft (7224m); max range 1390nm (2575km).

Weights: Empty 6202kg (13,674lb); max takeoff 9072kg (20,000lb).

Dimensions: Wing span 23.77m (78ft 0in); length 19.05m (62ft 6in); height 6.04m (19ft 10in); wing area 76.5m² (824sq ft).

Accommodation: 16-22 passengers.

Production: 12.

History: Designed and built by Douglas' El Segundo facility as a local service airliner for operation out of minor airports, the DC-5's career was thwarted by the outbreak of war. Of all metal construction, it was the only Douglas high wing commercial transport design and featured advanced features such as retractable tricycle undercarriage.

The DC-5's design and overall configuration owed more than a little to the Douglas Model 7 Havoc and Boston light bombers which were designed by the same team, headed by Ed Heinemann. Work on the DC-5 began in 1938 and the prototype first flew on 20 February 1939.

Early flight testing revealed aerodynamic problems include tail buffeting which was cured by giving the horizontal tail surfaces marked dihedral. Interestingly, the prototype was sold to William Boeing in April 1940 as a 16 seat executive aircraft for his personal use as the Boeing company had no equivalent aircraft in its product range.

Commercially, the DC-5 got off to a promising start with orders from KLM (4), Pennsylvania Central (6), SCADTA Colombia (2) and even Britain's Imperial Airways (9) for use on its planned London-Berlin route in 1939. In the event, all but the KLM order lapsed and only 12 DC-5s were built, the remaining seven aircraft delivered to the US Navy and Marine Corps as the R3D-1 and R3D-2 (with R-1820-44 engines), respectively, before the programme was cancelled.

All production aircraft were built in 1940, KLM receiving its first aircraft in April. Due to the war in Europe, the four DC-5s were diverted to overseas operations, two to the West Indies linking Curaçao and Surinam and the other pair to the Netherlands East Indies operating from Batavia.

All four were used to evacuate civilians from Java to Australia when the Japanese invaded in early 1942 but one was captured, evaluated by the Japanese and then displayed in Tokyo with other captured Allied aircraft.

The three survivors were operated in Australia by the Allied Directorate of Air Transport (ADAT) and given USAAF serial numbers. One of them was taken over by Australian National Airways and used on services between Melbourne and Tasmania from 1944. It was sold to New Holland Airways in 1947, another was scrapped in 1946 and the third was written off as a result of a landing accident in 1942. The surviving USN/USMC DC-5s were all retired in 1946.

Photo: KLM DC-5. (MDC)

Douglas DC-6

Country of origin: USA.

Powerplants: Four 2100hp (1566kW) dry or 2400hp (1790kW) with water injection Pratt & Whitney R-2800-CA15 Double Wasp 18-cylinder radials; three bladed propellers.

Performance: Max speed 307kt (568km/h); max cruise 274kt (507km/h); economical cruise 234kt (433km/h); initial climb 1070ft (326m)/min; max payload range 2442nm (4523km); max fuel range with no reserves 3893nm (7210km).

Weights: Empty equipped 24,948kg (55,000lb); max takeoff 44,090kg (97,200lb).

Dimensions: Wing span 35.81m (117ft 6in); length 30.66m (100ft 7in); height 8.66m (28ft 5in); wing area 135.9m² (1463sq ft).

Accommodation: Typically 52-58 first class passengers four abreast or 74 economy class; maximum 85 in high density layout.

Production: 704 DC-6/A/B/C-118s of all versions including 175 DC-6.

History: Fundamentally a more powerful, heavier, faster, longer ranging and pressurised development of the DC-4, the DC-6 nevertheless introduced some commercial aviation firsts including preloaded cargo containers, reversible propellers, thermal deicing systems, ground air conditioning and provision from the start for the fitting of weather radar.

The DC-6 was 2.03m (6ft 8in) longer than its predecessor allowing up to 74 economy class passengers to be carried originally, although later 'air coach' operations saw this increase to 85. Other external changes included the fitting of square rather than circular cabin windows and taller vertical tail surfaces. It was developed during the closing stages of WWII to a military requirement, the prototype (designated XC-112A) flying for the first time on 15 February 1946.

With the cessation of hostilities the immediate military requirement lapsed and Douglas began marketing the aircraft to airlines as the DC-6. Orders covering 70 aircraft had already been placed by American (50) and United (20) before the war ended and others were soon added to the list.

Initial deliveries to the original customers were made in November 1946, United inaugurating regular services on its transcontinental USA flights in April 1947. Including a single fuel stop en route, the DC-6 took 10 hours to complete the journey compared with 11 for rival TWA's Constellations and 14 for the DC-4. Several speed records for point-to-point flights within the USA were established in 1947-48.

The DC-6 survived an early scare when it was grounded for four months from November 1947 while the cause of two internal fuselage fires was investigated. This did little to inhibit sales, other customers for the original DC-6 including Pan American Grace, Delta, KLM, PAL, Aerolineas Argentinas, National, Sabena, Braniff, SAS, Linee Aeree Italiane (LAI – later merged with Alitalia) and Mexicana.

Production switched to the further developed DC-6B (see next entry) in 1951, with the last new basic DC-6 being handed over to LAI in May 1952. By then, production was at a slow rate as the bulk of aircraft had been delivered before 1950.

Photo: Douglas DC-6.

Douglas DC-6A/B

Country of origin: USA.

Powerplants: Four 2400hp (1790kW) Pratt & Whitney R-2800-CB16 or 2500hp (1864kW) R-2800-CB17 Double Wasp 18-cylinder radials; three bladed propellers.

Performance: DC-6B – max speed 313kt (579km/h); economical cruise 267kt (494km/h); initial climb 1120ft (341m)/min; max payload range 2611nm (4837km); range with typical load 3354nm (6213km); max fuel range with no reserves 4267nm (7900km).

Weights: DC-6B – empty equipped 26,597kg (58,635lb); max takeoff 45,360kg (100,000lb) or 48,082kg (106,000lb).

Dimensions: Wing span 35.81m (117ft 6in); length 32.18m (105ft 7in); height 8.66m (28ft 5in); wing area 135.9m² (1463sq ft).

Accommodation: DC-6B – typically 60-66 first class or 82 economy class passengers; maximum 102 in high density layout. DC-6A – max payload 12,928kg (28,500lb).

Production: 704 DC-6/A/B/C-118s of all versions including 74 DC-6A and 288 DC-6B.

History: The availability of the 'CB' series of Pratt & Whitney R-2800 Double Wasp engines with their water-methanol injection and more power allowed Douglas to develop a stretched and heavier development of the basic DC-6. A 1.52m (5ft 0in) longer fuselage allowed an extra two rows of seating in the passenger version but it was a dedicated freighter which appeared first.

The DC-6A Liftmaster first flew on 29 September 1949 and the first delivery was made to Slick Airways in March 1951. This version was optimised for freight operations with forward and aft loading doors on the port side of the fuselage, no cabin windows, strengthened flooring and an optional built in power lift system for freight loading and unloading. In May 1951 a Slick Airways DC-6A set a new world record for the largest single piece of cargo ever air lifted to that point, a 10,430kg (23,000lb) extrusion press from Philadelphia to Los Angeles.

The DC-6B passenger model was flown on 2 February 1951 and was the most numerous of all the DC-6 variants with 288 built. First deliveries were to United Air Lines in April 1951 and the long list of customers included most of those which had operated the original DC-6 plus many more.

DC-6Bs also set several records including the longest non stop commercial flight at the time, the 4950nm (9170km) between Los Angeles and Paris. This was achieved in May 1953 by a Transportes Aeriens Intercontinentaux aircraft. An SAS DC-6B undertook the first commercial flight over the North Pole from Los Angeles to Copenhagen via Greenland in November 1952.

Production ended in November 1958 with the delivery of a DC-6B to Yugoslavia's JAT. The overall production total of 704 includes 167 for the US military comprising C-118As general and VC-118A staff transports for the USAF and C/VC-118Bs for the US Navy (originally R6D), based on the DC-6A with large freight doors.

The final commercial version was the DC-6C, a mixed passenger-freight conversion of the DC-6A. By 1999 about 100 DC-6s remained in commercial service, mostly as freighters with smaller operators.

Photo: Douglas DC-6B.

Douglas DC-7 and DC-7B

Country of origin: USA.

Powerplants: Four 3250hp (2423kW) Wright R-3350-18DA-2 Turbo-Compound 18-cylinder radials; four bladed propellers.

Performance: DC-7 – max cruise 312kt (577km/h); max payload range 2476nm (4587km); max range with no reserves 3770nm (6983km). DC-7B – max cruise 312kt (577km/h); max payload range 2850nm (5279km); max fuel range with no reserves 4275nm (7918km).

Weights: DC-7 – empty 30,076kg (66,306lb); max takeoff 55,430kg (122,200lb). DC-7B – empty 30,843kg (67,995lb); max takeoff 57,154kg (126,000lb).

Dimensions: Wing span 35.81m (117ft 6in); length 33.20m (108ft 11in); height 8.71m (28ft 7in); wing area 135.9m² (1463sq ft).

Accommodation: 60-95 passengers.

Production: 338 DC-7s of all models including 105 DC-7 and 112 DC-7B.

History: The creation of the DC-7 was inspired by American Airlines, which needed a new airliner to compete with TWA's Lockheed Super Constellations on non stop transcontinental USA operations. The Super Constellation's highly complex and often cantankerous Wright R-3350 Turbo-Compound engines made this possible as they offered considerably improved performance through an exhaust driven turbocharging system.

Douglas was at first reluctant to develop such an aircraft but American's offer to pay $US40m for 25 examples to complement its DC-6/B fleet helped persuade the manufacturer to go ahead as this covered most of the development costs. The result was the DC-7 with Turbo-Compound engines driving four bladed propellers, a 1.02m (3ft 4in) longer fuselage than the DC-6B, increased weights and a cruising speed some 35kt (65km/h) faster. The DC-6B's fuel capacity was retained.

DC-7 development was approved in January 1952 and the first aircraft flown on 18 May 1953. American Airlines inaugurated daily non stop services between New York and Los Angeles in November of the same year. 'Standard' DC-7s were delivered exclusively to US trunk carriers – American (34), United (57), Delta (10) and National (4) between then and 1956.

The search for more range resulted in the DC-7B, similar to the basic DC-7 apart from the incorporation of increased fuel capacity in extended nacelle tanks and higher weights. Intended mainly for international operations it first flew in October 1954 and was introduced to service by Pan American in June 1955 when it inaugurated non stop New York-London services. Despite the increased fuel, the DC-7B's range was barely adequate for this route and the return journey (against the prevailing wind) required a stop.

Other DC-7B customers were Continental, Delta, National, Panagra and South African Airways. Some were built to a 'halfway' standard without the full weight and fuel capacity increases.

Many DC-7s of all versions were converted to freighters after their front line airline careers had ended and designated DC-7F, DC-7BF or DC-7(C)F depending on the base model.

Photo: Douglas DC-7. (Douglas)

Douglas DC-7C

Country of origin: USA.

Powerplants: Four 3400hp (2535kW) Wright R-3350-18EA1 Turbo-Compound 18-cylinder radials; four bladed propellers.

Performance: Max speed 352kt (652km/h); max cruise 308kt (570km/h); service ceiling 21,700ft (6614m); max payload range 4000nm (7409km); max fuel range with no reserves 4900nm (9076km).

Weights: Empty 33,005kg (72,763lb); max takeoff 64,865kg (143,000lb).

Dimensions: Wing span 38.86m (127ft 6in); length 34.21m (112ft 3in); height 9.70m (31ft 10in); wing area 152.1m² (1637sq ft).

Accommodation: 60-105 passengers.

Production: 338 DC-7s of all models including 121 DC-7C.

History: The need for more range resulted in development of the ultimate Douglas piston engined airliner, the DC-7C or 'Seven Seas' as it became known, the play of words on the designation appropriately reflecting its role as a long range, intercontinental airliner. Along with the final versions of the Lockheed Super Constellation, the DC-7C represented the pinnacle of piston engined airliner development, filling the gap for a few years until the Boeing 707 and Douglas DC-8 jets came into service.

The DC-7C was designed to overcome the marginal range performance of the DC-7B on the all important trans-Atlantic route and was capable of flying non stop services in both directions. Compared to its predecessor, the Seven Seas featured a further 1.02m (1ft 4in) increase in fuselage length, taller vertical tail surfaces, increased maximum weight and more powerful Turbo Compound engines.

The most significant modification was that to the wing, which until now had been basically unchanged since the DC-4. A 3.05m (10ft 0in) increase in span was introduced via a new centre section in which additional fuel capacity was housed, the result being a 21 per cent increase over the DC-7B.

The new centre section had the effect of moving the engines further outboard – resulting in a quieter cabin – while the increase in wing area reduced approach speeds and nullified the increased operating weights.

The first DC-7C flew on 20 December 1955 and Pan American introduced it into service on the trans-Atlantic route in June 1956, nearly a year ahead of rival TWA's Lockheed Starliner, the final expression of the Constellation design. Pan Am eventually received 26 DC-7Cs and other customers were Panair do Brasil (3), Swissair (3), Braniff (7), BOAC (10), Mexicana (4), Sabena (10), KLM (17), Northwest (19), Alitalia (6), SAS (9), TAI (3) and JAL (4). The final example was delivered to KLM in December 1958.

Once the jets entered service the DC-7C quickly disappeared from the major airlines' fleets, its high operating costs and fundamentally unreliable engines always making its economics questionable. A proposed further development with four 5730eshp (4273kW) Rolls-Royce Tyne turboprops was considered (as the DC-7D) but not proceeded with.

Photo: Douglas DC-7C. (Douglas)

Country of origin: USA.

Powerplants: Srs.10 – four 13,500lb (60.0kN) Pratt & Whitney JT3C-6 turbojets. Srs.20 – four 15,800lb (70.3kN) P&W JT4A-3 turbojets. Srs.30 – four 17,500lb (77.8kN) P&W JT4A-11 turbojets.

Performance: 10 – max cruise 471kt (872km/h); max fuel range with no reserves 3734nm (6920km). 20 – max cruise 503kt (932km/h); max payload range with no reserves 4045nm (7492km); max fuel range with no reserves 4790nm (8872km). 30 – max cruise 514kt (952km/h); max payload range with no reserves 4700nm (8705km); max fuel range with no reserves 5184nm (9602km).

Weights: 10 – operating empty 56,578kg (124,732lb); max takeoff 120,204-123,833kg (265,000-273,000lb). 20 – operating empty 57,632kg (127,056lb); max takeoff 125,194kg (276,000lb). 30 – operating empty 60,693kg (133,803lb); max takeoff 136,080-142,884kg (300,000-315,000lb).

Dimensions: Wing span 43.41m (142ft 5in); length 45.87m (150ft 6in); height 12.90m (42ft 4in); wing area 257.6m² (2773sq ft).

Accommodation: Typically 105-132 passengers in two classes or 144 in single class, maximum 179 six abreast.

Production: 556 DC-8s of all models including 28 Srs.10, 34 Srs.20 and 57 Srs.30.

History: Developed largely as a commercially necessary reaction to the Boeing 707, the DC-8 was always a little behind its rival from Seattle and also suffered as it didn't benefit from the amortisation of costs from associated military orders, as Boeing had been able to do with the KC-135 Stratotanker family.

Regardless, the DC-8 had considerable influence on the final 707 design (especially in the area of cabin width), was offered in domestic and overwater versions from the start (which the 707 wasn't) and finally entered service only 11 months after the Boeing despite its later start.

Formally launched in July 1955, the DC-8 was offered with only one fuselage length for the first decade of its life, variations occurring by varying engine power, fuel capacity and weights. The three initial versions were the domestic Srs.10 with JT3C turbojets; the 'hot and high' domestic Srs.20 with more powerful JT4As; and intercontinental Srs.30 with JT4As, increased weights and substantially more fuel. The Srs.40 with first generation Rolls-Royce conway turbofans was also in the early lineup but this is described in the next entry. Subvariant designations (eg DC-8-11, -12, -31, -32) indicated further variations in weights and fuel capacities.

The prototype DC-8-10 flew on 30 May 1958. Flight testing revealed the need to reduce drag and resulted in the incorporation of extended wing tips and other refinements from the DC-8-12 subvariant. Leading edge slots to improve low speed handling were also subsequently fitted. United Airlines took delivery of its first DC-8-11 in June 1959 followed by Delta the next month. Delta flew the first revenue service between New York and Atlanta in September.

Other first flights (and initial deliveries) were: Srs.20 – 29 November 1958 (Eastern Airlines January 1960) and Srs.30 – 21 February 1959 (Pan American February 1960). The first DC-8 export customers – KLM and SAS – began receiving Srs.30s in March 1960.

Photo: DC-8 Srs.11.

Country of origin: USA.

Powerplants: Srs.40 – four 17,500lb (77.8kN) Rolls-Royce Conway 509 turbofans. Srs.50 – four 17,000lb (75.6kN) Pratt & Whitney JT3D-1 or 18,000lb (80.1kN) JT3D-3/3B turbofans.

Performance: 43 – max cruise 509kt (943km/h); max payload range with no reserves 4857nm (8998km); max fuel range with no reserves 5300nm (9817km). 53 – max cruise 504kt (933km/h); max payload range with no reserves 5375nm (9955km); max fuel range with no reserves 6078nm (11,258km).

Weights: 40 – operating empty 62,461kg (137,700lb); max takeoff 136,080-142,884kg (300,000-315,000lb). 50 – operating empty 60,023kg (132,325lb); max takeoff 125,914-147,420kg (276,000-325,000lb).

Dimensions: Wing span 43.41m (142ft 5in); length 45.87m (150ft 6in); height 12.90m (42ft 4in); wing area 257.6m² (2773sq ft) or 266.4m² (2868sq ft).

Accommodation: 40/50 – typically 132 passengers mixed class or 144 economy class; maximum 179 six abreast. 50F – up to 189 passengers or 43.0 tonnes (94,800lb) max payload.

Production: 556 DC-8s of all models including 32 Srs.40, 89 Srs.50 and 54 Srs.50F.

History: Both Douglas and Boeing were quick to exploit the lower fuel consumption and noise benefits which could be gained from installing turbofan engines on their jet airliners, the early generation Rolls-Royce Conway equipping versions of the DC-8 and 707 from 1959.

The Conway powered DC-8 Srs.40 was similar to the intercontinental Srs.30 but for its engines, the first example flying 3 June 1959. As was standard procedure with the DC-8, subvariants with different weights, fuel capacities and detail changes were indicated by suffixes such as DC-8-41, -42 and -43. Ongoing aerodynamic improvements like a 1½ deg drooped flap cruise setting and a new wing leading edge extension appeared on the Srs.40. A DC-8-40 made history in August 1961 when it became the world's first supersonic transport, reaching Mach 1.012 during a carefully planned dive from 52,000ft (15,850m).

Only three customers purchased DC-8-40s – Alitalia, Canadian Pacific and Trans-Canada – most operators preferring to wait for the Srs.50 models with more efficient Pratt & Whitney JT3Ds. Offered in both standard passenger and freight (DC-8F Jet Trader) versions, the Srs.50 was marketed in direct competition with the Boeing 707-320B/C models.

The DC-8-50 was first flown on 20 December 1960 and initial delivery was to KLM in May 1961 immediately after certification. Many early model DC-8s were subsequently upgraded to the new standard.

The DC-8F-50 Jet Trader with large cargo door and aft pressure bulkhead moved rearwards to allow more cabin space first flew on 29 October 1962 and deliveries to launch customer Trans-Canada Airlines began in January 1963. The Jet Trader could be configured for all passenger, mixed passenger/freight or pure freight operations and was offered in two gross weight standards as the DC-8F-54 and -55.

A Jet Trader was the last 'short fuselage' DC-8 built (line number 410), handed over to United Air Lines in November 1968.

Photo: DC-8 Srs.52.

Douglas DC-8 Super 60 and 70

Country of origin: USA.

Powerplants: Srs.60/61 – four 18,000lb (80.1kN) Pratt & Whitney JT3D-3B turbofans. Srs.63 – four 19,000lb (84.5kN) JT3D-7 turbofans. Srs.71/72/73 – four 22,000lb (97.8kN) CFM International CFM56-2 turbofans.

Performance: 61 – max cruise 505kt (935km/h); economical cruise 470kt (870km/h); max payload range 3256nm (6031km); max fuel range 5730nm (10,614km). 62 – max cruise 510kt (944km/h); economical cruise 454kt (841km/h); max payload range 5210nm (9659km). 63 – max cruise 507kt (939km/h) economical cruise 455kt (843km/h); max payload range 4110nm (7613km).

Weights: 61 – operating empty 67,540kg (148,897lb); max takeoff 147,420kg (325,000lb). 62 – operating empty 64,367kg (141,903lb); max takeoff 151,956kg (335,000lb). 63 – operating empty 69,740kg (153,749lb); max takeoff 158,760-161,028kg (350,000-355,000lb).

Dimensions: 61/71 – wing span 43.41m (142ft 5in); length 57.10m (187ft 4in); height 12.93m (42ft 5in); wing area 266.4m² (2868sq ft). 62/72 – wing span 45.24m (148ft 5in); length 47.98m (157ft 5in); wing area 271.9m² (2927sq ft). 63/73 – wing span 45.24m (148ft 5in); length 57.10m (187ft 4in).

Accommodation: 61/71/63/73 – typically 210 passengers mixed class, maximum 269 passengers six abreast. 62/72 – maximum 189 passengers. 63AF – max payload 52.6 tonnes (117,000lb).

Production: 556 DC-8s of all models including 88 Srs.61, 67 Srs.62 and 107 Srs.63; 110 Srs.71/72/73 conversions.

History: The stretched DC-8 'Super Sixty' series was announced in April 1965, after Douglas belatedly realised that restricting the DC-8 family to a single fuselage length was inhibiting sales. The move proved successful as the new models nearly doubled the DC-8's sales tally.

Three models were announced: the Srs.61 (first flight 14 March 1966) mainly for US domestic operations with an 11.18m (36ft 8in) fuselage stretch for up to 269 passengers and the powerplants, fuel capacity and maximum weight of the DC-8-50; Srs.62 (first flight 29 August 1966) optimised for long range operations with increased fuel, a more modest 2.04m (6ft 8in) fuselage stretch, longer span wings, increased maximum weight and a more aerodynamically efficient engine pod/pylon design; and Srs.63 (first flight 10 April 1967, the same month Douglas and McDonnell merged) which combined the Srs.61's long fuselage with the fuel capacity, wings and aerodynamic refinements of the Srs.62 plus further increased weights. Convertible (CF) and pure freight (AF) versions were also offered.

Inaugural services were by United (Srs.61 February 1967), SAS (Srs.62 May 1967) and KLM (Srs.63 July 1968). The last DC-8 (a Srs.63) was delivered to SAS in May 1972.

McDonnell Douglas began a re-engining programme for the DC-8-60 models in the early 1980s under which the JT3D engines were replaced with more powerful, considerably quieter and more fuel efficient CFM56s. As the 70 series, the first conversion flew in August 1981 and the last was completed in April 1986. By 1999 about 250 DC-8s (mainly 60s and 70s) remained in service.

Photo: DC-8 Srs.73CF. (Lance Higgerson)

Embraer EMB-110 Bandeirante

Country of origin: Brazil.

Powerplants: EMB-110P1/P2 – two 750shp (559kW) Pratt & Whitney Canada PT6A-34 turboprops; three bladed propellers.

Performance: 110P2 – max cruise 225kt (417km/h); long range cruise 176kt (326km/h); initial climb 1787ft (545m)/min; service ceiling 22,500ft (6858m); range with 15 passengers and reserves 150nm (278km); max range 1025nm (1900km). 110P2/41 – range with 17 passengers and reserves 200nm (370km); range with nine passengers 800nm (1482km).

Weights: 110P1/2 – empty equipped 3516-3564kg (7751-7857lb); max takeoff 5670kg (12,500lb). 110P1/2/41 – max takeoff 5900kg (13,007lb).

Dimensions: 110P1/2 – wing span 15.32m (50ft 3in); length 15.10m (49ft 6¹/₂in); height 4.92m (16ft 2in); wing area 29.1m² (313sq ft).

Accommodation: 110P1/2 – 18 or 19 passengers three abreast.

Production: 502 EMB-110s of all models.

History: The cornerstone of the current success of the Brazilian aerospace industry due to its considerable export success, and the aircraft which introduced regional air services to the vast expanse of its home country, the Bandeirante (Pioneer) proved to be a versatile, multirole light utility transport for both civil and military applications.

Design work began in the late 1960s in response to a Brazilian Ministry of Aeronautics specification for an unpressurised general purpose light transport. The design was developed at the Brazilian Institute of Research and Development under the direction of famed French designer Max Holste. The three YC-95 prototypes (with 'port hole' cabin windows) were built by this organisation and the first of them flew on 26 October 1968.

Embraer (Empresa Brasilièra de Aeronáutica SA) was established the following year and took responsibility for development and production of the C-95 as the EMB-110. The first production standard Bandeirante (with 680shp/507kW PT6A-27s, slightly lengthened fuselage and square windows) first flew on 9 August 1972 and deliveries to the Brazilian Air Force began in January 1973. The first civil version, the 15 passenger EMB-110C, was delivered to Transbrasil in March 1973.

Other variants include the aerial photography EMB-110B, maritime patrol EMB-111, EMB-110E seven seat corporate transport, EMB-110P commercial transport with 18 seats and intended mainly for export (from 1975) and EMB-110K1 military transport with longer fuselage and more powerful PT6A-34 engines.

This formed the basis of the major commercial models, the 18-19 passenger EMB-110P1 convertible with large rear cargo door and the EMB-110P2 dedicated passenger transport with conventional doors fitted with air-stairs. These first appeared in 1977. Subsequent development resulted in the EMB-110P1/41 and P2/41 with increased maximum weight.

The final variants were the EMB-110P1A, P1A/41, P2A and P2A/41, introduced in 1983 and featuring interior improvements and tailplane dihedral. The last two Bandeirantes were flown in October 1992 and delivered to the Colombian Air Force.

Photo: EMB-110P1 Bandeirante.

Embraer EMB-120 Brasilia

Country of origin: Brazil.

Powerplants: Early EMB-120 – two 1500shp (1118kW) Pratt & Whitney Canada PW115 turboprops. EMB-120RT/ER two 1800shp (1342kW) PW118 or PW118A; four bladed propellers.

Performance: EMB-120 (PW118) – max cruise 300kt (557km/h); long range cruise 260kt (482km/h); initial climb 2120ft (646m)/min; service ceiling 30,000ft (9144m); range with 30 passengers 550nm (1019km). EMB-120 (PW118A) – max cruise 310kt (574km/h); service ceiling 32,000ft (9754m); range with 30 passengers 500nm (925km). EMB-120ER – max cruise 298kt (552km/h); long range cruise 264kt (489km/h); initial climb 2000ft (610m)/min; range with 30 passengers 840nm (1556km); max range 1640nm (3038km).

Weights: EMB-120 – empty equipped 7100kg (15,653lb); max takeoff 11,500kg (25,353lb). EMB-120ER – empty equipped 7170kg (15,807lb), max takeoff 11,990kg (26,433lb).

Dimensions: Wing span 19.78m (64ft 11in); length 20.00m (65ft 7 1/2in); height 6.35m (20ft 10in); wing area 39.4m² (424sq ft).

Accommodation: Normally 30 passengers three abreast.

Production: Approximately 350 ordered by early 1999 of which about 330 delivered.

History: Keen to build on the success of the Bandeirante in the turboprop regional airliner market, Embraer developed the EMB-120 Brasilia with an eye to capturing the market for operators wanting to step up from 19 seaters. The pressurised 30 seat category was chosen, the aircraft being slightly smaller and therefore less expensive to purchase and operate than 34-37 seat rivals such as the Dash 8 and Saab 340.

Embraer began design work on a new regional turboprop in 1975 when the company studied stretching its EMB-121 Xingu corporate turboprop into a 25 seat airliner. While this was the first aircraft to bear the EMB-120 designation (named Araguaia), the definitive EMB-120 is an all new aircraft. Development was formally launched in September 1979.

The PW115 powered first prototype flew on 27 July 1983 and the initial delivery was to Atlantic Southeast Airlines in August 1985.

Versions of the EMB-120 include the original production EMB-120 with PW115 engines and 10,800kg (23,809lb) maximum takeoff weight; EMB-120RT (Reduced Takeoff) of 1986 with more powerful PW118s, improved airfield performance and 11,500kg (25,353lb) maximum weight; EMB-120ER with further increased weights; EMB-120 Cargo freighter; mixed passenger/freight EMB-120 Combi; and EMB-120 Convertible. Hot and high versions of these models have PW118A engines, which retain their power ratings to a higher altitude. This option was first made available in late 1986.

The standard production version since 1994 has been the EMB-120ER Advanced with a range of external and interior improvements. A stretched version of the Brasilia's fuselage is used in the ERJ-135/145 regional jets.

Photo: EMB-120RT Brasilia. (Embraer)

Embraer ERJ-135 and 145

Country of origin: Brazil.

Powerplants: Two 7040lb (31.3kN) Allison AE 3007A or 7430lb (33.0kN) AE 3007A1 turbofans.

Performance: ERJ-145ER – max cruise 430kt (796km/h); range with 50 passengers 1320nm (2445km). ERJ-145LR – range with 50 passengers 1640nm (3037km). ERJ-135ER – range with 37 passengers 1430nm (2650km). ERJ-135LR – range with 37 passengers 1813nm (3358km).

Weights: 145ER – operating empty 11,667kg (25,721lb); max takeoff 20,600kg (45,415lb). 145LR – max takeoff 22,000kg (48,500lb). 135ER – empty equipped 10,684kg (23,554lb); max takeoff 19,000kg (41,887lb). 135LR – max takeoff 20,000kg (44,092lb).

Dimensions: 145 – wing span 20.04m (65ft 9in); length 29.87m (98ft 0in); height 6.75m (22ft 2in); wing area 51.2m² (551sq ft). 135 – length 26.34m (86ft 5in).

Accommodation: 145 – normally 50 passengers three abreast. 135 – normally 37 passengers three abreast.

Production: 145 – 295 firm orders (plus 288 options) by July 1999 with 130 delivered. 135 – 139 orders and 180 options by July 1999.

History: The ERJ-145 family of regional jets survived a difficult and ever changing early development to become a considerable commercial success. The original EMB-145 concept for a 50 seat regional jetliner was launched in mid 1989 and was rather different to the design which ultimately emerged. At that stage it was essentially a minimum change stretched and jet engined EMB-120 Brasilia with straight wings and two turbofans mounted above and forward of the wing leading edges.

By 1990 Embraer was proposing a modified design with less commonality to the Brasilia as wind tunnel testing revealed the original configuration would not reach its design performance objectives. Changes to this interim design included a mildly swept wing and conventional underwing mounted engines. This design needed a tall undercarriage and was changed again, settling on the current configuration ERJ-145 with rear mounted Allison AE 3007A turbofans in 1991. The Brasilia's three abreast fuselage cross section was retained.

The ERJ-145 first flew on 11 August 1995 with first deliveries to Continental Express occurring in December 1996. Two basic versions are offered, the standard ERJ-145LR and the heavier, longer range ERJ-145ER. Continental has ordered 75 ERJ-145s while other major customers include AMR Eagle (42) and France's Regional Airlines (17).

Embraer launched the 'destretched' ERJ-135 with 37 seats in September 1997, this featuring a 3.53m (11ft 7in) shorter fuselage and reduction in maximum weights. The AE 3007 engines are retained. Big sales were quickly recorded after the launch, early customers including American Eagle (75 firm plus 75 options) and Continental Express (25 firm plus 50 options).

The ERJ-135 (converted from the second ERJ-145 prototype) first flew on 9 October 1998 and initial delivery was in July 1999 to Continental Express.

The entirely new ERJ-170/190 family of 70-108 seat regional jets was launched in June 1999 with a firm order for 60 and up to 100 options from Crossair. Deliveries start in 2002.

Photo: ERJ-145. (Gary Gentle)

Fairchild FC.2 and Model 71

Country of origin: USA.

Powerplant: FC.2 – one 220hp (164kW) Wright Whirlwind seven cylinder radial. FC.2W – one 425hp (317kW) Pratt & Whitney Wasp nine cylinder radial. Model 71 – one 410hp (306kW) Wasp; two bladed propeller.

Performance: FC.2W – max speed 121kt (225km/h); range 870nm (1609km). Model 71 – max speed 123kt (228km/h) at 5000ft (1524m).

Weights: FC.2W – empty 1097kg (2418lb); max takeoff 2087kg (4600lb). Model 71 – empty 1495kg (3296lb); max takeoff 2495kg (5500lb).

Dimensions: FC.2 – wing span 15.24m (50ft 0in); length 9.45m (31ft 0in); height 2.74m (9ft 0in); wing area 17.1m^2 (184sq ft).

Accommodation: FC.2 – pilot and four passengers. Model 71 – pilot and six passengers.

Production: 100 FC.2/W, 90 Model 71.

History: The first major product from the recently established Fairchild Airplane Manufacturing Company, the FC.2 light commercial transport and its derivatives were pioneer US airliners which played an important part in the development of air transport in North America during the late 1920s.

The first of the line was the FC.2, a high wing monoplane capable of carrying a pilot and four passengers. Of mixed metal and wood construction it was powered by a Wright Whirlwind radial engine and was available in land and floatplane versions.

First flown in 1927, the FC.2 was used by Pan American Airways to conduct its inaugural air mail service between Key West (Florida) and Havana (Cuba) in October of the same year.

The more powerful FC.2W with Pratt & Whitney Wasp radial quickly followed, this and its predecessor also serving Pan American Grace Airways (Panagra) and Colonial Air Transport on passenger mail and cargo services throughout North, Central and South America. Panagra used the FC.2 to inaugurate a mail service which linked the Panama Canal Zone with Argentina via Chile and Peru.

An FC.2W was used by the Bell Telephone Laboratories for airborne radio communications experiments while in 1928 John Mears and Charles Collyer flew one around the world from New York in just under 24 days.

The slightly larger Model 71 appeared in 1928, featuring accommodation for seven, folding wings and interchangeable wheel, ski or float undercarriage. Widely used in Canada and Alaska (plus in Central America by Panagra) it was also manufactured in Canada by a Fairchild subsidiary company which had been established in Montreal in 1929. This division also developed and built an improved version with metal fuselage skinning, parasol wing and rear cockpit as the Super 71.

Three 1929 vintage Model 71s were impressed into US military service in early 1941 as the UC-96 and used for photographic survey duties. Not surprisingly, they were the Army Air Corps' oldest aircraft in service at the time!

Photo: FC-2W2 of the 1927 Byrd Antarctic expedition. (John Sise)

Fairchild F-27 and FH-227

Country of origin: USA/Netherlands.

Powerplants: FH-227 – two 2250eshp (1678kW) Rolls-Royce Dart 532-7 turboprops. FH-227B/C/D/E – two 2300eshp (1715kW) Dart 532-7L; four bladed propellers.

Performance: FH-227B – max cruise 255kt (472km/h); economical cruise 236kt (437km/h); service ceiling 28,000ft (8534m); max payload range 527nm (975km); max fuel range 1440nm (2667km).

Weights: FH-227B – operating empty 12,478kg (27,510lb); max takeoff 20,639kg (45,500lb).

Dimensions: FH-227 – wing span 29.00m (95ft 2in); length 25.50m (83ft 8in); height 8.41m (27ft 7in); wing area 70.0m^2 (754sq ft).

Accommodation: FH-227 – normally 48-52 passengers four abreast, maximum 56.

Production: 786 Fokker/Fairchild F27/F-27/FH-227s of all models including 207 by Fairchild comprising 129 F-27s and 78 FH-227s.

History: Fairchild acquired a licence to build the Fokker F27 Friendship regional turboprop (see separate entry) in March 1956, four months after the prototype had flown in the Netherlands. The US company assumed responsibility for both production and marketing in North America. Compared with the Dutch original, Fairchild F-27s had a lengthened nose for weather radar (later adopted by Fokker), US instrumentation and other detail changes.

Once the preliminary work had been done the project developed quickly, Fairchild flying its F-27 prototype on 12 April 1958 with another 32 flown by the end of the year. Remarkably, the service entry of the first Fairchild F-27 (on 27 November 1958 with West Coast Airlines) was nearly three weeks before the first Fokker built model entered service with Aer Lingus.

Fairchild's short fuselage F-27s followed some but not all of the Fokker models. The original F-27 was equivalent to the Fokker F27 Srs.100 and was followed by the F-27A (Srs.200), F-27B (Srs.300) and F-27F (corporate equivalent of the F-27A), but the F-27J (1965) and F-27M (1969) were unique to Fairchild in having more powerful Dart 532-7 or 532-7N engines in combination with the original fuselage length. Production ended in early 1968 and the last F-27M (for Lloyd Aereo Boliviano) was delivered in October 1969.

Fairchild also developed a stretched family called the FH-227, the 'FH' referring to Fairchild's takeover of Hiller in 1964 to form the Fairchild-Hiller Corporation. The FH-227 was 1.83m (6ft 0in) longer than the original models and could carry up to 56 passengers. It preceded the slightly shorter stretched Fokker F27-500 by nearly two years, first flying on 27 January 1966 and being first delivered to Mohawk Airlines in June 1966.

Several FH-227 variants were produced: the FH-227B with more powerful engines and larger diameter propellers; FH-227C (basic FH-227s converted to 'B' standards); FH-227D (anti skid brakes and other detail refinements) and FH-227E (earlier models upgraded to 'D' specifications).

Production of the FH-227 ended in December 1968 but a few were delivered from storage after that, the last (an FH-227D) going to Mexico in December 1972.

Photo: Fairchild FH-227E.

Fairchild (Swearingen) Metro

Country of origin: USA.

Powerplants: II – two 940shp (701kW) Garrett AiResearch TPE331-3UW-303G turboprops; three bladed propellers. III/23 – 1000shp (746kW) TPE331-11U-612G. 23 (optional) – 1100shp (820kW) TPE331-12-UHR; four bladed propellers.

Performance: II – max cruise 255kt (472km/h); range cruise 242kt (448km/h); range with 19 passengers 187nm (346km); range with 15 passengers 595nm (1006km). III – max cruise 278kt (515km/h); range cruise 256kt (474km/h); range with 19 passengers 575nm (1065km) standard or 1150nm (2130km) at optional weight. 23 – max cruise 290kt (537km/h); initial climb 2700ft (823m)/min; operational ceiling 25,000ft (7620m); max payload range 540nm (1000km).

Weights: II – empty 3379kg (7450lb); max takeoff 5670kg (12,500lb). III – operating empty 3963kg (8737lb); max takeoff 6577kg (14,500lb) or 7257kg (16,000lb). 23 – operating empty 4300kg (9480lb); max takeoff 7484kg (16,500lb).

Dimensions: II – wing span 14.10m (46ft 3in); length 59.35m (59ft 4¹/₄in); height 5.08m (16ft 8in); wing area 25.8m² (278sq ft). III/23 – wing span 17.37m (57ft 0in); wing area 28.7m² (309sq ft).

Accommodation: 19 passengers two abreast.

Production: Over 1020 ordered by early 1999.

History: The longest lasting of all the 19 seat regional turboprops, the Metro's lineage goes back to the Merlin I executive transport of 1964 (basically a Beech Queen Air with a new pressurised fuselage and more powerful engines) which was derived from Ed Swearingen's previous Queen Air modification programmes.

From there, Swearingen developed the turboprop powered Merlin II and III which formed the basis of the stretched Metro commuter airliner, fundamentally an all new design. The first SA-226TC Metro I flew on 26 August 1969, certification was awarded in June 1970 and first deliveries were made to Air Wisconsin in early 1971. Swearingen was taken over by Fairchild at around the same time and the Swearingen name was later dropped.

The Metro II with rectangular rather than circular cabin windows and cabin improvements was introduced in 1974, the equivalent executive version marketed as the Merlin IV. An increased gross weight version (Metro IIA) was introduced in 1980, followed in 1981 by the SA-227AC Metro III with more powerful engines, increased span wings, conical cambered wing tips to reduce drag, new landing gear doors, more streamlined engine cowlings and four bladed propellers. Two maximum weight options were offered as was the Expediter freighter version. The Metro IIIA with 1100shp (820kW) PWAC PT6A-45R engines was first flown in December 1981 but none were sold.

The current SA-227DC Metro 23 was certificated in June 1990 to FAR Part 23 regulations (thus the designation) allowing a further increase in maximum takeoff weight. Military versions have also been built as the C-26 while the Expediter 23 freighter is also in the current model lineup. The Metro V with T-tail and Metro 25 with 25 seats in the same fuselage length and the baggage hold moved to an underbelly compartment remained only as projects.

Photo: SA-227AC Metro.

Fairchild 328JET

Country of origin: Germany/USA.

Powerplant: Two 6050lb (26.9kN) Pratt & Whitney Canada PW306B turbofans.

Performance: Max cruise 408kt (756km/h); max operating altitude 35,000ft (10,668m); design range with 32 passengers 900nm (1667km).

Weights: Operating empty 9344kg (20,600lb); max takeoff 14,990kg (33,047lb) standard or 15,200kg (33,510lb) optional.

Dimensions: Wing span 20.98m (68ft 10in); length 21.28m (69ft 10in); height 7.24m (23ft 9in); wing area 40.0m² (431sq ft).

Accommodation: 32-34 passengers three abreast.

Production: 163 orders and options by August 1999.

History: By adding turbofan engines and creating the 328JET, Fairchild Aerospace has provided a new lease of life to the slow selling Dornier 328 regional turboprop airframe while at the same time pioneering a new class of airliner, the 30 seat regional jet.

Development of the 328JET was launched soon after Fairchild Aerospace took over Dasa's 80 per cent stake in Dornier in mid 1996. Soon after, what was then called Fairchild Dornier launched a market survey of 50 regional airlines worldwide which confirmed their customers' preference for jet equipment.

The airlines were therefore happy with the concept of a 30 seat regional jet providing the operating economics were competitive. Armed with this information, Fairchild Dornier launched the 328JET in February 1997 and by early 1999 had attracted orders from Aspen Mountain Air, Proteus, Tyrolean Jet Service, EuroCityLine, Modern Air and Express/Skyway.

The most obvious change to the 328 is the addition of Pratt & Whitney Canada PW306 turbofans mounted in underwing pods. Aside from this the 328JET was designed to be a minimum change development of the 328 turboprop to allow Fairchild to bring the aircraft to the market as quickly as possible.

Fairchild was able to achieve this because of the 328's conservative engineering and clean aerodynamic design. Just two fuselage frames (to which the wing and main undercarriage attach) required strengthening while a 10cm (4in) extension to the trailing edge flaps cuts aerodynamic drag.

Other changes include strengthened landing gear, upgraded brakes, slight changes to the Honeywell Primus 2000 EFIS avionics software, and the standard fitting of an auxiliary power unit (APU).

The 328JET prototype was converted from the second 328 turboprop and first flew in Munich, Germany, on 20 January 1998. Certification was achieved in June 1999 and first delivery to the USA's Skyway Airlines.

Fairchild has dropped development of the proposed 50 seat 528JET due to a congested marketplace and is instead concentrating on the stretched 42-44 seat 428JET. A completely different family of 55-95 seat regional jets has also been launched. The Envoy 3 10-14 seat corporate version of the 328JET has extra fuel and a range of up to 1650nm (3056km).

Photo: 328JET prototype.

Farman F.60 Goliath

Country of origin: France.

Powerplants: F.60 – two 230hp (172kW) Salmson/Canton-Unné 9Z or 260hp (194kW) Salmson 9Cm radials. F.60bis – two 300hp (224kW) Salmon 9Az radials. F.61 – two 300hp (224kW) Renault 12Fe inlines. F.63bis – two 380hp (283kW) Gnome-Rhône (Bristol) Jupiter 9Aa radials; two bladed propellers.

Performance: F.60 – max speed 76kt (140km/h); cruising speed 65kt (121km/h); range 216nm (400km). F.63bis – max speed 82kt (151km/h); range 216nm (400km).

Weights: F.60 – empty 2500kg (5511lb); max takeoff 4770kg (10,516lb). F.63bis – empty 3030kg (6680lb); max takeoff 5395kg (11,894lb).

Dimensions: Wing span 26.49m (86ft 11in); length 14.32m (47ft 0in); height 5.59m (18ft 4in); wing area 160.1m² (1733sq ft).

Accommodation: 12 passengers.

Production: Approximately 360 Goliaths of all versions including about 60 airliners.

History: One of the most important European airliners of the 1920s, the Goliath was built in commercial and bomber versions. Both stemmed from the FF.60 bomber developed during 1918 but with the end of WWI in November 1918 the nearly complete prototypes were converted to airliners and first flew in this guise (as the F.60) in January 1919. One cabin for four passengers was located in the nose and another for eight amidships, separated by an open cockpit for two crew.

The Goliath established several world records during testing in 1919 including a non stop flight of 1107nm (2050km) between Paris and Casablanca in 18hr 23min carrying a crew of eight. The Goliath entered service with Compagnie des Grands Express Aériens between Paris (Le Bourget) and London (Croydon) on 29 March 1920. Other French operators such as Compagnie des Messageries Aériennes, Société Generale des Transports Aériens (the Farman Line) and Aero Union flew Goliaths on numerous routes throughout Europe.

Foreign operators included Belgium's SNETA and Czechoslovakia's CSA, whose Goliaths were mainly built under licence by Avia and Letov. Some were also sold to South American airlines.

Several variants were produced with different engines including the basic Salmson powered F.60, the F.60bis with more powerful Salmson radials, F.61 with Renault inlines and F.63bis with Gnome-Rhône built Bristol Jupiters. Bomber versions went into production in 1922 and were supplied to France, Poland, Italy, Japan and the USSR.

Farman developed the F.160 Goliath series in 1928, an attempt to modernise the original design. Apart from more powerful 500hp (373kW) Farman or Jupiter engines, differences were few and only one civil version was built along with about 70 bombers.

The last Goliath was withdrawn from commercial service in 1933, the aircraft having meanwhile established many 'firsts'. An unfortunate one occurred over France in April 1922 when the world's first mid-air collision between airliners was recorded, involving a Compagnie des Grands Express Goliath and a Daimler Airways DH.18.

Photo: F.60 Goliath.

Farman Jabiru

Country of origin: France.

Powerplants: F.3X – four 180hp (134kW) Hispano-Suiza 8Ac V8s in tandem pairs. F.4X – three 300hp (224kW) Salmson 9Az nine cylinder radials; two bladed propellers.

Performance: F.3X – cruising speed 95kt (175km/h); range 351nm (650km).

Weights: F.3X – empty 3000kg (6614lb); max takeoff 5000kg (11,023lb).

Dimensions: Wing span 19.0m (62ft 4in); length 13.68m (44ft 10¹/₂in); wing area 81.0m² (872sq ft).

Accommodation: Up to nine passengers.

Production: 9 F.3X and 4 F.4X, total 13.

History: Generally and quite properly regarded as an aesthetic atrocity, the F.121 (or F.3X) Jabiru featured a slab sided fuselage with a tall flat nose, angular tail surfaces and an enormous wooden wing of very low aspect ratio – the root chord was no less than 6m (19ft 8in) and thickness nearly 76cm (2ft 6in).

Its engines were mounted in tandem pairs on a stub wing and joined to the wing struts, fuselage construction was of mixed steel and wood, and up to nine passengers could be accommodated in three compartments – two in the nose, one under the cockpit and six in the main cabin under the wing. An open cockpit for two crew was located at the top of the forward fuselage.

First flown in 1923, the Jabiru was designed specifically to win that year's Grand Prix des Avions Transports competition for airliners and its 50,000 francs prizemoney. The emphasis of the competition was on safety and the Farman entry's wing provided the key to it taking out first prize.

Testing revealed serious difficulties in cooling the rear pair of Hispano-Suiza V8 engines, these problems taking a considerable amount of time to resolve. They eventually were – in 1926 – by fitting a pair of radiators above each engine pair, but Farman in the meantime had developed an even uglier version – if that was possible – in an attempt to find an alternative solution to the problem.

Dubbed the F.4X, this Jabiru featured removal of the rear engines and two 300hp (224kW) Salmson radials placed on the leading edges of the stub wings. A third Salmson was then attached to the upper fuselage nose. Another experimental and undesignated version was powered by two 400hp (298kW) Lorraine-Dietrich V12s.

The F.121/F.3X Jabiru finally entered service in 1926 with the Farman Line, four serving the Paris-Brussels-Amsterdam route. Danish Air Lines (DDL) also had four for use on the Copenhagen-Amsterdam route, of which two were built under licence by Orlogsvaerftet. The F.4Xs served with Compagnie Internationale de Navigation Aérienne.

The F.121 design was developed into the smaller F.170 Jabiru, powered by a single 500hp (373kW) Farman 12WE engine driving a four bladed propeller. Accommodation was for eight passengers and the pilot sat in an open cockpit immediately forward of the wing leading edge. Thirteen of these were built plus four slightly larger F.170bis with nine passenger seats.

Photo: F.121 Jabiru.

Fiat G.12 and G.212

Country of origin: Italy.

Powerplants: G.12C – three 770hp (574kW) Fiat A.74 RC 42 14-cylinder radials. G.212CP – three 1065hp (794kW) Pratt & Whitney R-1830-S1C3-G Twin Wasp 14-cylinder radials; three bladed propellers.

Performance: G.12C – cruising speed 166kt (307km/h); service ceiling 26,247ft (8000m); range 940nm (1740km). G.212CP – cruising speed 162kt (300km/h); range 1620nm (3000km).

Weights: G.12C – empty 8890kg (19,600lb); max takeoff 12,800kg (28,219lb). G.212CP – empty 11,200kg (24,691lb); max takeoff 17,400kg (38,360lb).

Dimensions: G.12C – wing span 28.60m (93ft 10in); length 20.16m (66ft 2in); height 4.90m (16ft 1in); wing area 113.5m² (1222sq ft). G.212 – wing span 29.34m (96ft 3in); length 23.05m (75ft 7½in); height 6.50m (21ft 4in); wing area 116.6m² (1255sq ft).

Accommodation: G.12 – 14-22 passengers. G.212 – 34-40 passengers.

Production: 104 G.12 and 19 G.212.

History: This series of three engined transports had its beginnings with the G.12C, first flown on 15 October 1940 as a 14 seat high speed and long range commercial transport. Intended for Avio-Linee Italiane, its civil career was thwarted by Italy's involvement in WWII, it and other versions delivered to the Regia Aeronautica for military service instead. Some were also used by the Luftwaffe.

A small number were built postwar, including the commercial G.12CA for 18 passengers with Alfa Romeo 128 engines and the 22 seat G.12L models powered by a variety of engines including the Fiat A.74, Alfa Romeo 128, Bristol Pegasus and Pratt & Whitney Twin Wasp. Some flew with Italian airlines.

The larger G.212 was developed from the G.12, featuring increased wing span, wider and longer fuselage for three rather than two abreast seating, more powerful engines and increased weights. First flown on 19 February 1947, the prototype G.212CA was powered by three 860hp (641kW) Alfa Romeo 128 radials.

Two production versions were planned, the G.121CP Monterosa passenger model and the G.212TP Monviso freighter, both powered by Pratt & Whitney R-1830 Twin Wasps. Only the 34 seat G.121CP entered commercial service, initially with Avio-Linee Italiane which received six in 1947-48, of which four subsequently served with Ali Flotte Riunite.

The only other civil customer for new aircraft was Services Aériennes Internationaux d'Egypte (SAIDE) which operated three from 1948 on its Cairo to Tunis (via Benghazi and Tripoli) service. The Spanish freight company ESA was an operator of second hand aircraft in the late 1940s.

Six G.212CPs were purchased by the Italian Air Force for transport and training duties, the latter as flying classrooms for navigation (with 22 seats and tables) and bombing training with an underfuselage gondola for pupil and instructor. Another was equipped as a flying conference room. The last two G.212CPs were delivered in 1951.

Photo: Fiat G.212CP.

Focke-Wulf A 16

Country of origin: Germany.

Powerplant: A 16 – one 75hp (56kW) Siemens Sh 11 seven cylinder radial. A 16a – one 100hp (75kW) Mercedes D 1 six cylinder inline. A 16b – one 85hp (63kW) Junkers L 1a eight cylinder inline. A16c – one 100hp (75kW) Siemens Sh 12 nine cylinder radial. A16d – one 120hp (89kW) Mercedes D II six cylinder inline; two bladed propeller.

Performance: A16/A 16b – max speed 73kt (135km/h); service ceiling 2500m (8500ft); range 297nm (550km). A 16a – max speed 78kt (145km/h); service ceiling 3000m (9843ft); range 270nm (500km).

Weights: A 16/a 16b – empty 570kg (1257lb); max takeoff 970kg (2138lb). A 16a – empty 760kg (1675lb); max takeoff 1200kg (2645lb).

Dimensions: Wing span 13.90m (45ft 7¼in); length 9.10m (29ft 10¼in); height 2.30m (7ft 6½in).

Accommodation: Pilot and 3-4 passengers.

Production: 23 of all models comprising 2 A 16, 6 A 16a, 2 A 16b, 4 A 16c and 9 A 16d.

History: An important pioneering German commercial aircraft and the first design to emerge from the works of the newly established Focke-Wulf Flugzeugbau AZ, the A 16 light airliner was of all wood construction with plywood covering. The wing – which was similar in design to Taube practice – was subsequently used in several other Focke-Wulf designs.

The A16 featured a low slung fuselage which provided accommodation for three or four passengers with the pilot housed in an open cockpit cut into the leading edge of the wing. The main undercarriage units were attached to the bottom of the fuselage via short struts.

The prototype A 16 with a 75 hp (56kW) Siemens Sh 11 radial was flown on 23 June 1924 with company co-founder Georg Wulf at the controls. A second example flew two weeks later, this subsequently used by Bremer Luftverkehr to inaugurate a service between Bremen and Wangerooge in the East Friesian Islands.

Subsequent A 16 variants were the A 16a with 100hp (75kW) Mercedes D I six cylinder inline engine; A 16b (85hp/63kW Junkers L 1a eight cylinder inline); A 16c (100hp/75kW Siemens Sh 12 radial); and A16d (120hp/89kW Mercedes D II six cylinder inline). Several early models were later converted to A16c or A16d configuration with their increased weights and greater useful load.

Apart from Bremer Luftverkehr, A16s of the various models were delivered to seven German operators not only for regular passenger work but also for the joyriding activities which were popular at the time. The other operators were Junkers Luftverkehr, Deutsche Luft Hansa, Luftverkehr AG Niedersachsen, LVG Wilhelmshaven-Rüstringen, Flugverkehr Halle AG, Luftverkehr AG Westfalen and Norddeutsche Luftverkehr.

One of the former Junkers Luftverkehr A 16bs was purchased by the newspaper company Berliner Lokal Anzeiger to transport its products from Berlin to Hannover, Bremen and other centres in one of the first examples of this kind of operation.

Photo: Focke-Wulf A16b used for newspaper deliveries.

Focke-Wulf Möwe

Focke-Wulf Fw 200 Condor

Country of origin: Germany.

Powerplants: A 17 – one 480hp (358kW) Siemens (Bristol) Jupiter nine cylinder radial. A 29 – one 650hp (485kW) BMW VI V12. A 38 – one 400hp (298kW) Siemens Jupiter nine cylinder radial. A 38b – one 500hp (373kW) Siemens Sh 20u radial; two bladed propeller.

Performance: A 17 – max speed 109kt (201km/h); service ceiling 4500m (14,764ft); range 432nm (800km). A 29 – max speed 108kt (200km/h); service ceiling 4700m (15,420ft); range 700nm (1300km). A 38 – max speed 110kt (204km/h); service ceiling 5000m (16,404ft); range 864nm (1600km).

Weights: A 17 – empty 2450kg (5401lb); max takeoff 4000kg (8818lb). A 29 – empty 2710kg (5974lb); max takeoff 4400kg (9700lb). A 38 – empty 2200kg (4850lb); max takeoff 4400kg (9700lb).

Dimensions: All models – wing span 20.00m (65ft 7$^{1}/_{4}$in). A 17 – length 14.63m (48ft 0in); height 3.20m (10ft 6in). A 29 – length 14.80m (48ft 7in); height 4.00m (13ft 1$^{1}/_{2}$in). A 38 – length 15.39m (50ft 6in); height 5.30m (17ft 5in).

Accommodation: 8-10 passengers.

Production: 12 A 17, 5 A 29 and 4 A 38, total 21.

History: The successful Möwe (Seagull) series of eight passenger single engined transports had its origins in 1927 with the A 17, which utilised an enlarged version of the A 16's wooden wing in combination with a welded steel tube plywood and fabric covered fuselage.

The prototype was powered by a 420hp (313kW) Gnome-Rhône (Bristol) Jupiter radial and the 11 production aircraft had 480hp (358kW) Siemens built versions of the same engine.

The prototype was delivered to Norddeutsche Luftverkehr in 1928 and then to Deutsche Luft Hansa, which also received 10 others for use on its Berlin-Cologne and Berlin-Nuremburg services. The last A 17 went to the military.

The A 29 Möwe followed in 1929, basically an A 17 airframe fitted with a 650hp (485kW) BMW VI V12 and featuring increased weights. Only five were built, four of them for Luft Hansa which used them for services to Paris, Marienbad, Konigsburg and Berne until 1932 and secondary routes for two years after that. The fifth A29 was delivered to the German airline pilots' training school.

The final member of the Möwe family was the A 38, built in 1931. Like its predecessors, it retained the original wooden wing but had a more streamlined fuselage which was entirely fabric covered.

Powered by a 400hp (298kW) Siemens Jupiter radial, its tare weight was some 500kg (1100lb) less than the A 29's but its maximum weight remained the same. Four were built for Luft Hansa and all were subsequently modified to A 38b standards with a 500hp (373kW) Siemens Sh 20u radial.

Luft Hansa flew its A 38s on many major trunk routes including from Berlin to Paris (via Cologne and Leipzig), Berne, Munich, Vienna, Oslo and Saarbrücken. It was progressively replaced by the Junkers Ju 52/3m trimotor in 1933.

Photo: Focke-Wulf A17a Möwe.

Country of origin: Germany.

Powerplants: Fw 200A – four 720hp (537kW) BMW 132G-1 nine cylinder radials; two bladed propellers. Fw 200B – four 850hp (634kW) BMW 132DC or 830hp (619kW) BMW 132H; three bladed propellers.

Performance: Fw 200A – cruising speed 175kt (325km/h); service ceiling 21,980ft (6700m); range 675nm (1250km). Fw 200B – cruising speed 198kt (367km/h); range 810nm (1500km).

Weights: Fw 200A – empty 9800kg (21,605lb); max takeoff 14,600kg (32,187lb). Fw 200B – empty 11,300kg (24,912lb); max takeoff 17,000kg (37,478lb).

Dimensions: Wing span 33.00m (108ft 3$^{1}/_{4}$in); length 23.85m (78ft 3in); height 6.00m (19ft 8$^{1}/_{4}$in); wing area 120.0m^2 (1292sq ft).

Accommodation: 26 passengers.

Production: 276 Condors of all models including 14 commercial versions.

History: Although best remembered in its military guise as a maritime patrol bomber during World War II – Winston Churchill described it as "the scourge of the Atlantic" – the Fw 200 Condor began life as a commercial transport for Deutsche Luft Hansa.

Largely inspired by the threat to the airline and the German aircraft industry by the advanced Douglas DC-2 and forthcoming DC-3, Focke-Wulf's chief designer Kurt Tank presented his ideas for the four engined Fw 200 to Luft Hansa in July 1936.

Powered by four 875hp (652kW) Pratt & Whitney Hornet radials, the prototype first flew almost exactly a year later on 27 July 1937. An elegant, all metal monoplane with retractable undercarriage, variable pitch propellers and other modern features, it was configured to carry 17 passengers three abreast in the main cabin plus another nine in a forward smoking cabin.

Two more prototypes powered by BMW 132 radials (upgraded licence built Hornets) followed, the second of which later became Adolf Hitler's personal transport. The second prototype went to Luft Hansa along with four of an initial preproduction batch of nine Fw 200As from the second half of 1938 while others were delivered to DDL Danish Air Lines (2) and Syndicato Condor in Brazil (2), a Luft Hansa affiliate. The ninth Fw 200A was delivered to the Luftwaffe for use as a staff transport, while the Brazilian aircraft eventually went to Cruzeiro do Sol, where re-engined with Pratt & Whitney Twin Wasps, it remained in service until 1947.

The prototype (redesignated Fw 200S-1) made several long distance flights before the war, one of them in August 1938 a non stop, 25 hour journey from Berlin to New York. It also flew from Berlin to Tokyo via Basra, Karachi and Hanoi later in the year.

The final civil models before military needs took over were the Fw 200B-1 (one only for Luft Hansa) and Fw 200B-2 of which five were ordered by Japan's Dai Nippon and two by Finland's Aero OY. Both versions featured more powerful engines, increased weights and three bladed propellers. Only three B-2s were built, all of them diverted to Luft Hansa in 1939. Luft Hansa continued operating its Condors during the war, the final scheduled flight (between Barcelona and Berlin) taking place on 14 April 1945.

Photo: Focke-Wulf Fw 200S-1 (Berlin to New York non stop).

Fokker F.II

Countries of origin: Netherlands/Germany.

Powerplant: F.II – one 185hp (138kW) BMW IIIa six cylinder inline. Fokker-Grulich F.II – one 250hp (186kW) BMW IV six cylinder inline. Fokker-Grulich F.IIb – one 320hp (238kW) BMW Va six cylinder inline; two bladed propeller.

Performance: F.II – max speed 81kt (150km/h); cruising speed 65kt (121km/h); range 648nm (1200km). Fokker-Grulich F.II – range 324nm (600km).

Weights: F.II – empty 1200kg (2645lb); max takeoff 1900kg (4189lb). Fokker-Grulich F.II – empty 1650kg (3637lb); max takeoff 2300kg (5070lb).

Dimensions: Wing span 16.10m (52ft 10in); length 11.65m (38ft 2³/₄in); height 3.20m (10ft 6in); wing area 38.2m² (411sq ft).

Accommodation: Pilot and five passengers.

Production: Approximately 30 of all models.

History: Designed by the German Reinhold Platz, the concept which resulted in the F.II emerged over the winter of 1918-19 with a commercial aircraft based on the configuration of the Fokker D.VIII parasol wing fighter, also designed by Platz.

This design (called the F.I) featured an open cockpit for the passengers but was abandoned in favour of the F.II with the wing as originally planned in combination with a new fuselage accommodating four enclosed passengers. A fifth passenger sat alongside the pilot in the enclosed cockpit.

Unusual in being a monoplane in the age of biplanes, the first F.II flew in Germany in October 1919. By then, Anthony Fokker had decided to relocate his business to his native Netherlands and the first F.II was illegally flown out of Germany in March 1920.

The first F.IIs entered service with KLM in September 1920 and were used until 1927. Among other routes in Europe, they were used to fly the airline's Amsterdam-London service. Two KLM F.IIs were later sold to Belgium's Sabena for use on its Brussels-Antwerp service.

Only a handful of F.IIs were built in the Netherlands, production then lapsing for about six years before restarting in Germany, with Deutsche Luft-Reederei (DLR), Veere and Fokker's German factory at Schwerin, the latter building three for use in Poland's German enclave centred around Danzig and operated by Deutsche Luft Hansa.

The largest source of production – about 19 aircraft – was DLR, these Fokker-Grulich F.IIIs (named after the engineer responsible, Karl Grulich) having their wooden wings built by Albatross and the fabric covered steel tube fuselages by Deutsche Aero Lloyd (DAL). They were powered by more powerful 250hp (186kW) BMW IV engines which allowed increased weights. About 14 were subsequently re-engined with 320hp (238kW) BMW Va inlines.

The Grulich F.IIs were built mainly for DLR before passing to DAL and finally Luft Hansa on its formation in 1926. They were used on 13 routes, largely feeder services to centres such as Cologne, Aachen, Essen, Krefeld and Mülheim. Luft Hansa also had some Dutch built F.IIs and by 1934 10 still remained in service.

Photo: Fokker F.II.

Fokker F.III

Country of origin: Netherlands.

Powerplant: Various: one 240hp (179kW) Armstrong Siddeley Puma inline; 230hp (172kW) Hiero IVH; 185hp (138kW) BMW IIIa inline; 360hp (268kW) Rolls-Royce Eagle VIII; 400hp (298kW) Gnome-Rhône (Bristol) Jupiter VI radial; 240hp (179kW) Gnome-Rhône Titan radial; 250hp (186kW) BMW IV inline; or 320hp (238kW) BMW Va inline; two bladed propeller.

Performance: Puma engine – max speed 81kt (150km/h); cruising speed 73kt (135km/h); range 365nm (675km). BMW Va engine – cruising speed 81kt (150km/h); range 324nm (600km).

Weights: Puma – empty 1200kg (2645lb); max takeoff 2000kg (4409lb). BMW Va – empty 1550kg (3417lb); max takeoff 2300kg (5070lb).

Dimensions: 17.62m (57ft 9³/₄in); length 11.07m (36ft 3³/₄in); height 3.66m (12ft 0in); wing area 39.1m² (421sq ft).

Accommodation: Pilot and five passengers.

Production: Approximately 78 of all models by Fokker in the Netherlands (31) and Fokker-Grulich in Germany.

History: Developed from the F.II and like its predecessor, designed by Reinhold Platz, the F.III also carried five passengers but differed in having them all accommodated within the main cabin. The single seat cockpit was unusual in that it was offset to starboard and recessed into the cantilever wing's leading edge.

The prototype first flew in the Netherlands in early 1921 powered by a 185hp (138kW) BMW IIIa inline engine and entered service with KLM on the Amsterdam-Croydon (London) route the following April. The KLM aircraft were subsequently put to work on the airline's Hamburg-Bremen-Amsterdam-Rotterdam and Danzig-Memel routes.

KLM's 12 F.IIIs were powered by Armstrong Siddeley Puma engines while other operators used different engines. Deutsche Luft-Reederei's (DLR) aircraft had BMWs, while two of Hungarian operator Malert's four F.IIIs had BMWs and the other pair Hiero IVHs.

Other F.IIIs were built by Fokker for Russo-German operator Deruluft (Rolls-Royce Eagle) and others with a variety of powerplants. The last Dutch built F.III was completed in 1922, some of the later aircraft featuring a strut mounted parasol wing configuration.

As had been the case with the F.II, production of the F.III was then taken up in Germany by DLR as the Fokker-Grulich F.III. Deliveries began in 1923 with most aircraft powered by 250hp (186kW) BMW IV inline engines although some were completed with Armstrong Siddeley Pumas. Others were subsequently converted to 320hp (238kW) BMW Va engines and redesignated as the F.IIIc.

Deutsche Aero Lloyd was a major customer for Fokker-Grulich F.IIIs, taking 20, while Deutsche Luft Hansa took over 16 on its formation in 1926 for operation on its Hamburg and Amsterdam services before transferring them to shorter routes linking the coastal resorts in northern Germany. Croydon based British Airlines also purchased two Puma engined examples of this important European airliner in 1929.

Photo: Fokker F.III.

Fokker F.VII

Country of origin: Netherlands.

Powerplant: F.VII – one 360hp (268kW) Rolls-Royce Eagle IX. F.VIIa – various including one 400hp (298kW) Liberty 12 V12; 450hp (335kW) Gnome-Rhône (Bristol) Jupiter VI nine cylinder radial; or 500hp (373kW) Jupiter XI; two bladed propeller.

Performance: F.VIIa (Jupiter) – max speed 100kt (185km/h); cruising speed 83kt (154km/h); service ceiling 8530ft (2600m); max range 626nm (1160km).

Weights: F.VIIa (Jupiter) – empty 1950kg (4299lb); max takeoff 3650kg (8047lb).

Dimensions: Wing span 19.30m (63ft 4in); length 14.35m (47ft 1in); height 3.90m (12ft 9½in); wing area 58.2m² (626sq ft).

Accommodation: Eight passengers.

Production: 5 F.VII and approximately 48 F.VIIa.

History: The basis of a line of successful and in some cases individually famous commercial transports which made Fokker a major force in the 1920s and '30s, the original single engined F.VII first appeared in 1924. Based on the F.III, it was designed to carry eight passengers.

Only five F.VIIs were built and all were delivered to KLM and powered by Rolls-Royce Eagle engines. They were used on regular services between points in the Netherlands, Poland and Switzerland. One was subsequently flown by Mr C D Barnard from Karachi to London in 4½ days.

The improved F.VIIa with rounded wing tips, fully inset ailerons and redesigned undercarriage first flew on 12 March 1925. It featured the usual Fokker construction of wooden wing and fabric covered steel tube fuselage and was designed to be powered by a variety of engines of between 350 and 525hp (261-391kW). The prototype was powered by a 400hp (298kW) Liberty V12; some production versions had this powerplant as well as Gnome-Rhône (Bristol) Jupiter radials and others such as the 450hp (335kW) Lorraine-Dietrich.

The F.VIIa was sold to several airlines in Europe and the USA while two were supplied to the Royal Netherlands Air Force. KLM was a major European operator. Others were used for pioneering and exploratory flights, one by Sir Hubert Wilkins for his 1926 Arctic expedition, while several former KLM aircraft were flown by British pilots on long distance flights in the late 1920s.

Examples were G-EBTQ *St Raphael* (owned by Princess Alice of Lowenstein-Wertheim) lost on a trans-Atlantic flight in August 1927; and G-EBTS *Princess Xenia* used on the R H McIntosh/Fitzmaurice trans-Atlantic attempt of September 1927, the McIntosh/Bert Hinkler flight to India in the same year (as *The Spider*) and the C D Barnard/Duchess of Bedford flights to India and the Cape in 1929-30. Two other British registered aircraft were operated on behalf of the League of Nations in 1936.

Although the F.VII models were successful in their own right, true greatness was conferred on the aircraft by the expedient of fitting it with two extra engines and creating the F.VII/3m, as described in the next entry.

Photo: Fokker F.VIIa.

Fokker F.VII/3m

Country of origin: Netherlands.

Powerplants: Typically three 200hp (149kW), 220hp (164kW), 240hp (179kW), 300hp (224kW) or 330hp (246kW) Wright R-760 Whirlwind seven cylinder radials; or three 220hp (164kW) Armstrong Siddeley Lynx IVC seven cylinder radials; two bladed propellers.

Performance: F.VIIb/3m (Whirlwind) – max speed 112kt (208km/h); range 450-648nm (834-1200km).

Weights: F.VIIa/3m (Lynx) – empty 2146kg (4730lb); max takeoff 4100kg (9039lb). F.VIIb/3m (Whirlwind) – empty 3100kg (6834lb); max takeoff 5300kg (11,684lb).

Dimensions: F.VIIa/3m – wing span 19.30m (63ft 4in); length 14.50m (47ft 7in); height 3.91m (12ft 10in); wing area 58.5m² (630sq ft). F.VIIb/3m – wing span 21.72m (71ft 3in); wing area 67.7m² (729sq ft).

Accommodation: Up to 10 passengers.

Production: Approximately 145 plus 124 F.X/Xa in USA and 14 Avro Ten.

History: Fokker designer Reinhold Platz created one of the most important airliners of its era simply by adding two more engines to the single engined F.VII to produce the F.VII/3m trimotor. The nose engine was retained and the two additional powerplants located under the wings on steel tube mountings and above the vertical undercarriage struts.

The prototype was converted from a standard F.VII and first flown on 4 September 1925. Powered by three 200hp (149kW) Wright Whirlwind radials, this aircraft was taken to the USA later in the same month where it displayed excellent performance in the Ford Reliability Contest, creating considerable interest around the world. The prototype subsequently achieved fame when it became the first aircraft to fly over the North Pole, by Lt Cdr Richard Byrd USN and Floyd Bennett in May 1926.

The initial Netherlands built production model was designated F.VIIa/3m, followed in 1928 by the F.VIIb/3m with larger wing and increased weights. Both could be powered by a variety of radial engines. Fokker's US subsidiary built its own versions as the F.X and F.Xa with the first use of the larger wing, up to 12 passenger seats and power usually provided by three 425hp (317kW) Pratt & Whitney Twin Wasps. Production of these models reached 124 and operators included American, Pan American and Western Air Express. The F.VII/3m was also built under licence in Britain as the Avro Ten (which see).

The F.VII/3m's three engined reliability made it a popular choice with airlines around the world and also with long distance aviators. Its feats included flights from Amsterdam to Batavia, San Francisco to Honolulu, across the Atlantic, and most famously, across the Pacific from San Francisco to Brisbane by Charles Kingsford Smith and Charles Ulm in the *Southern Cross* between 31 May and 9 June 1928.

This pioneering flight covered 7288 miles (11,728km) in 83hrs 19min flying time with two intermediate stops at Hawaii and Fiji. Powered by 240hp (179kW) Whirlwinds, *Southern Cross* was a hybrid, combining an F.VIIa/3m fuselage with the larger wing of the American F.X.

Photo: Fokker F.VIIb/3m *Southern Cross* replica. (ARDU)

Fokker F.VIII

Country of origin: Netherlands.

Powerplants: Two 690hp (514kW) Wright R-1820 Cyclone; 500hp (373kW) Pratt & Whitney Wasp; or 450hp (335kW) Gnome-Rhône (Bristol) Jupiter VI radials; two bladed propellers.

Performance: Jupiter engine – max speed 108kt (200km/h); cruising speed 92kt (170km/h); service ceiling 18,045ft (5500m); range 564nm (1045km).

Weights: Jupiter – empty 3685kg (8124lb); max takeoff 5700kg (12,566lb). Wasp – empty 3357kg (7400lb); max takeoff 5806kg (12,800lb).

Dimensions: Wing span 23.00m (75ft 5$\frac{1}{2}$in); length 16.75m (54ft 11$\frac{1}{2}$in); height 4.19m (13ft 9in); wing area 83.0m^2 (893sq ft).

Accommodation: 15 passengers.

Production: 8 by Fokker and 2 by Manfred Weiss, total 10.

History: An enlarged and twin engined development of the previous F.VII models, the F.VIII was built to meet a KLM requirement for an airliner with greater passenger capacity than the earlier aircraft. It followed the by then well established Fokker method of construction with wooden wing and metal fuselage structure with fabric covering.

Compared to the F.VII, the F.VIII had a longer and wider fuselage capable of carrying up to 15 passengers and a wing which was of slightly greater span than the F.VIIb/3m models but with some 22 per cent more area.

Two crew members were carried and the nose of the aircraft – now without an engine attached to it – incorporated a hinged baggage compartment. The engines were mounted under the wings and on top of the main undercarriage vertical struts in a fashion similar to that applied to the underwing engines of the F.VII/3m.

The prototype was powered by two 450hp (335kW) Gnome-Rhône Jupiter VI radials built under licence from Bristol and first flew on 12 March 1927. This and six other Jupiter powered F.VIIIs were delivered to KLM in 1927-28.

Fokker production reached just eight aircraft – the KLM machines and a single example for Hungary's Malert in 1928. Two others were built under licence in that country by Manfred Weiss of Budapest, both for Malert.

The KLM F.VIIIs were subsequently re-engined with either 690hp (514kW) Wright Cyclone or 500hp (373kW) Pratt & Whitney Wasp radials. Two of the latter were purchased by British Airways Ltd for use on its cross-Channel services from London.

They were delivered in January and May 1937 but saw only relatively brief service with British Airways: one was withdrawn from use in May 1938 and the other sold to Sweden in April 1939.

This was the last Dutch built F.VIII and the only example to see military service. After being been sold to Sweden it was donated to the Finnish Air Force, with which it served in the Continuation War against the Soviet Union from 1941.

Photo: The Fokker F.VIII was originally powered by the Gnome-Rhône Jupiter engine built under licence from Bristol. This example has been re-engined with Pratt & Whitney Wasps.

Fokker F.XI Universal

Countries of origin: USA and Netherlands.

Powerplant: Universal – One 200hp (149kW) Wright R-760 Whirlwind J4 seven cylinder radial; 220hp (164kW) Whirlwind J5; or 330hp (246kW) Whirlwind J6. Super Universal – One 425hp (317kW) Pratt & Whitney Wasp or 450hp (335kW) Nakajima (Bristol) Jupiter IX; two bladed propeller.

Performance: Universal (Whirlwind J6) – cruising speed 85kt (158km/h); range 521nm (966km). Super Universal (Jupiter) – cruising speed 102kt (190km/h); range 586nm (1086km).

Weights: Universal – empty 953kg (2100lb); max takeoff 1900kg (4189lb). Super Universal – empty 1475kg (3252lb); max takeoff 2390kg (5269lb).

Dimensions: Universal – wing span 14.55m (47ft 9in); length 10.06m (33ft 0in). Super Universal – wing span 15.44m (50ft 8in); length 11.15m (36ft 7in); height 2.77m (9ft 1in); wing area 34.4m^2 (370sq ft).

Accommodation: Universal – up to four passengers. Super Universal – up to six passengers.

Production: 45 Universal, 3 F.XI, 123 Super Universal (Fokker Aircraft 94, Nakajima 29).

History: An important and widely used small airliner of the late 1920s, the Universal series was developed in North America for Fokker's US subsidiary, the Atlantic Aircraft Corporation of Teterboro, New Jersey. The company was renamed Fokker Aircraft from September 1925 and the aircraft was designed by Robert Noorduyn, founder of the Canadian company which bore his name.

With a wooden wing and fabric covered steel tube fuselage, the Universal could carry four passengers plus two crew. First flight was in 1925, shortly before the establishment of Fokker Aircraft. The Universal was operated by a number of airlines in the USA and elsewhere. Powered by the Wright Whirlwind radial, it featured an open cockpit in its initial version and remained in production until 1931.

It was followed by the larger, heavier and more powerful Super Universal (or 'Universal Special' as it was sometimes known) with enclosed cockpit in late 1927. Passenger accommodation for six was provided in a lengthened cabin and licence production was undertaken by Nakajima in Japan. US built Super Universals were powered by Pratt & Whitney Wasp radials while the Japanese version had a Bristol Jupiter radial also built under licence by Nakajima. Like its predecessor, the Super Universal also saw widespread service in the Americas and other parts of the world including Australia.

Fokker's parent organisation in the Netherlands eventually produced its own version of the aircraft as the F.XI. First flown in early 1929, it was in some ways a hybrid of the US built Universal and Super Universal. The four passenger prototype was powered by a 240hp (179kW) Lorraine 7A radial and after the completion of testing was delivered to Swiss operator Alpar.

Only two more F.XIs were built, for Hungarian airline Malert. Powered by a 500hp (373kW) Gnome-Rhône (Bristol) Jupiter VI radial, these could accommodate six passengers plus the usual two crew members.

Photo: Fokker F.XI Super Universal with Wasp engine.

Fokker F.XII

Country of origin: Netherlands.

Powerplants: Dutch built – three 425hp (317kW) Pratt & Whitney R-1340 Wasp C or 500hp (373kW) Wasp T1D1 nine cylinder radials. Danish built – three 465hp (347kW) Bristol Jupiter VI nine cylinder radials; two bladed propellers.

Performance: Max speed 124kt (230km/h); normal cruising speed 110kt (204km/h); range cruise 95kt (175km/h); service ceiling 11,155ft (3400m); range 702nm (1300km).

Weights: Empty 4350kg (9590lb); max takeoff 7750kg (17,086lb).

Dimensions: Wing span 23.01m (75ft 6in); length 17.80m (58ft 5in); height 4.72m (15ft 6in); wing area 83.0m² (893sq ft).

Accommodation: Up to 16 passengers.

Production: 11 by Fokker and 2 by Orlogsvaerftet (Denmark), total 13.

History: Designed to meet a KLM requirement for a medium capacity airliner, the 16 passenger F.XII trimotor was fundamentally a larger and more advanced development of the F.VII/3m and although meeting the aims set for it was nowhere near as commercially successful with only 13 built.

The prototype first flew at the beginning of 1931 and in March that year flew from the Netherlands to Batavia in the Netherlands East Indies on a route proving flight. This flight was successful and regular services on the route began in October 1931.

Fokker built 11 F.XIIs: eight for KLM, two for KNILM (the airline's Netherlands East Indies subsidiary) and one for Swedish operator AB Aerotransport.

The KLM/KNILM aircraft were powered by 425hp (317kW) Pratt & Whitney Wasp C engines and the Aerotransport example by more powerful 500hp (373kW) Wasp T1D1s.

The latter also featured Townend rings enclosing its engines, spatted undercarriage (both for reduced drag) and passenger capacity reduced from the normal 16 to 14.

The Danish airline DDL also selected the F.XII but its two aircraft were built under licence in Denmark by Orlogsvaerftet and differed in being powered by Bristol Jupiter engines. The first was delivered in May 1933 but the second didn't appear until two years later and featured aerodynamic improvements which allowed it to be about 11kt (20km/h) faster than the Dutch built aircraft. It was designated the F.XIIM.

The seven surviving KLM F.VIIIs were sold in 1936, one going to Air Tropic and the others to British Airways Ltd. Of these, one crashed while in service with British Airways, one survived until scrapped in 1940 and four were sold to the Spanish Government a few months after delivery to Britain.

Only two of the four were handed over to their new owner in Spain as one was damaged beyond repair in a landing accident at La Rochelle in fog during its delivery flight and another was burned out after a landing accident at Biarritz, also during the delivery flight.

The last survivors were the Swedish aircraft and the Danish built F.XIIM – both had been scrapped by 1947.

Photo: Fokker F.XII with Wasp engines.

Fokker F.XVIII and F.XX

Country of origin: Netherlands.

Powerplants: F.XVIII – three 420hp (313kW) Pratt & Whitney Wasp C nine cylinder radials; two bladed propellers. F.XX – three 640hp (477kW) Wright R-1820-9 Cyclone nine cylinder radials; two bladed propellers.

Performance: F.XVIII – max speed 129kt (240km/h); cruising speed 113kt (209km/h); service ceiling 15,750ft (4800m); range 983nm (1820km). F.XX – max speed 165kt (306km/h); cruising speed 135kt (249km/h); service ceiling 20,340ft (6200m); range 761nm (1410km).

Weights: F.XVIII – empty 4623kg (10,192lb); max takeoff 7850kg (17,306lb). F.XX – empty 6455kg (14,230lb); max takeoff 9400kg (20,723lb).

Dimensions: F.XVIII – wing span 24.70m (80ft 4½in); length 18.50m (60ft 8¼in); wing area 84.0m² (904sq ft). F.XX – wing span 25.70m (84ft 4in); length 16.70m (54ft 9½in); height 4.80m (15ft 9in); wing area 96.0m² (1033sq ft).

Accommodation: F.XVIII – 14 passengers. F.XX – 12 passengers.

Production: 5 F.XVIII and 1 F.XX.

History: The F.XVIII and F.XX were the last of Fokker's long line of trimotor airliners, the former continuing the construction methods, design philosophies and general appearance of earlier aircraft and the latter attempting to introduce some modern features including retractable undercarriage. Only five F.XVIIIs were built and the F.XX was a one-off.

The F.XVIII was a 14 seater built for KLM. Its heritage was obvious although there were some attempts to present a more modern appearance. The five F.XVIIIs were built in 1932 and all were put into service on KLM's Amsterdam-Batavia (Dutch East Indies) route, although passenger accommodation was usually reduced to only four on this service in sleeper seats.

The F.XVIIIs were withdrawn from KLM's long distance routes in 1935 and put to work on other services including in the West Indies where two remained until 1946. Two others were sold to Czechoslovakia's CSA for use on its services from Prague to Berlin and Vienna in the prewar years and the other aircraft went to French firm Air Tropic, acting on behalf of the Spanish Government.

The sole 12 passenger F.XX was a mixture of the old and the new, incorporating the traditional thick section wooden wing (in further enlarged form) and steel tube fabric covered fuselage but of rounded rather than the previous rectangular cross section. Much attention was paid to aerodynamic refinement including the incorporation of retractable main landing gear, a first for Fokker. The gear retracted rearwards into the enlarged underwing engine nacelles.

The F.XX first flew in 1933 and was delivered to KLM for use on its services from Amsterdam to London and Berlin. Despite the attempt to modernise what was by now an old design, the F.XX proved to be no match for the new generation of all metal, twin engined airliners coming out of the USA, the Douglas DC-2 and then DC-3 rendering it and many other airliner designs obsolete. The F.XX's last known tasks were performed with the Spanish Government on liaison duties between Madrid and Paris during 1937.

Photo: Fokker F.XX.

Fokker F.XXII and F.XXXVI

Fokker F.XXXII

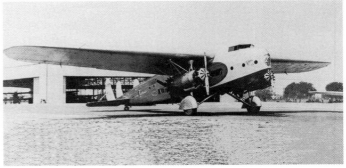

Country of origin: Netherlands.

Powerplants: F.XXII – four 500hp (373kW) Pratt & Whitney Wasp T1D1 nine cylinder radials; three bladed propellers. F.XXXVI – four 750hp (559kW) Wright R-1820-F2 nine cylinder radials; three bladed propellers.

Performance: F.XXII – max speed 154kt (285km/h); cruising speed 116-141kt (215-261km/h); service ceiling 16,076ft (4900m); range 850nm (1577km). F.XXXVI – cruising speed 129-143kt (240-265km/h); range 729nm (1350km).

Weights: F.XXII – empty 8100kg (17,857lb); max takeoff 13,000kg (28,660lb). F.XXXVI – empty 9900kg (21,825lb); max takeoff 16,500kg (36,376lb).

Dimensions: F.XXII – wing span 30.17m (99ft 0in); length 20.98m (68ft 10in); height 4.60m (15ft 1in); wing area 124.4m² (1339sq ft). F.XXXVI – wing span 33.00m (108ft 3in); length 23.98m (78ft 8in); height 6.00m (19ft 8in); wing area 170.0m² (1830sq ft).

Accommodation: F.XXII – 22 passengers. F.XXXVI – 32 passengers in four cabins.

Production: 4 F.XXII and 1 F.XXXVI.

History: Fokker's last two prewar airliners finally abandoned the trimotor concept and were of four engined cantilever high wing configuration but with fixed undercarriage. Neither were successful in terms of sales and both used the old construction methods – wooden wing and fabric covered steel tube fuselage. As such they were completely overshadowed by the new generation of Douglas Commercials, KLM itself becoming a major customer for these.

The F.XXII and F.XXXVI were closely related, the former being fundamentally a scaled down version.

The one-off, 32 passenger F.XXXVI appeared first, designed to meet a 1932 KLM requirement. Six were ordered but only one was built, this first flying on 22 June 1934. It was operated by KLM mainly on its London-Amsterdam-Berlin route from March 1935 but the appearance of the Douglas aircraft meant the airline abandoned its intention to operate the F.XXXVI to the Dutch East Indies and cancelled the other five orders. The aircraft was sold to Scottish Aviation in 1939 and used a trainee navigators' flying classroom until destroyed in a takeoff accident at Prestwick in May 1940.

The smaller, 22 passenger F.XXII first flew in early 1935 and only four were built, three of them for KLM (delivered in March and May 1935) and the other for Sweden's AB Aerotransport (delivered March 1935) for services between Malmö and Amsterdam. It crashed the following year. One KLM aircraft also crashed shortly after delivery but the other two were used on the airline's European routes for four years before being sold in Britain to British American Air Services and Scottish Aviation. Both were subsequently impressed into RAF service for wartime use as transports and navigation trainers.

The ex BAAS F.XXII crashed during the war but the Scottish Aviation aircraft returned to its former owner with the end of hostilities and survived until 1947 after having been used on services between Prestwick and Belfast before being grounded.

Photo: Fokker F.XXXVI.

Country of origin: USA.

Powerplants: Four 575hp (429kW) Pratt & Whitney R-1690 Hornet nine cylinder radials in tandem pairs; two bladed propellers.

Performance: Cruising speed 104-122kt (193-225km/h); range 435nm (805km).

Weights: Empty 6441kg (14,200lb); max takeoff 11,000kg (24,250lb).

Dimensions: Wing span 30.17m (99ft 0in); length 21.28m (69ft 10in); height 5.03m (16ft 6in).

Accommodation: 32 seated day passengers or 16 berthed night passengers.

Production: 10.

History: Designed and built wholly by the Fokker Aircraft Corporation of Teterboro, New Jersey – the Dutch company's US operation – the F.XXXII was developed to meet the requirements of Western Air Express.

This airline was itself a component of the General Aviation Manufacturing Corporation which had acquired a controlling interest in Fokker Aircraft during 1929. The company's name was subsequently changed to properly reflect its new ownership.

The out of sequence F.XXXII designation was given to the aircraft as a marketing device to indicate its 32 seat passenger capacity. Had the normal sequence been followed it would have been called the F.XII but this designation was instead allocated to the parent company's 1931 16 seat development of the F.VII/3m trimotor.

The F.XXXII was the last aircraft to emerge from Fokker's American operation and the first four engined airliner to be built in the USA. At the time of its introduction it was the world's largest civil airliner.

The F.XXXII employed the usual Fokker design philosophies of a thick wooden wing and fabric covered steel tube fuselage but it was different in firstly being four engined, and secondly having these engines mounted in tandem pairs on either side of the fuselage supported by a network of struts from the lower wing, fuselage and fixed undercarriage units. Braced triple vertical tail units completed the aerodynamic specification.

The powerplant and airframe configuration was inefficient, conspiring to produce high levels of drag (fitting various spat and trouser designs to the undercarriage didn't help) and the rear engines could never be properly cooled. An interesting feature of the fuselage's construction was the use of balsa wood layers in an attempt to provide soundproofing for the passengers.

The first F.XXXII was flown in 1929 and entered service with Western Air Express on April Fool's Day 1930. The airline used it on its Los Angeles-San Francisco route and despite its ongoing failings, the F.XXXII did make a substantial contribution in ensuring the continuation of mail and passengers services between the USA west coast and New York.

Despite this and the fact that passengers liked the F.XXXII, the engine cooling and other problems were serious and ongoing, Pacific Western substantially reducing its order and second customer Universal Air Lines System suffering the loss of its first aircraft shortly after delivery. The US Army Air Corps evaluated one example as the YC-20 but no orders were placed.

Photo: Fokker F.XXXII.

Fokker F27 Friendship Srs.100-400

Country of origin: Netherlands.

Powerplants: 100/300 – two 1742ehp (1299kW) Rolls-Royce Dart 511 or 1850ehp (1380kW) Dart 514-7 turboprops. 200/400/600 – two 2020ehp (1506kW) Dart 528, 2105ehp (1570kW) Dart 528-7E, 2230ehp (1663kW) Dart 532-7/536-P or 2320ehp (1730kW) Dart 536-7R; four bladed propellers.

Performance: 100 – cruising speed 231kt (428km/h); initial climb 1070ft (326m)/min; service ceiling 29,000ft (8840m); max payload range 673nm (1247km); max fuel range 1090nm (2020km). 200 – normal cruise 259kt (480km/h); initial climb 1475ft (450m)/min; service ceiling 29,500ft (8992m); range with 44 passengers and reserves 1194nm (2212km).

Weights: 100/300 – max takeoff 16,193-18,371kg (35,700-40,500lb). 200/400/600 – operating empty 11,159-11,567kg (24,600-25,500lb); max takeoff 20,412kg (45,000lb).

Dimensions: Wing span 29.00m (95ft 1³/₄in); length (radar nose) 23.56m (77ft 3¹/₂in); height 8.51m (27ft 11in); wing area 70.0m² (753sq ft).

Accommodation: Typically 40-44 passengers four abreast, maximum 52.

Production: 786 Fokker/Fairchild F27/F-27/FH-227s of all versions of which 579 by Fokker including 85 Srs.100, 138 Srs.200, 13 Srs.300 and 218 Srs.400/600.

History: The most commercially successful of the 'DC-3 replacement' turboprops developed by Western manufacturers during the 1950s, the F27 developed from design concepts started by Fokker in 1950 under the project number P.275.

Originally a pressurised 32 seater powered by Rolls-Royce Dart turboprops, the Dutch Government provided financial support for the programme in 1953, at which time it was designated F27 and had grown to carry 36 passengers. The name 'Friendship' was bestowed later.

The prototype F27 first flew on 24 November 1955 and the second aircraft (first flight January 1957) was representative of the initial production Series 100 with a 0.91m (3ft 0in) fuselage stretch, sufficient for an additional row of seats. The first production aircraft flew in March 1958 and was delivered to Aer Lingus in November of the same year. This F27 was still flying in Australia in 1999. The Series 300 (first flight May 1960) was similar but featured a large cargo door on the port side forward fuselage for mixed passenger/freight operations.

The prototypes and Srs.100/300 F27s were powered by Dart RDa.6 series engines; future versions had the more powerful RDa.7 family in combination with increased weights and fuel capacity. These were the Srs.200 (first flight September 1959); Srs.400 'Combiplane' (October 1961) with large cargo door and strengthened watertight floor; and Srs.600 (December 1966) with the large freight door but a standard floor and optional quick change configuration. Military versions were also built as the Srs.300M and 400M Troopship and specialist maritime patrol versions later emerged.

The Friendship was built under licence in the USA by Fairchild – see separate entry. The last 'short fuselage' F27 to fly was a Srs.200 in March 1985. It was delivered to Busy Bee of Norway in April 1986.

Photo: Fokker F27-200 Friendship.

Fokker F27 Friendship Srs.500

Country of origin: Netherlands.

Powerplants: Two 2105ehp (1570kW) Rolls-Royce Dart 528-7E, 2230ehp (1663kW) Dart 532-7/536-7P, 2280ehp (1700kW) Dart 552 or 2320ehp (1730kW) Dart 532-7R/536-7R turboprops; four bladed propellers.

Performance: Normal cruise 259kt (480km/h); long range cruise 232kt (430km/h); initial climb 1480ft (451m)/min; service ceiling 29,500ft (8990m); range with 56 passengers and reserves 862nm (1597km); range with 52 passengers and reserves 935nm (1732km); max fuel range with reserves 1017nm (1884km).

Weights: Operating empty 12,700kg (28,000lb); max takeoff 20,820kg (45,900lb).

Dimensions: Wing span 29.00m (95ft 1³/₄in); length 25.06m (82ft 2¹/₂in); height 8.51m (27ft 11in); wing area 70.0m² (753q ft).

Accommodation: Typically 52 passengers four abreast, maximum 60.

Production: 786 Fokker/Fairchild F27/F-27 and FH-227s of all models of which 579 by Fokker including 112 Srs.500.

History: Fokker was a relatively late starter in developing a stretched version of the Friendship, trailing its licencee Fairchild's FH-227 by nearly two years. What finally emerged as the F27 Series 500 featured a fuselage which was lengthened by 1.50m (4ft 11in) increasing normal accommodation to 52 or up to a maximum of 60 in a high density arrangement.

Maximum takeoff weight initially remained as before at 20,412kg (45,000lb) but increased slightly later on. Variants of the Rolls-Royce RDa.7 Dart family were fitted and the large freight door of the Srs.300, 400 and 600 was retained but without the Srs.400's strengthened and watertight floor.

Despite being first proposed as early as 1961, the first 500 was not flown until 15 November 1967 and initial deliveries were to KLM and Denmark's Sterling Airways in May 1968. Other early customers included Air Inter and Air France. Along with the other 'short fuselage' Friendships, the Srs.500 was developed over the years with different versions of the Dart engine offered along with upgraded systems, cockpits and cabins.

The final Srs.500 was also the last Friendship of any version to roll off Fokker's production line. First flown on 11 June 1986, it was delivered to Air Wisconsin later in the same month. The last Fairchild variant (see separate entry) had been built 18 years earlier in 1968.

As had been the case with the earlier F27 variants, the Srs.500 was also offered to the military market in transport and maritime patrol forms including as the armed Maritime Enforcer. Additional fuel capacity (including in underwing tanks) was provided.

As a member of the first generation of regional turboprop airliners it outsold its Western opposition (the HS.748 and Herald) by a considerable margin and brought pressurised comfort to many regional routes previously served by Douglas DC-3s. Some countries' airlines operated large fleets. Australian operators for example between them had more than 80 F27s in service over the years. By mid 1999 more than 300 F27s of all versions remained in commercial service.

Photo: Fokker F27-500 Friendship. (Rob Finlayson)

Fokker 50

Country of origin: Netherlands.

Powerplants: Srs.100 – two 2500shp (1864kW) Pratt & Whitney Canada PW125B turboprops. Srs.300 – two 2750shp (2050kW) PW127B; six bladed propellers.

Performance: 100 – max cruise 282kt (522km/h); economical cruise 245kt (454km/h); operational ceiling 25,000ft (7620m); range with 50 passengers 1110nm (2056km) standard or 1524nm (2823km) optional. 300 – range with 50 passengers 1097nm (2032km) standard or 1535nm (2843km) optional.

Weights: Operating empty 12,520kg (27,600lb); max takeoff 19,950kg (43,981lb) standard or 20,820kg (45,900lb) optional.

Dimensions: F50 – wing span 29.00m (95ft 1³/₄in); length 25.25m (82ft 10in); height 8.32m (27ft 3¹/₂in); wing area 70.0m² (753sq ft). F60 – length 26.87m (88ft 2in).

Accommodation: Typically 50 passengers four abreast, maximum 58.

Production: 205 Fokker 50s and 4 Fokker 60s.

History: Launched simultaneously with the Fokker 100 regional jet (which see) in November 1983, the Fokker 50 turboprop was developed as an upgraded successor to the successful F27 Friendship incorporating both new and old features.

The Fokker 50 combined the wing and basic fuselage of the F27-500 (albeit with a greater number of smaller rectangular cabin windows in the interest of layout flexibility instead of the previous and much liked distinctive large ovals) with new generation and much more efficient PW120 series engines driving advanced six bladed Dowty propellers. The result was higher cruising speeds, lower noise and greater fuel efficiency.

Under the skin the changes were substantial and the 50 retained only 20 per cent components commonality with the F27. Improvements included the fitting of an EFIS glass cockpit and digital avionics, a hydraulic rather than pneumatic landing gear and flap operating system, improved cabin environmental control system, upgraded cabin and the use composites throughout the airframe. Small winglets were fitted to the tips.

The first two Fokker 50s were converted from F27-500 airframes, the first of them flying on 28 November 1985. The first production model flew in February 1987 and deliveries to DLT (now Lufthansa CityLine) began in August 1987. The basic PW125B powered aircraft is also known as the Series 100, while the Fokker 50 High Performance with more powerful PW127Bs is referred to as the Series 300. This was first delivered to Avianca Colombia in April 1993. The Fokker 50 Utility with an additional multi purpose door and strengthened floor was sold to several military operators.

The only major development of the basic design was the Fokker 60 with 1.62m (5ft 4in) fuselage stretch, four of which were delivered to the Royal Netherlands Air Force between April and July 1996, after the company's financial collapse in March. A few Fokker 50s were also completed after then, the last example flown in April 1997 and delivered to Ethiopian Airlines the same month.

Photo: Fokker 50.

Fokker F28 Fellowship

Country of origin: Netherlands.

Powerplants: 1000/2000 – two 9850lb (43.8kN) Rolls-Royce Spey Mk.555-15 turbofans. 3000/4000 – two 9900lb (44.0kN) Spey Mk.555-15P.

Performance: 3000/4000 – max cruise 455kt (843km/h); economical cruise 366kt (678km/h); operational ceiling 35,000ft (10,668m). 3000 – range with 65 passengers 1480nm (2741km) at max cruise, 1710nm (3176km) at range cruise. 4000 – range with 85 passengers 1125nm (2084km).

Weights: 3000 – operating empty 16,965kg (37,400lb); max takeoff 33,113kg (73,000lb). 4000 – operating empty 17,645kg (38,900lb); max takeoff 33,113kg (73,000lb).

Dimensions: Wing span 1000/2000 – 23.58m (77ft 4¹/₂in); 3000/4000 – 25.07m (82ft 3in). Length 1000/3000 – 27.40m (89ft 11in); 2000/4000 – 29.61m (97ft 2in). Height 8.47m (27ft 9¹/₂in). Wing area 1000/2000 – 76.4m² (822sq ft); 3000/4000 – 79.0m² (850sq ft).

Accommodation: 1000/3000 – max 65 passengers five abreast. 2000 – max 79 passengers. 4000 – max 85 passengers.

Production: 98 Mk.1000, 2 Mk.1000C, 10 Mk.2000, 19 Mk.3000, 112 Mk.4000, 2 Mk.6000, total 243.

History: The world's first successful small capacity (for the time) jet airliner, the F28 Fellowship was developed to complement the F27 Friendship turboprop on regional routes.

As originally projected in 1962 the aircraft was a 50 seater powered by two Bristol Siddeley BS.75 turbofans but by the time of its launch in November 1965 (on the basis of an order from German inclusive tour operator LTU) the F28 had grown to a 65 seater powered by a simplified and lightened version of the Rolls-Royce Spey turbofan, at that time called the Spey Junior (later Spey Mk.550/555).

The prototype F28 first flew on 9 May 1967 and the first delivery of what was known as the Mk.1000 was to LTU in February 1969. Fokker also offered the 1000C convertible with large freight door. The first stretched Mk.2000 with accommodation for 79 passengers flew on 28 April 1971, converted from the prototype Mk.1000. The first production example flew in June 1972 and was delivered to Nigeria Airways the following October. Plans by Fairchild Hiller to build a shortened 55 seat version under licence in the USA (as the F-228) were abandoned.

The Mks.5000 (short fuselage) and 6000 (long fuselage) were intended to provide improved airfield performance by having increased span wings with leading edge slats. No Mk.5000s were built but the original prototype was converted to Mk.6000 standards, first flying in this form in August 1973. Two new airframes were built as Mk.6000s in 1975 and leased to Sweden's Linjeflyg but were soon converted to Mk.4000s.

The final versions were the short fuselage Mk.3000 and long fuselage Mk.4000 with the increased span wings but without the slats. Initial deliveries were to Garuda Indonesia (July 1977) and Linjeflyg (December 1976), respectively. The Mk.4000 could accommodate up to 85 passengers due to the introduction of additional overwing emergency exits. It remained the major production model until the final F28 was delivered (again to Linjeflyg) in July 1987.

Photo: Fokker F28-4000 Fellowship.

Fokker 70 and 100

Country of origin: Netherlands.

Powerplants: 70 – two 13,850lb (61.6kN) Rolls-Royce Tay Mk.620 turbofans. 100 – two 13,850lb (61.6kN) Tay Mk.620 or 15,100lb (67.2kN) Tay Mk.650.

Performance: 70 – max cruise 462kt (856km/h); operational ceiling 35,000ft (10,668m); range with 79 passengers 1080nm (2000km) standard or up to 1840nm (3408km) optional. 70ER – max range 3240nm (6000km). 100 – range with 107 passengers 1290nm (2390km) standard or up to 1680nm (3112km) optional.

Weights: 70 – operating empty 22,784kg (50,230lb); max takeoff 36,742-39,915kg (81,000-87,997lb). 100 – operating empty 24,747kg (54,558lb); max takeoff 43,092-45,814kg (95,000-101,000lb).

Dimensions: 70 – wing span 28.08m (92ft 1½in); length 30.91m (101ft 5in); height 8.51m (27ft 11in); wing area 93.5m² (1006sq ft). 100 – length 35.53m (116ft 7in).

Accommodation: 70 – typically 79 passengers five abreast. Executive Jet 70 – 30-52 passengers. 100 – typically 97 passengers in two classes or 107 single class, maximum 122.

Production: 48 Fokker 70 and 283 Fokker 100.

History: Launched in November 1983 (simultaneously with the Fokker 50 turboprop), the Fokker 100 regional jet (nominally a 100 seater, thus the designation) is based on the F28-4000 airframe but with a stretched fuselage, new generation Rolls-Royce Tay 620 turbofans, a revised and more efficient wing of greater span, larger tailplane, EFIS 'glass' flight deck and digital avionics, upgraded interior and a thorough update of systems and many components.

The two prototypes first flew on 30 November 1986 and 25 February 1987, certification was awarded in November 1987 and the first delivery was to Swissair in February 1988. Other early customers included International Lease Finance Corporation, KLM and USAir. Several maximum takeoff weight options were offered as was the choice of more powerful Tay 650 engines.

Fokker studied both further stretched and 'destretched' versions of the basic design, the longer, 137 seat Fokker 130 eventually being abandoned. The smaller 79 seat Fokker 70 did go ahead, however, formally launched in November 1992 (after construction of the prototype had begun – converted from the second Fokker 100) and first flown on 2 April 1993. The first production aircraft flew in July 1994 and was delivered to the Ford Motor Co as a corporate aircraft three months later. The first airline delivery was to Korean Air in December 1994.

Compared to the Fokker 100, the 70 was 4.62m (15ft 2in) shorter and standardised on the Tay 620 engine. Otherwise, there was a high degree of commonality with the 100. Three maximum weight options were offered as was the 70ER option with additional fuel tanks in the forward cargo hold (mainly for the Executive 70 version), increasing maximum range to over 3200nm (5925km) for intercontinental operations.

Despite selling strongly, the 70 and 100 fell victim to Fokker's ongoing financial problems and the company failed in March 1996. A few more were completed and delivered after that (the last in April 1997) but plans to reactivate the line have so far come to nothing.

Photo: Fokker 100.

Ford Tri-Motor

Country of origin: USA.

Powerplants: 4-AT/4-AT-A – three 200hp (149kW) Wright Whirlwind J4 radials. 4-AT-B – three 220hp (164kW) Whirlwind J5; 4-AT-C – one 400hp (298kW) Pratt & Whitney Wasp in nose and two Whirlwind J5s under wings; 4-AT-D – three various Whirlwinds. 4-AT-E – three 300hp (224kW) Whirlwind J6. 5-AT-A/B/C – three 420hp (313kW) Pratt & Whiney Wasp C or SC nine cylinder radials. 5-AT-D – three 450hp (335kW) Wasp C; two bladed propellers.

Performance: 4-AT-E – cruising speed 93kt (172km/h); range 495nm (917km). 5-AT-D – max speed 130kt (241km/h); cruising speed 106kt (196km/h); service ceiling 18,500ft (5640m); range 480nm (889km).

Weights: 4-AT-E – empty 2948kg (6500lb); max takeoff 4595kg (10,130lb). 5-AT-D – empty 3556kg (7840lb); max takeoff 6124kg (13,500lb).

Dimensions: 4-AT-E – wing span 22.55m (74ft 0in); length 15.19m (49ft 10in); height 3.58m (11ft 9in); wing area 72.9m² (785sq ft). 5-AT-D – wing span 23.72m (77ft 10in); length 15.32m (50ft 3in); height 3.86m (12ft 8in); wing area 77.6m² (835sq ft).

Accommodation: 4-AT – 11-15 passengers. 5-AT – 13-17 passengers.

Production: 78 4-AT, 117 5-AT, 4 6-AT, total 199.

History: One of the classic airliners of its time, the all metal cantilever monoplane Tri-Motor came about as the result of the Ford Motor Company purchasing the Stout Metal firm in 1925. William Stout immediately began developing a three engined version (the 3-AT) of his 2-AT twin, but a row between himself and Ford ended with his dismissal. The 3-AT was then subject to a substantial redesign by Ford, resulting in the 4-AT Tri-Motor.

This first flew on 11 June 1926 and at the time was the largest civil aircraft to be built in the USA. Capable of carrying eight passengers, it led to the initial production AT-4-A which entered service with the Ford Motor air service in August 1926. Following major versions featured a variety of powerplant options (as listed above) and were the 4-AT-B (1927, increased span wings, 11 passengers), 4-AT-C (mixed powerplants), 4-AT-D (up to 15 passengers) and 4-AT-E.

The larger 5-AT Tri-Motor was introduced in 1928 and was as much a commercial success as its predecessor, the two models being produced in parallel for a time. All 5-ATs were powered by Pratt & Whitney Wasps, the main variants (5-AT-A, -B, -C and -D) differing mainly in their seating capacity of between 13 and 17 passengers. The 6-AT-A was a lower powered version of the 5-AT-C with Wright Whirlwinds while several other variants were created by conversion, usually as a result of different engine configurations.

The Tri-Motor was also available on floats and skis and its versatility saw it used not only for airline operations but also for exploration, freighting, aerial tanking, paratrooping, fire fighting and even cropspraying. The US Navy and Army Air Corps between them received 22 as the JR-1/3 or RR-1/5 and C-3, respectively.

Affectionately nicknamed the 'Tin Goose', the rugged and reliable Tri-Motor was built until 1933 but continued earning its keep in some parts of the world until well into the 1970s.

Photo: Ford 5-AT-C. (RAAF)

GAF Nomad

Handley Page O/400 (civil conversions)

Country of origin: Australia.

Powerplants: Two 400shp (298kW) Allison 250-B17B or 420shp (313kW) 250-B17C turboprops; three bladed propellers.

Performance: N22B – max cruise 168kt (311km/h); economical cruise 153kt (283km/h); long range cruise 145kt (268km/h); initial climb 1460ft (445m)/min; service ceiling 21,000ft (6400m); max range 790nm (1463km) or 1070nm (1982km) with optional fuel. N24A – max cruise 173kt (320km/h); initial climb 1280ft (390m)/min; range with 11 passengers 780nm (1445km); max range with optional fuel 1080nm (2000km).

Weights: N22B – empty equipped 2286kg (5040lb); max takeoff 3856kg (8500lb). N24A – empty equipped 2389kg (5266lb); max takeoff 4264kg (9400lb).

Dimensions: N22B – wing span 16.46m (54ft 0in); length 12.57m (41ft 3in); height 5.53m (18ft 2in); wing area 30.10m² (324sq ft). N24A – length 14.36m (47ft 1in).

Accommodation: N22 – up to 12 passengers in cabin. N24A – up to 16 passengers in cabin.

Production: 127 N22 variants and 45 N24/A, total 172.

History: Developed by Australia's state owned Government Aircraft Factories (GAF) in the late 1960s, the Nomad was a multi purpose STOL light transport with both civil and military applications. The programme was thwarted by its political masters who failed to develop and market it properly, with the result that production was several hundred units fewer than it could have been.

Australia's foreign policies of the time precluded substantial sales to several military customers (eg South Africa and Portugal) while many were given away to Australia's northern neighbours under foreign aid programmes.

The Nomad had several interesting features, including the first production fixed wing application of the turboprop version of the Allison 250 turboshaft, an engine more usually associated with helicopters, and the use of full span double slotted flaps and drooping ailerons for low speed control. The 12 passenger N22 Nomad provided exceptional STOL performance while the stretched, 16 passenger N24 was optimised for commuter airline operations and sacrificed some STOL capability. Military, radar equipped maritime patrol, air ambulance, floatplane and other specialist versions were produced.

The short fuselage prototype first flew on 23 July 1971 with deliveries of the initial N22 Nomad beginning in early 1975. Production soon switched to the N22B with increased weights. Civil customers included Papua New Guinea's Douglas Airways, Club Air and the Royal Flying Doctor Service.

The first N24 flew on 17 December 1975 and production deliveries of the N24A with increased weights began in late 1977. Commercial customers included Alaska Central Air, Rhine Air, Skywest, Princeton Airways and Trans Micronesian.

Production of the Nomad was unceremoniously axed by the Australian Government in 1984. The N22B was recertified in 1985 as the N22C with increased 4060kg (8950lb) maximum weight and improved engine oil filter system.

Photo: GAF N24A (bottom) and N22B Nomad.

Country of origin: United Kingdom.

Powerplants: Two 360hp (268kW) Rolls-Royce Eagle VIII V12s; four bladed propellers.

Performance: Max speed 84kt (156km/h); service ceiling 8500ft (2590m); range 520nm (965km).

Weights: Empty 3777kg (8326lb); max takeoff 5466kg (12,050lb).

Dimensions: Wing span 30.48m (100ft 0in); length 19.16m (62ft 10¼in); height 6.70m (22ft 0in); wing area 153.1m² (1648sq ft).

Accommodation: 10-14 passengers.

Production: 43 O/400 civil conversions including 12 as O/7s, 10 as O/10s and 3 as O/11s.

History: British commercial aviation was able to develop in the immediate post-WWI period due to implementation in February 1919 of the Air Navigation Act, resulting in the civil conversion of several British ex military types as interim airliners.

One of them was the Handley Page O/400 heavy bomber, over 400 of which had been built by the time of the Armistice, when outstanding orders were cancelled. This in turn had been developed from the O/100 of late 1915, the designation reflecting the type's wing span in feet. Frederick Handley Page purchased an initial 16 O/400s for commercial use, at first for the delivery of newspapers.

Passenger conversions quickly followed with accommodation for 10 passengers in the rearranged but very draughty and cold interior plus another two in what had been the front (open) gunner's cockpit. Handley Page Transport Ltd performed the first commercial flight of the type on 1 May 1919 when chief pilot Lt Col W F Sholto Douglas (later Lord Douglas of Kirtleside) flew 10 passengers from Cricklewood to Manchester.

Improved versions quickly followed: the O/7 with a better appointed cabin for 14 passengers (complete with windows) and introduced in August 1919, the O/10 (March 1920) mainly for freight but with a small passenger cabin at the rear of the fuselage; and the O/11 ten seat all passenger version with full length cabin windows.

Handley Page Transport was the main user of the family, operating 34 of the 43 aircraft (some of which were built up from new but incomplete airframes) within Britain and to points in Europe. Six O/7s were sold to the Chinese Government in 1920. Some of the Handley Page Air Transport machines were operated by its Indo-Burmese Transport subsidary.

Late in its career, a plan to re-engine the O/10 with lighter and more powerful Bristol Jupiter radials was tested but a proposal to modify the fleet was cancelled due to the impending arrival of the new Handley Page W.8b (see next entry). Although limited by their modest performance, low standard of passenger comfort and to some extent reliability, the O/400 civil versions nevertheless filled a useful role in the early 1920s as interim types until better airliners could be developed.

Of note is the fact that the first O/400 was awarded the No.1 British Certificate of Airworthiness. The type's last commercial flight was performed in September 1923 when an O/10 flew from Zurich to London.

Photo: Handley Page O/7.

Handley Page W.8, W.9 and W.10

Country of origin: United Kingdom.

Powerplants: W.8 – two 450hp (335kW) Napier Lion IB W12s. W.8b – two 360hp (268kW) Rolls-Royce Eagle VIII V12s. W.8e/f – one 360hp (268kW) Eagle IX in nose and two 240hp (179kW) Armstrong Siddeley Pumas between wings. W.9 – three 385hp (287kW) Armstrong Siddeley Jaguar IV 14-cylinder radials. W.10 – two 450hp (335kW) Lion IIB or 480hp (358kW) Rolls-Royce F.XI inlines; two or four bladed propellers.

Performance: W.8 – max speed 100kt (161km/h); cruising speed 78kt (145km/h); initial climb 600ft (183m)/min; service ceiling 18,000ft (5485m); range 435nm (805km). W.8b – max speed 90kt (167km/h); cruising speed 78kt (145km/h); initial climb 550ft (168m)/min; service ceiling 10,600ft (3230m). W.8f – cruising speed 74kt (137km/h). W.9 – cruising speed 82kt (153km/h); initial climb 900ft (274m)/min; range 348nm (644km). W.10 – max speed 87kt (161km/h); range 435nm (805km).

Weights: W.8b – empty 3493kg (7700lb); max takeoff 5443kg (12,000lb). W.9 – empty 3794kg (8364lb); max takeoff 6577kg (14,500lb). W.10 – empty 3674kg (8100lb); max takeoff 6250kg (13,780lb).

Dimensions: W.8 – wing span 22.86m (75ft 0in); length 18.36m (60ft 3in); height 5.18m (17ft 0in); wing area 135.3m² (1456sq ft). W.8b – length 18.31m (60ft 1in). W.10 – length 17.78m (58ft 4in). W.9 – wing span 24.08m (79ft 0in); length 18.39m (60ft 4in).

Accommodation: 12-16 passengers.

Production: 20 W.8s of all models (Handley Page 7, SABCA 13), 1 W.9 and 4 W.10.

History: Handley Page continued development of its large airliner family using the O/400 bomber as the basis through more specialist versions with a redesigned fuselage which did away with the earlier aircraft's internal bracing and other protuberances to create a an unobstructed cabin. The new aircraft also incorporated the shorter span wings and new undercarriage design of the V/1500 bomber and the result was an outstanding airliner for its time.

Basic models were the W.8 with either two or three engines; the one-off W.9 Hampstead trimotor; and the more powerful W.10 twin, essentially an improved W.8. The first W.8 with Napier Lion W12s flew on 2 December 1919 and established a load to altitude record before entering service with Handley Page Transport on the Croydon-Paris route in October 1921.

W.8 production variants were the W.8b twin with R-R Eagle V12s (first flight April 1922, three for Handley Page Transport and one for Belgium's Sabena); W.8e mixed powerplant trimotor for Sabena (one built by Handley Page and three others under licence in Belgium by SABCA); and similar W.8f Hamilton (one built by Handley Page for Imperial Airways in 1923 and 10 others by SABCA for Sabena). The W.8g was a single W.8f converted to two 480hp (358kW) Rolls-Royce F.XIIA engines in 1929.

The sole W.9 Hampstead trimotor with three Armstrong Siddeley Jaguar radials initially (Bristol Jupiters later) first flew on 1 October 1925 and was used by Imperial Airways on its London-Paris service. The line ended with four W.10s with two Napier Lions or R-R F.XIs from March 1926 for Imperial Airways' European routes. The last W.10 survived until 1934.

Photo: Handley Page W.8.

Handley Page HP.42

Country of origin: United Kingdom.

Powerplants: HP.42E – four 490hp (365kW) Bristol Jupiter XIF nine cylinder radials. HP.42W – four 555hp (414kW) Jupiter XFBM; four bladed propellers.

Performance: HP.42E – max speed 104kt (193km/h); cruising speed 87kt (161km/h); initial climb 790ft (241m)/min; range 435nm (805km). HP.42W – max speed 110kt (204km/h); cruising speed 87kt (161km/h).

Weights: HP.42E – empty 8047kg (17,740lb); max takeoff 12,700kg (28,000lb). HP.42W – max takeoff 13,381kg (29,500lb).

Dimensions: Wing span 39.62m (130ft 0in); length 27.36m (89ft 9in); height 8.23m (27ft 0in); wing area 277.7m² (2989sq ft).

Accommodation: HP.42E – 18-24 passengers. HP.42W – up to 38 passengers.

Production: 4 HP.42E and 4 HP.42W, total 8.

History: Stately, comfortable, economical, safe and slow, the HP.42 in many ways epitomises British air travel in the 1930s. This successful and large airliner was built to meet Imperial Airways requirements for an aircraft to serve its Indian, South African and European routes.

Two versions were built: the HP.42E (Eastern) for use on Indian and South African services (under the class name *Hannibal)* and the HP.42W (Western, class name *Heracles*) with more powerful engines and increased maximum weight for service on European routes. Accommodation was for 18-24 passengers in the HP.42E in two cabins or up to 38 passengers in the HP.42W. Some historians have subsequently stated that the correct designation for the HP.42W was in fact HP.45. Four of each version was built.

A unequal span biplane with a pair of engines mounted on both sets of wings, the HP.42 featured a metal structure with metal skinning on the forward fuselage but fabric covering on the rear fuselage, wings and tail. The wings were braced by a massive Warren girder system of struts and the engines placed as close as possible to the centreline to help maintain symmetry in the case of engine failure.

The first aircraft – HP.42E *Hannibal* – flew on 14 November 1930 and after testing entered service on Imperial Airways' London-Paris route in June 1931 before it and its siblings began working the Cairo-Kisumu sector of the African route and Cairo-Karachi over the northern winter of 1931-32. The first HP.42W *Heracles* was delivered to Imperial Airways in September 1931 and the last of the line in early 1932.

The HP.42s proved to be reliable, economical and safe, the first fatal accident not occurring until March 1940 when *Hannibal* was lost in the Gulf of Oman while returning to Britain for RAF service. The only loss in airline service was in 1937 when one of the HP.42Ws was destroyed in a hangar fire at Karachi. For its time, the HP.42 was subject to very high utilisation and initial disrespect shown towards its Gothic appearance and 'built in headwinds' speed soon gave way to greater appreciation of its virtues.

The HP.42s were withdrawn from airline service with the outbreak of war in September 1939. Several were lost in unusual, weather related circumstances (mainly while on the ground) over the next few months, leaving three to be impressed into RAF service. None survived 1940.

Photo: Handley Page HP.42 prototype.

Handley Page Halifax and Halton

Country of origin: United Kingdom.

Powerplants: Halton – four 1765hp (1316kW) Bristol Hercules 100 14-cylinder radials; three bladed propellers.

Performance: Halton – cruising speed 226kt (418km/h); initial climb 740ft (225m)/min; service ceiling 21,000ft (6400m); range 2198nm (4072km).

Weights: Halton – empty 17,160kg (37,830lb); max takeoff 30,845kg (68,000lb).

Dimensions: Wing span 31.60m (103ft 8in); length 22.43m (73ft 7in); height 6.91m (22ft 8in); wing area 118.4m² (1275sq ft).

Accommodation: Halton – 10-12 passengers in cabin and 3629kg (8000lb) freight in underfuselage pannier.

Production: 12 Halton 1 and 1 Halton 2 conversions by Short and Harland. Approximately 120 other Halifax civil conversions by Aviation Traders, Short and Harland, Handley Page and others.

History: A general shortage of British transport aircraft in the period immediately after WWII resulted in the conversion of former bombers to interim transports to help fill the need. The Avro Lancastrian (from the Lancaster) and Handley Page Halton (from the Halifax) were important examples.

The HP.70 Halton designation was specifically applied to 13 conversions from Halifax C.VIII transports performed by Short & Harland at Belfast. The C.VIII transport had first flown in June 1945 with guns removed, turrets faired over and a detachable underfuselage pannier fitted for freight and mail.

The failure of the Avro Tudor left BOAC with a shortage of capacity with the result that it ordered 12 Halton 1s with cabin windows and a large loading door. The first of them was rolled out in July 1946 and the 12 aircraft flew between London and Accra for the next year on mixed passenger/freight services before they were disposed of for resale. The sole Halton 2 was originally intended as a VIP aircraft for Maharajah Gaekwar of Baroda but instead went to South Africa.

Civil conversions which retained the name 'Halifax' were the most numerous of the breed starting in February 1946 when Handley Page converted a Mk.III bomber into a 15 passenger transport. Many others followed, the aircraft flying around the world largely on freight charters such as London Aero and Motor Services, Skyflight, Lancashire Aircraft, Alpha Airways, Payloads, Bond Air Services, British American Air Services, Chartair, Air Freight, Eagle Aviation and Westminster Air Services. Most conversions were based on the Halifax C.VIII but Bristol Hercules powered former bombers were also involved.

The initial postwar British freight boom collapsed in 1948 but the Halifaxes and Haltons were pressed into service for extensive use on the Berlin Airlift. Between 24 June 1948 and 15 August 1949 41 operated around the clock into Gatow Airport, flying no fewer than 4653 freight and 3509 diesel fuel delivery sorties during that period.

The end of the Berlin Airlift also marked the end of the Halifax and Halton as commercial aircraft and most were scrapped shortly afterwards.

Photo: BOAC's first Halton conversion.

Handley Page Hermes

Country of origin: United Kingdom.

Powerplants: Hermes 4 – four 2100hp (1566kW) Bristol Hercules 763 14-cylinder radials; four bladed propellers.

Performance: Hermes 4 – max speed 304kt (563km/h); cruising speed 240kt (444km/h) at 10,000ft (3048m); initial climb 1030ft (314m)/min; service ceiling 24,500ft (7468m); max payload range 1738nm (3219km); max range 3040nm (5631km).

Weights: Hermes 4 – empty 25,107kg (55,350lb); max takeoff 39,010kg (86,000lb).

Dimensions: Hermes 4 – wing span 34.44m (113ft 0in); length 29.51m (96ft 10in); height 9.12m (29ft 11in); wing area 130.1m² (1408sq ft).

Accommodation: Hermes 4 – typically 40-63 passengers in BOAC service, up to 78 later.

Production: 1 Hermes 1, 1 Hermes 2, 25 Hermes 4, 2 Hermes 5, total 29.

History: The pressurised Hermes was the first new British aircraft to enter service with BOAC after WWII but it had a mixed career. The prototype HP.68 Hermes 1 with four 1650hp (1230kW) Hercules 101 radials and tailwheel undercarriage got the project off to the worst possible start when it crashed shortly after takeoff on its maiden flight on 3 December 1945, the result of elevator overbalance.

Development effort then concentrated on the Hastings military version for the RAF, but a second civil version, the HP.74 Hermes 2, was successfully flown on 2 September 1947. Also fitted with tailwheel undercarriage, this aircraft featured a 3.96m (13ft 0in) fuselage stretch and 1675hp (1249kW) Hercules 121s. It was used as a development aircraft for the only production variant, the similarly sized HP.81 Hermes 4 with more powerful Hercules 763s and tricycle undercarriage, 25 of which had been ordered by BOAC in April 1947.

The first Hermes 4 flew on 5 September 1948 and entered service with BOAC on its West African route to Tripoli, Kano, Lagos and Accra in August 1950. Services from London to Entebbe and Nairobi followed the next month and Johannesburg was soon added. The final delivery was in January 1951.

In service, the Hermes proved to have good payload-range characteristics but suffered ongoing problems with some systems. Always regarded as an interim type by BOAC, it began to be replaced by Canadair Argonauts during 1952. The discovery of fatigue cracks in one aircraft after only 3500 flying hours resulted in a resparring programme before most were cocooned, although after the Comet groundings some briefly returned to BOAC service in 1954.

Former BOAC aircraft found work with charter operators Airwork and Skyways initially (fitted with up to 78 seats) largely for commercial trooping flights; and operators such as Britavia/Silver City, Falcon Airways, Air Safaris and Bahamas Airways later on. As the Hermes 4A, several had their Hercules 763s (which used 115 octane fuel) replaced with Hercules 773s which ran on more readily available 100 octane. Most were scrapped in 1961-62 but Air Links recorded the last Hermes commercial flight in December 1964.

Two HP.82 Hermes 5s with 2490ehp (1857kW) Bristol Theseus turboprops were flown in 1949 and used for research flying.

Photo: Hermes 4A.

Handley Page Herald

Country of origin: United Kingdom.

Powerplants: Two 2105ehp (1570kW) Rolls-Royce Dart Mk.527 turboprops; four bladed propellers.

Performance: 200 – max cruise 238kt (441km/h); economical cruise 230kt (427km/h); service ceiling 27,900ft (8505m); max payload range 965nm (1787km); max range 1364nm (2526km).

Weights: 200 – operating empty 11,703kg (25,800lb); max takeoff 19,505kg (43,000lb).

Dimensions: 200/400 – wing span 28.88m (94ft 9in); length 23.01m (75ft 6in); height 7.31m (24ft 0in); wing area 82.3m² (886sq ft).

Accommodation: 100 – 44 passengers four abreast. 200 – up to 56 passengers.

Production: 2 HPR.3, 4 Srs.100, 36 Srs.200 and 8 Srs.400, total 50.

History: The Herald was the first of the major Western 'DC-3 replacement' regional airliners to be launched (in early 1954) but lost its early marketing advantage when the necessary decision to convert it from piston engine to turboprop power was taken.

As the HPR.3, the Herald was originally powered by four 870hp (649kW) Alvis Leonides radials and the first of two prototypes was flown on 25 August 1955. Despite strong early interest it was realised the success of the Vickers Viscount and its Dart turboprops plus the launch of the directly competitive Dart powered Fokker F27 meant it was essential that the Herald also utilise that powerplant.

Re-engined with Darts and with its fuselage lengthened by 50.8cm (20in) so the forward crew/baggage door would be clear of the propeller arc (and a fin fillet and larger cabin windows incorporated), the first prototype was reflown as the HPR.7 Dart Herald Srs.100 on 17 December 1958.

The first order was placed by BEA and the first production aircraft flown in October 1959. Only three others were built as Srs.100s and after development problems caused delays, deliveries to Jersey Airlines (brief leases pending the arrival of Srs.200s) began in May 1961. These aircraft soon found their way into BEA service.

The first Srs.200 (converted from the second prototype) with a further 1.07m (40in) fuselage stretch and increased weights flew on 8 April 1961 and the first production model was delivered to Jersey Airlines in January 1962. By then, sales momentum had been lost and only 36 examples of this major production variant were built.

The Herald 400 'tactical transport' with side loading doors and strengthened cabin floor was built only for the Royal Malaysian Air Force (eight from November 1963) and the Srs.700 was a still-born 60 seater with more powerful Dart 532s, increased weights and additional fuel. Brazil's VASP ordered 10 in 1965 but these were cancelled and partially completed airframes scrapped. The 50th and last Herald (a Srs.200 for Israel's Arkia) was flown and delivered in August 1968. Handley Page failed the following year.

Subsequently, second hand Heralds gave reliable service to many operators. Air UK flew the type's last passenger service from Leeds to Belfast in June 1985 and others continued as freighters. By 1999 only one remained in service, a Srs.400 with Channel Express and it was retired during the year.

Photo: Herald 200. (D Fraser)

Hawker Siddeley HS.748

Country of origin: United Kingdom.

Powerplants: Srs.1 – two 1740ehp (1297kW) Rolls-Royce Dart Mk.514 turboprops. Srs.2 – two 1910ehp (1424kW) Dart 531 or 2105ehp (1570kW) Dart 533. Srs.2A – two 2230ehp (1663kW) Dart 534. Srs.2B – two 2280ehp (1700kW) Dart 536 or 552; four bladed propellers.

Performance: Srs.2 – max cruise 232kt (430km/h); initial climb 1150ft (350m)/min; operational ceiling 25,000ft (7620m); max payload range 450nm (833km); max range 1310nm (2426km). Srs.2B/Super – max cruise 244kt (452km/h); initial climb 1420ft (433m)/min; max payload range 785nm (1454km); range with 40 passengers 1420nm (2630km).

Weights: Srs.1 – operating empty 10,258kg (22,614lb); max takeoff 17,237kg (38,000lb). Srs.2 – operating empty 11,149kg (24,580lb); max takeoff 19,732kg (43,500lb). Srs.2A/2B – operating empty 12,159-12,327kg (26,806-27,176lb); max takeoff 21,092kg (46,500lb).

Dimensions: Srs.1/2/2A – wing span 30.02m (98ft 6in); length 20.42m (67ft 0in); height 7.75m (24ft 10in); wing area 75.2m² (810sq ft). Srs.2B/Super – wing span 31.23m (102ft 5½in); wing area 77.0m² (829sq ft).

Accommodation: Typically 44-52 passengers four abreast, maximum 58.

Production: 381 of all models comprising 20 Srs.1, 85 Srs.2, 123 Srs.2A, 33 Srs.2B/Super and 31 HS.780/Andover C.1 in UK plus 4 Srs.1 and 85 Srs.2 by HAL in India.

History: Faced with uncertainties about future British defence spending in 1957, Avro decided to diversify and began development of a turboprop 'DC-3 replacement' regional airliner. The resultant Avro 748 (Hawker Siddeley HS.748 from 1963 and BAe 748 from 1977) found a steady civil and military market over more than a quarter of a century.

The prototype Srs.1 first flew on 24 June 1960 and deliveries to Skyways-Coach Air began in April 1962. Progressive development saw more powerful versions of the Dart and increased weights introduced for improved payload-range performance, subsequent versions being the Srs.2 (also with increased fuel, first flight November 1961); Srs.2A (September 1967); Srs.2B (June 1979) with increased span wing, more efficient engines, upgraded flight deck and other detail refinements; and finally the Super 748 (July 1984), an upgraded 2B with advanced flight deck, hushkitted engines, systems modifications and modernised 'widebody' interior.

The Srs.2C with large freight door was flown in December 1971, this subsequently proving to be a popular option with both civil and military customers. Aircraft fitted with the door had the designation suffix 'LFD' applied. The last 748 was a Super first flown in December 1988 and delivered to Makung International the following month.

Hindustan Aeronautics Ltd assembled 89 748s under licence for Indian civil and military operators between 1961 and 1984, 20 of them in LFD configuration. The specialised military tactical transport HS.780 Andover C.1 with more powerful Darts, 'kneeling' main undercarriage and a redesigned rear fuselage incorporating clamshell doors and a loading ramp was developed for the RAF. The prototype (converted from the first Srs.1) flew in December 1963 and 31 production aircraft were delivered 1965-68.

Photo: 748 2B Super. (BAe)

Hawker Siddeley Trident 1

Country of origin: United Kingdom.

Powerplants: 1C – three 9850lb (43.8kN) Rolls-Royce Spey 505-5 turbofans. 1E – three 11,400lb (50.7kN) Spey 511-5 turbofans.

Performance: 1C – max cruise 530kt (982km/h); economical cruise 503kt (932km/h); long range cruise 469kt (869km/h); range with 92 passengers 1290nm (2390km); max range 2220nm (4112km). 1E – max cruise 526kt (974km/h); range with 115 passengers 1564nm (2897km); max range 2216nm (4105km).

Weights: 1C – operating empty 30,890kg (68,100lb); max takeoff 52,164kg (115,000lb). 1E – operating empty 32,432kg (71,500lb); max takeoff 61,500kg (135,580lb).

Dimensions: 1C – wing span 27.38m (89ft 10in); length 34.98m (114ft 9in); height 8.23m (27ft 0in); wing area 126.2m² (1358sq ft). 1E – wing span 28.96m (95 ft 0in); wing area 134.3m² (1446sq ft).

Accommodation: 1C – typically 88 passengers in two classes or up to 103 passengers (payload limited) single class six abreast. 1E – normally up to 115 passengers six abreast, maximum 139.

Production: 117 Tridents of all versions including 24 Srs.1C and 15 Srs.1E.

History: A classic example of how to ruin the excellent commercial prospects of a design which should have thrived in the marketplace, the Trident was originally developed by de Havilland as the DH.121 to meet a 1956 British European Airways requirement for a 111-140 seater powered by the planned 12,000lb (53.4kN) Rolls-Royce RB.141 Medway turbofan. The aircraft was very close in specification to the Boeing 727-100 and more than a year ahead of it.

Even as the first metal was being cut, BEA insisted on a smaller, less flexible aircraft with lower weights and reduced range, at a stroke handing an enormous market to Boeing. Inexplicably, the de Havilland (later Hawker Siddeley) board agreed to this and the Spey powered HS.121 Trident was born. A sensational opportunity for the British industry was lost as a result and the final production numbers tell the story: Trident 117; 727 1832.

The name Trident was appropriate not only for the aircraft's three engined layout but also because of the triplication of major systems. The first aircraft was flown on 9 January 1962 and the only customer for the initial Srs.1C – BEA – put the first of its 24 aircraft into service in March 1964. Entirely predictably, BEA immediately started complaining that the Trident was too small and had too little range!

The Trident 1C was too closely tailored to BEA's needs to have any export appeal, so Hawker Siddeley developed the Srs.1E with increased span wing (with leading edge slats), more fuel capacity and improved payload-range performance. Although the fuselage and cabin dimensions remained as before, less harsh payload restrictions and a rearranged interior meant that up to 139 passengers could be accommodated. First flight was in June 1965.

Seven operators purchased new Trident 1Es but only in small numbers: Kuwait Airways (2), Iraqi Airways (4), Pakistan International (4), BKS Air Transport (2) and Channel Airways, Air Ceylon and Northeast one each. Meanwhile, the 727 was selling by the truckload.

Photo: Trident 1C. (Evan Jones)

Hawker Siddeley Trident 2 and 3

Country of origin: United Kingdom.

Powerplants: 2E/3B – three 11,930lb (53.1kN) Rolls-Royce Spey 512-5W turbofans. 3B – additional 5250lb (23.3kN) Rolls-Royce RB162-86 turbojet in tail.

Performance: 2E – max cruise 525kt (972km/h); economical cruise 518kt (960km/h); long range cruise 439kt (813km/h); range with 107 passengers 2110nm (3908km); max range 2346nm (4346km). 3B – max cruise 522kt (967km/h); economical cruise 463kt (858km/h); max payload range 1550nm (2871km); range with 141 passengers 2050nm (3797km).

Weights: 2E – operating empty 33,203kg (73,200lb); max takeoff 65,092kg (143,500lb). 3B – operational empty 37,309kg (82,250lb); max takeoff 68,040kg (150,000lb).

Dimensions: 2E – wing span 29.87m (98ft 0in); length 34.97m (114ft 9in); height 8.23m (27ft 0in); wing area 135.7m² (1461sq ft). 3B – wing span 29.87m (98ft 0in); length 39.98m (131ft 2in); height 8.61m (28ft 3in); wing area 138.7m² (1493sq ft).

Accommodation: 2E – up to 132 passengers six abreast in high density arrangement or 149 with some seven abreast rows. 3B – maximum 180 passengers.

Production: 117 Tridents of all versions including 50 Srs.2E, 26 Srs.3B and 2 Super 3B.

History: BEA quickly decided it needed a longer ranging Trident than the one it had originally specified for use on services between London and the Middle East. Hawker Siddeley responded with the Srs.2E with a further increase in wing span, fuel capacity and weights, the use of weight saving titanium in some parts of the structure and more powerful Speys. In BEA service the Trident had earned the nickname 'The Ground Gripper' because of its appetite for runway length – the new model with its extra power and larger wings was slightly better.

BEA took 15 Trident 2Es, the first flying on 27 July 1967 and entering service in April 1968. There were only two other customers: Cyprus Airways (2) and China's CAAC which ordered 33 and helped save the programme from being a total commercial disaster. They were delivered between November 1972 and June 1978, ending the Trident line.

The Trident really needed to be stretched early in its career but this option was limited by the power available from the Spey engine and the cost of installing a completely new powerplant. The problem was solved by introducing an auxiliary RB162 turbojet mounted in the tail for some extra boost when needed on takeoff. The resulting Trident 3B was therefore a four engined aircraft (the 'Quadrant', perhaps?) with a 5.00m (16ft 5in) fuselage stretch allowing up to 180 passengers in a high density layout. The wing had the same span as the 2E's but with slightly larger area and modified flaps.

BEA reluctantly ordered 26 Trident 3Bs in 1967 (it really wanted 727s), first flown on 11 December 1969. Final delivery was in April 1973. Two others were built as Super 3Bs for CAAC with extra fuel capacity and delivered in August and September 1975. British Airways' final Trident service was in May 1986, the aircraft's excessive noise finally killing it off as hushkitting was impractical. CAAC's last Trident flight was in late 1991 and the Chinese military's in June 1992.

Photo: Trident 3B. (Brian Chidlow)

Harbin Y-12

Country of origin: China.

Powerplants: Y-12 (II) – two 620shp (462kW) Pratt & Whitney Canada PT6A-27 turboprops. Y-12 (IV) – two 680shp (507kW) uprated PT6A-27s; three bladed propellers.

Performance: Y-12 (II) – max cruise 177kt (328km/h); economical cruise 135kt (250km/h); initial climb 1595ft (486m)/min; service ceiling 22,965ft (7000m); range 725nm (1343km).

Weights: Y-12 (II) – max takeoff 5300kg (11,684lb). Y-12 (IV) – max takeoff 5670kg (12,500lb).

Dimensions: Y-12 (II) – wing span 17.23m (56ft 6½in); length 14.86m (48ft 9in); height 5.68m (18ft 7½in); wing area 34.3m² (369sq ft).

Accommodation: Y-12 (II) – up to 17 passengers three abreast. Y-12 (IV) – 19 passengers.

Production: More than 100 by 1999.

History: A product of the Harbin aircraft factory in China's Heilongjiang Province, the Y-12 is a twin turboprop general purpose light utility transport suitable for a variety of civil and military roles in the vein of the de Havilland Canada Twin Otter. The 'Y' in the designation stands for *Yunshuji* or 'transport'.

The Y-12 has its origins in the smaller Y-11 piston engined transport with which it shares a similar overall configuration. In its original version powered by two 285hp (212kW) Jia Hou-sai 6itsi (AI-14R) nine cylinder radials, the prototype Y-11 first flew in 1975 as a replacement for Chinese built Antonov An-2s. Production began in 1980. The Y-11B with 350hp (261kW) Teledyne Continental TSIO-550-B turbocharged horizontally opposed sixes was first flown in late 1995. About 45 Y-11s had been built by 1999.

Work on a turboprop powered derivative began in 1980, the first of two prototypes flying on 14 July 1982 as the Y-11T1 (later Y-12 I). Apart from its engines and increased size, compared to the Y-11 the Y-12 features a new aerofoil section, the use of bonded construction instead of rivets in parts of the structure and integral rather than bag fuel tanks.

Three development Y-12 (II)s were then built, the first of them flying in June 1984 and used to obtain certification in the US FAR Part 23 and Part 135 categories. Chinese certification was awarded in December 1985 and deliveries began to local operators. Harbin worked in conjunction with the Hong Kong Aero Engineering Co (HAECO) to install western avionics and equipment in the aircraft to increase its sales appeal and sales to regional operators in Fiji, Laos, Nepal and elsewhere have been recorded. Military and government sales have been made in Africa and the Asia-Pacific region.

The Y-12 (IV) with uprated engines, modified wing tips, improved undercarriage and brakes, systems modifications and a redesigned interior for two extra passengers is designed specifically for the western market, especially the USA. It first flew on 30 August 1993 and was awarded FAA certification in March 1995. An agreement was struck with the Canadian Aerospace Group (CAG) covering licence production in that country as the Twin Panda with a high content of western equipment.

Photo: Harbin Y-12. (Keith Anderson)

Ilyushin Il-12

Country of origin: Soviet Union.

Powerplants: Two 1830hp (1365kW) Shvetsov ASh-82FNV 14-cylinder radials; four bladed propellers.

Performance: Max speed 220kt (407km/h) at 8200ft (2500m); cruising speed 189kt (250km/h); initial climb 900ft (274m)/min; service ceiling 21,980ft (6700m); range with 32 passengers and no reserves 675nm (1250km); max range 1620nm (3000km).

Weights: Empty 9000kg (19,841lb); max takeoff 17,250kg (38,029lb).

Dimensions: Wing span 31.70m (104ft 0in); length 21.31m (69ft 11in); height 8.00m (26ft 3in); wing area 100.0m² (1076sq ft).

Accommodation: 27-32 passengers.

Production: Approximately 3000 of which about 250 civil.

History: Soviet civil and military air transport was heavily dependent on the Lisunov Li-2 licence built version of the Douglas DC-3 (plus American built aircraft) from the late 1930s until the early postwar era, but in 1943 development of a more modern replacement was investigated.

An official requirement for such as aircraft was issued, the specification requiring the ability to operate from grass airfields. Ilyushin responded with the all metal, tricycle undercarriage Il-12 (NATO reporting name 'Coach') in both civil and military versions, the latter with a large cargo door on the rear port side fuselage and provision for machine guns to be fired from some of the cabin windows.

The aircraft was originally intended to be fitted with a pair of Charomsky diesel engines but all were fitted with Shvetsov ASh-82 radials.

The prototype first flew in early 1946. It was publicly revealed in August of the same year. Deliveries of both the civil and military versions began in 1947, operations with Aeroflot starting that August.

Initial operations were on Soviet internal routes but international services began in 1948. Commercial models were built for export to Czechoslovakia's CSA, Poland's LOT and the state run Chinese airline. The vast majority of the production run was of the military version which was supplied to the USSR and some of its Warsaw Pact allies. Production ended in 1953 in favour of the improved Il-14 (see next entry).

Modifications introduced to the Il-12 during its life included the fitting of a small dorsal fin fillet, lengthened nosewheel and improved de-icing system. Aircraft so modified were designated Il-12B, unmodified examples had the retrospective designation Il-12A applied.

Aeroflot Il-12s carried 27 passengers initially and a large flight deck crew of five. Passenger capacity was later increased to 32 and some were converted to mixed passenger/freight aircraft.

The Il-12's poor performance in the engine-out situation forced a reduction in maximum takeoff weight, this in turn necessitating a passenger capacity reduction to only 16 or 18, an obviously uneconomical load.

Photo: Ilyushin Il-12.

Ilyushin Il-14

Country of origin: Soviet Union.

Powerplants: Two 1900hp (1417kW) Shvetsov ASh-82T-7 14-cylinder radials; four bladed propellers.

Performance: Il-14M – max speed 225kt (417km/h); max cruise 208kt (385km/h); normal cruise 174kt (322km/h); initial climb 1220ft (372m)/min; service ceiling 22,000ft (6705m); max payload range 558nm (1034km); max range 945nm (1750km).

Weights: Il-14M – empty equipped 12,600kg (27,778lb); max takeoff 18,000kg (39,683lb).

Dimensions: Il-14M – wing span 31.70m (104ft 0in); length 22.30m (73ft 2in); height 7.90m (25ft 11in); wing area 99.7m² (1073sq ft).

Accommodation: Il-14P – 18-26 passengers. Il-14M – 30-36 passengers.

Production: Approximately 3500 of all versions including under licence by VEB Flugzeugwerke (80) and Avia (approx 120).

History: Experience with the Il-12 and its many operational flaws led Ilyushin to develop an improved version in the early 1950s combining the original fuselage length with a new wing incorporating an improved aerofoil section plus aerodynamic refinements, slightly more powerful engines, enlarged vertical tail surfaces and structural revisions. As the Il-14, the new aircraft first flew in 1952.

Like its predecessor, the Il-14 was built in large numbers for civil and military roles and was supplied to the operators and armed forces within the Soviet Union's sphere of influence for both purposes. The NATO reporting name 'Crate' was applied.

The initial civil model was the Il-14P (for *Passazhirkii* – passenger), this entering service with Aeroflot in November 1954. The military version was designated simply Il-14. Like the Il-12, the Il-14 suffered from marginal engine-out performance, resulting in a restricted maximum weight and the passenger payload reduced from 32 to only 18-26.

The stretched (by 1.00m/3ft 3½in) Il-14M (*Modifikatsirovanny* – modified) appeared in 1956 with accommodation for up to 36 passengers but 30 was the normal load. Il-14s converted to freighters were designated Il-14T while the specialist freighter Il-14G (*Gruzovoi* – freighter) was also produced.

East Germany's VEB built 80 Il-14s under licence from 1956, while Czechoslovakia's Avia started building the aircraft in 1957, becoming the sole source in 1958 when Soviet manufacture ended.

Several variants were produced as the Avia 14/14P, 14-32 (an Il-14M variant for 32 passengers), 14T freighter, 14FG aerial survey version, 14 Salon VIP aircraft and 14-40 Super (1960) with pressurised fuselage, accommodation for up to 42 passengers and circular cabin windows.

Despite its operational and safety problems and extremely poor operating economics (even by Soviet standards), the Il-14 was built in very substantial numbers and remained in widespread service well into the 1980s. By 1999 about 100 still remained in commercial service mainly for freight and charter work.

Photo: A CAAC Il-14 photographed at Shanghai in 1987 with an Il-18 in the background. (Julian Green)

Ilyushin Il-18

Country of origin: Soviet Union.

Powerplants: Il-18V – four 4015eshp (2994kW) Ivchenko AI-20K turboprops. Il-18D/E – four 4250eshp (3169kW) Ivchenko AI-20M turboprops; four bladed propellers.

Performance: Il-18D – max cruise 364kt (674km/h); economical cruise 337kt (624km/h); operational ceiling 32,810ft (10,000m); max payload range 1998nm (3700km); max range 3510nm (6500km). Il-18E – max payload range 1359nm (2500km).

Weights: Il-18D – operating empty 35,000kg (77,160lb); max takeoff 64,000kg (141,094lb). Il-18E – operating empty 34,630kg (76,345lb); max takeoff 61,200kg (134,920lb).

Dimensions: Wing span 37.40m (122ft 8½in); length 35.89m (117ft 9in); height 10.16m (33ft 4in); wing area 140.0m² (1507sq ft).

Accommodation: Il-18B – 84 passengers. Il-18V – up to 111 passengers. Il-18D/E – up to 122 passengers six abreast.

Production: Estimated 700-800 of all versions.

History: One of the new generation of airliners developed for Aeroflot in the 1950s, the Il-18 turboprop (NATO reporting name 'Coot') was designed to meet the airline's 75-100 seat medium range requirements. It went on to enjoy a long production and service life and was supplied to many Soviet bloc operators as well as a few outside that circle.

The prototype – named *Moskva* and powered by four 4000ehp (2983kW) Kuznetsov MK-4 turboprops – first flew on 4 July 1957. Two pre-production and a trials batch of twenty 75 seat aircraft followed, powered alternatively by the MK-4 and the Ivchenko AI-20, the latter adapted for series production aircraft. Early production aircraft were 84 seaters designated Il-18B and after service trials carrying mail and freight in the Ukraine, Aeroflot inaugurated passenger flights on the Moscow to Adler and Alma routes in April 1959. The first international service (Moscow-London) was flown in October 1959.

There were some serious early problems with AI-20 engine, modifications resulting in the Il-18V of 1961 with improved AI-20K powerplants and accommodation for up to 111 passengers. The other major versions included the Il-18D (1965) with more powerful AI-20Ms, substantially increased fuel capacity and passenger accommodation increased to a maximum of 122 by moving the rear cabin pressure bulkhead further aft. The Il-18E for domestic services was similar but lacked the additional fuel capacity and had a lower maximum weight. Both were developed via the Il-18I prototype. Many earlier models were upgraded to Il-18E standards.

The Il-18E was a mainstay of Aeroflot's internal services for some time and could be quickly reconfigured to various 'summer' and 'winter' layouts for between 90 and 122 passengers five or six abreast. The winter layouts had fewer seats because of the need to provide additional closet space for the passengers' very necessary heavy fur coats.

Il-18 production ended in 1968 and by 1999 more than 400 were still in service, mainly in the CIS and Eastern Europe but also in the Middle East and Caribbean. The Il-18 forms the basis of the maritime patrol and anti submarine warfare Il-38 'May'.

Photo: Ilyushin Il-18D. (Wally Civitico)

Ilyushin Il-62

Country of origin: Soviet Union.

Powerplants: Il-62 – four 23,150lb (103.0kN) Kuznetsov NK-8-4 turbofans. Il-62M/MK – four 24,250lb (107.9kN) Soloviev D-30KU turbofans.

Performance: Il-62 – cruising speed 442-486kt (819-900km/h); cruising altitude 32,800-39,400ft (10,000-12,000m); max payload range 3610nm (6685km); range with 110 passengers 4968nm (9200km). Il-62M – max payload range 4210nm (7800km); range with 110 passengers 5400nm (10,000km).

Weights: Il-62 – operating empty 69,400kg (153,000lb); max takeoff 162,000kg (357,143lb). Il-62M – operating empty 71,600kg (157,848lb); max takeoff 165,000kg (363,757lb). Il-62MK – max takeoff 167,000kg (368,166lb).

Dimensions: Wing span 43.20m (141ft 9in); length 53.12m (174ft 3½in); height 12.35m (40ft 6¼in); wing area 279.5m² (3009sq ft).

Accommodation: Il-62 – 168-186 passengers six abreast. Il-62M – maximum 174 passengers. Il-62MK – maximum 195 passengers.

Production: Approximately 250.

History: The Soviet Union's first long range jet airliner, the Il-62 was designed to provide Aeroflot with an aircraft suitable for international services and which was equivalent to Western types in terms of performance and passenger comfort.

Its configuration was similar to that of the British Vickers VC10 with rear mounted engines and T-tail, other features including double slotted flaps, three section ailerons, upper surface spoilers and a fixed leading edge extended droop on the wings' outer two-thirds.

The prototype first flew in January 1963 powered by 16,535lb (73.5kN) Lyulka AL-7 turbojets as the specified Kuznetsov NK-8 turbofans were not ready. NK-8s were fitted to the original Il-62 production model. A lengthy development programme followed due to problems with the aircraft's tendency to deep stall (from which recovery was impossible) when the wings blocked airflow to the tail at high angles of attack, and slow development of the NK-8.

Aeroflot finally put the Il-62 into international service in September 1967 on the Moscow-Montreal route and replaced the Tupolev Tu-114 on the Moscow-New York service in July 1968. It was subsequently flown on most of Aeroflot's long haul routes including Moscow-Paris, Moscow-Tokyo and Moscow-Havana. NATO's reporting name was 'Classic'.

Developed versions were the Il-62M (1971) with more fuel efficient Soloviev D-30 turbofans, modified wing spoilers, revised flight deck, increased fuel capacity and much improved payload-range capability; and Il-62MK (1978) with strengthened structure and landing gear to allow an increase in maximum weight. This and a redesigned 'widebody' interior permitted an increase in maximum passenger capacity. The last two Il-62s were completed in 1994 but production was sporadic and at a low rate in later years.

Other operators included CAAC, Interflug, Balkan Bulgarian, LOT, CSA and Cubana. About 160 remained in service in 1999, the vast majority in the CIS and Eastern Europe.

Photo: Ilyushin Il-62M. (Rob Finlayson)

Ilyushin Il-76

Country of origin: Soviet Union/Russia.

Powerplants: Il-76T – four 26,445lb (117.6kN) Aviadvigatel (Soloviev) D-30KP turbofans. Il-76TD – four 26,445lb (117.6kN) D-30KP-II turbofans.

Performance: Il-76T – cruising speed 405-432kt (750-800km/h); service ceiling 50,850ft (15,500m); max payload range 1970nm (3650km); max range 3600nm (6670km). Il-76TD – cruising speed 405-421kt (750-780km/h); max payload range 2052nm (3800km); range with 40.0 tonnes (88,183lb) payload 2570nm (4760km); range with 20.0 tonnes (44,092lb) payload 3942nm (7300km); max range 4212nm (7800km).

Weights: Il-76T – operating empty 89,000kg (196,208lb); max takeoff 170,000kg (374,780lb). Il-76TD – max takeoff 190,000kg (418,871lb).

Dimensions: Wing span 50.50m (165ft 8in); length 46.58m (152ft 10in); height 14.76m (48ft 5in); wing area 300.0m² (3229sq ft).

Capacity: Max payload 40.0 tonnes (88,183lb).

Production: More than 900 by 1999 including about 300 civil.

History: Design work on the Il-76 heavy freighter (NATO reporting name 'Candid') began in the late 1960s intended as a replacement for the Antonov An-12 in both military and civil roles. Most production has been for the Soviet (and subsequently Russian/CIS) military and its allies but about one-third have been manufactured for Aeroflot and other civilian operators, including in Western Europe.

The specification which resulted in the Il-76 was demanding and required the ability to lift specific items of civil and military equipment from rough fields and extreme climatic conditions such as those found in Siberia. The Il-76's configuration is conventional for this type of aircraft – high wing with four podded engines underneath, T-tail and rear loading ramp.

The prototype first flew on 25 March 1971 and the first production aircraft on 8 May 1973. Initial versions were the basic Il-76 and Il-76M military transports plus the civil Il-76T, the latter naturally lacking the defensive armament fitted to most military models and featuring additional fuel capacity and higher operating weights.

The military Il-76MD with increased fuel, higher weights, strengthened structure and D-30KP-II engines (which retain their power to higher altitudes and temperatures) formed the basis of the second civil model, the Il-76TD. Several other military and civil subvariants have been developed for specialist roles such as cosmonaut training, search and rescue, firefighting, electronic countermeasures, medivac and reconnaissance.

The latest version is the Il-76MF (Il-76TF in its civilian guise) with stretched fuselage, increased weights, upgraded avionics and more fuel efficient, Stage 3 noise regulations compliant 35,275lb (156.9kN) Aviadvigatel PS-90AN turbofans. This first flew on 1 August 1995 and is capable of lifting a payload of 52.0 tonnes (114,640lb) and carrying 40.0 tonnes (88,183lb) over a distance of 3132nm (5800km). The Il-76MF/TF forms the basis for a planned 'westernised' version powered by CFM International CFM56 turbofans.

Photo: Ilyushin Il-76MF.

Ilyushin Il-86

Country of origin: Soviet Union/Russia.

Powerplants: Four 28,660lb (127.5kN) KKBM (Kuznetsov) NK-86 turbofans.

Performance: Max cruising speed 512kt (948km/h); economical cruise 486kt (900km/h); service ceiling 36,090ft (11,000m); max payload range 1944nm (3600km); max fuel range 2484nm (4600km).

Weights: Max takeoff 208,000kg (458,554lb).

Dimensions: Wing span 48.06m (157ft 8in); length 59.94m (195ft 4in); height 15.81m (51ft 10½in); wing area 320.0m² (3444sq ft).

Accommodation: Typically 234 passengers in two classes or maximum 350 in single class nine abreast.

Production: 103.

History: Russia's first widebody airliner, the Il-86 has had a less than successful career, suffering from poor fuel economy and therefore failure to meet its design range, which was modest by Western standards anyway. It was therefore produced only in small numbers.

Il-86 development was announced at the 1971 Paris Air Show, the aircraft intended as a replacement for the Il-62 and prompted by the arrival of the Boeing 747. A protracted development programme followed, the prototype not flying until 22 December 1976 and the first production aircraft on 24 October 1977.

The Il-86 production line was established at Voronehz in Russia. Poland's PZL Mielec manufactured the tailplane, fin, engine pylons and wing slats. There were no variants, the only significant change being an increase in the maximum takeoff weight from the original 206,000kg (454,145lb) to the definitive 208,000kg (458,554lb).

The Il-86 began proving flights in September 1978 but did not enter scheduled service with Aeroflot until December 1980 on the Moscow-Tashkent route. The airline's aim to have the Il-86 in service in time for the 1980 Moscow Olympic Games was therefore not met. International services (initially Moscow-Berlin) started in July 1981.

The Il-86 was initially proposed in a similar configuration to the narrowbody Il-62, with four rear mounted turbofans and a T-tail. A rethink followed, resulting in the adoption of a conventional tail and underwing podded engines.

Although a conventional design, one unusual feature of the Il-86 is that – where airport aerobridges are not provided – passengers can board the aircraft via airstairs leading to a lower deck baggage area before climbing a fixed internal staircase to the main passenger cabin.

Plans to equip the Il-86 with CFM International CFM56 turbofans to dramatically improve fuel economy and range and reduce noise levels to within ICAO Stage 3 limits have been discussed at various times, but the cost of such an upgrade has proved prohibitive and is likely to remain so.

About 90 Il-86s remained in service by 1999 with Russian and CIS operators plus China's Xinjiang Airlines. Production ended in 1994.

Photo: Ilyushin Il-86. (Bruce Malcolm)

Ilyushin Il-96-300

Country of origin: Soviet Union/Russia.

Powerplants: Il-96-300 – four 32,275lb (156.9kN) Aviadvigatel (Soloviev) PS-90A turbofans. Il-96M/T – four 37,000lb (164.6kN) Pratt & Whitney PW2337 turbofans.

Performance: 96-300 – max cruise 486kt (900km/h); typical cruise 459kt (850km/h); max payload range 4050nm (7500km); range with 165 passengers 5940nm (11,000km). 96M – max cruise 469kt (869km/h); range with 330 passengers 6195nm (11,475km).

Weights: 96-300 – operating empty 117,000kg (257,937lb); max takeoff 216,000kg (476,190lb). 96M – operating empty 132,400kg (291,887lb); max takeoff 270,000kg (595,238lb).

Dimensions: 96-300 – wing span 60.11m (197ft 2½in); length 55.35m (181ft 7in); height 17.57m (57ft 8in); wing area 391.6m² (4215sq ft). 96M – length 63.93m (209ft 9in); height 15.72m (51ft 7in).

Accommodation: 96-300 – 235 passengers in three classes or 300 in single class nine abreast. 96M – 312 passengers in three classes, 335 in two classes or 375 in single class. 96T – max payload 92.0 tonnes (202,822lb).

Production: Il-96-300 – approximately 15 by early 1999. Il-96M/T – about 50 orders by early 1999.

History: Despite resembling the longer Il-86, the Il-96-300 is in many ways a new design, incorporating a number of advanced technologies and new engines aimed at improving the uncompetitive Il-86.

Advanced features include a triplex fly-by-wire flight control system, six screen EFIS flight deck (but with three crew members), some composite construction (including the flaps and main deck floors) and winglets. The PS-90 turbofans are designed to comply with ICAO Stage 3 noise limits and the Il-86's unique lower deck airstair feature is deleted.

Development began in the mid 1980s and first flight was on 28 September 1988. Two other flying prototypes were built, as were two airframes used for static and ground testing. Russian certification was awarded in December 1992 and the Il-96-300 entered service with Aeroflot Russian International Airlines in early 1993.

The stretched and further modernised Il-96M passenger transport and Il-96T freighter with Pratt & Whitney PW2337 engines, Collins digital avionics and other items of Western technology was developed in the early 1990s.

The prototype (converted from a new Il-96-300 airframe) first flew on 6 April 1993 and the first new build aircraft (an Il-96T freighter) was flown on 16 May 1997. Il-96M and T customers include Aeroflot (20), Transaero (6) and Partnairs of the Netherlands. US certification was awarded in June 1999, the first for a Russian aircraft.

Planned developments include the Il-96MK with ducted fan engines, Il-96-300D (a -300 re-engined with PW2337 engines), Il-96-500/550 double deckers and the twin engined Il-98 with two high thrust Western turbofans such as the Rolls-Royce Trent, General Electric GE90 or Pratt & Whitney PW4000.

Photo: Ilyushin Il-96-300.

Ilyushin Il-114

Country of origin: Soviet Union/Russia.

Powerplants: Two 2466shp (1839kW) Klimov TV7-117S turboprops; six bladed propellers.

Performance: Max cruise 270kt (500km/h); normal cruise 254kt (470km/h); operational ceiling 23,620ft (7200m); max payload range 540nm (1000km); max range 2592nm (4800km).

Weights: Operating empty 15,000kg (33,069lb); max takeoff 22,700kg (50,044lb) or 23,500kg (51,808lb).

Dimensions: Wing span 30.00m (98ft 5in); length 26.88m (88ft 2in); height 9.32m (30ft 7in); wing area 81.9m² (882sq ft).

Accommodation: 60-64 passengers four abreast.

Production: Approximately 15 built by early 1999.

History: The Ilyushin Il-114 was originally designed to fill the potentially large requirement for an Antonov An-24 replacement on Aeroflot's short haul internal routes. That requirement still exists but since the breakup of the Soviet Union, in Russia and other CIS states and for export.

Although starting to enter service with Uzbekistan Airways at the beginning of 1999, work on the Il-114's basic design and configuration began as early as 1986. The first of three flying prototypes (two static test airframes were also built) took to the air on 29 March 1990, the original intention being to achieve certification and service entry in 1993. The test programme was delayed, however, at least in part by the crash of one of the prototypes on takeoff during a test flight in mid 1993. The first production aircraft flew in August 1992 and Russian certification was finally awarded in April 1997.

The Il-114 is of conventional configuration, but 10 per cent of its structure by weight is of composites and advanced metal alloys, including titanium. It features low noise six blade composite construction propellers, built-in airstairs and can operate from unpaved airfields.

The Il-114 is the basic airliner model and forms the basis for several developments. The Il-114T is a freighter version developed for Uzbekistan Airlines with a large freight door in the rear port side fuselage, removable roller floor and increased maximum weight of 23,500kg; and the Il-114M will feature more powerful TV7M-117 engines and the increased maximum weight.

Like many current Russian airliner programmes, a Westernised version of the Il-114 has been developed. This is the Pratt & Whitney Canada PW127 powered Il-114-100 (formerly Il-114PC) with not only the new engines but also Western sourced avionics and equipment. The first Il-114-100 was flown on 26 January 1999 and its launch customer is Uzbekistan Airways.

Other planned versions are the Il-114P maritime patrol variant and the Il-114FK electronic intelligence gathering (Elint), reconnaissance and cartographic model with a glazed nose and raised flight deck.

The Il-114 has also been designed to be easily stretched so that 70-75 passengers can be carried. Although a Russian design, the Il-114 is assembled at Tashkent in Uzbekistan, while Romanian, Polish and Bulgarian aerospace companies are also responsible for some component manufacture.

Photo: Ilyushin Il-114. (Bruce Malcolm)

Junkers F 13

Country of origin: Germany.

Powerplant: Various including one 185hp (138kW) BMW IIIa six cylinder inline; 265hp (198kW) Junkers L.2 inline; 380hp (283kW) Junkers L.5 inline; 250hp (186kW) BMW IV six cylinder inline; or 360hp (268kW) BMW Va V12; two bladed propeller.

Performance: F 13a – max speed 95kt (177km/h); cruising speed 76kt (140km/h); range 350nm (648km). F 13fe – max speed 107kt (198km/h); cruising speed 92kt (171km/h).

Weights: F 13a – empty 1150kg (2535lb); max takeoff 1730kg (3814lb). F 13fe – empty 1510kg (3330lb); max takeoff 2703kg (5960lb).

Dimensions: Wing span 17.75m (58ft 3in); length 9.60m (31ft 6in); height 3.61m (11ft 10in); wing area 44.0m² (474sq ft).

Accommodation: Two crew and four passengers.

Production: 322.

History: The F 13 is assured of its place in commercial aviation history by being the world's first all metal purpose built airliner to enter service.

Apart from that significant fact, the F 13 was also notable for its time in being a monoplane rather than biplane, for having a semi enclosed (originally) and then fully enclosed cockpit for its crew and for having seat belts for the passengers.

The construction of the F 13 ensured strength and longevity, the wing – which lacked any external bracing – built around nine spars forming a metal girder and the fuselage built up from metal frames. Both were covered by the distinctive corrugated dural skinning which became a feature of Junkers transports.

The prototype was powered by a 160hp (119kW) Mercedes D.IIIa inline and first flew on 25 June 1919. The first 13 production aircraft were designated F 13a and powered by the more efficient BMW IIIa. Production continued until 1932, during which time some 70 variants were introduced with a wide variety of engines. Ski and float equipped models were also built.

Apart from the original production F 13a, the major variants were the F 13ba/ca/da/fa (Junkers L.2 engine), F 13be/ce/de/fe (Junkers L.5), F 13dle/fle/ge/he/ke (improved Junkers L.5), F 13bi/ci/di/fi (BMW IV) and F 13co/fo/ko (BMW Va). An F 13fe delivered to Britain in 1928 for the use of the Rt Hon F E Guest had its original Junkers L.5 engine replaced with a 450hp (335kW) Bristol Jupiter VI nine cylinder radial.

The F 13 played a significant role in the development of the air transport industry in Europe and elsewhere including South America, the USA and Soviet Union. Some of the major operators were Junkers Luftverkehr which had about 60 aircraft, Deutsche Luft Hansa (72), Poland's Aerolot (16), Romania's LARES (9), Sweden's AB Aerotransport (6) and Switzerland's Ad Astra Aero (6). Some F 13s were also delivered to military operators.

A good indication of the soundness of the F 13's basic design is provided by the original prototype – it was still being used for joyriding flights over Berlin in 1939, 20 years after first flight and capping an extraordinarily long career for an aircraft of that period.

Photo: Junkers F 13 floatplane.

Junkers G 23, G 24 and G 31

Country of origin: Germany.

Powerplants: G 24 – normally three 310hp (231kW) Junkers L.5 inlines. G 31 – three 450hp (335kW) Siemens (Bristol) Jupiter nine cylinder radials or three 525hp (392kW) BMW (Pratt & Whitney) Hornet nine cylinder radials; three bladed propellers.

Performance: G 24 – max speed 108kt (200km/h); range 702nm (1300km). G 31 – max speed 108kt (200km/h); cruising speed 92kt (170km/h); range with 1005kg (2216lb) payload 540nm (1000km).

Weights: G 24 – max takeoff 6500kg (14,330lb). G 31 – empty 5000kg (11,023lb); max takeoff 8500kg (18,739lb).

Dimensions: G 24 – wing span 27.76m (91ft 1in); length 15.70m (51ft 6in). G 31 – wing span 30.30m (99ft 5in); length 17.27m (56ft 8in); wing area 102.0m² (1098sq ft).

Accommodation: G 23/24 – nine passengers. G 31 – 12-15 passengers or 2500kg (5511lb) freight.

Production: 9 G 23, 56 G 24 and 13 G 31.

History: Junkers continued developing its commercial aircraft line with the nine passenger G 23, the world's first three engined all metal monoplane. It incorporated the corrugated metal skinning which was becoming a Junkers trademark.

The G 23 first went into service with Sweden's AB Aerotransport on its Malmö-Hamburg-Amsterdam route in May 1925. Only nine were built, powered by 160hp (119kW) Mercedes D.IIIa or 265hp (198kW) Junkers J.2 engines.

The similarly sized G 24 was the major production version of the basic design, differing in having more powerful engines and higher weights, these making it illegal under the terms of the Versailles Treaty affecting aircraft for service in Germany.

The G 24 first flew in 1925 and in July 1926 a Deutsche Luft Hansa aircraft flew from Berlin to Peking and back to assess the possibilities of starting a regular service across Asia.

Another aircraft set a world speed, distance and duration record in March 1927, carrying a 2000kg (4409lb) load over 550nm (1018km) in 7hr 52min.

Eleven G 24s were converted to single engined F 24 configuration from 1928 with the wing mounted engines removed. Nine of these were for Luft Hansa.

The larger G 31 with accommodation for up to 15 passengers appeared in 1926. The prototype was powered by three Junkers L.5 inlines but the production model with lengthened fuselage had Bristol Jupiters built under licence by Siemens or Gnome-Rhône; or BMW built Pratt & Whitney Hornets. The cabin was arranged in three compartments, any of which could be fitted with sleeping bunks for night flying.

The G 31 was originally operated by Luft Hansa (9), Österreichische Luftverkehr (1) and Guinea Airways (2), the latter operating on behalf of the Bulolo Gold Dredging Company in New Guinea. Used as heavy freighters, these aircraft were modified to incorporate a domed hatch on the forward upper fuselage through which freight was loaded. They were used from 1931 to 1942, their rugged construction and modest airfield requirements proving ideal for the terrain.

Photo: Junkers G 31 of Deutsche Luft Hansa.

Junkers G 38

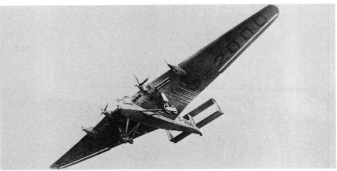

Country of origin: Germany.

Powerplants: Final configuration – four 750hp (559kW) Junkers Jumo 204 six cylinder inline diesel engines; four bladed propellers.

Performance: Cruising speed 112kt (208km/h); range 1026nm (1900km).

Weights: Empty 14,880kg (32,804lb); max takeoff 24,000kg (52,910lb).

Dimensions: Wing span 44.00m (144ft 4in); length 23.19m (76ft 1in); height 7.20m (23ft 7½in); wing area 300.0m² (3229sq ft).

Accommodation: Up to 34 passengers comprising 26 in fuselage, six in wing leading edges and two in nose.

Production: 2 by Junkers and 6 by Mitsubishi as Ki-20.

History: A remarkable four engined, all metal design, the G 38 was basically a flying wing with a relatively small fuselage. Although most of the passengers were accommodated in the fuselage (including two in the nose), three were seated in each wing leading edge inboard of the engines, complete with windows to provide an extraordinary view.

The enormous wing was 1.70m (5ft 7in) thick and had a chord of 10.00m (32ft 10in). Engines mounted on the wing leading edges, massive tandem wheel main undercarriage units, triple fins/rudders between biplane horizontal tail surfaces and use of characteristic Junkers slotted ailerons (or 'double wings') completed the aerodynamic configuration.

Only two G 38s were built in Germany, the first of them – named *Deutschland* – flying in 6 November 1929. Originally fitted with 400hp (298kW) Junkers L.8 inline engines outboard and 800hp (597kW) L.88 V12s inboard, it was subsequently fitted with four L.88s and finally with 750hp (559kW) Jumo 204 diesels in 1934.

Deutschland was handed over to Deutsche Luft Hansa for route proving trials in June 1930 but was never put into regular commercial service. It survived until 1936 when it crashed at Dessau in eastern Germany.

The second aircraft was named *Generalfeldmarschall von Hindenburg*. It featured several modifications over the original including fitting the slotted ailerons over the whole wing trailing edge rather than just outboard of the engines, and a modified fuselage. It also had its engines uprated over the years culminating in fitting the Jumo 204 diesels. The first aircraft was upgraded to the new standards. The retrospective designations G 38a (first aircraft) and G 38ce were applied in 1932 when modifications began.

Hindenburg did serve Luft Hansa on a regular basis after entering service in September 1931. It flew through the 1930s but was destroyed in an RAF bombing raid during 1940.

Six examples of a modified version of the G 38 were secretly built in Japan by Mitsubishi between 1931 and 1936 as the Ki-20 Type 92. Intended as a heavy bomber for the Imperial Japanese Army, the Ki-20 carried a crew of ten, eight defensive machine guns and one cannon, and a maximum bomb load of 5000kg (11,023lb) over short ranges. Slow and vulnerable, it was regarded as a failure and never used operationally.

Photo: G 38a *Deutschland*, the first aircraft with half span ailerons.

Junkers W 33 and W 34

Country of origin: Germany.

Powerplant: W 33 – normally one 310hp (231kW) Junkers L.5 inline. W 34 – various including one 420hp (131kW) Gnome-Rhône (Bristol) Jupiter VI nine cylinder radial; 540hp (403kW) Siemens Sh 20 (Jupiter) nine cylinder radial; 600hp (447kW) BMW (Pratt & Whitney) Hornet nine cylinder radial; or 660hp (492kW) BMW 132A nine cylinder radial; two bladed propeller.

Performance: W 34 (BMW 132A engine) – max speed 143kt (265km/h); cruising speed 95-126kt (176-233km/h); service ceiling 20,670ft (6300m); range 486nm (900km).

Weights: W 34 – empty 1700kg (3748lb); max takeoff 3200kg (7055lb).

Dimensions: W 34 – wing span 17.75m (58ft 3in); length 10.26m (33ft 8in); height 3.53m (11ft 7in); wing area 43.0m² (463sq ft).

Accommodation: Two crew plus freight or six passengers; cabin volume 4.78m³ (169cu ft).

Production: 199 W 33 and 1791 W 34.

History: The enormously successful W 33 and W 34 single engined light transports found acceptance in both civil and military roles. All metal monoplanes, they were basically the same aircraft but for their engines and were direct developments of the F 13 but with a lengthened version of the earlier aircraft's fuselage and the same wings in combination with more powerful engine options and increased weights. They were built using the same production line and jigs as the F 13.

The W 33 and W 34 both first flew in 1926 (the original W 33 converted from an F 13) and both were intended mainly for use as freighters. Most early aircraft were built to this standard and lacked fuselage windows but as more were put to use for carrying up to six passengers, windows began appearing, one at first and subsequently three per side. The W 34 was the version most used for passenger carrying. Skis and twin floats could be fitted to both models.

Various powerplants were fitted and there were some 30 W 33 and 70 W 34 subvariants including military models. About 900 served with the Luftwaffe mainly as navigation trainers and transports until the end of WWII. German production of the W 34 ended in 1934 while a specialist military bomber/reconnaissance version was built in Sweden as the K 43, from where it was exported to Finland and Colombia.

Where the F 13 had played a vitally important role in the development of commercial air transport in Europe and elsewhere, the W 33 and W 34 built on that, especially in the more remote parts of South America where they were extensively used.

Both types were involved in some notable long distance and endurance flights. A W 33 set a world endurance record of 52hr 23min in August 1927; another recorded the first east to west non stop crossing of the North Atlantic in April 1928, flying from Dublin (Ireland) to Greenly Island (off Labrador) in 37 hours.

The W 33 and W 34 inherited the rugged construction and longevity of their predecessor. The last one (a floatplane) was not retired by its Canadian operator until September 1962.

Photo: Luft Hansa Junkers W 34.

Junkers Ju 52/3m

Country of origin: Germany.

Powerplants: Prewar civil – typically three 600hp (447kW) BMW (P&W) Hornet or 660hp (492kW) BMW 132A-1 nine cylinder radials; two bladed propellers.

Performance: Max speed 149kt (275km/h); cruising speed 113-132kt (209-245km/h); service ceiling 19,360ft (5900m); max range 691nm (1280km).

Weights: Empty 5346kg (11,785lb); max takeoff 9200kg (20,282lb).

Dimensions: Wing span 29.25m (95ft 11½in); length 18.90m (62ft 0in); height 5.55m (18ft 2½in); wing area 110.5m² (1189sq ft).

Accommodation: 15-17 passengers two abreast.

Production: To 1945 – 4871 of all models (3234 in Germany, 26 in Hungary and 1611 by Amiot in France). Postwar – 400 AAC.1 in France and 170 CASA 352 in Spain; overall total 5441.

History: Although best known as the Luftwaffe's standard transport aircraft during WWII, the Ju 52/3m trimotor was also one of the most significant prewar airliners, over 200 flying with 30 airlines before 1940 including Deutsche Luft Hansa and numerous foreign operators. Luft Hansa had at least 120 which were responsible for carrying more than three-quarters of its European traffic in the 1930s.

Popularly known as *Tante Ju* ('Auntie Junkers') or 'Iron Annie', the Ju 52/3m was a simple three engined development of the single engined Ju 52 freighter, the first of which had flown in October 1930. Only six were built and the seventh airframe was converted to the first Ju 52/3m, flying in April 1931. This was powered by three BMW built Pratt & Whitney Hornet nine cylinder radials as were many of the early models, while the vast majority which followed had versions of the Hornet-derived BMW 132 fitted.

The Ju 52/3m had the trademark Junkers features including all metal construction with corrugated skinning and the patented 'double wing' full span slotted ailerons/flaps. The result was a rugged and dependable workhorse with modest airfield requirements and the ability to operate from wheels, floats or skis.

The first airline to put the Ju 52/3m into service was Lloyd Aereo Boliviano in early 1932. Other 1930s civil operators included Luft Hansa, Finland's Aero O/Y, Sweden's AB Aerotransport and British Airways. Numerous military versions quickly followed, Luftwaffe aircraft making their operational debut during the Spanish Civil War as a bomber and troop transport. The aircraft was prominent in all the major German campaigns of WWII including the 1940 Norway invasion which saw the first large scale use of air transport in war.

Postwar, production continued in France as the AAC.1 with 400 built for Air France and the French military, and in Spain as the CASA 352. The Ju 52/3m continued in service with commercial and military operators for many years, several examples remaining in full time use until the late 1970s. British European Airways used 12 ex Luftwaffe aircraft on internal services 1946-48. Spanish military versions were not withdrawn until 1975 while the Swiss Air Force did not retire its last example until 1981.

Photo: Junkers Ju 52/3m.

Junkers Ju 60 and Ju 160

Country of origin: Germany.

Powerplant: Ju 60 – one 600hp (447kW) BMW (Pratt & Whitney) Hornet C nine cylinder radial. Ju 160 – one 660hp (492kW) BMW 132E nine cylinder radial.

Performance: Ju 160 – max speed 183kt (339km/h); cruising speed 170kt (315km/h); service ceiling 17,060ft (5200m); range 550nm (1020km).

Weights: Ju 160 – empty 2320kg (5115lb); max takeoff 3550kg (7826lb).

Dimensions: Ju 160 – wing span 14.32m (47ft 0in); length 12.00m (39ft 4½in); height 3.92m (12ft 10½in); wing area 34.7m² (374sq ft).

Accommodation: Two crew and six passengers.

Production: 4 Ju 60 and 48 Ju 160.

History: The Ju 60 was developed to meet a Deutsche Luft Hansa requirement for a light single engined transport which was capable of matching the performance standards set by the Lockheed Orion. The catalyst which sparked its development was Swiss Air Lines' ordering of the Orion in 1931. The Heinkel He 70 was developed to the same specification.

The Ju 60 broke away from what had become the 'traditional' Junkers method of construction. Although remaining all metal, it dispensed with the multi spar/girder wing structure of the F 13/G 31/W 34/Ju 52 models and instead adopted a more conventional two spar design. The wing – which featured a distinct leading edge sweep back – remained covered in the familiar corrugated metal skinning but the fuselage was smooth skinned.

The two pilots sat in tandem in an enclosed cockpit, retractable undercarriage was fitted, the Junkers 'double wing' full span ailerons/flaps were installed and power was provided by a 600hp (447kW) BMW built Pratt & Whitney Hornet radial. The prototype flew in 1932 and only four were built. These saw limited service with Luft Hansa but the Ju 60 did not go into series production, this status falling to the improved Ju 160 instead.

Compared to its predecessor, the Ju 160 featured a more powerful BMW 132E radial (a development of the Hornet) housed in a more streamlined cowing, a modified wing plan form and smooth skinning instead of corrugated skinning on the wings and tail surfaces. A tail wheel (rather than skid) was fitted to production aircraft as was a modified fin and rudder. Accommodation was as before – two crew and six passengers.

The first Ju 160 was flown in June 1934 and immediately proved superior to the earlier aircraft, matching the Lockheed Orion in many respects.

The Ju 160 entered service with Luft Hansa in 1935, almost exclusively for use on the airline's German domestic services. By 1937 it was flying on more than a dozen routes throughout the country. Luft Hansa took about half of the 48 Ju 160s built and by the second half of 1939 still had about 16 in service. Others were operated by the German Air Ministry and two were sold to Manchurian Air Transport in 1937.

Surviving Ju 160s were impressed into Luftwaffe service at the outbreak of war in September 1939 and used for transport and communications duties.

Photo: Junkers Ju 160.

Junkers Ju 86

Country of origin: Germany.

Powerplants: Various on civil models including two 600hp (447kW) Junkers Jumo 205C six cylinder diesels; two 800hp (596kW) Pratt & Whitney Hornet S1E-G nine cylinder radials; two 770hp (574kW) BMW 132D or 810hp (604kW) BMW 132F nine cylinder radials; three bladed propellers.

Performance: Hornet engines – cruising speed 195kt (360km/h); range 594nm (1100km).

Weights: Hornet engines – empty 4960kg (10,935lb); max takeoff 8000kg (17,637lb).

Dimensions: Wing span 22.50m (73ft 10in); length 17.41m (57ft 1½in); height 4.70m (15ft 5in); wing area 82.0m² (883sq ft).

Accommodation: 10 passengers.

Production: Approximately 470 Ju 86s of all versions including about 44 civil models.

History: A contemporary of the Heinkel He 111 (which it beat into the air by three months), the Ju 86 was, like its rival, designed as both a civil airliner and bomber. Unlike the He 111, the Ju 86 quickly fell out of favour as a bomber due to various operational and performance shortcomings and apart from some combat use during the assault on Poland in 1939, had been relegated to secondary duties by the Luftwaffe when war broke out.

Although it was the first aircraft designed specifically for diesel power, the first of five Ju 86 prototypes was powered by Siemens SAM 22 radial piston engines when it first flew on 4 November 1934.

The first civil prototype (with Jumo diesels) flew in April 1935. Early production models were powered by Jumo 205C diesels and included the Ju 86A bomber, Ju 86B pre-production transport, and the major production Ju 86D bomber.

The commercial version could accommodate 10 passengers in the main cabin, basically two abreast but in staggered and turned inwards pairs to compensate for the cabin's lack of width. Deutsche Luft Hansa began operating Ju 86s on its domestic routes in 1936 but like the bomber versions, these proved to be not a great success.

Despite this, some were exported under the general designation Ju 86Z with a variety of powerplants including the Jumo diesel, Pratt & Whitney Hornet or BMW 132 radials.

Other operators were Swiss Air Lines (with Jumo and BMW engines), Sweden's AB Aerotransport (Hornets, for night mail services), LAN Chile (Jumos), Lloyd Aereo Boliviano (Hornets), Manchurian Air Services (BMWs, some later re-engined with Mitsubishi Kinsei radials) and Australia's Southern Airlines and Freighters, which briefly operated a Jumo engined Ju 86 from 1937.

Apart from Germany, military Ju 86s were sold to Hungary, Sweden (including 16 built under licence by Saab), South Africa, Portugal, Manchuria, Chile and Brazil. Luftwaffe Ju 86s were used mainly as trainers and transports (including during the 1942-43 Stalingrad airlift), while Hungary's saw some action on the Eastern Front 1941-42. South Africa's were mostly flown on coastal patrol duties but also flew against Italian forces in East Africa during 1941.

Photo: Junkers Ju 86B-0.

Junkers Ju 90

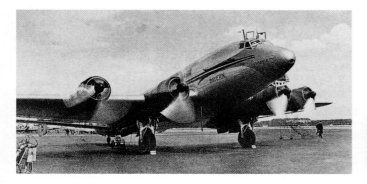

Country of origin: Germany.

Powerplants: Ju 90B – four 830hp (619kW) BMW 132H nine cylinder radials; three bladed propellers.

Performance: Ju 90B – max speed 189kt (349km/h) at 8200ft (2500m); cruising speed 173kt (320km/h); service ceiling 18,044ft (5500m); range 1080nm (2000km).

Weights: Ju 90B – empty 16,000kg (35,273lb); max takeoff 23,000kg (50,705lb).

Dimensions: Wing span 35.00m (114ft 10in); length 26.30m (86ft 3½in); height 7.30m (23ft 11½in); wing area 184.0m² (1981sq ft).

Accommodation: Up to 40 passengers.

Production: 14.

History: Junkers had developed the Ju 89 four engined bomber in 1935-36 to meet a Luftwaffe requirement. The prototype had flown in December 1936 and a second aircraft was completed, while the third was under construction the programme was cancelled. The company then decided to build a large transport derivative for Deutsche Luft Hansa, combining the wings and tail of the Ju 89 with a new fuselage for up to 40 passengers, creating the Ju 90.

Construction was all metal, the wing featuring a marked sweep back on the leading edges. The by then normal Junkers 'double wing' flaps and ailerons were fitted. The slab sided fuselage provided a wide cabin capable of a comfortable four abreast arrangement.

The prototype was powered by four 1100hp (820kW) Daimler-Benz DB 600 inverted V12 engines and first flew in mid 1937, although the aircraft broke up in flight early in its test programme. Development continued with another three prototypes built along with eight production standard Ju 90Bs with BMW 132H radials. Flight trials of the BMW powered models began in early 1938.

Two others were built as the Ju 90Z with Pratt & Whitney Twin Wasps for South African Airways but these were never delivered.

Luft Hansa began operating the Ju 90 on its Berlin to Vienna route in mid 1938 and a few flights were made to London before the war. The declaration of war resulted in the Ju 90s being taken over by the Luftwaffe, with which they served as transports between 1940 and 1943. They made their operational debut in the invasion of Norway in April 1940 and were subsequently employed in the Balkans, Mediterranean, Greek and Iraqi areas of operation. They were also flown in the southern part of the Russian Front during the Battle of Stalingrad.

The Ju 290 military transport and reconnaissance bomber was a direct development of the Ju 90. First flown in 1939 (the prototype built up from a Ju 90), the 290 was promoted as a replacement for the Focke-Wulf Fw 200 Condor and although it did operate in similar roles, never usurped it and was built in much smaller numbers (only 66 in several subvariants).

Compared to its predecessor, the Ju 290 featured more powerful BMW 801 14-cylinder radials, a larger wing and the ability to carry offensive and defensive armament. Deliveries began in 1943 and production was terminated in late 1944.

Photo: Junkers Ju 90B.

Kalinin K-4 and K-5

Country of origin: Soviet Union.

Powerplant: K-4 – one 240hp (179kW) BMW IV six cylinder inline or 290hp (216kW) M-6 V8. K-5 – one 525hp (391kW) M-15, 500hp (373kW) M-17F or 480hp (358kW) M-22 radial; two bladed propeller.

Performance: K-4 (BMW IV) – cruising speed 86kt (160km/h). K-5 – max speed 107-113kt (198-209km/h).

Weights: K-4 (BMW IV) – empty 1400kg (3086lb); max takeoff 2400kg (5291lb). K-5 – max takeoff 3500-4030kg (7716-8884lb).

Dimensions: K-4 – wing span 16.71m (54ft 10in); length 11.35m (37ft 3in); wing area 40.0m² (431sq ft). K-5 – wing span 20.50m (67ft 3in); length 15.70m (51ft 6in).

Accommodation: K-4 – pilot and six passengers. K-5 – two crew and eight passengers.

Production: K-4 – 22. K-5 – 260.

History: Konstantin Kalinin was a prolific Soviet designer of mainly light transport aircraft during the 1920s and 1930s and an advocate of the elliptical wing plan form as well as incorporating streamlining in his designs.

The K-1, K-2 and K-3 were 3-4 passenger strut braced high wing monoplanes which achieved some modest success, experience gained with them leading to the six passenger K-4 of 1928.

Construction comprised light alloy wings (including the skinning) and metal fuselage structure with metal skinning to the rear of the cabin area. The rear fuselage and tail section was built of wood.

The prototype was reportedly originally powered by a 300hp (224kW) BMW VI V12 engine but most of the 21 production models had the 240hp (179kW) BMW IV. A few – built as aerial ambulances – had more powerful M-6 V8s, a Soviet built Hispano-Suiza engine.

The K-4 was operated mainly by the Soviet Dobrolet and Ukrainian Ukrvozdukhput concerns, the two companies combining to form Dobroflot in 1929.

The K-5 was fundamentally a scaled up K-4 with two crew in an enclosed cockpit, accommodation for eight passengers, more powerful engine and increased weights.

It reverted to wings of wooden construction with fabric covering and was highly successful, production amounting to 260 aircraft between 1930 and 1934.

The prototype was powered by a 525hp (391kW) M-15 nine cylinder radial (licence built Bristol Jupiter) but production versions had either M-17F or M-22 engines. Dobroflot ordered 120 K-5s which were delivered from 1933 and the aircraft was extensively used on passenger services within the Soviet Union.

In 1933 Kalinin flew the prototype of the huge K-7 twin tailboom four engined heavy bomber. It crashed after structural failure later in the same year and plans to build a 120 passenger airliner version were abandoned.

Konstantin Kalinin did not survive to develop his career beyond 1938. In that year he fell victim to the Soviet purge – he was arrested and shot and his design bureau closed down.

Photo: Kalinin K-4.

Koolhoven FK.50

Country of origin: Netherlands.

Powerplants: Two 420hp (313kW) Pratt & Whitney Wasp Junior T1B nine cylinder radials; two bladed propellers.

Performance: Cruising speed 140kt (260km/h); range 540nm (1000km).

Weights: Empty 2505kg (5522lb); max takeoff 4100kg (9038lb).

Dimensions: Wing span 18.00m (59ft 1in); length 14.00m (45ft 11$\frac{1}{4}$in); height 3.70m (12ft 1$\frac{1}{2}$in); wing area 44.7m^2 (481sq ft).

Accommodation: Two crew and eight passengers.

Production: 3.

History: Frederick Koolhoven's company was one of the leading Dutch aircraft manufacturers in the 1920s and 1930s, its more successful products including the FK.33 ten seat twin engined commercial transport which flew with Deutsche Luft Hansa, German Aero and KLM (on its Amsterdam to Paris, London and Malmö services) and the FK.42/43 3-4 seat single engined monoplanes which found some favour with private and air taxi operators. The FK.41 was built under licence in Britain by Desoutter.

Military training and general purpose types were also built (and a fighter later on) as was the one-off FK.48 six passenger commercial twin of 1935. This was used by KLM on its Rotterdam-Eindhoven route.

The FK.50 was of similar high wing layout but larger and capable of carrying eight passengers. Construction comprised a wooden cantilever two spar wing and fabric covered metal fuselage and tail unit.

The cockpit was enclosed and six of the eight passengers sat on individual chairs with the remaining pair on a bench seat at the rear.

Only three were built, all powered by Pratt & Whitney Wasp Junior radials. The first was flown in September 1935 and delivered to Switzerland's Alpar Luftverkehrs later in the year. Two others joined the Alpar fleet, one in early 1936 and the other in 1938, this aircraft differing in having twin fins and rudders in place of the original single unit.

The third FK.50 also featured a modified cockpit, larger wheels, increased maximum weight and smaller engine nacelles replacing the earlier rather bulbous NACA cowlings. Sometimes referred to as the FK.50A, this aircraft was ordered to replace the second example which had crashed in September 1937.

The FK.50 displayed remarkable longevity despite its tiny production run and single operator. The two remaining aircraft survived the war and were operated on a Berne-London (Croydon) service during 1946. The first aircraft was broken up in 1947 but the third survived until 1962 when it crashed in Liberia and was destroyed.

Koolhoven proposed a military version as the FK.50B with more powerful Bristol Mercury radials, a crew of four, defensive guns and a 1000kg (2205lb) bomb load accommodated in a largely redesigned and deepened fuselage, but this never progressed beyond the drawing board.

Photo: The third Koolhoven FK.50 with twin fins.

Latécoère 28

Country of origin: France.

Powerplants: 28-0 – one 500hp (373kW) Renault 12Jb V12. 28-1 – 500hp (373kW) Hispano-Suiza 12Hbr V12. 28-3 – 600hp (447kW) Hispano-Suiza 12Lbr V12. 28-5 – 650hp (484kW) Hispano-Suiza 12Nb V12; two bladed propeller.

Performance: 28-0 – max speed 121kt (224km/h); service ceiling 17,060ft (5200m); range 513nm (950km). 28-3 – cruising speed 108kt (200km/h); max range 1728nm (3200km).

Weights: 28-0 – empty 2173kg (4790lb); max takeoff 3856kg (8500lb). 28-3 – empty 2637kg (5814lb); max takeoff 5017kg (11,060lb).

Dimensions: 28-0/1 – wing span 19.25m (63ft 2in); length 13.64m (44ft 9in); height 3.58m (11ft 9in); wing area 48.6m^2 (523sq ft).

Accommodation: Mail or eight passengers.

Production: Approximately 54.

History: The Latécoère company's aviation origins date back to 1919 with the establishment of the Lignes Aériennes Latécoère, one of the first French airlines and a specialist mail carrier operating largely from France to North Africa and South America. It built a series of single engined, parasol wing monoplane mailplanes for operation from wheels or floats to fill this role plus a flying boat design.

The successful Laté 26 (70 of which were built in 1928-30) led to the larger Laté 28, a single engined high wing braced monoplane designed to fill a requirement of the French mail service Aéropostale, which needed a modern aircraft to operate its joint mail services both within France and to Africa and South America.

Two models were initially developed for competitive evaluation, the Laté 28-0 with a Renault 12Jb engine and the Hispano-Suiza 12H powered Laté 28-1. Apart from their powerplants they were identical and could carry either mail or eight passengers. First flight was in 1929 and both were put into widespread service by Aéropostale including in the Mediterranean area and on charter operations. Production was 17 28-0s and 29 28-1s, although about 14 of the 28-0s were converted to 28-1 standards.

Other major versions were the Laté 28-3 and 28-5 mail carrying floatplanes with more powerful versions of the Hispano-Suiza engine and wings of increased area. Other variants were created mainly by conversion and included wheeled versions of the floatplanes (and *vice-versa*) and passenger versions of mailplanes. The designation Laté 28-6 was applied to three 'big wing' aircraft supplied to Aviacon Nacional Venezolana, which had previously received three 28-1s. Linea Aeropostal Venezolana and Aeroposta Argentina were other operators.

The Laté 28-3 and 28-5 floatplanes established no fewer than 19 speed with load over distance, closed circuit with load and endurance records in the early 1930s, the most celebrated involving renowned pilot Jean Mermoz flying a 28-3 from St Louis (Senegal) across the South Atlantic to Natal (Brazil) in May 1930. The 1713nm (3173km) journey was completed in 21 hours flying time and was part of the first air mail service between Toulouse and Rio de Janeiro.

Photo: Latécoère Laté 28-0.

Let L 410 and L 420

Country of origin: Czech Republic.

Powerplants: L 410 UVP-E – two 751shp (560kW) Motorlet M 601 E turboprops. L 420 – two 778shp (580kW) M 601 F turboprops; five bladed propellers.

Performance: L 410 UVP-E – max cruise 205kt (380km/h); economical cruise 197kt (365km/h); max climb 1420ft (433m)/min; service ceiling 23,785ft (7250m); max payload range 294nm (545km); max fuel range 711nm (1317km). L 420 – max cruise 210kt (389km/h); initial climb 1400ft (427m)/min; range with 17 passengers 367nm (680km); max fuel range 737nm (1365km).

Weights: L 410 UVP-E – operating empty 4120kg (9083lb); max takeoff 6400kg (14,109lb). L 420 – operating empty 4225kg (9314lb); max takeoff 6600kg (14,550lb).

Dimensions: Wing span 19.98m (65ft 6½in); length 14.43m (47ft 4in); height 5.83m (19ft 1½in); wing area 35.2m² (379sq ft).

Accommodation: 17-19 passengers three abreast.

Production: Over 1000 of all versions by 1999.

History: Designed to meet the small regional airliner requirements of Eastern Europe and the Soviet Union's Aeroflot, development of the pressurised L 410 Turbolet began in 1964. The intention was for the aircraft to be powered by the indigenous Walter (Motorlet) M 601 turboprop but as this was not ready in time, the first 31 aircraft (designated L 410A) were powered by 715shp (533kW) Pratt & Whitney Canada PT6A-27 engines driving four bladed propellers. The prototype XL 410 was first flown on 16 April 1969.

Services were inaugurated by Czech domestic operator Slov-Air in late 1971. The Motorlet engine became available in 1973, resulting in the L 410M, deliveries of which began in 1976. The original L 410M had 550shp (410kW) M 601 A turboprops; this was followed by the L 410MA with 691shp (515kW) M 601Bs and L 410-MU with different equipment as specified by Aeroflot. Production of all L 410M models was 110.

Aeroflot criticism of the L 410M's handling characteristics resulted in the L 410 UVP with larger wings and vertical tail surfaces, modified spoilers and flaps and slightly lengthened fuselage. This first flew in November 1977 and was in turn replaced by L 410 UVP-E (first flight December 1984) with five bladed propellers, tip tanks, reconfigured interior and more powerful M 601 E engines. Aeroflot continued as by far the major customer and had taken delivery of 872 L 410s of all models by 1991.

The L 420 with M 601 F engines and increased weights flew in November 1993. Intended mainly for export, it received US certification in May 1998. The chances of the aircraft achieving success in the international market improved in September 1998 when it was announced the USA's Ayres Corporation was to take a majority interest in Let, with the intention of developing the L 410/420 and larger L 610 lines. Seattle based Pan Pacific Airways became the L 420's first US customer in June 1999, ordering five and optioning 15.

Let's facilities in Czechoslovakia – which have been substantially under utilised since the collapse of the Soviet Union – will also be used to build components for the Ayres LM 200 Loadmaster freighter/utility aircraft.

Photo: Let L 420.

Let L 610

Country of origin: Czech Republic.

Powerplants: L 610G – two 1750shp (1305kW) General Electric CT7D-9D turboprops; four bladed propellers.

Performance: L 610G – max cruise 237kt (439km/h); long range cruise 152kt (175km/h); initial climb 1673ft (510m)/min; service ceiling 27,560ft (8400m); range with 40 passengers 664nm (1230km); max fuel range 1280nm (2370km).

Weights: L 610G – operating empty 9220kg (20,326lb); max takeoff 14,500kg (31,996lb).

Dimensions: Wing span 25.60m (84ft 0in); length 21.72m (71ft 3in); height 8.19m (26ft 10½in); wing area 56.0m² (603sq ft).

Accommodation: 40 passengers four abreast.

Production: 4 prototypes and 9 production L 610Ms by 1999.

History: Although similar in configuration to the earlier L 410, the L 610 is a larger and entirely new design, conceived in the mid 1980s mainly to meet an Aeroflot requirement for a 40 seat regional airliner capable of operating from rudimentary airfields over stage lengths of 215-325nm (400-600km).

Aeroflot needed 600 aircraft in that category but the collapse of the Soviet Union also saw the major market for the L 610 disappear with the result that by 1999 none had been delivered to airline customers.

The prototype L 610 with 1822shp (1358kW) Motorlet M 602 turboprops flew on 28 December 1988, followed by two more flying and two structural test prototypes. As the L 610M, the aircraft was awarded Czech certification in December 1994 but deliveries were restricted to nine to the Czech Air Force for evaluation and trials.

The L 610G is an attempt to widen the type's international appeal in a crowded marketplace by fitting General Electric CT7D engines, Hamilton Standard propellers and western avionics. It first flew on 18 December 1992 and despite a strong sales push, no firm orders were forthcoming although CSA Czech Airlines placed options.

Until 1998 the future of the L 610 appeared to rest on the success of negotiations aimed at achieving a joint production programme with the Smolensk plant in Russia, either with the Motorlet engine, a Russian turboprop or the Pratt & Whitney Canada PT6 built under licence by Klimov.

These plans came to nought, but the probability of the L 610 programme succeeding increased in September 1998 when it was announced that US manufacturer Ayres was taking over Let Kunovice (and its long term debt), purchasing 93.8 per cent of its stock from the Czech Republic's Aero Holding and the state owned Konsolidacni Bank. The remainder of the company stays with small shareholders.

Let will manufacture components for the forthcoming Ayres LM-200 Loadmaster utility/freighter aircraft and the L 610G (plus the smaller L 410) will be further developed under Ayres' stewardship and actively marketed in the West. Seattle based Pan Pacific Airways ordered two in June 1999.

Photo: Let L 610G. (L Stloukal)

Lioré et Olivier LeO H.242 and H.246

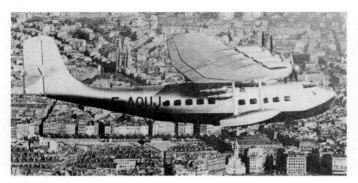

Country of origin: France.

Powerplants: H.242 – four 420hp (313kW) Gnome-Rhône Titan Major 7Kd seven cylinder radials; two bladed propellers. H.246 – four 720hp (537kW) Hispano-Suiza 12X V12s; three bladed propellers.

Performance: H.242 – cruising speed 97kt (180km/h); range 405nm (750km). H.246 – max speed 178kt (330km/h); service ceiling 22,965ft (7000m); range 1080nm (2000km).

Weights: H.242 – empty 5056kg (11,146lb); max takeoff 8400kg (18,518lb). H.246 – empty 9800kg (21,605lb); max takeoff 15,000kg (33,069lb).

Dimensions: H.242 – wing span 28.00m (91ft 10¹/₂in); length 18.47m (60ft 7in); height 6.10m (20ft 0in); wing area 116.2m² (1251sq ft). H.246 – wing span 31.95m (104ft 1in); length 21.18m (69ft 6in); height 7.16m (23ft 6in); wing area 131.0m² (1410sq ft).

Accommodation: H.242 – 15 passengers. H.246 – 26 passengers.

Production: H.242 – 14. H.246 – 7.

History: Ordered in 1932 by Air Union (which merged with Air Orient, CIDNA and SGTA in August 1933 to form Air France), the LeO H.242 monoplane flying boat was designed as a replacement for the all wooden CAMS 53 biplane 'boat and featured a metal hull in combination with a wooden monoplane cantilever wing. The four Gnome-Rhône 7Kd radial engines were mounted in tandem pairs on struts above the wing centre section.

Capable of carrying 15 passengers, the first H.242 flew in 1933 and entered service the following year. The first two aircraft featured uncowled engines and flat sided nacelles but the following 12 H.242.1s had increased weights and range, circular nacelles and NACA cowlings on the front engines originally, later replaced with exhaust collector rings.

The H.242s provided Air France with reliable service on its Marseilles-Algiers, Marseilles-Ajaccio-Tunis and Marseilles-Athens-Tripoli-Beirut services until September 1939 when war intervened. The survivors were mostly taken over by the Italians.

The much larger H.246 was designed to a 1935 requirement for an H.242 replacement for use on Air France's Mediterranean routes. Derived from the H.47 which was intended for the trans-Atlantic route but never entered airline service, the H.246 featured a two step metal hull, accommodation for 26 passengers and a parasol wooden wing with the four Hispano-Suiza 12X V12 engines mounted on the wing's leading edges.

The prototype H.246.01 first flew on 30 September 1937 and Air France ordered six production H.246.1s in January 1938. Service on the Marignane-Algiers route was about to start when war broke out. It was then intended that all the H.246s would be impressed into French Navy service for use as maritime patrol aircraft but only one was used in this role, armed with bombs and defensive machine guns.

The others operated to Algiers until November 1942 when they were seized by the Luftwaffe and used as troop transports and air ambulances. Postwar, two were operated for a short time by Air France between Marignane and Algiers.

Photo: LeO H.246.

Lockheed Vega

Country of origin: USA.

Powerplant: Model 1 – one 225hp (168kW) Wright J-5 Whirlwind seven cylinder radial. Model 2 – one 300hp (224kW) Whirlwind J-6. Model 5 – one 410hp (306kW) Pratt & Whitney R-1340 Wasp A, 420hp (313kW) Wasp C1 or 450hp (335kW) Wasp B nine cylinder radial; two bladed propeller.

Performance: Model 5 – max speed 155kt (286km/h); cruising speed 135kt (249km/h); service ceiling 18,000ft (5485m); range 478-608nm (885-1126km).

Weights: Model 5 – empty 1130-1163kg (2491-2564lb); max takeoff 1935-2155kg (4265-4750lb).

Dimensions: Wing span 12.50m (41ft 0in); length 8.38m (27ft 6in); height 2.59m (8ft 6in); wing area 25.5m² (275sq ft).

Accommodation: Pilot and four-six passengers.

Production: 128 of all models.

History: Designed by Jack Northrop with assistance from Gerald Vultee (both of whom went on to achieve fame with their own companies), the five-six seat Vega set a new standard for single engined performance at the end of the 1920s and as such found favour with many US airlines (including Pan American and Braniff), air taxi operators and record breaking flyers.

Constructed almost entirely of wood (the monocoque fuselage built up from two pressure formed plywood half shells), the Vega was highly streamlined for its day, aided by a cantilever wing devoid of struts and bracing. The major drag inducing components were the uncowled engine and fixed, unspatted undercarriage of early aircraft; later examples had wheel spats and a NACA engine cowling.

The first Model 1 Vega was powered by a 225hp (168kW) Wright J-5 Whirlwind radial and flew on 4 July 1927. Built for newspaper owner George Hearst to sponsor competing in the Oakland to Hawaii air race, it and pilots Jack Forst and Gordon Scott disappeared without trace en route.

Subsequent versions were the Model 2 with a 300hp (224kW) Whirlwind and the major production Model 5 series with 410-450hp (306-335kW) Pratt & Whitney Wasp engines. Subvariants were the Vega 5A Executive with plush interior, 5B seven seater for commercial operators with increased maximum weight, and 5C with revised vertical tail surfaces. Many were converted to other models and there were several floatplane conversions. Nine were built by the Detroit Aircraft Corporation (Lockheed's owner 1929-31) as the DL-1, these featuring a duralumin fuselage. Production ended in 1932.

Vegas were used for several record breaking flights: the first trans-Arctic and Antarctic exploratory flights (Wilkins and Eilson); the first solo trans-Atlantic flight by a woman (Amelia Earhart, Newfoundland to Ireland in May 1932); and the first solo around the world flight by Wiley Post (July 1933) in his Vega 5B *Winnie Mae*. Two years earlier, Post and navigator Harold Gatty completed a record breaking around the world flight in 8 days, 15 hours and 51 minutes.

Photo: Vega in Varney Speed Line colours.

Lockheed Air Express

Country of origin: USA.

Powerplant: One 410hp (306kW), 425hp (317kW) or 450hp (335kW) Pratt & Whitney R-1340 Wasp nine cylinder radial; two bladed propeller.

Performance: Max speed 145kt (269km/h).

Weights: Empty 1149kg (2533lb); max takeoff 1985kg (4375lb).

Dimensions: Wing span 12.95m (42ft 6in); length 8.38m (27ft 6in); height 2.55m (8ft 4$^{1}/_{4}$in); wing area 26.7m^2 (288sq ft).

Accommodation: Pilot and 4-6 passengers or 2.83m^3 (100cu ft) of mail; max payload 454kg (1000lb).

Production: 7 Air Express Model 3s and 1 Air Express Special, total 8.

History: Despite not being intended for airline operations, the Lockheed Vega had found a small market among commercial operators mainly because of its speed and its timing, appearing just when US airlines were entering into something of a boom period.

This started as a natural occurrence of increasing interest in the commercial possibilities of aviation but was further boosted in 1926 when the United States Government passed the Air Commerce Act.

The Air Express Model 3 was designed by Jack Northrop specifically for Western Air Express, which had asked that some of its own design ideas be incorporated into a development of the Vega for use on the air mail route between Salt Lake City (Utah) and Los Angles (California).

Despite its origins, the Air Express differed from the Vega in several substantial ways. The basic moulded plywood fuselage, powerplant, undercarriage, tail unit and wooden cantilever wing were retained but with the latter in extended span form and mounted in parasol fashion on short struts above the fuselage.

The fuselage was itself modified with the original enclosed forward flight deck changed to an open cockpit (to meet the preference of air mail pilots of the day) relocated to the rear fuselage, behind the cabin and the trailing edge of the wing.

The enclosed cabin provided accommodation for a 454kg (1000lb) mail load or four-six passengers, or a combination of both. The Vega's Pratt & Whitney Wasp nine cylinder radial was retained, most Air Expresses being fitted with the 410hp (306kW) version when built.

The first Air Express was flown in the first half of 1928 and despite Western Air Transport providing the catalyst for its development, this was the only example it operated.

The other six were built for New York, Rio, and Buenos Aires Line (2), Pan American Airways (2), American Airways (1) and Texas Air Transport (1).

The eighth and final aircraft was dubbed the Air Express Special and was built for Laura Ingalls' 1931 attempt to fly New York to Paris non stop and create a new record for women. Delays prevented her from taking that particular record but in 1934 she made an important and successful flight around South America in the Air Express.

Further development of the Vega theme led to the Orion low wing monoplane of 1930 (see next entry).

Photo: Air Express prototype.

Lockheed Orion

Country of origin: USA.

Powerplant: Orion 9 – one 450hp (335kW) Pratt & Whitney R-1340 Wasp C nine cylinder radial. 9D – one 550hp (410kW) Wasp S1D1. 9B – one 575hp (429kW) Wright R-1820-E Cyclone nine cylinder radial; two bladed propeller.

Performance: 9D – max speed 196kt (364km/h); cruising speed 178kt (330km/h); service ceiling 22,000ft (6705m); range 650nm (1204km).

Weights: 9D – empty 1851kg (3640lb); max takeoff 2449kg (5400lb).

Dimensions: Wing span 13.05m (42ft 10in); length 8.48m (27ft 10in); height 2.95m (9ft 8in); wing area 27.3m^2 (294sq ft).

Accommodation: Pilot and six passengers.

Production: 35 of all models.

History: Lockheed continued its range of high performance single engined monoplanes firstly with the Sirius (first flight late November 1929) and the Altair (September 1930), both two seat (rear cockpit) mail carrying or sporting monoplanes based around the Vega/Air Express fuselage but with a low wooden cantilever wing. The Sirius was originally developed for Charles Lindbergh for his Pacific and Atlantic air routes surveys; the Altair was similar but with retractable undercarriage.

Pioneering Australian airman Charles Kingsford Smith used an Altair named *Lady Southern Cross* for his successful Brisbane-San Francisco flight in November 1934. Kingsford Smith and navigator J T Pethyridge were lost over the Bay of Bengal in this aircraft while attempting a UK-Australia record in November 1935, their bodies never recovered.

To meet airline requirements, Lockheed designed the Model 9 Orion which combined the Vega fuselage (with forward enclosed cockpit) with the Altair's low wing and retractable undercarriage. Accommodation was provided for six passengers in the cabin.

The first Orion flew in early 1931 and versions were offered with either the Pratt & Whitney Wasp or Wright Cyclone engines. Thirty-five were built comprising 14 Orion 9 (Wasp), one 9A Special (Wasp and airframe revisions), two 9B (Cyclone, for Swissair), 13 9D (Wasp and minor airframe changes), three 9E (similar to 9), and two 9F (650hp/485kW Cyclone, executive aircraft). The one off Orion 9C was an Altair converted to the new configuration.

Fort Worth (Texas) based operator Bowen Air lines introduced the Orion to airline service in May 1931. The aircraft was used by 12 other US airlines including Air Express, American Airways, Varney Speed Lines, Northwest Airways, Wyoming Air Service and Transcontinental & Western Air (subsequently Trans World Airlines). Air Express used its Orions on trans-continental USA services in 1933-34.

Swissair's two Orion 9Bs were the first fitted with Wright Cyclone engines and entered service in May 1932 on the airline's Zürich-Munich-Vienna route. From late 1936 about a dozen Orions found their way into Spanish Republican air force service after the outbreak of the Spanish Civil War.

Photo: The one-off Lockheed Orion 9C Special, converted from an Altair to the new configuration.

Lockheed L.10 Electra

Country of origin: USA.

Powerplants: L.10A – two 450hp (335kW) Pratt & Whitney R-985-SB Wasp Junior nine cylinder radials. L.10B – two 440hp (328kW) Wright R-975-E3 Whirlwind nine cylinder radials. L.10C – two 450hp (335kW) Wasp Junior SC1. L.10E – two 600hp (447kW) Pratt & Whitney R-1340-S3H1 Wasp nine cylinder radials; two bladed propellers.

Performance: L.10A – max speed 175kt (325km/h); max cruise 169kt (314km/h); normal cruise 161kt (298km/h); service ceiling 19,400ft (5913m); range 704nm (1304km).

Weights: L.10A – empty 2927kg (6454lb); max takeoff 4672kg (10,300lb).

Dimensions: Wing span 16.76m (55ft 0in); length 11.76m (38ft 7in); height 3.07m (10ft 1in); wing area 42.6m² (458sq ft).

Accommodation: Two crew and 10 passengers two abreast.

Production: 101 L.10A, 18 L.10B, 8 L.10C, 15 L.10E, 1 XR2O-1, 1 XR3O-1, 1 XC-35, 3 C-36, total 148.

History: Lockheed had achieved some success with its Vega and Orion single engined commercial transports in the late 1920s and early 1930s but realised it needed to develop more modern and capable designs if that success was to continue.

The result of its investigations was the Model 10 Electra, a low wing, monoplane, retractable undercarriage and all metal design powered by two Pratt & Whitney Wasp radial engines driving constant-speed propellers. Capable of seating 10 passengers, the Electra was a commercial success for Lockheed and helped establish the company internationally.

The prototype first flew on 23 February 1934 and although some operators found its 10 passenger capacity too small, others were attracted by its speed, modern features and sizing below the 14 passenger Douglas DC-2. It was proportionately cheaper and as such complemented the larger aircraft in many fleets.

Northwest Airlines was the first to put the Electra into service in August 1934 and an impressive list of customers was quickly built up including Pan American, Braniff, Continental, Mid-Continent and National in the USA, British Airways in the UK, LOT and Aeroput in Europe, Trans-Canada Airlines (which used Electras as its initial equipment on formation in 1937), and Australia's Ansett and Guinea Airways. Others were sold in South America.

The major production version was the initial L.10A with R-985 Wasp Juniors along with smaller numbers of the L.10B (Cyclones), L.10C (Wasp Juniors) and L.10E (R-1340 Wasps). The XR2O-1 and -2 were one-off transports for the US Navy and Coast Guard, respectively, the XC-35 was an experimental version with pressurised cabin, and the C-36 models for the USAAC comprised three aircraft purchased new and others subsequently impressed into military service.

Electras were also used as corporate aircraft and for long distance flights. In 1936 Major James Doolittle set a new Chicago-New Orleans record and in July 1937 famed aviatrix Amelia Earhart and her navigator Fred Noonan perished when their L.10E disappeared without trace over the Pacific during an around the world flight attempt.

Photo: Lockheed L.10B.

Lockheed L.12 Electra Junior

Country of origin: USA.

Powerplants: Two 450hp (335kW) Pratt & Whitney R-985-SB Wasp Junior nine cylinder radials; two bladed propellers.

Performance: L.12A – max speed 195kt (362km/h); cruising speed 184kt (341km/h); service ceiling 22,900ft (6980m); range 695nm (1288km).

Weights: L.12A – empty 2740kg (6040lb); max takeoff 3924-4173kg (8650-9200lb).

Dimensions: Wing span 15.09m (49ft 6in); length 11.07m (36ft 4in); height 2.97m (9ft 9in); wing area 32.7m² (352sq ft).

Accommodation: Two crew and six passengers.

Production: 130.

History: Although some airlines felt the 10 passenger L.10 Electra was too small to meet their main services needs, others also considered the aircraft too big for economical use on feeder services to small communities.

Lockheed responded with the L.12 Electra Junior, basically a scaled down and lighter six passenger version of the L.10 which retained the original's powerplants and as a consequence offered higher performance. The result was an aircraft which sold nearly as well as its predecessor with 130 manufactured. Of those, a fair proportion were purchased by the US military and other nations' air arms.

The first L.12 was flown on 27 June 1936. The major production model was the standard L.12A, delivered to airlines in the USA, Britain, Europe and elsewhere.

US military versions were C-40 and C-40A (later UC-40/A) for the USAAC (13 aircraft) and JO-1 (US Navy) and JO-2 (US Marine Corps), one of each being purchased. The XJO-3 was an experimental model with fixed tricycle undercarriage for carrier deck landing trials and the designation C-40D/UC-40D was applied to 10 L.12As impressed for wartime USAAF service.

Other nations to purchase L.12s for military use included Argentina, Canada, Cuba and the Netherlands East Indies Army which had 36. Of these, 16 were converted Model 212 crew trainers with dorsal gun turret and provision to carry bombs under the wings. One L.12A was acquired by the National Advisory Committee for Aeronautics (NACA – the predecessor of today's NASA) for testing a wing de-icing system utilising hot engine exhaust gasses.

One of the more interesting uses to which an L.12 was put occurred during the three months leading up to the outbreak of WWII in September 1939. As an executive of the British based Dufaycolour company, Australian Sidney Cotton (who was involved in the development of colour photography and largely responsible for modern aerial photography techniques) flew his aircraft ostensibly on business and other trips into Europe. Cotton's L.12 was equipped with cameras and the aircraft used to surreptitiously photograph German military installations as it flew overhead.

The information provided was invaluable to the war effort and Cotton's activities led to the formation of the RAF Photo Reconnaissance Unit.

Photo: Lockheed L.12A. (David Foote)

Lockheed L.14 Super Electra

Country of origin: USA.

Powerplants: L.14-H/H2 – two 750hp (559kW) Pratt & Whitney R-1690-S1E2G Hornet nine cylinder radials. L.14-WF62/14-WG3B – two 900hp (671kW) Wright R-1820-F62 or -G3B nine cylinder radials; three bladed propellers.

Performance: L.14-H – max speed 215kt (398km/h); max cruise 200kt (370km/h); service ceiling 24,300ft (7405m); normal range 870nm (1610km); max range 1790nm (3315km).

Weights: L.14-H – empty 4672kg (10,300lb); max takeoff 7938kg (17,500lb).

Dimensions: Wing span 10.96m (65ft 6in); length 13.51m (44ft 4in); height 3.48m (11ft 5in); wing area 51.2m² (551sq ft).

Accommodation: 12-14 passengers.

Production: 112 by Lockheed and 119 in Japan by Tachikawa and Kawasaki (plus 2941 military Hudson/A-28/A-29/AT-18).

History: Lockheed expanded its range of twin engined transports with the 12-14 passenger L.14 Super Electra, this differing considerably from its predecessors by being larger with a new, deepened fuselage, mid rather than low mounted wings of modified design, slots in the outer wing, integral fuel tanks, more powerful engines, increased weights, baggage holds below the cabin floor and in the nose, fully feathering propellers and area increasing Fowler flaps.

The first aircraft flew on 29 July 1937, by which time Lockheed held 30 orders. Two basic versions were offered, the L.14-H models with Pratt & Whitney Hornet engines and the L.14-W variants with Wright R-1820 Cyclones. Northwest Airlines was the first to put the Super Electra into service, on its Twin Cities-Chicago route in October 1937. Other airlines in the USA, Australia, Britain, Canada, Asia and Europe also ordered L.14s.

Licence production was undertaken in Japan by Tachikawa and Kawasaki which between them built 119 powered by Mitsubishi Ha-26-II engines as the LO. A further developed version was manufactured in Japan as the Ki-56, 121 of these leaving the factories.

The L.14 was used for several notable flights including one by millionaire aviator and industrialist Howard Hughes when he and his crew flew a 12,853nm (23,803km) circuit of the northern hemisphere (often incorrectly dubbed an 'around the world' flight) in 3 days 19 hours 8 minutes in July 1938. Also in 1938, British Prime Minister Neville Chamberlain flew to Germany in an L.14 for his ill fated meeting with Adolf Hitler.

The L.14's other major claim to fame resulted from its selection in June 1938 by the British Purchasing Commission as a reconnaissance bomber for the RAF. The order for 200 as the Model 414 Hudson severely stretched Lockheed, which had hitherto been only a small to medium sized firm. The company was reorganised and recapitalised to meet the demanding delivery schedule and the Hudson and its derivatives were subsequently built in large numbers for the British, Commonwealth, US and other air arms for extensive WWII service.

Postwar, many demobbed Hudsons found their way into commercial roles as transports and survey aircraft.

Photo: Lockheed L.14.

Lockheed Lodestar

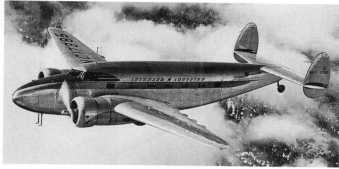

Country of origin: USA.

Powerplants: Depending on version – two 750-875hp (559-652kW) Pratt & Whitney R-1690 Hornet; or two 900-1200hp (671-895kW) Wright R-1820 Cyclone nine cylinder radials; or two 900-1200hp (671-895kW) Pratt & Whitney R-1830 Twin Wasp 14-cylinder radials; three bladed propellers.

Performance: L.18-07 (750hp Hornets) – max speed 189kt (351km/h); service ceiling 20,400ft (6220m); range 1564nm (2897km). C-60A (1200hp Cyclones) – max speed 231kt (428km/h); cruising speed 174kt (322km/h); service ceiling 30,000ft (9145m); range 1442nm (2671km).

Weights: L.18-07 – empty 5103kg (11,250lb); max takeoff 8709kg (19,200lb). C-60A – empty 5477kg (12,075lb); max takeoff 5639kg (18,500lb).

Dimensions: Wing span 19.96m (65ft 6in); length 15.18m (59ft 10in); height 3.61m (11ft 10in); wing area 51.2m² (551sq ft).

Accommodation: Normally 14 passengers two abreast, maximum 26 on bench seats along cabin sides in high density layout.

Production: 625 of all models including approximately 145 commercial.

History: A direct development of the Model 14 Super Electra/Hudson series, the Model 18 Lodestar was initially built as a civil transport offering greater passenger capacity than its predecessor. First flown on 21 September 1939, the Lodestar combined the powerplants of the Model 14 (Pratt & Whitney Hornets initially, Wright Cyclones and Pratt & Whitney Twin Wasps later) with a 1.71m (5ft 7in) longer fuselage, a wing of similar span but revised planform and increased weights.

US airlines were not overly interested in the Lodestar as they were queuing to buy the Douglas DC-3, but it was nevertheless purchased by operators such as Continental, Pan American and National. Exports were reasonably strong with 96 ordered by 1941 for customers in Canada, Australia, South Africa, Brazil, Africa, France, the Netherlands, Norway, Britain and Venezuela. Six basic models were produced differing mainly in their powerplants: L.18-07 (Hornet); L.18-08 and -14 (Twin Wasps); and L.18-40/50/56 (Cyclones).

US military interest in the Lodestar began in May 1941 when an initial single C-56 with Cyclone engines and three C-57s with Twin Wasps were ordered. With the USA joining the war in December 1941 many were impressed into service with different powerplants and interior fittings under the designations C-56A/E, C-57B, C-59, C-60, C-66 and C-111.

The major new build military version was the C-60A (325 manufactured) with Cyclones and equipped to carry 18 paratroops. US Navy versions were designated R5O-1 to -6, the latter equivalent to the C-60A.

The RAF's aircraft were all impressed ex civil aircraft supplied mainly from the USA under Lend-Lease and designated Lodestar I, IA (equivalent to the C-59) and II (C-60). The Lodestar performed a myriad of invaluable transport duties in WWII including general, paratroop, VIP, ambulance, cargo and as a glider tug and was put to widespread postwar commercial use.

Photo: Lockheed L.18 prototype.

Lockheed L.049-749 Constellation

Country of origin: USA.

Powerplants: L.049 – four 2200hp (1640kW) Wright R-3350-C18-BA1 Cyclone 18-cylinder radials. L.649/749 – four 2500hp (1864kW) Wright R-3350-C18-BD Cyclones; three bladed propellers.

Performance: L.049 – max cruise 272kt (504km/h); service ceiling 25,300ft (7710m); max payload range 1990nm (3686km); max range 3472nm (6430km). L.749A – cruising speed 259kt (480km/h); max payload range 2260nm (4185km); max range 4210nm (7798km).

Weights: L.049 – empty 22,408kg (49,400lb); max takeoff 39,123kg (86,250lb). L.649 – empty 24,948kg (55,000lb); max takeoff 42,638kg (94,000lb). L.749A – empty 27,280kg (60,140lb); max takeoff 48,535kg (107,000lb).

Dimensions: Wing span 37.49m (123ft 0in); length 29.03m (95ft 3in) or 29.67m (97ft 4in) with radar nose; height 7.21m (23ft 8in); wing area 153.3m² (1650sq ft),

Accommodation: L.049 – typically 43-48 passengers, maximum 60. L.649/749 – typically 48-64 passengers, maximum 81.

Production: 856 Constellations, Super Constellations and Starliners of all models including 233 L.049-749s comprising 88 C-69/L.049, 14 L.649, 60 L.749, 59 L.749A, 10 C-121A/B and 2 PO-1W.

History: Design work on the Lockheed Model 049 Constellation pressurised large transport began in 1939 to meet a TWA requirement.

TWA ordered an initial nine in early 1940 with Pan American, KLM and others soon adding to the tally. The war intervened, however, and the Constellation was taken over by the USAAF. The first aircraft flew on 9 January 1943 and as the C-69, 22 were built for the USAAF (first delivery July 1943) of which only 15 were taken on charge. Orders for more than 200 were cancelled on VJ Day.

The remaining seven C-69/L.049s were delivered to TWA, Pan American and BOAC after the cessation of hostilities, the distinctively styled airliner's commercial career finally getting under way in February 1946 on Pan Am's New York-Bermuda route. TWA began USA-Europe (Paris) services in the same month, while BOAC inaugurated a London-New York service in July 1946.

The L.049s were followed by the first true postwar versions: the L.649 (14 for Eastern Air Lines, first flight 19 October 1946) with more powerful engines, numerous systems and equipment modifications and increased weights which allowed more passengers to be carried; the L.749 of 1947 with the more powerful engines and increased fuel capacity; and L.749A (1949) with strengthened undercarriage and further increased maximum weight.

Pan Am inaugurated the world's first around the world service in June 1947 with the L.749. Other airlines which purchased this model and the 749A included KLM, TWA, Qantas, Air France, Air India, South African Airways and Eastern Air Lines.

Postwar military versions of the Constellation were the C-121A (9 delivered from December 1948) and C-121B VIP transport (1) for the USAF and two PO-1W early warning aircraft for the US Navy. The last L.749A was delivered to Air France in September 1951.

Photo: L.049 Constellation. (Lockheed)

Lockheed L.1049 Super Constellation

Country of origin: USA.

Powerplants: L.1049 – four 2500hp (1864kW) Wright R-3350-C18-BD1 or 2700hp (2013kW) R-3350-C18-CA1 Cyclone 18-cylinder radials. L.1049C-H – four 3250hp (2423kW) Wright R-3350-TC18-DA1 Turbo Compound 18-cylinder radials; three bladed propellers.

Performance: L.1049G – max speed 321kt (595km/h); max cruise 308kt (571km/h); normal cruise 270kt (500km/h); service ceiling 22,800ft (6950m); max payload range 3620nm (6704km); max range 4184nm (7750km).

Weights: L.1049C – empty 31,790kg (70,083lb); max takeoff 60,329kg (133,000lb). L.1049G – empty 33,120kg (73,016lb); max takeoff 62,370kg (137,500lb).

Dimensions: Wing span 37.49m (123ft 0in) or 37.62m (123ft 5in) with tip tanks; length 34.62m (113ft 7in) or 35.41m (116ft 2in) with radar nose; height 7.54m (24ft 9in); wing area 153.3m² (1650sq ft).

Accommodation: 69-95 passengers.

Production: 856 Constellations, Super Constellations and Starliners of all models including 265 commercial Supers comprising 24 L.1049, 48 L.1049C, 4 L.1049D, 28 L.1049E, 102 L.1049G and 59 L.1049H; also 320 military versions.

History: The need for greater seating capacity to reduce seat-mile operating costs resulted in Lockheed developing a stretched Constellation in 1949. As the L.1049 Super Constellation, this featured a 5.59m (18ft 4in) longer fuselage allowing up to 95 passengers to be carried, larger fins, redesigned windscreen, improved pressurisation system, rectangular rather than circular cabin windows, increased fuel and weights and more powerful R-3350 engines.

The first L.1049 was converted from the original L.049/C-69 prototype – no mean feat given the aircraft's curved and complex fuselage design – and first flew in its new form on 13 October 1950. Only two airlines – TWA and Eastern – ordered the original Super Constellation for use mainly on domestic routes. Eastern inaugurated services (between New York and Miami) in December 1951.

The company designation L.1049B was applied to the many military versions built for the USAF and US Navy, while the L.1049C was the first to have the more powerful Wright Turbo Compound engines installed. These complex and temperamental powerplants (three engined journeys were common) utilised power recovery turbines fed by the exhaust, feeding it back through the engine to increase power.

The first L.1049C flew in February 1953 and was put into service by KLM on its Amsterdam-New York route five months later. Subsequent versions with Turbo Compounds were the L.1049D convertible passenger/freighter with cargo doors (four built for Seaboard & Western in 1954); L.1049E (a C with higher weights); and the major production L.1049G with wing tip tanks and increased weights. First flown on 17 December 1954, this was ordered by 16 major international airlines, the first going to Northwest in January 1955. The L.1049H was a passenger/freight version of the G. The last Super Constellation (an H) was delivered to Flying Tiger in October 1958.

Photo: L.1049G Super Constellation. (Lockheed)

Lockheed L.1649A Starliner

Country of origin: USA.

Powerplants: Four 3400hp (2535kW) Wright R-3350-TC18-EA2 Turbo Compound 18-cylinder radials; three bladed propellers.

Performance: Max speed 328kt (607km/h); max cruise 297kt (550km/h); initial climb 1080ft (329m)/min; service ceiling 23,700ft (7223m); max payload range 4293nm (7950km); max range 5983nm (11,080km).

Weights: Empty 38,675kg (85,262lb); max takeoff 70,762kg (156,000lb).

Dimensions: Wing span 45.72m (150ft 0in); length 35.41m (116ft 2in); height 7.14m (23ft 5in); wing area 171.9m^2 (1850sq ft).

Accommodation: 71 passengers in two classes or 92 in single class.

Production: 856 Constellations, Super Constellations and Starliners of all models including 43 Starliners.

History: The ultimate development of the basic Constellation design, the L.1649A Starliner was built in response to the ever increasing rivalry between Lockheed and Douglas with their piston engined airliners, in particular the final version of the DC-7, the long range DC-7C 'Seven Seas' which had been ordered by a dozen airlines for international routes.

Development of the Starliner began in May 1955 and the aircraft was fundamentally the Super Constellation's fuselage, tail unit and powerplants with an entirely new wing of considerably greater span and area and higher aspect ratio. The new wing allowed a fuel capacity that was nearly double the L.1049G's and also permitted moving the engines further outboard to reduce cabin noise. Additional soundproofing and synchophasing of the propellers also contributed to a much improved cabin environment.

More powerful Turbo Compound engines were installed and higher weights permitted, the result being an aircraft with greater range than the DC-7C. Unfortunately, the Starliner's relatively late start meant it entered service nearly a year behind its rival and was built only in modest numbers. By then, the airlines were starting to order the new jets in numbers.

The prototype was first flown 10 October 1956 and the Starliner entered service with TWA in May 1957 on the prestigious 'Blue Riband' North Atlantic route. Major rival Pan American had introduced the DC-7C on that route in June 1956.

TWA received most of the Starliner production run, taking delivery of 29. The only other customers were Air France (9) and Lufthansa (4). The prototype was retained by Lockheed, four ordered by Alitalia were cancelled and transferred to TWA and Brazil's Varig cancelled its order for three in favour of additional Super Constellations. The last Starliner was handed over to Air France in February 1958.

Second hand Starliners were subsequently flown by operators such as Aero Condor Colombia, the Flying Ambassadors Travel Club, International Travel Club, Holiday Wings, World Airways, Trans Atlantica Argentina, Air Afrique, Trek Airways, Condor Flugdienst, and Luxair. Most had been retired by the late 1960s but a couple survived until the early 1980s.

Photo: L.1649 Starliner. (Lockheed)

Lockheed L.188 Electra

Country of origin: USA.

Powerplants: Four 3750shp (2796kW) Allison 501-D13 or 4050shp (3020kW) 501-D15 turboprops; four bladed propellers.

Performance: L.188A – max cruise 352kt (652km/h); initial climb 1670ft (509m)/min; service ceiling 27,000ft (8230m); max payload range 1912nm (3540km); range with 8165kg (18,000lb) payload 2407nm (4458km). L.188C – range with 9980kg (22,000lb) payload 2172nm (4024km); max range 3000nm (5557km).

Weights: Operating empty 27,896kg (61,500lb); max takeoff 51,257kg (113,000lb) or 52,617kg (116,000lb).

Dimensions: Wing span 30.17m (99ft 0in); length 31.86m (104ft 6¹/₂in); height 10.01m (32ft 10in); wing area 120.8m^2 (1300sq ft).

Accommodation: L.188A/C – typically 65-81 passengers, maximum 98 in high density layout.

Production: 115 L.188A and 55 L.188C, total 170.

History: The only 'large' US designed turboprop airliner to achieve production (the Fairchild F-27 was licence built and the Convair 580/600 models were conversions), the Electra was developed to meet a 1954 American Airlines requirement for a short-medium range 75-100 seat domestic airliner.

The programme got off to a good start with American ordering 35 in 1955, quickly followed by Eastern Air Lines with 40. By the time the prototype first flew on 6 December 1957 the order book was a healthy 144 aircraft from several operators including export orders from KLM, Cathay Pacific, Ansett and Trans-Australia Airlines. Deliveries of the initial L.188A began to American in December 1958 but Eastern had the honour of inaugurating services (due to a pilots' strike at American) on its New-York Miami route in January 1959.

The promising early career of the Electra was thwarted by several fatal crashes in 1959-60, two of which involved the aircraft breaking up in flight. Speed restrictions were imposed and a painstaking investigation revealed a design defect in the engine mountings which allowed a potentially disastrous engine/propeller oscillation (called 'whirl mode') to develop, resulting in the wing eventually shaking itself to pieces.

A major (and hugely expensive) modification programme followed. This solved the problem and the Electra went on to give many years of safe and reliable service, but the delays in combination with the arrival of jets conspired to keep sales down to only a few more than had originally been ordered.

The longer range 'overwater' L.188C with additional fuel entered service later in 1959, customers including Northwest, KLM, Qantas and TEAL (Air New Zealand). The last Electra built was an L.188C delivered to Garuda Indonesia in January 1961. Lockheed introduced a freighter conversion of the Electra with large cargo door, strengthened floor and 11,800kg (26,000lb) payload in 1967 as the L.188AF or CF, 41 conversions being performed. Many remain in service.

The Electra formed the basis of the P-3 Orion maritime patrol aircraft, the aerodynamic prototype (converted from an L.188) first flying in August 1958.

Photo: L.188A Electra.

Lockheed L-100 Hercules

Country of origin: USA.

Powerplants: L-100 – four 4050shp (3020kW) Allison 501-D22 turboprops. L-100-20/30 – four 4508shp (3362kW) Allison 501-D22A turboprops; four bladed propellers.

Performance: L-100-20 – max cruise 315kt (583km/h); economical cruise 300kt (557km/h); initial climb 1900ft (579m)/min; max payload range 2100nm (3890km); max range (zero payload) 4250nm (7872km). L-100-30 – max payload range 1363nm (2525km).

Weights: L-100-20 – operating empty – 32,935kg (72,607lb); max takeoff 70,308kg (155,000lb). L-100-30 – operating empty 35,236kg (77,680lb); max takeoff 70,308kg (155,000lb).

Dimensions: L-100 – wing span 40.41m (132ft 7in); length 29.79m (97ft 9in); height 11.66m (38ft 3in); wing area 162.1m^2 (1745sq ft). L-100-20 – length 32.33m (106ft 1in). L-100-30 – length 34.37m (112ft 9in).

Capacity: L-100-20 – max payload 21,497kg (47,393lb). L-100-30 – max payload 23,183kg (51,110lb); hold volume 171.5m^3 (6057cu ft).

Production: Over 2200 Hercules of all models built by 1999 including 22 L-100, 27 L-100-20 and 66 L-100-30.

History: The world's most successful and prolific postwar military transport, the Hercules has been delivered to over 60 nations. The prototype YC-130 first flew on 23 August 1954 and deliveries of the initial production C-130A began in late 1956. The many subsequent variants are based around four major versions, the C-130B (1959), C-130E (1962), C-130H (1975) and new generation C-130J (first flight April 1996, deliveries from 1999 after substantial delays) with new engines, propellers and extensive systems upgrades.

Lockheed developed a civil version based on the C-130E as the Model 382B (marketing name L-100), the first converted prototype flying on 21 April 1964. Civil certification was awarded in February 1965 and early deliveries were made to Alaska Airlines, Continental Air Services and Zambia Air Cargoes.

The problem of 'cubing out' – volumetric capacity being reached before weight limits – resulted in the stretched by 2.54m (8ft 3in) Model 382E/L-100-20 with more powerful engines. Deliveries began in late 1968 to Interior Airways and Southern Air Transport.

The further stretched Model 382G/L-100-30 first flew in August 1970, developed for Saturn Airways which had a contract to carry a 'ship set' of three Rolls-Royce RB211 engines from England to California for the Lockheed L-1011 TriStar airliner. This fuselage length subsequently became a standard option for military versions of the Hercules. A commercial version of the C-130J is also offered as the L-100J.

The -30 is the most numerous of the civil Hercules although deliveries have been sporadic since the early 1980s and the most recent examples delivered in 1992. Some have been sold to air forces despite their civil designations. Indonesia's Pelita Air Services received six L-100-30s in 1979-82, three of which were used for a government transmigration programme under which 12,000 families per month were moved from overpopulated Java and Bali to other areas. Each Hercules could carry 128 passengers in this role.

Photo: Passenger carrying L-100-30 Hercules.

Lockheed L-1011-1/100/200 TriStar

Country of origin: USA.

Powerplants: L-1011-1/100 – three 42,000lb (186.8kN) Rolls-Royce RB211-22B turbofans; 43,500lb (193.5kN) RB211-22Fs optional on -100. L-1011-200 – three 48,000lb (213.5kN) RB211-524 turbofans.

Performance: L-1011-1 – max cruise 525kt (972km/h); economical cruise 463kt (857km/h); range 3110nm (5760km). L-1011-100 – range 3820nm (7075km). L-1011-200 – range 3864nm (7157km). L-1011-250 – range 4533nm (8396km).

Weights: L-1011-1 – operating empty 109,045kg (240,400lb); max takeoff 195,048kg (430,000lb). L-1011-100/200 – max takeoff 211,377kg (466,000lb). L-1011-250 – max takeoff 224,985kg (496,000lb).

Dimensions: Wing span 47.34m (155ft 4in); length 54.17m (177ft 8¹/₂in); height 16.86m (55ft 4in); wing area 321.1m^2 (3456sq ft).

Accommodation: Typically 256 passengers in two classes six and nine abreast, maximum 400 passengers ten abreast in high density arrangement.

Production: 250 TriStars of all models including 163 L-1011-1s, 13 L-1011-100s and 24 L-1011-200s.

History: Developed to meet the same 1966 American Airlines requirement which resulted in the McDonnell Douglas DC-10, the Lockheed L-1011 (Model 385) TriStar widebody was originally intended as a twin but emerged as a trijet in order meet airfield requirements.

The chosen – and exclusive – powerplant, the Rolls-Royce RB211, came very close to bringing Lockheed down in February 1971 when the engine manufacturer went bankrupt due to the development costs of the RB211. The British Government rescued Rolls-Royce by nationalising it and the TriStar programme went ahead.

American Airlines chose the DC-10 but the TriStar was launched by orders from TWA and Eastern Air Lines in March 1968. The first aircraft flew on 16 November 1970 – just three months before Rolls-Royce's bankruptcy – and after those problems had been sorted and certification awarded, Eastern began revenue services with the aircraft in April 1972.

The initial domestic version was designated L-1011-1 and made up the bulk of standard 'long fuselage' TriStar production. This was followed by two longer range models: L-1011-100 with increased weights and fuel capacity and the L-1011-200 which combined those features with more powerful engines. Initial deliveries of both models were to Saudia in June 1975 (100) and May 1977 (200). The longer range, short fuselage TriStar 500 is described in the next entry.

Other versions were conversions of the L-1011-1: the L-1011-250 (from 1986 mainly for Delta Air Lines) with the more powerful RB211-524B4 engines, increased maximum takeoff weight and greater fuel capacity of the L-1011-500; the L-1011-50 with increased maximum weight; and the L-1011-150 with longer range.

Sales of the TriStar failed to match expectations as it and the DC-10 fought over a relatively limited market. It nevertheless earned a good reputation in the following years and by 1999 more than 180 of all models remained in service, mostly with charter airlines.

Photo: L-1011-100 TriStar. (Scott Allen)

Lockheed L-1011-500 TriStar

Martin 130

Country of origin: USA.

Powerplants: Three 50,000lb (222.4kN) Rolls-Royce RB211-524B turbofans.

Performance: Max cruise 518kt (959km/h); economical cruise 483kt (895km/h); initial climb 2820ft (860m)/min; service ceiling 43,000ft (13,105m); range with max passenger load 5297nm (9812km); max fuel range 6100nm (11,300km).

Weights: Operating empty 111,359kg (245,500lb); max takeoff 231,336kg (510,000lb).

Dimensions: Wing span 50.09m (164ft 4in); length 50.05m (164ft 2½in); height 16.86m (55ft 4in); wing area 329.0m² (3541sq ft).

Accommodation: Typically 246 passengers in two classes six and nine abreast, maximum 330 passengers ten abreast in high density layout.

Production: 250 TriStars of all models including 50 L-1011-500s.

History: Launched in August 1976, the L-1011-500 was developed as a derivative of the -200 TriStar in order to achieve the longer ranges demanded by some airlines. Key changes were a 4.11m (13ft 6in) shorter fuselage which reduced maximum seating capacity from 400 to 330 passengers, more powerful RB211-524B turbofans, increased fuel capacity and greater maximum takeoff weight.

Also included in the specification were improved wing to fuselage and fuselage to rear intake fairings, automatic braking, an advanced flight management system and replacement of the earlier TriStars' unusual below deck galleys with conventional main deck units.

A significant feature introduced to all but the first few TriStar 500s was the incorporation of automatic active ailerons to reduce wing bending moments (and saving weight by eliminating the need for a stronger structure in the process), this resulting in the incorporation of longer span wings (for lower drag) and smaller horizontal tail surfaces.

These, the more powerful engines and other features were tested on the original L-1011 prototype which became known as the Advanced TriStar.

The first TriStar 500 (with standard wings) flew on 16 October 1968 and the first with all the new features in November 1979. The interim model had meanwhile entered service with British Airways in May 1979 while Pan American introduced the full specification version to service in early 1980.

Production of the L-1011-500 amounted to 50 aircraft for BA, Pan Am, Delta, BWIA International, LTU, Air Canada, Alia Royal Jordanian, Air Lanka, TAP Air Portugal and the Algerian Government, the latter receiving the last of the line in August 1984, ten months after it had first flown. The L-1011 programme proved expensive for Lockheed (as did its previous airliner, the Electra) and the company has not returned to the civil market since the last TriStar was built.

Six former British Airways L-1011-500s were delivered to the Royal Air Force in the early 1980s and subsequently converted to tanker/transports by Marshall Aerospace with in-flight refuelling capability. Three ex Pan Am -500s were also acquired, these used as troop transports.

Photo: L-1011-500 TriStar. (Julian Green)

Country of origin: USA.

Powerplants: Four 830hp (619kW) Pratt & Whitney R-1830-S1A4G Twin Wasp 14-cylinder radials; three bladed propellers.

Performance: Max speed 156kt (290km/h); cruising speed 136kt (253km/h); range with 2188kg (4824lb) payload 2780nm (5150km); max range 3475nm (6437km).

Weights: Empty 11,164kg (24,611lb); max takeoff 23,587kg (52,000lb).

Dimensions: Wing span 39.62m (130ft 0in); length 27.61m (90ft 7in); height 7.49m (24ft 7in); wing area 201.6m² (2170sq ft).

Accommodation: Up to 48 seated day passengers or 18 berths for night passengers.

Production: 3.

History: The three famed Martin 130 flying boats (class name *China Clipper*) were developed for Pan American for use on its trans-Pacific routes which – for the time – involved very long overwater stage lengths. By 1934 the airline had already established a network of services in South America and the Caribbean and was keen to develop additional routes from the USA across the Atlantic and Pacific Oceans.

Charles Lindbergh conducted survey flights on both routes and recommended a northern route across the Pacific. This proved to be unfeasible because of political considerations, leaving Pan American with no choice but to take its flights across the vast expanses of the Pacific.

Pan Am conducted its own route surveys in 1935 using a Sikorsky S-42 but this had insufficient payload-range performance. Anticipating this, Pan Am had meanwhile issued a specification for a flying boat able to carry four crew and a minimum 136kg (300lb) mail load for 2500 statute miles (4023km) against a 30mph (48km/h) headwind.

Martin responded with the 130, a large four engined, metal flying boat with strut braced monoplane wing. The advanced two step hull design resulted from extensive testing of models and lateral stability was provided by two large sponsons or 'sea wings'.

The first aircraft (*China Clipper*) flew on 30 December 1934 followed by two others – *Hawaii* (later *Hawaiian*) *Clipper* and *Philippine Clipper* during 1935. *China Clipper* inaugurated services from San Francisco to the Philippines in November 1935, the first journey taking just under 60 hours elapsed time. The first air services from the USA to China were flown by the Martin flying boats.

Hawaiian Clipper was lost in 1938 and in 1942 the two survivors were impressed into US Navy service for use on trans-Pacific routes. No military designation was applied. *Philippine Clipper* was lost while in USN service and *China Clipper* returned to Pan Am in 1943 where it was put to work on South Atlantic operations. It too was lost, in a night landing accident at Trinidad in January 1945.

Martin flew the larger M-156 with four 1000hp (746kW) Wright Cyclones and twin fins and rudders in 1937 but the outbreak of war in Europe saw the company concentrating on military orders from France and Britain. The M-156 remained a one-off but went to the Soviet Union where it was operated by Aeroflot as the PS-30.

Photo: Martin 130 *China Clipper*. (Pan Am)

Martin 2-0-2 and 4-0-4

Country of origin: USA.

Powerplants: 2-0-2 – two 2100hp (1566kW) Pratt & Whitney R-2800-CA18 Double Wasp 18-cylinder radials. 2-0-2A/4-0-4 – two 2400hp (1790kW) R-2800-CB16 Double Wasps; three bladed propellers.

Performance: 4-0-4 – max speed 271kt (502km/h); normal cruise 240kt (444km/h); initial climb 1905ft (580m)/min; service ceiling 29,000ft (8840m); range with 40 passengers 938nm (1738km); max range 1738nm (3219km).

Weights: 2-0-2 – empty 11,379kg (25,086lb); max takeoff 18,099kg (39,900lb). 4-0-4 – empty 13,212kg (29,126lb); max takeoff 20,367kg (44,900lb).

Dimensions: 2-0-2 – wing span 28.42m (93ft 3in); length 21.74m (71ft 4in); height 8.66m (28ft 5in); wing area 80.3m^2 (864sq ft). 4-0-4 – length 22.73m (74ft 7in).

Accommodation: 2-0-2 – 36-40 passengers four abreast. 4-0-4 – 40 passengers.

Production: 34 2-0-2, 12 2-0-2A, 1 3-0-3 and 101 4-0-4.

History: The first US twin engined transport aircraft of entirely post-war design, the Martin 2-0-2 was developed for the 'DC-3 replacement' market and as such was a competitor to the Convair CV-240. The two aircraft were similar in their general configurations but the Martin product lacked the cabin pressurisation of its rival.

The prototype first flew on 22 November 1946 (four months before the CV-240), with Northwest inaugurating 2-0-2 services in November 1947, beating American Airlines' Convair by some six months. Orders for 2-0-2s were also placed by LAN Chile, Linea Aeropostal Venezolana and TWA.

The 2-0-2's early success was short lived when the investigation into the loss of a Northwest aircraft over Minnesota in August 1948 revealed structural failure of the wing to be the cause. All were withdrawn from service for modification and the final 12 aircraft (delivered between July and September 1950) were completed as 2-0-2As with the structural upgrades and more powerful R-2800-CB16 engines.

These dramas meant that sales momentum shifted to the Convairs, several customers changing allegiances of which United Airlines was a significant example. Martin had meanwhile developed the similar but pressurised 3-0-3 (first flight 3 July 1947) but abandoned that after a single prototype had been built in favour of the definitive 4-0-4 with modified structure. This was also pressurised and had the 2-0-2A's CB16 engines and a 0.99m (39in) longer fuselage.

The first 4-0-4 was flown on 21 October 1950 and ordered only by TWA (61) and Eastern (40), although these numbers assured a reasonable production run. The 4-0-4 entered service with Eastern in October 1951 and with the structural problems sorted out they proved to be reliable in service.

The last two 4-0-4s were built as RM-1 (later VC-3A) staff transports for the US Coast Guard, delivered in October and November 1952 and subsequently transferred to the US Navy before retirement in 1969. The third from last 4-0-4 was actually the final example to be delivered, to Eastern in February 1953.

Photo: Martin 4-0-4.

McDonnell Douglas DC-9 Srs.10-30

Country of origin: USA.

Powerplants: Srs.10 – two 12,250lb (54.5kN) Pratt & Whitney JT8D-5 turbofans. Srs.20 – two 14,500lb (64.5kN) JT8D-9s or 15,000lb (66.7kN) JT8D-11s. Srs.30 – two JT8D-9s, JT8D-11s, 15,500lb (68.9kN) JT8D-15s or 16,000lb (71.2kN) JT8D-17s.

Performance: 10 – max cruise 488kt (904km/h); max payload range 570nm (1056km). 30 – max cruise 490kt (907km/h); range cruise 443kt (820km/h); initial climb 2900ft (884m)/min; cruising altitude 30,000-35,000ft (9145-10,670m); range with 80 passengers 1670nm (3093km); max range 1980nm (3668km).

Weights: 10 – empty 22,635kg (49,900lb); max takeoff 41,141kg (90,700lb). 20 – empty 23,986kg (52,880lb); max takeoff 44,453kg (98,000lb). 30 – empty 25,941kg (57,190lb); max takeoff 48,989-54,885kg (108,000-121,000lb).

Dimensions: 10 – wing span 27.25m (89ft 5in); length 31.82m (104ft 5in); height 8.38m (27ft 6in); wing area 86.8m^2 (934sq ft). 20 – wing span 28.47m (93ft 5in); wing area 93.0m^2 (1001sq ft). 30 – wing span 28.47m (93ft 5in); length 36.36m (119ft 3^1/$_2$in).

Accommodation: 10/20 – 80-90 passengers five abreast. 30 – 105-115 passengers five abreast.

Production: 976 DC-9s of all models including 137 Srs.10, 10 Srs.20 and 662 Srs.30 (incl 41 C-9A/B).

History: The last airliner designed and built by Douglas Aircraft before the company's 1967 merger with McDonnell, the DC-9 resulted from a Delta Air Lines requirement for a Convair CV-440 replacement on short haul routes. Developed as the Model 2086, the DC-9 was launched in April 1963 when Delta ordered 15. The rival BAC One Eleven first flew four months later, both aircraft sharing a similar configuration with T-tail and rear mounted engines.

The first DC-9 flew on 25 February 1965, by which time the disappointing total of 58 had been ordered, Douglas at that stage showing concern about the aircraft's future. It need not have worried, the aircraft and its MD-80/90/717 derivatives going on to become the most successful Douglas airliner with more than 2400 sold by 1999.

The initial 80-90 seat DC-9 Srs.10 entered service with Delta in December 1965. Douglas had always planned a family of DC-9s with different fuselage lengths and the next to appear was the best selling Srs.30 (first flight August 1966) with a 4.54m (14ft 10^1/$_2$in) fuselage stretch for 105-115 passengers, an extended span wing with full span leading edge slats for improved airfield performance, more powerful engines, increased weights and greater fuel capacity. The designation suffixes -31, -32, -33 etc reflected different powerplant, weight and fuel options.

Eastern Air Lines inaugurated DC-9-30 services in early 1967 and the same model formed the basis of the C-9A/B for the US Air Force and Navy. The Srs.20 combined the original short fuselage with the DC-9-30's engines and wing (10 built for SAS in 1968-69), and the Srs.15 was a longer range version of the -10 with more fuel and higher weights.

Convertible and pure freighter versions were also offered, Continental receiving the first DC-9-10C in March 1966 and Alitalia the first DC-9-30F in May 1968.

Photo: DC-9 Srs.10.

McDonnell Douglas DC-9 Srs.40 and 50

Country of origin: USA.

Powerplants: Srs.40 – two 14,500lb (64.5kN) Pratt & Whitney JT8D-9, 15,500lb (68.9kN) JT8D-15 or 16,000lb (71.2kN) JT8D-17 turbofans. Srs.50 – two JT8D-15s or JT8D-17s.

Performance: 40 – max cruise 489kt (906km/h); range cruise 443kt (820km/h); cruising altitude 30,000-35,000ft (9145-10,670m); initial climb 2850ft (868m)/min; range with 87 passengers 1555nm (2880km); max range 1850nm (3427km). 50 – max cruise 501kt (928km/h); range cruise 443km/h (820km/h); initial climb 2600ft (792m)/min; range with 97 passengers 1795nm (3325km); max range 2185nm (4047km).

Weights: 40 – empty 26,613kg (58,670lb); max takeoff 54,886kg (121,000lb). 50 – empty 28,069kg (61,880lb); max takeoff 54,886kg (121,000lb).

Dimensions: 40 – wing span 28.47m (93ft 5in); length 38.28m (125ft 7in); height 8.53m (28ft 0in); wing area 93.0m² (1001sq ft). 50 – length 40.72m (133ft 7in).

Accommodation: 40 – up to 125 passengers five abreast. 50 – up to 139 passengers.

Production: 976 DC-9s of all models including 71 Srs.40 and 96 Srs.50.

History: Development of the DC-9 continued in the mid 1960s with further stretched versions planned and implemented. The first was the Srs.40, developed specifically to meet the requirements of SAS, which wanted greater seating capacity.

Compared to the Srs.30, the 40 featured a 1.93m (6ft 4in) longer fuselage able to accommodate up to 125 passengers. Engine options were as per the DC-9-30 and the first aircraft was flown on 28 November 1967. Certification was awarded in February 1968 and SAS put the Srs.40 into service the following month. The only other customer for new DC-9-40s was Japan's TOA Domestic Airlines, both airlines operating large fleets. The last was delivered to SAS in March 1979.

In 1973 Swissair became the launch customer for the final and longest version of the aircraft to carry the DC-9 name. The Srs.50's fuselage was stretched a further 2.44m (8ft 0in) allowing up to 139 passengers to be carried. Other significant changes included the first use of improved JT8D-15 and -17 engines which were then also made available for the Srs.30 and 40. These were smokeless and quieter than previous JT8Ds thanks to the incorporation of sound absorption materials developed for the DC-10. They also had redesigned thrust reversers which reduced the possibility of exhaust gas ingestion.

Other improvements incorporated into the Srs.50 included an improved anti skid braking system and a redesigned 'widebody' interior with enclosed overhead baggage racks, sculptured wall panels, acoustically treated ceiling panels and indirect lighting.

The first Srs.50 was flown on 17 December 1974 and deliveries to Swissair began in August 1975. Other customers included Austrian, Allegheny, Hawaiian, Finnair, North Central, Linea Aeropostal Venezolana, Eastern and BWIA. The last DC-9-50 was delivered to North Central in June 1979 but the final aircraft to carry the name 'DC-9' (following models were MD-80s) was a DC-9-32 first flown in July 1979 and delivered to Texas International Airlines the next month.

Photo: DC-9 Srs.41. (Gerard Frawley)

McDonnell Douglas MD-80

Country of origin: USA.

Powerplants: MD-81 – two 18,500lb (82.3kN) Pratt & Whitney JT8D-209 turbofans. MD-82/88 – two 20,000lb (89.04kN) JT8D-217A/C. MD-83 – two 21,000lb (93.4kN) JT8D-219.

Performance: All models – max cruise 499kt (924km/h); range cruise 440kt (815km/h). MD-81 – range with 155 passengers 1563nm (2895km). MD-82/88 – range with 155 passengers 2049nm (3795km). MD-83 – range with 155 passengers 2500nm (4630km).

Weights: MD-81 – operating empty 35,329kg (77,886lb); max takeoff 63,504kg (140,000lb). MD-82/88 – max takeoff 67,813kg (149,500lb). MD-83 – max takeoff 72,576kg (160,000lb).

Dimensions: Wing span 32.87m (107ft 10in); length 45.06m (147ft 10in); height 9.02m (29ft 7in); wing area 112.3m² (1209sq ft).

Accommodation: Typically 144 passengers in two classes, maximum 172 five abreast.

Production: 1191 MD-80s of all versions (incl MD-87) ordered by May 1999 of which 1169 delivered. MD-81 – 132 ordered and all delivered; MD-82 – 562 ordered and all delivered; MD-83 – 264 ordered and 242 delivered; MD-88 – 158 ordered and all delivered by May 1999.

History: The MD-80 series is a stretched and upgraded development of the DC-9. Its origins lie in 1975 testing when a standard DC-9 was fitted with improved, more efficient, higher bypass ratio JT8D-200 series turbofans. McDonnell Douglas originally proposed fitting the new engines (which meet Stage 3 noise limits) to a development designated the DC-9-55 with two JT8D-209s and a 3.86m (12ft 8in) longer fuselage than the DC-9-50.

Instead, the DC-9 Super 80 (or DC-9-80) was developed, combining the JT8D-200 with a further stretched fuselage, increased span wing and other improvements. Launched in October 1977, the Super 80 first flew on 18 October 1979. Certification for the initial Super 80 model, the -81, was awarded in August 1980 and Swissair inaugurated services two months later.

McDonnell Douglas renamed the DC-9-80 the MD-80 in 1983, the designation a generic one for the series. Individual MD-80 variants are the initial MD-81; the MD-82 with more powerful JT8D-217 engines and increased maximum weight (first delivery to Republic Airlines in August 1981); the extended range MD-83 with extra fuel, higher weights and more efficient JT8D-219s (Alaska Airlines, May 1986); and the MD-88 (Delta, December 1987), basically an MD-82 with an EFIS flight deck, redesigned cabin and other improvements. The shorter fuselage MD-87 is described separately.

Initial sales of the Super 80 were slow until American Airlines placed an initial order for 67 MD-82s (with options on 100) in early 1984, kickstarting what went on to become a highly successful programme. American eventually acquired a fleet of 260 MD-80s. The 1000th MD-80 was delivered in March 1992.

Following the late 1997 takeover of McDonnell Douglas by Boeing, the future of the Douglas airliners was reviewed, Boeing announcing in December 1997 its decision to drop the MD-80 and MD-90 once current orders were filled. An April 1998 TWA order for 24 MD-83s ensured the MD-80 would remain in production until January 2000.

Photo: McDonnell Douglas MD-82. (MDC)

McDonnell Douglas MD-87

Country of origin: USA.

Powerplants: Two 20,000lb (89.0kN) Pratt & Whitney JT8D-217C turbofans.

Performance: Max cruise 500kt (926km/h); long range cruise 438kt (811km/h); range with 130 passengers 2371nm (4392km) standard or 2833nm (5248km) optional; max range 3650nm (6760km).

Weights: Operating empty 33,237-33,965kg (73,274-74,879lb); max takeoff 63,504kg (140,000lb) standard or 67,813kg (149,500lb) optional.

Dimensions: Wing span 32.87m (107ft 10in); length 39.75m (130ft 5in); height 9.30m (30ft 6in); wing area 112.3m² (1209sq ft).

Accommodation: Typically 117 passengers in two classes, maximum 139 passengers five abreast.

Production: 1191 MD-80s of all models ordered by March 1999 of which 1169 delivered. MD-87 – 75 ordered and all delivered.

History: The McDonnell Douglas MD-87 is a shortened, smaller capacity version of the successful MD-80 series, featuring a fuselage 'destretched' by 5.31m (17ft 5in). The MD-87 combines the advanced features introduced on the MD-80 (most notably the Pratt & Whitney JT8D-200 engines) into a fuselage length slightly longer than that of the best selling DC-9 variant, the Series 30.

The MD-87 was the first of the MD-80 series to introduce an EFIS 'glass' cockpit with two flight management systems and an optional Sundstrand Head Up Display (HUD); Pratt & Whitney JT8D-217C turbofans (which are approximately 2 per cent more efficient than the -217A); the cruise performance package improvements introduced on late production MD-80s (including an extended low drag tail cone, fillet fairing between the engine pylons and the fuselage and low drag flap hinge fairings); and increased height fin to compensate for the loss of moment arm due to the shorter fuselage.

The MD-87 was optionally available with extra front and rear cargo compartment auxiliary fuel tanks to extend range, and other engines in the JT8D-200 series. In other respects it is similar to other members of the MD-80 family.

McDonnell Douglas launched development of the MD-87 in January 1985, following the placing of initial orders by Finnair and Austrian Airlines the previous month. The prototype first flew on 4 December 1986, US FAA certification was awarded in October 1987 and Austrian and Finnair received their first aircraft in November 1987.

MD-87 sales have been modest by DC-9/MD-80 standards and mainly to traditional Douglas customers. Notable operators include Iberia (24), SAS (18) and Japan Air System (8). Other smaller operators include Aero Lloyd, Aeromexico, Great American, Austrian and Reno Air (now part of American Airlines). A corporate version was also offered.

By the time Boeing had taken over McDonnell Douglas in late 1997 all MD-87 orders had been filled and the type has not been actively marketed since then.

Photo: McDonnell Douglas MD-87. (Gerard Frawley)

McDonnell Douglas MD-90

Country of origin: USA.

Powerplants: MD-90-30 – Two 25,000lb (111.2kN) International Aero Engines V2525-D5 turbofans. MD-90-55 – Two 28,000lb (124.5kN) V2528-D5s.

Performance: MD-90-30 – typical cruising speed 437kt (809km/h); range with 152 passengers 2085nm (3862km). 30ER – range with 152 passengers 2172nm (4023km) standard or 2389nm (4425km) optional. MD-90-50 – range with 152 passengers 3022nm (5598km). MD-90-55 – range with 187 passengers 2700nm (5000km).

Weights: MD-90-30 – operating empty 39,917kg (88,000lb); max takeoff 70,762kg (156,000lb). MD-90-50/55 – operating empty 41,686kg (91,900lb); max takeoff 78,246kg (172,500lb).

Dimensions: Wing span 32.87m (107ft 10in); length 46.51m (152ft 7in); height 9.33m (30ft 7in); wing area 112.3m² (1209sq ft).

Accommodation: MD-90-30/50 – typically 152 passengers in two classes, maximum 172 in single class five abreast. MD-90-55 – maximum 187 passengers five abreast.

Production: 134 MD-90s of all models ordered by March 1999 of which 99 delivered. MD-90 – 114 ordered and 99 delivered; MD-90T – 20 ordered by March 1999.

History: The MD-90 is the largest member of the Douglas/McDonnell Douglas/Boeing DC-9/MD-80/MD-90/717 family, and is a stretched, higher technology and IAE V2500 powered development of the MD-80. Combined sales of all these aircraft exceeded 2400 by March 1999, second only to the Boeing 737.

The MD-90 programme was launched in November 1988, first flight occurred on 22 February 1993, and certification was awarded in November 1994. Launch customer Delta Airlines (which ordered 31) inaugurated MD-90 services on its Dallas/Fort Worth-Newark route in April 1995. Other major customers include Saudi Arabian Airlines and Japan Air System.

The most important of the changes introduced on the MD-90 are the two V2500 turbofans with greater efficiency than the MD-80's JT8D-200s and the 1.37m (4ft 6in) fuselage stretch, allowing an extra two rows of seating. Other changes include an EFIS glass cockpit based on that in the MD-88, the MD-87's taller tailfin, digital environmental control system, improved brakes, modified flight controls and improved cabin interior.

The basic MD-90 model is designated the MD-90-30 which was also offered in MD-90-30ER extended range form with additional fuel. The MD-90-50 has increased maximum weight and extra fuel, and the MD-90-55 high capacity variant is capable of seating 187 passengers in a single class thanks to the addition of two doors in the forward fuselage to meet emergency evacuation requirements although neither were built.

An agreement signed in November 1994 covers the production of 20 MD-90T Trunkliners in China with Shanghai Aviation Industrial Corporation (SAIC) as the prime contractor. The MD-90T is similar to the MD-90-30 but with double bogey main landing gear. Following Boeing's late 1997 takeover of McDonnell Douglas, it was announced that MD-90 production would cease once existing orders were filled.

Photo: McDonnell Douglas MD-90-30. (MDC)

McDonnell Douglas DC-10

Country of origin: USA.

Powerplants: Srs.10 – three 40,000lb (177.9kN) General Electric CF6-6D or 41,000lb (182.4kN) CF6-6D1 turbofans. Srs.30 – three 49,000lb (217.9kN) CF6-50As, 51,000lb (226.8kN) CF6-50Cs, 52,500lb (233.5kN) CF6-50C1/2s or 54,000lb (240.2kN) CF6-50C2Bs. Srs.40 – three 49,400lb (219.7kN) Pratt & Whitney JT9D-20 or 53,000lb (235.7kN) JT9D-59A turbofans.

Performance: Srs.10 – max cruise 490kt (907km/h); normal cruise 470kt (870km/h). Srs.30 – max payload range 4000nm (7410km); max range (zero payload) 6504nm (12,047km). Srs.30ER – max payload range 5730nm (10,614km). Srs.40 – max payload range 3500nm-4050nm (6483-7502km).

Weights: Srs.10 – max takeoff 185,976kg (410,000lb) or 206,388kg (455,000lb). Srs.30 – empty 121,200kg (267,197lb); max takeoff 259,460-263,088kg (572,000-580,000lb). Srs.40 – max takeoff 251,748-259,459kg (555,000-572,000lb).

Dimensions: Wing span 50.40m (165ft 4¹/₂in); length 55.50m (182ft 1in); height 17.70m (58ft 1in); wing area 367.7m² (3958sq ft).

Accommodation: Typically 255-270 passengers in two or three classes, maximum 380 in single class nine abreast. DC-10-30F – max payload 80,283kg (176,993lb).

Production: 386 civil models plus 60 KC-10A tankers.

History: Designed to meet the same American Airlines requirement which also spawned the Lockheed TriStar, the DC-10 was, like its rival, originally intended as a twinjet but airfield performance requirements necessitated three engines. The DC-10 was launched in February 1968 with orders from American and United and first flight took place on 29 August 1970.

The first transcontinental range DC-10 Srs.10s entered service with American in August 1971 on the Los Angeles-Chicago route. Subsequent versions were the Srs.15 for Aeromexico with improved airfield performance (combining the Srs.10's weights with more powerful CF6-50C2 engines, first flight January 1981); the intercontinental Srs.30 with more powerful engines, increased weight and fuel capacity options and a third main undercarriage unit under the centre fuselage (first flight June 1972, initial deliveries to KLM and Swissair); and Srs.40 (originally named Srs.20), similar but powered by JT9D engines (first flight February 1972, first delivery to Northwest). The Srs.30 was the most produced and was also built in -30ER extended range, -30CF convertible freighter and -30F pure freighter versions.

Sixty KC-10A Extender tanker/transports were built for the USAF between 1980 and 1988, while the last of the line – a DC-10-30 – was flown in December 1988 and subsequently delivered to Nigeria Airways.

Several accidents damaged the DC-10's reputation in the 1970s, but the causes were found and overcome, the aircraft going on to operate reliably and safely with a large number of airlines.

The Boeing MD-10 conversion for Federal Express involves fitting DC-10s (both current freighters and 'new' ex airliner freighter conversions) with an advanced two crew EFIS flight deck. The MD-10 conversion is also on offer to other DC-10 freighter operators.

Photo: McDonnell Douglas DC-10 Srs.30. (MDC)

McDonnell Douglas MD-11

Country of origin: USA.

Powerplants: Three 60,000lb (266.9kN) Pratt & Whitney PW4460, 62,000lb (275.8kN) PW4462 or 61,500lb (273.6kN) General Electric CF6-80C2D1F turbofans.

Performance: MD-11 – max cruise 511kt (946km/h); economical cruise 473kt (876km/h); range with 298 passengers 6835nm (12,660km). MD-11ER – range with 298 passengers 7245nm (13,420km). MD-11F – max payload range 3948nm (7313km). MD-11 Combi – range with 183 passengers and six freight pallets 5736nm (10,625km).

Weights: Operating empty 130,167-131,770kg (286,965-290,498lb); max takeoff 273,319kg (602,555lb) standard or 285,995kg (630,500lb) optional.

Dimensions: Wing span 51.77m (169ft 10in); length 61.37m (201ft 4in); height 17.60m (57ft 9in); wing area 338.9m² (3648sq ft).

Accommodation: MD-11 – typically 285-298 passengers in three classes or 323 in two classes; maximum 410 in single class nine abreast. MD-11F – max payload 90.8 tonnes (200,150lb).

Production: 200 of all models ordered by March 1999 and 186 delivered. MD-11 – 136 ordered and all delivered; MD-11C – 5 ordered and all delivered; MD-11F – 59 ordered and 45 delivered by March 1999.

History: The MD-11 is a modernised, stretched, re-engined and longer range development of the DC-10 trijet. Launched in December 1986 after 12 airlines had placed firm orders for 52 aircraft, the MD-11 was the result of a several years' investigation into various advanced DC-10 derivatives. The first of five development aircraft flew on 10 January 1990, certification was awarded in November 1990 and Finnair inaugurated services the following month.

Compared to the DC-10, the MD-11 features a 5.71m (18ft 9in) fuselage stretch, increased span wing with winglets, modified tail, an advanced two crew six screen EFIS flight deck, restyled main cabin interior, increased fuel capacity and weights and new engine options. Variants offered include the longer range MD-11ER (first delivery to World Airways in March 1996); MD-11F freighter (FedEx, September 1991); MD-11 Combi (Alitalia, November 1991); and MD-11CF convertible passenger/freighter (Martinair, December 1994).

The MD-11 failed to meet its performance guarantees and was subject to an extensive Performance Improvement Programme (PIP) to reduce weight and drag and increase range. Conducted in several phases, the programme involved numerous aerodynamic modifications.

Various developments aimed at increasing seating through stretches and underfloor panorama deck seating were examined and in 1996 MDC looked closely at the MD-XX, basically a rewinged MD-11 with two fuselage length choices. None left the drawing board.

Always a relatively slow seller, the MD-11 became part of the Boeing line-up following its 1997 takeover of McDonnell Douglas. In November of that year, Boeing surprised many observers by announcing the MD-11 would be retained in production, primarily as a freighter. That decision was reversed in June 1998, Boeing saying that due to a lack of market demand the last MD-11 would be delivered in February 2000.

Photo: McDonnell Douglas MD-11. (MDC)

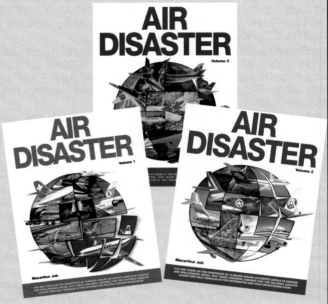

Messerschmitt M.20

Country of origin: Germany.

Powerplant: M.20a/b – one 500hp (373kW) BMW VIa V12. M.20b2 – one 640hp (477kW) BMW VIu; two bladed propeller.

Performance: M.20b – max speed 95kt (175km/h); range 540nm (1000km).

Weights: M.20b – empty 2800kg (6173lb); max takeoff 5600kg (12,345lb).

Dimensions: Wing span 25.50m (83ft 8in); length 15.90m (52ft 2in); height 4.19m (13ft 9in); wing area 65.0m² (700sq ft).

Accommodation: Two crew and 10 passengers two abreast or 1500kg (3307lb) payload.

Production: 2 M.20a and 12 M.20b, total 14.

History: The Messerschmitt M.20 single engined, 10 passenger airliner was fundamentally a scaled up development of the eight passenger M.18d, itself the result of an evolutionary process which began in 1925 with the five seat M.18. The small number built served with Luft Hansa throughout the 1930s on both passenger and freight carrying duties.

The wooden M.18 was powered by an 80hp (60kW) Siemens and Halske Sh 11 radial and was a one-off. The mixed metal and wood M.18a was put into production and the series ended with the M.18d with various modifications including an improved main undercarriage with vertical shock absorbers running up into the wing and a variety of powerplants ranging from the 150hp (112kW) Walter Mars to the 325hp (242kW) Wright Whirlwind.

The M.20 closely resembled the M.18d but differed in being of mainly metal construction, having the considerably more powerful BMW VI V12 engine installed and being fitted with a much larger wing of some 9.90m (32ft 6in) greater span. That and the new engine allowed a substantial increase in maximum takeoff weight.

The prototype M.20 first flew on 26 February 1928 but crashed during that maiden flight. Messerschmitt was suffering cashflow problems at the time with the result that the second aircraft didn't fly until July 1928.

This and the first aircraft were both designated M.20a but the remaining 12 for Luft Hansa were dubbed M.20b with a deeper fuselage, strut braced tailplane, reshaped fin and rudder and raked back (rather than forward) windscreen.

Luft Hansa introduced the M.20 to service in 1929, initially operating from Stuttgart to Barcelona via Geneva and Marseilles, and from Basle to Amsterdam via Mannheim, Frankfurt, Cologne and Essen. The M.20 was also used as a freighter and mailplane by Luft Hansa and some aircraft continued flying on scheduled services until as late as 1937.

After that, a few remained in service until the war on the seasonal routes carrying holidaymakers from the major cities to Germany's coastal resorts. A couple of M.20s continued flying with Luft Hansa until late 1942.

Some of the M.20b models were re-engined with 640hp (477kW) BMW VIu engines in 1932 and redesignated M.20b2. Messerschmitt also produced the M.24 high speed passenger and M.28 mail carriers up until 1931.

Photo: Messerschmitt M.20b.

Miles Aerovan

Country of origin: United Kingdom.

Powerplants: Mks.1-4 – two 155hp (116kW) Blackburn Cirrus Major III four cylinder inverted inlines; two bladed propellers.

Performance: Mk.4 – max speed 110kt (204km/h); cruising speed 97kt (180km/h); initial climb 625ft (190m)/min; service ceiling 13,250ft (4040m); range 347nm (644km).

Weights: Mk.4 – empty 1393kg (3070lb); max takeoff 2631kg (5800lb).

Dimensions: Wing span 15.24m (50ft 0in); length 10.97m (36ft 0in); height 4.11m (13ft 6in); wing area 36.2m² (390sq ft).

Accommodation: One pilot and 6-9 passengers.

Production: 1 Mk.1, 1 Mk.2, 7 Mk.3, 43 Mk.4, 1 Mk.5 and 1 Mk.6, total 54.

History: Designed in 1944, the M.57 Aerovan was intended as literally a 'flying van' capable of carrying a tonne of freight or eight passengers over short ranges on the modest power of two 155hp (116kW) Blackburn Cirrus Major piston engines.

The boxy fuselage provided 15.0m³ (530cu ft) of space – sufficient for a small car – and was of plastic bonded wood construction. A hinged rear section allowed easy access. The wing was of wood with auxiliary aerofoil flaps and the tail boom was metal. Tricycle undercarriage ensured there was sufficient headroom for the loading of freight under the tail boom.

The prototype Aerovan 1 first flew on 26 January 1945 and was a one-off. The Aerovan 2 with a 46cm (18in) longer fuselage and round instead of square cabin windows followed in March 1946. Seven similar production Aerovan 3s were built during 1946, five of them delivered to Air Contractors for cross-Channel freight work, one to Liverpool based Skytravel for passenger charters and the other to Jersey based Island Air Charters. Several Mk.3s subsequently went to Beirut for service with the Arab Contracting and Trading Co, from where they operated over large areas of the Near East.

The major production Aerovan 4 was similar to its predecessors and delivered to a variety of customers in 1946-47. These included Air Contractors, Spain's Aerotechnica, Jersey's Air Transport (Charter), Lockwood Flying Services, British Nederland Air Services, East Anglian Flying Services, North Sea Air Transport, Ulster Aviation and others. Ulster Aviation's fleet was the largest with five Aerovans operated mainly on the Isle of Man tourist run.

Later in their careers, several second hand Aerovans found their way to the Channel Islands for charter and joyriding operations. Two went to New Zealand in 1949 for the RNZAF's Research and Development Flight, one for cropdusting trials.

Two prototype Aerovan models were built: the Mk.5 with two 145hp (108kW) de Havilland Gipsy Major 10 engines; and the Mk.6 with a pair of 195hp (145kW) Lycoming O-435-A flat sixes. One Mk.4 was fitted with a Hurel-Dubois high aspect ratio metal wing in 1957 and redesignated the HDM.105. Miles flew a prototype of the similarly configured but much larger all metal M.71 Merchantman in 1947, this featuring four 250hp (186kW) Gipsy Queen engines and a Marathon wing.

Photo: Aerovan 4.

Miles/Handley Page Marathon

Country of origin: United Kingdom.

Powerplants: Four 340hp (253kW) de Havilland Gipsy Queen 70-3 or 70-4 inverted six cylinder inlines; three bladed propellers.

Performance: HPR.1 – max speed 202kt (374km/h); cruising speed 152-175kt (281-324km/h); initial climb 595ft (181m)/min; service ceiling 18,000ft (5486m); range 812nm (1505km).

Weights: HPR.1 – empty 5302kg (11,688lb); max takeoff 8278kg (18,250lb).

Dimensions: Wing span 19.81m (65ft 0in); length 15.93m (52ft 3in); height 4.29m (14ft 1in); wing area 46.3m^2 (498sq ft).

Accommodation: 18-20 passengers.

Production: 3 prototypes by Miles and 40 HPR.1 Marathon 1 by Handley Page (Reading), total 43.

History: Designed to meet the Brabazon Committee's Specifications 5A and 18/44 for a postwar feederliner, the M.60 Marathon was the first all metal aircraft designed by Miles Aircraft and its first with four engines and retractable tricycle undercarriage. Three prototypes were ordered, the first of them flying on 19 May 1946.

Despite being adjudged suitable, official vacillation delayed orders being placed and Miles meanwhile suffered the double blow of getting into financial difficulties in 1947 and losing the prototype Marathon in a crash in May 1948. Miles went into liquidation during 1948 and the Marathon programme was taken over by Handley Page subsidiary, Handley Page (Reading) Ltd and redesignated the HPR.1 Marathon 1. The third prototype was completed by HPR as the sole Marathon 2 testbed with two 1010ehp (753kW) Armstrong Siddeley Mamba turboprops in place of the standard four Gipsy Queen piston engines. It first flew in July 1949.

Handley Page (Reading) received orders for 50 Marathon 1s from the Ministry of Supply for British European Airways (30) and BOAC's subsidiaries and associated companies around the world (20). BEA intended using Marathons (as the *Clansman* Class) to replace Dragon Rapides on its Scottish services but decided it was unsuitable and reduced the order to firstly 25, then seven and finally none in February 1952. BOAC interest also declined.

Production of 40 Marathon 1s (and 1As when fitted with Gipsy Queen 70-4 engines) had meanwhile begun in 1949 and although several flew in BEA colours, the type never entered regular service with the airline. Twenty-eight Marathons were diverted to the RAF for use as navigation trainers as the Marathon T.11. The others found their way into commercial service, deliveries being made to West African Airways (6), Union of Burma Airways (3), Far East Airlines (2) and King Hussein of Jordan (1).

Other subsequent operators included the West German Civil Aviation Board for radio calibration duties and All Nippon Airways. The RAF operated the Marathon T.11 only briefly, the aircraft replaced by the Vickers Varsity in 1958 and in most cases consigned to the scrapyard. The Mamba powered Marathon 2 was re-engined with two 870hp (649kW) Alvis Leonides Major radials in 1955 as the HPR.5 as a testbed for the forthcoming HPR.3 Herald.

Photo: Second prototype M.60 Marathon.

Nakajima AT-2

Country of origin: Japan.

Powerplants: Prototype – two 580hp (432kW) Nakajima Kotobuki 2-1 radials. Production – two 710hp (529kW) Nakajima Kotobuki 41 or Ha-1b nine cylinder radials; two bladed propellers.

Performance: Max speed 195kt (360km/h) at 11,025ft (3360m); cruising speed 168kt (310km/h); time to 9840ft (3000m) 6.7min; service ceiling 22,965ft (7000m); max range 648nm (1200km).

Weights: Empty 3500kg (7716lb); max takeoff 5250kg (11,574lb).

Dimensions: Wing span 19.81m (65ft 0in); length 15.29m (50ft 2in); height 4.15m (13ft 7^1/$_2$in); wing area 49.2m^2 (530sq ft).

Accommodation: 8 passengers two abreast.

Production: 33 AT-2 plus 318 Ki-34 by Nakajima and Tachikawa, total 351.

History: Nakajima began the design of a small twin engined commercial aircraft in 1935 under the designation AT-1 for use on Japanese air routes with limited traffic which did not require an aircraft such as the larger, 14 passenger Douglas DC-2 for which Nakajima had acquired a manufacturing licence.

The AT-1 was in some ways a scaled down version of the American aircraft, incorporating its multi-cellular cantilever wing construction designed by Jack Northrop. It was all metal except for plywood covered flying controls.

The design underwent extensive changes as it was developed, resulting in the new designation AT-2 by the time the prototype was first flown on 12 September 1936.

This was powered by two 580hp (432kW) Nakajima Kotobuki 2-1 radials driving fixed pitch wooden propellers but civil production aircraft would have more powerful Kotobuki 41 engines and variable pitch metal propellers.

Nakajima built 32 production AT-2s for the commercial market, delivering them to Dai Nippon Koku KK (Greater Japan Air Lines) and Manchuria Air Transport.

They remained in commercial service until 1945 operating within Manchuria and on services such as Tokyo-Hsinking and Tokyo-Tienstin.

Military interest in the AT-2 resulted in the placing of orders in 1937 for the Imperial Japanese Army Air Force under the designation Ki-34 or Army Type 97.

Powered by Nakajima Ha-1b radials, 19 were initially built by the parent company before production of another 299 was undertaken by Tachikawa.

The final example was delivered in 1942 and the Allied code name was 'Thora'.

In Army service the Ki-34 was used mainly for paratroop training and communications.

Some of the Ki-34s were transferred to the Imperial Japanese Navy Air Force during the war for service as communications and general transports. They were redesignated Navy Type AT-2 Transport or Nakajima L1N1.

Several Ki-34s which had been based in China were supplied to the Japanese puppet Cochin Chinese Air Force in 1942.

Photo: Nakajima AT-2.

NAMC YS-11

Country of origin: Japan.

Powerplants: Two 3060shp (2282kW) Rolls-Royce Dart Mk.542-10K turboprops; four bladed propellers.

Performance: YS-11A-200 – max cruise 253kt (487km/h); economical cruise 244kt (452km/h); service ceiling 22,900ft (6980m); max payload range (with reserves) 270nm (500km); max fuel range (no reserves) 1736nm (3215km).

Weights: YS-11A-200 – operating empty 15,419kg (33,993lb); max takeoff 24,500kg (54,012lb). YS-11A-500/600/700 – max takeoff 25,000kg (55,115lb).

Dimensions: Wing span 32.00m (104ft 11¾in); length 26.30m (86ft 3½in); height 8.98m (29ft 5½in); wing area 94.8m² (1020sq ft).

Accommodation: 60 passengers four abreast.

Production: 50 YS-11-100, 94 YS-11A-200, 16 YS-11A-300, 8 YS-11A-400, 5 YS-11A-500 and 9 YS-11A-600, total 182.

History: The only indigenous Japanese airliner to enter production since WWII, the YS-11 60 passenger twin turboprop was conceived mainly to meet the requirements of Japanese domestic carriers although it did achieve a number of export sales including to the USA.

The Nihon Aircraft Manufacturing Co (NAMC) consortium was established in 1957 to design and build the aircraft, members including Fuji (tail unit), Kawasaki (wings and engine nacelles), Mitsubishi (forward fuselage and final assembly), Nippi (ailerons and flaps), Shin Meiwa (rear fuselage) and Showa (light alloy components such as doors).

The two prototype YS-11s were flown on 30 August and 28 December 1962 followed by the first of 48 initial production YS-11-100s from October 1964. Japanese certification was awarded in August 1964 and US FAA certification in March 1965. First delivery was to the Japanese Civil Aviation Bureau in March 1965, followed by initial airline deliveries to Toa Airways, Japan Domestic and All Nippon between April and July.

The first YS-11A with higher operating weights flew in November 1967 and was made available in several subvariants: the -200 standard passenger model; -300 mixed passenger-freight version with large cargo door; and -400 military version with freight door for the JASDF.

YS-11A deliveries began in 1968, customers including Piedmont Airlines, Toa, Olympic, Japan Domestic, All Nippon, Pelita, the Japanese military, Southwest, Argentina's ALA, Brazil's Cruzeiro del Sol, Hawaiian, VASP, and Transair.

NAMC introduced the YS-11A-500/600/700 models in early 1970s, these equivalent to the 200/300/400 (respectively) but with a further increase in maximum weight. Production was limited to five -500s (two of them for Olympic Airways) and nine -600s for the JMSDF, Reeve Aleutian, Pelita Air Service and the Gabon Air Force. The last YS-11 was a -600 delivered to the JMSDF in February 1974.

Some 60 civil and military operators have flown new and used YS-11s over the years and by 1999 over 60 aircraft remained in commercial service.

Photo: NAMC YS-11A-300.

Nord (Aerospatiale) 262

Country of origin: France.

Powerplants: 262A/B – two 1080ehp (805kW) Turboméca Bastan VIC turboprops. 262C/D two 1145ehp (854kW) Bastan VIIC; three bladed propellers. Mohawk 298 – two 1180shp (880kW) Pratt & Whitney Canada PT6A-45 turboprops; five bladed propellers.

Performance: 262A – max cruise 208kt (385km/h); range with 26 passengers 626nm (975km). 262C – max cruise 220kt (407km/h); initial climb 1380ft (420m)/min; service ceiling 28,500ft (8685m); range with 26 passengers 550nm (1019km); max range 985nm (1825km).

Weights: 262A – operating empty 6763kg (14,910lb); max takeoff 10,600kg (23,369lb). 262C – operating empty 7225kg (15,928lb); max takeoff 10,800kg (23,810lb).

Dimensions: 262A/B – wing span 21.89m (71ft 10in); length 19.28m (63ft 3in); height 6.20m (20ft 4in); wing area 55.0m² (592sq ft). 262C/D – wing span 22.60m (74ft 10in); wing area 55.8m² (601sq ft).

Accommodation: 26-29 passengers three abreast.

Production: 4 262, 69 262A, 4 262B, 10 262C, 24 262D, total 111.

History: The Nord 262 pressurised 26-29 passenger regional turboprop was based on the unpressurised Max Holste MH.250 Broussard prototype (first flight May 1959) powered by two Pratt & Whitney Wasp radial piston engines, this in turn leading to the MH.260 Super Broussard with Turboméca Bastan turboprops. The first of 10 MH.260s flew in July 1960.

Nord began development of a pressurised version with circular rather than square section fuselage in early 1961 as the 262, the aircraft retaining the MH.260's high wing, Bastan turboprops and main undercarriage retracting into lower fuselage blisters. The prototype first flew on 24 December 1962 and was followed by three pre-production models. The first production version was designated the 262B. Powered by 1080ehp (805kW) Bastan VICs, only four were built for launch customer Air Inter and delivered between July 1964 and January 1965.

Paradoxically, the second and major production version was designated the 262A. Similarly powered to the 'B', the first of this model flew in May 1965 and deliveries to the USA's Lake Central Airlines (later merged with Allegheny Airlines) began three moths later. Other 262A customers included Japan Domestic, Alisarda, Air Ceylon, Linjeflyg, Cimber Air, Tunis Air, Air Ceylon and the French military.

The next models were the 262C (civil) and 262D (military) Frégate with more powerful Bastan VIIC engines, longer wing tips and increased maximum weight. The prototype 262C flew on 9 July 1968 and deliveries began in 1970, by which time Nord had been absorbed into Aerospatiale. Most of the 34 Frégates went to military customers including all 24 262Ds to the Armee de L'Air. The last aircraft (a 262D) was delivered in March 1977.

Allegheny Airlines upgraded nine of its 262As to Mohawk 298 standards – the designation resulting form Mohawk Air Services performing the conversions to FAR Part 298 regulations – with Pratt & Whitney PT6A-45 engines driving five bladed propellers. Avionics and other systems were also upgraded and the first conversion was flown in January 1975.

Photo: Mohawk 298. (Julian Green)

Northrop Alpha

Country of origin: USA.

Powerplant: Alpha 1-4 – one 420hp (313kW) Pratt & Whitney R-1340-C Wasp C nine cylinder radial. Alpha 4-A – one 450hp (335kW) Wasp SC1; two bladed propeller.

Performance: Cruising speed 126kt (233km/h); range 521nm (966km).

Weights: Empty 1207kg (2660lb); max takeoff 2041kg (4500lb).

Dimensions: Wing span 12.75m (41ft 10in); length 8.65m (28ft 4¹/₂in); height 2.74m (9ft 0in); wing area 27.4m² (295sq ft).

Accommodation: Pilot and 6-7 passengers or mixed passengers/freight.

Production: 17.

History: Designed by John ('Jack') Northrop, the all metal stressed skin and cantilever low wing monoplane Alpha is regarded by many as the first 'modern' airliner due to its method of construction which included the multi-cellular wing design later incorporated in the Douglas DC-2 and DC-3. The divided main undercarriage was fixed and subsequently enclosed in streamlined fairings to reduce drag, while the single pilot open cockpit was located aft of the circular enclosed cabin.

Northrop's company was part of the United Aircraft and Transport Corporation (UATC) when the Alpha first flew in May 1930, other members including Boeing, Chance Vought, Pratt & Whitney, Hamilton Standard and Transcontinental and Western Air (TWA). The Alpha was designed primarily for TWA, which purchased 13 of the 17 built after placing an initial order for five.

TWA launched Alpha services in April 1931 between San Francisco and New York with 13 stops en route. The journey took just over 23 hours to complete and the aircraft were configured to carry three passengers and a 211kg (465lb) load of freight and mail.

To ensure the necessary reliability of service at night and in all weathers was achieved, they were equipped with the most modern available radio aids and from 1932 the Alpha became the first commercial aircraft to be fitted with Goodrich rubber deicing boots on the wing and tail surface leading edges.

National Air Transport (part of United Airlines) and the US Assistant Secretary of Commerce for Aeronautics were among the other users, the latter's aircraft – the third built – also serving with the Ford Motor Company, National Air Transport and TWA. It is now preserved in the Smithsonian Institution's National Air and Space Museum. The US Army Air Corps was another operator, receiving three for evaluation.

Production variants differed mainly in their interior configurations. The Alpha 2 could be arranged as either an all passenger or all cargo aircraft; the Alpha 3 was the mixed passenger/freight model but the Alpha 4 of late 1931 had a new cantilever main undercarriage design and the more powerful 450hp (335kW) Wasp SC1 engine which was retrofitted to several earlier aircraft. The Alpha 4-A was a pure freighter with its cabin windows blanked out. It could carry a 567kg (1250lb) payload.

Photo: Alpha 4.

Percival Prince

Country of origin: United Kingdom.

Powerplants: Mks.1/2 – two 520hp (388kW) Alvis Leonides 501/4 nine cylinder radials. Mks.3/4 – two 550hp (410kW) Leonides 502/4 or 560hp (418kW) Leonides 502/5; three bladed propellers.

Performance: 1/2 – max speed 188kt (348km/h); cruising speed 155kt (288km/h); initial climb 1110ft (338m)/min; service ceiling 23,500ft (7160m); range 817nm (1513km). 3/4 – max speed 199kt (368km/h); cruising speed 171kt (317km/h); initial climb 1100ft (335m)/min; service ceiling 23,400ft (7130m); range 777nm (1439km).

Weights: 1/2 – empty 3340kg (7364lb); max takeoff 4835-4990kg (10,659-11,000lb). 3/4 – empty 3646kg (8038lb); max takeoff 4990-5216kg (11,000-11,500lb).

Dimensions: 1/2/3/4 – wing span 17.07m (56ft 0in); length 13.06m (42ft 10in); height 4.90m (16ft 1in); wing area 33.9m² (365sq ft).

Accommodation: 8-10 passengers.

Production: 1 P.48 Merganser, 24 P.50 Prince, 7 P.66 President plus 7 Sea Prince and 51 Pembroke.

History: The line of development which led to the P.50 Prince feederliner began on 9 May 1947 with the first flight of the P.48 Merganser, an all metal high wing light transport with a roomy fuselage for five passengers.

Powered by two 296hp (221kW) de Havilland Gipsy Queen 51 inline engines, development was abandoned as production of the engine was discontinued.

Instead, Percival designed the similarly configured but larger P.50 Prince for 8-10 passengers and powered by Alvis Leonides radial engines. The prototype first flew on 13 May 1948 and an initial production of batch of 10 laid down.

Despite being built in modest numbers, several versions of the Prince were developed, all powered by Leonides engines. They included the Mk.2 with the Mk.1's vertical windscreen replaced with a more aesthetically pleasing sloping unit, the Mk.3 with more powerful engines and the similar Mk.4. Subvariants of these were also built including the P.54 Survey Prince with lengthened and glazed nose.

The ultimate civil version was the P.66 President (originally Prince Mk.5) with longer span wings, increased weights and lengthened nose. This was also built for the RAF as the Pembroke and Royal Navy as the Sea Prince C.2. Three Sea Prince C.1s were also delivered, based on the short span P.50.

In commercial service, Princes were operated by Transportes Aereos Norte do Brasil, Polynesian Airways and others but most were delivered to corporate customers such as Shell (eight for its operations around the world), whose Aviation Department was headed by WWII fighter ace Douglas Bader. Bader personally collected the Princes delivered to the company.

Other Prince operators included the Sudanese Air Force, Hunting Surveys, the Standard Motor Co, Martin-Baker Ltd and the Tanganyika Government. The last civil Prince was built in 1953, Pembroke production continued until 1958.

Photo: P.50 Prince prototype.

Potez 62

Country of origin: France.

Powerplants: 62-0 – two 870hp (649kW) Gnome-Rhône 14Kirs Mistral 14-cylinder radials. 62-1 – two 720hp (537kW) Hispano-Suiza 12Xrs V12s; three bladed propellers.

Performance: 62-0 – max speed 175kt (325km/h); cruising speed 151kt (280km/h); service ceiling 24,605ft (7500m); range 540nm (1000km).

Weights: 62-0 – empty 4895kg (10,791lb); max takeoff 7500kg (16,534lb).

Dimensions: 62-0 – 22.45m (73ft 8in); length 17.32m (56ft 10in); height 3.90m (12ft 9^1/$_2$in); wing area 76.0m^2 (818sq ft).

Accommodation: 14-16 passengers two abreast.

Production: 12 62-0s and 13 62-1s, total 25 (plus 15 Potez 65 military transport derivatives).

History: A significant element of Air France's fleet in the second half of the 1930s, the twin engined, 14-16 passenger Potez 62 was developed from the Potez 54 bomber of 1933, combining that aircraft's strut braced high wing and engines mounted on a structure attached to the fuselage with a new and aerodynamically efficient fuselage.

The rectangular section fuselage was of ply covered wooden construction, the wings were metal with mainly fabric covering and the tail surfaces were wood with fabric covering. The main undercarriage units retracted into the engine nacelles. The passengers were accommodated in two cabins.

The prototype first flew on 28 January 1935 as the Potez 62-0 with Gnome-Rhône Mistral radial engines and this became the initial production version. Air France began operations with the aircraft on its Paris-Marseilles-Rome service in June 1935.

The Potez 62-1 with Hispano-Suiza V12 engines was introduced later in 1935, this version also featuring a slightly swept back wing. Three of Air France's 62-1s were subsequently re-engined with Hispano-Suizas and the remaining nine with 900hp (671kW) Gnome-Rhône 14N 16/17 radials.

The Potez 62s operated on many of Air France's European services in the years before the outbreak of WWII plus to the Far East and on the Buenos Aries to Santiago route, which involved crossing the Andes. They were beginning to be replaced by more modern types as the war approached but had proved reliable and safe with only one lost, in India during 1938.

The Potez 65 military transport variant was first flown in June 1937. Powered by Hispano-Suiza 12X engines, it featured increased weights and a lower fuselage trap door which allowed large items such as aero engines to be winched aboard. Fourteen fully equipped troops or six stretcher cases and four seated casualties (plus a medical attendant) could be accommodated. In an emergency, the Potez 65 could also be adapted to carry a reasonable bomb load.

Prewar, the Potez 65 originally served with France's two paratroop units but the aircraft was subsequently used on general transport duties. At least one of the former Air France Potez 62s flew with the Free French during the war.

Photo: Potez 62-1.

Saab 90 Scandia

Country of origin: Sweden.

Powerplants: Two 1800hp (1342kW) Pratt & Whitney R-2180-E1 14-cylinder radials; four bladed propellers.

Performance: Max speed 243kt (450km/h); cruising speed 210kt (389km/h); initial climb 1350ft (411m)/min; service ceiling 24,605ft (7500m); range 800nm (1482km).

Weights: Empty 9960kg (21,958lb); max takeoff 16,000kg (35,273lb).

Dimensions: Wing span 28.00m (91ft 10^1/$_2$in); length 21.30m (69ft 10^1/$_2$in); height 7.09m (23ft 3in); wing area 85.6m^2 (922sq ft).

Accommodation: 24-36 passengers.

Production: 18.

History: Saab broke with its traditional activity of designing and building military aircraft to produce the Saab 90 Scandia, a twin piston engined airliner intended to fill the postwar 'DC-3 replacement' market, competing with the Convair CV-240 and Martin 2-0-2. The Scandia was an all metal, low wing cantilever monoplane with tricycle undercarriage. Its oval section stressed skin fuselage was unpressurised.

Saab had high hopes that the Scandia would achieve substantial sales in the postwar market but strong opposition from the American manufacturers and a glut of war surplus DC-3s meant that only one prototype and 17 production aircraft were built for just two customers.

Development began in 1944 under the project name CT. The prototype was powered by a pair of 1350hp (1007kW) Pratt & Whitney R-2000 Twin Wasp radials and first flew on 16 November 1946. Production aircraft were designated the Saab 90A and differed in having 1800hp (1342kW) R-2180s, the only application for this particular variant of the Twin Wasp.

The first order wasn't placed until two years after the prototype's first flight, AB Aerotransport (Swedish Airlines) contracting for 10. When this airline was absorbed into Scandinavian Airlines System (SAS) the order was reduced to six and the first four production Scandias were delivered to Aerovias Brazil. The first of these flew on 12 November 1949 and deliveries began June 1950.

Aerovias was absorbed into VASP which ordered five additional aircraft and also purchased the prototype in March 1950. Deliveries to SAS began in October 1950.

SAS subsequently ordered two additional aircraft, these and the extras for VASP built after a three year break in production. The final Scandia was flown in November 1954 and delivered to SAS the same month. Perhaps ironically given the Scandia's poor sales record, the last six aircraft were in effect built by Fokker (Aviolanda and de Schelde were also involved) due to Saab's heavy military aircraft commitments at the time.

SAS sold its Scandias to VASP in 1957-58, the Brazilian operator therefore owning the entire production run. After providing many years of useful service, the fleet was retired and scrapped between 1964 and 1968 with one preserved in the Bededouro Museum. The projected Saab 90B Scandia with pressurised cabin was not built.

Photo: Scandia prototype.

Saab 340

Country of origin: Sweden.

Powerplants: 340A – two 1735shp (1294kW) General Electric CT7-5A2 turboprops. 340B – two 1750shp (1305kW) CT7-9Bs; four bladed propellers.

Performance: 340A – max cruise 272kt (504km/h); range cruise 250kt (463km/h); initial climb 1800ft (548m)/min; operational ceiling 25,000ft (7620m); range with 35 passengers 630nm (1167km); range with 30 passengers 940nm (1741km). 340B – max cruise 282kt (522km/h); range cruise 252kt (467km/h); initial climb 2000ft (610m)/min; range with 35 passengers 935nm (1732km).

Weights: 340A – operating empty 7900kg (17,416lb); max takeoff 12,700kg (28,000lb). 340B – operating empty 8225kg (18,133lb); max takeoff 13,154kg (29,000lb).

Dimensions: Wing span 21.44m (70ft 4in); length 19.73m (64ft 9in); height 6.97m (22ft 10$^{1}/_{2}$in); wing area 41.8m^2 (450sq ft). 340B Plus – optional wing span 22.75m (74ft 8in).

Accommodation: 33-37 passengers four abreast.

Production: 159 340A and 299 340B, total 458.

History: The first collaborative venture of its kind between European and US manufacturers, the aircraft originally known as the SF-340 was conceived as a 'new generation' regional turboprop by Saab and Fairchild in 1979, their joint venture agreement signed in January 1980. Both manufacturers were to produce components for the aircraft with final assembly taking place in Sweden.

The first of three prototypes flew on 25 January 1983. The initial SF-340A was certified in May 1984, early aircraft featuring 1630shp (1215kW) CT7-5A engines instead of the standard CT7-5A2s. They were subsequently upgraded, the 340's first revenue services meanwhile having been flown by Switzerland's Crossair in June 1984.

Other early customers included Birmingham Executive, Swedair, Australia's Kendell Airlines and the USA's Comair and Air Midwest. A quick change (340QC) version was introduced, the first going to Finnaviation in 1986. Corporate and Combi models were also sold.

The 340 programme had meanwhile become an entirely Saab affair, Fairchild dropping out from November 1985, the aircraft's designation subsequently becoming simply Saab 340.

Aircraft from the 160th onwards (first flight April 1989) were completed as 340Bs with slightly more powerful CT7-9B engines with greater power reserve for improved hot and high performance, increased maximum weight, increased span tailplane and better payload-range performance. Crossair was the first to introduce the 340B to service in September 1989. American Eagle became the major customer, ordering well over 100.

Development continued with the 340B Plus from March 1994 with upgraded interior, optional active cabin noise control system and optional wing tip extensions which permit a 680kg (1500lb) increase in maximum weight. Despite the 340 selling well, Saab found it was losing money on its regional airliners and in late 1997 announced the termination of both the 340 and 2000 (see next entry) programmes. The final 340 was delivered in 1999.

Photo: Saab 340B.

Saab 2000

Country of origin: Sweden.

Powerplants: Two 4152shp (3096kW) Allison AE 2100A turboprops; six bladed propellers.

Performance: Max cruise 368kt (682km/h); range cruise 321kt (595km/h); initial climb 2250ft (686m)/min; operational ceiling 31,000ft (9450m); range with 58 passengers 935nm (1732km) at max cruise, 1045nm (1935km) at range cruise; range with 50 passengers 1180nm (2185km) at max cruise, 1425nm (2640km) at range cruise.

Weights: Operating empty 13,800kg (30,423lb); max takeoff 22,800kg (50,265lb).

Dimensions: Wing span 24.76m (81ft 3in); length 27.28m (89ft 6in); height 7.72m (25ft 4in); wing area 55.7m^2 (600sq ft).

Accommodation: 50-58 passengers three abreast.

Production: 63.

History: Wanting to capitalise on the success of the 340 and reading the trend towards larger capacity regional airliners, Saab began development of a stretched 340 capable of carrying 50 passengers at speeds high enough to achieve similar block times to jets but with turboprop fuel economy.

The result was the Saab 2000 which combined the 340's basic fuselage stretched by 7.54m (24ft 9in) with heavily derated Allison AE 2100 engines driving advanced, slow turning six bladed propellers (for minimum noise), a larger wing, an active cabin noise reduction system, glass cockpit and advanced avionics and systems. The 2000 was the first civil application for the AE 2100 engine derived from the military T406 developed for the V-22 Osprey tiltrotor.

Launched in December 1988 with an order for 15 from Switzerland's Crossair, the programme was given the formal go ahead in May 1989. Risk sharing partners in project were CASA (wings), Westland (rear fuselage) and Valmet (tail).

The prototype 2000 first flew on 26 March 1992 and European JAA certification was awarded in March 1994. US FAA certification was gained the following month, both of these dates rather later than planned due to problems with the 2000's high speed longitudinal stability. This was overcome by the development of a Powered Elevator Control System (PECS) first flight tested in May 1994 and certified later in the year. Aircraft already flying had PECS retrofitted.

Crossair put the 2000 into service in September 1994 followed by Deutsche BA, Air Marshall Islands, General Motors (which received three corporate models) and Scandinavian Airlines System (SAS).

Unfortunately for Saab, the high speed turboprop concept was not a winner and sales of the 2000 were poor, most airlines preferring to opt for the new generation of small capacity jets. It's interesting to note that whereas a very high proportion of Saab 340 sales were to US operators, the only 2000s sold to that market were General Motors' three corporate aircraft.

Faced with ongoing losses on its regional airliner programmes, Saab announced in late 1997 that production of both the 340 and 2000 would end. The last 2000 was delivered to Crossair in April 1999.

Photo: Saab 2000.

Saunders ST-27

Country of origin: Canada.

Powerplant: Two 783ehp (584kW) Pratt & Whitney Canada PT6A-34 turboprops; three bladed propellers.

Performance: Max cruise 200kt (370km/h); economical cruise 182kt (337km/h); initial climb 1600ft (488m)/min; service ceiling 25,000ft (7620m); max payload range with reserves 100nm (185km); max fuel range 710nm (1315km).

Weights: Operating empty 3583kg (7900lb); max takeoff 6124kg (13,500lb).

Dimensions: Wing span 21.79m (71ft 6in); length 17.98m (59ft 0in); height 4.75m (15ft 7in); wing area 46.4m² (499sq ft).

Accommodation: Up to 23 passengers two abreast.

Production: 13 ST-27 conversions and 1 ST-28.

History: The growth of the third level/commuter airline market in North America and elsewhere during the 1960s inspired Canadian aeronautical engineer David Saunders to develop a stretched, turboprop powered conversion of the de Havilland Heron Srs.2.

He established the Saunders Aircraft Corporation in May 1968 to develop and manufacture the ST-27, with a 2.59m (8ft 6in) longer fuselage than the Heron enabling 23 rather than 17 passengers to be carried (the nose was also lengthened to provide space for radar) and the original four 250hp (186kW) Gipsy Queen piston engines replaced by two PT6A-34 turboprops. The wing, tailplane and undercarriage remained as per the Heron albeit with a strengthened main wing spar and reshaped rudder.

Most of the original design work was carried out by Aviation Traders (Engineering) in Britain but manufacturing and assembly was performed in Canada. Most of the finance was provided by the Manitoba Provincial Government's taxpayers.

The first ST-27 (converted from a former Cimber Air Heron) flew on 28 May 1969 and the first delivery was to ACES of Colombia in January 1972. Sales were sluggish and the final tally of 13 ST-27 conversions over six years (mostly for small Canadian operators) indicates the tough market and that the ST-27 was always enormously inhibited by the fact it could not be certified in the USA as merely a modified Heron (with a Supplemental Type Certificate) but needed a full new Type Certificate. The substantial cost of this was beyond Saunders' resources.

Saunders had always realised that converting Herons was a limited and temporary measure and began developing a new build version called the ST-28 (originally ST-27B). Although of similar appearance to its predecessor with minor external modifications, the ST-28 was a very different aircraft under the skin and was intended to be lightly pressurised. It took considerable resources to develop and by the time the one and only example first flew on 12 December 1975 the Manitoba Government had withdrawn its support for the company.

That was the end for Saunders, which shut down on 31 December 1975. Its assets were finally sold to Canadian ST-27 operator Air Atonabee in January 1979, the package including 10 ST-27s of which three were already leased by the airline.

Photo: Saunders ST-27.

Saunders-Roe Princess

Country of origin: United Kingdom.

Powerplants: Ten 3780ehp (2819kW) Bristol Proteus 600 turboprops – eight in coupled pairs with eight bladed counter-rotating propellers, two single units with four bladed propellers.

Performance: Cruising speed 313kt (579km/h); range 4580nm (8484km).

Weights: Empty 86,638kg (191,000lb); max takeoff 149,688kg (330,000lb).

Dimensions: Wing span 66.90m (219ft 6in); length 45.11m (148ft 0in); height 17.37m (57ft 0in); wing area 466.3m² (5019sq ft).

Accommodation: Up to 200 passengers.

Production: 3 (only 1 flown).

History: The last gasp of the big flying boats, the Saunders-Roe (Saro) SR.45 Princess was conceived during World War II to meet perceived postwar requirements for international air travel, especially for BOAC's trans-Atlantic services. As such, its concept was obsolete even before the sole example to fly did so, because wartime activities had seen the building of thousands of new airfields all over the world, more than enough to meet the needs of more economical landplanes.

Perhaps those who approved the Princess had their judgement clouded by dreams of continuing the success of the old Empire boats, because by the time the it received official interest in July 1945 – when Saro was asked to tender for a very large commercial flying boat – the trend towards landplanes was irreversible. There was still time to realise the folly of the project before three were ordered for BOAC by the Ministry of Supply in May 1946 but it went ahead regardless.

A huge aircraft for its time with a 'double bubble' fuselage design with the upper lobe intended to be pressurised, the Princess's main technical interest lay in its use of ten Bristol Proteus turboprop engines, five per wing mounted in two coupled pairs inboard (driving contra-rotating propellers) and one outboard.

After a lengthy building time, the first Princess was finally flown on 22 August 1952, by which time the concept of the aircraft was well and truly out of date. A litany of problems mainly relating to the gearboxes for the contra-rotating propellers was revealed in flight testing and it was decided to abandon the programme at an early stage.

The first aircraft appeared at the 1952 and 1953 Farnborough Air Shows before being grounded and cocooned at Cowes in 1954, BOAC not surprisingly having lost interest and cancelled its order some time earlier.

The second and third Princesses were launched in 1953 and immediately cocooned and beached before having been flown. All three languished in this state for another 14 years before finally being scrapped in 1967.

There were suggestions that the RAF could find a use for the Princess and installing Bristol Orion turboprops was looked at, but the Princess was destined to join the Bristol Brabazon as one of the two major 'white elephants' of postwar British commercial aviation.

Photo: The only Princess completed and flown.

Savoia-Marchetti S.66

Country of origin: Italy.

Powerplants: Three 750hp (559kW) Fiat A.24R V12s; four bladed propellers.

Performance: Max speed 129kt (238km/h); cruising speed 120kt (222km/h); service ceiling 17,550ft (5350m); range 648nm (1200km).

Weights: Empty 7450kg (16,424lb); max takeoff 10,950kg (24,140lb).

Dimensions: Wing span 33.00m (108ft 3in); length 16.64m (54ft 7in); height 4.93m (16ft 2in); wing area 126.7m^2 (1364sq ft).

Accommodation: Up to 18 passengers.

Production: 24.

History: The twin hulled, three engined S.66 flying boat was designed as a larger replacement for the S.55 torpedo bomber and 10 seat civil transport of 1925, of which 31 commercial versions (S.55C and S.55P) were built up to 1932. This also featured a twin hull design and was powered by two 510hp (380k) Isotta-Fraschini Asso 500 or 700hp (522kW) Fiat A.24R inline engines mounted in tandem above the centre section.

The S.55 achieved fame for several long distance flights but mainly for the extraordinary mass formation flights led by Italo Balbo.

The first one (begun in December 1930) saw a formation of S.55s fly the 5615nm (10,400km) from Italy to Brazil while the second involved 24 aircraft departing Italy and travelling across the Alps to Chicago via Greenland, Iceland and Labrador for the 1933 Century of Progress Exhibition. Mass formations of aircraft have been called 'Balbos' ever since.

The S.66's hulls and large wing were of wooden construction and the rear booms fabric covered metal. The three pusher engines were mounted on struts above the wings.

The enclosed cockpit was located in the wing centre section with the passengers accommodated in the hulls, initially seven seats, two sleeping couches and a lavatory per side but later nine seats in each of the structures.

The first S.66 with 550hp (410kW) Fiat A.22R engines flew in 1931. Production models were all powered by the more powerful A.24R. The type was used by Aero Expresso Italiana, SA Navigazione Aerea (SANA) and their successor Ala Littoria on various Mediterranean services including Rome-Tripoli, Rome-Tunis and Brindisi-Athens-Rhodes-Haifa.

The S.66 was also used by Italo Balbo and another by Benito Mussolini. Sixteen of the 24 were still in service by 1939 and when Italy joined the war in 1940, five passed into Regia Aeronautica service for transport and air-sea rescue duties, remaining there until about 1943.

An improved version – the SM.77 with three tractor 800hp (596kW) Alfa Romeo 126 RC10 radials – was developed in 1936 and although two were laid down, only one was completed and delivered to the Regia Aeronautica in 1937. The design was considered too outdated for commercial use and Ala Littoria's S.66s were replaced in service by other types.

Photo: Savoia-Marchetti S.66.

Savoia-Marchetti SM.73

Country of origin: Italy.

Powerplants: Various – three 600hp (447kW) Gnome-Rhône 9Kfr Mistral Major, 700hp (522kW) Piaggio Stella X.RC, 800hp (596kW) Alfa Romeo 126 RC.10, 760hp (568kW) Wright GR-1820 Cyclone or 615hp (459kW) Walter (Bristol) Pegasus IIM2 radials; three bladed propellers.

Performance: Stella engines – cruising speed 151kt (280km/h); range 864nm (1600km). Alfa engines – max speed 196kt (364km/h); service ceiling 22,965ft (7000m); range 540nm (1000km).

Weights: Stella engines – empty 6930kg (15,278lb); max takeoff 10,430kg (22,994lb). Alfa engines – empty 7300kg (16,093lb); max takeoff 10,800kg (23,810lb).

Dimensions: Wing span 24.00m (78ft 9in); length 17.45m (57ft 3in); height 4.60m (15ft 1in); wing area 93.0m^2 (1001sq ft).

Accommodation: 18 passengers two abreast.

Production: 47.

History: The first of the Savoia-Marchetti series of cantilever low wing three engined transports and bombers which included the SM.79 Sparviero (Sparrowhawk), SM.81 Pipistrello (Bat) and SM.82 Canguru (Kangaroo) of WWII fame, the SM.73 was designed as an airliner and found reasonably widespread use in the 1930s.

Accommodating 14 passengers in the main cabin and four in a small cabin immediately behind the raised cockpit, the SM.73 featured a three spar wooden wing with wood covering, metal ailerons and flaps with fabric covering and welded steel tube fabric covered fuselage. The undercarriage was fixed.

The prototype first flew on 4 June 1934 and differed from production aircraft in having a continuous row of cabin windows (rather than individual units), a four (rather than three) bladed propeller on the centre engine and taller tail. It was powered by Gnome-Rhône Mistral Major engines, as were the early production models.

The first aircraft were delivered to Sabena in 1935 for use on its European services. Sabena operated 12 SM.73s of which seven were built under licence in Belgium by SABCA.

These also had Mistral Major engines and some were used to replace Fokker F.VII/3ms on the airline's Brussels-Belgian Congo route.

Other major commercial operators were Italy's Ala Littoria and Avio Linee Italiane, whose aircraft were powered by a variety of powerplants.

Czechoslovakia's CSA received three SM.73s in 1937 with Walter built Bristol Pegasus powerplants.

Some Italian SM.73s served with the Regia Aeronautica during WWII, while seven of the Sabena aircraft found their way to Britain in May 1940 where they were impressed into the RAF. They were subsequently sent to North Africa and later taken over by the Regia Aeronautica.

Four SM.73s remained at the time of Italy's 1943 surrender, three of them flying with the Allies and one with the pro Axis forces after that. None survived the war.

Photo: Savoia-Marchetti SM.73.

Savoia-Marchetti SM.83

Country of origin: Italy.

Powerplants: Three 750hp (559kW) Alfa Romeo 126 RC.34 or 1000hp (746kW) Wright GR-1820-G2 nine cylinder radials; three bladed propellers.

Performance: SM.83 (Alfa engines) – max speed 240kt (444km/h); cruising speed 216kt (400km/h); range 1080nm (2000km). SM.83A/T – max range 2592nm (4800km).

Weights: Empty 6800kg (14,991lb); max takeoff 12,165kg (26,819lb).

Dimensions: Wing span 21.20m (69ft 6¹/₂in); length 16.20m (53ft 23in); height 4.60m (15ft 1in); wing area 60.0m² (646sq ft).

Accommodation: 10 passengers.

Production: 23.

History: A civil airliner development of the Regia Aeronautica's SM.79 Sparviero (Sparrowhawk) trimotor medium bomber – about 1370 of which were built from late 1934 and widely used during WWII – the 10 passenger SM.83 first flew on 19 November 1937.

Powered by Alfa Romeo 126 RC.34 engines, the SM.83 resembled the earlier SM.73 but was smaller. The wing was of the traditional Savoia-Marchetti three spar wooden construction but featured Handley Page leading edge slats and the welded steel tube fuselage structure was covered by a mixture of plywood, fabric and metal.

One major difference between the SM.83 and the earlier aircraft was the incorporation of retractable rather than fixed undercarriage.

Three SM.83 variants were built within the 23 aircraft production run: the standard 10 passenger model for European services; the SM.83A long range version with increased fuel and passenger capacity reduced to six; and the similar SM.83T for long range mail carrying, it and the SM.83A developed for use on services between Italy and South America.

Sixteen Alfa Romeo powered aircraft were built for Ala Littorio SA Linee Atlantiche and Linee Aeree Transcontinentali Italiane (LATI), the latter inaugurating a mail service between Rome and Rio de Janeiro in December 1939 and maintaining it until 1942.

The other seven SM.83s were exported – three for Romanian airline LARES, one for Prince Bibesco of Romania and three for Sabena for use on its Brussels-Belgian Congo route. The Sabena aircraft were powered by Wright Cyclone engines.

About 16 of the SM.83s were absorbed into the Regia Aeronautica in 1940 when Italy entered the war, sourced from LATI, Sabena and Romania. Operated by a unit called the Nucleo Communicazione LATI and flown mainly by the original airline crews, this unit continued operations basically as an airline but under military control, performing passenger flights to East Africa and Libya, as well as the mail service to Rio de Janeiro. The last SM.83 was withdrawn from service in 1945.

Transport versions of the SM.79 bomber were also produced including the SM.79C VIP aircraft with 1000hp (746kW) Piaggio P.XI radials and the long range Alfa Romeo 126 powered SM.79T with additional fuel capacity, this forming the basis for the SM.83A and SM.83T.

Photo: Savoia-Marchetti SM.83.

Savoia-Marchetti SM.95

Country of origin: Italy.

Powerplants: Four 860hp (641kW) Alfa Romeo 128RC.18 or 740hp (552kW) Bristol Pegasus 48 nine cylinder radials, or 1050hp (783kW) Pratt & Whitney R-1830-S1C3-G Twin Wasp 14-cylinder radials; three bladed propellers.

Performance: Max speed 216kt (400km/h); cruising speed 170-187kt (315-356km/h); service ceiling 21,325ft (6500m); range 1080nm (2000km).

Weights: Empty 12,800-14,500kg (28,219-31,966lb); max takeoff 21,600-24,000kg (47,619-52,910lb).

Dimensions: Wing span 34.28m (112ft 5¹/₂in); length 24.77m (81ft 3¹/₄in); height 5.70m (18ft 8¹/₂in); wing area 128.3m² (1381sq ft).

Accommodation: 18-30 passengers.

Production: Approximately 16.

History: Savoia-Marchetti began investigations into a four engined transport aircraft for both civil and military applications in the early 1940s as the SM.95. A cantilever low wing monoplane of mixed construction, the aircraft featured retractable undercarriage.

The prototype first flew in May 1943 powered by Alfa Romeo 131 RC.14 engines. Four aircraft were on order for the Regia Aironautica at that stage but development was slowed by Italy's military situation of the time and its surrender just four months after the SM.95's first flight.

Despite this, two other SM.95s were built after the surrender, both of them by SAI Ambrosini and powered by Alfa Romeo 128 RC.18 engines. Fitted out as 18 seaters and intended for use on trans-Atlantic services, they were requisitioned by the Luftwaffe. One of them was operated by the postwar Italian Air Force (Aeronautica Militare Italiana) and flown between Europe and Britain in 1945-46.

Limited production of the SM.95 resumed after WWII, these aircraft featuring a 2.51m (8ft 3in) longer fuselage and accommodation for up to 30 passengers. A choice of engines was offered – Alfa Romeo 128, Bristol Pegasus or Pratt & Whitney R-1830 radials. Opinions vary as to how many postwar SM.95s were built up to 1949, ranging from 12 to 20 and resulting in a total production run of between 15 and 23.

Commercial operators of the SM.95 were the newly created Italian national airline Alitalia (6), Linee Aeree Transcontinentali Italiane (3), and the Egyptian national airline SAIDE (4). Ala Littoria was a subsequent operator, its and SAIDE's powered by Bristol Pegasus engines while LATI's had Twin Wasps. Alitalia's aircraft were dubbed SM.95C. The SAIDE SM.95s were equipped to carry 38 passengers in a high density layout.

An SM.95C named *Marco Polo* inaugurated the first Alitalia international service from Rome to Oslo in August 1947 with Rome to London (Northolt) added in April 1948 and Caracas (Venezuela) in July 1949. Alitalia also acquired three SM.95s from LATI and continued operating the last of the Savoia-Marchetti airliners until 1951.

Photo: Savoia-Marchetti SM.95.

Short Calcutta

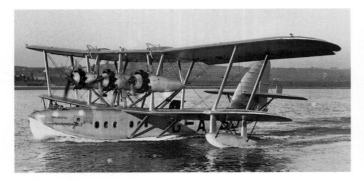

Country of origin: United Kingdom.

Powerplants: Three 540hp (403kW) Bristol Jupiter XIF nine cylinder radials; four bladed propellers.

Performance: Max speed 102kt (190km/h); cruising speed 84kt (156km/h); initial climb 750ft (228m)/min; service ceiling 13,500ft (4115m); range 565nm (1046km).

Weights: Empty 6280kg (13,845lb); max takeoff 10,206kg (22,500lb).

Dimensions: Wing span 28.35m (93ft 0in); length 20.35m (66ft 9in); height 7.24m (23ft 9in); wing area 169.5m² (1825sq ft).

Accommodation: 15 passengers.

Production: 7 as S.8 Calcuttas and 6 as military S.8 Rangoons by Shorts (total 13) plus 4 by Breguet.

History: The first commercial flying boat with a stressed skin metal hull, the S.8 Calcutta resulted from the formation of Imperial Airways in April 1924 and the need for an aircraft to fly the Mediterranean section of the airline's route to India. The Calcutta's entire structure was of metal with only the flying and control surfaces fabric covered. The 15 passengers were provided with luxurious accommodation for the day.

The Calcutta was derived from the RAF's Short S.5 Singapore flying boat but with a deeper and wider hull, three 540hp (403kW) Bristol Jupiter XIF radials instead of two 650hp (485kW) Rolls-Royce Buzzard inlines and wings of slightly greater area. Imperial Airways ordered an initial two in June 1926, the airline eventually receiving five.

The first Calcutta was flown on 21 February 1928 and Imperial Airways began scheduled proving flights to the Channel Islands and other local destinations in August before putting the aircraft into regular service from April 1929 on its major route between Genoa and Alexandria, a sector of the London to Karachi route.

By then, three Calcuttas had been delivered, the second introducing Handley Page automatic slats on the upper wing leading edges.

Four other Calcuttas were built: two for Imperial Airways in 1929-30, one for French manufacturer Breguet as a prelude to licence production of four in France and another to the French Navy, this differing in having supercharged 555hp (414kW) Jupiter XFBM engines and increased fuel capacity.

A military version called the Rangoon was first flown in September 1930 and six were delivered to the RAF for service in the Far East. These had the increased fuel capacity of the French Navy Calcutta and could be armed with defensive machine guns and a 454kg (1000lb) bomb load under the wings. They remained in RAF service until 1936, with one of them sold to civilian training organisation Air Pilots Training Ltd in the same year.

Imperial Airways' Calcuttas were largely redeployed on African services (mainly Khartoum-Kisumu) from 1933 and in 1936 the three survivors were sold to Air Pilots Training, the prototype re-engined with 840hp (626kW) Armstrong Siddeley Tiger radials. The last Calcutta was scrapped in 1939.

Photo: S.8 Calcutta.

Short Kent and Scylla

Country of origin: United Kingdom.

Powerplants: Four 555hp (414kW) Bristol Jupiter XFBM nine cylinder radials; four bladed propellers.

Performance: Kent – max speed 119kt (220km/h); cruising speed 91kt (169km/h); initial climb 840ft (256m)/min; service ceiling 17,500ft (5335m); range 391nm (724km). Scylla – cruising speed 91kt (169km/h); range 391nm (724km).

Weights: Kent – empty 9280kg (20,460lb); max takeoff 14,515kg (32,000lb). Scylla – empty 10,274kg (22,650lb); max takeoff 15,196kg (33,500lb).

Dimensions: Kent – wing span 34.44m (113ft 0in); length 23.90m (78ft 5in); height 8.53m (28ft 0in); wing area 245.2m² (2640sq ft). Scylla – length 25.55m (83ft 10in).

Accommodation: Kent – 16 passengers. Scylla – up to 39 passengers.

Production: 3 S.17 Kent and 2 L.17 Scylla.

History: An enlarged, four engined development of the Calcutta, the S.17 Kent was ordered by Imperial Airways for use on the Empire route to Cairo following the politically motivated closure of the Italian seaports to the airline in late 1929.

The first of three Kents (named *Scipio*) flew on 24 February 1931 followed by *Sylvanus* on 31 March and *Satyrus* on 2 May. Despite the larger internal and external size of the Kent compared to its predecessor, passenger capacity remained the same but in considerable comfort. The most important aspect of the Kent's payload was the mail, housed in a large hold capable of carrying up to two tonnes.

Imperial Airways inaugurated its modified Genoa-Alexandria service in May 1931, operating in conjunction with four Calcuttas. *Sylvanus* was sabotaged and burnt out at Brindisi in November 1935, *Scipio* was lost after a fatal heavy landing at Crete in August 1936, and *Satyrus* continued in service for two months after that until replaced by Empire flying boats. *Satyrus* was subsequently used for survey flights to Africa and Singapore and was broken up in Britain in June 1938.

Faced with a shortage of aircraft for its European routes, Imperial Airways in 1933 asked Short to build a landplane version of the Kent. The result was the L.17 (originally S.17/L), combining the powerplants, wings and tailplane of the Kent with a new rectangular section fuselage and fixed undercarriage. Up to 39 passengers could be accommodated.

The first aircraft (carrying the class name *Scylla*) flew on 26 March 1934 and the second and last example (*Syrinx*) on 1 May. Both entered Imperial Airways service in June on the Croydon-Paris route. *Syrinx* was fitted with Bristol Perseus radials on its two inboard positions in June 1935 and after being flipped onto its back during a gale at Brussels in October 1935 all four engines were replaced with 660hp (492kW) Pegasus XCs during the rebuild.

Both L.17s were used to transport stores and personnel to France after the outbreak of war in September 1939 and were then requisitioned by the RAF. Neither survived 1940, *Scylla* wrecked in a gale and *Syrinx* scrapped.

Photo: L.17 Scylla.

Short Scion and Scion Senior

Country of origin: United Kingdom.

Powerplants: Scion 1 – two 85hp (63kW) Pobjoy Niagara I or II seven cylinder radials. Scion 2 – two 90hp (67kW) Niagara IIIs; two bladed propellers. Scion Senior – four Niagara IIIs.

Performance: Scion 2 – max speed 111kt (206km/h); cruising speed 101kt (187km/h); initial climb 625ft (190m)/min; service ceiling 13,000ft (3960m); range 339nm (628km). Scion Senior (floatplane) – cruising speed 100kt (185km/h); range 348nm (644km).

Weights: Scion 1 – empty 776kg (1710lb); max takeoff 1383kg (3050lb). Scion 2 – empty 803kg (1770lb); max takeoff 1451kg (3200lb). Scion Senior (floatplane) – empty 1763kg (3886lb); max takeoff 2608kg (5750lb).

Dimensions: Scion – wing span 12.80m (42ft 0in); length 9.60m (31ft 6in); height 3.16m (10ft 4½in); wing area 23.7m² (255sq ft). Scion Senior – wing span 16.76m (55ft 0in); length 12.80m (42ft 0in); wing area 37.2m² (400sq ft).

Accommodation: Scion – pilot and 5-6 passengers. Scion Senior – 9 passengers.

Production: Scion – 1 prototype, 4 Scion 1 and 11 Scion 2 by Short plus 6 by Pobjoy, total 16. Scion Senior – 6 by Short.

History: Perceiving the need for a low cost, five passenger light transport in the early 1930s, Short broke away from its normal large flying boat product to produce the S.16 Scion. Economy ruled the Scion's design with power provided by a pair of tiny Pobjoy Niagara radials under the wings. The fuselage was of fabric covered steel tube construction, the wings were a fabric covered single spar metal design and either floats or wheels could be fitted.

The prototype with 75hp (56kW) Pobjoy R radials first flew on 18 August 1933. The initial production Scion 1 of 1934 had 85hp (63kW) Niagara I or II engines and raised rear fuselage top decking while the Scion 2 (1935) featured 90hp (67kW) Niagara IIIs remounted to produce a raised thrust line, increased maximum weight and accommodation for a sixth passenger. Short built 16 Scions of all models but Pobjoy then took over production so that Short could concentrate its resources on the 'C' Class (Empire) flying boats. Pobjoy built six Scions in 1936-37.

Scions flew with companies including Southend Flying Services, West of Scotland Airways, Aberdeen Airways, Olley Air Service, Sierra Leone's Elders Colonial Airways and Palestine Air Transport. Several found their way to Australia for operators such as Adelaide Airways, Australian National Airways, Guinea Airways and Connellan Airways. One of the Adelaide Airways Scion 2s flew with all of the above, surviving two crashes and rebuilds before finally being removed from the Australian civil register in early 1965. This aircraft also had 90hp (67kW) de Havilland Gipsy Minor engines fitted in 1946.

Short also developed the larger S.22 Scion Senior with four Niagara III engines and accommodation for nine passengers. Available as either a landplane or seaplane, five of the six built were in the latter configuration. The first aircraft flew on 22 October 1935 and deliveries made to West of Scotland, Elders Colonial and Burma's Irrawaddy Flotilla Company.

Photo: S.16 Scion.

Short Empire

Country of origin: United Kingdom.

Powerplants: S.23/33 – four 920hp (686kW) Bristol Pegasus XC or 1010hp (753kW) Pegasus XXII nine cylinder radials. S.30 – four 890hp (664kW) Bristol Perseus XII nine cylinder radials; three bladed propellers.

Performance: S.23 – max speed 174kt (322km/h); cruising speed 143kt (266km/h); initial climb 950ft (290m)/min; service ceiling 20,000ft (6096m); normal range 660nm (1223km) or 2868nm (5310km) in trans-Atlantic models. S.30 – normal range 1130nm (2092km).

Weights: S.23 – empty 10,660kg (23,500lb); max takeoff 19,732kg (43,500lb). S.30 – empty 12,323kg (27,180lb); max takeoff 21,773kg (48,000lb). S.33 – max takeoff 24,041kg (53,000lb).

Dimensions: Wing span 34.75m (114ft 0in); length 26.82m (88ft 0in); height 9.70m (31ft 10in); wing area 139.4m² (1500sq ft).

Accommodation: 16 berthed or 24 seated passengers.

Production: 31 S.23, 9 S.30 and 2 S.33, total 42.

History: In many ways the epitome of prewar British commercial aviation, the Empire (C-class) flying boats resulted from the British Government's 1934 Empire Air Mail Programme to allow the carriage of first class mail throughout the Empire without surcharge. As a result, Imperial Airways called for a flying boat capable of carrying 24 passengers and 1½ tonnes of mail over 800 statute mile (1290km) stages at a speed of 150mph (241km/h).

The result was the S.23, a highly advanced all metal monoplane powered by four Bristol Pegasus radials. Passengers were accommodated on the lower deck (complete with promenade lounge) while the upper level housed the spacious flight deck and mail hold. Imperial Airways was so impressed it took the unprecedented step of ordering 28 off the drawing board.

The first S.23 (*Canopus*) flew on 4 July 1936 and went into service on 30 October on a scheduled flight between Alexandria and Brindisi. *Canopus* also flew the first Southampton-Durban service in June 1937. By then the order had been increased to 31 of which nine were allocated to Qantas to fly the last sectors of the England-Australia route. Two S.23s were built with additional fuel capacity for long range trans-Atlantic air mail trials.

Nine S.30s with Perseus sleeve valve radials, increased fuel and strengthened structure for higher weights followed, the first of them (*Champion*) flying on 28 September 1938. Four were fitted with flight refuelling equipment for trans-Atlantic services (a significant first using Handley Page Harrow tankers) and made 16 crossings before the war. Two S.30s were delivered to New Zealand's Tasman Empire Airways Ltd (TEAL) for use on the Auckland-Sydney route.

The final C-class variant was the S.33, a hybrid combining the S.23's powerplants and fuel capacity with the S.30's strengthened hull and higher weights. Three were ordered but only two were completed for BOAC in 1940 as the last of the line.

The Empire boats saw extensive wartime service on transport duties and were involved in some courageous evacuations and other actions, especially in the Pacific. The last one was scrapped in Sydney in December 1947.

Photo: S.23 *Canopus.*

Short-Mayo S.20/S.21 Composite

Country of origin: United Kingdom.

Powerplants: S.20 – four 370hp (276kW) Napier Rapier VI 'H' inlines; two bladed propellers. S.21 – four 920hp (686kW) Bristol Pegasus XC nine cylinder radials; three bladed propellers.

Performance: S.20 – max speed 180kt (333km/h); cruising speed 156kt (280km/h); range 3300nm (6112km). S.21 – max speed 174kt (322km/h); cruising speed 143kt (266km/h); range 738nm (1368km).

Weights: S.20 – empty 4536kg (10,000lb); normal max takeoff 7031kg (15,500lb); air launched max takeoff 9300kg (20,500lb). S.21 – empty 10,886kg (24,000lb); normal max takeoff 17,237kg (38,000lb).

Dimensions: S.20 – wing span 22.25m (73ft 0in); length 15.54m (51ft 0in); wing area 56.8m² (611sq ft). S.21 – wing span 34.75m (114ft 0in); length 25.88m (84ft 11in).

Accommodation: S.20 – mail and freight. S.21 – 24 passengers or none if part of composite.

Production: 1 S.20 and 1 S.21.

History: The long distances involved with the important trans-Atlantic route led Imperial Airways to look at various ways of extending the range of its flying boats including the use of aerial refuelling (see previous entry) and the Short-Mayo composite. The brainchild of the airline's General Manager (Technical), Major Robert Mayo, the aircraft were built to test the theory of launching a heavily loaded mailplane from the back of a larger, lightly loaded 'mother' aircraft once cruising height was reached. The lower component would then return to base to pick up the next mailplane.

The upper component of the composite was the S.20 (named *Mercury*), a four engined all metal twin float seaplane which first flew on 5 September 1937. The lower component was the S.21 (named *Maia*), a derivative of the S.23 Empire flying boat with a wider planing hull, modified floats, engines located further outboard and modified fin. It first flew on 27 July 1937.

The composite began taxiing trails on 1 January 1938, first flight was on 20 January and the first separation achieved on 6 February. Trials were successfully completed in May 1938 and the aircraft handed over to Imperial Airways. The first commercial separation was recorded on 21 July 1938 when *Mercury* flew non stop to Montreal – a distance of 2546nm (4716km) – in 20hrs 20min carrying a 272kg (600lb) payload. The skipper was Captain (later Air Vice Marshal) Donald Bennett, subsequently of Pathfinders fame.

In October 1938 Bennett took *Mercury* 5253nm (9730km) non stop to the mouth of the Orange River in South Africa, setting a world distance record for seaplanes. The last commercial separation was in January 1939 when Bennett carried Christmas mail the 1912nm (3541km) from Southampton to Alexandria.

Mercury flew with the RAF's No 320 (Netherlands) Squadron, a seaplane reconnaissance unit, in 1940-41 but was scrapped in August of the same year; *Maia* was operated as a navigation trainer after the outbreak of war but destroyed by enemy action in Poole Harbour in May 1941.

Photo: S.21 *Maia* (lower) and S.20 *Mercury* Mayo composite. (Short)

Short S.26

Country of origin: United Kingdom.

Powerplants: Four 1380hp (1029kW) Bristol Hercules IV or XIV 14-cylinder radials; three bladed propellers.

Performance: Max speed 182kt (336km/h); cruising speed 156kt (290km/h); range 2780nm (5150km).

Weights: Empty 17,100kg (37,700lb); max takeoff 33,340kg (73,500lb).

Dimensions: Wing span 40.94m (134ft 4in); length 30.89m (101ft 4in); height 11.45m (37ft 7in); wing area 200.7m² (2160sq ft).

Accommodation: Up to 40 passengers.

Production: 3.

History: The success of the S.23 Empire flying boats in Imperial Airways service led to the airline discussing with the Air Ministry in 1937 a larger and longer range aircraft capable of flying the Atlantic. The concept was prompted by the development of the more powerful Bristol Hercules 14-cylinder radial, which allowed greater fuel load and higher weights.

Short responded with the S.26, three of which were ordered by Imperial Airways in February 1938 as the G-class and named *Golden Hind*, *Golden Fleece* and *Golden Horn*. Although bearing a strong resemblance to the S.23, the S.26 was substantially larger with considerably improved payload/range capability and intended to carry a 2 tonnes load over a range of 2500 statute miles (4023km).

Apart from the more powerful engines (driving three bladed de Havilland constant-speed propellers) and increased size, weight and fuel capacity, the S.26 differed from its predecessor by including some of the Sunderland military flying boat's features including its four crew flight deck and tall vertical rear step and taller stern.

Golden Hind was the first to fly on 21 July 1939 and was handed over to Imperial Airways for crew training on 24 September, three weeks after the outbreak of WWII. The other two followed quickly but none entered commercial service before they were impressed into RAF service. Under the designation S.26/M they were converted for military use in early 1940, the conversion including fitting radar, provision for the carriage of depth charges and three Boulton Paul gun turrets – two on the upper fuselage and one in the tail.

The S.26s served with No 119 Squadron until late 1941 when the two survivors returned to civil operations with BOAC. *Golden Fleece* had been lost in August 1941 after a double engine failure near Cape Finisterre resulted in a forced alighting. In BOAC service the two S.26s had their military equipment removed and 40 passenger seats fitted. Based at Poole, they were used mainly on the route to Lagos via Lisbon, Bathurst, Accra and Freetown.

Golden Horn was lost off Lisbon in January 1943 due to an engine fire during a test flight. *Golden Hind* soldiered on through and after the war, the latter after refurbishment to full civil standards and mainly on BOAC's Poole-Athens-Cairo service. Retired in September 1947, various plans for further use came to nought and she was sunk in a gale in May 1954.

Photo: S.26 *Golden Hind*.

Short Sandringham

Country of origin: United Kingdom.

Powerplants: Mks.2-7 – four 1200hp (895kW) Pratt & Whitney R-1830 Twin Wasp 14-cylinder radials; three bladed propellers.

Performance: Mks.5/7 – max speed 179kt (332km/h); cruising speed 153kt (283km/h); initial climb 840ft (256m)/min; service ceiling 17,900ft (5455m); range 2120nm (3927km).

Weights: Mks.5/7 – empty 17,916kg (39,498lb); max takeoff 27,216kg (60,000lb).

Dimensions: Wing span 34.38m (112ft 9½in); length 26.29m (86ft 3in); height 6.97m (22ft 10½in); wing area 156.7m² (1687sq ft).

Accommodation: Typically 16-30 passengers depending on day/night layout, maximum 45.

Production: 1 Mk.1, 3 Mk.2, 2 Mk.3, 4 Mk.4, 9 Mk.5, 5 Mk.6 and 3 Mk.7, total 27 conversions.

History: The S.25 Sunderland military flying boat's cavernous interior made it an obvious candidate for conversion to passenger and freight carrying duties. The first conversion programme was conducted between 1942 and 1944 when 25 Sunderland IIIs were converted for BOAC on the production line, the aircraft retaining the original Bristol Pegasus engines, bench seats were fitted, the guns and military equipment removed, and the turrets replaced by fairings.

Mainly used on services from Britain to West Africa and India, 18 of them were further modified for civil operations after VE Day as the *Hythe* class with accommodation for 24 day or 16 night passengers plus a 2948kg (6500lb) mail load. They plied the Empire routes to India, Singapore, Australia and New Zealand and were joined by two new conversions postwar plus two for Uruguay's CAUSA.

A more comprehensive conversion for civil use resulted in the S.25/V Sandringham, the sole Sandringham 1 prototype (converted from a Pegasus powered Sunderland III) first flying in November 1945. The conversion was extensive with reshaped S.26 G-class type nose and tailcone plus rectangular windows and a remodelled interior with two decks and spacious accommodation for 16 night or 24 day passengers, complete with dining room and cocktail bar.

All other Sandringhams converted between 1945 and 1948 were powered by Pratt & Whitney Twin Wasp engines regardless of the Sunderland mark (either III or V) from which they were derived.

Designations were applied to versions developed for specific operators: Mk.2 (Argentina's Dodero with accommodation for 45 passengers); Mk.3 (also for Dodero); Mk.4 (New Zealand's Tasman Empire Airways Ltd – TEAL); Mk.5 (BOAC 16-22 seaters); Mk.6 (Norway's DNL, radar equipped 37 seaters); and Mk.7 (BOAC *Bermuda* class as 30 seaters).

BOAC began replacing its 'boats with Constellations and Canadair Fours in 1949 and ended flying boat operations completely in November 1950. Its fleet of Sandringhams and Sunderlands was dispersed to operators such as Aquila Airways, CAUSA and Qantas.

The final conversion was carried out long after the others, in 1963 when Australia's Ansett modified a former RNZAF Sunderland GR.5 to near Sandringham standards at its flying boat base in Sydney.

Photo: Sandringham 4. (Eric Allen)

Short Solent

Country of origin: United Kingdom.

Powerplants: Solent 2/3 – four 1690hp (1260kW) Bristol Hercules 637 14-cylinder radials. Solent 3 – four 2040hp (1521kW) Hercules 733; four bladed propellers.

Performance: 2 – max speed 237kt (439km/h); cruising speed 212kt (393km/h); initial climb 925ft (282m)/min; service ceiling 17,000ft (5180m); range 1564nm (2897km). 3 – cruising speed 205kt (380km/h); range 1903nm (3525km). 4 – cruising speed 218kt (404km/h); range 2607nm (4828km).

Weights: 2 – empty 21,664kg (47,760lb); max takeoff 35,381kg (78,000lb). 3 – empty 21,868kg (48,210lb); max takeoff 35,653kg (78,600lb). 4 – empty 22,292kg (49,145lb); max takeoff 36,288kg (80,000lb).

Dimensions: Wing span 34.38m (112ft 9½in); length 26.72m (87ft 8in); height 10.44m (34ft 3in); wing area 156.7m² (1687sq ft).

Accommodation: Up to 44 passengers.

Production: 12 Solent 2, 6 Solent 3 and 4 Solent 4, total 22 (see text).

History: Short's last large commercial flying boat, the S.45 Solent had its origins in the Seaford (originally Sunderland IV) military 'boat intended for service in the Pacific.

An enlarged Sunderland, the Seaford retained the early aircraft's wing but with a longer and wider planing bottom on the standard width hull, increased weights, the use of heavier gauge metal, more powerful Bristol Hercules engines and larger vertical and horizontal tail surfaces.

The prototype first flew on 30 August 1944 but the type was too late to see service in WWII and the original order for 30 was reduced to six. One of these was loaned to BOAC in 1946 for evaluation, resulting for an order for 12 being placed as the Solent 2 with accommodation for 34 day passengers on two decks connected by a spiral staircase. Lounge, dining, promenade, library and cocktail bar facilities were provided. The originally proposed Solent 1 with day or night accommodation was not built.

The first Solent 2 was launched on 11 November 1946 and the 12th and last on 8 April 1948. The Solents were leased by BOAC from the Ministry of Civil Aviation, entering service on the South Africa route in April 1948. BOAC ended its flying boat operations in November 1950 but six 39 passenger Solent 3s had meanwhile entered service from early 1949, these converted on the production line from Seafords originally intended for the RAF.

The final version was a quartet of Solent 4s ordered by New Zealand's Tasman Empire Airways Ltd (TEAL) in September 1947 and built during 1949. These featured more powerful engines, increased weights and longer range. Accommodating 44 passengers, they went into service on the Auckland-Sydney route in November 1949 and from June 1950 to Fiji.

Most BOAC Solents were scrapped after withdrawal from service but some went to Australia's Trans-Oceanic Airways and Britain's Aquila Airways which operated its final Solent service to Madeira in September 1958. TEAL retained one until September 1960 when the last service from Fiji to Tahiti was flown.

Photo: Solent 4.

Short Skyvan

Country of origin: United Kingdom.

Powerplants: Srs.3 – two 715shp (533kW) Garrett-AiResearch TPE331-201 turboprops; three bladed propellers.

Performance: Srs.3 – max cruise 175kt (324km/h); economical cruise 150kt (278km/h); initial climb 1640ft (500m)/min; service ceiling 22,500ft (6860m); range with 1814kg (4000lb) payload and reserves 162nm (300km); max fuel range 600nm (1111km).

Weights: Srs.3 – operating empty (passenger version) 3674kg (8100lb); max takeoff 5670kg (12,500lb).

Dimensions: Wing span 19.79m (64ft 11in); length 12.22m (40ft 1in) or 12.60m (41ft 4in) with radome; height 4.60m (15ft 1in); wing area 35.1m² (378sq ft).

Accommodation: 19 passengers three abreast or up to 2086kg (4600lb) freight.

Production: 1 Srs.1, 13 Srs.2, 85 Srs.3, 50 Srs.3m, total 149 (plus one incomplete airframe).

History: The concept behind the SC.7 Skyvan was a continuation of that begun in the mid 1940s by Miles Aircraft with its Aerovan, literally a 'flying van' with capacious fuselage for its modest size and rear loading capability. One Aerovan had been experimentally fitted with the very high aspect ratio Hurel Dubois wing in 1957 as the HDM.105.

Short acquired the larger HDM.106 Caravan's design rights in 1958 and extensively reworked it, producing the utilitarian Skyvan built around a 1.98 x 1.98m (6ft 6in x 6ft 6in) fuselage box for 19 passengers and/or freight with rear loading door and a reduced span version of the Hurel Dubois wing. Construction of the prototype began in 1960 but due to the workload associated with the Belfast military transport it didn't fly until 17 January 1963, powered by two 390hp (291kW) Continental GTSIO-520 turbocharged six cylinder piston engines.

It had already been decided that turboprop power was the way to go and in October 1963 the first aircraft was reflown with two 529ehp (394kW) Turboméca Astazou Xs and lowered tailplane. Production Skyvan Srs.2s had 730eshp (544kW) Astazou XIIs, square cabin windows, modified nose and a single rather than twin nosewheel. The first Srs.2 flew in October 1965 and customers included Aeralpi, Emerald Airways and Northern Consolidated.

The Astazou suffered some performance deficiencies in hot and high conditions and lacked appeal to American operators, resulting in another engine change to the definitive Srs.3 with Garrett-AiResearch TPE331s. A Srs.2 was converted to the new engine and flown in December 1967 and deliveries began the following year, early customers including Cherokee Airlines, Continental Air Services, Papuan Air Transport, Wien Consolidated and Loganair.

The military Skyvan 3M with optional increased maximum weight and accommodation for up to 22 troops was introduced in 1969 and sold to several air arms. A purely passenger carrying version with a higher standard of interior furnishings and air-stair door appeared in 1971 as the Skyliner and was sold to Malaysia Air Charter, Gulf Aviation and BEA. Skyvan production was sporadic from the late 1970s, the last one (for the United Emirates Air Force) flown in January 1986 and delivered three months later.

Photo: Skyvan 3M. (Alan Scoot)

Short 330

Country of origin: United Kingdom.

Powerplants: 330-100 – two 1173shp (875kW) Pratt & Whitney Canada PT6A-45A/B turboprops. 330-200 – two 1198shp (893kW) PT6A-45R; five bladed propellers.

Performance: 330-200 – max cruise 190kt (352km/h); economical cruise 160kt (296km/h); initial climb 1180ft (360m)/min; max payload range 473nm (876km); range with 22 passengers 915nm (1695km).

Weights: 330-100 – empty equipped (airliner) 6577kg (14,500lb); max takeoff 10,292kg (22,690lb). 330-200 – empty equipped (airliner) 6680kg (14,727lb); max takeoff 10,387kg (22,900lb).

Dimensions: Wing span 22.76m (74ft 8in); length 17.69m (58ft 0½in); height 4.95m (16ft 3in); wing area 42.1m² (453sq ft).

Accommodation: 30 passengers three abreast or mixed passengers/freight.

Production: 141 of all models including 9 330-UTT and 34 C-23.

History: Affectionately known as 'The Shed' by some, development of the Short SD.3-30 (later simply 330) began in the early 1970s to capture the emerging commuter or regional airline market. Intended as a simple, unpressurised and inexpensive to buy and operate aircraft, the aim was to produce a 30 seat airliner with a price of less than £400,000 ($US1,000,000) in 1973 values.

The resulting design shared many of the features of the Skyvan including a stretched by 3.78m (12ft 5in) version of its square section fuselage, the same outer wing panels attached to longer inner panels and similar but larger twin tail surfaces. Completely new features included a longer nose (incorporating a baggage hold), increased fuel capacity and weights, deletion of the Skyvan's rear loading ramp, retractable undercarriage and more powerful Pratt & Whitney Canada PT6A-45 turboprops driving advanced five bladed propellers.

Project go-ahead was given in May 1973. The first prototype flew on 22 August 1974, the second on 8 July 1975 and the first production example on 15 December 1975. The first delivery was to Canada's Time Air in August 1976.

Early 330s were powered by 1173shp (875kW) PT6A-45A or B engines and dubbed either simply the 330 or 330-100. The definitive commercial version, the 330-200 with more powerful PT6A-45Rs, increased fuel capacity and higher weights appeared in 1978. After a slow start sales gradually picked up including to many US regional operators. Customers included Golden West Airlines, DLT, Hawaiian Airlines, Henson Airlines, Suburban Airlines, Metro Express, Atlanta Express, Thai Airways, Aer Lingus Commuter, Air UK and Jersey European.

Freighter and special missions versions of the 330 were offered including the Sherpa with rear loading ramp (34 built for the USAF/Army as the C-23A/B) and the 330-UTT which was sold in small numbers to the Thai Police and others. The last new airline 330 was delivered to Sweden's Syd-Aero in March 1984, the final civil model was a UTT for the Quebec Government in June 1991 and the last of the line was a C-23B for the USAF delivered in September 1992.

Photo: Short 330-200.

Short 360

Country of origin: United Kingdom.

Powerplants: 100 – two 1327shp (990kW) Pratt & Whitney Canada PT6A-65R turboprops. 200 – two 1424shp (1062kW) PT6A-65AR; five bladed propellers. 300 – two 1424shp (1062kW) PT6A-67R; six bladed propellers.

Performance: 100 – max cruise 210kt (389km/h); range with 36 passengers at max cruise 230nm (426km). 300 – max cruise 216kt (400km/h); initial climb 952ft (290m)/min; range at max cruise 402nm (745km) with 36 passengers or 636nm (1178nm) with 31 passengers.

Weights: 100 – operating empty 7530kg (16,600lb); max takeoff 11,658kg (25,700lb). 300 – operating empty 7870kg (17,350lb); max takeoff 12,293kg (27,100lb).

Dimensions: Wing span 22.80m (74ft 9¹/₂in); length 21.58m (70ft 9¹/₂in); height 7.26m (23ft 10in); wing area 42.2m² (454sq ft).

Accommodation: 36 passengers three abreast.

Production: 80 360-100, 36 360-200 and 48 360-300, total 164.

History: A stretched, larger capacity and upgraded 36 seat derivative of the 330, development of the 360 (originally SD.3-60) was prompted by the reasonable success of the earlier aircraft in the regional airliner market, especially in the USA, and the deregulation of the US industry in 1978 which relaxed the rule that aircraft flown by commuter operators should have no more than 30 passenger seats.

Short had already been studying an improved 330 with more powerful PT6A-65 engines and higher weights but in July 1980 released details of the 360 with accommodation for 36 passengers and the new engines. The aircraft's appearance was 'modernised' by replacing the earlier twin tails with a conventional design with single fin and rudder mounted on a redesigned rear fuselage which removed the option of a rear loading ramp. The new rear fuselage allowed two more seat rows to be fitted and reduced drag, providing increased speed. The cabin remained unpressurised.

Formal go-ahead was given in January 1981 and the first aircraft flown on 1 June of the same year, this short gestation period indicating the high degree of commonality between the 360 and 330. The first production 360 (later 360-100) flew in August 1982 and the first delivery was to Pennsylvania based Suburban Airlines in November 1982.

The improved 360 Advanced (later 360-200) with more powerful PT6A-65R engines flew in October 1985 and initial deliveries to Thai Airways began the following month.

The final version was the 360-300 (first flight February 1987) with PT6A-67Rs of similar power (but greater derating for improved hot and high performance) driving six bladed propellers, modified wing struts, low drag exhaust stubs, increased maximum weight, an optional autopilot (offered for the first time, interestingly) and improved interior. Philippine Airlines was the initial customer, receiving its first aircraft in April 1987.

The 360 remained in production until 1989 but the last example for Rheinland Air Service wasn't assembled and flown until June 1991. Seven other airframes were not completed.

Photo: Short 360-100.

Sikorsky S-38

Country of origin: USA.

Powerplants: S-38A – two 410hp (306kW) Pratt & Whitney R-1340 Wasp nine cylinder radials. S-38B/C – two 420hp (313kW) Pratt & Whitney Wasps; two bladed propellers.

Performance: S-38B – max speed 108kt (200km/h); cruising speed 95kt (176km/h); range 517nm (958km).

Weights: S-38B – empty 2948kg (6500lb); max takeoff 4754kg (10,480lb).

Dimensions: Wing span 21.84m (71ft 8in); length 12.27m (40ft 3in); height 4.22m (13ft 10in); wing area 66.9m² (720sq ft).

Accommodation: S-38A/B – 6-10 passengers. S-38C – up to 12 passengers.

Production: 1 S-38, 11 S-38A, 75 S-38B and 33 S-38C, total 120.

History: Although mainly remembered for his pioneering work in developing the concept of the helicopter as a practical proposition, Igor Sikorsky also made a significant contribution to commercial air transport after he emigrated from Russia to the USA during the 1917 revolution.

Flying boats were his speciality in the 1920s and '30s beginning with the experimental S-34 and production S-36 of 1927, an eight passenger amphibian powered by two 220hp (164kW) Wright Cyclone radials. Five were built, one of which was used by Pan American on scheduled services for a short time.

The S-38 was Sikorsky's first commercial success in the USA. A twin engined sesquiplane with a pod-like hull and twin booms leading from the upper wings to the tail unit, the S-38's hull was constructed of a wooden frame covered with duralumin. Power was provided by two Pratt & Whitney Wasps, accommodation was for typically eight passengers and the main landing gear units could be retracted or extended independently to assist water manoeuvring.

The first S-38 flew on 25 June 1928 and was followed by the initial production S-38A which was operated by several airlines including Pan American in the Caribbean, Western Air Express and New York, Rio & Buenos Aires Line (NYRBA).

The major production S-38B featured increased fuel capacity and a variety of interior layouts for up to 10 passengers. A 6-8 seat executive 'air yacht' layout was offered and all configurations had provision for a toilet at the rear of the cabin.

The S-38C was a short range version with accommodation for up to 12 passengers and reduced fuel capacity. Hawaii's Inter-Island Airways (later Hawaiian Airlines) was a major operator and others were flown by Colonial Western Airways.

Pan American was the largest operator of the overall series with more than 30 of the various models while the S-38 was also flown by operators in South America, West Africa and the Dutch East Indies. The US Navy acquired two S-38As as the XPS-2 (later XRS-2) and seven S-38Bs (PS-3 then RS-3) while the USAAC had 11 as the C-6 and C-6A.

The S-39 was a smaller, five seat and single engined version of the S-38 and the S-41 a larger development for 15 passengers powered by three 575hp (429kW) Pratt & Whitney Hornets.

Photo: Sikorsky S-38B.

Sikorsky S-40

Country of origin: USA.

Powerplants: Four 575hp (429kW) Pratt & Whitney R-1690 Hornet nine cylinder radials; two bladed propellers.

Performance: Cruising speed 110kt (185km/h); normal range 486nm (900km).

Weights: Empty 9526kg (21,000lb); max takeoff 15,422kg (34,000lb).

Dimensions: Wing span 34.75m (114ft 0in); length 23.37m (76ft 8in); height 7.26m (23ft 10in); wing area 161.6m² (1740sq ft).

Accommodation: 28-32 passengers.

Production: 3.

History: The largest amphibian in the world when it first appeared, the S-40 continued the design concepts of the S-38 but on a larger scale, resulting in a four engined airliner capable of carrying 32 passengers.

The basic elements were as before – a relatively short hull above which was placed a high, strut mounted wing from which twin booms led to the tail unit with twin fins and rudder. One significant difference was that the lower stub wing of the S-38 (making it a sesquiplane) was replaced with struts on which the wing bracing and stabilising floats were attached. The four Pratt & Whitney Hornet radials were strut mounted below the leading edge of the wing.

The two step design metal hull was divided into seven watertight compartments. The wings were metal with fabric covering, except for the metal leading edges. The retractable undercarriage was later removed in order to save weight, converting the S-40s into flying boats. The passengers were accommodated in a high degree of luxury and had a separate smoking room available to them.

The S-40 was developed to meet the requirements of Pan American, which needed a larger aircraft than the S-36, S-38s and S-41s (see previous entry) it had already operated. The S-40 appeared after the S-41.

Pan American ordered three S-40s in December 1929 and the first aircraft was completed in early 1931. A naming ceremony was held in October 1931, the aircraft christened *American Clipper* by Mrs Herbert Hoover. The other two S-40s were named *Caribbean Clipper* and *Southern Clipper*, the first Pan American aircraft to carry the long running *Clipper* title.

The first S-40 passenger carrying service was conducted on 19 November 1931 from Miami to the Panama Control Zone via Barranquila (Colombia), Cienfuegos (Cuba) and Kingston (Jamaica), the last leg from Kingston involving a 520nm (965km) overwater sector.

A certain Colonel Charles Lindbergh was in command of the flight and one of the passengers was Igor Sikorsky. From Panama, Consolidated Commodores continued on to Buenos Aires, resulting in a relatively fast and comfortable air service between the USA and Argentina.

The three aircraft were redesignated S-40A in 1935 when they were fitted with more powerful 660hp (492kW) Hornet T2D1 engines. All three remained in Pan American service throughout the 1930s. *Caribbean Clipper* later flew with the US Navy as a navigation trainer.

Photo: Sikorsky S-40 *Southern Clipper.*

Sikorsky S-42

Country of origin: USA.

Powerplants: S-42 – four 700hp (522kW) Pratt & Whitney R-1690-S5D1-G Hornet nine cylinder radials. S-42A/B – four 750hp (559kW) Hornet S1EG; three bladed propellers.

Performance: Max speed 163kt (302km/h); cruising speed 148kt (274km/h); range 1043nm (1931km).

Weights: S-42 – empty 10,886kg (24,000lb); max takeoff 17,237kg (38,000lb). S-42A – max takeoff 18,144kg (40,000lb). S-42B – max takeoff 19,051kg (42,000lb).

Dimensions: S-42 – wing span 34.80m (114ft 2in); length 21.08m (69ft 2in); height 5.28m (17ft 4in); wing area 124.5m² (1340sq ft). S-42A/B – wing span 36.02m (118ft 2in).

Accommodation: Up to 32 passengers.

Production: 10.

History: Pan American Airways issued a specification for a new, modern and long range flying boat in August 1931, the requirement calling for the capability to carry a crew of four and at least 12 passengers over a range of 2500 statute miles (4023km) at a speed of 145mph (233km/h).

Sikorsky responded with the S-42 which differed from the company's earlier amphibians and flying boats by dispensing with their 'pod and booms' design and adapting a more conventional configuration with full length, two step hull above which a strut braced parasol wing was mounted on a short superstructure. The four Pratt & Whitney Hornet radials were mounted on the wing leading edges, construction was all metal and the 32 passengers were accommodated in four compartments.

Pan American ordered an initial three S-42s in November 1932, the first of which was 'properly' flown on 30 March 1934, following a short hop the previous day. The S-42 entered service with Pan American on 16 August 1934 on its Miami-Rio de Janeiro route. In 1935 the S-42 pioneered the Pacific route from San Francisco to Manila. It was not entirely suitable for the long distances involved in the Pacific as payload-range performance was poor.

Pan American took delivery of seven other S-42s, four as S-42As with more powerful engines, longer span wings and increased maximum weight; and three S-42Bs with a further weight increase, some aerodynamic refinements (especially associated with hull and fairings design) and constant-speed propellers.

An S-42B surveyed the San Francisco to New Zealand (via Honolulu) route in 1937 and this variant was also used to inaugurate the Manila-Hong Kong service, and from June 1937 the New York-Bermuda passenger and mail service shared with Imperial Airways. North Atlantic survey flights were undertaken during 1937 and Pan American introduced Seattle-Alaska services in 1940.

Negotiations for production of the S-42A in Britain by British Marine Aircraft reached an advanced stage with ground being cleared for the factory at Hamble on Southampton Water before the project was shelved. The last S-42s were scrapped in 1946.

Photo: Sikorsky S-42 of Pan American Airways.

Sikorsky S-43

Country of origin: USA.

Powerplants: Two 750hp (559kW) Pratt & Whitney R-1690 Hornet nine cylinder radials; three bladed propellers.

Performance: Max speed 165kt (306km/h); cruising speed 144kt (267km/h); initial climb 1000ft (305m)/min; service ceiling 19,000ft (5790m); range 673nm (1247km).

Weights: Empty 5783kg (12,750lb); max takeoff 8845kg (19,500lb).

Dimensions: Wing span 26.21m (86ft 0in); length 15.60m (51ft 2in); height 5.38m (17ft 8in); wing area 72.5m² (781sq ft).

Accommodation: Up to 18 passengers.

Production: 53.

History: Despite resembling a scaled down version of the four engined S-42 flying boat, the twin engined 15-18 passenger S-43 amphibian was a rather more advanced design, although the general characteristics of the larger aircraft – all metal construction, parasol wing etc – were retained.

The two Pratt & Whitney Hornet nine cylinder radial engines drove constant-speed propellers and were mounted on the wing leading edges.

Single rather than twin vertical tail surfaces were fitted, the wing struts were of more compact design and the mainwheels retracted into cutouts on the sides of the two-step hull with the tailwheel located behind the rear step.

A feature of the S-43 was its large flaps which covered nearly half the wing span and about one-fifth of the chord. The underwing stabilising floats were fixed.

The first S-43 flew in 1935 and Pan American purchased 14 for itself and associate airline Panair do Brasil (nicknaming them *Baby Clippers*), putting them into service in April 1936 in Brazil and the Caribbean where they replaced Consolidated Commodore flying boats. In August 1938 Pan American used the S-43 for proving flights between Seattle and Juneau in Alaska.

Several other operators also purchased S-43s, among them Inter-Island Airways (later Hawaiian Airlines) which had four, Aéromaritime (four in West Africa), DNL-Norwegian Air Lines (1), Iloilo-Negros Air Express of the Philippines and Alaska's Reeve Aleutian Airways (1).

Others were flown in China, Russia and other parts of South America including being used for the transport of rubber in Brazil during WWII.

There were no S-43 variants as such, although military versions were purchased by the USAAC (five Y1OA-8s in 1937 plus one impressed OA-11 in 1941) and 17 as the JRS-1 delivered to the US Navy (15) and Marine Corps (2) between 1937 and 1939.

The USAAC's Y1OA-8s were slightly modified for military service with the seats removable for the carriage of cargo; the OA-11 was briefly used as a personnel transport before crashing on a journey to Trinidad. The US Navy's JRS-1s served with a single Utility Squadron (VJ-1) based at San Diego while the type was operated by two Marine Corps units. They were all out of service by mid 1942.

Photo: Preserved Sikorsky S-43.

Sikorsky VS-44A Excalibur

Country of origin: USA.

Powerplants: Four 1200hp (895kW) Pratt & Whitney R-1830-S1C3-G Twin Wasp 14-cylinder radials; three bladed propellers.

Performance: Max speed 197kt (365km/h); cruising speed 152kt (282km/h); initial climb 600ft (183m)/min; service ceiling 23,100ft (7040m); max range 3950nm (7315km).

Weights: Empty 11,978kg (26,407lb); max takeoff 22,018kg (48,540lb).

Dimensions: Wing span 37.80m (124ft 0in); length 23.22m (76ft 2in); height 8.41m (27ft 7in); wing area 155.1m² (1670sq ft).

Accommodation: Initially 16, later 47 passengers.

Production: 1 XPBS-1 and 3 VS-44A.

History: The VS-44A had its origins in a 1935 US Navy requirement for a long range, four engined patrol flying boat, ordering a single prototype as the XPBS-1. Powered by four 1050hp (783kW) Pratt & Whitney R-1830-68 14-cylinder radials, it flew for the first time on 13 August 1937. Armament was a single 0.50in machine gun in the nose and tail and a 0.30in machine in each of the two waist positions. The XPBS-1 was the first US military aircraft to incorporate a tail turret.

Although tested successfully, the XPBS-1 was not ordered into production but the prototype remained in US Navy service until 1942 when it sank in San Francisco Bay. The aircraft's commercial career began in May 1939 when major US shipping company American Export Line formed American Export Airlines (AEA) to operate a trans-Atlantic flying boat service from New York to Britain and France.

AEA ordered three in 16 passenger long range configuration as the VS-44A Excalibur, the 'VS' in the designation reflecting the proper name of the company at the time – Vought-Sikorsky Aircraft, a division of the United Aircraft Corporation.

Powered by more powerful R-1830-S1C3-G Twin Wasps, the first VS-44A was flown on 18 January 1942 and all three had been delivered by the following June, although by then the war had changed AEA's situation. The outbreak of war in Europe in September 1939 ended plans to operate to Britain and France but in June 1940 permission was granted to start services from New York to Lisbon.

The USA's entry to the war in December 1941 changed it again, AEA then contracted by the US Navy to operated its Naval Air Transport Service on the North Atlantic route, the first such flight between New York and Foynes (Ireland) occurring in June 1942. The VS-44As were allocated the military designation JR2S-1 but carried civil markings. More than 400 Atlantic crossings were made between then and October 1945.

AEA then sold the two surviving VS-44As (one had crashed in October 1942), Antilles Air Boats and Avalon Air Transport continuing operations of the type with seating for up to 47 passengers on short haul flights.

A former Antilles Air Boats VS-44A survives in a museum at Windsor Locks, Connecticut.

Photo: Sikorsky VS-44A.

Stinson Model A

Country of origin: USA.

Powerplants: Three 260hp (194kW) Lycoming R-680-5 nine cylinder radials; two bladed propellers.

Performance: Cruising speed 136kt (253km/h); range 348nm (644km).

Weights: Empty 3184kg (7020lb); max takeoff 4513kg (9950lb).

Dimensions: Wing span 18.29m (60ft 0in); length 11.23m (36ft 10in); height 3.89m (12ft 9in); wing area 46.4m² (500sq ft).

Accommodation: Two pilots and 8-10 passengers.

Production: 35.

History: Formed in 1926 by pioneer pilot Eddie Stinson, the company initially known as the Stinson Aircraft Syndicate made its name in the late 1920s and early 1930s through a long line of single engined high wing cabin monoplanes, notably the Detroiter and Junior series.

By 1930 the company had decided to branch out into the airliner market, building a number of high winged three engined transports starting with the 10 passenger SM-6000 Airliner first flown in July 1930. Variations included the SM-6000-A, B, B1, B2 and Model U, production of these models reaching a combined total of about 80.

The company's next and final trimotor airliner was the Model A which was very different in featuring a strut braced low wing with retractable undercarriage. The Stinson A was of fabric covered all metal construction featuring a single spar wing with unusual inverse taper on the centre section inboard of the two wing mounted engines (the third was nose mounted), and trailing edge flaps. The main undercarriage retracted into the engine nacelles with the wheels partially protruding to minimise damage in a wheels up landing.

The Model A came about as the result of American Airways issuing a requirement for a nine passenger airliner costing no more than $US35,000 and with modest runway requirements, a takeoff run of no more than 244m (800ft) being specified. The Model A's three 260hp (194kW) Lycoming R-680 radials helped it easily meet this limitation and the aircraft was ordered into production.

The Model A's first 'proper' flight (after a few test hops) was made on 27 April 1934, although changes demanded by American resulted in Delta Air Corporation putting it into service first in July 1935 on its Dallas-Atlanta-Charleston route. Other US operators included Central Air Lines and of course American, which received 15. Both American and Delta had withdrawn their Model As from service by 1938.

Export sales were made to Airlines of Australia (4) and China's CNAC as well as some private operators. Tata Air Lines (later Air India) acquired four second hand examples in 1941. Two of the Australian Stinsons were lost in accidents, one of them (in February 1937) prompting an extraordinary rescue of the survivors in inhospitable terrain after the wreckage was spotted 10 days after the crash. The two surviving Model As subsequently passed to Australian National Airways which re-engined them with two Pratt & Whitney Wasp radials.

Photo: Stinson Model A.

Sud-Est (Bloch) SE.161 Languedoc

Country of origin: France.

Powerplants: Four 1150hp (857kW) Gnome-Rhône 14N-44/45 14-cylinder radials or four 1200hp (895kW) Pratt & Whitney R-1830-S1C3-G Twin Wasp 14-cylinder radials; three bladed propellers.

Performance: Gnome-Rhône engines – max speed 219kt (405km/h); range 540nm (1000km). Twin Wasp engines – max speed 237kt (439km/h); cruising speed 202kt (375km/h).

Weights: Empty 12,651kg (27,890lb); max takeoff 22,940kg (50,573lb).

Dimensions: Wing span 29.38m (96ft 5in); length 24.25m (79ft 6in); height 5.13m (16ft 10in); wing area 111.3m² (1198sq ft).

Accommodation: 33-44 passengers.

Production: 100.

History: The Languedoc all metal four engined airliner had a somewhat convoluted formative history, its origins going back to September 1939 and the first flight of the Bloch MB.160 prototype. A short range airliner intended for Air Afrique, the MB.160 was powered by four 720hp (537kW) Hispano-Suiza 12 X engines but did not enter production in its original form.

Instead, development concentrated on a larger variant designated the MB.161. The occupation of France resulted in the project being taken over by the Germans and 20 were ordered for Deutsche Luft Hansa, the aircraft to be built in the Société Nationale de Constructions Aéronautiques de Sud-Est (SNCASE) factory at Toulouse.

As it happened, none were delivered during the war, largely as a result of delaying tactics by the French industry which wanted to cause as many problems for the Germans as possible.

The first example of what was now called the SE.161.1 finally flew on 17 September 1945 powered by four Gnome-Rhône 14N radials and providing typical seating for 33 passengers. Keen to modernise its air services in the postwar world, Air France ordered 40 under the name Languedoc for use on its European and North African routes.

Air France began Languedoc services on its Paris-Algiers, Paris-Oran-Casablanca and Paris-Marseilles routes between June and August 1946 but most had been temporarily withdrawn from service by October to solve ongoing undercarriage problems and an unsuitability for winter operations.

Several modifications were incorporated including the installation of de-icing equipment and cabin heating and at the same time the opportunity was taken to replace the Gnome-Rhône engines with Pratt & Whitney Twin Wasps. The new designation SE.161.P7 was applied to the modified aircraft.

Some of Air France's Languedocs were modified to seat 44 passengers in 1951, the airline retaining a proportion of its fleet of aircraft well into the 1950s. Other operators included Poland's LOT, Tunis Air, Air Atlas, Iberia, Egypt's Misrair and the French military. By 1960 only Spain's Aviaco retained the SE.161 in commercial service.

Photo: MB.161 Languedoc.

Sud-Est SE.2010 Armagnac

Country of origin: France.

Powerplants: Four 3500hp (2610kW) Pratt & Whitney R-4360-B13 Wasp Major 28-cylinder radials; four bladed propellers.

Performance: Max speed 268kt (495km/h); cruising speed 245kt (454km/h); service ceiling 22,310ft (6800m); max payload range 1323nm (2450km); max range 2765nm (5120km).

Weights: Empty 44,922kg (99,035lb); max takeoff 77,500kg (170,855lb).

Dimensions: Wing span 48.95m (160ft 7in); length 39.62m (130ft 0in); height 13.50m (44ft 3^1/$_2$in); wing area 235.6m^2 (2536sq ft).

Accommodation: Typically 84 passengers in two classes or 107 in single class, maximum 160 in high density arrangement.

Production: 9.

History: The French aviation industry continued design work on numerous civil and military aircraft projects during WWII despite operating under German occupation.

One of those projects was the Société Nationale de Constructions Aéronautiques de Sud-Est (SNCASE) SE.2000 four engined airliner intended for the trans-Atlantic route and powered by four 2100hp (1566kW) Gnome-Rhône 18R 18-cylinder radials.

Full scale development began in 1945 but it was quickly realised that a more modern aircraft would be required. The result was the larger and pressurised SE.2010 Armagnac with tricycle undercarriage, four Pratt & Whitney Wasp Major 28-cylinder radials and accommodation for 64 passengers for the trans-Atlantic run (many with sleeping berths) or 107 on shorter stages. Up to 160 passengers could be squeezed into a high density layout.

At the time of its appearance the Armagnac was the largest commercial transport in the world (notably larger than the USA's Lockheed Super Constellation, Douglas DC-7 or Boeing Stratocruiser, for example) and remained so for several years.

The prototype first flew on 2 April 1949 and production of 15 was initiated to meet the anticipated Air France requirement. Unfortunately, and after a thorough evaluation of the prototype, Air France rejected the Armagnac, citing poor operating economics.

Sud-Est decided to build another eight aircraft regardless, four of the first six going to Transports Aériens Intercontinentaux (TAI) which inaugurated services in December 1952 but quickly discovered why Air France had decided not to purchase the aircraft – the operating economics were extremely poor.

TAI returned the aircraft to Sud-Est after less than eight months of service and they were put into storage.

A reprieve came later in 1953 when the war in French Indo-China (now Vietnam) created the need for considerable airlift capability. The Société Auxiliaire de Gerence et de Transports Aériens (SAGETA) was formed especially to carry troops, cargo and mail between Toulouse and Saigon via Beirut, Karachi and Calcutta and took over seven Armagnacs to perform that role.

Despite its considerable carrying capacity, production of the Armagnac reached just nine aircraft and SAGETA's use was its swansong. A planned turboprop powered version was not built.

Photo: SE.2010 Armagnac.

Sud-Aviation (Aerospatiale) Caravelle I-VI

Country of origin: France.

Powerplants: III – two 11,400lb (50.7kN) Rolls-Royce Avon Mk.527 turbojets. VI-N – two 12,200lb (54.3kN) Avon Mk.531. VI-R – two 12,600lb (56.0kN) Avon Mk.532R or 533R.

Performance: III – max cruise 434kt (804km/h); economical cruise 391kt (724km/h); range with 80 passengers 995nm (1843km). VI-N – max cruise 456kt (845km/h); economical cruise 426kt (789km/h); range with 80 passengers 1350nm (2500km). VI-R – max cruise 456kt (845km/h); economical cruise 424kt (785km/h); range with 80 passengers 1380nm (2556km).

Weights: III – operating empty 27,210kg (59,987lb); max takeoff 46,000kg (101,411lb). VI-N – operating empty 27,330kg (60,251lb); max takeoff 47,620kg (104,982lb). VI-R – operating empty 28,655kg (63,172lb); max takeoff 50,000kg (110,229lb).

Dimensions: Wing span 34.29m (112ft 6in); length 32.00m (105ft 0in); height 8.71m (28ft 7in); wing area 146.7m^2 (1579sq ft).

Accommodation: Typically 64 passengers in two classes or up to 80 passengers five abreast.

Production: 282 Caravelles of all models including 2 prototypes, 32 Caravelle I/IA, 78 III, 53 VI-N and 56 VI-R.

History: A 1951 French Ministry of Civil Aviation requirement for a turbine powered airliner capable of carrying a 6-7 tonnes payload over a range of up to 2000km (1080nm) at a speed of 700km/h (378kt) led to the Sud Caravelle, the world's first short-medium range jet airliner, the first to use the widely copied rear mounted engines configuration and the first with a rear airstair door under the tail.

The Sud-Est X.210 (later SE.210) design was selected for further development in September 1952. Originally a trijet with three Snecma Atar turbojets grouped around the tail (as in the Boeing 727), it was decided during 1953 to use two more powerful and proven Rolls-Royce Avons. Two prototypes were ordered and the name Caravelle selected.

The first prototype flew on 27 May 1955 with 10,000lb (44.5kN) Avon 521s, revealing an elegant design with distinctive 'rounded triangle' cabin windows. The nose and cockpit section was directly from the de Havilland Comet, for which a royalty was paid to the British manufacturer. The first production standard Caravelle I with 10,500lb (46.7kN) Avon 522s and slightly lengthened fuselage flew on 18 May 1958 (by which time Sud-Est and Sud-Ouest had merged to form Sud-Aviation) and Air France put the aircraft into service a year later. Other early customers included SAS and Finnair. The Caravelle IA had Avon 526 engines.

The Caravelle III with more powerful engines and increased weights flew in December 1959 (first delivery to Alitalia, April 1960) and all but one of the earlier models were upgraded to the new standard. The final Avon powered Caravelles were the VI-N (Sabena, January 1961) with more power and greater weights and VI-R with further power and weight increases plus engine thrust reversers, wing spoilers, modified windscreen and improved brakes. The VI-R was significant because it was sold to United Airlines in the USA (20), delivered from June 1961. Remarkably, the final Avon powered Caravelle was a 'first generation' III for Tunis Air first flown in June 1970.

Photo: Caravelle VI-R.

Sud-Aviation (Aerospatiale) Caravelle 10-12

Country of origin: France.

Powerplants: Two 14,000lb (62.3kN) Pratt & Whitney JT8D-7 or 14,500lb (64.5kN) JT8D-9 turbofans.

Performance: 10R – max cruise 432kt (800km/h); economical cruise 405kt (750km/h); range with 80 passengers 1780nm (3297km). 10B – max cruise 445kt (824km/h); economical cruise 432kt (800km/h); range with 84 passengers 1758nm (3256km). 12 – range with 94 passengers 1478nm (2738km).

Weights: 10R/B/11R – operating empty 29,075-30,055kg (64,098-66,259lb); max takeoff 52,000-54,000kg (114,638-119,048lb). 10B – optional max takeoff 56,000kg (123,457lb). 12 – operating empty 31,800kg (70,106lb); max takeoff 56,000kg (123,467lb).

Dimensions: 10R – wing span 34.29m (112ft 6in); length 32.00m (105ft 0in); height 8.71m (28ft 7in); wing area 146.7m² (1579sq ft). 11R – length 32.71m (107ft 4in). 10B – length 33.01m (108ft 3¹/₂in); height 9.02m (29ft 7in). 12 – length 36.23m (118ft 10¹/₂in); height 9.02m (29ft 7in).

Accommodation: 10R – max 80 passengers five abreast. 10B – max 104 passengers. 12 – typically 104 passengers in two classes or 118-128 in single class.

Production: 282 Caravelles of all models including 1 10A, 20 10R, 22 10B, 6 11R and 12 Caravelle 12.

History: By the late 1950s Sud-Aviation had realised that a second generation of turbofan powered Caravelles was necessary to maintain sales and to increase the type's appeal to US operators. A newly built Caravelle III was converted to 16,100lb (71.6kN) General Electric CJ805-23C turbofans, first flying on 29 December 1960 as the Srs.VII.

Sometimes known as the Caravelle Horizon, the VII generated an order from TWA (as the Horizon 10A) but this was subsequently cancelled. One 10A was built new and flown in August 1962 but later scrapped. This aircraft also featured a 1.00m (3ft 3¹/₂in) longer fuselage and a number of aerodynamic and structural refinements (extended wing leading edge near the roots, double slotted flaps, bullet fairing at the rudder/elevators intersection, increased tailplane span etc), which would appear on some later models.

Future Caravelle developments used the Pratt & Whitney JT8D turbofan and were generally known as the Super Caravelle. The 10R was basically a VI-R airframe modified to accept the new engines and with some structural changes allowing an increase in the lower baggage hold capacity. First delivery was to Alia-Royal Jordanian in July 1965. The Caravelle 11R (Air Afrique July 1967) was a mixed passenger/freight version of the 10R with large freight door, strengthened floor and small fuselage stretch.

These were preceded by the 10B (or Super B) which evolved from the 10A with its lengthened fuselage and aerodynamics refinements. First flown in March 1964, Finnair took first delivery three months later. The final model was the further stretched and heavier Caravelle 12 with accommodation for up to 128 passengers. First flown in October 1970 (10 months after Sud had become part of Aerospatiale), it was delivered to Sterling Airways and Air Inter from May 1971 with the last of the line following in March 1973.

Photo: Caravelle Super 10B. (Rob Finlayson)

Sud-Ouest SO.30P Bretagne

Country of origin: France.

Powerplants: SO.30P-1 – two 2000hp (1491kW) Pratt & Whitney R-2800-B42 Double Wasp 18-cylinder radials. SO.30P-2 – two 2400hp (1790kW) R-2800-CA18 Double Wasp; three or four bladed propellers.

Performance: 30P-2 – max speed 250kt (463km/h); max cruise 232kt (430km/h); economical cruise 210kt (389km/h); normal range 648nm (1200km); max range 1517nm (2810km).

Weights: 30P-2 – empty 13,600kg (29,982lb); max takeoff 19,500kg (42,989lb).

Dimensions: Wing span 26.87m (88ft 2in); length 18.95m (62ft 2in); height 5.89m (19ft 4in); wing area 85.9m² (925sq ft).

Accommodation: 30-43 passengers.

Production: 45 of all models.

History: Germany's occupation of France from 1940 had little effect on French efforts to continue designing and developing new aircraft, although in most cases these had to wait until France's liberation before they could be built or flown.

One of those was the SO.30, conceived by its designers as the first French pressurised transport aircraft and featuring retractable tricycle undercarriage. The group responsible for its design comprised a number of Sud-Ouest engineers from factories in the occupied zone who got together in May 1941 to create the Groupe de Technique de Cannes as a clandestine operation. It was – naturally enough – based in Cannes on the French Riviera.

The original version was designated SO.30N for 23 passengers and a 1200kg (2645lb) freight load. Powered by two 1600hp (1193kW) Gnome-Rhône 14R radials, it was ready for flight testing in late 1942 but the Italo-German Armistice Commission refused to give permission for it to fly and this was delayed until 26 February 1945.

The interim SO.30R Bellatrix with 1650hp (1230kW) Gnome-Rhônes and various modifications including replacing the original twin fin and rudder tail design with a single unit flew in March 1946 but from 1948 the production standard SO.30P Bretagne was rolling off the production line.

This was built in two versions: the SO.30P-1 with 2000hp (1491kW) Pratt & Whitney R-2800 Double Wasp radials and three bladed Curtiss Electric propellers; and the SO.30P-2 with 2400hp (1790kW) versions of the same engine driving four bladed Hamilton Standard propellers. The original twin fin tail design was reverted to.

The SO.30P-2 was ordered by Air France with normal seating for 30 passengers in considerable luxury although 43 could be accommodated in a less spacious arrangement. Air France operated its Bretagnes from 1951 to the end of the decade while other civil users included Air Algérie and some small airlines in the French colonies.

Most, however, were either delivered to or taken over by the French military, the Aéronavale receiving 20 from the production line of which 10 were mixed passenger/freight aircraft and the remainder personnel transports.

Photo: SO.30P-2 Bretagne.

Tupolev ANT-3

Country of origin: Soviet Union.

Powerplant: One 400hp (298kW) M-5 (Liberty) V12 or 450hp (335kW) Lorraine-Dietrich V12; two bladed propeller.

Performance: M-5 engine – max speed 110kt (204km/h); range 378nm (700km).

Weights: M-5 engine – max takeoff 2085kg (4596lb).

Dimensions: Wing span 13.21m (43ft 4in); length 9.91m (32ft 6in); height 3.90m (12ft 9½in).

Capacity: Two crew and 300kg (661lb) mail load.

Production: Approximately 300 including about 80 civil models.

History: After co-founding the Central Aero-Hydrodynamic Institute (TsAGI) in Moscow during 1918, Andrei Nikolayevich Tupolev moved on to establish his own design bureau in 1925, this going on to be one of the Soviet Union's major design establishments. Tupolev's previous experience as the head of the State Committee examining the use of metal in aircraft construction – pioneered by Junkers – meant it was natural his own designs would reflect that.

The first aircraft to emerge from the Tupolev bureau was the technology demonstrator ANT-1 single seat biplane which incorporated many aluminium alloy components, specifically Kolchugalumin, claimed by the Russians to be stronger than the more common duralumin. The ANT-2 light transport followed. Another one-off, this featured an all Kolchugalumin airframe with corrugated metal skinning in the style of many Junkers designs.

The ANT-3 (military designation R-3) was the first of Tupolev's new designs to achieve production and the first of aluminium alloy construction to be purchased by the Soviet military. It was developed to meet a requirement for a light bomber and reconnaissance aircraft and emerged as an unequal span biplane with an unusual inverted triangle fuselage section which provided a superior downwards view.

The first ANT-3 flew in September 1925 powered by a 400hp (298kW) Liberty engine. Many production aircraft were fitted with the Soviet built version of the same engine, the M-5, some (with the military designation R-3NL) had a 450hp (335kW) Napier Lion W12, and others a 450hp (335kW) Lorraine-Dietrich installed as the R-3LD. Flight testing was successfully completed in May 1926 and production got underway, initially for the Soviet military.

ANT-3s were used for several notable long distance flights in 1926-27 including one skippered by M M Gromov from Moscow to Warsaw via Königsberg, Berlin, Paris, Rome and Vienna. For this flight the ANT-3 was powered by a Napier Lion. Another important flight which proved the ruggedness and reliability of the ANT-3 was conducted by V P Chkalov and his mechanic, who flew the 11,880nm (22,000km) from Moscow to Tokyo and back in mostly appalling weather over a flying time of 153 hours.

These flights helped prove the ANT-3's suitability as a civil mailplane, where reliability and punctuality were of prime importance. In this role, the aircraft was extensively used carrying two crew and mail load of 300kg (661lb) and usually operating out of unprepared airstrips. One ANT-3 was tested with a 680hp (507kW) BMW VI V12 installed.

Photo: Tupolev ANT-3.

Tupolev ANT-9 and PS-9

Country of origin: Soviet Union.

Powerplants: ANT-9 – three 300hp (224kW) M-26 or 365hp (272kW) Wright Whirlwind J6 radials; two or three bladed propellers. PS-9 – two 680hp (507kW) Mikulin M-17F (BMW VI) V12s; two bladed propellers.

Performance: ANT-9 (Whirlwind) – max speed 110kt (205km/h); range 378nm (700km). PS-9 – max speed 116kt (215km/h); range 540nm (1000km).

Weights: ANT-9 – max takeoff 6000kg (13,227lb); PS-9 – empty 4400kg (9700lb); max takeoff 6200kg (13,668lb).

Dimensions: ANT-9 – wing span 23.85m (78ft 3in); length 16.65m (54ft 7½in). PS-9 – wing span 23.72m (77ft 10in); length 17.00m (55ft 9in); height 5.51m (18ft 1in); wing area 84.0m² (904sq ft).

Accommodation: Two crew and nine passengers.

Production: Approximately 12 ANT-9s and 70 PS-9s.

History: The ANT-9 high wing monoplane transport continued the Tupolev design philosophy of all metal construction (using the Kolchugalumin aluminium alloy) with corrugated metal skinning, reflecting the Junkers influence of the time. Accommodation was provided for two crew members and nine passengers with a toilet and baggage hold in the rear fuselage.

The prototype first flew May 1929 powered by three 230hp (171kW) Gnome-Rhône Titan radials built under licence from Bristol. This aircraft was extensively demonstrated including during a tour of the Soviet Union in June 1929 and in July-August 1930 when it completed a 4860nm (9000km) journey around Europe carrying the name *Krilya Soveto* – Wings of the Soviets.

Early production ANT-9s were powered by 300hp (224kW) M-26 radials but these were quickly replaced by more powerful Wright Whirlwinds as performance was found to be wanting. The Whirlwinds added about 11 knots (20km/h) to the aircraft's speed. ANT-9s were operated by Soviet-German airline Deruluft on the Moscow-Berlin service while some were flown by the Soviet military as troop and VIP transports.

From 1932 a revised version was introduced, the PS-9 (or ANT-9-M-17) with the three radial engines replaced by two 680hp (507kW) Mikulin M-17F V12s, a licence built BMW VI. The PS-9 had greater power available than its trimotor predecessor and exhibited superior performance as a result. It was also able to operate at a higher maximum weight. Widely used on passenger services by Aeroflot and Deruluft it was – like the earlier aircraft – able to operate from either wheels or skis.

Perhaps the best known example was the PS-9 flown by the Soviet Union's propaganda squadron. Named *Krokodil* (Crocodile), its nose was suitably decorated with painted teeth. The one-off ANT-14 *Pravda* was a very much enlarged development of the ANT-9 with accommodation for 36 passengers, wing span of 40.40m (132ft 6½in) and five 480hp (358kW) Bristol Jupiter radials. It served as the propaganda squadron's flagship between 1931 and 1941, its cabin serving as a cinema!

Photo: Tupolev PS-9.

Tupolev ANT-35

Country of origin: Soviet Union.

Powerplants: Two 800hp (597kW) M-85 (Gnome-Rhône 14K) 14-cylinder or 1000hp (7846kW) M-62IR (Wright Cyclone) nine cylinder radials; three bladed propellers.

Performance: M-62IR engines – max speed 200kt (370km/h); cruising speed 189kt (350km/h); range 885nm (1640km).

Weights: Empty 4710kg (10,384lb); max takeoff 6620kg (14,594lb).

Dimensions: Wing span 20.80m (68ft 3in); length 15.00m (49ft 2½in); wing area 58.0m² (624sq ft).

Accommodation: 10 passengers.

Production: 11.

History: Incorporating some of the features of the Tupolev SB-2 twin engined medium bomber of 1934 (the Soviet Union's first monoplane and retractable undercarriage bomber of stressed skin metal construction), the ANT-35 followed by being the nation's first similarly configured transport aircraft.

Designed by A A Arkangelskii (despite the designation, which reflected Andrei Tupolev's initials), the ANT-35 carried 10 passengers in a circular section cabin and as such was of similar capacity to the contemporary Lockheed L.10 Electra. The prototype was powered by a pair of 800hp (597kW) Gnome-Rhône 14K 14-cylinder radials and subsequently re-engined with the Soviet built M-85 development of the French engine.

The first aircraft flew on 20 August 1936 and the following month proved its capabilities by flying from Moscow to Leningrad and back in just over 3½ hours at an average speed of 203kt (376km/h). Its first appearance outside the Soviet Union was at the Paris Salon later in 1936.

Despite this, it was felt that better performance was required and the second aircraft was an improved version powered by two 1000hp (746kW) M-62IR radials (based on the Wright Cyclone). Dubbed the ANT-35bis.

The ANT-35bis was slightly heavier than the prototype and sacrificed some of its range performance in favour of the ability to carry a greater payload.

Nine series production ANT-35bis were built between 1937 and 1939, Aeroflot designating them PS-35 and introducing them to service on the Moscow-Riga-Stockholm route from July 1937 and subsequently on the Moscow-Prague route.

Although fast and reasonably comfortable, the PS-35 was regarded as being uneconomic due to its modest passenger load, although the few built remained in service until as late as 1941 including on Aeroflot's Moscow-Lvov and Moscow-Odessa routes. After that, several were used by the Soviet government and military for VIP and liaison duties.

The SB-2 bomber which provided the basis for the ANT-35 had largely been relegated to secondary roles such as training and target towing by 1943, although light transport versions (the PS-40 and PS-41) were also developed and saw some limited operational service. These were powered by Soviet built versions of the Hispano-Suiza 12Y V12 series of engines.

Photo: Tupolev ANT-35 prototype.

Tupolev Tu-104

Country of origin: Soviet Union.

Powerplants: Tu-104 – two 14,880lb (66.2kN) Mikulin AM-3 turbojets. Tu-104A – two 19,180lb (85.3kN) AM-3Ms. Tu-104B – two AM-3Ms or 21,385lb (95.1kN) AM-3-M-500s.

Performance: Max cruise 486kt (900km/h); economical cruise 432kt (800km/h). Tu-104 – max payload range 1095nm (2028km); max range 2160nm (4000km). Tu-104B – service ceiling 37,730ft (11,500m); max payload range 1134nm (2100km); range with 66 passengers 1674nm (3100km).

Weights: Tu-104A – empty 41,600kg (91,710lb); max takeoff 76,000kg (167,548lb). Tu-104B – empty 42,500kg (93,695lb); max takeoff 76,000kg (167,548lb).

Dimensions: Tu-104/A – wing span 34.54m (113ft 4in); length 38.85m (125ft 5½in); height 11.90m (39ft 0½in); wing area 183.5m² (1975sq ft). Tu-104B – length 40.05m (131ft 5in).

Accommodation: Tu-104 – typically 50 passengers. Tu-104A – typically 70 passengers in two classes. Tu-104B – 100 passengers in high density arrangement.

Production: 200-250.

History: Designed in 1953 as part of a major programme intended to modernise Aeroflot's fleet, the Tu-104 was significant because it was the world's second jet airliner to enter service (after the de Havilland Comet) and the Soviet Union's first.

In order to expedite development, the Tu-104 was largely based on the Tu-16 'Badger' twin engined jet bomber of 1952, incorporating that aircraft's wing (with 35deg sweep), powerplants and undercarriage with a new pressurised fuselage. The two Mikulin AM-3 turbojets were mounted at the wing roots and like the Tu-16, the main undercarriage retracted into large wing trailing edge fairings.

The prototype Tu-104G (for *Grazdhanskii* – civil) first flew on 17 July 1955 and entered service on Aeroflot's Moscow-Irkutsk route in September 1956, travelling via Kazan, Sverdlovsk, Omsk and Novosibirsk. International services to centres such as Paris and Amsterdam followed.

The initial production model was designated as simply the Tu-104 and carried 48-50 passengers in a four abreast arrangement. About 20 were built. The Tu-104A with more powerful AM-3M engines and a rearranged cabin for 70 passengers in two classes was introduced into service in early 1958, followed in April 1959 (on the Moscow-Leningrad route) by the Tu-104B with a slightly longer fuselage, seating for up to 100 passengers and – after the first few had been delivered – more powerful AM-3M-500 engines. Production ended in 1960.

Versions created by the conversion were the Tu-104D and V, Tu-104As modified to carry 100 and 85 passengers, respectively, within the original fuselage length. The Tu-110 was a one-off prototype powered by four 12,125lb (53.9kW) Lyulka AL-5 turbojets and flown in 1957.

The only export order was for six Tu-104As delivered to Czechoslovakia's CSA. The Tu-104's NATO reporting name was 'Camel' and the aircraft operated reliably in Aeroflot service until 1981.

Photo: Early production Tupolev Tu-104.

Tupolev Tu-114 Rossiya

Country of origin: Soviet Union.

Powerplants: Four 14,795eshp (11,032kW) Kuznetsov NK-12M or 15,000eshp (11,185kW) NK-12MV turboprops; eight bladed contra-rotating propellers.

Performance: Max cruise 416kt (770km/h); economical cruise 387kt (716km/h); service ceiling 39,370ft (12,000m); max payload range 3348nm (6200km); range with 170 passengers 4833nm (8950km).

Weights: Operating empty 93,000kg (205,026lb); max takeoff 171,000kg (376,984lb).

Dimensions: Wing span 51.10m (167ft 8in); length 54.10m (177ft 6in); height 15.49m (50ft 10in); wing area 311.1m² (3349sq ft).

Accommodation: Typically 120 passengers in three classes or 170 two classes six abreast, maximum 220 seven or eight abreast.

Production: Approximately 30.

History: Developed in parallel with the Tu-20 'Bear' long range strategic bomber, the Tu-114 Rossiya was essentially a civil development of that aircraft employing its wings, powerplants, tail, undercarriage and a widened version of its fuselage. A remarkable aircraft, it was the largest and heaviest airliner in the world when introduced, the world's fastest turboprop and the only propeller driven civil aircraft with swept wings.

The prototype (designated Tu-116) first flew in late 1956 and was a minimum change demilitarised Tu-20 used as a 'proof of concept' test aircraft.

Two other similar aircraft appeared during 1957 and under the designation Tu-114D were used by Aeroflot for route proving flights and other trials.

The first 'proper' Tu-114 flew on 3 October 1957 and the aircraft later proved its capabilities by setting a number of speed-payload records, including carrying a 25,000kg (55,115lb) load over a 5000km (3107 statute mile) circuit at a staggering 877.2km/h (545.1mph). The NATO reporting name 'Cleat' was applied.

Despite these successes, the Tu-114's Kuznetsov NK-12M engines were causing problems, overheating and fires delaying introduction to service until April 1961, initially between Moscow and Khabarovsk and about 18 months behind schedule. Aeroflot subsequently used the aircraft on its long range domestic services and on international routes such as Moscow-Havana as well as to Canada, India and Japan.

The emergence of jet airliners quickly rendered the Tu-114 obsolescent with the result that production was limited to only about 30. Aeroflot began to withdraw the Tu-114 from service in 1971, finally retiring it completely in October 1976.

The Tu-114 lived on for a time, however, in the form of the Tu-126 'Moss' airborne warning and control (AWACS) aircraft with large rotating radome pylon mounted above the fuselage and aerial refuelling equipment fitted. First flown circa 1963, about 15 Tu-126s were converted. The last examples were retired from Soviet military service in the early 1990s, replaced by the Beriev A-50 'Mainstay', based on the Ilyushin Il-76MD transport.

Photo: Tupolev Tu-114.

Tupolev Tu-124

Country of origin: Soviet Union.

Powerplants: Two 11,905lb (53.0kN) Soloviev D-20P turbofans.

Performance: Max cruise 470kt (870km/h); economical cruise 432kt (800km/h); service ceiling 39,010ft (11,890m); max payload range 659nm (1220km); range with 39 passengers 1134nm (2100km).

Weights: Empty 22,500kg (49,603lb); max takeoff 38,000kg (83,774lb).

Dimensions: Wing span 25.54m (83ft 9½in); length 30.58m (100ft 4in); height 8.08m (26ft 6in); wing area 119.0m² (1281sq ft).

Accommodation: 44-56 passengers four abreast initially, 68 later.

Production: About 150.

History: Although superficially a scaled down Tu-104, the short range Tu-124 twinjet was in reality almost an entirely new design, although Aeroflot's original requirement called for a smaller version of the earlier aircraft capable of operating from shorter and rougher runways. Intended to replace the piston engined Ilyushin Il-14, the Tu-124 was developed as part of Aeroflot's overall modernisation scheme.

Features included a relatively high thrust to weight ratio, robust undercarriage, double slotted flaps and combined airbrake/spoiler/lift dump surfaces on the wings. A notable feature was the incorporation of Soloviev D-20P turbofans, the first application of this type of engine in a short-medium range airliner.

The passengers (44 originally, then 56 and up to 68 later on) were accommodated in three cabins, an inefficient arrangement resulting from the need to raise part of the cabin floor over the wing centre section structure. This characteristic was shared with the Tu-104, as were the aft wing blisters into which the main undercarriage retracted.

The first Tu-124 flew in June 1960 and after testing Aeroflot inaugurated services on the Moscow-Tallinn route on 2 October 1962. This event has often been incorrectly described as the world's first commercial service using a turbofan powered aircraft but ignores the fact that the Rolls-Royce Conway powered Boeing 707-420 and Douglas DC-8-40 entered service in 1960.

The standard production version was designated Tu-124V but two special models with higher levels of accommodation were also built: the Tu-124K and K2 with seating for 36 and 22 passengers, respectively. These were used as VIP transports for the carriage of government and communist party officials within the Soviet Union and were mechanically identical to the standard model.

Production of the Tu-124 is thought to have reached only about 150 aircraft – the total was certainly fewer than 200. Of these, the vast majority were delivered to Aeroflot with others going to Czechoslovakia's CSA (3), East Germany's Interflug (2) and the Indian Air Force (3). Production ended in 1966 and the NATO reporting name was 'Cookpot'.

Aeroflot still had about 90 Tu-124s in service by 1980, operating on secondary routes, but these were retired over the next few years.

Photo: Tupolev Tu-124V.

Tupolev Tu-134

Country of origin: Soviet Union.

Powerplants: Tu-134A – two 14,490lb (64.4kN) Soloviev D-30 turbofans. Tu-134A – two 14,990lb (66.7kN) Soloviev D-30 Series II turbofans.

Performance: Tu-134/A – max cruise 486kt (900km/h); economical cruise 405kt (750km/h); operational ceiling 39,040ft (11,900m). Tu-134 – initial climb 2913ft (888m)/min; max payload range 1295nm (2400km); range with max fuel and 33 passengers 1890nm (3500km). Tu-134A – max payload range 1020nm (1890km); range with max fuel and 55 passengers 1630nm (3020km).

Weights: Tu-134 – operating empty 27,500kg (60,626lb); max takeoff 44,500kg (98,104lb). Tu-134A – operating empty 29,050kg (64,043lb); max takeoff 47,000kg (103,616lb).

Dimensions: Tu-134 – wing span 29.00m (95ft 2in); length 34.34m (112ft 8in); height 9.14m (30ft 0in); wing area 127.3m² (1370sq ft). Tu-134A – length 37.05m (121ft 6½in).

Accommodation: Tu-134 – 64 passengers in two classes or 72 in single class four abreast. Tu-134A – up to 84 passengers four abreast, 90 with galley removed or 96 five abreast.

Production: Over 700.

History: Even before the Tu-124 (see previous entry) had entered service in October 1962, Tupolev had begun development of an improved successor, aimed at bridging the gap in standards between Soviet and western airliners. The new aircraft's original designation was Tu-124A, indicating the intention to base it as much as possible on the earlier aircraft.

Although retaining a lengthened version of the Tu-124's fuselage and a longer span version of its wing, the changes were extensive and the Tu-134 as it emerged was revealed as a substantial redesign with rear mounted engines and T-tail in the style of the contemporary BAC One Eleven and Douglas DC-9. The Tu-134's wing box passed through the fuselage below floor level, eliminating one of the Tu-124's major flaws where the cabin had to be divided into sections to cater for the raised floor in its centre.

The first Tu-134 flew on 29 July 1963 and was followed by five pre-production models. After completing a series of proving flights, Aeroflot operated the first Tu-134 commercial service between Moscow and Stockholm in September 1967.

The only other production model was the Tu-134A (service entry November 1970) with more powerful D-30 Series II engines, improved systems and avionics, structural modifications and replacement of the traditional Soviet 'bomber' glazed nose with a solid unit containing weather radar on all but the earliest aircraft. NATO's reporting name was 'Crusty'.

Production ended in 1978 but other versions were created by conversion including the Tu-134A-3 with increased passenger capacity and Tu-134B (May 1980) also with more seats and improved Series III engines. The Tu-134 was widely used by Aeroflot and about 170 were exported to airlines in most East European and Soviet Bloc countries. More than 350 remained in service in 1999, most of them in Russia and the CIS. Elsewhere, the Tu-134 was already largely replaced by western airliners.

Photo: Tupolev Tu-134A. (Paul Merritt)

Tupolev Tu-144

Country of origin: Soviet Union.

Powerplants: Tu-144 – four 44,080lb (196.1kN) with reheat Kuznetsov NK-144 turbofans. Tu-144D/LL – four Kolesov RD36-51A turbofans of similar thrust but without reheat.

Performance: Tu-144 – max cruise Mach 2.35 or 1350kt (2500km/h); operating ceiling 59,055ft (18,000m); range 3510nm (6500km).

Weights: Tu-144 – empty 85,000kg (187,390lb); max takeoff 180,000kg (396,825lb).

Dimensions: Wing span 28.80m (94ft 6in); length 65.70m (215ft 6½in); wing area 438.0m² (4715sq ft).

Accommodation: 140 passengers.

Production: 1 Tu-144 prototype, 11 production Tu-144 and 5 Tu-144D, total 17.

History: The world's first supersonic transport aircraft to fly (31 December 1968), exceed Mach 1 in level flight (June 1969), exceed Mach 2 (May 1970) and enter service – of sorts – in December 1975, the Tu-144 holds a significant place in aviation history.

Despite that, it cannot be regarded as a success because it never achieved the regular passenger services for which it was designed and was quietly withdrawn after a series of problems. Many of these stemmed from the programme being rushed and corners cut in order to gain the prestige associated with beating the Anglo-French Concorde.

Due to its overall similarity to Concorde the Tu-144 was quickly dubbed 'Concordskii' by the western press but there were many significant differences. The fuselage was wider for five (rather than four) abreast seating; reheated 38,580lb (171.6kN) NK-144 turbofans were used instead of turbojets, the engines grouped together and close to the centreline in a single large nacelle (with individual intakes and compartments); and the wing – although superficially similar to Concorde's – lacked its subtle camber, droop and twist. The NATO reporting name was 'Charger'.

The production standard Tu-144 began a series of 50 cargo flights over the 1800nm (3300km) between Moscow and Alma Ata in December 1975 (the month before Concorde entered scheduled passenger carrying service) and the first passenger flights between the same two points started in November 1977. These were terminated in June 1978 after a fatal accident.

A substantially redesigned Tu-144 appeared at the 1973 Paris Air Show with uprated NK-144A engines more widely spaced in separated nacelles, a 10.7m (35ft 0in) longer fuselage, increased span fully cambered delta wings and retractable canard foreplanes just behind the cockpit. Tragically, the aircraft crashed during the show.

Unable to achieve its design goals, and despite development of the Tu-144D with more efficient Kolesov turbofans, the Tu-144 programme had been effectively abandoned by 1984.

It was given something of a reprieve between November 1996 and February 1998 when one Tu-144 performed 19 flights on behalf of a US aerospace industry and NASA team to assist in the development of the proposed High Speed Civil Transport (HSCT) programme. The aircraft used was a Tu-144D first flown in April 1981 and redesignated Tu-144LL (*Letayushchye Laboratorii* – flying laboratory) for the trials.

Photo: Tupolev Tu-144 in its proposed production form.

Tupolev Tu-154

Country of origin: Soviet Union/Russia.

Powerplants: Tu-154 – three 20,950lb (93.2kN) Kuznetsov NK-8-2 turbofans. Tu-154A/B – three 23,146lb (102.9kN) NK-8-2Us. Tu-154M – three 23,380lb (104.0kN) Aviadvigitel (Soloviev) D-30KU-154-II turbofans.

Performance: Tu-154 – typical cruise 486kt (900km/h); max payload range 1360nm (2520km). Tu-154A – typical cruise 486kt (900km/h); max payload range 1728nm (3200km). Tu-154B – range with max fuel and 63 passengers 2700nm (5000km). Tu-154M – max cruise 505kt (935km/h); max payload range 2052nm (3800km); range with 143 passengers 2754nm (5100km).

Weights: Tu-154 – operating empty 43,500kg (95,900lb); max takeoff 90,000kg (198,413lb). Tu-154A – max takeoff 94,000kg (207,231lb). Tu-154B – max takeoff 98,000kg (216,050lb); Tu-154M – operating empty 55,300kg (121,914lb); max takeoff 100,000kg (220,458lb).

Dimensions: Wing span 37.55m (123ft 2½in); length 47.90m (157ft 2in); height 11.40m (37ft 5in); wing area 201.4m² (2168sq ft).

Accommodation: Tu-154/A – up to 158 passengers six abreast. Tu-154B/M – up to 180 passengers.

Production: 1030 of all models by 1999.

History: The Tu-154 trijet is the standard medium range airliner within many states of the former Soviet Union plus China and parts of Eastern Europe and remained in production in 1999. Like many of Aeroflot's airliners, the Tu-154 was designed to operate from short and poorly surfaced strips. Its power-to-weight ratio is high and the low footprint triple bogey main undercarriage units retract into characteristic Tupolev fairings aft of the wing.

Early Tu-154s were powered by Kuznetsov NK-8 turbofans. The prototype first flew on 4 October 1968 and Aeroflot began proving and *ad hoc* passenger flights in 1971 before putting the Tu-154 into regular scheduled service in February 1972, initially on the Moscow-Mineralnye Vody route. International services started in August 1972 between Moscow and Prague.

Subsequent MK-8 powered versions were the Tu-154A (service entry April 1974) with more power, additional fuel and increased weights and the Tu-154B (1977) with improved high lift devices, further increased weights and French Thomson CSF avionics. The Tu-154C is a freighter conversion of the Tu-154B with large cargo door. It appeared in 1981.

The current production Tu-154M (initially designated Tu-164) with more efficient Soloviev D-30KU turbofans, increased weights and numerous other refinements first flew in 1982 and was delivered to Aeroflot from December 1984. Projects under development in 1999 included the Tu-154-100 with upgraded interior and avionics, and the Tu-154M2 with two PS-90 engines. Versions powered by ducted propfans and cryogenic fuel engines (Tu-155 and -156) were also being examined.

Named 'Careless' by NATO, some 160 Tu-154s had been exported to 17 countries by 1999, recent orders including 20 for Iranian carriers and four VIP configured aircraft for Slovakia.

Photo: Tupolev Tu-154M. (Andrew Briggs)

Tupolev Tu-204

Country of origin: Soviet Union/Russia.

Powerplants: Tu-204 – two 35,580lb (158.3kN) Aviadvigatel PS-90A turbofans. Tu-204-120/220 – two 43,100lb (191.7kN) Rolls-Royce RB211-535E4 or -535F5 turbofans.

Performance: Tu-204-100 – cruising speed 437-459kt (809-850km/h); range with 214 passengers 2645nm (4900km). Tu-204-200 – range with 212 passengers 3415nm (6325km). Tu-204-220 – max payload range 2484nm (4600km).

Weights: Tu-204 – operating empty 58,300kg (128,527lb); max takeoff 94,600kg (208,554lb). Tu-204-100 – operating empty 58,800kg (129,630lb); max takeoff 103,000kg (227,072lb). Tu-204-220 – operating empty 59,000kg (130,070lb); max takeoff 110,750kg (244,158lb).

Dimensions: Wing span 42.00m (137ft 10in); length 46.00m (150ft 11in); height 13.90m (45ft 7in); wing area 182.4m² (1963sq ft).

Accommodation: Up to 214 passengers in single class six abreast.

Production: About 35 of all models by 1999.

History: The Tupolev Tu-204 medium range narrowbody twinjet was the first Russian airliner to fly with western engines. Tupolev began development of the Tu-204 to meet an Aeroflot requirement for a replacement for the medium range Tu-154 trijet. This all new twin featured a supercritical wing, while engine designer Soloviev (now Aviadvigatel) specifically developed the PS-90 turbofan for the aircraft. Other Tu-204 design features include fly-by-wire and a six screen EFIS flight deck. First flight was on 2 January 1989.

The Tu-204 is offered in a myriad of versions: the basic Tu-204; Tu-204-100 (certified December 1994) and -200 (first flight March 1996, marketed as the Tu-214) with higher maximum takeoff weights and additional fuel; Tu-204C and Tu-204-100C convertibles with a forward main deck freight door; and Tu-204-100F pure freighter.

The Tu-204's first revenue passenger flight (by Vnukovo Airlines) was between Moscow and Mineralnye Vody in February 1996. Other CIS operators by 1999 included Aeroflot, Uzbekistan Airways and Kazakhstan Airlines with others showing interest. Up to 500 Tu-204s are expected to be built for CIS airlines over the years. Production is planned to increase to 35 per annum from two factories, Aviastar at Ulyanovsk (100 and 300 series) and Kazan (200s).

Keen to broaden the Tu-204's international market appeal, Tupolev developed 'westernised' versions of the Tu-204, its efforts resulting in the Rolls-Royce RB211-535 powered Tu-204-120 (first flight 14 August 1992). Production models feature a Honeywell VIA 2000 EFIS avionics suite and RB211 powered subvariants include the Tu-204-120C freighter, -122 with Rockwell Collins avionics, the increased weight -220 (or Tu-224) and equivalent cargo -220C; -222 with Collins avionics and -223 with Sextant Avionique avionics. Egypt's Air Cairo received the first production Tu-204-120 in November 1998.

Tupolev is also developing shortened versions as the Tu-234 (or Tu-204-300 series) with 166 seats and a choice of powerplants. The prototype (converted from a Tu-204) was displayed at the 1995 Moscow Aeroshow but it had not flown by 1999.

Photo: Tupolev Tu-204. (Keith Anderson)

Tupolev Tu-334

Country of origin: Russia

Powerplants: Tu-334-100 – two 16,535lb (73.5kN) Ivchenko Progress D-436T1 turbofans.

Performance: (provisional) Tu-334-100 – cruising speed 432-443kt (800-820km/h); cruising altitude 34,770-36,420ft (10,600-11,100m); range with 102 passengers 972nm (1800km).

Weights: Tu-334-100 – empty 30,050kg (66,248lb); max takeoff 46,100kg (101,630lb).

Dimensions: Tu-334-100 – wing span 29.77m (97ft 8in); length 31.27m (102ft 7in); height 9.37m (30ft 9in); wing area 83.2m² (896sq ft).

Accommodation: 72-92 passengers in two classes or up to 102 passengers in single class six abreast.

Production: Prototype first flew February 1999.

History: The advanced technology Tu-334 100 seat twinjet has been developed as a replacement for the ageing Tu-134 on CIS domestic routes. Development began in late 1989 but was a somewhat protracted affair due to a severe funding shortage, the first prototype rolled out in August 1995 at Zhukovsky during the 1995 Moscow Aeroshow but not flying until 3½ years later on 8 February 1999.

The Tu-334 is to some extent based on the Tu-204 twinjet using as many of its systems as possible in order to reduce costs and time including an identical EFIS flight deck and a substantially shortened version of the Tu-204's fuselage. The supercritical wing (itself derived from Tu-204 technology) is swept at 24 degrees and fitted with winglets, while composites and other lightweight materials comprise about 20 per cent of the airframe's weight and fly-by-wire controls are fitted.

The Tu-334 is being developed in a number of versions apart from the basic Tu-334-100 as flown in February 1999. Planned standard fuselage length variants are the Tu-334-100C passenger/freight convertible; Tu-334-120 with BMW Rolls-Royce BR710-48 engines; and Tu-334M with increased weight and a 1685nm (3120km range).

Tu-334-100D (also known as the Tu-354) has the standard passenger capacity of 102 but with modest 0.48m (1ft 7in) fuselage stretch, more powerful, 18,078lb (80.4kN) D-436T2 engines, increased weights, longer span wing, additional fuel and a range of 2214nm (4100km) with full passenger load.

Planned Tu-334-200 models with a 3.90m (12ft 9½in) fuselage stretch and accommodation for up to 126 passengers are the basic model with D-436T2 engines, increased weights and fuel and a range of 1188nm (2200km); the -200C convertible; and -220 with BMW Rolls-Royce BR715-55 engines.

There are grand plans for the Tu-334 including manufacture at no fewer than three sites – Moscow, Kiev and the Aviakor facility in Samara, the latter concentrating on the Tu-334-100D/Tu-354. Discussions with Iran on the subject of licence manufacture were held in 1997, these also covering the Tu-204, but nothing has been heard since.

The Russian market is estimated at 160 aircraft and about 14 options had been placed by 1999.

Photo: Tupolev Tu-334 prototype.

VEB BB 152

Country of origin: East Germany.

Powerplants: 152A (proposed) – four 6940lb (30.9kN) Pirna Type 014 turbojets.

Performance: 152A (estimated) – cruising speed 432kt (800km/h); initial climb 4330ft (1320m)/min; range with 57 passengers 1042nm (1930km); range with 48 passengers 1350nm (2500km).

Weights: Operating empty 30,390kg (66,997lb); max takeoff 50,945kg (112,313lb).

Dimensions: Wing span 27.00m (88ft 7in); length 31.39m (103ft 0in); height 8.99m (29ft 6in); wing area 138.0m² (1485sq ft).

Accommodation: 48-73 passengers five abreast.

Production: 2 prototypes flown.

History: This curiosity of postwar commercial aviation took the aviation world completely by surprise when revealed in 1958. Previously unknown or even rumoured in the west, the four jet VEB BB 152 was and remains the only airliner designed and built in the former German Democratic Republic, or East Germany. The 'BB' in the designation reflect the initials of chief designer Brunolf Baade.

The BB 152's origins go back to the Soviet Alekseyev Type 150 jet bomber of 1951, an unsuccessful contender for the order eventually won by the Tupolev Tu-16, which also formed the basis of the Tu-104 airliner.

The Type 150 had been designed by a group of captured German engineers in the Soviet Union and when they were allowed to return to (East) Germany in 1953 they established VEB Flugzeugwerke at Dresden and set about developing an airliner derivative of the bomber.

The original Type 151 designs were superceded by the improved Type 152, a high wing aircraft with four underwing engines in podded pairs on large pylons and tandem 'bicycle' undercarriage assisted by outrigger stabilising units which retracted into wing tip pods. Power was planned to be provided by the locally designed Pirna Type 014 turbojet (probably derived from the wartime Junkers Jumo 012) but this was not available by the time of first flight.

The prototype BB 152-I (with Tumansky RD-9 engines reportedly taken from MiG-19s) flew on 4 December 1958 and numerous problems were quickly revealed. It crashed in March 1959 during rehearsals for an important display in front of senior communist party officials at the Leipzig trade fair.

The second aircraft (BB 152-II) flew on 26 August 1960 and differed in having a solid (rather than glazed) nose, more conventional tricycle undercarriage in which the main four wheel bogey units retracted into fairings behind the engine pods, and additional fuel in the wing tip pods previously occupied by the outriggers.

By now, components for production BB 152s were being built at the VEB factory but the aircraft continued to suffer problems as well as making no economic sense.

As a result, the programme was cancelled in April 1961 by the Politburo when there were 14 incomplete airframes on the assembly line. Some fuselage sections were discovered after the reunification of Germany.

Photo: VEB BB-152 first prototype.

VFW 614

Country of origin: West Germany.

Powerplants: Two 7473lb (33.2kN) Rolls-Royce/Snecma M45H Mk.501 turbofans.

Performance: Max cruise 380kt (704km/h); economical cruise 339kt (628km/h); long range cruise 319kt (590km/h); initial climb 3100ft (945m)/min; max operating altitude 25,000ft (7620m); range with 40 passengers 645nm (1195km).

Weights: Operating empty 12,179kg (26,850lb); max takeoff 19,958kg (44,000lb).

Dimensions: Wing span 21.50m (70ft 6½in); length 20.60m (67ft 7in); height 7.82m (25ft 8in); wing area 64.0m² (689sq ft).

Accommodation: 40-44 passengers four abreast.

Production: 19.

History: Often described as being ahead of its time, the VFW 614 was a brave but ultimately unsuccessful attempt to build and market a small capacity regional jet, a category only recently conquered by aircraft such as the Canadair CRJ and Embraer ERJ-135/145.

Intended for the 'DC-3 replacement' market, the 614 was originally proposed in 1961 by the Entwicklungsrinf Nord (ERNO) group comprising Focke-Wulf, Hamburger Flugzeugbau (HFB) and Weser as the E.614, a 36-40 seater powered by two Lycoming PLF1B-2 turbofans. The West German industry was subsequently reorganised and Vereinigte Flugtechnische Werke (VFW) established at Bremen. Development of what was now the VFW 614 continued.

The project was given the go ahead in 1968 with 80 per cent of the financial backing coming from the West German Government. Full scale production was approved in June 1970, by which time VFW and Fokker had merged (an unhappy arrangement which lasted only a decade) and risk sharing agreements had been concluded with SIAT in Germany, Fairey and SABCA in Belgium and Shorts in the UK. Final assembly was at Bremen.

The first of three prototypes flew on 14 July 1971, the aircraft revealed to be of unconventional configuration with two quiet, smoke free but untried Rolls-Royce/Snecma M45H turbofans mounted on pylons above the wings to avoid the structural weight penalties of rear mounted engines and the potential ingestion problems of engines mounted under the modestly swept wings.

Development was protracted and the receipt of orders slow despite a strong marketing campaign – the former not helped by Rolls-Royce's bankruptcy in 1971 which threatened the supply of engines and the loss of the prototype in February 1972 due to elevator flutter. By February 1975 only 10 had been ordered. The first production VFW 614 flew in April 1975 and was delivered to Denmark's Cimber Air four months later.

In the end only Cimber Air (5), France's Air Alsace (3), Germany's Touraine Air Transport (2 leased) and the Luftwaffe (3) received new 614s. Three others were flown but never delivered and four airframes were dismantled before completion. The programme was cancelled in 1977 and the last (unsold) aircraft flown in July 1978. Most had been broken up by 1981, only the Luftwaffe aircraft remaining in service and they were being disposed of in 1999.

Photo: Second production VFW 614.

Vickers Vimy Commercial

Country of origin: United Kingdom.

Powerplants: Two 360hp (268kW) Rolls-Royce Eagle VIII V12s; four bladed propellers.

Performance: Max speed 85kt (158km/h); cruising speed 73kt (135km/h); initial climb 375ft (114m)/min; service ceiling 10,500ft (3200m); range 390nm (722km).

Weights: Empty 3534kg (7790lb); max takeoff 5670kg (12,500lb).

Dimensions: Wing span 20.47m (67ft 2in); length 13.00m (42ft 8in); height 4.76m (15ft 7½in); wing area 123.6m² (1330sq ft).

Accommodation: 10 passengers.

Production: 43.

History: Immortalised by Alcock and Brown and their first non stop crossing of the Atlantic by air in June 1919, the Vickers FB.27 Vimy was a capable heavy bomber but too late to see service in WWI. First flown on 30 November 1917, it was of fabric covered mixed construction and in its military form capable of carrying a 1123kg (2476lb) bomb load.

Vimy bomber production reached 239 aircraft with more than 400 others cancelled at the end of the war, Vickers then taking the decision to develop a commercial version in order to exploit its load carrying capabilities. Dubbed the Vimy Commercial, the aircraft differed from most contemporary minimum change transport conversions of bombers by having a radically modified forward fuselage in which the original slim structure was replaced with a completely new and spacious oval section plywood monocoque fuselage with no internal obstructions. Individual wicker or leather chairs provided good comfort for the 10 passengers.

The first aircraft flew on 20 September 1919, subsequent modifications including replacing the original circular cabin windows with larger rectangular units and adding an 'air-stair' door to the rear fuselage.

Although faster than the bomber, the Vimy Commercial proved to be deficient in payload-range due to the extra drag created by the new fuselage. This necessitated a fuel stop on the relatively short hop between London and Paris and worked against sales to British and European operators.

The bulk of production went to the Chinese government which ordered 40 in 1919 for use on a mail service between Peking and Tsinan. After sorting out the financial arrangements, these were built between April 1920 and February 1921. The service was inaugurated but most of the Vimys remained in their crates, unpacked, unassembled and unused.

Only one Vimy Commercial entered service with a British airline, the 41st aircraft delivered to S Instone and Co Ltd in time for its inaugural flight from London (Croydon) to Brussels in May 1920. It reliably plied the airline's Paris, Brussels and Cologne routes before being handed over to Imperial Airways in April 1924. It was scrapped in 1926.

One was fitted with 400hp (298kW) Lorraine-Dietrich engines for France's Grands Express Aériennes in late 1921 and the last aircraft went to Russia in September 1922. This was powered by 450hp (336kW) Napier Lion engines and as such was similar to the Vernon military transport version of the Vimy Commercial, 55 of which were built for the RAF from 1921.

Photo: Vimy Commercial.

Vickers Vulcan

Country of origin: United Kingdom.

Powerplant: One 360hp (268kW) Rolls-Royce Eagle VIII V12 or 450hp (336kW) Napier Lion; two bladed propeller.

Performance: Eagle engine – max speed 91kt (169km/h); cruising speed 78kt (145km/h); initial climb 450ft (137m)/min; range 313nm (579km). Lion engine – max speed 97kt (180km/h); range 374nm (692km).

Weights: Eagle – empty 1712kg (3775lb); max takeoff 2790kg (6150lb). Lion – empty 1996kg (4400lb); max takeoff 3062kg (6750lb).

Dimensions: Eagle – wing span 14.93m (49ft 0in); length 11.43m (37ft 6in); height 4.34m (14ft 3in); wing area 78.0m^2 (840sq ft). Lion – length 11.58m (38ft 0in).

Accommodation: Pilot and 6-8 passengers.

Production: 8.

History: Once accurately described as being 'spectacularly ugly', the Vickers Vulcan was an attempt by the manufacturer to build a commercial aircraft capable of being operated without subsidy. Low acquisition and running costs were the priority at the expense of performance, this reflected in the decision to power the aircraft with a cheap, war surplus Rolls-Royce Eagle engine and to use a plywood fuselage similar to that developed for the Vimy Commercial.

The cabin provided accommodation for six-eight passengers and the pilot was accommodated in what has been noted as 'lordly splendour', high up in an open cockpit above the cabin and immediately in front of the upper wing. The Vulcan's appearance quickly gave rise to the nickname 'Flying Pig'.

The first Type 61 Vulcan flew in May 1922, testing revealing directional instability and extremely poor performance thanks to insufficient power and including a reluctance to take off at the intended maximum weight! These characteristics later contributed to several accidents and one aircraft delivered to QANTAS in late 1922 for evaluation on the Charleville-Cloncurry (Queensland) route was quickly returned and an order for two cancelled. The second QANTAS Vulcan was not completed.

Five Vulcans were built to Type 61 standards including the prototype and the QANTAS aircraft. Three were delivered to Instone Air Line for use on its Brussels route and one to Douglas Vickers MP to compete in the 1922 King's Cup race, finishing 7th. Another Vulcan was completed as a Type 63 windowless freighter for evaluation by the Air Council.

The Vulcan's poor performance led to development of the Type 74 with more powerful Napier Lion engine. Two were built to this standard, the first of them flying on 3 March 1923 and delivered to Douglas Vickers for the 1923 King's Cup race. It retired on the first leg. This and the second Type 74 then passed on to Imperial Airways for use on its scheduled European services. One of them was withdrawn from service in 1926, leaving only the other Type 74 and Douglas Vickers' Type 61 airworthy. Both were then leased out for charter work, the 61 crashing in May 1926 and the 74 in July 1928.

Photo: Imperial Airways Vulcan.

Vickers Viking

Country of origin: United Kingdom.

Powerplants: Two 1690hp (1260kW) Bristol Hercules 630 or 634 14-cylinder radials; four bladed propellers.

Performance: 1/1A – max speed 219kt (406km/h); cruising speed 182kt (338km/h); initial climb 1390ft (424m)/min; service ceiling 22,000ft (6705m); max range 1629nm (3018km). 1B – max speed 228kt (423km/h); cruising speed 182kt (338km/h); initial climb 1275ft (388m)/min; service ceiling 23,750ft (7240m); max payload range 450nm (833km); max range 1477nm (2736km).

Weights: Empty 10,392-10,546kg (22,910-23,250lb); max takeoff 15,422kg (34,000lb).

Dimensions: 1/1A – wing span 27.20m (89ft 3in); length 19.18m (62ft 11in); height 5.94m (19ft 6in); wing area 81.9m^2 (882sq ft). 1B – length 19.86m (65ft 2in).

Accommodation: 1/1B – originally 24 passengers three abreast. 1B – originally 27 passengers, later up to 36.

Production: 163 Vikings of all models plus 251 Valettas.

History: Often overlooked when the history of British commercial aviation is discussed, the Viking was an important part of the story as it was Britain's first postwar airliner and provided the basis of British European Airways' operations until the Viscount began to replace it 1954.

After that, British independent airlines such as Channel Airways, Airwork, Eagle Aviation, Autair and Air Safaris found the Viking a reliable and useful part of their fleets until the last example was retired in 1971. Also of importance was the Viking's contribution to Britain's postwar export drive. Of the 163 built, some 65 were sold to overseas operators including DDL Danish Air Lines, South African Airways, Aer Lingus, Indian National Airways and Iraqi Airways. Others found their way into military service including with the King's Flight.

The Viking was regarded as an interim type and therefore not part of the Brabazon Committee's plans. Instead, it was designed to Air Ministry Specification 17/44 under the company designation VC1 (Vickers Commercial 1).

Owing more than a little to the Wellington bomber, it combined that aircraft's Bristol Hercules powerplants, nacelles, undercarriage, outer wings (with their geodetic structure) and tail surfaces from the Wellington derived Warwick with a new stressed skin fuselage.

The first Viking flew on 22 June 1945 and the last in April 1949. Twenty-four were built as Viking 1As with the original fabric covered geodetic wings, 15 as Viking 1s with conventional metal wings, and the remainder Viking 1Bs (service entry April 1947) with slightly longer fuselages and space for an extra row of seats.

The newly established BEA operated 49 Vikings from September 1946, the first service flown between Northolt and Copenhagen. By the time the airline started replacing its Vikings with Viscounts they had flown 65 million statute miles (104.6m kilometres) and carried more than 2.7 million passengers, Vickers also built 251 military transport and navigation trainer versions for the RAF as the Valetta. From that Vickers developed the tricycle undercarriage Varsity.

Photo: Viking 1B.

Vickers Viscount 700

Country of origin: United Kingdom.

Powerplants: Four 1547ehp (1154kW) Rolls-Royce Dart Mk.505 or 506 turboprops; four bladed propellers.

Performance: Max cruise 282kt (522km/h); economical cruise 275kt (509km/h); initial climb 1200ft (366m)/min; service ceiling 28,500ft (8690m); max payload range 844nm (1563km); range with 40 passengers 1044nm (1932km) or 1260nm (2028km) with optional fuel.

Weights: Empty 16,719kg (36,859lb); max takeoff 27,216-28,577kg (60,000-63,000lb).

Dimensions: Wing span 28.56m (93ft 8½in); length 24.74m (81ft 2in) or 24.94m (81ft 10in) with radar nose; height 8.15m (26ft 9in); wing area 89.5m² (963sq ft).

Accommodation: 40-53 passengers four/five abreast, up to 63 passengers five abreast later.

Production: 444 Viscounts of all models including 2 prototypes and 138 V.700.

History: Britain's most commercially successful airliner and the first turboprop airliner to enter production, the Viscount was responsible for a revolution in air transport, offering a combination of speed, operating economics and passenger appeal which saw it used as the primary medium range equipment of many major airlines during the 1950s and 1960s until jets began to take over.

The Viscount came from the wartime Brabazon Committee's Type 2B requirement for a postwar DC-3 replacement for European and Empire routes carrying 20 passengers up to 1750 statute miles (2800km) at 200mph (320km/h). Vickers' design evolved into a 32 seat four engined, pressurised turboprop powered by Armstrong Siddeley Mamba engines as the Type 609 Viceroy. By 1947 Rolls-Royce Dart engines had been substituted and the aircraft known as the Type 630 Viscount.

Two prototypes were ordered by the Ministry of Supply, the first of which flew on 16 July 1948. Ironically considering the aircraft's later success, this was the lowest point of the Viscount programme as its major potential customer, British European Airways, was showing little interest and had ordered piston engined Airspeed Ambassadors instead. The second aircraft was therefore completed as the V.663 testbed with two Rolls-Royce Tay turbojets. It first flew in March 1950.

The promise of more power from the Dart encouraged development of a 40-53 seater as the V.700 with stretched fuselage and increased span wings, despite there still not being a customer for the aircraft. The V.700 first flew on 28 August 1950 but by then its virtues had been recognised and BEA had placed an order for 27. Others quickly followed. The first V.700 was used by BEA for route proving flights and also won the transport section of the 1953 England to New Zealand Air Race.

The first production V.701 (Vickers allocated individual type numbers to customers) for BEA flew in August 1952 and the airline inaugurated services in April 1953. Other early customers included Air France, Trans-Australia Airlines and Aer Lingus while constant product improvement (increased fuel capacity including optional slipper tanks, increased weights, more efficient engines, anti skid brakes etc) ensured a steady stream of customers. A late 1952 order from Trans-Canada Airlines allowed the Viscount into the important North American market.

Photo: V.701 Viscount. (Stewart Wilson)

Vickers Viscount 700D

Country of origin: United Kingdom.

Powerplants: Four 1740ehp (1297kW) Rolls-Royce Dart Mk.510 turboprops; four bladed propellers.

Performance: Max cruise 290kt (537km/h); economical cruise 282kt (521km/h); initial climb 1400ft (426m)/min; service ceiling 27,500ft (8382m); max payload range 1157nm (2140km); range with 43 passengers 1496nm (2768km); range with slipper tanks 1627nm (3010km); max range with slipper and fuselage tanks 2131nm (3943km).

Weights: Empty 17,200kg (37,918lb); max takeoff 29,257kg (64,500lb).

Dimensions: Wing span 28.56m (93ft 8½in); length 24.74m (81ft 2in) or 24.94m (81ft 10in) with radar nose; height 8.15m (26ft 9in); wing area 89.5m² (963sq ft).

Accommodation: Initially 40-53 passengers four/five abreast, 60-63 passengers later.

Production: 444 Viscounts of all models including 150 V.700.

History: The generic designation V.700D was applied to Viscount 700 series aircraft with more powerful 1740ehp (1297kW) Rolls-Royce Dart 510 turboprops driving more efficient paddle bladed propellers, the combination allowing higher cruising speeds and a further increase in maximum takeoff weight. This in turn resulted in improved payload-range performance.

Other generic designations associated with the series were the V.770D for the North American market and V.771D executive version. As before, each customer was allocated an individual type number for its aircraft.

The 700D's first customer was a vitally important one as it represented a breakthrough into the US market. Capital Airlines placed a series of orders in 1954 for no fewer than 60 aircraft, at the time the biggest ever placed with a British manufacturer. As the V.745D, the first of them flew on 3 November 1955 (the airline had earlier received three standard models) and deliveries began immediately.

Capital's Viscounts incorporated other modifications which would subsequently be offered as standard equipment including a fuel jettison system (a mandatory US requirement), weather radar, hydraulically operated forward airstairs, air conditioning and stronger lower spar booms to cope with the high number of operating cycles associated with short stages.

Numerous other orders for the 700D followed, customers including Central African Airways, Braathens-SAFE, MEA, Union of Burma, Hunting Clan, Trans-Australia Airlines, Indian Airlines, Alitalia and PAL. Several military and corporate orders were also placed, the latter usually taking advantage of the availability of an additional fuel tank in the belly. Many ex airline Viscounts were later converted to corporate transports.

The last 700D (and the final Viscount 700 of any model) was delivered to Turkey's THY in December 1958 at a time when Viscount production was just starting its rapid decline from the peak of 111 built in 1957 in two factories. The production figure had doubled to 82 in 1956, reached 93 in 1958 and then fell to 38 in 1959. After that it was single figures until the final example flew in 1964.

Photo: V.745D Viscount.

Vickers Viscount 800 and 810

Country of origin: United Kingdom.

Powerplants: V.800 – four 1740ehp (1297kW) Rolls-Royce Dart Mk.510 turboprops. V.810 – four 1990ehp (1484kW) Dart Mk.525; four bladed propellers.

Performance: V.800 – max cruise 283kt (523km/h); economical cruise 270kt (499km/h); initial climb 1220ft (372m)/min; max payload range 600nm (1110km); range with 43 passengers 1165nm (2156km). V.810 – max cruise 318kt (587km/h); economical cruise 305kt (565km/h); initial climb 1650ft (503m)/min; service ceiling 27,000ft (8230m); range with 65 passengers 1110nm (2052km); range with 50 passengers and slipper tanks 1523nm (2816km).

Weights: V.800 – empty 18,688kg (41,200lb); max takeoff 29,257kg (64,500lb). V.810 – empty 19,596kg (43,200lb); max takeoff 32,886kg (72,500lb).

Dimensions: Wing span 28.56m (93ft 8½in); length 25.91m (85ft 0in) or 26.11m (85ft 8in) with radar nose; height 8.15m (26ft 9in); wing area 89.5m² (963sq ft).

Accommodation: 52-71 passengers five abreast.

Production: 444 Viscounts of all models including 68 V.800 and 86 V.810.

History: Thoughts of an enlarged Viscount first emerged in 1952 when Rolls-Royce announced the more powerful R.Da.5 family of Dart engines. Development began under the Type 800 designation, initial investigations centring around a 4.04m (13ft 3in) fuselage stretch over the Viscount 700 and accommodation for up to 86 passengers.

The design involved numerous unacceptable compromises including a substantial reduction in speed and payload-range performance. Despite this, BEA ordered 12 in 1953 as the V.801 but further studies resulted in a new 800 series with the Viscount 700D's Dart 510 engines and its maximum takeoff weight in combination with a modest 1.17m (3ft 10in) fuselage stretch. Inside, the cabin was lengthened by 2.82m (9ft 3in) by moving the rear pressure bulkhead aft.

Accommodation was for 52-65 passengers (up to 71 later) and although payload-range performance was still only fair, it was adequate for BEA's purposes. A visible change was replacing the oval passenger doors with rectangular ones. BEA changed its order to the new model (V.802) in 1954 and eventually purchased 24. It first flew on 29 September 1956 and services between London and Paris began in February 1957.

The next development was the V.806 with 1890ehp (1409kW) Dart 520s (first flight 9 August 1957) which was ordered by BEA, New Zealand National Airways and Aer Lingus, while the final Viscount version to achieve production was the V.810. This had the carrying capacity of the 800 without the payload-range compromises thanks to more powerful Dart 525s and increased operating weights. The structure was strengthened to cope.

The first Viscount 810 flew on 23 December 1957 and launch customer Continental Airlines began services with its V.812s between Chicago and Los Angeles in May 1958. Other customers included South African Airways, Lufthansa, TAA, Pakistan International, Ansett-ANA, All Nippon and Austrian. The last Viscount (a V.843 for China's CAAC) was delivered in April 1964. Only about 10 remained in service by 1999, all in Africa.

Photo: V.806 Viscount.

Vickers Vanguard

Country of origin: United Kingdom.

Powerplants: V.951/953 – four 4985ehp (3717kW) Rolls-Royce Tyne Mk.506 turboprops. V.952 – four 5545ehp (4135kW) Tyne Mk.512; four bladed propellers.

Performance: V.952 – Max cruise 369kt (684km/h); economical cruise 363kt (673km/h); initial climb 3360ft (1024m)/min; service ceiling 30,000ft (9145m); max payload range (no reserves) 1590nm (2945km); max range (no reserves) 2694nm (4990km). V.953 – normal cruise 358kt (663km/h); range 1800nm (3334km).

Dimensions: Wing span 35.97m (118ft 0in); length 37.45m (122ft 10½in); height 10.64m (34ft 11in); wing area 142.0m² (1529sq ft).

Weights: V.952 – operating empty 38,556kg (85,000lb); max takeoff 66,452kg (146,500lb).

Accommodation: Up to 139 passengers. V.953C – max payload 16.8 tonnes (37,000lb).

Production: 1 V.950, 6 V.951, 23 V.952 and 14 V.953, total 44.

History: Conceived as a second generation, large capacity turboprop airliner for British European Airways, the Vanguard was intended to provide low seat-mile operating costs on medium range routes but was overtaken by the arrival of pure jets which could perform the same function. The result was that only 44 were built including the prototype, sold to just two airlines.

Investigations began in 1953, the design evolving from high wing 60 seat concepts to the Vickers Type 870, a 93 seater powered by four Rolls-Royce Tyne engines with a 'double bubble' fuselage cross section to allow considerable space for underfloor freight. This characteristic was influenced by Trans-Canada Airlines, which was coincidentally looking for a similar aircraft.

The V.870 evolved into the larger V.950 Vanguard for 126 passengers, BEA ordering 20 in July 1956 as the V.951 with Tyne 506 engines. In January 1957 TCA also ordered 20 (plus another three later on) as the V.952 with more powerful Tyne 512s, increased maximum weight and accommodation for up to 139 passengers. BEA later amended its order to cover six V.951s and 14 V.953s, the latter still with Tyne 506s but featuring increased weights and the ability to carry 139 passengers.

The prototype V.950 Vanguard first flew on 20 January 1959 followed by the first V.951 three months later. Deliveries to BEA began in December 1960 and service on the airline's European routes began in March 1961. The first V.953 flew in May 1961. TCA put the V.952 into service in February 1961. The last was flown in June 1962

TCA's successor Air Canada had sold all its Vanguards by 1974 while by 1968 BEA (later British Airways) had begun converting nine of its V.953s to V.953C Merchantman freighters with large cargo door. The conversions were performed by Aviation Traders and the last of the type was retired from British Airways service in 1979.

Operators of second hand Vanguards included Indonesia's Merpati, Hunting Cargo, Air Bridge Carriers, Europe Aero Service, Invicta International, Air Trader and Air Gabon. The last Vanguard flight was recorded on 17 October 1996 when a Hunting Cargo V.953C flew into the Brooklands Museum at Weybridge, the place of its birth.

Photo: V.953C Merchantman. (Bruce Malcolm)

Vickers Standard VC10

Country of origin: United Kingdom.

Powerplants: Four 21,000lb (93.4kN) Rolls-Royce Conway Mk.540 turbofans.

Performance: Max cruise 502kt (939km/h); economical cruise 480kt (889km/h); initial climb 1920ft (585m)/min; operational ceiling 38,000ft (11,580m); max payload range (no reserves) 4380nm (8112km); max fuel range (no reserves) 5275nm (9765km).

Weights: Operating empty 66,670kg (146,980lb); max takeoff 141,523kg (312,000lb).

Dimensions: Wing span 44.55m (146ft 2in); length 48.36m (158ft 8in); height 12.04m (39ft 6in); wing area 264.8m² (2851sq ft) or 272.4m (2932sq ft).

Accommodation: Typically 109 passengers in two classes, maximum 151 passengers in single class six abreast.

Production: 54 VC10s of all models including 18 Standards and 14 VC10 C.1.

History: Loved by its passengers and crews but a commercial failure and purchased new by only five airlines, the VC10 was too late to challenge the Boeing 707 and Douglas DC-8 in the marketplace and was severely hampered by the customer for which it was designed, BOAC. The airline constantly cancelled or changed its orders and then seemed to delight in publicly criticising the aircraft.

Originally designed for service on BOAC's routes to Africa and the Far East, the specification demanded excellent airfield performance. This was achieved in the original short fuselage Standard VC10 but at the expense of operating economics. The BOAC specification which resulted in the VC10 called for a Comet and Britannia replacement capable of carrying a 15,876kg (35,000lb) payload of a range of 2500 statute miles (4023km).

The design evolved from a jet powered version of the Vanguard turboprop to the final configuration with four rear mounted Rolls-Royce Conway turbofans and T-tail. BOAC ordered 35 plus 20 options in May 1957: after all the changes it finally received 12 Standard VC10s and 17 stretched Supers (see next entry).

The prototype V.1100 VC10 first flew on 29 June 1962 followed by the first production V.1101 for BOAC on 8 November. Flight testing resulted in fitting extended wing tips to reduce drag, increasing the wing chord by 4 per cent, moving the engines slightly outboard and increasing their incidence. BOAC's aircraft lacked the extended tips.

BOAC put the VC10 into service in late April 1964. The only other airline customers were Ghana Airways (two V.1102s with large freight doors) and British United (three V.1102s also with freight doors). The prototype was sold to Laker Airways in 1968 and other airlines which operated second hand or leased Standards included MEA, British Caledonian, Nigeria Airways, Gulf Air, Air Ceylon and Air Malawi plus three Middle East heads of state.

The last Standard VC10 was delivered to BUA in July 1965 and 14 VC10 C.1 hybrids (with the Standard's fuselage and the Super's engines plus increased weights and fuel capacity) were delivered to the RAF in 1967-68. The BOAC/British Airways Standards were withdrawn in 1974 and sold to some of the operators listed above. Others were later converted to K.2 tankers for the RAF.

Photo: V.1101 Standard VC10. (Peter Keating via Eric Allen)

Vickers Super VC.10

Country of origin: United Kingdom.

Powerplants: Four 22,500lb (100.1kN) Rolls-Royce Conway Mk.550 turbofans.

Performance: Max cruise 505kt (935km/h); economical cruise 478kt (885km/h); initial climb 2300ft (700m)/min; operational ceiling 38,000ft (11,580m); max payload range (no reserves) 4100nm (7595km); max fuel range (no reserves) 6195nm (11,475km).

Weights: Operational empty 71,137kg (156,828lb); max takeoff 151,956kg (335,000lb).

Dimensions: Wing span 44.55m (146ft 2in); length 52.32m (171ft 8in); height 12.04m (39ft 6in); wing area 272.4m² (2932sq ft).

Accommodation: Typically 139 passengers in two classes or maximum 174 passengers in single class six abreast.

Production: 54 VC10s of all models including 22 Supers.

History: Studies into a higher capacity version of the VC10 were instigated early in the development programme, one version – the Super 200 with accommodation for 191-212 passengers – looked at as early as 1958. This was adjudged too big for the market, efforts then concentrating on the V.1150 Super VC10 as it finally emerged.

Compared to the Standard VC10, the Super featured a 3.96m (13ft 0in) fuselage stretch, more powerful Conway 550 engines, higher weights and increased fuel capacity via an extra tank in the fin. The aerodynamic improvements developed as a result of the original VC10 flight test programme were incorporated. The result was a superb aircraft which sacrificed some of the Standard VC10's airfield performance for greater efficiency including lower seat-mile operating costs.

There was no prototype Super VC10, the first aircraft also the first V.1151 for BOAC. It flew on 7 May 1964 (eight days after the Standard had entered service) and BOAC inaugurated services on the North Atlantic route on 1 April 1965. It was soon used all over the BOAC network and proved to be even more popular with passengers than the Standard had been.

BOAC's 17th and last Super VC10 was delivered in May 1969 and the airline's successor, British Airways, started to withdraw them from service in March 1980. The last BA Super VC10 scheduled flight was on 29 March 1981 followed by a farewell charter for enthusiasts the following day.

The only other airline to order the Super VC10 was East African Airways, which took delivery of five V.1154s with large freight doors between December 1966 and February 1970, the last of the order also the final VC10 built. EAA's Supers operated to various points in Africa and the Middle East until 1977 when the four survivors were repossessed by British Aerospace following the airline's collapse.

They – along with other Standard and Super VC10s – ended up in Royal Air Force service as tankers. The VC10 tanker conversion programme ran from 1979 to 1996 and covered 14 aircraft – five K.2s (ex BOAC/Gulf Air Standards), four K.3s (ex EAA Supers) and five K.4s (ex BA Supers). In addition, 13 of the RAF's 14 VC10 C.1s were converted to C.1(K) tanker/transports.

Photo: V.1151 Super VC10. (BAe)

Westland IV and Wessex

Country of origin: United Kingdom.

Powerplants: IV – three 95hp (71kW) ADC Cirrus III or 105hp (78kW) Cirrus Hermes I four cylinder inlines. Wessex – three 105hp (78kW) Armstrong Siddeley Genet Major five cylinder radials or 140hp (104kW) Genet Major 1A seven cylinder radials; two bladed propellers.

Performance: IV – max speed 90kt (167km/h); range 455nm (843km). Wessex (Genet Major) – max speed 102kt (190km/h); cruising speed 87kt (161km/h); initial climb 600ft (183m)/min; service ceiling 12,300ft (3750m); range 450nm (834km). Wessex (Major 1A) – max speed 106kt (196km/h); cruising speed 87kt (161km/h); initial climb 680ft (207m)/min; service ceiling 14,900ft (4540m); range 365nm (676km).

Weights: IV – empty 1429kg (3150lb); max takeoff 2495kg (5500lb). Wessex – empty 1728-1765kg (3810-3891lb); max takeoff 2608-2858kg (5750-6300lb).

Dimensions: Wing span 17.53m (57ft 6in); length 11.58m (38ft 0in); height 2.90m (9ft 6in); wing area 45.5m² (490sq ft).

Accommodation: Normally six seats including pilot, eight on some aircraft.

Production: 2 Westland IV and 8 Wessex.

History: The Westland IV six seat trimotor was designed in 1928 as an air taxi or feederliner, the choice of three small engines intended to reduce the risk of a forced landing in the event of an engine failure. The outer ADC Cirrus III engines were mounted beneath the wings on the wing and undercarriage struts.

Constructed of fabric covered wood, the first aircraft flew on 22 February 1929 followed by the second a few months later. This featured slightly more powerful Cirrus Hermes engines and a metal rear fuselage. It went into service with Imperial Airways' private hire department.

Orders for single examples were received from Shell in Australia and Kenya's Wilson Airways but these subsequently fell through. Testing had revealed the original inline engines to be unsuitable resulting in the third aircraft being completed as the first Wessex with Armstrong Siddeley Genet Major radials.

This first flew in May 1930 and along with three others was delivered to Belgium's Sabena for use on its short haul European routes. The original prototype was converted to Wessex standards and used as a company demonstrator.

The last four Wessexes built in 1931-34 had more powerful Genet Major 1A radials installed and metal skinning on the forward fuselage. The first one was used for charter operations before being transferred to Imperial Airways, another was delivered to the Egyptian Air Force and the remaining pair went to Portsmouth, Southsea and Isle of Wight Aviation for its Portsmouth-Ryde and Portsmouth-Shoreham services. These aircraft featured dural instead of wooden wing structures, raised cockpit, strengthened undercarriage, larger rudder and provision for an extra two passengers by reducing the baggage space.

The three surviving Sabena Wessexes returned to Britain in 1935 and were purchased by Cobham Air Routes for use on its Portsmouth-Christchurch-Guernsey service.

Photo: Westland Wessex.

Wibault 280-283T

Country of origin: France.

Powerplants: Three 350hp (261kW) Gnome-Rhône Titan Major 7Kd seven cylinder radials; two bladed propellers.

Performance: 282T.12 – cruising speed 108kt (200km/h); range 567nm (1050nm). 283T.12 – max speed 135kt (251km/h); service ceiling 17,060ft (5200m); range 605nm (1120km).

Weights: 282T.12 – empty 4097kg (9032lb); max takeoff (13,668lb). 283T.12 – empty 4500kg (9920lb); max takeoff 6350kg (14,000lb).

Dimensions: Wing span 22.61m (74ft 2in); length 17.00m (55ft 9in); height 5.56m (18ft 3in); wing area 64.4m² (693sq ft).

Accommodation: 10-12 passengers.

Production: 2 prototypes, 6 Wib.282T.12 and 10 Wib.283T.12, total 18.

History: Considered an advanced design for its day – a cantilever low wing all metal monoplane when biplanes still largely dominated airliner design – the Wibault 280-283 trimotor became a familiar sight throughout Europe during the 1930s, operated mainly by Air Union and subsequently Air France.

The prototype Wibault 280 – powered by 300hp (224kW) Hispano-Suiza 9Qa radials – first flew in November 1930 but was soon re-engined with Gnome-Rhône Titan Majors, this changing the designation to Wib.281T.10. The Titan Major became the standard powerplant for the production versions which followed.

The second aircraft was similarly powered and both prototypes were purchased by the French Government. The prototypes were originally fitted with divided type main undercarriages with exposed struts but these were later modified to production standard 'trousered' streamlined units. The aircraft also flew with these removed.

In 1931 the Societé des Avions Michel Wibault was taken over by the Chantiers de Saint-Nazaire Penhoët shipyard and finance provided to begin series production of the new airliner as the 282T.12. It accommodated 12 passengers and differed from the earlier aircraft in having fully cowled engines, although as was the case with the undercarriage fairings, these were sometimes removed.

The CIDNA company flew one of the 282T.12s on the Paris-Prague-Istanbul route and most of the other five served with Air Union on its Paris-London *Voile d'Or* (Golden Clipper) service. Air Union merged into Air France in October 1933 and the fleet taken over by the new French national airline. One 282T was fitted with experimental retractable undercarriage.

Air France took delivery of the first of 10 283T.12s in early 1934, these featuring increased weights and fuel capacity and mainly operated on the airline's services to London and Berlin.

The outbreak of war in September 1939 saw 12 Wibaults impressed into Armeé de l'Air service for use as transports between then and mid 1940.

Their visual similarity to the Junkers Ju 52 resulted in all of them suffering damage from friendly anti-aircraft fire during the Battle of France and one was shot down as a result.

Photo: Wib.282T.

Yakovlev Yak-40

Country of origin: Soviet Union.

Powerplants: Yak-40 – Three 3307lb (14.7kN) Ivchenko AI-25 turbofans. Yak-40V – three 3858lb (17.2kN) AI-25T turbofans.

Performance: Yak-40 – max cruise 297kt (550km/h); economical cruise 254kt (470km/h); initial climb 1575ft (480m)/min; range with 32 passengers 783nm (1450km); max range 972nm (1800km).

Weights: Yak-40 – operating empty 9400kg (20,723lb); max takeoff 16,000lb (35,273lb). Yak-40V – max takeoff 16,500kg (36,375lb).

Dimensions: Wing span 25.00m (82ft 0in); length 20.36m (66ft 9¹/₂in); height 6.50m (21ft 4in); wing area 70.0m² (753sq ft).

Accommodation: 27-32 passengers three abreast.

Production: Over 1000.

History: The world's first small capacity regional jet to achieve other than limited production, the Yak-40 was designed to meet an early 1960s Aeroflot requirement to replace the many Lisunov Li-2s (licence built DC-3s) still in service.

The Yak-40 needed to operate from short unprepared airfields, hence the three engined configuration, chosen because the calculation of takeoff lengths and weights could be based on two-thirds of total power being available in the event of engine failure rather than half in the case of a twin. The three engines also provide a high level of redundancy.

The Ivchenko AI-25 small turbofan was developed specifically for the Yak-40, the unswept high aspect ratio wing illustrating the emphasis on short field performance rather than speed and the rear fuselage ventral airstair and auxiliary power unit (APU) providing operational autonomy at remote strips.

The numerical success of the Yak-40 compared with contemporary western attempts at small capacity jets (such as the VFW 614) is tempered to a large extent by the fact that the vast majority of production went to Aeroflot or other Soviet *Bloc* airlines.

It must be remembered that at the time, these operators did not have their equipment choice decisions encumbered by troublesome and inconvenient economic issues such as the need to make a profit! Regardless of this, it must also be recognised that the Yak-40 performed its design role well.

The prototype Yak-40 first flew on 21 October 1966 and the aircraft was assigned the NATO reporting name 'Codling'.

Aeroflot began services in September 1968 and apart from adding a clamshell thrust reverser to the centre engine during the production run, the Yak-40 remained basically unchanged.

The designation Yak-40V was applied to export aircraft with more powerful AI-25T engines and increased maximum weight. These were sold to Afghanistan, France, West Germany and several Eastern European countries. Production ended in 1978.

Proposed developments which failed to materialise included the stretched, 40 seat Yak-40M, the Yak-40TL twin with two Lycoming LF507s, and US company ICX Aviation's version with Garrett TFE731 turbofans and western avionics.

Photo: Yakovlev Yak-40.

Yakovlev Yak-42

Country of origin: Soviet Union/Russia

Powerplants: Three 14,330lb (63.7kN) ZMKB Progress D-36 Series 1 turbofans.

Performance: Yak-42 – max cruise 437kt (810km/h); economical cruise 405kt (750km/h); service ceiling 31,500ft (9600m); range with 120 passengers 1026nm (1900km); range with 104 passengers 1242nm (2300km). Yak-42D – max cruise 437kt (810km/h); economical cruise 400kt (740km/h); range with 102 passengers 1505nm (2788km); range with 120 passengers 1185nm (2195km).

Weights: Yak-42 – operating empty 33,000kg (72,750lb); max takeoff 57,000kg (125,661lb). Yak-42D – operating empty 34,515kg (76,091lb); max takeoff 57,500kg (126,763lb).

Dimensions: Wing span 34.88m (114ft 5in); length 36.38m (119ft 4in); height 9.83m (32ft 3in); wing area 150.0m² (1615sq ft).

Accommodation: Typically 102 passengers in two classes or up to 120 in single class six abreast.

Production: About 200 by 1999 including approximately 125 Yak-42Ds.

History: Development of the Yak-42 trijet began in the early 1970s as a replacement for Aeroflot's Tupolev Tu-134 twinjets, Antonov An-24 turboprops and Ilyushin Il-18 turboprops on Soviet domestic routes. Modest airfield requirements and the ability to operate in remote regions with minimal support were key requirements, resulting in features such as an APU and a rear fuselage ventral airstair.

In order to find the best configuration, the unusual step of ordering prototypes with different wing sweeps (11deg and 23deg) was taken. The first one flew on 7 March 1975, testing revealing the 23deg sweep to be best with the result that the third prototype and production models were built to this standard. The first production aircraft flew in November 1976.

The sweepback issue in combination with development problems associated with the new D-36 three shaft turbofan caused delays, Aeroflot not inaugurating services (between Moscow and Krasnodar) until December 1980. A 1982 incident saw the Yak-42 temporarily withdrawn from service and production but both resumed in 1984, Aeroflot adding Moscow-Pykovo and Leningrad-Saratov to the aircraft's schedules. Apart from the Soviet Union/CIS, Yak-42s have also been delivered to operators in Lithuania, China, Central America, the Far East, Africa and Cuba. NATO's reporting name was 'Clobber'.

The initial Yak-42 was replaced in production by the Yak-42D with increased fuel and maximum weight in 1988, this becoming the standard production model. Other proposed or offered versions include the Yak-42T freighter design study with main deck large cargo door and 12 tonnes (26,455lb) payload; Yak-42D-100 with a four screen AlliedSignal EFIS cockpit (certified July 1997) and Yak-42ML VIP/corporate version.

The Yak-142 (originally Yak-42A) also has western digital avionics plus increased fuel and other modifications (flown December 1992), while the Yak-42-200 (Yak-42M) is a proposed stretched version for up to 150 passengers powered by D-436 turbofans.

Photo: Yakovlev Yak-42D. (Bruce Malcolm)

INDEX

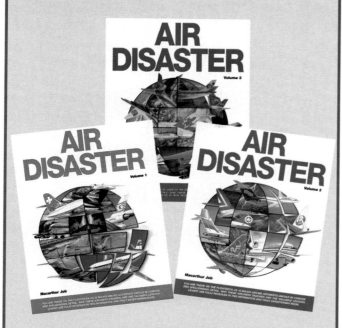
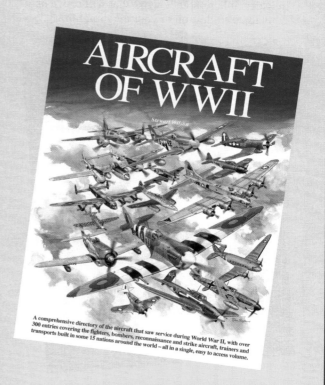

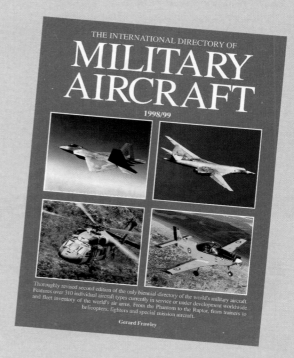